Writing Poems

Second Edition

Robert Wallace
Case Western Reserve University

Little, Brown and Company

BOSTON  TORONTO

for Sharon

Library of Congress Cataloging-in-Publication Data

Wallace, Robert, 1932–
  Writing poems.

  Bibliography: p. 424
  Includes indexes.
  1. Poetry—Authorship.   I. Title.
PN1059.A9W34   1986   808.1   86-7418
ISBN 0-316-92000-2

Library of Congress Catalog Card No. 86-7418

ISBN 0-316-92000-2

9 8 7 6 5 4 3

MV

Published simultaneously in Canada
by Little, Brown & Company (Canada) Limited

Printed in the United States of America

ACKNOWLEDGMENTS

Aal, Katharyn Machan, "Hazel Tells Laverne." Copyright © 1981 by Katharyn Machan Aal. Reprinted by permission.
Aberg, W. M., "The Lark and the Emperor." Copyright © 1980 by W. M. Aberg. Reprinted by permission.
Adrian, Vonna, "St. Jerome." Copyright © 1986 by Vonna Adrian. Reprinted by permission.
Armour, Richard, "Going to Extremes." From *Light Armour* by Richard Armour. Reprinted by permission of the author and McGraw-Hill Book Company.
Ashbery, John, "These Lacustrine Cities." From *Rivers and Mountains* by John Ashbery. Copyright © 1962 by John Ashbery. Reprinted by permission of John Ashbery and Georges Borchardt, Inc.
Azusenis, Pamela, "Salvation." Copyright © 1978 by Pamela Azusenis. Reprinted by permission.
Basho, "Breaking the silence. . . ." From *The Narrow Road to the Deep North & Other Travel Sketches*, translated by Nobuyuki Yuasa. Copyright © 1966 by Nobuyuki Yuasa. Reprinted by permission of Penguin Books, Ltd.
Bennett, Bruce, "Smart." Copyright © 1978 by Bruce Bennett. "Sort of a Sestina." Copyright © 1980 by Bruce Bennett. Reprinted by permission.
Bishop, Elizabeth, "First Death in Nova Scotia." From *The Complete Poems* by Elizabeth Bishop. Copyright © 1969 by Elizabeth Bishop. Reprinted by permission of Farrar, Straus and Giroux, Inc.
Bliss, Deborah, "Van Busbeke Discovers the Tulip, 1550." Copyright © 1967 by Deborah Bliss. Reprinted by permission.
Bly, Robert, "Looking at a Dead Wren in My Hand." From *The Morning Glory* by Robert Bly. Copyright © 1970 by Robert Bly. "Come with Me." From *The Light Around the Body* by Robert Bly. Copyright

(Continued on page 438)

FOREWORD

Do Poets Need
to Know Something?

One of the advantages to being a poet, says an elder statesman among poets, Robert Francis, is that you aren't required to know anything in particular.

Not that Francis believes that for a minute. Slyly, he is just stating a prevalent misconception: the view of the poet as an empty-headed blatherer of beautiful words. When you reflect about it, though, most poets have to soak up a great deal that needs knowing. First, they must learn to strum that colossal and resonant harp, the English language, a temperamental instrument that calls for practiced fingering. Perhaps a good half of the poet's art consists in knowing exactly how to proceed and exactly when. At times, the poet barges ahead with confidence, setting down words as surely and rapidly as a Japanese master brush artist draws a leaping carp upon paper so porous that a second's hesitation may run the ink to the tip of his brush, producing a botch. At other times, the poet slows down and takes pains, casting and recasting a line of a poem till it hooks fast. All this is only basic working knowledge, to which poets add anything they can learn. Just for fun, W. H. Auden drew up the curriculum for an imaginary college for poets that encompassed such matters as archaeology, mathematics, cooking, gardening, and the care of chickens and goats. Auden's point, I take it, was that poetry may thrive on any old soil of learning. Quality of observation, not mere breadth of experience, seems to be what makes poetry out of what a poet knows. To find the raw material for poems, you don't need to backpack to Katmandu. No doubt some have done so and returned knowing less than Emily Dickinson knew from watching humming-birds and garter snakes in the meadow across the road past her home.

That in order to be a poet you have to know something, college students have long taken for granted. At least, they keep signing up for courses in writing poetry as if they expect such studies to impart something valuable. Nowadays, with the tendency of basic composition courses to include a unit or two of creative writing, it is a rare student who escapes being asked to write a poem at some moment in the college experience. Things were not always so. When, in 1931, Paul Engle founded his celebrated Writers' Workshop at the University of Iowa, academic traditional-ists (as Engle later recalled) thought the term "creative writing" an obscenity. (To me, the term seems closer to blasphemy. In a sense, only the Unmoved Mover creates; all a writer does is assemble things from words.)

In colleges today, the titular poet in residence doesn't ever simply reside, but has to teach, like the rest of the faculty. But in most departments of English, the teacher of poetry writing is generally envied. Peers look upon this teacher in much the way that musicians in a band, struggling to pack their amplifiers and timpani after a concert is over, cast jealous eyes upon the piano player, who casually picks up the sheet music and goes home. To the instructor of composition—*prose* composition—struggling to reread "On Civil Disobedience" before the next bell for class and groaning under four sets of essays on Thoreau's nonconformity, it would appear that the poetry writing teacher has a racket. The latter, having asked students to run off copies of a poem or two they have written, apparently strolls into class without a preparation in mind, has the students read aloud their poems, and chats about them.

But this is another misconception. Like the piano player, a teacher of poetry writing has to possess innate ability, devotion to craft, and the strength to endure a professional training that never ends. I doubt that even a brain surgeon, who (these are Richard Brautigan's delectable words) removes "with a sudden but delicate motion . . . a disordered portion of the imagination," puts longer hours or finer skill into the art than does the instructor who detaches a rickety line from a student poem and suggests how to tighten it. To ferret out the weakness in a poem—or the strength—may take far more time and thought than to fathom a student essay. A deep satisfaction of the job, and yet a continuing responsibility, is that the student-teacher relationship often lasts. Although students of freshman composi-tion, after their onerous course is through, don't usually want anything further to do with their instructors, students of poetry writing may persist for years in looking to their instructors for support and encouragement. A decade after the poetry workshop has disbanded, the instructor may still be asked to criticize a book manuscript, or to testify on a former student's behalf to some grant-giving institu-tion.

However hard they toil, instructors of poetry writing continually feel expected to justify their existence. Most often, they defend their profession in one of two ways. Either they claim that, by trying to write poems, students come to understand poetry from the inside, and so become more astute readers; or else they argue that the attempt to write poetry benefits the students' more mundane writing, enabling them to wield words with greater skill and keener sensitivity when they write term papers and job applications. Both these reasons make pretty good sense to me, but I would add still another. Although it happens rarely, sometimes a workshop in poetry brings together an inspired teaching poet and an inspired student poet— mind to mind, face to face. And when any such situation brings John Crowe Ransom together with Robert Lowell, or Robert Lowell together with Sylvia Plath and Anne Sexton, it achieves something unique and remarkable. Perhaps, in a relatively small way, it even strengthens the flickering light of civilization.

I would say, then, that courses in the writing of poetry are, by and large, wholesome and morally sweet activities. They wouldn't be were they to make huge and misleading claims, but they never do. They don't offer, directly, practical and remunerative job training. They don't even promise to usher the student's writings into print. No self-respecting instructor of poetry writing pretends to ready the young for a money-making future in literature—a profession that, Wallace Stegner said, barely exists. Robert Wallace makes all this clear in his chapter "Oddments" in *Writing Poems*. He offers the young poet this frank and succinct advice: "Get a job."

Designed to help a student write poetry—financially unprofitable poetry— Wallace's textbook isn't a usual one at all. Until I met it, I had seen one or two other textbooks purporting to aid the novice poet in writing poems, but none that I thought would greatly help anybody. That we have not previously had a really useful textbook in the subject isn't hard to explain. It is demonstrably impossible to tell another human being how to write a poem, and even to suggest how to get ready to write poetry is a task fraught with boobytraps and complexities. Moreover, instructors of poetry writing usually know their own minds. As often as not, they have favorite teaching techniques, and it is a brave and foolhardy textbook author who would push techniques on them.

Like most who have taught courses in poetry writing, I had thought I knew how to do it decently, and so, when the publisher first asked me to look at Wallace's book in manuscript, I began to read with skepticism. I was won over. Wallace doesn't tell the student how to write a poem; he doesn't lay down arbitrary laws. Instead, he carefully arrays all the possibilities. Starting with the assumption that the student, in order to write a poem, would do well to read poetry and see what goes on in it, he sets forth poems, elements of poetry, suggestions for writing, and a generous bag of wisdom and advice. Soon I was turning his pages in astonishment, nodding in doglike assent, struck many times by insights that had never occurred to me. Whatever the instructor's persuasions, this book is a flexible instrument. Some matters will seem basic (the line, the metaphor), and the instructor may care to take them up with the entire class. Other matters may seem of limited interest (say, how to write in syllabics), and the instructor may wish simply to point them out to the student who asks about them. In a single book, Wallace gives us a highly teachable classroom text; a compact and lively anthology including greats such as Shakespeare, Donne, Walt Whitman, and Anonymous; a work of reference; a worldly-wise companion; and a poetical *Guide to the Perplexed.* Instructors can employ it how they will.

As a writer of prose, Wallace knows how to put subtle matters clearly, and he radiates forthrightness, modesty, and good cheer. That he is himself a fine poet who has taught the writing of poetry for a long time and thought hard about it, his every page reveals. No doubt being a poet helps a teacher of poetry writing. Still, I can't agree with Ezra Pound's counsel to pay no heed to the criticism of anyone who hasn't written a notable work. In one respect, the teaching of poets is like the training of boxers. There are distinguished instructors whose own poems haven't stood up for three rounds, yet who have nurtured champions.

Lately, some observers have blamed creative writing programs for the sort of poetry that now clutters our little magazines: a poetry that seems composed by a word processor smothered in mothballs, a poetry lacking in music and grace, in passion and intelligence. Such observers assume that there once was a golden age when every poem in the little magazines shone like a risen sun, and that in these degenerate days we have fallen from that primal glow. But a browse through an old file of *Poetry* from the 1930s or *Evergreen Review* from the 1960s will puncture this illusion in a hurry. I suspect that our current poetry glut (as Karl Shapiro calls it) or superabundance (as I'd rather call it) may have resulted from forces at work in our civilization at large. Today, more and more Americans seem driven to switch off their television sets and proclaim that they are individuals, not consumers. Evidently, one way to declare their individuality is to publish poetry. The urge to charge headfirst into print with a signed lyric, no matter how poor, has been facilitated by the cheapness and convenience of offset printing. Anyone with a hundred dollars in hand can quickly bring out a chapbook of poems or a new little magazine. Perhaps some teachers of creative writing have egged their students on to premature and reckless publication. Still, the best teachers, aware that good poets take time to arrive, don't try to accelerate them. If anything, such teachers gently apply the brakes by insisting on excellence.

Nowadays, when creative writing seems lodged securely in most college curricula, a discipline nearly as respectable as anthropology, we sometimes hear its professors accused of making the writing of poetry into an arcane exercise, referring neither to the world at large nor to other humane studies. That is another reason for liking *Writing Poems*, in whose pages writing is pursued side by side with reading, and neither the world at large nor its varied knowledge is ever far from sight. Robert Wallace reminds us of an essential quest: to make creative writing more demanding, more nearly central to the humanities, more large-minded, more generously informative.

First of all, to be sure, it has to serve the student—to whom a good poetry workshop is useful as a sounding board. Face to face with readers, the fledgling poet well knows that he or she writes to be understood and appreciated. Although this living audience is likely to be more attentive, more caring, than readers in the world at large tend to be, such human concern, at an early stage in a poet's development, sometimes makes the difference between ceasing to write and continuing. As Sylvan Barnet has remarked, how hard poets work may be the best test of their sincerity. In a creative writing class, the most valuable participants tend also to be the most sincere readers.

From Robert Wallace's *Writing Poems,* with the instructor's help, students will surely learn much about poetry from the inside, will acquire more sensitivity to words, and almost certainly will learn a good deal that will be useful in writing poems, should they write any. If, in this second edition and future editions, Wallace's book continues to have a benevolent effect, then magazines, both little and large, will be printing more and more new poems we will remember. To help a single memorable poem come into the world—what instructor wouldn't call that ample reward for a lifetime of reading manuscripts? That would be justification enough for a thousand creative writing courses.

X. J. Kennedy

PREFACE

I am not sure writing poems can be taught, but I know it can be learned. This book is intended to help provide the circumstances for that learning.

I have tried to write it simply, but without simplifying. Because poetry happens all at once in writing a poem—as it does in reading a poem—the division into sections on form, content, and process; and of these sections into chapters, is primarily a convenience of exposition, not an implicit theory. Readers, or teachers, are invited to skip around freely, following their own direction or interest. Partly to spread out the clumps of very technical information in Chapters 2 (on free verse), 3 (on meter), and 4 (on diction, syntax, alliteration, assonance, rhyme, and texture), I might assign Chapters 1, 2, 6, and 10 first; then 3, 7, and 11—more or less raising simultaneous matters simultaneously. Establishing a different emphasis, another teacher might begin with Chapter 8 (on metaphor). In a short-format course (a one-semester introduction to creative writing, for instance, in which half the course will be spent on the short story), some chapters might not be assigned at all or might be assigned only selectively. The sections within chapters are handy in this way. In such a course I might choose only *Syntax* from Chapter 4 and *Symbols* from Chapter 7. If something else seemed relevant to a particular student or student's poem—like *Rhyme*, say—I could assign or refer to it in conference.

In creative writing courses, far more than in subject matter courses, one is teaching not material but *students*. Because so much class time is (and should be) devoted to discussing students' writing, a significant value of this book will be to let the teacher put the exposition of technical matters on automatic pilot. It is discouraging, after an especially exciting semester, to recall that a class never really got to metaphor, or to the basics of meter.

Since reading poems naturally stimulates and guides writing poems, this book is also, in effect, a mini-anthology. The selection of course favors the modern and contemporary. I have included a number of poems written by students (whose names are marked by asterisks) both because they are good poems and because they may serve as friendly models of what beginning poets can accomplish. A few of my own poems are here because I can bear witness about them. *Questions and Suggestions* are intended to supplement, not replace, the instigations a thoughtful teacher can supply. This or that exercise will often be more relevant to a particular student than to a whole class.

A rule I have rarely broken is not to use "bad" examples. All poets write (and learn from) their own bad poems, and the beginning poet will be able to do so without unhappy illustrations. Early versions of poems, particularly in Chapters 11 and 12 (on revising), offer instances of clumsiness or wrongheadedness—as well as the assurance that problems can be solved.

Writing poems—trying to handle one's deepest feelings and to present one's most serious view of the world—is always an intimate, vulnerable activity. In a sense, all good poems are lucky hits. Beginning poets, then, especially those faced with deadlines, should always consider the poems they present as *experiments*, valuing those which succeed, letting go of those which do not. One doesn't grade all the poems, only the best.

Everything I know about writing poetry I have learned from somebody. I am grateful to all the teachers, poets, editors, students, and colleagues whose touch is on this book.

A Word on the Second Edition

Chiefly, there are more *Poems to Consider* and more *Questions and Suggestions*. A few topics have been added to the discussion; a reader of the first edition will note especially *Balance, Imbalance* in Chapter 1, *Negative Capability* in Chapter 7, *A Note on Humor* in Chapter 9. Nearly everywhere, however, I have followed my own advice by tightening.

The rearrangement into thirteen (instead of fifteen) chapters will, I hope, be clarifying. Essentials in the vanished chapters have been moved elsewhere.

I am indebted for suggestions and complaints to Clemewell Young, Gary Pacernick, Robert D. Sutherland, Bonnie Jacobson, Vivian Shipley, Patrick Bros-towin, Roger Weaver, Diana Abu-Jaber, Brendan Galvin, Ben Wilson, and Bonnie L. Bedford, and to Joseph Opiela and Nancy DeCubellis at Little, Brown. None of them can be blamed, however, where I may have continued willfully to stray.

The young never know how deeply we are concerned for them. It is far more than a cliché that, as we must, we entrust to them the future of everything, including poetry. For we have seen our own mentors and especially older poets and poet-friends, who we thought would always be there to advise and to set the example, begin to fall away and vanish. "Timor mortis conturbat me" (The fear of death troubles me), as William Dunbar (1465–1520?) puts it in "Lament for the Makaris" (Makers). It is a heavy responsibility we pass along to the young, hoping that among them poets as fine, and poet-friends as selfless and lovely, as Dick Lattimore (1906–1983) will emerge.

Robert Wallace

CONTENTS

I Form: The Necessary Nothing

5   *Stanzas and Fixed Forms: Rooms, Houses, and an Old Man of Nantucket*   117

II   Content: The Essential Something

6   *Subject Matter: Roses and Fried Shoes*   157

III Process: Making the Poem Happen

I

Form:
The Necessary Nothing

Verse Is:
Catsup and Diamonds

Shakespeare was seventeen. None of his great poems was written, nor even imagined. That year—perhaps a year or two earlier or later—admiring a poem, he wrote one similar to it. Possibly his wasn't a very good poem, but it pleased him. He enjoyed having written it, enjoyed saying it over to himself aloud as he walked along. When the occasion arose, he wrote another poem, then another. Like him, all poets begin. Like them, Shakespeare had chosen to write in a form called verse.

He might as easily have chosen to write in prose since it is more akin to both the ordinary and the elevated speech of everyday affairs. Prose, too, may be impassioned, complex, and finely wrought, as is that of Shakespeare's contemporary, John Lyly. Some writers are drawn to prose and to the essays, stories, and novels for which prose is suitable. Others, electing the odd and ancient conventions of verse, write the poems that verse makes possible. What is verse, then? What are the substantial differences between verse and prose?

We may begin to answer that question by identifying the obvious difference. When you open a book, how do you know whether you are looking at prose or verse? Prose always continues across the printed page from left margin to an even right margin set arbitrarily, *externally*, by the printer. The printer determines when a new line begins, and the wider the page, the longer the line. On a page wide enough, an entire book of prose theoretically could be printed on one line.

Verse, however, is a system of writing in which the right margin, the line-turn, is determined *internally* by a mechanism contained within the line itself. Thus, no matter how wide the page, a poem is always printed in the same way. The poet, not the printer, determines line length, or measure.

The Greek word for measure is *meter* (as in *thermometer*, "heat measure"). In poetry the word *meter* traditionally refers to the conventions of verse by which poets measure their lines (for instance, iambic pentameter). *All* verse, though, even free verse, has some kind of measure—some rationale or system by which the poet breaks or ends lines. The choice of the measure may be intuitive or trained, but the nature of verse demands that the poet have a clear perception of the identity of each line, even if he or she cannot articulate the reasons.

This crucial aspect of verse is hidden in the etymology of the word itself. *Verse* comes from the Latin *versus*, which derives from the verb *verso, versare*, meaning "to turn." (This root appears in such familiar words as *reverse*, "to turn back.") Originally the past participle, *versus* literally meant *"having turned."* As a noun it came to mean *the turning of the plough*, hence *furrow*, and ultimately *row* or *line*. Thus, the English word *verse* refers to the *deliberate turning from line to line* that distinguishes verse from prose.

This deliberate turning of lines adds an element to verse that prose does not possess. The rhythm of prose is simply the linear cadence of the voice; in verse, however, this cadence constantly plays over the relatively fixed unit of **line.** The element of line gives verse an extraordinary, complex rhythmic potential of infinite variation.

Line-breaks may coincide with grammatical or syntactical units. This reinforces their regularity and emphasizes the normal speech pauses.

How many times,
I thought,
must winter come
and with its chill whiteness
slip-cover
field and town.

Line-breaks also may occur between grammatical or syntactical units, creating pauses and introducing unexpected emphases.

How
many times, I thought, must
winter
come and with its chill
whiteness
slip-cover field and
town.

When the end of a line coincides with a normal speech pause (usually at punctuation), the line is called **end-stopped,** as in these lines by John Milton (1608–1674) from *Paradise Lost:*

> As killing as the canker to the Rose,
> Or taint-worm to the weanling Herds that graze,
> Or Frost to Flowers, that their gay wardrobe wear

Lines that end without any parallel to normal speech pause are called **run-on** or **enjambed** (noun: **enjambment**), as in these lines of Milton:

> Of man's first disobedience, ‖ and the Fruit
> Of that forbidden Tree, ‖ whose mortal taste
> Brought Death into the World, ‖ and all our woe.

A **caesura** (‖), a normal speech pause that occurs within a line, may produce further variations of rhythm and counterpoint not possible in prose.

By varying the use of end-stop, run-on, and caesura and by playing sense, grammar, and syntax against them, the poet may produce an infinite range of effects. In the following passage note how Milton creates an effect of free-falling with these devices:

> Men called him Mulciber: and how he fell
> From Heaven they fabled, thrown by angry Jove
> Sheer o'er the crystal battlements: from morn
> To noon he fell, from noon to dewy eve,
> A summer's day, and with the setting sun   5
> Dropt from the zenith, like a falling star,
> On Lemnos, th' Aegean isle.

The emphatic pauses, or divisions of the action, occur within the lines; and the line-ends are primarily run-on.

Line

Line is the essence of verse. The poet's sensitivity to line, an awareness of its effect on the other elements of a poem, is central to craftsmanship. Consider this poem by an anonymous poet (ca. 1300), born more than two centuries before Shakespeare. Probably young and in love, he composed a quatrain now called "Western Wind."

> Western wind, when wilt thou blow,
>   The small rain down can rain?
> Christ, if my love were in my arms
>   And I in my bed again!

Perhaps a sailor away from home and missing his girl, the poet longs impatiently for spring when he will return to her. In prose he might have written something like this:

> I long for spring to come, with its westerly wind and its fine, nurturing rain; for then at last I will again hold my love in my arms and we will be in bed together!

Compare the poem and its prose imitation. What makes the poem especially effective?

Speaking *to* the wind, for instance, suggests isolation as well as loneliness, whereas in prose we address inanimate objects only rarely (as a man who has just struck his thumb with a hammer may address the hammer). In the poem both wind and the "small rain" are personified—**personification** is treating something inanimate as if it had the qualities of a person, such as sex or (here) volition—and "can rain" suggests that the rain shares the speaker's impatience for spring. By parallel, the direct address to the wind suggests that the exclamatory "Christ" in line 3 is also, in part, a prayer. The sailor's world (if a sailor he was) is a world of forces—wind, rain, and Christ—as the merely human world of my prose statement is not. The poem expresses the natural procreativity of the speaker's desire more passionately than the prose version does, so that the human in the poem seems, too, a force among forces. The incomplete conditional of lines 3–4 conveys more by ellipsis than the prose's explicit but flat "we will be in bed together." What is longed for is simply beyond words. The poem's singular "I in my bed again!" seems at once more vigorous and, because it is in some measure joking, less intimidated by circumstance than does the rather passive prose.

All of this—the dramatization, personification, implication—might be presented in prose, but it occurs more naturally, more succinctly in verse. The compression of verse calls for an alertness of attention, word by word, line by line, that we rarely give to prose. More happens in less space (and fewer words) in verse than in prose, which is habitually discursive and given to adding yet something further, drawing us onward to what is next and then next, and next again. We half expect the prose to continue, whereas the poem seems finished, complete, inviting us again and again to explore it. Prose, like a straight line, extends to the horizon. Verse, like a spiral, draws us into itself.

This reflexiveness of verse causes us to attend to, hear, *feel*, the poem's rhythm as we do not the prose's rhythm. Only two syllables in lines 1–2 (the second syllable of "Western" and "The") are not heavy. The lines are slow, dense, clogged, expressing the speaker's anguish and the ponderousness of waiting. By contrast, filled with light syllables (only "Christ," "love," "arms," "I," and "bed" have real weight), lines 3–4 seem to leap forward, expressing the speaker's eagerness for the eventual release of longing into forthright action. The poem's measuring of lines is also a measuring of feeling. Rhythm is meaning. The "equal" lines of verse differ more tellingly from one another than the elements of the freer, looser prose can do. The young sailor's desire, carrying its own music with it, is less a speech than a song.

Inviting attention line by line, verse holds a spatial dimension that prose cannot imitate. Consider "Me up at does" by E. E. Cummings (1894–1962).

Me up at does

out of the floor
quietly Stare

a poisoned mouse

still who alive   5

is asking What
have i done that

You wouldn't have

Here is the prose translation:

From the floor, a poisoned mouse, which is still alive, stares up at me quietly, asking, "What have I done that you wouldn't have?"

Note that the lines of the poem break the flow of the statement, isolating its elements for emphasis. Despite the poem's odd syntax, the scene seems easier to visualize in verse than in prose. The poem's verticality aids us in perceiving the ironic verticality of the exchange between the two protagonists: the "Me" appropriately stands above the "poisoned mouse." Like the speaker's gaze, the lines of the poem travel downward to the mouse. But the mouse's stare, and more-than-human indignation, travel up. It is as if the force of this counterface not only disconcerts the speaker but causes the poem's dislocations of syntax as well. In a sense the poem happens all at once on the page, while the coherently linear prose does not.

The disordered language registers the speaker's discomposure and simultaneously allows the poet to present the pieces of the scene in a dramatically effective sequence. He begins with the self-conscious, tense "Me up at does" and concludes with the mouse's silent question (which interestingly does not exhibit the rattled incoherence of the speaker's observation). The poem's four capitalized words ("Me," "You," "Stare," "What") sum up the little drama: the human arrogance of the poison, the bewildered dignity of the question. The lower-case "i" of the mouse's question underlines the simplicity of the animal in the face of the human. The speaker's "who" in line 5, instead of "which," suggestively registers his guilt.

The poem seems spontaneous, a fragmentary and unpremeditated evocation of the dramatic moment. But it is, in fact, carefully and very precisely structured. Every line has exactly four syllables. In effect, there are two stanzas, half-rhymed: *a b b a* ("does-floor-Stare-mouse" and "alive-What-that-have"). Each stanza, with its open lines, seems an eye. There are two eyes—an eye above, an eye below. There are two *I*'s, too—two creatures regarding one another across an irredeemable distance.

Ultimately, the inimitable effect of the poem derives from the *lines* of its verse. Cutting across the scene and feeling at mechanical intervals, the line-breaks bring the poem to life. As must be obvious from both "Western Wind" and "Me up at does," having something to say is only half of writing a poem, and may be the easier half. In everyday situations we value what is being said, not the way it is said. We require only that language be reasonably clear and informative. Even in newspapers and best sellers, we pay attention to **content** (the what-is-being-said), not to **form** (the way-it-is-said).

Literature, however—prose or verse—is language in which form is equal in importance to content. Poetry joins perfectly these two invariable halves: form and content, mode and meaning. We value a poem as we value a diamond for the form that the carbon takes under pressure. "What oft was thought, but ne'er so well expressed," said Alexander Pope. Shakespeare's *King Lear*, for example, is not only a great statement about the *human condition*, it is also a *great statement* about the human condition. The difference between someone handsome or pretty and someone not so handsome or pretty is a matter of the arrangement of features, the form of content.

Form

Why do we value form? Perhaps the answer lies in the secrets of our musculature, in our dark roots. Why do we live in square rooms? Why do we draw mechanical doodles when we are bored? Why do we tap our feet to music? Perhaps there is a profound link between the meter of verse and the human pulse, the rhythm of life itself—*te TUM te TUM te TUM*. The rhythmical impulse runs deep in us, and it is the basis of all the arts. We are pleased by symmetry, whether as children delighting in colored blocks of wood or as poets needing to make words rhyme. Hanging around language, seeing what tricks it can perform, is a crucial fascination for the poet. W. H. Auden says:

As a rule, the sign that a beginner has a genuine original talent is that he is more interested in playing with words than in saying something original; his attitude is that of the old lady, quoted by E. M. Forster—"How can I know what I think till I see what I say?"

Form is valuable because it preserves content, like our use of verse to remember which months have thirty days. We write a poem to keep fresh an experience or a person we care about; thus, the motive for writing a poem or story is not unlike that for taking photographs. We want to retain, however dimly or crudely, the light and the look of the moment. In a poem the thing is fixed, tied down, in the tightness of lines and rhymes. "Form alone," Henry James said, "*takes, and holds and preserves substance*—saves it from the welter of helpless verbiage that we swim in as in a sea of tasteless, tepid pudding."

When we try to express the thought, feeling, or event so well that it lasts as long as language itself, we escape (a little) the unremitting passage of all things into time, and we escape (a little) the endless bombardment of our senses. Works of art are machines for saving and clarifying experience. Robert Frost thought of a poem as "a momentary stay against confusion."

As simply as possible, form is the nothing, the magic or pressure, that is necessary to transform the ordinary carbon of experience into the forever-diamonds of art. Consider this simple case:

Going to Extremes
RICHARD ARMOUR   (b. 1906)

Shake and shake
    The catsup bottle.
None'll come—
    And then a lot'll.

That catsup bottles are poorly designed and blurt out gobs of the red goo is all too ordinary, familiar information. What makes us laugh is Armour's clever rhyme ("bottle-lot'll") with the contraction's surprising imitation of catsup's last-second, unexpected blurting. Form more than the content here is meaning.

Of course, form and content are inseparable in practice. Any utterance has both, and it is impossible to distinguish precisely between them. As consciousness is always embodied, every idea or feeling, when stated, has only the shape of the words used. Even the telephone book has form and rhythm ("Anderson, D. D., Anderson, D. R., Anderson, D. S., Anderson, E. B., Anderson, George"); but in a poem that pleases us, what works is the concord of the two, form and content. Often, when a poem "doesn't work," there may be a discord; an elegy written in galloping rhythm is ludicrous:

My old Harry is dead and is gone to his rest,
Who was always in all ways the bravest and best.

Fluid and Solid Forms

Poetic form may be thought of as being of two general kinds. In "A Retrospect," Ezra Pound distinguishes between what he calls **"fluid"** and **"solid" forms.** Some poems, he says, "may have form as a tree has form, some as water poured into a vase." Mighty literary quarrels have been fought over the preference, movements have been formed, manifestoes hurled. But both sorts of poetic form make good poems. Fluid (or **open**) form is organic, like a tree's growth. Solid (or **closed**) form is symmetrical, like water poured into a vase. Both are natural, and so long as the poet is willing not to be theory-bound, he or she may use whichever a given poem wants.

Fluid, organic form, in which the form "only" expresses the content, is an ideal no one could disagree with. Emerson suggested succinctly, "Ask the fact for the form." Charles Olson, elder statesman of the "Beats" and proponent of fluid form, presents the ideal this way in his famous essay "Projective Verse":

> FORM IS NEVER MORE THAN AN EXTENSION OF CONTENT. (Or so it got phrased by one R. Creeley, and it makes absolute sense to me, with this possible corollary, that right form, in any given poem, is the only and exclusively possible extension of content under hand.)

In practice, however, it must remain a dangerous matter of faith or pride for a poet to conclude that he or she has found the "only and exclusively possible" form for what he or she is saying. A poet's freedom to invent or discover a poem's form experimentally is also a hard discipline. Fluid form has made possible poems as finely wrought as Walt Whitman's "A Noiseless Patient Spider" (page 13), Ezra Pound's exquisitely conversational "The Garden" (page 22), and Charles Simic's magical "Stone" (page 24). But it has also, unhappily, justified a deluge of sloppy, raggedy, cavalier poems, more fluid than form—as many, surely, as there have been sloppy, overstuffed, padded sonnets or villanelles.

The problem with wanting form to be nothing more than expression of content is that it is impossible. Beginning poets might pin to the lampshades on their desks this poem by Robert Francis (b. 1901):

Glass

Words of a poem should be glass
But glass so simple-subtle its shape
Is nothing but the shape of what it holds.

A glass spun for itself is empty,
Brittle, at best Venetian trinket.   5
Embossed glass hides the poem or its absence.

Words should be looked through, should be windows.
The best word were invisible.
The poem is the thing the poet thinks.

If the impossible were not   10
And if the glass, only the glass,
Could be removed, the poem would remain.

Ideally, form is the necessary nothing.

Whether fluid or solid, form must express content. Because each poem is a new creation, one ideally gives it the form it needs, without regard to theory. Invented forms are neither better nor worse, in general, than adapted forms, only better or worse for the job at hand.

The sonnet, for instance, is one of the most difficult fixed forms, but its structure may well *help* the poet write a poem, just as a good interviewer's questions draw a coherent account from a witness. Consider how the material of Sonnet 73 by William Shakespeare (1564–1616) fills and fits the three quatrains and single couplet of the Elizabethan sonnet:

That time of year thou mayst in me behold
When yellow leaves, or none, or few, do hang
Upon those boughs which shake against the cold,
Bare ruined choirs° where late the sweet birds sang.   *choirlofts*
In me thou see'st the twilight of such day   5
As after sunset fadeth in the west,
Which by-and-by black night doth take away,
Death's second self that seals up all in rest.
In me thou see'st the glowing of such fire
That on the ashes of his youth doth lie,   10
As the deathbed whereon it must expire,
Consumed with that which it was nourished by.
  This thou perceiv'st, which makes thy love more strong,
  To love that well which thou must leave ere long.

The theme is the poet's aging. In the three quatrains he compares his age to three things: autumn, the dying of the year; twilight, the dying of the day; and glowing ashes, the dying of the fire. Because the fixed quatrains emphasize the threefold comparison, Shakespeare has accurately used an Elizabethan sonnet (three quatrains and a couplet) rather than a Petrarchan sonnet (octave and sestet). The couplet at the end, with its difference in tone, presents a resolving statement of the problem offered in the quatrains. Form and content are in harmony.

Note that the order of the quatrains corresponds to a mounting anguish of feeling. The movement is, in the first place, from a bare winter-daylight scene to a twilight scene, and then to a night scene, the time when a fire is usually allowed to die. The progression from day to dusk to night emphasizes and supports the image of night as "Death's second self" and possibly suggests night as the time one most fears dying.

Another progression is at work in the three images: each of the *dyings* is shorter and more constricted than the last, as though the speaker were aware of the quickening of death's approach. The first comparison is to a season's dying, the second to a day's dying, and the third to a fire's dying. In its preoccupation with time, the first quatrain looks backward to summer, when "late the sweet birds sang." The second looks forward to "Death" explicitly and inevitably ("by-and-by"). The third imagines the coming night/death, when death is no longer a prospect but a reality: "deathbed." The increasingly narrow, bleak images of the three quatrains enhance the speaker's sense of loss and depletion in aging. There echoes throughout the poem's images a story of an old man's death during the night after a cold winter day.

The constraint of the sonnet form dramatically matches that of the speaker. He addresses the trouble of aging only indirectly, through inanimate images, as though he held its personal implications at a distance. The apparent composure is, however, deceptive. Each of the three images begins with a more positive tone than it ends with. The increasingly self-diminishing revisions in line 2 offer a clear example: "yellow leaves, or none, or few." The yellow leaves, like the "twilight" and the "glowing" of the fire, are attempts at an optimism that the speaker cannot maintain. In each of the images he is compelled to say what he originally seems to have wanted to withhold, even from his own consciousness.

Intended as a compliment to the lover on the strength of her love, the couplet begins on a positive note: "This thou perceiv'st, which makes thy love more strong." But the next line betrays the speaker's fears because he does not say, as we might expect, "To love that well which thou must *lose* ere long"; rather, "To love that well which thou must *leave* ere long." He sees his death as *her* leaving him, not the other way around. Throughout the poem, the speaker has expressed, not his self-image, but what he imagines to be his lover's image of him: "thou mayst in me behold," "In me thou see'st," and "This thou perceiv'st." By "leave" in line 14 he need not mean more than "leave behind," but the bitter taste of jealousy is on the word. He does not say, "To love *me* well *whom*," nor even "To love *him* well *whom*," but "To love *that* well *which*." The poet refers to himself as a thing, as though time had robbed him, in his lover's eyes, of manhood. Thus, the full weight of his fear of being rejected, replaced, falls on his odd choice of the word "leave." The complimentary statement of the poem stands, of course, but we feel the swirl of dramatic currents beneath its surface.

Such delicate precision of content in form is equally possible in fluid forms.

A Noiseless Patient Spider
WALT WHITMAN   (1819–1892)

A noiseless patient spider,
I marked where on a little promontory it stood isolated,
Marked how to explore the vacant vast surrounding,
It launched forth filament, filament, filament, out of itself,
Ever unreeling them, ever tirelessly speeding them.   5

And you O my soul where you stand,
Surrounded, detached, in measureless oceans of space,
Ceaselessly musing, venturing, throwing, seeking the spheres to connect
    them,
Till the bridge you will need be formed, till the ductile anchor hold,
Till the gossamer thread you fling catch somewhere, O my soul.   10

The spacious lines, unreeling loosely out across the page, correspond to the long filaments the spider strings out into the wind when it is preparing to construct a web. The two equal stanzas, one for the description of the spider, one for the soul's "musing, venturing, throwing, seeking," perfectly shape the poem's central comparison.

The comparison of the spider's "unreeling" and the soul's "throwing" is not presented mechanically. The spider's activities, described in stanza 1, are neither explained nor resolved until the last line of stanza 2. The success of the soul's "gossamer thread," catching and anchoring, implies a similar success for the spider. Notice the verbal echoes between various words in the two stanzas: "stood"/ "stand," "surrounding"/"Surrounded," "tirelessly"/"Ceaselessly." Similar links bridge the images, as in the contrast of small to grand scale with "on a little promontory," followed in stanza 2 by "measureless oceans of space." After "promontory" (a headland or cliff jutting out into the ocean), the images of "oceans of space," "bridge," and "anchor" lend unity to the comparison. Like the spider's action, the poem's apparent randomness is in fact careful and purposeful.

Alliteration and assonance give some of the lines a unity of sound and emphasize the linear, filamentlike structure: *m*'s in line 2, *f*'s in line 4, and long *e*'s in "unreeling" and "speeding" in line 5. The half-hidden rhyme in lines 9–10 ("hold"/"soul") suggests the success of both the spider's and the soul's ventures. The caesural pause after "somewhere," so near the end of the last line, also suggests that the long line makes contact with something akin, not alien.

Although Shakespeare's Sonnet 73 is an example of solid form and Whitman's "A Noiseless Patient Spider" of fluid form, these poems are more alike, as verse, than different. Both demand and reward careful attention. There need be no war to the death between fluid and solid form, between sonnets and free verse. Practically, there is a richness of choice for the poet concerned with writing his or her next poem. Classic forms such as sonnets are new and contemporary when they are used for fresh purposes, as in E. E. Cummings's "next to of course god america i" (page 130) or Robert Frost's "Design" (page 344). The poet, writing as one must in the language and styles of a particular time, but keeping an eye on what poets of the past have done, must neither accept the moment's fashions too easily nor fear them.

Balance, Imbalance

Form is a poem's—a poet's—way of letting us notice things. The packed, heavy syllables of lines 1–2 of "Western Wind," for instance, contrast with the quick, lighter syllables of lines 3–4, showing at least two different tones or elements of the speaker's complex feelings (sadness, elation in prospect). A single line may, in its balance or imbalance, make us aware rhythmically of something unstated or only implicit in its meaning. So the last line of "A Noiseless Patient Spider," in its two very uneven parts: the long wavering "Till the gossamer thread you fling catch somewhere" and the short, ending fixity of "O my soul." Similarly, the imbalances of Milton's lines about Mulciber help give the illusion of falling in space.

A line, being the unit of verse, may have its own inner structure of relationships. One feels, for example, the antitheses or strict balancing of parts in these lines from Alexander Pope's "The Rape of the Lock" (1714):

> Whether the nymph shall break Diana's Law,
> Or some frail *China* Jar receive a Flaw,
> Or stain her Honour, or her new Brocade,
> Forget her Pray'rs, or miss a Masquerade,
> Or lose her Heart, or Necklace, at a Ball . . .

II, 105–109

The irony of course is in the apparent treating of the important and the trivial with equal significance: to lose her chastity or to crack a China jar, to stain her honor or a mere brocade, and so on. The first contrast balances in two lines, but then the madness of misplaced values escalates and each line contains its own pithy contrast. Two heavily accented syllables on each side of the caesuras underline the balance rhythmically:

> Or stain her Honour, ‖ or her new Brocade,
> Forget her Pray'rs, ‖ or miss a Masquerade,
> Or lose her Heart, ‖ or Necklace, at a Ball . . .

The balance or imbalance may be—usually is—a good deal subtler than in Pope's lines; and it may function equally in poems in meter or in poems in free verse. In an elegant essay, "Listening and Making," Robert Hass points out the rhythmical imbalance in these lines (4–5) from Whitman's "Song of Myself":

> I loáf and invíte my soúl,
> I leán and loáf at my éase‖obsérving a spéar of súmmer grás.

The rhythm of the first line (three accents) is essentially repeated by the first part of the second line (three accents); but the second part not only extends the line but does so by *four* accents. Hass's notation of the accents by line, with a single slash showing caesura: 3, 3/4. He comments: "Had Whitman written *observing a spear of grass*, all three phrases would be nearly equivalent . . .; instead he adds *summer*, the leaning and loafing season, and announces both at the level of sound and of content that this poem is going to be free and easy."

As a further example Hass offers this little poem by Whitman:

A Farm Picture

Through the ample open door of the peaceful country barn,
A sunlit pasture field with cattle and horses feeding.
And haze and vista, and the far horizon fading away.

Each line has six accents, divided (by a light phrasal pause or caesura in lines 1–2) in this way:

    3 / 3
    3 / 3
    2 / 4

The asymmetry of line 3 (2/4) effectively resolves the pattern (as a 3/3 version of the line might not), releasing the tension, letting the rhythm come to rest in the longer, four-accent phrase, "and the far horizon fading away." (Hass's argument takes him in a different direction, so let it be clear that he is not to blame for the rest of this commentary. But do look up his essay in *Twentieth Century Pleasures*, Ecco, 1984.)

Each of the poem's three lines presents an element in the "Picture": line 1, the close-up frame of the peaceful barn's doorway; line 2, the cattle and horses in the middle distance; and line 3, the distant—"and the far horizon fading away." What's *seen* in any particularity are the cattle and horses in the "sunlit pasture field." Curiously, the barn isn't really seen: the epithet "peaceful" is abstract and we only look *through* the open doorway; the distance is utterly indefinite. "Peaceful" does, ironically, characterize the speaker's vantage point—things in their places, order, ampleness. The barn is the cattle's and horses' home or storehouse, from which they go only a short way, to the pasture, to feed. The asymmetry of line 3, however, helps to make this implicit point: the speaker's attention is drawn beyond the peaceful and ample to the doubtful and far-off. For the pretty scene is felt as melancholy, whether because the horizon ("vista") implies an elsewhere to which the speaker could go or because it ("fading") implies some threat in the solidity of the peaceful near-at-hand. After the slight caesuras (unmarked by punctuation) in lines 1–2, the more decisive caesura in line 3 helps give a sense of incompleteness, of division, in the perception of the distant and vaguer haze, vista, and horizon. Lines 1–2 are joined by a comma into a single sentence. Line 3 stands as a sentence by itself.

Moreover, we feel the poem as static. Neither sentence has a main verb. The speaker does not mention himself (as he might: "I see a sunlit pasture . . ."), but he is present *as an absence*, for he is strongly implied by his vantage point ("Through the ample open door . . ."). This detachment from the near and ample scene perhaps suggests his dissatisfaction with it. Probably, we sense, the poem's un-expected air of sadness arises from an unfulfilled and perhaps not yet even focussed longing. The poem's last and longest phrase, "and the far horizon fading away," lets it end with a lingering attention to what is both distant and vanishing. The line's imbalance fixes its emphasis.

Look again at the couplet of Shakespeare's Sonnet 73. Its peculiar dolefulness no doubt comes in part from the lines' succession of virtually heavy, monosyllabic accents. (It would be hard not to count "thy" and "ere.")

This thóu perceív'st,‖which mákes thý lóve móre stróng,
To lóve that wéll‖which thóu múst leáve ére lóng.

The sense of unresolved feeling no doubt comes also in part from the pattern of accents:

3 / 5
3 / 5

(Metrically, both lines pause exactly between the second and third foot.) The lack of change leaves the tension unrelieved. There is a certain grimness, too, in the unrelenting parallel of the two "which" clauses.

Space and Object

Because nothing in a poem is waste, even the space between the lines or stanzas may be significant. As in Cummings's "Me up at does" or Whitman's "A Noiseless Patient Spider," the relationship between space and object is no less the concern of the poet than it is of the sculptor. Consider this sometimes mis-understood poem by Robert Frost (1874–1963):

Dust of Snow

The way a crow
Shook down on me
The dust of snow
From a hemlock tree

Has given my heart   5
A change of mood
And saved some part
Of a day I had rued.

The division of the poem into two stanzas reveals the balance of the two elements in its statement: subject and predicate; the scene and the feeling it produced; cause, effect. The symmetry draws attention to the fact that the poem's statement is a paradox.

A crow is negative, a bad omen. The image "dust of snow" is unpleasant, suggesting disuse, neglect, or even a kind of baptism in the cold of death or ruin; and the hemlock, a cemetery tree, as well as one from which a poison is made, suggests death. Thus, the event described in stanza 1 is unpleasant, and ought to make the speaker miserable. Surprisingly, the feeling produced is cheering: "saved some part / Of a day" he would otherwise have regretted.

Frost doesn't say anything so banal as that something good happened to him and made him feel good. Rather, something uncomfortable made him, strangely enough, feel better. The most significant detail in the poem may well be that space between the quatrains, the two parts of the speaker's thought, that makes us balance and compare. "Dust of Snow" leaves unanswered the question of why the speaker was cheered by a disagreeable experience. But the mystery makes us puzzle over the poem and pushes us back to the first line: "The *way* a crow." How might a crow shake snow from a tree so that someone would feel his day had been "saved"? By alighting, by resettling, or by departing? The poem seems to hint that any reader should be able to imagine which of these it was.

A good poem nearly always lets the reader complete it by suggesting, implying more than it states.

QUESTIONS AND SUGGESTIONS

1. Here are two poems printed as prose. Experiment with turning them into verse by dividing the lines in different ways for different effects. The originals, as well as all further notes to the Questions and Suggestions, will be found in Appendix I.

   a) *For a Lady I Know*

   She even thinks that up in heaven her class lies late and snores, while poor black cherubs rise at seven to do celestial chores.

   b) *Potatoes*

   Grandpa said potatoes reminded him of school. Potatoes and school. He said he'd wake nearly freezing, kindle a fire and throw two potatoes on. Going to school he carried them to warm his hands. To warm his feet he ran. He said by noontime those potatoes almost froze, said he ate a lot of cold potatoes for lunch.

2. Compare the next poem with Whitman's "A Noiseless Patient Spider" (page 13). How has what the poet is saying influenced her formal decisions? Perhaps write a poem of your own about a spider, choosing the form carefully.

Spider

JAN M. W. ROSE*

Afraid for both of them,
her movements, uncertain,
she lightfoots it between

twelve intersections of thread
and an odd collector's item: 5
a strange dark bug she keeps

knotted in a silk pouch
tight as a cherry pit.
Gnats hover in the moist air

languorous with conversation.   10
"She's strange" they murmur,
riding tiny currents of air.

About her are slung
a dozen males,
bulging in their white hammocks,   15

shimmering in porch light.
Even as she wanders,
legs tapping the wires

like piano strings,
they bob up and down,   20
suspended hard in sleep.

But her long worn Utility
chooses none; the captive males
curl tighter in their nets;

and dropping her blue-white line,   25
for a moment—she fidgets—
then turns into shadow.

*Throughout *Writing Poems,* an asterisk following the poet's name indicates that the
poem was written when the poet was a student.

3. Consider how much "In the Morning, In the Morning," written in 1895 by
A. E. Housman (1859–1936), depends on implication. How do we know that the
characters are lovers? How are we led to understand what has happened? What lets
us know that they are regretful?

In the morning, in the morning,
    In the happy field of hay,
Oh they looked at one another
    By the light of day.

In the blue and silver morning
    On the haycock as they lay,
Oh they looked at one another
    And they looked away.

4. Study the line-breaks of this poem. Is any principle of division deducible from
the length or handling of line or from the poem's appearance? Why has the poet
not used stanzas?

Move into the Wheat

SUZANNE RASCHKE*

Blond heads of grain gods
Loll on the hills.
Farmers understand.
The rest of us keep
Small towns between these hills,   5
Watch the sway of hair,
And try to brush off
Our ripening desire
To move into the wheat
And sleep among gods.   10

Like golden bodies from the black
Earth, sun-bleached tassels stretch
Into August. It is September,
Still they sleep until
Farmers go to wake them,   15
Turn the golden bodies,
Toss back their heads and comb
Hair from their faces.
We see their eyes,
Black as the empty beds   20
Where they slept until harvest.
Later, when I watch
Grains of gold in your eyes
Hide, at dark, I see
Their eyes. Tonight   25
While you sleep my desire
Ripens. I tell myself, "Tomorrow
I will move into the wheat."

5. In the spring of 1854 Henry David Thoreau (1817–1862) jotted down a couplet in his journal. He gave it *two* last lines, and himself never chose between them. If it were your poem, which version of the second line would you choose? Why?

    a) When the toads begin to ring,
       Then thinner clothing bring.

    b) When the toads begin to ring,
       Off your greatcoat fling.

6. In his essay Robert Hass considers these possible versions of the last line of Whitman's "A Farm Picture." (The last is, of course, the original.) What differences in meaning *and* in rhythm do these variations produce? In each, how is the lines' balance/imbalance working?

Through the ample open door of the peaceful country barn,
A sunlit pasture field with cattle and horses feeding.
And haze, and vista.

Through the ample open door of the peaceful country barn,
A sunlit pasture field with cattle and horses feeding.
And haze and vista, and the far horizon.

Through the ample open door of the peaceful country barn,
A sunlit pasture field with cattle and horses feeding.
And haze and vista, and the far horizon fading.

Through the ample open door of the peaceful country barn,
A sunlit pasture field with cattle and horses feeding,
And haze and vista, and the far horizon fading away.

7. Look ahead to Shakespeare's Sonnets 55 (page 111), 30 (page 239), and 130 (page 247). In the lines of each final couplet, what rhythmical balance/imbalance do you find? How is the feeling or mood of the poems' endings affected? Read them aloud several times before deciding.

8. Choose a simple object—a stone, a twig, a leaf, a wristwatch, for example—and study it slowly and carefully with each of your five senses (sight, hearing, smell, taste, touch) in turn. Don't be shy about tasting a watch or listening to a twig! Then write a sentence or two of description for each sense. Comparisons are fine. ("It feels like a flat, closed bowl or box. Heavy. There's a little button on the side that probably opens the lid.")

   Any surprises? Might there be a poem in it? Have a look at Charles Simic's "Stone" (page 24). (This exercise is based on a suggestion by poet-teacher Clemewell Young.)

POEMS TO CONSIDER

The Girl in the Red Convertible   *1971*

GARY GILDNER   (b. 1938)

The girl in the red convertible
with the heater going full blast
and her throat knocking
turns off the lights
on the road to Winterset   5
and rolls toward the moon
resting expressionless
on the next hill.

When the car stops coasting
it is still June, and   10
she is at the edge

of a field, waiting . . .
She has a
"fifty-fifty chance." It—
that expression—is quietly   15
eating her eyeballs . . .

At dawn a cow appears; then
another. Taking all the time
they need. If only something
would break—break open   20
so she could scream—
Finally there are nine lined up
along the fence—
like visitors to the zoo.

The Garden   *1916*

En robe de parade.
       SAMAIN

EZRA POUND (1885–1972)

Like a skein of loose silk blown against a wall
She walks by the railing of a path in Kensington Gardens°,   *park in London*
And she is dying piece-meal
    of a sort of emotional anæmia.

And round about there is a rabble   5
Of the filthy, sturdy, unkillable infants of the very poor.
They shall inherit the earth.

In her is the end of breeding.
Her boredom is exquisite and excessive.
She would like some one to speak to her,   10
And is almost afraid that I
    will commit that indiscretion.

Player Piano

JOHN UPDIKE   (b. 1932)

My stick fingers click with a snicker
And, chuckling, they knuckle the keys;
Light-footed, my steel feelers flicker
And pluck from these keys melodies.

My paper can caper; abandon   5
Is broadcast by dint of my din,
And no man or band has a hand in
The tones I turn on from within.

At times I'm a jumble of rumbles,
At others I'm light like the moon,   10
But never my numb plunker fumbles,
Misstrums me, or tries a new tune.

Loving in Truth, and Fain
in Verse My Love to Show

SIR PHILIP SIDNEY   (1554–1586)

Loving in truth, and fain in verse my love to show,
That she, dear she, might take some pleasure of my pain,
Pleasure might cause her read, reading might make her know,
Knowledge might pity win, and pity grace obtain,
I sought fit words to paint the blackest face of woe,   5
Studying inventions fine, her wits to entertain,
Oft turning others' leaves, to see if thence would flow
Some fresh and fruitful showers upon my sunburnt brain.
But words came halting forth, wanting Invention's stay;
Invention, Nature's child, fled step-dame Study's blows;   10
And others' feet still seemed but strangers in my way.
Thus great with child to speak, and helpless in my throes,
Biting my truant pen, beating myself for spite:
"Fool," said my Muse to me, "look in thy heart and write."

Stone

CHARLES SIMIC   (b. 1938)

Go inside a stone
That would be my way.
Let somebody else become a dove
Or gnash with a tiger's tooth.
I am happy to be a stone.   5

From the outside the stone is a riddle:
No one knows how to answer it.
Yet within, it must be cool and quiet
Even though a cow steps on it full weight,
Even though a child throws it in a river;   10
The stone sinks, slow, unperturbed
To the river bottom
Where the fishes come to knock on it
And listen.

I have seen sparks fly out   15
When two stones are rubbed,
So perhaps it is not dark inside after all;
Perhaps there is a moon shining
From somewhere, as though behind a hill—   20
Just enough light to make out
The strange writings, the star-charts
On the inner walls.

Howard

GLENN BROOKE*

A fisherman, Howard goes down to the Ohio River
every day; there is nothing else.
He cuts a fresh willow rod, and settles himself
by the same muddy pool below the B&O tracks,
on his usual knob of damp slate.   5

Howard never baits his hook. He waits.
He looks at the dimple where his twill line
disappears into the brown water,
hardly looking up or down or away.
"Tis enough," he says.   10

My mother says Howard is crazy;
our preacher, who has prayed earnestly,
says Howard is the greatest fisherman in the world.
We accept Howard with the patience of farmers,
with the faith of great depths in rivers.   15

Howard has never caught a fish.
There, in his cord coat and patch cap,
he endures season upon season, the comings and goings
of barges and children, and the backwater fogs
drifting in and out, like doubts, like legends.   20

Hamlen Brook   1982

RICHARD WILBUR   (b. 1921)

   At the alder-darkened brink
 Where the stream slows to a lucid jet
I lean to the water, dinting its top with sweat,
   And see, before I can drink,

   A startled inchling trout   5
 Of spotted near-transparency,
Trawling a shadow solider than he.
   He swerves now, darting out

   To where, in a flicked slew
 Of sparks and glittering silt, he weaves   10
Through stream-bed rocks, disturbing foundered leaves,
   And butts then out of view

   Beneath a sliding glass
 Crazed by the skimming of a brace

Of burnished dragon-flies across its face,   15
    In which deep cloudlets pass

    And a white precipice
Of mirrored birch-trees plunges down
Toward where the azures of the zenith drown.   20
    How shall I drink all this?

    Joy's trick is to supply
Dry lips with what can cool and slake,
Leaving them dumbstruck also with an ache
    Nothing can satisfy.

The Idea of Order at Key West   1934

WALLACE STEVENS   (1879–1955)

She sang beyond the genius of the sea.
The water never formed to mind or voice,
Like a body wholly body, fluttering
Its empty sleeves; and yet its mimic motion
Made constant cry, caused constantly a cry,   5
That was not ours although we understood,
Inhuman, of the veritable ocean.

The sea was not a mask. No more was she.
The song and water were not medleyed sound
Even if what she sang was what she heard,   10
Since what she sang was uttered word by word.
It may be that in all her phrases stirred
The grinding water and the gasping wind;
But it was she and not the sea we heard.

For she was the maker of the song she sang.   15
The ever-hooded, tragic-gestured sea
Was merely a place by which she walked to sing.
Whose spirit is this? we said, because we knew
It was the spirit that we sought and knew
That we should ask this often as she sang.   20

If it was only the dark voice of the sea
That rose, or even colored by many waves;
If it was only the outer voice of sky
And cloud, of the sunken coral water-walled,
However clear, it would have been deep air,   25
The heaving speech of air, a summer sound
Repeated in a summer without end
And sound alone. But it was more than that,
More even than her voice, and ours, among
The meaningless plungings of water and the wind,   30
Theatrical distances, bronze shadows heaped
On high horizons, mountainous atmospheres
Of sky and sea.
                        It was her voice that made
The sky acutest at its vanishing.
She measured to the hour its solitude.   35
She was the single artificer of the world
In which she sang. And when she sang, the sea,
Whatever self it had, became the self
That was her song, for she was the maker. Then we,
As we beheld her striding there alone,   40
Knew that there never was a world for her
Except the one she sang and, singing, made.

Ramon Fernandez°, tell me, if you know,   *a French critic*
Why, when the singing ended and we turned
Toward the town, tell why the glassy lights,   45
The lights in the fishing boats at anchor there,
As the night descended, tilting in the air,
Mastered the night and portioned out the sea,
Fixing emblazoned zones and fiery poles,
Arranging, deepening, enchanting night.   50

Oh! Blessed rage for order, pale Ramon,
The maker's rage to order words of the sea,
Words of the fragrant portals, dimly-starred,
And of ourselves and of our origins,
In ghostlier demarcations, keener sounds.   55

Free Verse:
Invisible Nets and Trellises

Fluid form has several names, including organic or open form. The most familiar name, of course, is **free verse**. Borrowed from the French *vers libre*, the term means verse written without a particular or recognizable meter. Since verse requires some system of measure, some internal signal when a new line should begin, the term *free verse* may seem self-contradictory. Indeed, verse that really is free of any measure often ends up as arbitrary, random, "chopped-up prose." Robert Frost compares such verse to playing tennis without a net—too easy, no fun. W. H. Auden describes the problem:

> The poet who writes "free" verse is like Robinson Crusoe on his desert island: he must do all his cooking, laundry and darning for himself. In a few exceptional cases, this manly independence produces something original and impressive, but more often the result is squalor—dirty sheets on the unmade bed and empty bottles on the unswept floor.

Even Ezra Pound, who championed free verse in 1912, was very soon complaining about the sloppy free verse being written:

> Indeed *vers libre* has become as prolix and as verbose as any of the flaccid varieties that preceded it. It has brought faults of its own. The actual language and

phrasing is often as bad as that of our elders without even the excuse that the words are shovelled in to fill a metric pattern or to complete the noise of a rhyme-sound.

He concluded:

Eliot has said the thing very well when he said, No *vers* is *libre* for the man who wants to do a good job.

Despite the dangers of slackness, free verse is a useful form. *The Princeton Encyclopedia of Poetry and Poetics* notes that free verse "has become so common as to have some claim to being the characteristic form of the age." Many finely wrought, even formal poems have been written in free verse; and finally that must be the test—the form is good that works.

There is, however, little practical theory of free verse. Poets who have written successfully have done so largely through intuition. A well-tuned ear—a delicate sensitivity to language—finds the right form, right rhythm, which, in Pound's words, "corresponds exactly to the emotion or shade of emotion to be expressed." Poets often do this without being able to explain how, just as readers may respond to such rhythms without knowing, technically, why. Charles Olson's view, passed along by Allen Ginsberg, that length of line is somehow determined by the poet's breath, seems purely impressionistic and of little use in practice. (Do poets who write very short lines, for instance, suffer from emphysema?) William Carlos Williams's notion of the "variable foot," suggestive though it is, is also vague. His rhythms and forms may be imitated, but there is no satisfactory account of the principles underlying them.

To discover what will be useful to you as a beginning poet, you must find tempting models and work experimentally from them in developing your own free verse. And, until there is an adequate theory (and historical account), you may find a few rough distinctions valuable. Three basic types of free verse, I think, can be distinguished. They may be called end-stopped, run-on, and spatial, though, of course, any given poem may be a mixture of these and there are a number of subtypes of each.

End-Stopped Free Verse

The father of modern end-stopped free verse is Walt Whitman (1819–1892), although there are historical antecedents in the "verse" of the King James Bible of 1611 (especially in Psalms, Ecclesiastes, and chapter 38 of Job), in Christopher Smart's *Rejoice in the Lamb,* and in William Blake's prophetic poems in the eighteenth century. Walt Whitman's "A Noiseless Patient Spider" (page 13) exemplifies end-stopped free verse, as does the first section of "Song of Myself" (1855):

I celebrate myself, and sing myself,
And what I assume you shall assume,
for every atom belonging to me as good belongs to you.

I loaf and invite my soul,
I lean and loaf at my ease observing a spear of summer grass.   5

My tongue, every atom of my blood, formed from this soil, this air,
Born here of parents born here from parents the same, and their
                                          parents the same,
I, now thirty-seven years old in perfect health begin,
Hoping to cease not till death.

Creeds and schools in abeyance,   10
Retiring back a while suffced at what they are, but never forgotten,
I harbor for good or bad, I permit to speak at every hazard,
Nature without check with original energy.

In this passage the line-breaks occur at syntactical or grammatical pauses or
intervals; that, simply, identifies end-stopped free verse. Although the lines vary
considerably in length, they are generally long and loose, allowing for great variety
in rhythm with or without internal pauses (caesuras). They are essentially in prose
rhythm, that is, rangy and irregular, but are heightened by recurring phrases, as in
lines 7–8, or by recurring parallel structures, as in lines 4–5. Whitman's rhythms
and patterns of rhythms are often oratorical and prophetic, as are the rhythms in
the later end-stopped free verse of Carl Sandburg or Allen Ginsberg. Typically, the
Whitman manner and gesture are grand. It is interesting that the first line is
written in traditional iambic pentameter:

I célĕbráte mўsélf, ănd síng mўsélf.

Whitman's use of that meter seems to imply that his free verse was essentially an
opening up of the traditional line of English metrical verse.

    End-stopped free verse tends toward long lines because they permit internal
pauses and greater internal rhythmic variation. When there are pauses and syntactical intervals that do not fall at line-ends, those that do are doubly emphatic,
whereas the internal pauses are minimized and lightly passed over. The muscular
cadence of end-stopped free verse derives in large part from the tension between
these two kinds of pauses.

    Short lines of end-stopped free verse diminish the possibility of internal pause
and variation. In the logical extreme—where every syntactical unit is given an
individual line—the tension disappears and all that remains is chopped prose.
Suppose the sixth line of the passage were rearranged:

My tongue,
every atom of my blood,
formed from this soil,
this air . . .

The result merely parallels the phrasal pauses of a prose statement. Beginners often mistakenly divide lines this way, and the impact is about as arresting, in its lack of variety, as a stack of lumber or dishes. Line in verse, however one measures or defines it, must somehow *cut across* the natural flow of sentences, at least often enough to allow one to distinguish its rhythm from prose.

End-stopped free verse may, of course, be written in lines shorter than Whitman's. "The Garden" by Ezra Pound (page 22) is an instance, as is this very droll poem of his:

The Three Poets

Candidia has taken a new lover
And three poets are gone into mourning.
The first has written a long elegy to 'Chloris,'
To 'Chloris chaste and cold,' his 'only Chloris.'
The second has written a sonnet   5
            upon the mutability of woman,
And the third writes an epigram to Candidia.

The syntactical units are long enough to allow for rhythmical variation, and Pound has treated the end of the very long line 5 as a "dropped" line ("upon the mutability of woman") to provide further variation and indicate subordination. While this phrase is long enough to justify a line of its own, note how wooden the movement is when the line begins at the left margin:

The second has written a sonnet
Upon the mutability of woman,
And the third writes an epigram to Candidia.

The dropped-line not only adds flexibility but also prepares, like a whip whirling backwards, for the rhythmic decisiveness and snap of the last line. After the first three lines, each of which contains a simple sentence structure (subject, verb, object), the fourth line ("To 'Chloris chaste . . .' ") is a subordinate appositional clause on a line by itself—and with a caesural pause as well. Throughout, not one of the poem's three sentences lies across the verse lines in the same way. As a consequence, the pace is lithe and sinewy, suitable to the poem's satiric point.

Each of the first two poets is mocked, in different ways. The triple repetition of the first poet's fancy literary name for Candidia—"Chloris," handled in quotation marks like tongs—underlines his tedious pomposity and indirection. His elegy is "long." The second poet's sonnet, albeit brief enough, is pompously on an inappropriately huge and abstract theme, "the mutability of woman." The dropped line transforms that otherwise weighty phrase into a sardonic aside. The comma at the end of line 6, where we might expect a period, hurries the voice on to the last line where the wit seems quick and offhand. The shift to the present tense— "writes"—indicates that Pound's speaker *is* the third poet, and that this poem is his "epigram to Candidia." Far from being soulful, the epigram *to* Candidia is not even about her, but about the two silly poets—which is perhaps his way of registering how little he is hurt by her having taken (note the word!) a new lover.

Other poems in end-stopped free verse to which an interested reader may want to look ahead are J. D. Reed's "The Weather Is Brought to You" (page 208) and Kenneth Koch's "You Were Wearing" (page 265).

Run-On Free Verse

Along with others, most notably William Carlos Williams and Marianne Moore, Ezra Pound explored and enhanced the possibilities of run-on free verse. The first stanza of his "The Return" exemplifies the form:

> See, they return; ah, see the tentative
> Movements, and the slow feet,
> The trouble in the pace and the uncertain
> Wavering!

The rhythmic character of the passage primarily derives from the very strong run-on lines broken between the adjectives and the nouns: "the tentative / Movements" and "the uncertain / Wavering!" Both force a slightly abnormal pause, and this extra hesitation evokes rhythmically the tentative, uncertain feeling. Given a line by itself, "Wavering!" unexpectedly ends the stanza's flow, leaving it on an appropriately awkward diminuendo.

Since no formal meter determines where the lines must end, the choice is arbitrary in run-on free verse. Line-breaks tend to occur where there is no major grammatical or syntactical pause. Of course, the last line of a poem is inevitably end-stopped, and other lines may be. The texture of run-on free verse may vary, not only with the mixing in of end-stopped lines but also with the differences in "pull" of the various run-ons.

Pull is the force or speed of the line's turn—or, really, the force of the sentence's flow that the line-break ever so slightly interrupts. The eye or voice, reading, tends to pause *and* then hurry on somewhat more than if one were reading the passage as prose. This jog or awareness is the *metrical* element of run-on free verse. Try reading aloud the run-on in

> . . . ah, see the tentative
> Movements,

which divides an adjective from its noun, making the wrench or pull very strong. You should feel, first, the slightest *pause* as voice and eye reach the unexpected break in the sentence's flow; then, second, as if to catch up, a slightly muscular *speeding up* as the voice turns the corner. Both the pause and the consequent release of energy give the run-on its rhythmic flavor. (Contrast the effect with a reading of the lines as prose, which is continuous and simply lets "tentative" flow into "movements." No pause, no energy.)

The dual quality of a run-on allows either pause or energy to seem predominant: as here, the effect is a pause, *hesitation*, which seems to imitate the meaning. Similarly, the strong run-ons (between preposition and the rest of the phrase, between adjective and noun) in

> into the pit of
> the empty
> flowerpot

help induce an impression of pause, *slowness*. But another, equally strong run-on may give the impression of speed or energy, as in

> a flight of small
> cheeping birds
> skimming
> bare trees

Many run-ons (including most of those in metered verse) are relatively weak, occurring, for example, between a verb and its adverb or between two prepositional phrases as in Milton's

> thrown by angry Jove
> Sheer o'er the crystal battlements: from morn
> To noon he fell . . .

The pull or imbalance seems only a much slighter dislocation among related *phrases* lying across the line-break. In context, of course, such run-ons are effective.

A simple scale of pull will help: three slashes (///) for strong pull; two (//) for moderate pull; one (/) for weak pull; and zero (0) for end-stopped lines. Here is a primary example of run-on free verse:

To Waken an Old Lady

WILLIAM CARLOS WILLIAMS   (1883–1963)

Old age is	//	
a flight of small	//	
cheeping birds	/	
skimming	//	
bare trees	/	5
above a snow glaze.	0	
Gaining and failing	/	
they are buffeted	/	
by a dark wind—	0	
But what?	0	10
On harsh weedstalks	/	
the flock has rested,	0	
the snow	/	
is covered with broken	///	
seedhusks	/	15
and the wind tempered	//	
by a shrill	///	
piping of plenty.	0	

The short, oddly broken lines convey the speed and skittery movement of the small birds. (As always, the criterion is whether the form, free or strict, expresses its content.)

Of the poem's eighteen lines, thirteen are run-on and only five end-stopped. Seven lines have weak run-ons; four, moderate run-ons; and two, strong run-ons. Relative to run-ons, the poem has three movements. Lines 1–5 are moderately active (//-//-/-//-/). Lines 6–13 are weakly active (0-/-/-0-0-/-0-/). Lines 14–18 are strongly active (///-/-//-///-0). These relative movements correspond to the three phases of the poem. In lines 1–6 the birds are active and mobile, in flight, "skimming." In lines 7–13, they are defeated by the dark wind—the weak run-ons of lines 7–8 suggest their efforts ("Gaining") and their unsuccess ("and failing")—and come to rest on the "harsh weedstalks." The defeat, however, is temporary, for in lines 14–18 the activity is resumed, even increased, as they feed. The strong run-on of line 14—"is covered with broken /// seedhusks"—suggests or imitates the breaking open of the husks; and the strong run-on of line 17, again separating adjective and noun, emphasizes the activity of "shrill /// piping of plenty."

No doubt Williams felt the rightness of the rhythms not by calculation but intuitively, which is what having a good ear means. Counting the syllables per line confirms just how good Williams's ear is. Lines range in length from two to six syllables. Lines in the middle of the poem, where action is diminished, are generally longer than those at the beginning or end. Around the stark interrogative at the poem's center ("But what?") are six lines of four or five syllables, while shorter lines are characteristic of the more active parts of the poem.

Local effects of the rhythm are also telling. The only two syllable lines that come together—"skimming // bare trees"—give an impression of the swiftness of the birds' flight. In:

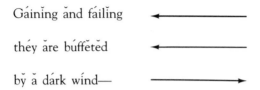

Gáinǐng ănd fáilǐng

théy ǎre búffětěd

bў ǎ dárk wínd—

the "drag" or backward leaning of the first two lines (accented followed by unaccented syllables) suggests their difficulty in making headway, whereas the advance or forward leaning of the third line (unaccented syllables running to accented) suggests the irresistible force of the wind. I have marked this drag or advance with arrows alongside the scansion.

The similarly short, oddly broken lines of Williams's "Poem" offer an interesting contrast, conveying rather than speed and skittery movement a feeling of catlike hesitancy and care.

Poem

As the cat
climbed over
the top of

the jamcloset
first the right   5
forefoot

carefully
then the hind
stepped down

into the pit of   10
the empty
flowerpot

Short lines do not necessarily produce rhythmic speed, any more than long lines necessarily produce slowness or ponderousness (Whitman's spider works rapidly), but in most cases they do. How, then, does Williams achieve the virtual slow-motion of "Poem"?

The use of stanzas, none of which is end-stopped, clearly slows and tends to accentuate the very deliberate rhythm, as does the fact that the poem is all one fairly long sentence. Moreover, the stronger syllabic norm may contribute. Line-length varies only from two to five syllables, and eight of the twelve lines have three syllables. (Only two have two syllables, and only one each has four or five.)

Neither of these explanations seems sufficient, however, to account for the slow-motion rhythm. The marking of run-ons shows that the poem is strongly run-on; only two lines are end-stopped. (I have counted the end of the subordinate clause after "jamcloset" as end-stopped, though Williams omits the expected comma.) Generally, the run-ons are strongest where the action of the cat is least decisive, most slow-motion; and are weakest in lines 5–8 where the actual steps of the cat are described. The strongest run-ons—between preposition and object, or between adjective and noun—occur in lines 2, 3, 5, and 10. Strangely, these seem to produce the effect of the least movement, the reverse of what we might expect.

The explanation becomes clear from a scansion of syllables:

Ăs thĕ cát	/	————————→
clímbed óvĕr	///	←————————
thĕ tóp ŏf	///	←————————→
thĕ jámclósĕt	0	←————————→
fírst thĕríght	///	←————————→
fórefóot	//	←————————→
cárefúllў	/	←————————
thén thĕ hínd	/	←————————→
stépped dówn	/	←————————→
ĭntŏ thĕ pít ŏf	///	————————→
thĕ émptў	//	←————————→
flówĕrpót	0	←————————→

Only three of the poem's twelve lines show either drag or advance (lines 1–2 and 7). Nine of the lines are balanced, or static (shown by the double-headed arrows).

In "To Waken an Old Lady" only six lines are in balance, with five showing drag and seven showing advance. In "Poem" the preponderance of lines in balance causes a feeling of stasis, which even the sentence's momentum can scarcely overcome. Perhaps Williams, a doctor, wrote the poem as he wrote so many others, on the back of a sheet from his prescription pad, between patients. No doubt he wrote it rapidly, and certainly—the beginning poet will be relieved to remember!—he didn't write it by conducting any such complicated metrical analysis. Unquestionably, though, he was *listening* to the words and recognizing, as he set them down, the little slow, careful rhythm the poem needed. The secret is listening to the words, and arranging, and listening, and listening again.

Run-on free verse continually plays its line structure against the speech flow of the poem. Other poems in run-on free verse include Gerald Costanzo's "Potatoes" (page 413) and John Ciardi's "Counting on Flowers" (page 55).

Just as end-stopped free verse tends to longer lines, run-on free verse characteristically tends to shorter lines. In the long lines which allow for caesural pauses and for any number of rational places to break lines (essential to end-stopped free verse), the speed or pull of run-ons would be obtrusive and seem abnormal, competing with the slower, deliberate pace of the main part of the line. Indeed, when free verse mixes very short and very long lines, it is often unsuccessful—bumpy and unpaced. Thus, some roughly equal line-length seems necessary to unify a poem or passage.

This daring poem by Louise Glück (b. 1943) shows the odd effect of longer lines in run-on free verse:

The Racer's Widow

The elements have merged into solicitude.
Spasms of violets rise above the mud
And weed and soon the birds and ancients
Will be starting to arrive, bereaving points
South. But never mind. It is not painful to discuss   5
His death. I have been primed for this,
For separation, for so long. But still his face assaults
Me, I can hear that car careen again, the crowd coagulate on asphalt
In my sleep. And watching him, I feel my legs like snow
That let him finally let him go   10
As he lies draining there. And see
How even he did not get to keep that lovely body.

Line length ranges from eight to nineteen syllables, and the pattern of run-ons is strong: 0-//-/-///-//-0-///-//-/-/-//-0. The widow's assertion that "It is not painful to discuss // His death" is contradicted not only by the imagery that suggests how distraught she really is ("Spasms of violets"; "I can hear . . . the crowd coagulate on asphalt"), but also by the run-ons that flow to or from caesuras very near the line-ends. Run-ons into lines 3 ("above the mud // And weed"), 5 ("bereaving points /// South"), 6 ("to discuss // His death"), 8 ("his face assaults /// Me"), and 9 ("on asphalt // In my sleep"), and from line 11 ("And see // How even he") conform to this pattern. The effect is an odd starting and stopping, a smooth assertiveness and an odd careening around corners. The repetition in line 10—"That let him finally let him go"—sounds natural but of course is not. The sentence fragment at poem's end has the same effect: "And see . . ." which is by ellipsis parallel to "I feel my legs. . . ." The poem's rhythm, jerking forward in very forced run-ons and smoothing in the relatively long lines, appropriately conveys the widow's repressed but unconcealed emotional turmoil.

Many poems are a mixture of end-stopped and run-on free verse. Each free verse poem establishes its own norms, one of which is the range of line-length. Once a pattern of lines of relatively consistent length has been established, it should be maintained. Lines very much shorter, or longer, than the norm stand out and may seem awkward or contrived. A one-word line in "The Racer's Widow," for example, would seem out of place, as would a very long line in Williams's "To Waken an Old Lady."

Visible Stanzas

Historically, before the invention of printing in the fifteenth century, poetry was primarily an oral art, rather than a written one. It was heard, rather than seen. Songs were sung; epics and narratives were declaimed by traveling bards. Formal meters, clearly accented and countable, allowed a poem's form to be followed by its hearers—just as rhyme, aside from its musical qualities, served to mark the turn from line to line like a typewriter bell. Since the sixteenth century, and especially after the rise of general literacy in the nineteenth century, poetry has become ever more a visual art through almost imperceptible evolution. Today we are more accustomed to seeing a poem than to hearing it, and students must be reminded to read poems aloud, particularly older poems, lest they miss an essential element.

The rise of free verse in the twentieth century corresponds, I suspect, to the acceleration of the evolution of poetry toward the visual. Free verse permits us to *see* the difference from prose. More in run-on than in end-stopped free verse, this visual quality represents the development of new formal possibilities, of visual forms. The visual will not replace the oral (poetry always relies on speech for its vigor) but will complement it, enriching and widening the poet's resources. William Carlos Williams is unquestionably the American master of run-on free verse, his poems a virtual library of effects. One of his significant innovations is free verse in stanzas of the same number of lines, and frequently of the same shape, as in "Poem." Such stanzas provide a regularity in visual form on the page, within which the language and the content can ebb and flow. The stanzaic regularity, reassuringly suggesting order and decisiveness to the eye, complements or counterpoints the freedom of speech inside the form. In the case of one poem, as Williams reports in *I Wanted To Write a Poem,* he changed a stanza of five lines to four to match the poem's other stanza. The original version:

The Nightingales

My shoes as I lean
unlacing them
stand out upon
flat worsted flowers
under my feet.

Nimbly the shadows
of my fingers play
unlacing
over shoes and flowers.

The revision:

My shoes as I lean
unlacing them
stand out upon
flat worsted flowers.

Nimbly the shadows
of my fingers play
unlacing
over shoes and flowers.

"See," he says, "how much better it conforms to the page, how much better it looks?" Aside from the symmetry of stanzas of an identical number of lines, the poem is tighter without losing anything; line 5 in the original was weak and redundant.

Traditionally, stanzas are structural units of thought and are end-stopped, as in "The Nightingales." They may be run-on as well, however, as in Williams's poem about the cat or Frost's "Dust of Snow." As with lines, stanzas provide an additional element of modulation and flow. Late in his career, Williams often used an indented pattern of three lines, as in this excerpt from "Asphodel, That Greeny Flower":

The sea! The sea!
       Always
              when I think of the sea
there comes to mind
        the *Iliad*   5
              and Helen's public fault
that bred it.
        Were it not for that
              there would have been
no poem but the world   10
        if we had remembered,
              those crimson petals
spilled among the stones,
        would have called it simply
              murder.   15

These triads gave Williams a fixed but flexible medium for longer poems—for starting and stopping, speeding and slowing the voice. Notice the quickness with which, in line 10, the second part of the compound sentence begins, prompting a momentarily mistaken but relevant reading of "no poem but the world" as a syntactical unit (with "but" as preposition, in the sense of "except," rather than as conjunction). Notice also the weight with which the sentence comes to its end on the one-word line, "murder." (See page 392 for another excerpt from this poem.) Similarly, lines of regularly *differing* lengths, repeated from stanza to stanza, as in "The Double Play" (page 56) or "The Girl Writing Her English Paper" (page 378) offer, on Williams's model, any number of fresh possibilities for the control and organization of free verse.

Free verse stanza patterns such as Williams's are trellises; they are the framework of visual regularity on which the morning glory of the new poem fluidly and freely twines. An alliance with form does not necessarily imply the loss of freedom. Even when the choice of stanza length or shape seems arbitrary, its uses may be organic and expressive of the content. Stanza structure may produce run-on free verse as precise and formally made as a metrical poem.

Robert Creeley (b. 1926) deftly develops free-flowing content on the arbitrary trellis of stanzas in this dramatic poem:

I Know a Man

As I sd to my
friend, because I am
always talking,—John, I

sd, which was not his
name, the darkness sur-   5
rounds us, what

can we do against
it, or else, shall we &
why not, buy a goddamn big car,

drive, he sd, for
christ's sake, look
out where yr going.

10

Both lines and stanzas are strongly run-on, with line-breaks occurring at awkward places: "my /// friend" or "I /// sd" or "against /// it." Even the word "sur- /// rounds" is broken. The effect is a feeling of disorder, confusion, haste. Abbreviations ("sd" for "said," "yr" for "you're," "&" for "and") support this impression of flurry. The speaker is highly agitated, rattled. Realizing that the "darkness" in line 5 is not merely physical (one can't *do* anything against merely physical darkness), we also know that the speaker's agitation is a kind of frantic, desperate outburst about the negative circumstances of life. In the last stanza, his friend recalls him from this general complaint to an immediate danger: "drive, he sd." This makes the poem's point that it is better to deal practically with real problems than to worry about abstract, symbolical issues of good and evil. In this context, "for /// christ's sake" takes on a deeper meaning, suggesting perhaps that goodness consists not in generalizations but in specific acts, not in vague, ineffective opposition to evil but in particular resistance. Here the specific resistance is to the temptation of despair ("& /// why not, buy a goddamn big car") or of being careless of others.

A major part of the poem's effect comes from the choice of a form in which the run-on lines imitate the confusion, haste, and irrationality of the speaker. Breaking "sur- /// rounds," for instance, emphasizes the sense of being surrounded by appearing to point both right and left; the "turn" of the line seems a gesture in all directions. Further, note that the poem is one long sentence. The mere comma after "car" in line 9 does not prepare us for the change of speaker, as would the normal period or dash. Our sudden realization in line 10—"drive, he sd"—that the voice has changed imitates the suddenness of danger, the unexpectedness with which an "accident" can occur when one is morally off guard. The terse urgency of the warning reinforces this abruptness. That comma after line 9 is a master stroke.

The title, "I Know a Man," which at first seems emptily descriptive, comes finally to mean something like "I know a *real* man, one who isn't flustered by moral complaint or danger." The overtone of both "goddamn" and "for /// christ's sake," which at first seem mere vulgarity, suggests that manliness may be very much a moral or spiritual matter. The regular three-line stanzas contain, box in, and so *measure* the frustrations and confusion of the speaker. Like the "friend," they are a reminder of restraint and, thus, stand as a formal expression of the poem's theme. (**Theme** is what a poem *as a whole* says, or more often implies, about its subject matter. That is, it is the poem's central thought, its drift, its consensus of meaning.)

The use of a visual, stanzaic form explains the popularity of this strangely effective little poem by William Carlos Williams:

The Red Wheelbarrow

so much depends
upon

a red wheel
barrow

glazed with rain   5
water

beside the white
chickens

The stanzas focus on each detail separately, giving the poem its intense, painterly concentration—and emphasizing the important first statement which, so isolated, can't just be passed over. Then, convinced by the color and clarity of the images, we wonder how such details are significant. The poem's theme resonates with possibilities: the natural fecundity of land and rain and labor on which we depend for food; the ancient human inventiveness ("wheel," perhaps "glaze") of which the simple farmyard scene reminds us and on which our sophisticated civilization thoughtlessly depends; the enduring values of a plain and honest daily life, which the unmentioned farmer, whose tools and concerns they are, represents; and not least (because it is Williams's poem) the spiritually nutritious perception of the beauty of the ordinary.

Each stanza is, indeed, shaped roughly like a wheelbarrow, with the longer first line suggesting the handle. Less obviously, the second line of each couplet is reached by a very strong run-on. In the first couplet the forced run-on causes the voice to come down on the preposition "upon" more heavily than the word normally deserves and so emphasizes it. In the last three couplets the line-break divides an adjective from its noun: "a red wheel /// barrow," "glazed with rain /// water," "beside the white /// chickens." In stanza 2 the run-on in fact divides, though without hyphen, the single word "wheelbarrow." That both "wheel" and "rain" are nouns used as adjectives reinforces the pull of the run-ons. Rhythmically, we might illustrate these strong run-on lines this way:

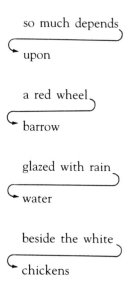

so much depends

upon

a red wheel

barrow

glazed with rain

water

beside the white

chickens

If the stanzas are shaped like tiny wheelbarrows, it is not too fanciful to suggest that these turning run-ons rhythmically suggest the wheels. Probably, the fascination of this apparently quiet little poem comes from the way its combined visual and oral form mirrors its subject. This tiny still-life catches energy in stasis, a complex vitality only momentarily at rest.

Like a vine that goes up and spreads on its trellis instead of blooming in a heap on the ground, the free verse in all these poems uses visual form—stanza shapes and relative line-lengths—to express the inner shape or movement of their subjects and feelings. What is important is not the stanza forms (they are empty shapes) but the way they are used, the way the vine of the language has been trained upon them. Any form, any measure, whether free or conventionally metrical—or something else—is only as valuable as the use that is made of it.

Syllabics

That something else might be **syllabics:** a formal measure in which only the number of syllables in each line is counted. Strictly speaking, syllabics is not free verse. (Compare Dylan Thomas's "Fern Hill," p. 188.) But neither, strictly, are the fixed shape stanzas we have been discussing. Both are, nonetheless, more than anything else, forms of free verse; and recognizing them as such is a further step toward an adequate theory of the major verse form of the twentieth century. Since the counting of syllables in English syllabic verse cannot be done by ear (that is, syllabics is not a measure or rhythm we can hear), syllabics is merely mechanical form. It is a development of free verse, as is the measure of counting the number of *words* per line (pioneered by Robert Francis) or, indeed, the counting of any other nonrhythmical element or feature of the language. Like shape-stanzas, such forms provide a trellis for the rhythmically free cadence. Like William Carlos Williams, Marianne Moore (1887–1972) must be regarded as one of the masters of free verse. Here is her syllabic poem,

To a Steam Roller

The illustration
is nothing to you without the application.
    You lack half wit. You crush all the particles down
        into close conformity, and then walk back and forth on them.

Sparkling chips of rock   5
are crushed down to the level of the parent block.
    Were not "impersonal judgment in aesthetic
        matters, a metaphysical impossibility," you

might fairly achieve
it. As for butterflies, I can hardly conceive   10
    of one's attending upon you, but to question
        the congruence of the complement is vain, if it exists.

Each first line has five syllables; each second line, twelve; each third line, twelve; and each fourth line, fifteen. Especially in stanzas 1 and 3, the longer last lines mimic, both visually and rhythmically, the effect of something rolled over and flattened by a steam roller. And the rhyme in each stanza's lines 1–2 (on top, where the too mechanical steam roller would be) is followed by the *lack* of rhymes in lines 3–4, as if the last two lines had been squashed. Even the mechanical chopping off of the run-on "achieve / it" in lines 9–10 seems something the steam roller would do. "To a Steam Roller" is a graceful and sardonic poem in syllabic run-on free verse.

Spatial Free Verse

A spatial or visual element has been important in a number of the poems already discussed, such as "Me up at does" or "The Red Wheelbarrow." In these poems the visual quality remains subordinate to the aural. In other poems, however, the visual predominates; and even the elementary structure of line becomes secondary or may disappear. A simple case:

> The
>
>   ball
>
>   bumps
>
>   down
>
>   the
>
>   steps . . .

Here the lines themselves are clearly secondary to the visual image they create. A poem like this one by Kenneth Patchen (1911–1972) can't in any normal sense be *read*, but is perceived:

The Murder of Two Men by a Young Kid Wearing Lemon-Colored Gloves

    Wait.

               Wait.

        Wait.

     Wait. Wait.

  Wait.

             Wait.

       W a i t.

  Wait.

         Wait.

           Wait.

     Wait.

          Wait.

 Wait.

    NOW.

E. E. Cummings, who brilliantly wrote "mOOn," has been the most influential experimenter with visual effects in poetry and with spatial free verse. In
poems like "chanson innocente" (page 143), Cummings uses spacing as a sort of
musical notation for emphasis, for speeding or slowing the voice. Consider, for
instance, the differences in the three repetitions of the phrase "far and wee" in
"chanson innocente." But he also writes poems in which the oral is effectively
replaced by the visual or spatial as the primary medium. This fine little poem,
whose first line is "l(a," defies reading aloud. Study it carefully so as not to let me
ruin the surprise.

l(a

le
af
fa

ll

s)
one
l

iness

The poem is the word "loneliness" and, inside it, parentheses containing the image
of a single leaf falling as an example of loneliness. The poem is symmetrical,
alternating stanzas of one line and three lines; and the broken way the image of the
leaf twists down from line to line perhaps suggests the turning descent of the leaf,
rocking as it drops. Compare this commonplace rearrangement:

loneliness
(a leaf falls)

Cummings's version of the identical statement is visually textured and, because it
requires us to puzzle it out, fresh. The vital and startling detail of the poem is not
found in the rearrangement: in the formal splintering of the word "loneliness," we
are shown an almost heartbreaking accident of the language. The lower case "l" and
the arabic numeral "1" are designed the same way (one key serves for both on the
standard typewriter). What the poem's form unmistakably tells us is that loneliness
is "1-one-1-iness." That is what loneliness is, one-one-one-iness.

Another rearrangement of the poem—omitting the stanza breaks—suggests
how much its form is its necessary nothing. The poem seems to lose its precision,
feels cluttered:

l(a

le

af

fa

ll

s)

one

l

iness

Spatial poetry may be as simple as this visually punning poem by Barry Spacks (b. 1931):

In the Fields

Rainingrainingraining.

Or it may be as complex as **picture poems,** which use the shape of an object as their form. Picture poems are an old tradition. "Easter Wings" by George Herbert (1593–1633), written in meter, is an early example:

Lord, who createdst man in wealth and store,
Though foolishly he lost the same,
Decaying more and more
Till he became
Most poore;
With thee
O let me rise
As larks, harmoniously,
And sing this day thy victories;
Then shall the fall further the flight in me.

My tender age in sorrow did beginne;
And still with sicknesses and shame
Thou didst so punish sinne,
That I became
Most thinne.
With thee
Let me combine,
And feel this day thy victorie;
For if I imp my wing on thine,
Affliction shall advance the flight in me.

19 *imp:* to engraft feathers on a damaged wing (term from falconry).

Decreasing and then increasing the lines of each stanza by one foot, Herbert not only makes the poem look like two pairs of angels' wings but also embodies the poem's theme of personal diminution and regrowth.

Twentieth-century picture poems have been written in the shape of Coca-Cola bottles, traffic cloverleafs with Model T's and Model A's circling them, and umbrellas. In 1969 John Hollander (b. 1929) published *Types of Shape*, in which there are poems shaped like a key, a light bulb, a bell, a heart, New York State, and even a swan and its shadow. Here is "Eskimo Pie":

```
                      I shall
                   never pretend
                 to have forgotten
               such loves as those
               that turned the dying
              brightness at an end of
              a childs afternoon into
              preludes To an evening of
              lamplight To a night dark
              with blanketing To mornings
              of more and more There deep
              in the old ruralities of play
              the frosted block with papery
              whisps still stuck to it kissed
              me burningly as it arose out of
              dry icy stillnesses And there now
              again I taste first its hard then
              its soft Now I am into the creamy
              treasure which to have tasted is to
              have begun to lose to the heat of a
              famished sun But O if I break faith
              with you poor dreadful popsicle may
              my mouth forget warm rains a tongue
              musty Pauillac cool skin all tastes
                      I see
                      sweet
                      drops
                      slide
                      along
                      a hot
                      stick
                      It is
                      a sad
                      sorry
                      taste
                      which
                      never
                      comes
                      to an
                      end
```

Pauillac: a very fine French wine.

So-called **"concrete poems"** lie halfway between poetry and graphics. Here is one of the most famous, by Reinhard Döhl (b. 1934). *Apfel* is German for apple.

```
          ᴀpfelApfelApfelApfeᴉ,
        ᴐfelApfelApfelApfelApfelA,
       ,felApfelApfelApfelApfelApfe
      ApfelApfelApfelApfelApfelApfᴜ
      pfelApfelApfelApfelApfelApfelʌ
      ᴉApfelApfelApfelApfelApfelApfe
      pfelApfelApfelApfelApfelApfelA
      ApfelApfelApfelApfelApfelApfe
      ᴐfelApfelApfelApfelApfelApfel/
      \pfelApfelApfelApfelApfelApf
       ᴈlApfelApfelApfelWurmApᴐ
       ᶠelApfelApfelApfelApfel/
        ᴐfelApfelApfelApfel/
         ᴧfelApfelApfelAᴦ
          ᴧ ᴐfelAnfelᴧ
```

Whatever its form, free verse—because it may be invented to suit its occasion or subject—is always changing and fresh. It is not merely poetry written any-old-which-a-way.

QUESTIONS AND SUGGESTIONS

1. Using a recent free verse poem of your own with which you aren't really satisfied, experiment with arranging it in stanzas. Don't spare the paper.

2. Write a poem in syllabics. Or write a picture poem about a carrot, a hat, an alarm clock, or some other common object. Or write an acrostic poem, using your own name or the name of someone you know. An **acrostic** is a poem in which the first letters of each line have a meaning when read downward, like:

Here lies an
English teacher who was
Never
Really
Young at heart.

Let him rest in peace:
Every word spelled right,
Every period in its place.

Probably the most dizzying acrostic ever is George Starbuck's poem of 156 lines, "A Tapestry for Bayeux," in *Bone Thoughts* (Yale University Press, 1960). Its subject is the Allied landings in Normandy in 1944. But the lines' first letters spell out this epigram about a well-known anthologist: "Oscar Williams fills a need, but a Monkey Ward catalog is softer and gives you something to read. We treasure his Treasuries, most every pominem. Our remarks are uncouth or unjust or ad hominem."

3. How have these student-poets reinvented and used free verse for their purposes?

a) FRANCES SLACK·

> I think the needle is stuck
> ink the needle is stu
> ink the needle is stu
> ink the needle is stu
> ink the needle is stu
> ink the needle is stu
> ink the needle is stu

b) *disappearances*

SHEILA HEINRICH·

> was a man of many disguises
> was a man of few words and
> one day when they looked where he had been
> they found
>
> and no one said
> so no one ever

c) *Working Men*

BRAD GERMAN·

> The man in charge is stealing my wallet
>   and the money I made hauling bricks.
> Who put him in charge? Who said
>   he could have this job?
> He was a stranger,   5
>   like I was, a moment ago,
> now he's my boss:
>   a cool authority, a specialist, with
>   finger soft tools searching my
>   pockets like a hungry spider.   10
> Across the faces of the street are
> curtains, covering their eyes like cataracts.

The children on the corner,
   they aren't even looking!
What of those other men in charge,   15
the elected bosses? Will they take charge
   when I'm back hauling bricks,
and protect me? Or,
      did they give this man his job too?
He shoves me aside,   20
         and vanishes in a haze of footsteps.
My eyes are averted to the ground;
in this old neighborhood, I know
      my place.

d) *Onset*

WILLIAM R. JOHNSON *

Again, the fields gave
all the way to the tree line.
The cornstalks are humbled to stubs now
their sun-blanched roots
in a mâché grasp of land.

Plowing, over his flat-red tractor
bends my father. His jaw set tight.
Indian summer's final sweat gathers
in small streams that search
the creases in his muscled neck.

I imagine somewhere in the distance,
perhaps Hudson Bay,
delicate ice forming among the reeds.
The lines like cobwebs stretching southward.

4. In "Smart" by Bruce Bennett (b. 1940) what *gestures* do you find the poet
making in his choice of line-breaks and stanzas? Does Bennett's omission of
capitalization and punctuation help his fable?

Smart

like the fox
who grabs a stick
and wades
into the water

deep   5
and deeper
till only his muzzle's

above it
his fleas

leap   10
up and up
onto his head
out onto the stick

which he lets go

off it floats   15
as he swims back
and shakes himself dry

5. In this poem by James Laughlin (b. 1914), can you discover the principle by which he "measures" the line-length? Read the poem aloud two or three times. What is the effect of treating it as if it were a single long sentence without internal punctuation (there is a final period)? Is there a significance in a poem of two-line stanzas ending with a stanza of one line?

The Goddess

I have seen the goddess
with my mortal eyes they

were filming down the
street and it was Meryl

Streep she was attended   5
by five trailers eight

trucks thirty technici-
ans and four policemen

the whole street was il-
lumined with a heavenly   10

blaze she walked up the
steps of the house four

times and I know that she
saw me and smiled at me

she knew that I was her   15
devotee she went into

the house and they said
the next scene was in-

side and I couldn't go
in will I ever see her   20

again my goddess but it
doesn't really matter I

saw her and she knew me.

6. Poet Robert D. Sutherland suggests this exercise. To test the integrity and possible effect of lines, try out as many free-versed versions of a prose sentence as you can think of. The sentence he uses: "Bob and Sarah, my friends of many years, have come back in time for tea." Literally, of course, there are dozens of possibilities. The range is from phrasal units (omitting internal punctuation):

> Bob and Sarah
> my friends of many years
> have come back
> in time for tea.

—to off-the-wall arrangements (mechanically, two words per line):

> Bob and
> Sarah my
> friends of
> many years
> have come
> back in
> time for
> tea.

—or to indented versions, like:

> Bob and Sarah
>   my
>   friends of many
> years
>   have come back
>   in time for tea.

Play around further with this sentence, or make up an interesting sentence of your own to use. Do type the versions, so you get an approximation of how they would look in print. Observe especially how the variations bring out emphases or potential hidden in the sentence. In the indented version above, for instance, the subsentence "years have come back," buried in the original, appears and perhaps suggests some of the meaning of the event to the speaker. Are there other buried subsentences or subphrases?

7. Choose a very short poem in meter (or a stanza from one) and experiment with rearranging it as free verse. What seems gained? lost? (Lines 1–4 of Shakespeare's Sonnet 73, page 11, or Frost's "Dust of Snow," page 17, would do nicely.)

Kidnaper

1976

TESS GALLAGHER   (b. 1943)

He motions me over with a question.
He is lost. I believe him. It seems
he calls my name. I move
closer. He says it again, the name
of someone he loves. I step back pretending   5

not to hear. I suspect
the street he wants
does not exist, but I am glad to point
away from myself. While he turns
I slip off my wristwatch, already laying a trail   10
for those who must find me
tumbled like an abandoned car
into the ravine. I lie

without breath for days among ferns.
Pine needles drift   15
onto my face and breasts
like the tiny hands
of watches. Cars pass.
I imagine it's him
coming back. My death   20
is not needed. The sun climbs again
for everyone. He lifts me
like a bride

and the leaves fall from my shoulders
in twenty-dollar bills.   25
"You must have been cold," he says
covering me with his handkerchief.
"You must have given me up."

A Reason for Moving

1964

MARK STRAND   (b. 1934)

In a field
I am the absence
of field.
This is
always the case.   5
Wherever I am
I am what is missing.

When I walk
I part the air
and always   10
the air moves in
to fill the spaces
where my body's been.

We all have reasons
for moving.   15
I move to keep things whole.

Counting on Flowers

1962

JOHN CIARDI   (1916–1986)

Once around a daisy counting
she loves me / she loves me not
and you're left with a golden
button without a petal left to
it. Don't count too much on   5
what you count on remaining
entirely a flower at the end.

The Double Play   1961

ROBERT WALLACE   (b. 1932)

In his sea-lit
distance, the pitcher winding
like a clock about to chime comes down with

the ball, hit
sharply, under the artificial   5
banks of arc lights, bounds like a vanishing string

over the green
to the shortstop magically
scoops to his right whirling above his invisible

shadows   10
in the dust redirects
its flight to the running poised second baseman

pirouettes
leaping, above the slide, to throw
from mid-air, across the colored tightened interval,   15

to the leaning-
out first baseman ends the dance
drawing it disappearing into his long brown glove

stretches. What
is too swift for deception   20
is final, lost, among the loosened figures

jogging off the field
(the pitcher walks), casual
in the space where the poem has happened.

Jump Cabling

1984

LINDA PASTAN   (b. 1932)

When our cars   touched
When you lifted the hood   of mine
To see the intimate workings   underneath,
When we were bound   together
By a pulse of pure   energy,   5
When my car like the   princess
In the tale woke with a   start,
I thought why not ride the rest of the way together?

Short-order Cook

1985

JIM DANIELS   (b. 1956)

An average joe comes in
and orders thirty cheeseburgers and thirty fries.

I wait for him to pay before I start cooking.
He pays.
He ain't no average joe.   5

The grill is just big enough for ten rows of three.
I slap the burgers down
throw two buckets of fries in the deep frier
and they pop pop spit spit . . .
psss . . .   10
The counter girls laugh.
I concentrate.
It is the crucial point—
they are ready for the cheese:
my fingers shake as I tear off slices   15
toss them on the burgers/fries done/dump/
refill buckets/burgers ready/flip into buns/
beat that melting cheese/wrap burgers in plastic/
into paper bags/fries done/dump/fill thirty bags/

bring them to the counter/wipe sweat on sleeve   20
and smile at the counter girls.
I puff my chest out and bellow:
"Thirty cheeseburgers, thirty fries!"
They look at me funny.
I grab a handful of ice, toss it in my mouth   25
do a little dance and walk back to the grill.
Pressure, responsibility, success,
thirty cheeseburgers, thirty fries.

Ruby Tells All   1985

MILLER WILLIAMS   (b. 1930)

When I was told, as Delta children were,
that crops don't grow unless you sweat at night,
I thought that it was my own sweat they meant.
I have never felt as important again
as on those early mornings, waking up,   5
my body slick, the moon full on the fields.
That was before air conditioning.
Farms girls sleep cool now and wake up dry,
but still the cotton overflows the fields.
We lose everything that's grand and foolish;   10
it all becomes something else. One by one,
butterflies turn into caterpillars
and we grow up, or more or less we do,
and, Lord, we do lie then. We lie so much
the truth has a false ring and it's hard to tell.   15

I wouldn't take crap off anybody
if I just knew that I was getting crap
in time not to take it. I could have won
a small one now and then if I was smarter,
but I've poured coffee here too many years   20
for men who rolled in in Peterbilts,
and I have gotten into bed with some
if they could talk and seemed to be in pain.
I never asked for anything myself;

giving is more blessed and leaves you free.   25
There was a man, married and fond of whiskey.
Given the limitations of men, he loved me.
Lord, we laid concern upon our bodies
but then he left. Everything has its time.
We used to dance. He made me feel the way   30
a human wants to feel and fears to.
He was a slow man and didn't expect.
I would get off work and find him waiting.
We'd have a drink or two and kiss awhile.
Then a bird-loud morning late one April   35
we woke up naked. We had made a child.
She's grown up now and gone though god knows where.
She ought to write, for I do love her dearly
who raised her carefully and dressed her well.

Everything has its time. For thirty years   40
I never had a thought about time.
Now, turning through newspapers, I pause
to see if anyone who passed away
was younger than I am. If one was
I feel hollow for a little while   45
but then it passes. Nothing matters enough
to stay bent down about. You have to see
that some things matter slightly and some don't.
Dying matters a little. So does pain.
So does being old. Men do not.   50
Men live by negatives, like don't give up,
don't be a coward, don't call me a liar,
don't ever tell me don't. If I could live
two hundred years and had to be a man
I'd take my grave. What's a man but a match,   55
a little stick to start a fire with?

My daughter knows this, if she's alive.
What could I tell her now, to bring her close,
something she doesn't know, if we met somewhere?
Maybe that I think about her father,   60
maybe that my fingers hurt at night,
maybe that against appearances
there is love, constancy, and kindness,
that I have dresses I have never worn.

Meter:
Genie-Bottles
and Spiderwebs

Solid form includes poem forms (like sonnets), stanza forms (like couplets or quatrains), and conventional meter, the basic underlying rhythmic pattern of the *line* of verse in English for about five hundred years. This chapter describes the mechanics of meter. While free verse is more formal than its name indicates, meter is happily less formal than it may seem—and less complicated than its thicket of terminology suggests.

Meter means "measure." Some recurring element of the language is used as the unit of measurement. As the music of speech varies with each language, each uses distinctive elements as the basis for poetic meter. Latin verse, for example, used the duration of vowels, long or short, as the measuring element. Chinese, in which all words are monosyllabic, uses syllables as the measuring element. More strongly accented in the manner of the Germanic languages, English has always used **accent** as the measuring element. Accent is the emphasis—in loudness, pitch, or duration—with which a syllable is spoken, relative to adjacent syllables. For metrical purposes only two levels of accent (or **stress**) are counted: relatively *heavily* accented syllables (called accented) and relatively *lightly* accented syllables (called unaccented).

Anglo-Saxon (Old English) meter used two simple elements, accent and alliteration. A line of verse had four main accents, two on each side of a heavy caesura; and at least three of the four accented syllables were alliterated (usually with a consonant). Unaccented syllables were not counted. In the twentieth century Richard Wilbur has employed this meter in a poem called "Junk." Notice the splitting of each line into distinct halves and the alliterated accent-syllables "axe, angles, ashcan" in line 1, "Hell's, handiwork, hickory" in line 2, and so on.

Junk

> *Huru Welandes*
> > *worc ne geswiceð*
> *monna ænigum*
> > *ðara ðe Mimming can*
> *heardne gehealdan.*
>
> WALDERE

An axe angles
             from my neighbor's ashcan;
It is hell's handiwork,
             the wood not hickory,
The flow of the grain
             not faithfully followed.
The shivered shaft
         rises from a shellheap
Of plastic playthings,
             paper plates,   5
And the sheer shards
         of shattered tumblers
That were not annealed
             for the time needful.
At the same curbside,
         a cast-off cabinet
Of wavily-warped
       unseasoned wood
Waits to be trundled
             in the trash-man's truck.   10
Haul them off! Hide them!
             The heart winces
For junk and gimcrack,
             for jerrybuilt things
And the men who make them
             for a little money,
Bartering pride
         like the bought boxer
Who pulls his punches,

or the paid-off jockey

Who in the home stretch

        holds in his horse.

Yet the things themselves

        in thoughtless honor

Have kept composure,

        like captives who would not

Talk under torture.

        Tossed from a tailgate

Where the dump displays

        its random dolmens,   20

Its black barrows

        and blazing valleys,

They shall waste in the weather

        toward what they were.

The sun shall glory

        in the glitter of glass-chips,

Foreseeing the salvage

        of the prisoned sand,

And the blistering paint

        peel off in patches,   25

That the good grain

        be discovered again.

Then burnt, bulldozed,

        they shall all be buried

To the depth of diamonds,

        in the making dark

Where halt Hephaestus°

        keeps his hammer

And Wayland's work

        is worn away.   30

29 *Hephaestus:* lame Greek god, patron of artists who worked in iron or metal.

The epigraph, from an Anglo-Saxon poem about the legendary smith Wayland, reads, as Wilbur translates it: "Truly, Wayland's handiwork—the sword Mimming which he made—will never fail any man who knows how to use it bravely." The choice of the archaic Anglo-Saxon alliterative form for this poem is a good one, because it emphasizes the theme: contrasting the well-made old with modern plastic, mismade "junk."

Accentual-Syllabic Meter

Later, more or less during Chaucer's time, when modern English influenced by French (brought by the Normans to England) was emerging, the old alliterative meter disappeared. It gave way to what is called **accentual-syllabic meter,** which has been standard in English since the sixteenth century. Accentual syllabic has been a rich metrical tradition, as varied as the poets who have used it: Shakespeare, Donne, Milton, Pope, Wordsworth, Keats, Yeats, Frost, Stevens, and in recent decades Richard Wilbur, Robert Lowell, Howard Nemerov.

In theory both the number of accents and the number of syllables are counted, and it is the *pattern* of accented and unaccented syllables that forms the meters. The elementary unit is called a **foot** (note the analogy to dance). The basic metrical unit is the *iambic foot,* or **iamb,** which is an unaccented followed by an accented syllable: tĕ TÚM, as in "avoid" or "to break" or "the time|less trees." Note, as in the third example, that a word may be part of two separate feet.

Lines may be composed of any given number of feet, though lines of four or five feet (eight or ten syllables) have been the norm. **Monometer** is a line consisting of one foot:˘ ´. It is rarely used; however, Robert Herrick (1591–1674) provides an example:

Upon His Departure Hence

Thŭs Í
Passe by,
And die:
As One,
Unknown,   5
And gon:
I'm made
A shade,
And laid
I'th grave,   10
There have
My Cave.
Where tell
I dwell,
Farewell.   15

Dimeter, also rare, is a line consisting of two feet: ˘ ´ | ˘ ´. Although it deviates a little from strict iambic dimeter, here is a twentieth century example. (Note: a final unaccented syllable at the end of the line—a "feminine" ending—is not counted and does not charge the meter.)

Hŏw tíme | rĕvér|sĕs

Thĕ próud | ĭn héart!

Ĭ nów | măke vér|sĕs

Whŏ áimed | ăt árt.

Here is the poem:

For My Contemporaries
J. V. CUNNINGHAM   (1911–1985)

How time reverses
The proud in heart!
I now make verses
Who aimed at art.

But I sleep well.   5
Ambitious boys
Whose big lines swell
With spiritual noise,

Despise me not!
And be not queasy   10
To praise somewhat:
Verse is not easy.

But rage who will.
Time that procured me
Good sense and skill   15
Of madness cured me.

Trimeter is a line consisting of three feet: ˘ ´ | ˘ ´ | ˘ ´ , as in these wonderfully waltzing lines:

Thĕ whís|kĕy ŏn | yŏur bréath

Cŏuld máke | ă smáll | bŏy díz|zy̆;

Bŭt Í | hŭng ón | lĭke déath:

Sŭch wáltz|ĭng wás | nŏt éas|y̆.

The poem:

My Papa's Waltz

THEODORE ROETHKE   (1908–1963)

The whiskey on your breath
Could make a small boy dizzy;
But I hung on like death:
Such waltzing was not easy.

We romped until the pans   5
Slid from the kitchen shelf;
My mother's countenance
Could not unfrown itself.

The hand that held my wrist
Was battered on one knuckle;   10
At every step you missed
My right ear scraped a buckle.

You beat time on my head
With a palm caked hard by dirt,
Then waltzed me off to bed   15
Still clinging to your shirt.

Tetrameter, very common and serviceable, is a line consisting of four feet: ˘ ´ |
˘ ´ | ˘ ´ | ˘ ´, as in:

Lóvelĭest | ŏf treés, | thĕ chér|rў nów

Ĭs húng | wĭth blóom | ălóng | thĕ bóugh,

Ănd stánds | ăbóut | thĕ wóod|lănd ríde

Wéar|ĭng whíte | fŏr Éas|tertíde.

The poem:

Loveliest of Trees

A. E. HOUSMAN

Loveliest of trees, the cherry now
Is hung with bloom along the bough,

And stands about the woodland ride
Wearing white for Eastertide.

Now, of my threescore years and ten,   5
Twenty will not come again,
And take from seventy springs a score,
It only leaves me fifty more.

And since to look at things in bloom
Fifty springs are little room,   10
About the woodlands I will go
To see the cherry hung with snow.

Pentameter is a line consisting of five feet: ˘ ´ | ˘ ´ | ˘ ´ | ˘ ´ | ˘ ´. Iambic pentameter has been the standard line of verse in English from Shakespeare to Frost. When it is unrhymed, it is also called **blank verse,** as in:

All out|-of-doors | looked dark|ly in | at him

Through the | thin frost | almost | in sep|arate stars,

That gath|ers on | the pane | in emp|ty rooms.

What kept | his eyes | from giv|ing back | the gaze . . .

The poem:

An Old Man's Winter Night

ROBERT FROST

All out-of-doors looked darkly in at him
Through the thin frost almost in separate stars,
That gathers on the pane in empty rooms.
What kept his eyes from giving back the gaze
Was the lamp tilted near them in his hand.   5
What kept him from remembering what it was
That brought him to that creaking room was age.
He stood with barrels round him—at a loss.
And having scared the cellar under him
In clomping here, he scared it once again   10
In clomping off;—and scared the outer night,
Which has its sounds, familiar, like the roar
Of trees and crack of branches, common things,

But nothing so like beating on a box.
A light he was to no one but himself   15
Where now he sat, concerned with he knew what,
A quiet light, and then not even that.
He consigned to the moon, such as she was,
So late-arising, to the broken moon
As better than the sun in any case   20
For such a charge, his snow upon the roof,
His icicles along the wall to keep;
And slept. The log that shifted with a jolt
Once in the stove, disturbed him and he shifted,
And eased his heavy breathing, but still slept.   25
One aged man—one man—can't keep a house,
A farm, a countryside, or if he can,
It's thus he does it of a winter night.

Hexameter (or **Alexandrine**) is a line consisting of six feet: ˘ ´ | ˘ ´ | ˘ ´ | ˘ ´ |
˘ ´ | ˘ ´. Because it tends to be long and sluggish in practice, it is rare. Howard
Nemerov (b. 1920) uses it deftly, however, in this epigram:

Power to the People

Why̆ are | thĕ stámps | ădórned | with kíngs | ănd prés|ĭdénts?

Thăt wĕ | măy líck | thĕir hínd|ĕr párts | ănd thúmp | thĕir héads.

Heptameter, a line consisting of seven feet, is awkward and very rare. The example
is from "The Book of Thel" by William Blake (1757–1827):

Thĕ Lí|ly̆ ŏf | thĕ vál|ley̆, bréath|ĭng 'ĭn | thĕ húm|blĕ gráss,

Ánswĕred | thĕ lóve|ly̆ máid | ănd sáid: | "Ĭ ám | ă wát|'ry̆ wéed,

Ănd Í | ăm vér|ly̆ smáll | ănd lóve | tŏ dwéll | ĭn lów|ly̆ váles;

Sŏ wéak, | thĕ gíld|ĕd bút|tĕrfly̆ | scárce pérch|ĕs ŏn | my̆ héad.
Yet I am visited from heaven, and he that smiles on all   5
Walks in the valley, and each morn over me spreads his hand,
Saying, 'Rejoice, thou humble grass, thou new-born lily flower,
Thou gentle maid of silent valleys and of modest brooks;
For thou shalt be clothed in light, and fed with morning manna,
Till summer's heat melts thee beside the fountains and the springs,   10
To flourish in eternal vales.' "

Over the centuries, tetrameter and pentameter lines have become the norm; they are neither too short and clipped nor too long and clumsy. Monometer or dimeter lines tend to occur only in stanzaic poems of varying line lengths, such as George Herbert's "The Collar" (page 118) or John Donne's "Song" (page 119).

The iamb (tĕ TÚM) is the basic foot. But, as suggested by anomalies in the scansions already marked, five other feet may be substituted for iambs without changing the metrical pattern. They are:

> **Trochee** (trochaic): accented followed by unaccented syllable: TÚM tĕ.
> ónlў   tótăl   ców ănd   the | fárm bĕ|low
>
> **Anapest** (anapestic): two unaccented followed by an accented: tĕ tĕ TÚM.
> intĕrvéne   fŏr ă while   lŏv|ĕr ŏf mine
>
> **Dactyl** (dactylic): accented followed by two unaccented: TÚM tĕ tĕ.
> mérrĭlў   tíme fŏr ă   lóvĕr ŏf | mine
>
> **Spondee** (spondaic): two accented syllables together: TÚM TÚM.
> bréad bóx   in the | swéet lánd   stróng fóot
>
> **Double-iamb:** two unaccented followed by two accented: tĕ tĕ TÚM TÚM.
> ŏf thĕ swéet lánd   in ă gréen sháde

Instead of the double-iamb, most accounts include the **pyrrhic** foot, two unaccented syllables: tĕ tĕ. But since it contains no accent, the pyrrhic is awkward to hear as a unit, and it is almost invariably followed by a spondee. This pattern is so frequent that it seems simpler and more natural to think of it as a double-iamb. A double-iamb, of course, counts as two feet.

Substitution and Variations

Any of these other feet—trochees, anapests, dactyls, spondees, or double-iambs—may be *substituted* for iambs in the norm line. (The noun is **substitution**.) "Slid from" is a trochee substituted as the first foot in the second line of "My Papa's Waltz" (page 65):

Wĕ rómped ŭntíl thĕ páns

Slíd frŏm | thĕ kítch|ĕn shélf

The slightly unexpected tipping in the rhythm imitates (perhaps) the described action of pans sliding from a shelf. A trochee, an anapest, and a spondee are substituted in lines 13–14:

You beat | time on | my head

With a palm | caked hard | by dirt

"Why are" is a trochaic substitution in Nemerov's "Why are | the stamps | adorned | with kings | and pres|idents?" Note the double-iamb and the anapest substituted in the second line of Frost's "An Old Man's Winter Night" (page 66):

Through the thin frost, | almost | in sep|arate stars

Substitution allows an almost infinite rhythmical variety, and it is frequently the means of imitative, expressive effects. Used heavily or awkwardly, of course, it can break the flow of the meter. But used deftly, it is the freedom of the formal poem. Meter might best be thought of, not as something that must be rigidly followed, but as something the poet is free to vary whenever it suits his or her purpose.

Substitution of anapests or dactyls (feet of three syllables) tends to simplify accentual-*syllabic* meter toward what may be called **accentual meter,** in which the syllables of a line are less strictly counted. When unaccented syllables are not counted at all, accentual meter in effect escapes the conventions and approaches a loosely patterned free verse, as in the seventeen-line opening passage of T. S. Eliot's *The Waste Land* (1922). Although a number of Eliot's lines may be scanned with conventional substitution, lines like "Dull roots with spring rain" and "I read, much of the night, and go south in the winter" make any system unintelligible. Similarly idiosyncratic are lines of what Gerard Manley Hopkins called "sprung rhythm," such as "As a skate's heel sweeps smooth on a bow-bend: the hurl and gliding" in "The Windhover."

Three further aspects of the metrical system are important. First, meter is a simplification of what we actually hear. In speech it is possible to distinguish a wide and subtle range of accents. In metered verse, however, the distinction is narrow and clear-cut: syllables are counted as either **accented** or **unaccented.** That meter is two-valued, for counting, does not of course reduce the variety of accents of natural speech that play over it. Thus, regular meter need never be goose-step or wooden. Further, the distinction between accented and unaccented syllables is relative; that is, we count a syllable as accented or unaccented *in relation to* the syllables next to it, not by an absolute measurement. The first line of "An Old Man's Winter Night" is scanned this way:

All out|-of-doors | looked dark|ly in | at him

We can hear the meter ticking along regularly under the speech rhythm. Although "looked" counts as an unaccented syllable (being next to the more heavily accented "dark-") and although "in" counts as an accented syllable (being next to the still slightly less accented "-ly" and "at"), purely objectively "looked" is more accented than "in."

A second important aspect is that a line may be scanned—that is, interpreted or heard—somewhat differently by different readers. A single reader may often be aware of more than one obvious possibility. In the Frost line, for instance, I can also hear "looked dark-" as a spondee; it is the ominous center of the statement and both words might be read as equally heavily accented. Another reader might hear, and mark, the first foot in the line as a spondee, too: "All out-." In scanning, parentheses are often useful to call attention to such other obvious possibilities, so that the rhythmical flexibility of a line won't be lost in the description of it. Similarly, parentheses mark what may be called **"courtesy" accents:** syllables that should be treated as accented even though they barely deserve it, like "in" in "dark|ly in | at him." The parentheses indicate that, although the scanner primarily hears a line in a certain way, he or she is also aware of other ways of hearing it. As the accents of meter are essentially relative, **scansion** should be wisely tentative and undogmatic. In scanning, we do not seek the "correct" answer, but a notation of accents that allows us to perceive and discuss accurately the subtleties of the line.

A third aspect of the metrical system is the **feminine ending,** a final unaccented syllable at the end of the line, as in Roethke's

Could make | a small | boy diz|zy

or in Frost's

The log | that shift|ed with | a jolt

Once in | the stove, | disturbed | him and | he shift|ed.

Because they are unaccented, feminine endings are regarded metrically as extras and are uncounted; thus, these lines remain iambic trimeter (Roethke) and iambic pentameter (Frost). Feminine endings may, however, be rhythmically useful for expressive or imitative effects. In Frost's lines the nearly unaccented syllable "with" lets the voice speed toward the abrupt "jolt," and the trochaic substitution "Once in" helps to mimic the loose and jolting motion of the log in the fire. The trochaic substitution that puts two unaccented syllables together—"him and | he shift-"—helps to suggest the old man's restiveness resulting from the fire's disturbing noise. The feminine ending "and | he shift|ed" completes the effect by also suggesting the old man's restlessness and the unfinished, unsatisfying, indecisive quality of his movement as contrasted with the abrupt, finished movement of the log's "jolt" at the (so-called) **masculine ending**—on an accented syllable—of the preceding line. The feminine ending lets the line end with four syllables, only one of which ("shift-") is accented, giving an effect of slight but unresolved movement. Contrast the effect of the same line with a masculine ending: "Once in the stove, disturbed | him and | he stirred."

Metrical verse may be more or less strict, depending on: 1) how closely the rhythm approximates the meter's beat; 2) the occurrence of substitutions and feminine endings; and 3) the frequency of caesural pauses and run-on lines. Strict meter would avoid anapestic or dactylic substitutions, which add syllables to a line. More leisurely meter might use these substitutions for loosening or variation. The poet's problem of how to choose and use a conventional meter is similar to the problem of how to choose and use a free verse measure. Meter is (simply) a more complex trellis. In his deceptively offhand way, Frost summed up the matter when he remarked that there are really only two meters in English, strict iambic and loose iambic.

Rhythm

Meter is a purely mechanical pattern of unaccented and accented syllables: te TUM te TUM te TUM, always *exactly* regular and arbitrary. An iamb is an iamb, just as an inch is an inch. But something happens when the words of a poem are laid over meter. The result is never precisely regular, is no longer mechanical. The usual stresses of words, their varying importance or placement in the statement, their sounds, as well as the pauses and syntactical connections between them, all work to give the line an individual movement, flavor, weight. This we call **rhythm:** the play of the words across the rigid metrical pattern.

Meter measures speech, the varied flow of a voice. Rhythm is the result of blending the fixed (meter) with the flexible (speech). The result isn't exactly the te TUM te TUM of meter nor a reproduction of actual speech. A poem is read neither as inflexible meter nor as wholly flexible speech, but always as something between the two.

Although all iambic pentameter lines have exactly the same meter, no two lines have exactly the same rhythm. Variations in rhythm can never be exhausted. The poet, thus, need not fear being trapped by the regularities of meter, but may delight in the freedom of searching out the qualities of rhythm that will make each line unique.

Consider a simple example, the sentence which is part of the first line of Richard Wilbur's "Juggler" (page 84): "A ball will bounce, but less and less." It is as inaccurate to read the line mechanically by the meter ("a BALL will BOUNCE, but LESS and LESS") as it is to read it as one might speak it ("a ball will BOUNCE, but less and less"). In speech, we usually dash off everything but the most emphatic part. In fact, depending on the intention, we might place the primary accent on *any* of the eight words in the sentence. If we are distinguishing a ball from a glass bottle, for instance, we might well say, "a BALL will bounce, but less and less." If we are distinguishing a single ball from a box of balls, we might well say, "A ball will bounce, but less and less." Similarly, in speech, we might find a perfectly good reason for saying "a ball WILL bounce, but less and less" or "a ball will bounce, BUT less and less," and so on, depending on what we are trying to say in a particular context.

We read this sentence in "Juggler" neither according to the rigid meter nor according to any of those possible speech emphases. In the poem the meter changes the speech-run a little, giving the sentence a more measured movement; and the speech-run of the sentence loosens the march-step of the meter. The result is distinctive—rhythm. Speech flowing over meter produces rhythm.

Normally, the unique qualities of rhythm, especially in its imitative potential, occur where the strength of the speech-run dislodges the meter, that is, where substitution occurs. When the poet is doing his or her job, substitutions and the consequent variations in rhythm will be significant, as in the Frost and Roethke lines discussed. Almost every substitution in the poems cited has some useful expressive effect. Consider the second stanza of Cunningham's "For My Contemporaries" (page 64):

But Í sleep well.

Ămbitious boys

Whose big lines swell

With spiritual noise,

Line 3, with its four heavy syllables (two spondees), suggests the pompous, proud rhetoric of the poets Cunningham is describing; and the alliterated b's of "Ambitious boys" climax emphatically in "big," reenforcing the rhythmical effect. Line 4 is particularly interesting. The anapestic second foot—"-itual noise"—is made rather gummy due to the already elided "-ual" of normal pronunciation, though it might be enunciated as "-ual." This possibility of four syllables in the foot—"-itual noise"—makes us somewhat mouth the line to keep on track. The little muddle is deliberate: it is Cunningham's rhythmic imitation of, and comment on, the muddled intellect he finds in such pompous poetry. The contempt is conveyed by more than the choice of the word "noise."

In Roethke's "My Papa's Waltz" (page 65) note the probable spondee in line 2—"Could make | a small | boy diz|zy"—three accents together, which, along with the feminine ending syllable of "diz|zy," might suggest force and the twisting movement that is described. Notice in line 3—"But Í | hung on | like death"— the imitative "hanging on" of the spondaic "hung on." All three feet in that line might almost be read as spondees: the voice maintains a nearly even pitch throughout the line.

Another common variation is the omission of the initial unaccented syllable at the beginning of a line. In Housman's "Loveliest of Trees" (page 65) this occurs three times: in lines 4 ("Wear|ing white | for Eas|tertide"), 6 ("Twen|ty will | not come | again"), and 10 ("Fif|ty springs | are lit|tle room"). If such monosyllabic feet occurred elsewhere in the line, they would mark a major hiatus in the rhythm; but, occurring innocuously at the beginning of lines, they scarcely disturb the flow. In two of these three instances in "Loveliest of Trees," in lines 6 and 10, this almost unnoticeable metrical shortening emphasizes the brevity of the "Twenty" years that "will not come again" and of the "Fifty springs" which are "little room."

Typically, the unique qualities in rhythm occur where substitutions occur. (One purpose of scansion is to locate such qualities so that they can be discussed accurately.) Even a perfectly regular line, however, may have its own deliciously characteristic, even imitative rhythm. Consider again Wilbur's "A ball will bounce, but less and less," containing four perfectly regular iambs, te TUM te TUM te TUM te TUM. Within that regularity or, rather, precisely because of it, small differences in stress give the effect of less and less force and so seem to imitate the way a ball dribbles to a stop in smaller and smaller hops. The first two accents are made fairly forceful by the alliterated *b*'s—"A *b*all will *b*ounce"—while the liquid *l*'s of "*l*ess and *l*ess" are softer and the *s*'s seem to stretch. The second "less" naturally gets less force than the first, but it is the difference in the accents that is crucial in establishing the line's rhythm. The first iamb is strongest because the contrast between the negligible "A" and the sharp "ball" is very large: "a BALL." Comparatively, the second iamb seems less forceful because the unaccented syllable—"will"—gets some emphasis from its near-rhyme with "ball" and is much less sharply contrasted, in force, with "bounce." The second iamb, "will bounce," is more evenly spread, softer. The same is true of the third iamb, "but less": "but" picks up a little extra emphasis from the already alliterated *b*'s of "ball" and "bounce"; thus the contrast of the unaccented syllable with the accented syllable seems more muted still than in "will bounce." The fourth iamb, "and less," is weaker in both parts. In short, the *difference* between each unaccented syllable and its accented syllable diminishes with each foot. We might show it pictorially, imagining each foot as a piece of string proportionally arranged according to accent:

A ball will bounce, but less and less.

Or we could simply draw the relative rise in each foot:

A ball will bounce, but less and less.

This is rhythmical mastery of a high order, like performing a magic trick without props. Such effects are possible with meter, which tunes the ear to careful measurements. "The strength of the genie," Wilbur has said, "comes of being confined in the bottle."

Just as a taut web allows the spider to feel the slightest disturbance, tight metrical structures let us perceive the slightest variation as significant. Tuned to that expectation—te TUM te TUM—we can respond sensitively to the smallest subtleties or counterpoint. Alexander Pope's justly famous "sound of sense" passage from *An Essay on Criticism* (page 83) is a treasury of metrical effects. Here, for instance, is the couplet about the Greek hero in the Trojan War, Ajax:

When Ájax strives sŏme róck's vást weĭght tŏ thrów,

The lĭne tóo labŏrs, ănd thĕ wórds mŏve slów

Pope uses several spondaic substitutions to produce the feeling of weight and then of effort. In the second line, in addition to the two spondees—"too lab-" and "move slow"—the third foot is broken by the caesura—"-ors, ‖and"—so that the somewhat forced accent on "and" seems itself slow and effortful. In the first line the two spondees (or near spondees) put five heavy syllables together and so weight the center of the line, as Ajax lifts the boulder he means to hurl. The secret of the line, however, isn't merely a matter of dumping a heavier foot or two into it. The craft lies in the perfectly regular iamb in the fifth foot, "to thrów." It is in that small te TUM gesture that we *feel* Ajax's effort. After five nearly even strong syllables, the contrast in weight between "to" and "throw" rhythmically mimics Ajax's gesture:

When Ajax strives some rock's vast weight to throw

Pope's skill is evident in his having varied slightly the normal word order of the sentence. If we move "to throw" back to its normal place, the effect disappears, and Ajax is left standing there with the rock sagging in his hands:

When Ájax strives to throw some rock's vast weight

Read the two versions of the line aloud. The little fillip of a perfectly regular foot makes us feel the actual attempt to heave the rock. The embodiment of content in form could hardly be more remarkable.

Scansion

"Excellence" by Robert Francis is a subtle example of rhythmic sleight-of-hand:

Excellence is millimeters and not miles.

From poor to good is great. From good to best is small.

From almost best to best sometimes not measurable.

The man who leaps the highest leaps perhaps an inch

Above the runner-up. How glorious that inch   5

And that split-second longer in the air before the fall.

Try your hand at scanning this poem to see what its meter is and how it works. Mark the meter with a pencil or on a separate sheet before you look at the scansion that follows. (*Note:* Omitting the unaccented syllable from the *first* foot of a line is a very normal variation. Here, the first foot is "Éx-." The effect is to push the poem off to a sharp, confident start. When such a defective foot occurs *within* a line, however, it is called a **"lame" foot** and usually suggests disorder or a dramatic break. The first line of William Butler Yeats's "After Long Silence" (page 353), for instance, may be scanned correctly two ways:

Spéech af|tér lóng | sílence; | ˣít | is ríght,

or:

ˣSpéech | after | lóng si|lence; it | is ríght,

Both scansions suggest the abruptness of beginning to speak after a long silence—the first in the trochaic substitution, the second in the normal variation of the omitted first unaccented syllable. Both record the halting, jerky rhythm—only two regular iambic feet in the line. But the second seems less revealing, since it suggests iambic smoothness in the last two feet. In the first, the glitch of the lame fourth foot, coinciding with the caesura, suggests not only the abrupt starting of speech, but its starting and stopping . . . and resuming awkwardly, ambiguously (the uncertainty of accent on "it"). To my ear, the first scansion is a better record of the line's dramatic rhythm as I hear it. (Note: the missing syllable is indicated by an *x*.)

In scanning, listen to the poem without imposing a metrical pattern on it. Read each line aloud slowly and more than once. It may also be a good idea to scan several lines tentatively before marking them, to determine what the *norm* of the poem is. Having that norm in mind may help you resolve difficult or ambiguous spots in the rhythm. Since unique qualities most readily appear in variations from the norm, don't *te TUM* so hard that you miss something interesting. Mark ambiguous syllables (those you can imagine two ways) with your preferred interpretation in parentheses. Like substitutions, such feet will very likely lead to a secret of the rhythm.

Éx|cellénce | is mil|limét|ers and | not miles.

From poor | to good | is great. | From good | to best | is small.

From al|most best | to best | sometimes | not mea|surab|le.

The man | who leaps | the high|est leaps | perhaps | an inch

Above | the run|ner-up. | How glor|ious | that inch

And that | split-sec|ond long|er in | the air | before | the fall.

The norm meter in "Excellence" is iambic hexameter, which may appear an odd choice for a poem about legerity, the lightness of the high-jumper. Perhaps the poet's first line—"Excellence is millimeters and not miles"—gave him the meter. Having said that to himself, or written it down, he had at least to consider writing the poem in hexameters, "sluggish" as they may seem (Pope's characterization). He might have changed the line to "Excellence is inches and not miles" and had a lighter, pentameter line. Since he uses "inch" later in the poem, it wouldn't have been out of place to make that change. But probably he liked the *feel* of "is millimeters and not miles," as the alliterated *m*'s contrast the tiny and vast units of measure.

However accidental, hexameters were an excellent choice. The poem is less interested in the jumper's lightness or ease than in his difficulty, the extra push or effort that earns excellence, that buys the additional "inch / And that split-second longer in the air." Possibly because hexameter feels as though it goes on a little beyond the pentameter norm of English—seems to have to somehow push its way to its end—it was a perfect choice. Having made that choice, the poet exploits it beautifully, especially in the poem's last line where, after we have become accustomed to lines of six feet, he pushes it just a little farther and ends with a heptameter. We don't see that extra length because the words are shorter, but we hear it, even if we don't count the feet. The line itself lasts in the ear just a second longer than the others.

Something subtle, and perhaps not very noticeable to a casual reader, is going on rhythmically in every line of "Excellence." In the first line, the almost spondaic "not miles" provides a rhythmical emphasis on the line's contrast between millimeters and miles, tiny and large, as do the short "i" of "mil-" and the long "i" of "miles." In line 2, the unrelenting monosyllables and the caesural pause may suggest the distance between "poor" and "best," a distance that can be crossed only by such a dogged pace as the line itself has. In line 3 the main effect is in the last foot, where the almost completely unaccented secondary accent of the word "meas|urab|le," followed by the unaccented feminine syllable, blurs the beat so much that we almost have to force the voice to record it. (We can't bring ourselves to say "MÉAS-ur-ÁB-le.") And so the line's end perfectly mimes the meaning of "not measurable." This effect is heightened, too, by the temptation to hear an off-rhyme between the last syllable of "measurable" and "miles" and "small," and so to displace the accent falsely onto that last syllable.

Like line 2, line 4 is metrically regular; but the movement is not broken by a caesura. It continues without pause to its end, where, after three end-stopped lines, the run-on to line 4 suggests the leap itself. In line 5 a light secondary accent on the last syllable of "glor|ious" hurries us along to the poem's second run-on. This run-on and the spondee of "split-sec-" in line 6 appropriately hold the voice a bit longer than we expect. The very light accent on "in" perhaps suggests the momentary suspension of the jumper "before the fall."

Metrical Potential

Of all the qualities meter may be said to provide, including our pleasure in symmetry, the focusing of attention, or the lull of the trance it may induce, none is more important than its stretching the web tight so that every effect may be felt. But there is one function the poet will be aware of, and a reader perhaps not. Once chosen, meter, like stanza shape in free verse, provides a trellis for the tendrils of the unfolding poem to wind around. Though a good poet takes advantage of rhythmical possibilities and imitative effects, every phrase, every line cannot be jeweled. There will be flat portions—necessary exposition, transition, or preparation for effects to come—and for these the poet will be grateful that the meter, the form, is simply *there*. Its presence allows her or him, without being particularly brilliant, to keep the poem going, the voice talking, the ball in the air. Often enough, the real magic is the unnoticed craft with which the poet gets the rabbit *into* the hat.

Look back to Miller Williams's moving "Ruby Tells All" (page 58). Did you notice when you first read it that the norm is iambic pentameter? A poem in meter may be as natural and speech-like as a poem in free verse, and a reader (unless he or she is interested) needn't pay attention to which it is. Rhythm, of course, *works* without having to be analyzed. A student of "Ruby Tells All," though, would notice the lines where Williams has varied from the iambic pentameter norm, and would be interested in how and why.

As a beginning poet you may find meter hard to manage at first; it may seem wooden, mechanical. As Pope says, however,

> True ease in writing comes from art, not chance,
> As those move easiest who have learned to dance.

With practice, meter becomes second nature. It is really a rule-of-thumb, simple, binary system; it usually bends, through substitution, to fit any purpose. Like the skillful tennis player who no longer has to think about form and so can concentrate on the ball and the game, as a skillful poet you will have your eye on the subject, your mind on the poem.

Once the form, whether metrical or stanzaic, is launched in a poem, it will suggest possibilities for dealing with the subject that might never have occurred to the poet otherwise. This must have happened in the writing of Francis's "Excellence" and perhaps happens in the writing of nearly every good poem. You cannot know the potential until you get there. Rhythmical discoveries result from intuition or trial-and-error. The poet says something and tests it across the meter; it doesn't feel right so she or he restates it and tries again until the right rhythm just "happens." Persistence can make one lucky.

QUESTIONS AND SUGGESTIONS

1. Scan the following poems, considering the significance of rhythmical variations. (For comparison, my scansions are in Appendix I.) *Clue:* Larkin's "First Sight" is iambic tetrameter with the first unaccented syllable of each line "omitted." How is the resulting line-by-line, halting rhythm appropriate to the poem?

a) *Epigram: Of Treason*

SIR JOHN HARINGTON   (1561–1612)

Treason doth never prosper, what's the reason?

For if it prosper, none dare call it treason.

b) *Death of the Day*

WALTER SAVAGE LANDOR   (1775–1864)

My pictures blacken in their frames

    As night comes on,

And youthful maids and wrinkled dames

    Are now all one.

Death of the day! a sterner Death

    Did worse before;

The fairest form, the sweetest breath,

    Away he bore.

c) *Tribute*

JOHN FANDEL   (b. 1925)

What the bee knows

Tastes in the honey

Sweet and sunny.

O wise bee. O rose.

d) *First Sight*

PHILIP LARKIN   (1922–1985)

Lambs that learn to walk in snow

When their bleating clouds the air

Meet a vast unwelcome, know

Nothing but a sunless glare.

Newly stumbling to and fro   5

All they find, outside the fold,

Is a wretched width of cold.

As they wait beside the ewe,

Her fleeces wetly caked, there lies

Hidden round them, waiting too,   10

Earth's immeasurable surprise.

They could not grasp it if they knew,

What so soon will wake and grow

Utterly unlike the snow.

Some other interesting poems for practicing scansion: Robert Francis's "Pitcher" (norm, iambic pentameter; page 109), John Milton's "On His Blindness" (page 129), Theodore Roethke's "I Knew a Woman" (page 148), Peter Klappert's "The Invention of the Telephone" (page 149).

2. Translate the following passage from Lewis Thomas's *The Lives of a Cell* into blank verse (unrhymed iambic pentameter). As much as possible, use the language of the prose. But stretch or compress and, where necessary, add your own touch. For comparison, a version in rhymed couplets is in Appendix I.

A solitary ant, afield, cannot be considered to have much of anything on his mind: indeed, with only a few neurons strung together by fibers, he can't be imagined to have a mind at all, much less a thought. He is more like a ganglion on legs. Four ants together, or ten, encircling a dead moth on a path, begin to look more like an idea. They fumble and shove, gradually moving the food toward the Hill, but as though by blind chance. It is only when you watch the dense mass of thousands of ants, crowded together around the Hill, blackening the ground, that you begin to see the whole beast, and now you observe it thinking, planning, calculating. It is an intelligence, a kind of live computer, with crawling bits for its wits.

3. Consider, in these poems by students, how appropriate is the choice of a very loose meter, bouncy with anapests? Do the rhythms enhance and convey the poems' tones?

a) *Cherries Jubilee*

—*Meditations while pie-eating*

JOSEPH URBAN·

The cherries in pies are all gooey and soft
unlike the firmness of little red buttocks
that float in fruit cocktail and bob upside down
or the round maraschino my father will munch
having drained a Manhattan on our kitchen barstool.   5
There are cherries in ice cream and cherry preserves
to spread on hot muffins on cold winter mornings.
The proverbial cherry has always been found
at the top of the heap of whipped cream on a sundae.
Cough syrup is cherry and Smith Brothers' drops.   10
Pink popsicles. Pastries with cherry insides.
Down on the corner the barber who slicks
the cowlicks on little boys' heads with hair tonic
gives the ones who don't cry a surprise lollipop
and cherry is always the flavor as well   15
as those little red boxes of Christmas hard candies
handed out as a prize by department store Santas
to cherry-eyed three-year-olds slobbering kisses
on his big cherry nose with their small cherry lips
like holiday cherubs with little round faces   20
and cheeks cherry red from the chill of December.
In fifth grade Fat Freddy whom everyone hated
was caught lighting cherry bombs in the boys' room
and sent to Miss Wakeley who wore cherry rouge,
the cherry bun tied on her head with red ribbon.   25
There are cherries on trees (which is where they all started)
that blossom on Washington's streets during April
like the one that our country's father chopped down
and couldn't lie to *his* father about.
But now boys his age have no trouble lying   30
about all the cherries they've popped in their time.
The name of the Cherry's been taken in vain.
I can't even drink a bottle of pop
without conjuring visions of sexual conquest.
Ma Chérie, my dear one, I'm still on your side.   35
I still eat my pie with a fork and yet this
even this that was once just an act pure and simple
has somehow turned phallic. I stab through the crust

piercing five at a time and savor the flavor—
the only known fruit so exquisite and tiny   40
to serve as the one word summation of all
our most infinite innocence, intimate drives.

b) *Belfast Ballad*

TIM LUCAS*

I was born on the rug of a two-story snug
And fueled up with heroic desires.
For old Ireland's cause I'd have broken all laws
And perished in Protestant fires.

Mum weaned me on stories of the Catholic glories   5
Of Charlie Parnell and his men.
I wanted the same for it seemed a grand game
For a lad and his mates to be in.

So I dreamed of the day when I'd join in the fray
And the English limbs I'd dismember;   10
That when Ireland was free, I'd sit—lads on knee—
Spinning legends in which I'm a member.

While wearing the green I caressed my machine
Gun and kept it ready and loaded;
And to my Priest's horror, I screamed "Faith Begorra!"   15
On learning Mountbatten° exploded.

But last Sunday I made my first Belfast raid
And didn't get on with the gore.
'Twas Sean Riley's arm that caused my alarm
As it fell, in three parts, to the floor.   20

16 *Mountbatten:* Lord Louis Mountbatten (1900–1979), killed by IRA terrorists.

4. Try making the rhythm and syntax, flow and pauses, of a long *prose* sentence imitate the movement of a skier (mountain climber, bowler, or quarterback fading back to pass). Try the same in a few lines of free verse, then in a few lines of iambic tetrameter.

5. Here are the first two stanzas of "The Garden Seat" by Thomas Hardy (1840–1928). Carefully assessing both the form and the idea or direction of the poem thus far, write the missing third (last) stanza. When you are satisfied with yours, compare it with Hardy's (in Appendix I).

Its former green is blue and thin,
And its once firm legs sink in and in;

Soon it will break down unaware,
Soon it will break down unaware.

At night when reddest flowers are black
Those who once sat thereon come back;
Quite a row of them sitting there,
Quite a row of them sitting there.

6. Transcribe the lyrics of a popular song you enjoy. What formal devices do you find?

7. How much of the fun of the following poem comes from its meter and rhyme? Experiment by trying a rhymeless, free verse version. (Rearrange, use synonyms like "found" for "discovered.") Invent a character with an amusing name and write a funny quatrain of your own.

Miss Twye

GAVIN EWART   (b. 1916)

Miss Twye was soaping her breasts in her bath
When she heard behind her a meaning laugh
And to her amazement she discovered
A wicked man in the bathroom cupboard.

POEMS TO CONSIDER

from An Essay on Criticism   1711

ALEXANDER POPE   (1688–1744)

But most by numbers judge a poet's song;
And smooth or rough, with them, is right or wrong:
In the bright muse though thousand charms conspire,
Her voice is all these tuneful fools admire;
Who haunt Parnassus° but to please their ear,   5
Not mend their minds; as some to church repair,
Not for the doctrine, but the music there.
These equal syllables alone require,
Though oft the ear the open vowels tire;

While expletives their feeble aid do join;   10
And ten low words oft creep in one dull line:
While they ring round the same unvaried chimes,
With sure returns of still expected rhymes;
Where'er you find "the cooling western breeze,"
In the next line, it "whispers through the trees":   15
If crystal streams "with pleasing murmurs creep,"
The reader's threatened (not in vain) with "sleep":
Then, at the last and only couplet fraught
With some unmeaning thing they call a thought,
A needless Alexandrine ends the song,   20
That, like a wounded snake, drags its slow length along.
Leave such to tune their own dull rhymes, and know
What's roundly smooth, or languishingly slow;
And praise the easy vigor of a line,
Where Denham's° strength, and Waller's° sweetness join.   25
True ease in writing comes from art, not chance,
As those move easiest who have learned to dance.
'Tis not enough no harshness gives offense,
The sound must seem an echo to the sense:
Soft is the strain when Zephyr° gently blows,   *the west wind*   30
And the smooth stream in smoother numbers flows;
But when loud surges lash the sounding shore,
The hoarse, rough verse should like the torrent roar:
When Ajax° strives some rock's vast weight to throw,
The line too labors, and the words move slow;   35
Not so, when swift Camilla° scours the plain,
Flies o'er th' unbending corn, and skims along the main.

5 *Parnassus:* Greek mountain, sacred to the Muses.   25 *Denham:* poet Sir John Denham (1615–1669); *Waller:* poet Edmund Waller (1606–1687).   34 *Ajax:* Greek warrior in *The Iliad.*   36 *Camilla:* ancient Roman queen, reputed to run so swiftly that
she could skim over a field of grain without bending the stalks, over the sea without
wetting her feet.

Juggler   1950

RICHARD WILBUR (b. 1921)

A ball will bounce, but less and less. It's not
A light-hearted thing, resents its own resilience.

Falling is what it loves, and the earth falls
So in our hearts from brilliance,
Settles and is forgot.
It takes a sky-blue juggler with five red balls   5

To shake our gravity up. Whee, in the air
The balls roll round, wheel on his wheeling hands,
Learning the ways of lightness, alter to spheres
Grazing his finger ends,   10
Cling to their courses there,
Swinging a small heaven about his ears.

But a heaven is easier made of nothing at all
Than the earth regained, and still and sole within
The spin of worlds, with a gesture sure and noble   15
He reels that heaven in,
Landing it ball by ball,
And trades it all for a broom, a plate, a table.

Oh, on his toe the table is turning, the broom's
Balancing up on his nose, and the plate whirls   20
On the tip of the broom! Damn, what a show, we cry:
The boys stamp, and the girls
Shriek, and the drum booms
And all comes down, and he bows and says good-bye.

If the juggler is tired now, if the broom stands   25
In the dust again, if the table starts to drop
Through the daily dark again, and though the plate
Lies flat on the table top,
For him we batter our hands
Who has won for once over the world's weight.   30

Learning by Doing   1967

HOWARD NEMEROV (b. 1920)

They're taking down a tree at the front door,
The power saw is snarling at some nerves,
Whining at others. Now and then it grunts,
And sawdust falls like snow or a drift of seeds.

Rotten, they tell us, at the fork, and one   5
Big wind would bring it down. So what they do
They do, as usual, to do us good.
Whatever cannot carry its own weight
Has got to go, and so on; you expect
To hear them talking next about survival   10
And the values of a free society.
For in the explanations people give
On these occasions there is generally some
Mean-spirited moral point, and everyone
Privately wonders if his neighbors plan   15
To saw him up before he falls on them.

Maybe a hundred years in sun and shower
Dismantled in a morning and let down
Out of itself a finger at a time
And then an arm, and so down to the trunk,   20
Until there's nothing left to hold on to
Or snub the splintery holding rope around,
And where those big green divagations were
So loftily with shadows interleaved
The absent-minded blue rains in on us.   25

Now that they've got it sectioned on the ground
It looks as though somebody made a plain
Error in diagnosis, for the wood
Looks sweet and sound throughout. You couldn't know,
Of course, until you took it down. That's what   30
Experts are for, and these experts stand round
The giant pieces of tree as though expecting
An instruction booklet from the factory
Before they try to put it back together.

Anyhow, there it isn't, on the ground.   35
Next come the tractor and the crowbar crew
To extirpate what's left and fill the grave.
Maybe tomorrow grass seed will be sown.
There's some mean-spirited moral point in that
As well: you learn to bury your mistakes,   40
Though for a while at dusk the darkening air
Will be with many shadows interleaved,
And pierced with a bewilderment of birds.

Song from *Twelfth Night*

1601/2

WILLIAM SHAKESPEARE (1564–1616)

O mistress mine, where are you roaming?
O, stay and hear, your true love's coming,
  That can sing both high and low.
Trip no further, pretty sweeting;
Journeys end in lovers meeting,   5
  Every wise man's son doth know.

What is love? 'Tis not hereafter.
Present mirth hath present laughter;
  What's to come is still unsure.
In delay there lies no plenty;   10
Then come kiss me, sweet and twenty,
  Youth's a stuff will not endure.

Act II, Scene iii

When I Set Out for Lyonnesse

1870

THOMAS HARDY (1840–1928)

When I set out for Lyonnesse,
  A hundred miles away,
  The rime was on the spray,
And starlight lit my lonesomeness
When I set out for Lyonnesse   5
  A hundred miles away.

What would bechance at Lyonnesse
  While I should sojourn there
  No prophet durst declare,
Nor did the wisest wizard guess   10
What would bechance at Lyonnesse
  While I should sojourn there.

When I came back from Lyonnesse
  With magic in my eyes,

All marked with mute surmise   15
My radiance rare and fathomless,
When I came back from Lyonnesse
    With magic in my eyes!

Adam's Curse   1904

WILLIAM BUTLER YEATS   (1865–1939)

We sat together at one summer's end,
That beautiful mild woman, your close friend,
And you and I, and talked of poetry.
I said: 'A line will take us hours maybe;
Yet if it does not seem a moment's thought,   5
Our stitching and unstitching has been naught.
Better go down upon your marrow-bones
And scrub a kitchen pavement, or break stones
Like an old pauper, in all kinds of weather;
For to articulate sweet sounds together   10
Is to work harder than all these, and yet
Be thought an idler by the noisy set
Of bankers, schoolmasters, and clergymen
The martyrs call the world.'

                        And thereupon
That beautiful mild woman for whose sake   15
There's many a one shall find out all heartache
On finding that her voice is sweet and low
Replied: 'To be born woman is to know—
Although they do not talk of it at school—
That we must labour to be beautiful.'   20

I said: 'It's certain there is no fine thing
Since Adam's fall but needs much labouring.
There have been lovers who thought love should be
So much compounded of high courtesy
That they would sigh and quote with learned looks   25
Precedents out of beautiful old books;
Yet now it seems an idle trade enough.'

We sat grown quiet at the name of love;
We saw the last embers of daylight die,
And in the trembling blue-green of the sky   30
A moon, worn as if it had been a shell
Washed by time's waters as they rose and fell
About the stars and broke in days and years.

I had a thought for no one's but your ears:
That you were beautiful, and that I strove   35
To love you in the old high way of love;
That it had all seemed happy, and yet we'd grown
As weary-hearted as that hollow moon.

The Sound of Sense:
Of Pitchers and Petticoats

In the "sound of sense" passage (page 83) Pope is having fun with the possibilities of language, showing the tricks it can be made to perform. But the fun has a serious side, for smooth "numbers," regularity of meter, is not enough. Nor is avoiding the common faults he mocks—though what were laughable blunders in 1711 aren't likely to seem nimble graces two and a half centuries later. The crux is that "The sound must seem an echo to the sense." The rest of the passage is a library of effects.

When he mentions the gluey effect of open vowels, he provides a line of them: "Though oft the ear the open vowels tire." He illustrates how filler words like "do" make awkward lines: "While expletives their feeble aid do join." Or how monotonously monosyllables can move: "And ten low words oft creep in one dull line." He makes an illustrative hexameter sinuously sluggish:

A needless Alexandrine ends the song,
That, like a wounded snake, drags its slow length along.

He contrasts the "roundly smooth" with the "languishingly slow," and shows how quick and easy a line can be: "And praise the easy vigor of a line." He makes sound imitate the difference between a "smooth stream" and "loud surges," or between weight or effort and speed or agility:

Soft is the strain when Zephyr gently blows,
And the smooth stream in smoother numbers flows;
But when loud surges lash the sounding shore,
The hoarse, rough verse should like the torrent roar.
When Ajax strives some rock's vast weight to throw,
The line too labors, and the words move slow;
Not so, when swift Camilla scours the plain,
Flies o'er th' unbending corn, and skims along the main.

Like the line showing the hexameter's snakelike slowness, the line showing Camilla's speed is a hexameter! Plainly, it isn't so much the metrical *what* as the rhythmical *how*.

A number of other things are at work in the sound effects of the passage, and this chapter will have a look at these cogs in the rhythmical machinery: *diction, syntax, alliteration and assonance,* and *rhyme.*

Diction

The precise choice of words for what you want to say is more important than sound. Meaning itself must be overriding—the exact word, not merely something near it. Poetry has no room for the *I mean's* and *you know's* by which, in everyday conversation, we stumble toward being understood. The poet, like his or her best reader, will have keen antennae for the overtones and nuances, the connotations and suggestions that most words carry with them. Connotations are the feelings, the approval or disapproval, that go along with essentially the same denotative information in different words. Consider S. I. Hayakawa's amusing example: the difference between *Finest quality filet mignon* and *first-class piece of dead cow.* Or the difference between *slim* or *slender* (approving), *thin* (approximately neutral), and *skinny* (disapproving). The language is happily full of words that are near but slightly differing in meaning, and a good thesaurus (like *Roget's New Pocket Thesaurus in Dictionary Form,* edited by Norman Lewis) is one of the handiest books a poet can own. When you are stuck for a word, a look in the thesaurus can set you off in a fresh direction. Often the overtones or nuances of a word come from its etymological derivation, as the word *thesaurus* itself comes from a Greek word meaning "treasury" or as our word *verse* has hidden in it the Latin root "to turn."

Under *old,* Roget cites some eighty-seven adjectives, including *aged, elderly, ancient, hoary, antiquated, archaic, antique, timeless, geriatric, senile, timeworn, worm-eaten, old-fashioned, out-of-date, outmoded, passé, stale, veteran, experienced, seasoned.* Several basic meanings of *old* appear among these, applying, for instance, to people (*elderly, senile*) or to things and manners (*archaic, antique, old-fashioned, stale*). Depending on how we felt about him, the same old man might be described as *old-fashioned* or *seasoned* or as *timeless* or *timeworn.*

As we choose words, we should consider more than meaning and nuance. A word, in general, ought to be of the same level as the other words in the context. A fancy polysyllable, for example, might not fit among more everyday words. We wouldn't say, "Mr. Jones was senectuous"; we would say simply, "old." Sometimes, however, an odd word, from another level or range of meaning, provides exactly the sense and the surprise the poet wants, as with Larkin's "vast unwelcome" in "First Sight" or Cunningham's "spiritual noise." In "My Papa's Waltz," Roethke chooses the less predictable word "countenance" rather than "face":

> My mother's countenance
> Could not unfrown itself

The greater formality and strangeness of "countenance" emphasize the stiffness and the oddness, to the boy, of her expression, as the word "face" could not. Countenance is also a shade more precise, since it primarily connotes the look or appearance of a face. (Lurking behind it, perhaps, is "countenance" as a verb.) The surprise of an unexpected word when it turns out to be especially appropriate to the poet's intention is exemplified by Robert Herrick's choice of "liquefaction" in "Upon Julia's Clothes" (page 126) or by X. J. Kennedy's use of "instruments" in "First Confession" (page 126) where he describes, from the point of view of a small boy, a little girl's genitals.

> I'd bribed my girl to pee
> That I might spy her instruments.

The witty "instruments" suggests both the sexual neutrality of the boy's interest and, along with "spy," implies the almost scientific quality of his curiosity.

Clichés—stale, timeworn, too familiar words and phrases—are best avoided in favor of freshness. The language of poetry pays attention, and it is the nature of a cliché not to pay attention. Recently a newspaper carried this sentence: " 'I think we are enjoying the backlash of the moral decline that peaked in Watergate,' Dr. Weber said." Enjoying a lash of any kind seems unlikely; and the *peak* of a *decline* is language that isn't listening to itself at all.

Poetry often generates a kind of cliché all its own, **"poetic diction,"** which is fancy, pompous, or ornate language that gets used and reused until it becomes simply dull. Contractions like *o'er* for *over* or *ere* for *before* and elegant pronouns like *thou* are examples. So are such eighteenth-century elegant variations as *finny tribe* for *fish*, or such twentieth-century buzz words as *ceremony, stardust,* or *parameters.* The best rule is never to use in a poem a word that you wouldn't use in speech.

So, roundabout, we come to the sound of words, which is a secondary but important property of diction. In general, the sounds of the words in a passage should be cleanly enunciated, smooth, and easy to say; or, when they are awkward, clogging, and hard to say, it should be for a reason related to the sense, as with Pope's deliberately clumsy "Though oft the ear the open vowels tire" or deliberately harsh "The hoarse, rough verse should like the torrent roar." The effect of a word on the other words near it, both in rhythm and in music (euphony or cacaphony), is basic. In the line about Ajax, for example, Pope might have chosen other words: "When Ajax *tries*," instead of "*strives*." But not only is "strives" more intense in meaning (suggesting "strife"), it is also a little harder to enunciate; "tries" would lose the slight difficulty of the two s-sounds, "A-jacks strives," a clear enunciation of which requires a small but effortful pause. Or he might have written, instead of "some rock's vast weight," "a boulder's weight." But the line would lose the massing of accents for the merely regular. And it would lose the further s-sound difficulty of "strives some," as well as the heavy clotting of consonants in "some rock's vast weight." Try saying the two versions of the line:

When Ajax tries a boulder's weight to throw

When Ajax strives some rock's vast weight to throw

Some words have their own sound effects built in: words like *hiss, buzz, snap, pop, smash, whisper, murmur, shout*. Such words are called *onomatopoetic* (noun: **onomatopoeia**). Never mind the Greek name, but keep your ear tuned for such inherent sound effects. More words than one might think have something of this quality. Notice the light vowels in *thin, skinny, slim, slender, spindly*. Or the long vowels or clotting consonants in *fat, hefty, gross, huge, stout, pudgy, thick*. Notice how lightly "*delicate*" hits its syllables, how heavily "*ponderous*" does. Feel how your mouth says *pinched, tight, open, round, hard, soft, smooth*.

It isn't that particular sounds, particular vowels or consonants, have meanings as such; *slight* and *threadlike* don't sound much like their meanings. Often, though, there seems to be some at least latent correlation between the meaning and the noise of words that the poet can use. The most familiar example of onomatopoeia is Tennyson's

The moan of doves in immemorial elms
And murmuring of innumerable bees

"Moan" and "murmur" are onomatopoetic, and the rather slurred, hard-to-count syllables of "innumerable" might also qualify. The hum of the lines, the alliterated m's, n's, and r's that pick up the sounds of "moan" and "murmuring," seems imitative throughout.

Such effects should be used sparingly. In the extreme they quickly become silly or obtrusive and overwhelm meaning, as in "The Bells" by Edgar Allan Poe (1809–1849):

Hear the sledge with the bells—
Silver bells!
What a world of merriment their melody foretells!
How they tinkle, tinkle, tinkle,
In the icy air of night!   5
While the stars that oversprinkle
All the heavens, seem to twinkle
With a crystalline delight;
Keeping time, time, time,
In a sort of Runic rhyme,   10
To the tintinnabulation that so musically wells
From the bells, bells, bells, bells,
Bells, bells, bells—
From the jingling and the tinkling of the bells.

And so it goes for a further ninety-nine lines, which we can do Poe the favor of ignoring.

Syntax

Syntax is the way that words are put together to form phrases, clauses, or sentences. The poet can take advantage of a language's many alternative patterns for formulating or constructing sentences. Placement of modifiers, apposition, series, restrictive or nonrestrictive clauses, active or passive voice, and inversion are obvious formulas. The word *syntax* comes from the Greek *syn* ("together") and *tassein* ("to arrange"): "to arrange together." Also from *tassein* we get the word *tactics,* a military image that may suggest the value of syntax to the poet in deploying his or her forces.

The syntactical qualities of good writing in general, with main ideas in main clauses and subordinate ideas in subordinate clauses, apply in poetry. Pope's "some rock's vast weight to throw," instead of "to throw some rock's vast weight," is a simple example of the reenforcement of meaning by syntax—by **inversion** of normal word order. So is the fussiness implied by the overcarefully inserted "with them" in:

But most by numbers judge a poet's song,
And smooth or rough, with them, is right or wrong

The syntax, not the statement itself, communicates the slight contempt, as if Pope were holding the words "with them" away from his nose. In "Excellence" (page 75) Robert Francis achieves a syntactical effect simply by choosing to make two sentences of the line "From poor to good is great. From good to best is small." The syntactical ambiguity of Laughlin's "The Goddess" (page 52) is part and parcel of the subject's tentative, excited, breathless quality. As with every aspect of form, the very arrangement of words into clauses and sentences can be useful.

In these lines from John Donne's "Satire III," the complex and entwined syntax, played skillfully over the line-breaks, rhythmically suggests the difficulty through which "Truth" is approachable.

> On a huge hill,
> Cragged, and steep, Truth stands, and he that will
> Reach her, about must, and about must go;
> And what the hill's suddenness resists, win so

Syntactical displacement and inversions constantly impede the lines' movement. Compare a more normal prose version:

> On a huge, cragged, and steep hill, Truth stands, and he that will reach her must go about and about, and in that way win what the hill's suddenness resists.

The effect is supported by the passage's metrical roughness and irregularity through-out, especially by the forced anapest in line 4:

And what | the hills sud|denness resists, win so

The voice wants to read "hill's" as accented but must push on to the syllable "sud-" before it finds the line's pattern. This rhythmic drag over "hill's" produces a feeling of the steepness or the abruptness of the slope, which cannot be gone up directly but only by a circling sideward path. Throughout the line the voice seems almost literally to be working against gravity.

In "The Frog" the anonymous poet uses syntactical patterning to produce, in spite of the apparent illiteracy, a very subtle formal structure:

> What a wonderful bird the frog are!
> When he stand he sit almost;
> When he hop he fly almost.
> He ain't got no sense hardly;
> He ain't got no tail hardly either.   5
> When he sit, he sit on what he ain't got almost.

Two sets of parallel sentences ("When . . . almost" in lines 2–3 and "He ain't got . . ." in lines 4–5) adroitly set up the last line which gathers both patterns in its climactic syntax.

Frequently, when someone talks of the speaking "voice" being caught in the words of a poem, it is the syntax that is giving the effect. Robert Frost was a master of coaxing both music and meaning out of syntax. Listen again to the repetitions and emphases of these lines from "An Old Man's Winter Night":

> What kept his eyes from giving back the gaze
> Was the lamp tilted near them in his hand.
> What kept him from remembering what it was
> That brought him to that creaking room was age.
> He stood with barrels round him—at a loss.   5
> And having scared the cellar under him
> In clomping here, he scared it once again
> In clomping off;—and scared the outer night,
> Which has its sounds, familiar, like the roar
> Of trees and crack of branches, common things,   10
> But nothing so like beating on a box.

Even the four *him*'s in lines 3–6—the first three unaccented—work to a minor climax within the turning and returning syntax that gives a rhythm to the old man's habitual, now meaningless, movements in the house.

How central to a poem's strategy syntax—"the muscle of thought"—can be is clear in Whitman's

When I Heard the Learn'd Astronomer

> When I heard the learn'd astronomer,
> When the proofs, the figures, were ranged in columns before me,
> When I was shown the charts and diagrams, to add, divide, and
> measure them,
> When I sitting heard the astronomer where he lectured with much
> applause in the lecture-room,
> How soon unaccountable I became tired and sick,   5
> Till rising and gliding out I wander'd off by myself,
> In the mystical moist night-air, and from time to time,
> Look'd up in perfect silence at the stars.

We, too, instantly prefer that "perfect silence" to the astronomer's blab, and the real stars to any talk about them. It is a point, however, the poet can't make by means of adjectives or a metaphor—they are simply "the stars." The closest he comes to being "poetic" is the alliterating phrase in line 7, "the mystical moist night air," which puns on *mist-mystical* and in "moist" contrasts to the lecturer's dry discussion. And we may recall that the verbs for the speaker's actions in line 6, "rising," "gliding," and "wander'd," are proper for describing the motions of heavenly bodies. (Our word *planet* comes from a Greek root meaning "wanderer.")

The poem's force and especially that of the chillingly beautiful last line come from Whitman's manipulation of syntax. Lines 1–4, describing the lecture, have no main clause, and so seem indecisive; and they are long, prosy, choppy, repetitous, clogged with lists and details—in perfect imitation of the lecture. Even the verbs in lines 2–3 are passive. The redundant thump of "where he *lectured* with much applause in the *lecture*-room" seems banal and clumsy. The effect on the listener is also recorded in the syntax. The placement of "sitting"—"I sitting heard"—suggests awkwardness and discomfort. In the contortion of line 5, the adjective "unaccountable" is misplaced; it doesn't really modify the speaker, and should be an adverb: I became unaccountably tired and sick. (The suggestion of course is that he, as a living being, is no more *countable* in figures and columns than the natural stars.)

In contrast, everything in lines 6–8 is shorter, simpler, more active. Unlike the dangling and restarting "when" clauses, the balanced prepositional phrases of line 7 give a sense of leisure and space, with "and" easily linking "I wander'd" and "Look'd." Beginning with a verb, line 8 flows with a sense of syntactical resolution. It is also the shortest and (in syntax) most direct line in the poem. This culminating impression of clarity is reenforced by rhythm: line 8 (in a poem of rangy free verse) happens to be perfect iambic pentameter!

Look'd úp | ĭn pér|fečt sí|lĕnce ˘at | thĕ stárs.

It is not only freedom we feel, but order, unity.

Alliteration and Assonance

Alliteration is the repetition of consonant sounds in several words in a passage; **assonance,** the repetition of vowel sounds. The *b*'s in these lines of "An Old Man's Winter Night" are alliteration:

> . . . like the roar
> Of trees and crack of *b*ranches, common things,
> But nothing so like *b*eating on a *b*ox.

Also alliterated, less emphatically, are the *r*'s, the hard *c*'s (including of course "box"—"bocks"), and the *n*'s. Assonance appears in the identical vowels of "crack" and "branches," of "common" and "box," and perhaps, muted by the distance of their separation, of "roar" and "so." The *b*'s are clearly onomatopoetic, suggesting the sounds of the old man's clomping about. The *r*'s may suggest the storm, much as in Pope's "But when loud surges lash the sounding shore, / The hoarse, rough verse should like the torrent roar." Other alliteration in the passage functions musically, linking sounds to thread the lines together so that they are tight and harmonious.

The assonance of "common" and "box," along with the climaxing of the string of *b*'s and hard *c*'s in "box," gives the word something very near the emphatic finality of rhyme. Every element of "box" repeats sounds heard earlier in the lines.

Given the limited number of common sounds in English, both alliteration and assonance would be hard to avoid. Using them is more discovering, or taking advantage of, than imposing them. Their main value, often more subliminal than obvious, is the linking of sounds that give a passage its autonomy or harmony. In Milton's "Men called him Mulciber; and how he fell / From Heaven they fabled" (page 5), the alliterated *m*'s and then *h*'s and *f*'s, and *l*'s throughout, give the clauses a musical unity. The assonance of "Men" and "fell" helps to frame the line. Similarly, in Williams's "The Red Wheelbarrow" (page 42), stanzas 2 and 3 are linked by the *r*'s of "*r*ed" and "*r*ain," stanzas 3 and 4 by the *w*'s of "*w*ater" and "*w*hite." The vowels of "depends" in stanza 1 reappear in "red wheel" in stanza 2. And stanzas 1, 3, and 4 have internal assonance: "m*u*ch" and "*u*pon," "glazed" and "rain," "beside" and "white." One by one, these assonances and alliterations are trivial; together they provide an aural undertone that helps to unify the poem. The four *b*'s in the last two quatrains of Roethke's "My Papa's Waltz" (page 65)— "*b*attered," "*b*uckle," "*b*eat," and "*b*ed"—thread the poem's climaxing music. The *s*'s frame the poem's last line—"Still clinging to your shirt"—and the short *i*'s and internal rhyme of "St*i*ll cl*i*nging" are onomatopoetic.

Alliteration and assonance also serve to emphasize or pair related words or phrases. The *s*'s in Pope's "The *s*ound must *s*eem an echo to the *s*ense" unify and also sharply emphasize the central meaning. Such emphatic pairing underlines comparison or contrast, as in Francis's "Excellence is *m*illimeters and not *m*iles" or in Nemerov's "That we may lick their *h*inder parts and thump their *h*eads." How potent such alliteration may be can be seen by comparing the last two lines of this stanza of Poe's "To Helen"—

> On desperate seas long wont to roam,
>> Thy hyacinth hair, thy classic face,
> Thy Naiad airs have brought me home
>> To the glory that was Greece
>> And the grandeur that was Rome.

—to an earlier version of the same lines, which are flat and insipid:

> To the beauty of fair Greece
> And the grandeur of old Rome.

Rhyme

By definition, **rhyme** is an identity in two or more words of vowel sound and of any following consonants (or syllables in the case of two- or three-syllable rhymes).

Exact rhymes: *gate-late; own-bone; aware-hair; applause-gauze; go-throw.* Rhymes normally fall on accented syllables. Double (or feminine) rhymes normally fall on an accented and unaccented syllable: *going-throwing; merry-cherry; army-harm me;* but they may fall on two accented syllables, as in p*ing-pong, sing-song* or *breadbox-head locks.* Triple rhymes are *merrily-warily;* admonish *you*—astonish *you;* head *you off*—instead *you scoff.* There are a few natural four-syllable or perhaps even five-syllable rhymes, like c*riticism-witticism.* For the most part, multiple rhymes seem comic. Clever, show-off rhymes are obtrusive and, thus, appropriate to light or humorous verse.

English is not an easy language to rhyme. (The problem in Italian is to keep from rhyming.) There are a number of familiar words for which there are no natural rhymes, like "circle" or "month." For some words there is only one natural rhyme: "strength-length," "fountain-mountain." And a word as much used as "love" offers only meager possibilities: *above, dove, glove, shove, of.* Despite a poet's best contortions, it is hard to make such rhymes fresh; consequently, *u*nrhymed verse is standard, as the much-used blank verse of Shakespeare's plays and many of Frost's dramatic monologues. Other properties of sound, like alliteration and assonance, can make unrhymed verse as musical or effective as need be.

The difficulty of rhyme in English has opened up a wide variety of inexact rhyme—**off-** or **slant-rhymes**—that the poet may use with considerable freshness. One device is terminal alliteration, as in *love-move, bone-gone, what-bat,* or "chi*ll-full.*" Another is consonance (identity of consonants with different main vowels), as in *bad-bed, full-fool, fine-faun,* or *summer-simmer;* or near consonance as in fi*rm-room, past-pressed,* or *shadow-meadow.* There is assonance, of course, as in *bean-sweet* or h*ow-cloud;* and Emily Dickinson has even made length of vowel work, as in "be-fly" or the fainter "day-eternity."

Rhyming accented with unaccented (or secondarily accented) syllables is also a frequent method of off-rhyme, as in "*see*-pretty," "*though*-fellow," "*full*-eagle," "*fish*-polish," "*them*-solemn," "*under*-stir." There is no need to be systematic about the varieties of off-rhyme. Anything will do in the right context. In this World War I poem by Wilfred Owen (1893–1918), off-rhyme becomes nearly as formal as exact rhyme. The persistent refusal to rhyme gives a slightly awry sound to the poem in keeping with its highly ironic theme.

Arms and the Boy

Let the boy try along this bayonet-blade
How cold steel is, and keen with hunger of blood;
Blue with all malice, like a madman's flash;
And thinly drawn with famishing for flesh.

Lend him to stroke these blind, blunt bullet-leads   5
Which long to nuzzle in the hearts of lads,

Or give him cartridges of fine zinc teeth,
Sharp with the sharpness of grief and death.

For his teeth seem for laughing round an apple.
There lurk no claws behind his fingers supple;   10
And God will grow no talons at his heels,
Nor antlers through the thickness of his curls.

In Marianne Moore's syllabic "The Fish," by contrast, the mingling of exact and inexact rhymes, along with the heavily run-on rhythm, gives a feeling of loose shifting, appropriate to its watery underseascape. This effect is reenforced by the surprising lack of rhyme in the last line of each stanza—which may suggest to the ear the openness of the long, yet unsettled, struggle of sea and rock-coast. The title is part of the poem's first sentence:

The Fish

wade
through black jade.
   Of the crow-blue mussel-shells, one keeps
   adjusting the ash-heaps;
      open and shutting itself like   5

an
injured fan.
   The barnacles which encrust the side
   of the wave, cannot hide
      there for the submerged shafts of the   10

sun
split like spun
   glass, move themselves with spotlight swiftness
   into the crevices—
      in and out, illuminating   15

the
turquoise sea
   of bodies. The water drives a wedge
   of iron through the iron edge
      of the cliff; whereupon the stars,   20

pink
rice-grains, ink-
   bespattered jelly-fish, crabs like green

lilies, and submarine
    toadstools, slide each on the other. 25

All
external
    marks of abuse are present on this
    defiant edifice—
      all the physical features of 30

ac-
cident—lack
    of cornice, dynamite grooves, burns, and
    hatchet strokes, these things stand
      out on it; the chasm-side is 35

dead.
Repeated
    evidence has proved that it can live
    on what can not revive
      its youth. The sea grows old in it. 40

The inventive rhyming is extraordinary. Expectation makes us hear the subtle double off-rhyme in "swiftness-crevices." A slight emphasis on the unaccented article "an" is achieved by setting it in a line by itself; and this gives the run-on an awkward, "injured" movement. Similarly, the rhyme on the first syllable of the broken "ac- / cident" seems ingeniously suggestive. The rhymes may be as heavy as "wade-jade" in the rhythmically viscous "wade / through black jade," or as light and merely touched-on as "the-sea" in the rhythmically shifting and quick "illuminating // the / turquoise sea / of bodies." The pattern of unrhymed fifth lines is resolved in the last stanza; there by assonance the light *i* of "it" picks up the light *i* of "live" (which is rhymed with "revive" only by terminal alliteration of *v*'s) and so brings the poem to a fulfilled musical stop. The interface of sea and rock is amusingly suggested in the poet's saying that the barnacles "encrust the side / of the *wave*," rather than the side of the rock. The color and suspense of the endless warfare between these entities is deftly presented in every detail of varying line-length, run-on, and rhyme.

    Rhyme works in a number of ways. It may serve simply as a formal device: musically pleasurable, part of the poem's tune. It may, in its sharpness and precision, reenforce the poem's "bite," closing the box up tight, as in epigrams. It may be charming and graceful as in Blake's "The Lamb" (page 179), grand and sonorous as in Shakespeare's Sonnet 55 ("Not marble, nor the gilded monuments," page 111), or unremitting and abrasive as the triple rhymes in Frost's sardonic "Provide, Provide" (page 112). Like alliteration, rhyme may be emphatic, underlining comparisons or contrasts. The juxtaposition "chance-dance" almost sums up the opposition in Pope's

> True ease in writing comes from art, not chance,
> As those move easiest who have learned to dance.

So far we have been considering *end*-rhyme, that is, rhyme occurring at line-ends as part of the formal organization of the poem. Rhyme may also be **internal,** occurring anywhere within lines, musically "accidental." Internal rhyme may be as obvious as in the line of the popular song, "the *lazy, hazy, crazy, days* of summer," or as in Algernon Swinburne's "*Sister,* my *sister,* O *fleet sweet swallow,*" where along with the alliteration it perhaps suggests the quick, darting flight of a swallow. Or it may be as casual as it appears in Howard Nemerov's "Learning by Doing" (page 85), where it works almost secretly among the alliteration and assonance that thread the tight lines:

> Maybe a hundred years in sun and shower
> Dismantled in a morning and let down
> Out of itself a finger at a time
> And then an arm . . .

Richard Wilbur's stately "Year's End" (page 115) exemplifies the masterly control of sound. Note the second stanza:

> I've known the wind by water banks to shake
> The late leaves down, which frozen where they fell
> And held in ice as dancers in a spell
> Fluttered all winter long into a lake;
> Graved on the dark in gestures of descent,
> They seemed their own most perfect monument.

The lovely whirling sound within the "which" clause is mainly the result of the internal rhyme of "held," which attaches to the end-rhyme "fell" and unexpectedly spins the voice toward the end-rhyme "spell." That quick movement is intensified by the only technically accented "in" of "as dancers in a spell," with three essentially unaccented syllables speeding the line. Although hardly noticeable, the "rhyme" of two in's—one unaccented, the other technically accented, "in ice as dancers in a spell"—also contributes to the magical feeling of whirling, as does the light, hidden rhyme in "And" and "dancers."

Part of the effect, too, comes from syntactical suspension. We wait a line and a half for the clause's subject, "which," to find its verb, "Fluttered." This suspension mirrors the suspended motion of the leaves (dancers) as, in ice, they *seem* to be still turning but are not. The alliterated *f*'s of "frozen," "fell," and "Fluttered" help mark off this suspension within the continuing *l*'s that begin with "late leaves" in line 2 and culminate with "*long into a lake*" in line 4. The trochaic substitution "Fluttered" signals the resumption of reality. Motion in stasis—leaves in ice, dancers in a spell.

Playing with sounds to see what they can be made to do may be serious work for the poet; it can also be plain fun, especially in comic poems. Rhymes can be both funny and effective, like Richard Armour's "bottle-lot'll." The more outrageous, the better. In *Don Juan* Lord Byron (1788–1824) offered up such rhymes as "fellows-jealous," "the loss of her—philosopher," and

> But—Oh! ye lords of ladies intellectual,
> Inform us truly, have they not hen-peck'd you all?

The twentieth-century master of outlandish rhyme was Ogden Nash (1902–1971), who reported that kids eat spinach "inach by inach," who advised "if called by a panther / Don't anther," and who said of "The Cobra":

> This creature fills its mouth with venum
> And walks upon its duodenum.
> He who attempts to tease the cobra
> Is soon a sadder he, and sobra.

The English Jesuit Gerard Manley Hopkins rhymed "Saviour—gave you a" in his serious sonnet "Hurrahing in Harvest" (page 110). But such multiple and contrived rhymes are best avoided in poems that don't intend to be funny.

Too much rhyme is like too much lipstick. Robert Frost's test for rhymes was to see if he could detect which had occurred to the poet first. Both rhyme words had to seem equally natural, equally called for by what was being said. If one or the other seemed dragged in more for rhyme than sense, the rhyming was a failure. This is a good test and a hard one. If you sometimes have to settle for a slightly weak rhyme, put the weaker of the pair *first*; then, when the rhyme-bell sounds in the ear with the second, it will be calling attention to the more suitable and natural word. Rhyming is easier in couplets, where rhymes come closer together, than in quatrains or other stanzaic forms, where it is more difficult to project ahead and know whether a suitable rhyme may be found or fitted in. At least the poet doesn't have to go back so far if he or she meets difficulty.

Rhyming a whole poem on one sound, like playing a tune on one note, makes an amusing puzzle for the poet:

Myth, Commerce, and Coffee on United Flight #622 from Cleveland to Norfolk

> Clouds, like bird-tracked snow,
> spread to dawn-sun five miles below,

while businessmen (& poets) flow
on air streams, to and fro.

Now, of course, we know   5
Icarus could have made a go,

formed Attic Airways Co.,
expanded, advertised, and so

have carried Homer and Sappho
from Athens to Ilo   10

on reading tours—with, below,
clouds spread out like bird-tracked snow.

Texture

All of the things this chapter has been about, diction, syntax, alliteration and assonance, and rhyme, function together, along with rhythm, to give a poem its **texture.** As cloth gets its texture or character from the quality of the interwoven strands, so a poem has a texture or "feel" that comes from the interweaving of its technical elements and its meanings. Consider how these elements mingle in this poem by Robert Herrick. (A *lawn* is a fine scarf; a *stomacher,* a bodice; and *ribbands,* ribbons.)

Delight in Disorder

A sweet disorder in the dress
Kindles in clothes a wantonness;
A lawn about the shoulders thrown
Into a fine distraction,
An erring lace, which here and there   5
Enthralls the crimson stomacher,
A cuff neglectful, and thereby
Ribbands to flow confusedly,
A winning wave, deserving note,
In the tempestuous petticoat,   10
A careless shoe-string, in whose tie
I see a wild civility,
Do more bewitch me than when art
Is too precise in every part.

Here is a scansion:

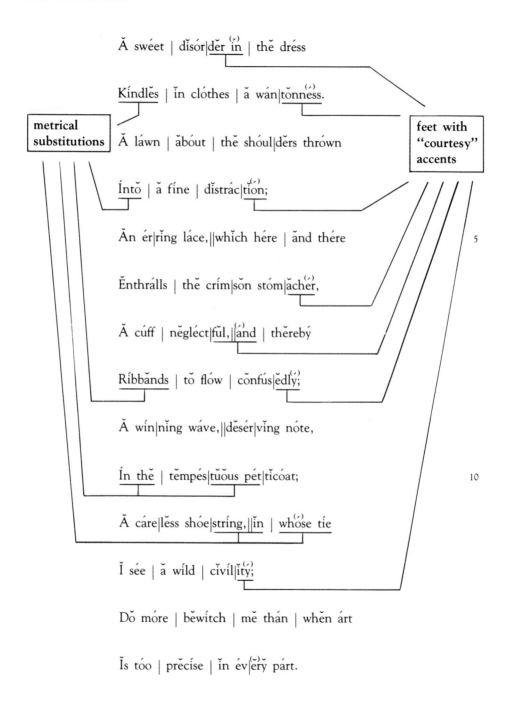

Ă swéet | dĭsór|dĕr ĭn | thĕ dréss

Kíndlĕs | ĭn clóthes | ă wán|tŏnnĕss.

metrical substitutions

Ă láwn | ăbóut | thĕ shóul|dĕrs thrówn

feet with "courtesy" accents

Íntŏ | ă fíne | dĭstrác|tĭon;

Ăn ér|rĭng láce, ‖ whĭch hére | ănd thére   5

Ĕnthrálls | thĕ crím|sŏn stóm|ăchĕr,

Ă cúff | nĕgléct|fŭl, ‖ ănd | thĕrebý

Ríbbănds | tŏ flów | cŏnfús|ĕdlý;

Ă wín|nĭng wáve, ‖ dĕsér|vĭng nóte,

Ín thĕ | tĕmpés|tŭŏus pét|tĭcóat;   10

Ă cáre|lĕss shóe|stríng, ‖ ĭn | whóse tíe

Ĭ sée | ă wíld | cĭvíl|ĭtý;

Dŏ móre | bĕwítch | mĕ thán | whĕn árt

Ĭs tóo | prĕcíse | ĭn év|ĕrÿ párt.

Every formal element of the poem bends to support Herrick's theme that we don't like things too neat, too mechanical, but enjoy a little spontaneity. Regularities and irregularities play against one another throughout. Only in the final couplet—when he mentions the opposite of charming casualness, "too precise in every part"—do the formal elements rigidify, in imitation of the idea.

Before the final couplet, the rhythm varies considerably over the tetrameter base. Seven lines have light, "courtesy" accents, five of them coming at line-ends where full accents would be normal. There are seven metrical substitutions. The little rhythmical flutters in line 10 are particularly imitative. Five lines have strong caesuras, two of which occur in the middle of feet. Five lines (1, 3, 5, 7, and 11) are run-on, so that the sense repeatedly flows and stops in a varied way down the trellis of lines.

Only in the final couplet does the rhythm at last march strictly by meter. The suppressed extra syllable in "every," usually elided in speech, underscores the marchlike effect, as the meter, like Marianne Moore's steam roller, crushes "all the particles down / into close conformity."

Something similar happens in the rhymes. Of the first six couplets, only the fifth is exactly rhymed ("note" and "-coat"). The others are off-rhymed in various ways, the least variation being the rhyme on a secondary accent in "dress" and "wantonness." The slightly awkward separation of syllables we normally elide in "dis-trac-ti-on" increases the irregularity. Only in the final couplet is the rhyme at last monosyllabic, hard, and exact: "art-part."

Alliteration and assonance add touches of casual order. The d's of line 1 link the words most essential to the sense: "disorder" and "dress," as do the hard c's in "Kindles" and "clothes" in line 2. In lines 3–4, "lawn" and "fine" add off-rhyme; and in lines 5–6, "err-" and "there," internal rhyme. Alliterations in lines 6–12 weave a continuous undersong. Noteworthy assonances occur in "shoulders thrown," "in the tempestuous petticoat," and "in whose tie / I see a wild civility."

By contrast, alliteration and assonance in the final couplet seem to increase its formality. Metrical rigidity comes from the relative evenness of the syllables; there is hardly a truly light unaccented syllable in the two lines:

Do more bewitch me than when art

Is too precise in every part.

Packed meaning, long vowels, and consonant-thick words join the effect, as do the internal rhymes ("Do," "too"; "be-," "me," "pre-," "-ry").

The syntax also contributes. After the first couplet, which concisely states the theme, the poem is a single rather disorderly, random sentence. The multiple subjects appear one after another, untidily: a lawn, a lace, a cuff, a wave, a shoestring. Four are garments or parts of garments, but the wave is a property, so even the subjects are not quite parallel. Other parts of garments appear in subsidiary phrases or clauses: a stomacher, ribbands. The subjects are variously modified by prepositional phrases, subordinate clauses, and adjective clauses, which slop over from line to line. Adjectives appear before ("erring lace") and after nouns ("cuff neglectful").

With all the asides (and asides of asides) even the direction of this wandering sentence is not clear until, with the last couplet, it reaches the main verb ("Do more bewitch"). Then the sudden syntactical focus of the sentence reenforces the rhythmical stiffness of the couplet.

Every formal element is working, albeit apparently casually, to mirror meaning. Herrick's point is not wildness but a wild *civility*. A disheveled woman isn't attractive, nor is one who is overly neat. A hint of disorder, a suggestion of wantonness—natural, spontaneous, well-mannered—is what makes a woman's dress delightful. The same quality in its texture makes this poem delightful. "*Ars celare artem*," as Horace's famous dictum says: the art is to hide the art.

QUESTIONS AND SUGGESTIONS

1. One adjective has been omitted in A. E. Housman's "Bredon Hill," in line 8. Housman himself deliberated long over the choice, trying out a number of words before he found the one he wanted to characterize the English countryside. What possibilities would you suggest? (Housman's successive notions appear in Appendix I.)

Bredon Hill

In summertime on Bredon
    The bells they sound so clear;
Round both the shires they ring them
    In steeples far and near,
    A happy noise to hear.   5

Here of a Sunday morning
    My love and I would lie,
And see the _____ counties,

And hear the larks so high
  About us in the sky.

The bells would ring to call her
  In valleys miles away:
"Come all to church, good people;
  Good people, come and pray."
  But here my love would stay.

And I would turn and answer
  Among the springing thyme,
"Oh, peal upon our wedding,
  And we will hear the chime,
  And come to church in time."

But when the snows at Christmas
  On Bredon top were strown,
My love rose up so early
  And stole out unbeknown
  And went to church alone.

They tolled the one bell only,
  Groom there was none to see,
The mourners followed after,
  And so to church went she,
  And would not wait for me.

The bells they sound on Bredon,
  And still the steeples hum.
"Come all to church, good people,"—
  Oh, noisy bells, be dumb;
  I hear you, I will come.

2. Think up some comic rhymes for these hard-to-rhyme words. Consider ways of working them into contexts that would make them seem natural. Then check your versions with those in Appendix I.

circle	*rhinoceros*	*broccoli*	*umbrella*
stop-sign	*evergreen*	*pelican*	

3. In "Pitcher," Robert Francis uses rhyme to express the baseball pitcher's art of deception and variation. Like a batter, the reader is tempted to perceive the poem as not really rhymed. In the first couplet, for instance, the way the second line pulls on to "at"—"to aim at"—not only imitates the sense (passing the rhyme or identity he might have seemed to aim at) but also suggests an uncertainty as to whether the lines are intended to rhyme. Study the way the poet keeps the reader mystified until, in the last couplet, he or she understands "too late"—when the curve catches the plate.

Pitcher

His art is eccentricity, his aim
How not to hit the mark he seems to aim at,

His passion how to avoid the obvious,
His technique how to vary the avoidance.

The others throw to be comprehended. He   5
Throws to be a moment misunderstood.

Yet not too much. Not errant, arrant, wild,
But every seeming aberration willed.

Not to, yet still, still to communicate
Making the batter understand too late.   10

4. Here is a rough paraphrase of a poem called "The Fourth of July." Following the development of its general sense as closely as possible, but choosing your own form, lineation, diction, syntax, images, and elaborations, *write* the poem. Compare your version with the real poem, by Howard Nemerov, which may be found in Appendix I.

> Having happened to drink too much tonight, I see from a hill the town's fireworks at a distance, fine rockets exploding slowly and very colorfully over the harbor. I also happen to be crying, because I remember the various fireworks we could purchase during my boyhood and use by ourselves—dangerously no doubt. Now there are laws of course, by means of which we are prevented from the harms and abuses that former freedom sometimes caused. And now the town's government can put on an entirely safe display, which can be far more grand than any single person could afford then (small pinwheels, a few firecrackers—one of which might have got tied to a dog's tail—and the like). In fact, this public display is gorgeous: giant rockets bursting in the sky like flowers, or showers and fountains of precious or semiprecious stones, with huge booms resounding long afterward. Tears of happiness fill my eyes. On such a night I fervently hope that God will bless this country of ours and that He will also bless the town's responsible and well-paid authorities who are in charge of this celebration of our independence.

5. Consider the structure of the ever-branching sentence of the first twelve lines of this poem by Richmond Lattimore (1906–1983). What is the effect? Also, what is the effect of the stanzas? of the single last line? (If line 13 were prose, wouldn't we expect a comma after "station"?)

Catania to Rome

The later the train was at every station,
the more people were waiting to get on.
and the fuller the train got, the more time it lost,

and the slower it went, all night, station to station,
the more people were on it, and the more people   5
were on it, the more people wanted to get on it,

waiting at every twilight midnight and half-daylight
station, crouched like runners, with a big suitcase
in each hand, and the corridor was all elbows armpits

knees and hams, permessos and per favores, and a suitcase   10
always blocking half the corridor, and the next station
nobody got off but a great many came aboard.

When we came to our station we had to fight to get off.

6. Using these rhyme words: *box-side-locks-wide*, write a reasonably coherent quatrain (*a b a b*). Then, reordering, rhyme: *box-locks-side-wide* (*a a b b*). Could you also do *wide-locks-side-box* and so on? (See Appendix I for possible versions.)

7. Look back at John Updike's "Player Piano" (page 23). Can you tabulate the variety of sound devices by which he imitates the tinkly quality of a mechanical piano?

8. Look back at Walt Whitman's "A Farm Picture" (page 15). Note the alliteration, assonance, and off-rhyme, considering how they help to organize the poem.

POEMS TO CONSIDER

Hurrahing in Harvest   1877

GERARD MANLEY HOPKINS   (1844–1889)

Summer ends now; now, barbarous in beauty, the stooks° arise   *stalks of grain*
  Around; up above, what wind-walks! what lovely behaviour
  Of silk-sack clouds! has wilder, wilful-wavier
Meal-drift moulded ever and melted across skies?

I walk, I lift up, I lift up heart, eyes,   5
  Down all that glory in the heavens to glean our Saviour;
  And, eyes, heart, what looks, what lips yet gave you a
Rapturous love's greeting of realer, of rounder replies?

And the azurous hung hills are his world-wielding shoulder
    Majestic—as a stallion stalwart, very-violet-sweet!—   10
These things, these things were here and but the beholder
    Wanting; which two when they once meet,
The heart rears wings bold and bolder
    And hurls for him, O half hurls earth for him off under his feet.

Sonnet 55   1609

WILLIAM SHAKESPEARE   (1564–1616)

Not marble, nor the gilded monuments
Of princes, shall outlive this powerful rhyme;
But you shall shine more bright in these contents
Than unswept stone°, besmeared with sluttish time.   *gravestone or monument*
When wasteful war shall statues overturn,   5
And broils root out the work of masonry,
Nor Mars° his sword nor war's quick fire shall burn   *Roman god of war*
The living record of your memory.
'Gainst death and all-oblivious enmity
Shall you pace forth; your praise shall still find room   10
Even in the eyes of all posterity
That wear this world out to the ending doom.
So, till the judgment that yourself arise,
You live in this, and dwell in lovers' eyes.

During Wind and Rain   1917

THOMAS HARDY   (1840–1928)

    THEY sing their dearest songs—
    He, she, all of them—yea,
    Treble and tenor and bass,
        And one to play;
    With the candles mooning each face. . . .   5

Ah, no; the years O!
How the sick leaves reel down in throngs!

They clear the creeping moss—
Elders and juniors—aye,
Making the pathways neat   10
    And the garden gay;
And they build a shady seat. . . .
    Ah, no; the years, the years;
See, the white storm-birds wing across!

They are blithely breakfasting all—   15
Men and maidens—yea,
Under the summer tree,
    With a glimpse of the bay,
While pet fowl come to the knee. . . .
    Ah, no; the years O!   20
And the rotten rose is ript from the wall.

They change to a high new house,
He, she, all of them—aye,
Clocks and carpets and chairs
    On the lawn all day,   25
And brightest things that are theirs. . . .
    Ah, no; the years, the years;
Down their carved names the rain-drop ploughs.

Provide, Provide   1936

ROBERT FROST   (1874–1963)

The witch that came (the withered hag)
To wash the steps with pail and rag,
Was once the beauty Abishag°,

The picture pride of Hollywood.
Too many fall from great and good   5
For you to doubt the likelihood.

Die early and avoid the fate.
Or if predestined to die late,
Make up your mind to die in state.

Make the whole stock exchange your own!   10
If need be occupy a throne,
Where nobody can call *you* crone.

Some have relied on what they knew;
Others on being simply true.
What worked for them might work for you.   15

No memory of having starred
Atones for later disregard,
Or keeps the end from being hard.

Better to go down dignified
With boughten friendship at your side   20
Than none at all. Provide, provide!

3 *Abshag:* the name of a fictional movie star, borrowed from the biblical account of a
beautiful young woman in I Kings, 1:3.

A Classic Situation   1960

JANE FLANDERS·

What's pat in the Latin
And chic in the Greek
I always distinguish
More clearly in English.

Very Like a Whale   1934

OGDEN NASH   (1902–1971)

One thing that literature would be greatly the better for
Would be a more restricted employment by authors of simile and metaphor.
Authors of all races, be they Greeks, Romans, Teutons or Celts,
Can't seem just to say that anything is the thing it is but have to go out of their
    way to say that it is like something else.
What does it mean when we are told   5
That the Assyrian came down like a wolf on the fold?
In the first place, George Gordon Byron had had enough experience
To know that it probably wasn't just one Assyrian, it was a lot of Assyrians.
However, as too many arguments are apt to induce apoplexy and thus hinder
    longevity,
We'll let it pass as one Assyrian for the sake of brevity.   10
Now then, this particular Assyrian, the one whose cohorts were gleaming in
    purple and gold,
Just what does the poet mean when he says he came down like a wolf on the
    fold?
In heaven and earth more than is dreamed of in our philosophy there are a
    great many things,
But I don't imagine that among them there is a wolf with purple and gold
    cohorts or purple and gold anythings.
No, no, Lord Byron, before I'll believe that this Assyrian was actually like a
    wolf I must have some kind of proof;   15
Did he run on all fours and did he have a hairy tail and a big red mouth and big
    white teeth and did he say Woof woof woof?
Frankly I think it very unlikely, and all you were entitled to say, at the very
    most,
Was that the Assyrian cohorts came down like a lot of Assyrian cohorts about
    to destroy the Hebrew host.
But that wasn't fancy enough for Lord Byron, oh dear me no, he had to invent
    a lot of figures of speech and then interpolate them,
With the result that whenever you mention Old Testament soldiers to people
    they say Oh yes, they're the ones that a lot of wolves dressed up in gold
    and purple ate them.   20
That's the kind of thing that's being done all the time by poets, from Homer to
    Tennyson;
They're always comparing ladies to lilies and veal to venison,
And they always say things like that the snow is a white blanket after a winter
    storm.
Oh it is, is it, all right then, you sleep under a six-inch blanket of snow and I'll

sleep under a half-inch blanket of unpoetical blanket material and we'll
     see which one keeps warm,
And after that maybe you'll begin to comprehend dimly   25
What I mean by too much metaphor and simile.

Year's End   1950

RICHARD WILBUR   *(b. 1921)*

Now winter downs the dying of the year,
And night is all a settlement of snow;
From the soft street the rooms of houses show
A gathered light, a shapen atmosphere,
Like frozen-over lakes whose ice is thin   5
And still allows some stirring down within.

I've known the wind by water banks to shake
The late leaves down, which frozen where they fell
And held in ice as dancers in a spell
Fluttered all winter long into a lake;   10
Graved on the dark in gestures of descent,
They seemed their own most perfect monument.

There was perfection in the death of ferns
Which laid their fragile cheeks against the stone
A million years. Great mammoths overthrown   15
Composedly have made their long sojourns,
Like palaces of patience, in the gray
And changeless lands of ice. And at Pompeii

The little dog lay curled and did not rise
But slept the deeper as the ashes rose   20
And found the people incomplete, and froze
The random hands, the loose unready eyes
Of men expecting yet another sun
To do the shapely thing they had not done.

These sudden ends of time must give us pause.   25
We fray into the future, rarely wrought

Save in the tapestries of afterthought.
More time, more time. Barrages of applause
Come muffled from a buried radio.
The New-year bells are wrangling with the snow.   30

The Universe   1963

MAY SWENSON   (b. 1919)

                    What
                       is it about,
                    the universe,
                    the universe about us stretching out?
    We, within our brains,   5
                within it,
                       think
    we must unspin
    the laws that spin it.
                    We think *why*   10
                because we think
                because.
                Because we think,
                    we think
                    the universe about us.   15

            But does it think,
                    the universe?
                    Then what about?
                            About us?
                    If not,   20
        must there be cause
                    in the universe?
    Must it have laws?
                    And what
                if the universe   25
                    is not about us?
                Then what?
                    What
                       is it about?
                And what   30
                    about *us?*

5

Stanzas and Fixed Forms:
Rooms, Houses, and
an Old Man of Nantucket

The etymology of the word **stanza**—a group of lines, usually of a fixed (and repeated) number and pattern of lines—takes us to an Italian word that means, among other things, a room. Stanzas are rooms, and a poem of them, a house. As there are one-room houses, there are one-stanza poems; and there are mansionlike poems of many stanzas. There are small rooms, spacious rooms, narrow rooms, ballrooms, living rooms, sunrooms, and, of course, closets. Stanzas come in all shapes and sizes, and, if need be, the poet can always invent a new one.

We may distinguish between "closed" and "open" stanzas: between stanzas that are end-stopped, closing with the end of a sentence and a period, and run-on stanzas, those from which a sentence continues across the stanza-break. Closed stanzas, like paragraphs in prose, correspond to units of meaning or segments of an argument. Francis's "Glass" (page 10) and Williams's "The Nightingales" (page 39) use closed stanzas. Frost's "Dust of Snow" (page 17) and Williams's "The Red Wheelbarrow" (page 42) use open stanzas. Marianne Moore's "To a Steam Roller" (page 44) and Cunningham's "For My Contemporaries" (page 64) mix open and closed stanzas. Such choices, made in the writing of a poem, have to do with the flow or structure, poised balance or imbalance of the statement. For a poem like Moore's "The Fish" (page 100), given its fluid and shifting subject matter, open stanzas seem obvious, as does her choice of varying line lengths.

Line-Length and Stanzas

In the main (exceptions pop up like dandelions) verse lines of even length convey more poise than do verse lines of uneven length, which suggest agitation. George Herbert's "The Collar," with its lines of various lengths and its irregular rhymes, shows what can be done. The speaker is a devout but rebellious Christian who is feeling cheated by the life of sacrifice he leads. The food imagery, including the board (table) he strikes, is a metaphorical reference to communion. Notice how, as the internal conflict climaxes, the alternation of long and short lines becomes more pronounced.

The Collar

I struck the board and cried, "No more;
 I will abroad!
What? shall I ever sigh and pine?
My lines and life are free, free as the road,
 Loose as the wind, as large as store°.   *abundance* 5
  Shall I be still in suit°?   *in someone's service*
Have I no harvest but a thorn
To let me blood, and not restore
What I have lost with cordial fruit?
  Sure there was wine   10
Before my sighs did dry it; there was corn
 Before my tears did drown it.
Is the year only lost to me?
 Have I no bays° to crown it,   *wreaths*
No flowers, no garlands gay? All blasted?   15
  All wasted?
Not so, my heart; but there is fruit,
 And thou hast hands.
Recover all thy sigh-blown age
On double pleasures: leave thy cold dispute   20
Of what is fit and not. Forsake thy cage,
 Thy rope of sands,
Which petty thoughts have made, and made to thee
 Good cable, to enforce and draw,
 `And be thy law,   25
While thou didst wink and wouldst not see.
  Away! take heed;
  I will abroad.
Call in thy death's-head° there; tie up thy fears.   *skull*
  He that forbears   30

To suit and serve his need,
      Deserves his load."
But as I raved and grew more fierce and wild
      At every word,
Methought I heard one calling, *Child!*   35
      And I replied, *My Lord.*

Something similar happens in the stanzas of "Song" by John Donne (1572–
1631). The indented lines, particularly the two short lines near the end of each
stanza, and the triple rhyming give the poem a rapid, frenetic feeling.

Song

Go and catch a falling star,
   Get with child a mandrake root°,   *forked root*
Tell me where all past years are,
   Or who cleft the Devil's foot,
Teach me to hear mermaids singing,   5
Or to keep off envy's stinging,
      And find
      What wind
Serves to advance an honest mind.

If thou beest born to strange sights,   10
   Things invisible to see,
Ride ten thousand days and nights,
   Till age snow white hairs on thee.
Thou, when thou return'st, wilt tell me
All strange wonders that befell thee,   15
      And swear
      Nowhere
Lives a woman true, and fair.

If thou find'st one, let me know,
   Such a pilgrimage were sweet;   20
Yet do not, I would not go,
   Though at next door we might meet;
Though she were true when you met her,
And last till you write your letter,
      Yet she   25
      Will be
False, ere I come, to two, or three.

The speaker's changeableness—"If thou find'st one . . . Yet do not"—also indicates how upset he is. His statement is bitter and extreme. It is also inaccurate: "Nowhere / Lives a woman true, and fair." Presented with measured calm, such a statement would find little sympathy. But we are able to sympathize because we feel the speaker's agitation. We can guess that he has just been betrayed by a woman, and we may realize how much he really wishes that what he is saying were not so. The poem is a dramatic monologue, belonging to a moment, arising out of an implied dramatic situation, not a considered pronouncement.

In contrast, consider Theodore Roethke's "My Papa's Waltz" (page 65) with its lines of even length. The plight of the boy is surely as upsetting as that of Donne's unhappy lover. Frightened by his father's roughness, divided in feeling between his father's strange gaiety and his mother's frowning disapproval, he is doubtless agitated and upset. Yet the lines are even, the poem's stanzas closed. The difference is that the voice in Donne's poem is inside the situation dramatically, and the voice in Roethke's, recalling the situation, is outside it. Roethke's speaker is not the boy but the man the boy has become, the man who has survived and who can remember with understanding and affection. The voice is at some distance, time, from the event, not (as Donne's speaker is) still within it.

Usually shorter lines lend themselves to lightness, ease, delicacy, speed, intricacy. Remember William Carlos Williams's "Poem" (page 35) about the cat? Longer lines tend toward weight, substance, difficulty, seriousness, like the pentameters of Shakespeare's Sonnet 55 (page 111). Shorter lines also lend themselves to wit. It is difficult to imagine Herrick's tetrameter "Delight in Disorder," which tumbles and falls so freely from line to line, in hexameters. In general, what is true of shorter or longer lines holds for longer or shorter stanzas. Couplets step more quickly than quatrains or nine-line Spenserian stanzas.

In starting a poem, the poet must very soon sense what sort of lines and stanzas it calls for. Here is a poem of mine about a bay-creek behind one of New Jersey's sand-spit islands. In choosing the length of lines—or letting the poem choose—I was aware of the linear, vertical, staccato nature of rain, so that shorter, quicker lines seemed appropriate. I also wanted a light touch, a fanciful tone. When I began to jot down my earliest impression in the first draft, I began with trimeter lines of six or seven syllables:

> No one but him to see
> the rain begin—a fine scrim
> far down the bay, like smoke,
> smoking and hissing its way

After eight or ten lines, I sensed that the poem was moving too slowly. Noticing the accidental rhyme of "him-scrim," I began the second draft by changing to dimeter lines of four or five syllables. Although I soon abandoned the rhyming, the poem had discovered its form. Because substitutions in dimeter radically vary the norm, I had the quick, jerky movement the poem wanted. The verticality remains in the fairly long stanzas.

Swimmer in the Rain

No one but him
seeing the rain
start—a fine scrim
far down the bay,
smoking, advancing 5
between two grays
till the salt-grass rustles
and the creek's mirror
in which he stands
to his neck, like clothing 10
cold, green, supple,
begins to ripple.

The drops bounce up,
little fountains
all around him, 15
swift, momentary—
every drop tossed back
in air atop
its tiny column—
glass balls balancing 20
upon glass nipples,
lace of dimples,
a stubble of silver
stars, eye-level,
incessant, wild. 25

White, dripping, tall,
ignoring the rain,
an egret fishes
in the creek's margin,
dips to the minnows' 30
sky, under which,
undisturbed, steady
as faith the tide pulls.
Mussels hang
like grapes on a piling. 35
Wet is wet.

The swimmer settles
to the hissing din—
a glass bombardment,
parade of diamonds,   40
blinks, jacks of light,
wee Brancusi's°, chromes   *modern sculptures*
like grease-beads sizzling,   *like those of Constantin*
myriad—and swims   *Brancusi (1876–1957)*
slowly, elegantly,   45
climbing tide's ladder
hand over hand
toward the distant bay.

Hair and eye-brows
streaming, sleek crystal   50
scarving his throat—
no one but him.

The choice of both line and stanza length opens up possibilities the poet will be able to exploit.

Consider the little stanza Marianne Moore has invented for this poem:

Nevertheless

you've seen a strawberry
    that's had a struggle; yet
    was, where the fragments met,

a hedgehog or a star-
    fish for the multitude   5
    of seeds. What better food

than apple-seeds—the fruit
    within the fruit—locked in
    like counter-curved twin

hazel-nuts? Frost that kills   10
    the little rubber-plant-
    leaves of *kok-saghyz*-stalks, can't

harm the roots; they still grow
    in frozen ground. Once where
    there was a prickly-pear-   15

leaf clinging to barbed wire,
    a root shot down to grow
    in earth two feet below;

as carrots form mandrakes
    or a ram's-horn root some-   20
    times. Victory won't come

to me unless I go
    to it; a grape-tendril
    ties a knot in knots till

knotted thirty times,—so   25
    the bound twig that's under-
    gone and over-gone, can't stir.

The weak overcomes its
    menace, the strong over-
    comes itself. What is there   30

like fortitude! What sap
    went through that little thread
    to make the cherry red!

Given Marianne Moore's style, we might expect the meter to be syllabics, and a quick test shows that the lines count out to six syllables. But as we read, an iambic beat quickly establishes itself. Except for "-bérrȳ" (where we expect ˘ ´) the opening lines are normal enough iambic trimeter:

you've seen a strawberry

    that's had a struggle; yet

    was, where the fragments met,

a hedgehog or a star-

    fish for the multitude

    of seeds. What better food

than apple-seeds—the fruit

    within the fruit . . .

We may count "-berry" as a trochaic substitution, albeit a very abnormal one (lines usually end with feet of culminating accent: iambs, anapests, or spondees). The metrical difficulty seems appropriate, rhythmically suggesting the "struggle" the misformed strawberry has had; "-berry" may also signal that the poem will not be bound by conventional meter and that other unusual metrical variations will be allowed. This idiosyncrasy is not, of course, irrelevant to the theme. If defining things were as important as understanding, we might decide that the meter of "Nevertheless" is something of a cross between syllabics and iambic trimeter, leaving the poet free to slip out of either and back at need.

The management of meter and rhythm is very interesting. For the moment, however, notice the stanzas. Moore has used a simple but startlingly effective device: although all the lines are the same length (iambically or syllabically), the second and third lines of each stanza are indented. Only these lines are rhymed. It is as if each stanza must work its way forward against some invisible resistance until, in the second and third lines, the rhyme can click into place. The sense of difficulty overcome is also exemplified in the careful, exacting syntax by which, in each stanza, the sentence finds or fulfills its precise intention:

What better food

than apple-seeds—the fruit
    within the fruit—locked in
    like counter-curved twin

hazel-nuts?

Notice the locked-in repetions of "fruit / . . . fruit" and of "within . . . in / . . . twin," and of course the alliteration of "counter-curved." The breaking of words across line-ends, with hyphens—"star- / fish," for example—reenforces both the poem's air of precision and its sense of difficulty overcome.

The individuality of the invented stanza confirms the poem's theme. In stanzas 8–10, the playfulness about "over" and "under" gathers some of its complexity from the stanza shape. In these stanzas, starting with the word "tendril," the rhythm almost reverses itself; trochees, rather than iambs, become the norm.

Víctŏry̆ wŏn't cóme

tŏ mé ŭnléss Ĭ gó

    tŏ ít; ă grápe-téndrĭl

    tíes ă knót ĭn knóts tĭll

knŏttĕd thírtў tímes,—sŏ (˘)

thĕ bóund twíg thăt's úndĕr-

góne ănd óvĕr-góne, cán't stír.

Thĕ wéak óvĕrcómes ĭts

ménăce, thĕ stróng óvĕr-

cómes ĭtsélf. Whăt (˘) ĭs thĕre

lĭke fórtĭtúde!

The sturdy march of the iambs resumes, as the poem comes to its fully resolved conclusion. The "knotting" feeling comes from this succession of "backward" trochees and from the repetition of the words "knot" three times and "-gone" twice. It also comes from the strongly forced run-ons from "till," "so," and the broken "under-"; from the internal rhymes of "thir-" and "over," which pick up the end-rhymes of "under" and "stir"; from the adjacent accented syllables of "bound twig" and "-gone, can't stir"; from the extra syllable (and extra accent) of the line "gone and over-gone, can't stir," which both stiffens and extends the line; and, finally, from the syntactical suspension, reenforced by the comma, between the subject, "bound twig," and its predicate, "can't stir."

It is a dazzling passage and surely would have pleased Pope. (If there were a heaven poets go to, we might find that bewigged eighteenth-century Englishman and Miss Moore, late of Brooklyn, discussing just such matters over watercress sandwiches—her favorite.) The sense of difficulty, of realizing one's nature against difficulties, which we have been shown in a strawberry, apple-seeds, rubber-plants, a prickly-pear-leaf, carrots, and a ram's-horn root, could scarcely be summed up more rhythmically. The poem's last example—the cherry—is no anticlimax. It is the ordinary which, we perceive, is extraordinary. As Moore says in another poem: "Ecstasy affords / the occasion and expediency determines the form."

Elementary Forms

The mechanics of the usual stanza forms are simple, and their potential variations and uses too many to begin counting. The **couplet** is the most elementary stanza: two lines, and when it is rhymed, *a a.* In any of its variations, the couplet tends to succinctness. Rhymed, it is capable of epigrammatic punch. Consider Pope's

> The hungry judges soon the sentence sign
> And wretches hang that jurymen may dine.

A flexible form, it has been serviceable for narratives (Pope's "The Rape of the Lock" or Chaucer's *The Canterbury Tales*).

Triplets (tercets) are stanzas of three lines. They may be rhymed *a a a* as in Robert Herrick's lovely

Upon Julia's Clothes

> Whenas in silks my Julia goes
> Then, then, methinks, how sweetly flows
> That liquefaction of her clothes.
>
> Next, when I cast mine eyes, and see
> That brave vibration, each way free,   5
> O, how that glittering taketh me!

Triple-rhyming can easily become monotonous and is difficult to maintain. Rhyming *a b a* or *a b b* (Moore's "Nevertheless") are alternatives. The well-known Italian form, **terza rima,** follows the *a b a* scheme *and* uses the unrhymed line in the immediate stanza for the double-rhyme of the next stanza: *a b a, b c b, c d c,* and so on; Shelley's "Ode to the West Wind" is the most familiar example in English.

Quatrains are stanzas of four lines. The usual schemes are: *a b c b* (rhyming only two of the four lines, the easiest; often used in ballads, hymns, popular songs), *a b a b, a a b b,* and *a b b a.* A familiar children's rhyme uses the first scheme:

> There's music in a hammer,
> There's music in a nail,
> There's music in a pussy cat,
> When you step upon her tail.

An example of the more difficult *a b a b* scheme is the funny and touching "First Confession" by X. J. Kennedy (b. 1929). Note, though, that although he maintains exact rhymes for the second and fourth lines, the poet accepts off-rhymes for the first and third lines.

First Confession

> Blood thudded in my ears. I scuffed,
>   Steps stubborn, to the telltale booth

Beyond whose curtained portal coughed
    The robed repositor of truth.

The slat shot back. The universe   5
    Bowed down his cratered dome to hear
Enumerated my each curse,
    The sip snitched from my old man's beer,

My sloth pride envy lechery,
    The dime held back from Peter's Pence°   *Catholic offering* 10
With which I'd bribed my girl to pee
    That I might spy her instruments.

Hovering scale-pans when I'd done
    Settled their balance slow as silt
While in the restless dark I burned   15
    Bright as a brimstone in my guilt

Until as one feeds birds he doled
    Seven Our Fathers and a Hail
Which I to double-scrub my soul
    Intoned twice at the altar rail   20

Where Sunday in seraphic light
    I knelt, as full of grace as most,
And stuck my tongue out at the priest:
    A fresh roost for the Holy Ghost.

In a further example, Robert Frost uses a difficult *a a b a* rhyme scheme. The difficulty is redoubled by Frost's picking up the unrhymed line for the triple rhymes of the next stanza, and so on.

Stopping by Woods on a Snowy Evening

Whose woods these are I think I know.
His house is in the village though;
He will not see me stopping here
To watch his woods fill up with snow.

My little horse must think it queer   5
To stop without a farmhouse near
Between the woods and frozen lake
The darkest evening of the year.

He gives his harness bells a shake
To ask if there is some mistake.   10
The only other sound's the sweep
Of easy wind and downy flake.

The woods are lovely, dark and deep,
But I have promises to keep,
And miles to go before I sleep,   15
And miles to go before I sleep.

Frost's commentary is illuminating:

I can have my first line any way I please. But once I say a line I am committed. The first line *is* a commitment. *Whose woods these are I think I know.* Eight syllables, four beats—a line—we call it iambic. I'm not terribly committed there. I can do a great many things. I did not choose the meter. What we have in English is mostly iambic anyway. When most of it is iambic, you just fall into that. *His house is in the village though*—the second line. I might be committed to couplets. If I had made another couplet beside that—a rhyme pair—I'd be in for it. I'd have to have couplets all the way. I was dancing still. I was free. Then I committed a stanza:

> Whose woods these are I think I know.
> His house is in the village though;
> He will not see me stopping here
> To watch his woods fill up with snow.

He will not see me stopping here is uncommitted. For the three rhymes in the next stanza, I picked up the unrhymed line in the first stanza and rhymed its end-rhyme "here" with "queer," "near" and "year," and for the third stanza I picked up "lake" from the unrhymed line in the second stanza and rhymed it with "shake," "mistake" and "flake." For the fourth stanza I picked up "sweep" from the unrhymed line in the third stanza, to rhyme with "deep" and "sleep."

Every step you take is a further commitment . . . How was I going to get out of that stanza?

He gets out of it brilliantly, resolving the form by keeping the "sweep" rhyme throughout the last stanza, *d d d d,* and repeating "And miles to go before I sleep" so that we feel both the weariness and the determination of the man stopped by the lonely, lovely woods. The monotony of the five rhymes—"sweep," "deep," "keep," "sleep," "sleep"—gives sound to these feelings.

Complex Forms

Beyond the quatrain, the possibility of stanzaic variation increases exponentially. Three longer stanzas have been employed with some frequency: **rime royal** (seven lines of iambic pentameter, *a b a b b c c*), **ottava rima** (eight lines of iambic pentameter, *a b a b a b c c*), and the **Spenserian stanza** (nine lines, eight of iambic pentameter and one of iambic hexameter, *a b a b b c b c c*). Working with such complex rhyme schemes can be like putting the pieces into a mosaic. The poet must be continually looking forward for possible rhymes in the sense that lies ahead, and backward to bring other rhyme-words into place, as he or she laces each stanza together. The craft of inventing complex forms like the one Donne uses in "Song" (page 119) isn't in doing it once, but in then being able to repeat it, naturally and effectively, throughout the poem.

Three complex stanza-poem forms should also be mentioned: sonnet, villanelle, and sestina. The **sonnet** is easily the most familiar and useful: fourteen lines of rhymed iambic pentameter. The **Shakespearean** (or **Elizabethan**) **sonnet** is rhymed in three quatrains and a couplet: *a b a b, c d c d, e f e f, g g.* Shakespeare's Sonnet 73 (page 11) is a good example, in which the sense corresponds to the four divisions. The **Italian** (or **Petrarchan**) **sonnet** is rhymed: *a b b a a b b a, c d e c d e* (or *c d c d c d*). Harder because of its fewer and more interlocking rhymes, the Italian sonnet falls into only two divisions, of eight and six lines: **octave** and **sestet.** The sense, statement and resolution, usually conforms to this division. Although its "turn" does not come exactly between the octave and the sestet, Milton's sonnet typifies the form:

On His Blindness

When I consider how my light is spent,
Ere half my days, in this dark world and wide,
And that one talent which is death to hide,
Lodged with me useless, though my soul more bent
To serve therewith my Maker, and present   5
My true account, lest he returning chide;
Doth God exact day-labor, light denied?
I fondly ask. But patience to prevent
That murmur, soon replies, God doth not need
Either man's work or his own gifts; who best   10
Bear his mild yoke, they serve him best; his state
Is kingly. Thousands at his bidding speed
And post o'er land and ocean without rest:
They also serve who only stand and wait.

Poets have worked any number of successful variations on the rhyme schemes of both kinds of sonnet. Edmund Spenser used an interlocking *a b a b, b c b c, c d c d, e e*. Frost, who wrote more sonnets than might be supposed, tried numerous variations, including: *a a a b b b c c c d d d e e*. His "Acquainted with the Night" is a variation on *terza rima*, with the final couplet made by simply "omitting" the unrhymed line in the last "triplet": *a b a, b c b, c d c, d e d, e e*.

How far the form will stretch can be observed in many of E. E. Cummings's sonnets. Here is his satire on patriotic platitudes and a politician's Fourth of July speech. Note how he solved a problem in rhyming lines 9 and 13:

> "next to of course god america i
> love you land of the pilgrims' and so forth oh
> say can you see by the dawn's early my
> country 'tis of centuries come and go
> and are no more what of it we should worry   5
> in every language even deafanddumb
> thy sons acclaim your glorious name by gorry
> by jingo by gee by gosh by gum
> why talk of beauty what could be more beaut-
> iful than these heroic happy dead   10
> who rushed like lions to the roaring slaughter
> they did not stop to think they died instead
> then shall the voice of liberty be mute?"
>
> He spoke. And drank rapidly a glass of water

The **villanelle,** borrowed from the French, is a poem of six stanzas—five triplets and a quatrain. It employs only *two* rhymes throughout: *a b a, a b a, a b a, a b a, a b a, a b a a*. Moreover, the first and third lines are repeated entirely, three times, as a refrain. Line 1 appears again as lines 6, 12, and 18. Line 3, as lines 9, 15, 19. Dylan Thomas (1914–1953) casts the masterful elegy for his father as a villanelle:

Do Not Go Gentle into That Good Night

Do not go gentle into that good night,
Old age should burn and rave at close of day;
Rage, rage against the dying of the light.

Though wise men at their end know dark is right,
Because their words had forked no lightning they   5
Do not go gentle into that good night.

Good men, the last wave by, crying how bright
Their frail deeds might have danced in a green bay,
Rage, rage against the dying of the light.

Wild men who caught and sang the sun in flight,
And learn, too late, they grieved it on its way,
Do not go gentle into that good night.

Grave men, near death, who see with blinding sight
Blind eyes could blaze like meteors and be gay,
Rage, rage against the dying of the light.

And you, my father, there on the sad height,
Curse, bless, me now with your fierce tears, I pray.
Do not go gentle into that good night.
Rage, rage against the dying of the light.

There are enough villanelles in English to convince us that poets like to make trouble for themselves.

Incidentally, the device of **refrain**—a phrase, line, or group of lines repeated from stanza to stanza, usually at the end—recalls one of the origins of the short poem: in song. It is a small step from the merry "Hey nonny nonny" of a Shakespearean song to the deliciously somber "Litany for a Time of Plague" by Thomas Nashe (1567–1601), of which this is a stanza:

Beauty is but a flower
Which wrinkles will devour;
Brightness falls from the air;
Queens have died young and fair;
Dust hath closed Helen's eye.
I am sick, I must die.
   Lord, have mercy on us!

Or to the sophistication of this witty poem by Andrew Marvell (1621–1678). Notice how the long refrain-line imitates the sweep of the scythe.

The Mower's Song

My mind was once the true survey
Of all these meadows fresh and gay;
And in the greenness of the grass
Did see its hopes as in a glass;
When Juliana came, and she
What I do to the grass, does to my thoughts and me.

But these, while I with sorrow pine,
Grew more luxuriant still and fine;
That not one blade of grass you spied,
But had a flower on either side;   10
When Juliana came, and she
What I do to the grass, does to my thoughts and me.

Unthankful meadows, could you so
A fellowship so true forego,
And in your gaudy May-games meet,   15
While I lay trodden under feet?
When Juliana came, and she
What I do to the grass, does to my thoughts and me.

But what you in compassion ought,
Shall now by my revenge be wrought: 20
And flowers, and grass, and I and all,
Will in one common ruin fall.
For Juliana comes, and she
What I do to the grass, does to my thoughts and me.

And thus, ye meadows, which have been   25
Companions of my thoughts more green,
Shall now the heraldry become
With which I shall adorn my tomb;
For Juliana comes, and she
What I do to the grass, does to my thoughts and me.   30

In the twentieth century, Yeats is the master of the refrain; a reader might usefully search out "Two Songs of a Fool," "For Anne Gregory," or "Long-Legged Fly."

Borrowed from the French and (if possible) even more difficult than the villanelle is the **sestina**: six six-line stanzas and one three-line stanza. Instead of rhyme, the *six words* at the ends of lines in the first stanza are repeated in a specific, shifting order as line-end words in the other five six-line stanzas. Then all six words are used again in the final triplet, three of them at line-ends, three of them in midline. The order of the line-end words in the stanzas may be transcribed this way: 1-2-3-4-5-6, 6-1-5-2-4-3, 3-6-4-1-2-5, 5-3-2-6-1-4, 4-5-1-3-6-2, 2-4-6-5-3-1; and in the triplet, (2)-5-(4)-3-(6)-1. Poets from Sir Philip Sidney until now have used the sestina successfully. In this playful one, note the round and round, spiraling-in quality of the form:

Sort of a Sestina

BRUCE BENNETT

In Partial Fulfillment of the Requirements

"What? You've never written a sestina?"
You gazed incredulous across your coffee.
"But I should think you'd take it as a challenge;
I mean, with all your fancy-work in form.
Well, if you ever write one, let me see it."   5
"I will," I promised. Here. I've kept my promise.

The thing is, I don't write things for the challenge.
Of course, when something's done I like to see it,
And once I start, it's sort of like a promise:
For instance, if I said, "We'll meet for coffee,"   10
We'd meet for coffee. It's like that with form,
And that's the way it is with this "sestina."

Don't get me wrong. I love to play with form,
And there's a certain pleasure in a challenge.
Again for instance, I've included "coffee,"   15
A word that doesn't have a lot of promise,
To say the least, for use in a sestina.
Once having used it, I'm obliged to see it

Through. Okay. Let's say I'm stuck with "coffee."
I need a spot to stick it, then I see it   20
And bang! (as right above) I've met that challenge.
That's what you've got to do with a sestina.
You pounce on any opening with promise
And score your piddling points against the form.

But having seized those openings with promise   25
And being well along in one's sestina
And every time it comes around to coffee
Sneaking another by to beat the form
's not such a grand achievement, as I see it.
Suppose you prove you're equal to the challenge—   30

The point is, what's the point? Who's going to see it
As anything but diddling with a form?

That's *why* I've never written a sestina.
It's always seemed a wholly senseless challenge.
But I remembered what you said at coffee;   35
And also, since a promise is a promise

(Even when it takes form as a sestina),
I'm hoping you may see it as a challenge
To promise we will meet again for coffee.

For the poet who enjoys the challenge of complicated forms, there are many more, like the French rondeau and rondel, the Malayan pantoum, or the Welsh cywydd llosgyrnog, all of which have been successfully adapted to English. The place to look these up is Lewis Turco's *The New Book of Forms.*

Short Forms

The **haiku** (or hokku) is a Japanese form: three lines of five, seven, and five syllables. The essence of the haiku, however, is less in its syllabic form than in its tone or touch. Consequently, given the differences in the languages, observing the five-seven-five syllabification in English isn't particularly valuable. The essence of the haiku is elusive, very deeply embedded in its culture and strongly influenced by Zen Buddhism. Haiku are, in general, very brief natural descriptions or observations that carry some implicit spiritual insight—in short, meditative nuggets.

The most famous of all haiku is by Matsuo Basho (1644–1694), translated by Nobuyuki Yuasa (into *four* lines although the original is three):

Breaking the silence
Of an ancient pond,
A frog jumped into water—
A deep resonance.

Nearly as famous is this tender poem by Kobayashi Issa (1763–1827), translated by Robert Bly:

Cricket, be
careful! I'm rolling
over!

Another by Issa, also translated by Bly:

The old dog bends his head listening . . .
I guess the singing
of the earthworms gets to him.

Because of the spiritual, cultural overtone of the form, original haiku in English often seem precious or phony, especially when they call attention to themselves by a title like "Haiku." The lesson of the haiku, though—brevity, pith, the force of an image presented without moralizing—is well taken. This poem by Ezra Pound, although directly influenced by the haiku, is entirely a Western poem:

In a Station of the Metro

The apparition of these faces in the crowd;
Petals on a wet, black bough.

A kindred tradition from Greek and Latin is the **epigram**: a very brief, aphoristic, and usually satiric poem like Pound's "The Bath Tub" (page 384) or Alexander Pope's

Epigram from the French

Sir, I admit your gen'ral rule
That every poet is a fool.
But you yourself may serve to show it,
That every fool is not a poet.

Samuel Taylor Coleridge (1772–1834) characterized the form:

What is an epigram? a dwarfish whole,
Its body brevity, and wit its soul.

Anonymous described it thus:

Three things must epigrams, like bees, have all,
A sting, and honey, and a body small.

The Greek word *epigramma* meant "inscription," as on a tomb or statue, and primarily implies brevity and pithiness. An **epitaph** (literally, "on a tomb") is a commemoration suitable for inscribing on a gravestone. But epitaphs, especially comic ones, are a literary convention that has little to do with real chisels or real marble—as in Thomas Hardy's

Epitaph on a Pessimist

I'm Smith of Stoke, aged sixty-odd,
    I've lived without a dame
From youth-time on; and would to God
    My dad had done the same.

Technically, a one-line poem can't be verse—it doesn't "turn." One-liners, nonetheless, make a delightful mini-genre. Since poetry is an art of concentration or compression, these tiny poems must be close to the center of it. This one by W. S. Merwin (b. 1927) is startling:

Elegy

Who would I show it to

So swift and fleeting are one-line poems that it often takes a minute for them to sink in. With Merwin's "Elegy," the silence, we may say, completes the poem. The title also provides an essential juxtaposition—and so the gap across which the spark can leap—in this poem by Eric Torgersen (b. 1943):

Wearing Mittens

You remember the sea.

"Frankenstein in the Cemetery" by Mike Finley (b. 1950) has a lovely comic pathos: "Here is where I ought to be. And here. And here. And here. And here. And here." Tiniest of these tiny knots is by Joseph Napora (b. 1944), with a palindromic title:

Sore Eros

tOUCH

(A **palindrome** is a word, phrase, or sentence that reads the same backward as forward: "Rats live on no evil star" or "Madam, I'm Adam.")

PROSE POEMS

Borrowed from the French, the **prose poem** is a short composition in prose that asks for the concentrated attention usually given to poetry rather than the more discursive attention usually given to prose. It is normally shorter in length than the short story or essay. This one by Robert Bly (b. 1926), for instance, acts in subject, tone, and imagery as we expect a poem to act:

Looking at a Dead Wren in My Hand

Forgive the hours spent listening to radios, and the words of gratitude I did not say to teachers. I love your tiny rice-like legs, that are bars of music played in an empty church, and the feminine tail, where no worms of Empire have ever slept, and the intense yellow chest that makes tears come. Your tail feathers open like a picket fence, and your bill is brown, with the sorrow of an old Jew whose daughter has married an athlete. The black spot on your head is your own mourning cap.

LIMERICKS

Easily the most popular verse form in English, the **limerick** is a five-line poem, rhymed *a a b b a.* The first, second, and fifth lines are trimeter; the third and fourth, dimeter. The dominant rhythm is anapestic. The skeleton looks like this:

˘ ˘ ´ ˘ ˘ ´ ˘ ˘ ´

˘ ˘ ´ ˘ ˘ ´ ˘ ˘ ´

  ˘ ˘ ´ ˘ ˘ ´

  ˘ ˘ ´ ˘ ˘ ´

˘ ˘ ´ ˘ ˘ ´ ˘ ˘ ´

Fleshed out, and with an occasional iamb substituted for an anapest, the limerick goes like this one by the versatile Anonymous:

There was a young fellow named Hall,
Who fell in the spring in the fall;
  'Twould have been a sad thing
  If he'd died in the spring,
But he didn't—he died in the fall.

Part of the fun often is using a proper name, preferably polysyllabic, to end the first line and then getting the second and fifth lines to rhyme with it. Anonymous also wrote:

There was an old man of Nantucket
Who kept all his cash in a bucket;
  But his daughter, named Nan,
  Ran away with a man,
And as for the bucket, Nantucket.

Punning will never be cleverer than in this one, also by Anonymous, about a famous nineteenth-century clergyman, the Reverend Henry Ward Beecher:

Said a great Congregational preacher
To a hen, "You're a beautiful creature."

And the hen, just for that,
Laid an egg in his hat,
And thus did the hen reward Beecher.

Titles

Like houses for sale, poems usually have a sign out front—**titles.** Primarily, titles announce the poem's subject or theme, as in "My Papa's Waltz" or "Delight in Disorder." But they may work more obliquely, addressing someone or something, as "To a Steam Roller"; emphasizing a main image, as "Dust of Snow"; or adding a note, as "To Waken an Old Lady." Sometimes titles function as the poem's real first line, as in Moore's "The Fish." Not infrequently, the title is the hardest part of a poem to write. Sometimes a poem seems complete in itself, and the title must be an afterthought. The poet at a loss for a title can often find one by looking back through the poem's worksheets for a good phrase or image or detail he or she had discarded. The title may sometimes be a convenient place to tuck information that will not fit easily *within* a poem, as in "Myth, Commerce, and Coffee on United Flight #622 from Cleveland to Norfolk."

Because the title is the first part of a poem the reader encounters, there is every reason to make it interesting—lest, thumbing through magazine or anthology, the reader just pass it by. Wallace Stevens was a master of the intriguing title. How could a reader resist poems called "Invective Against Swans," "The Emperor of Ice-Cream," or "The Revolutionists Stop for Orangeade"? Notice, moreover, how skillfully he uses a title as an active part of a poem:

A Rabbit as King of the Ghosts

The difficulty to think at the end of day,
When the shapeless shadow covers the sun
And nothing is left except light on your fur—

There was the cat slopping its milk all day,
Fat cat, red tongue, green mind, white milk   5
And August the most peaceful month.

To be, in the grass, in the peacefullest time,
Without that monument of cat,
The cat forgotten in the moon;

And to feel that the light is a rabbit-light,   10
In which everything is meant for you
And nothing need be explained;

Then there is nothing to think of. It comes of itself;
And east rushes west and west rushes down,
No matter. The grass is full   15

And full of yourself. The trees around are for you,
The whole of the wideness of night is for you,
A self that touches all edges,

You become a self that fills the four corners of night.
The red cat hides away in the fur-light   20
And there you are humped high, humped up,

You are humped higher and higher, black as stone—
You sit with your head like a carving in space
And the little green cat is a bug in the grass.

A satiric account of the danger of a solipsistic view of the world, Stevens's poem is
as deliciously colored and witty as a painting by Paul Klee. The speaker is a rabbit,
weary of being on guard against a cat, imagining himself safe at twilight, feeling
that the light of the moon is "a rabbit-light" and swelling up with his own image of
himself, while "the little green cat" seems only "a bug in the grass." The poem stops
there, and a reader who didn't recall the title might not understand how this ironic
tale of self-delusion ends.

Indentation and Dropped-Line

On the model of the Greek elegaic couplet (hexameter followed by pentameter), a convention of English verse allows the **indentation** of shorter lines, as in
the alternating tetrameter and trimeter lines of the **ballad stanza**:

The king sits in Dumferling toune°,	*town*
Drinking the blude-reid° wine:	*blood-red*
"O whar will I get guid° sailor	*good*
To sail this schip of mine?"	

Similarly, the longer and shorter lines of limericks are indicated by indentation.
This convention may be observed in metered poems like Herbert's "The Collar"
(page 118), in syllabics like Moore's "Critics and Connoisseurs" (page 175), or
more arbitrarily, for visual purposes, in free-verse stanzas like Williams's in
"Asphodel, That Greeny Flower" (page 40). Indentation may also be used very
flexibly, in free verse, as an open-ended musical notation to indicate subordination

or the speeding and bunching of the voice flow—as in Kenneth Patchen's "The Murder of Two Men . . ." (page 45) or May Swenson's "The Universe" (page 116).

The convention of indentation crosses and mingles with another convention: that of the **dropped-line,** which perhaps originated in dramatic usage. In printing Shakespeare, for instance, when a single pentameter line is divided between two speakers, the second part of the line is shown as "dropped":

> *Brutus:*   What means this shouting? I do fear, the people
>   Choose Caesar for their king.
> *Cassius:*   Ay, do you fear it?
>   Then must I think you would not have it so.

> *The Tragedy of Julius Caesar,* I,ii,79–81

On this model, for rhythmical emphasis, Richard Wilbur uses dropped-lines in "Love Calls Us to the Things of This World" (page 325); for instance,

> And the heaviest nuns walk in a pure floating
> Of dark habits,
>   keeping their difficult balance.

Another model for the dropped-line is the Greek stanza called Sapphics, which consisted of—to simplify—three lines of eleven syllables followed by an indented line of five syllables. Ezra Pound imitated this form in an early poem, "Apparuit," and on that model developed the dropped-line as a resilient technique in English. He uses it in "The Garden" (page 22) and in "The Three Poets" (page 31), and it is a major device in both "Homage to Sextus Propertius" (page 407) and *The Cantos.* Here is a passage from *Canto* II, spoken by Acoetes, the pilot of a ship whose crew had kidnapped the slumbering god Bacchus. The ship was whelmed in vines and in the lynxes and panthers that were Bacchus's attendant beasts; and the guilty mariners were changed into dolphins.

> Aye, I, Acœtes, stood there,
>   and the god stood by me,
> Water cutting under the keel,
> Sea-break from stern forrards,
>   wake running off from the bow,   5
> And where was gunwale, there now was vine-trunk,
> And tenthril where cordage had been,
>   grape-leaves on the rowlocks,
> Heavy vine on the oarshafts,
> And, out of nothing, a breathing,   10
>   hot breath on my ankles,

Beasts like shadows in glass,
    a furred tail upon nothingness.
Lynx-purr, and heathery smell of beasts,
    where tar smell had been,   15
Sniff and pad-foot of beasts,
    eye-glitter out of black air.

Both indentation and the dropped-line, in varying forms, open fresh possibilities for rhythmical innovation.

A related, *accidental* dropped-line may occur when, in printing, a longer line will not fit in the margins of a given page-space. The printer then "drops" (and indents) the part of the line leftover. This fine poem by Arthur Smith (b. 1948), for example, is clearly written in stanzas of three lines. But only once, in the next-to-last, does a stanza actually end up with only three printed lines. In every other stanza at least one, and sometimes all three lines, run-over and are dropped. The poem is printed here, as printers say, "line for line" from the book in which it originally appeared. Notice that the margins of the present text are somewhat wider and could have allowed more of each line to be printed before the dropping—and several lines, like line 1 in stanza 4, might well have fitted without dropping at all.

Extra Innings

Back then the ballpark grass was so overgrown
    and sweet-smelling, I think
I could have bellied down near the dugout
And drowsed away the afternoon. He was, then, simply

Someone on the mound. I went one-for-three—
The single, along with a strikeout and a towering pop-up
    that was, as one wit quipped,   5
A home run in an elevator shaft. Four months later

He was called up by the Mets. The rest, as we say,
    is history. We say a lot
Of stupid things. We know our bodies are not luminous
    like the stars,
And so we make amends: we think ourselves luminous
    the moment

Sleep comes on, or after loving someone loved—
    that warmth   10
Radiating out like sound, a name called and carried off
    on the air—or,
Better, and far richer, because it happened once,
    after breaking up

A no-hitter by Tom Seaver, with two out in the ninth.
That was almost twenty years ago, and here I am again
    rounding first, braking,
The dust whirled into a flurry at my feet and the relay
    coming back in   15

To the pitcher, who has turned away, his face now blurred
    beyond recognition.
Whoever he is, Seaver, or someone nameless like myself—
    a landscaper, perhaps,
As good as any other, catching his breath under an ash tree
    on a new-mown lawn—if he remembers anything,

He'll remember the sun flowing the length of his arm
    before flaring out
Into a slider no one could touch all afternoon.   20
He'll remember his no-hitter as precisely

And firmly as I remember spoiling it, and neither of us
    is wrong. Seaver has his stats,
And the rest of us are stuck with rearranging, cutting
And mixing, working day and night, in dreams, in the dark
    of a warehouse

Stacked with the daily, disintegrating rushes of 20 and 30
    and 40 years ago,   25
Trying to make it right, remixing, trying to accommodate
    what happened with what
Might have happened. And it never turns out true,

The possibilities not to be trusted but, rather,
Believed in against the facts—whatever they are:
    the low liner hanging
Long enough for the left fielder to dive for, tumbling,   30

And the graceful pop-up
To his feet, the ball visible, clearly,
In the webbing of the glove held

High over his head, the third out, the proof
That this, ah, yes, this is what happened, the fans in
    his memory standing,   35
Roaring in disbelief, and the lovely applause lasting
    till he's off the field.

The long lines (and their run-overs) suit the speaker's rambling, shifting recollection and meditation. And it is worth considering how that one, next-to-last stanza (with no dropped lines) especially focusses and clarifies the poem by its emphasis.

A poet writing in longer lines should be aware of the problems and possibilities of such accidental dropped lines, and certainly in correcting proof should steer the printer to the best way of dropping his or her lines. In "Extra Innings," notice, the word "and" *could* have been printed on the very first line—resulting in a less desirable line-break. E. E. Cummings, whose poems often use the page visually, was extremely fussy about how his poems were translated into print, and for his books worked directly with the typesetter.

QUESTIONS AND SUGGESTIONS

1. Write a sonnet, selecting all the rhyme words first and arranging them on the page. Then fill it in, keeping the meter. Write *anything,* don't worry whether it makes much sense. Read it aloud. How does it sound? Are there parts of it you like?

2. Write a *serious* limerick. What problems do you find?

3. Study the stanzas and spacing of E. E. Cummings's "chanson innocente." How has he kept, and varied, the form he chose?

in Just-
spring   when the world is mud-
luscious the little
lame balloonman

whistles   far   and wee   5

and eddieandbill come
running from marbles and
piracies and it's
spring

when the world is puddle-wonderful   10

the queer
old balloonman whistles
far   and   wee
and bettyandisbel come dancing

from hop-scotch and jump-rope and   15

it's
spring
and
    the

        goat-footed   20

balloonMan   whistles
far
and
wee

4. How does the poet Conrad Hilberry (b. 1928) achieve the feeling of slow
motion in "Storm Window"? What do syntax, repetitions, run-on lines, and the
lack of stanzas contribute to the effect?

> At the top of the ladder, a gust catches the glass
> and he is falling. He and the window topple
> backwards like a piece of deception slowly
> coming undone. After the instant of terror,
> he feels easy, as though he were a boy   5
> falling back on his own bed. For years,
> he has clamped his hands to railings, balanced
> against the pitch of balconies and cliffs
> and fire towers. For years, he has feared falling.
> At last, he falls. Still holding the frame,   10
> he sees the sky and trees come clear
> in the wavering glass. In another second
> the pane will shatter over his whole length,
> but now, he lies back on air, falling.

5. What possibilities can you foresee for a sestina using these line-end words:
popcorn, explosions, salt, lamplight, hungry, and *old maids?* How might it develop?
(Then have a look at David Evett's splendid "Popcorn," page 150.) Taking into
account the sestina's essential round-and-round-ness, make your own list of six
words. Give them a try.

6. Consider the usefulness of the stanza George Herbert has invented for this
poem-prayer. How do metrical effects reenforce the pattern of unrhymed and
rhymed fifth lines?

The Denial

> When my devotions could not pierce
>   Thy silent ears;

Then was my heart broken, as was my verse:
 My breast was full of fears
   And disorder.   5

My bent thoughts, like a brittle bow,
   Did fly asunder:
Each took his way; some would to pleasures go,
   Some to the wars and thunder
     Of alarms.   10

As good go anywhere, they say,
   As to benumb
Both knees and heart, in crying night and day,
   Come, come, my God, O come,
     But no hearing.   15

Therefore my soul lay out of sight,
   Untun'd, unstrung:
My feeble spirit, unable to look right,
   Like a nipt blossom, hung
     Discontented.   20

O cheer and tune my heartless breast,
   Defer no time;
That so thy favors granting my request,
   They and my mind may chime,
     And mend my rhyme.   25

7. As Michael Heffernan points out in *Poet & Critic* (Spring 1986), it seems as if, in this prose poem, James Wright (1927–1980) has hidden a rhymed (and off-rhymed) *sonnet.* When you are sure you see it, consider which version of the poem you prefer. Why?

May Morning

   Deep into spring, winter is hanging on. Bitter and skillful in his hopelessness, he stays alive in every shady place, starving along the Mediterranean: angry to see the glittering sea-pale boulder alive with lizards green as Judas leaves. Winter is hanging on. He still believes. He tries to catch a lizard by the shoulder. One olive tree below Grottaglie welcomes the winter into noontime shade, and talks as softly as Pythagoras. Be still, be patient, I can hear him say, cradling in his arms the wounded head, letting the sunlight touch the savage face.

The poem is also a good example of personification: both winter and the olive tree near the Italian village of Grottaglie are personified. What wisdom is there in the comforting advice the olive tree offers, that justifies its being compared to the philosopher Pythagoras (died about 497 B.C.)?

8. Make up three or four interesting, off-the-wall titles. Try to write a poem to follow one of them.

9. Compare the triple-rhyming in Frost's "Provide, Provide" (page 112) and in Herrick's "Upon Julia's Clothes" (page 126). How do the poets make it, in one poem, harsh, grating, and in the other, smooth? (Another point: in stanza 2, is Julia wearing anything? Critics disagree.) Look ahead to Robert Francis's "Cadence" (page 247). How does he use (and modulate) quadruple-rhyming in this poem which has a quite different tone?

POEMS TO CONSIDER

Nuns Fret Not at Their Convent's Narrow Room

1807

WILLIAM WORDSWORTH (1770–1850)

Nuns fret not at their convent's narrow room;
And hermits are contented with their cells;
And students with their pensive citadels;
Maids at the wheel, the weaver at his loom,
Sit blithe and happy; bees that soar for bloom,   5
High as the highest Peak of Furness-fells,
Will murmur by the hour in foxglove bells:
In truth the prison, into which we doom
Ourselves, no prison is: and hence for me,
In sundry moods, 'twas pastime to be bound   10
Within the sonnet's scanty plot of ground;
Pleased if some souls (for such there needs must be)
Who have felt the weight of too much liberty,
Should find brief solace there, as I have found.

Grief

1844

ELIZABETH BARRETT BROWNING   (1806–1861)

I tell you, hopeless grief is passionless;
That only men incredulous of despair,
Half-taught in anguish, through the midnight air
Beat upward to God's throne in loud access
Of shrieking and reproach. Full desertness,   5
In souls as countries, lieth silent-bare
Under the blanching, vertical eye-glare
Of the absolute Heavens. Deep-hearted man, express
Grief for thy Dead in silence like to death:—
Most like a monumental statue set   10
In everlasting watch and moveless woe
Till itself crumble to the dust beneath.
Touch it; the marble eyelids are not wet;
If it could weep, it could arise and go.

Sonnet: The Last Things

1971

GAVIN EWART   (b. 1916)

Of course there's always a last everything.
The last meal, the last drink, the last sex.
The last meeting with a friend. The last
stroking of the last cat, the last
sight of a son or daughter. Some would be more   5
charged with emotion than others—if one knew.
It's not knowing that makes it all so piquant.
A good many lasts have taken place already.

Then there are last words, variously reported,
such as: Let not poor Nelly starve. Or: 10
I think I could eat one of Bellamy's veal pies.
If there were time I'd incline to a summary:
Alcohol made my life shorter but more interesting.
My father said (not last perhaps): Say goodbye to Gavin.

I Knew a Woman   1954

THEODORE ROETHKE   (1908–1963)

I knew a woman, lovely in her bones,
When small birds sighed, she would sigh back at them;
Ah, when she moved, she moved more ways than one:
The shapes a bright container can contain!
Of her choice virtues only gods should speak,   5
Or English poets who grew up on Greek
(I'd have them sing in chorus, cheek to cheek).

How well her wishes went! She stroked my chin,
She taught me Turn, and Counter-turn, and Stand;
She taught me Touch, that undulant white skin;   10
I nibbled meekly from her proffered hand;
She was the sickle; I, poor I, the rake,
Coming behind her for her pretty sake
(But what prodigious mowing we did make).

Love likes a gander, and adores a goose: 15
Her full lips pursed, the errant note to seize;
She played it quick, she played it light and loose;
My eyes, they dazzled at her flowing knees;
Her several parts could keep a pure repose,
Or one hip quiver with a mobile nose   20
(She moved in circles, and those circles moved).

Let seed be grass, and grass turn into hay:
I'm martyr to a motion not my own;
What's freedom for? To know eternity.
I swear she cast a shadow white as stone.   25
But who would count eternity in days?
These old bones live to learn her wanton ways:
(I measure time by how a body sways).

The Invention of the Telephone

PETER KLAPPERT   (b. 1942)

The time it took he could have
crawled—on the hairs of his knuckles,
on his eyelids, on his teeth.

He could have chewed his way.
In a place without friction   5
he could have re-invented the wheel.

But he wanted you to be
proud of him, so he invented
the telephone before he called.

Poet and Critics

JOHN FREDERICK NIMS   (b. 1914)

One hound that trots. A thousand fleas that ride.
Which way? A vote for each. The fleas decide?

Birthday Quatrain to a Beautiful Lady

for Astra

F. C. ROSENBERGER   (b. 1915)

Grieve not the summer fled.
The snow and holly berry
Are as white and red
As cherry bloom and cherry.

Poems to Consider   149

The Battle of Muldoon's

TOM RILEY (b. 1958)

What are you lily-livered rascals at?
Just because Casey's down you're running off?
You cannot be such little girls as that.

Too bad if one guy's got a baseball bat.
It's when fists fail that bellies must be tough.   5
What are you lily-livered rascals at?

This isn't just some private household spat.
Our Casey's down. Now isn't that enough?
You cannot be such little girls as that,

to leave him on the floor alone. You sat   10
with him tonight and drank his drinking stuff.
What are you lily-livered rascals at,

thinking that you can quick put on your hat
and take your leave with just a nervous cough?
You cannot be such little girls as that.   15

Hell swallow every damn ungrateful rat
that scurries off when things start getting rough.
What are you lily-livered rascals at?
You cannot be such little girls as that.

Popcorn

DAVID EVETT (b. 1936)

It seems so right to sit here eating some popcorn,
dipping out handfuls of gentle white explosions,
relishing the contrast between cold bourbon and warm salt,
at ease with the world here within this ring of lamplight,
not yet satisfied but certainly no longer hungry,   5
selecting a last few morsels from among the old maids.

Another nice contrast: the small smooth brown old maids
against the white puffed irregularity of the popcorn.
When they're all that's left I'm glad I'm not hungry—
taut they are, swollen, threatening small explosions,   10
but held in by the comfortable circle of lamplight,
and the bowl, and pacified by fine small jewels of salt.

Of course, one of you is bound to observe that so much salt
provokes high blood pressure, and that hard old maids
break teeth, that scarce fuels burned to make my lamplight   15
and were processed into fertilizer to grow the popcorn.
While I indulge myself, the population explosion
booms: my pleasure against the misery of the truly hungry.

Of course, about now some woman among you's hungry
for justice, every word I say rubbing coarse salt   20
into an old wound, on the verge of a real explosion
at my thoughtless endorsement of the phrase "old maid":
a long history of exploitation trivialized by popcorn,
suffering in the shadows beyond the comfy male lamplight.

To say nothing of that definitive intense lamplight   25
ready to gather in its expanding ring both hungry
and fed, ready to shadow under clouds like monster popcorn
all of us, ready when we're finally sick of futile SALT
talks to gather us by handfuls, young, old, maids
and men, dissolving all contrast in one ghastly explosion.   30

All right, all right: I'll try to stop the explosion,
illuminate that darkness there beyond my lamplight.
But don't the rest of you in contrast sit there like old maids:
get out there, heal the sick, clothe the naked, feed the hungry,
battle indifference and injustice and discrimination, assault   35
fear, persuade the Others to trade guns for buttered popcorn.

First, though, we old maids and health freaks are a bit hungry.
Gathering forces by lamplight, even the very best, the salt
of the earth's explosion, can use the sustenance of a little popcorn.

Strawberry Moon

MARY OLIVER   (b. 1935)

I
My great-aunt Elizabeth Fortune
stood under the honey locust trees,
the white moon over her and a young man near.
The blossoms fell down like white feathers,
the grass was warm as a bed, and the young man   5
full of promises, and the face of the moon
a white fire.
Later,
when the young man went away and came back with a
    bride,
Elizabeth   10
climbed into the attic.

II
Three women came in the night
to wash the blood away,
and burn the sheets,
and take away the child.   15

Was it a boy or girl?
No one remembers.

III
Elizabeth Fortune was not seen again
for forty years.
Meals were sent up,   20
laundry exchanged.

It was considered a solution
more proper than shame
showing itself to the village.

IV
Finally, name by name, the downstairs died   25
or moved away,
and she had to come down,
so she did.

At sixty-one, she took in boarders,

washed their dishes,
made their beds,
spoke whatever had to be spoken,
and no more.   30

          V
I asked my mother:
what happened to the man? She answered: 35
Nothing.
They had three children.
He worked in the boatyard.

I asked my mother: did they ever meet again?
No, she said,   40
though sometimes he would come
to the house to visit.
Elizabeth, of course, stayed upstairs.

          VI
Now the women are gathering
in smoke-filled rooms,
rough as politicians,   45
scrappy as club fighters.
And should anyone be surprised

if sometimes, when the white moon rises,
women want to lash out   50
with a cutting edge?

II

Content:
The Essential Something

Subject Matter:
Roses and Fried Shoes

Content, the other half of the indivisible equation that defines poetry, is harder to describe systematically than form. There was a time when certain subjects were thought to be "poetic" and others not. Today almost nothing is off-limits to the poet. As Louis Simpson (b. 1923) says in his poem of that title, "American Poetry" must be able to "digest / Rubber, coal, uranium, moons, poems"—even, like the shark, "a shoe." Poems can be about anything. If someone says that one can't start a poem with "fried shoes," a poet will almost certainly start a poem with "fried shoes." (Gregory Corso said it, and John Hollander wrote the poem.)

More than responding to a challenge is reflected in this poem by Ronald Wallace (b. 1945):

"You Can't Write a Poem
About McDonald's"

Noon. Hunger the only thing
singing in my belly.
I walk through the blossoming cherry trees
on the library mall,
past the young couples coupling,   5

by the crazy fanatic
screaming doom and salvation
at a sensation-hungry crowd,
to the Lake Street McDonald's.
It is crowded, the lines long and sluggish.   10
I wait in the greasy air.
All around me people are eating—
the sizzle of conversation,
the salty odor of sweat,
the warm flesh pressing out of   15
hip huggers and halter tops.
When I finally reach the cash register,
the counter girl is crisp as a pickle,
her fingers thin as french fries,
her face brown as a bun.   20
Suddenly I understand cannibalism.
As I reach for her,
she breaks into pieces
wrapped neat and packaged for take-out.
I'm thinking, how amazing it is   25
to live in this country, how easy
it is to be filled.
We leave together, her warm aroma
close at my side.
I walk back through the cherry trees   30
blossoming up into pies,
the young couples frying in
the hot, oily sun,
the crowd eating up the fanatic,
singing, my ear, eye, and tongue   35
fat with the wonder
of this hungry world.

The challenge reminds the poet to pay attention to a part of his or her experience—a part of our experience—which we all usually drift through without realizing that it has significance. But of course it has. For we are constantly being moved, bombarded in our senses, and half-fantasizing through all, even the most trivial, parts of our lives.

It is useful to remind the beginning poet, even these days, of this freedom of subject matter. Any of several assumptions—the dead hand of convention—may be keeping her or him blindfolded. The assumption that poems should be about certain traditional subjects, for instance: the seasons, love (especially a lost love), "life" in general. Or the assumption that poetry should be, somehow, *grand*—high flown, solving all the world's problems at once, full of important pronouncements. Or the corollary assumption that the ordinary, everyday things he or she knows—things close to the nose, as Williams says: a particular flower on a particular morning, people in his or her hometown, a cat carefully stepping down into an empty flowerpot, a McDonald's—aren't proper subjects.

Equally blinding is the assumption that poetry is mainly direct self-expression: what happened to *me*, what *I* saw, and mostly, what *I* feel this morning (this afternoon, tonight). Poets become ancient mariners, endlessly reporting their own experience (because it is their own experience), unaware that it is boring the listener. This unrelentingly looking inward, of course, also keeps such poets from looking outward. If they notice the cat, flower, or neighbor, it is only to rush on to what they feel or think about them. The poem that begins, "I *watch* the kids in the park, / pushing their sailboats on a pond . . .," is going to be more about the poet's feelings than about the kids (who may in fact be interesting, though the poet won't really notice that) and will almost surely end with a pronouncement about life.

We're all tempted to write such poems. And poets, of course, do express themselves, though rarely as directly as it may seem.

The point is that **poems must be interesting.** Whether or not they elucidate one of the great human truths, they had better be interesting—or we are likely to leave them half-read and turn the page. Poems compete with everything else in the world for our attention. As E. E. Cummings says, "It is with roses and locomotives (not to mention acrobats Spring electricity Coney Island the 4th of July the eyes of mice and Niagara Falls) that my 'poems' are competing. They are also competing with each other, with elephants, and with El Greco."

Poems must be interesting. And there is nothing like *subject matter* to do the job. Subject matter is up front, obvious, able to draw a reader into a poem, like a story that begins, "He undid her blouse." Subject matter differentiates one poem from another. Especially for the beginning poet, a good subject, interesting, fresh, specific, can make up for any number of technical blunders.

It needn't be a big subject, I hasten to add. It may be something seen (a cat, a double play, kids playing by a pond in a park). It may be something personal, recalled, as in this poem by Peter Meinke (b. 1932), which records a painful little family drama from the early days of World War II:

Stille Nacht, Heilege Nacht

At Christmas, my sisters and I
learned to sing carols in German:
Grandpa would give us a quarter
apiece for performing, though
only Carol could carry a tune.   5
After the start of the War
Father forbid us to practice

and when Grandpa asked for his songs
we told him they weren't allowed.
You are German, he shouted. Sing! 10

Singt, meine Kinder, für mich!

We stood mute, unhappy, ashamed,
between father and son locking eyes
while the U-boats were nosing the currents
and propellers coughed in the skies 15
like angels clearing their throats.

A good subject may be virtually anything: an old news photograph (Sharon Olds's
"Photograph of the Girl," page 186), two ponies in a pasture (James Wright's "A
Blessing," page 339), or bits of broken bottles washed up in the surf:

Beach Glass

AMY CLAMPITT (b. 1920)

While you walk the water's edge,
turning over concepts
I can't envision, the honking buoy
serves notice that at any time
the wind may change, 5
the reef-bell clatters
its treble monotone, deaf as Cassandra
to any note but warning. The ocean,
cumbered by no business more urgent
than keeping open old accounts 10
that never balanced,
goes on shuffling its millenniums
of quartz, granite, and basalt.
                  It behaves
toward the permutations of novelty—
driftwood and shipwreck, last night's 15
beer cans, spilt oil, the coughed-up
residue of plastic—with random
impartiality, playing catch or tag
or touch-last like a terrier,
turning the same thing over and over, 20
over and over. For the ocean, nothing
is beneath consideration.

                    The houses
of so many mussels and periwinkles
have been abandoned here, it's hopeless
to know which to salvage. Instead   25
I keep a lookout for beach glass—
amber of Budweiser, chrysoprase
of Almadén and Gallo, lapis
by way of (no getting around it,
I'm afraid) Phillips'   30
Milk of Magnesia, with now and then a rare
translucent turquoise or blurred amethyst
of no known origin.
                    The process
goes on forever: they came from sand,
they go back to gravel,   35
along with the treasuries
of Murano, the buttressed
astonishments of Chartres,
which even now are readying
for being turned over and over as gravely   40
and gradually as an intellect
engaged in the hazardous
redefinition of structures
no one has yet looked at.

Discovering a subject may be partly luck, but the luck will come to the poet
who is alert, watches, keeps his or her antennae out. All of us have seen the
sea-smoothed bits of old Budweiser or Phillips' Milk of Magnesia bottles, but who
would have thought to connect them to the eroding stones and stained glass of the
cathedral at Chartres? Subjects are there plentifully, as other poets' poems remind
us; a poem may bloom from a noticed detail, a stray connection, something
forgotten. The need is to try to see everything freshly, with a cleansed eye. Look at
things. Notice. Study a slice of bread, really study it, and then write about what
you see. Forget about the staff of life and shimmering fields of golden grain. Look at
the bread. Like the purloined letter in Poe's story, this is a secret hidden in the
open. *Look. Notice.*

It is easy to see only what everybody sees, notice only what everybody notices.
The result is **clichés**—not only clichés of language, but clichés of observation, of
thinking, and even of feeling. We all fall victim to them. But the vision to see
something anew, singularly, is at the center of making good poems. Insights don't
have to be grand. Indeed, most of the original ones are small. In "The Black Snake"
(page 183) Mary Oliver mentions that the dead snake in the road "lies looped and
useless / as an old bicycle tire." In "In a Prominent Bar in Secaucus One Day" (page

192) X. J. Kennedy mentions "lovely white clover that rusts with its grass." In "A Blessing" (page 339) James Wright describes a pony's "long ear" as being "delicate as the skin over a girl's wrist." These small insights are triumphs of observation. The term **image** (or imagery) is sometimes used to refer to such visual detail and the mental pictures it evokes, even when it is simply literal ("the white diagonal lines in an empty parking lot"). But the term is also used for comparisons ("like fishbones") which reenforce such visual perceptions.

"Nor," as Marianne Moore might say, "is it valid / to discriminate against 'business documents and / school-books.' " An interesting subject may come as an anecdote in a biography or history the poet is reading (Deborah Bliss's "Van Busbeke Discovers the Tulip," page 184). A poem may start while the poet is watching a horror movie (Edward Field's "Curse of the Cat Woman," page 179) or reading a poem (Anthony Hecht's "The Dover Bitch," page 315). Consider Conrad Hilberry's poem about Houdini, which symbolically illuminates both the simplicity and the difficulty of noticing:

The Vanishing Horseman

Magnificent in his blue uniform,
Harry Houdini rides a fine white horse
onto the stage, surrounded by attendants

dressed in white. Two of them lift up
a huge fan, hiding Houdini   5
for a moment. When they lower it,

he has vanished. The horse stamps and rears—
but no blue rider. Where has he gone?
There is no trap door. He is not clinging

to the far side of the horse. Instead,   10
while the fan protected him, he tore off
the blue uniform, made of paper, tucked it

inside his white clothes, dismounted,
and became one of the attendants, one
of the uncounted retinue turning   15

the empty horse and running to the wings.

A good subject, stumbled on at the right moment, becomes a way of expressing our ideas and feelings. It can release, shape, focus them, as we might not be able to do directly. So it was for me when I chanced upon this anecdote about the

French painter Henri de Toulouse-Lautrec (1864–1901) in the foreword to a book of his drawings of animals, *A Bestiary* (Fogg Museum, 1954):

> A friend sent him in a hat box, from L'Isle Adam, a large toad (plate 11) which hopped about his apartment for days, becoming quite a pet. At last it escaped into the "wilderness" of the rue Caulaincourt (Montmartre quarter, in Paris). Toulouse-Lautrec, a far more affectionate and soft hearted man than some biographers have represented him, was desolate. When the rumor came later that the toad had been seen on the Avenue Frochot, he spent hours searching for him—the length of that street!

Adding what I knew of toads, Paris, and Lautrec—the painter we associate with can-can dancers and sophisticated scenes of Parisian night life near the turn of the century—I retold the story, in order to make my own quite different point.

Ungainly Things

A regular country toad—pebbly,
    squat,
        shadow-green

as the shade of the spruces
    in the garden   5
        he came from—rode

to Paris in a hatbox
    to Lautrec's
        studio (skylights

on the skies of Paris);   10
    ate
        cutworms from a box,

hopped
    occasionally
        among the furniture and easels,   15

while the clumsy little painter
    studied
        him in charcoal

until he was beautiful.
    One day   20
        he found his way

down stairs toward the world
   again,
      into the streets of Montmartre°,   *district of Paris*

and, missing him, the painter-dwarf   25
   followed,
      peering among cobbles,

laughed at, searching
   until long past dark
      the length of the Avenue Frochot,   30

over and over,
   for the fisted, marble-eyed
      fellow

no one would ever see again
   except   35
      in sketches that make ungainly things beautiful.

Presenting

Emotions, in themselves, are not subject matter. Being in love, or sad, or lonely, or feeling good because it is spring, are common experiences. Poems that merely say these things, *state* these emotions, won't be very interesting. We respect such statements, but we can't be moved by them.

The *circumstances* of the emotion, the scene or events out of which it comes, however, are subject matter. Don't tell the emotion. Tell the causes of it, the circumstances. Presented vividly, they will not only convince us of its truth but will also make us dramatically *feel* it. Theodore Roethke doesn't state his feeling about his father in "My Papa's Waltz." He lets us feel it for ourselves by presenting us with the particular scene out of which the feeling came. In "Dust of Snow" Robert Frost communicates the feeling by telling us about the crow, the hemlock, and the chill sprinkling of snow. In "Nevertheless" Marianne Moore presents her theme— admiration for fortitude, overcoming obstacles—by presenting a number of examples that surprise us because we don't usually think of strawberries and grape vines as courageous. Often, as in William Carlos Williams's "Poem" about the cat or in E. E. Cumming's "next to of course god america i," the poet simply gives us the facts and trusts them to elicit the proper feeling. Frequently, presenting the facts will be the only way to describe an emotion adequately. What word, or list of words, that describes the emotions of love, fear, pain, mischief, panic, delight, and helplessness could begin to sum up what the boy (and the grown man) feel in (and about) the little scene in "My Papa's Waltz"?

The key is **presenting;** not to tell about, but to show. Put the spring day or the girl or the father *into* the poem. Put the mountain *into* the poem. As Wallace Stevens urges in "The Poem That Took the Place of the Mountain," the poem not only can save and remember experience, but also can bring to exactness, because we can imagine it, the world that is always incomplete and transitory in reality. The experience has become permanent, even in the absence of the mountain: the pines "recomposed," the rock "exact," the oxygen in the air breathable "Even when the book lay turned in the dust of his table."

We have already looked at some of the ways in which imitative elements of form (shape, sound, rhythm) help in *presenting*. In Chapter 8 we will consider metaphor. For the moment, let's examine the management of subject matter, some of the ways in which a poet may arrange or dispose it in a poem to make it effective.

It almost goes without saying that subject matter should be presented accurately. Accuracy of information, of detail, of terminology tends to make the presentation convincing. Whether writing about antiques, rocking chairs, leopards, Denver, black holes in space, or the physiology of the grasshopper, the poet should know enough, or find out enough, to be reasonably authoritative. Tulips don't bloom in July. Whales are mammals, not fish. Ernie Banks played shortstop for the Chicago Cubs. Common knowledge and plain observation are usually sufficient, but sometimes the poet will come upon a subject that takes her or him to the library and requires becoming something of a specialist. Ezra Pound notes, in *ABC of Reading*, a physician's claim that the accuracy of medical information in *The Iliad* proved that Homer was an army doctor!

In presenting subject matter, **particulars** in and of themselves are frequently a source of vividness. Gerard Manley Hopkins both praises and exemplifies the effect of colorful and idiosyncratic detail:

Pied Beauty

Glory be to God for dappled things—
    For skies of couple-colour as a brinded° cow;   *brindled, streaked*
        For rose-moles all in stipple° upon trout that swim;   *stippled, dotted*
Fresh-firecoal chestnut-falls; finches' wings;
    Landscape plotted and pieced—fold, fallow and plough,   5
        And áll trádes, their gear and tackle and trim.
All things counter, original, spare, strange;
    Whatever is fickle, freckled (who knows how?)
        With swift, slow; sweet, sour; adazzle, dim;
He fathers-forth whose beauty is past change: 10
        Praise him.

Specific details add overtones as well as color. Suppose, in "Dust of Snow," Frost had said merely "tree" instead of "hemlock": the picture is vaguer, and the deadly suggestions of the funereal hemlock are lost. In Roethke's "My Papa's Waltz" the detail about the "pans" sliding from the "kitchen shelf" does more than indicate the rowdiness of the drunken father's dancing. It tells us something about the middle-class or lower-middle-class family—the kitchen described is neither large nor very elegant. More important, it sets the scene in the kitchen. Suggestions abound. The father, who works with his hands ("a palm caked hard by dirt"), has come home late from work, having stopped off for his whiskey. He has come in by the back door, into the kitchen. Dinner is over and the pans back on the shelf, but the boy and his mother are still in the kitchen. That they have not waited dinner, or waited it longer, measures the mother's stored-up anger, as does the word "countenance," which suggests how formidably she has prepared herself. The incongruity of the father's merriment is all the stronger because the waltzing begins, so inappropriately, in the kitchen.

This poem by William Stafford (b. 1914) shows a perfect articulation of details:

Traveling Through the Dark

Traveling through the dark I found a deer
dead on the edge of the Wilson River road.
It is usually best to roll them into the canyon:
that road is narrow; to swerve might make more dead.

By glow of the tail-light I stumbled back of the car   5
and stood by the heap, a doe, a recent killing;
she had stiffened already, almost cold.
I dragged her off; she was large in the belly.

My fingers touching her side brought me the reason—
her side was warm; her fawn lay there waiting,   10
alive, still, never to be born.
Beside that mountain road I hesitated.

The car aimed ahead its lowered parking lights;
under the hood purred the steady engine.
I stood in the glare of the warm exhaust turning red;   15
around our group I could hear the wilderness listen.

I thought hard for us all—my only swerving—,
then pushed her over the edge into the river.

Some of the details, like "the Wilson River road," attest to the reality of the incident. The speaker has seen dead deer along the road before and is not sentimental ("It is usually best to roll them into the canyon"). The most effective detail, perhaps, is the "glow of the tail-light," which bathes the whole scene an eerie red. Everything about the car is made to participate. The glow is red, like blood. The parking lights are "lowered," as if in respect or recognition of the tragedy. The engine "purred" like an animal, and the exhaust is "warm." The doomed warmth and life of the fawn could not be more ironically emphasized. Stafford has not added these details to the grim tableau—they are all naturally a part of it—but he *uses* them superbly to illuminate the event.

Absent specifics, left-out particulars that are natural parts of the material all too often result in missed opportunities. That occurs in this sonnet, submitted in a writing workshop I conducted once upon a time.

To One Who Shed Tears at a Play

Because I hold that fleeting moment dear
I prison it within each shining word
As fragile as the flight of startled bird,
Yet strong as iron bands. I still can hear
The actors speak their lines. The climax near,   5
They find frustration, sorrow, and they gird
Themselves for bitter loss. And you who heard
Pay them the priceless tribute of a tear.

O, gentle heart! May that day never come,
When you are heedless of the sight of grief,   10
Though only grief that mimics. For the sum
Of your vicarious sharing brings relief.
The callous heart is like a broken drum,
A bitter fruit, a sere and withered leaf.

The group concluded that the sonnet form is well managed, though at the price of the rather archaic rhyme-word "gird" and the padded "For the sum / Of your vicarious sharing" instead of simply "For your vicarious sharing." (The fact, not the amount, is the point.) The main problem, however, seemed to be a curious abstractness about its subject matter, someone who cries at a play. A surprising proportion of the poem does not deal directly with the subject at all. The first three and a half lines are about the writing of the poem, and the images in the last two lines are, oddly, about the "callous heart" rather than the "gentle heart" of the person who wept.

Consider the missing particulars, the missed opportunities. About the person who cries, we know nothing: not age, nor sex, nor any other detail, although such information might considerably affect our responses. Nor do we know anything about the speaker's relationship to this person. Was it a stranger who happened to be in the next seat? a friend? a relative? perhaps a son or daughter? Why did that person's sympathetic reaction strike the speaker as valuable? We don't even know what the play was, though that detail might have been useful. We are strangely barred from the very event that is supposed to move us. Its color and convincingness are left out.

Of course, all poems do not need description equally. Some require little or none, such as J. V. Cunningham's "For My Contemporaries." With poems that depend on description, the *selection* of particulars is more to the point than a mere piling up of them. There is no way to include everything about anything. Too many particulars may be as ineffective as too few. Dylan Thomas's lyric evocation of the childhood experience of a farm, "Fern Hill" (page 188), manages its rich profusion of detail without losing its thematic thread. The past tense—"Now as I *was* young and easy under the apple boughs"—is an implicit reminder throughout that the paradise of boyhood ends; and the emphatic fourth lines in stanzas 1 and 2—"Time let me hail and climb" and "Time let me play and be"—keep the poem's dizzyingly lovely detail always in perspective.

In writing, jot down every item that comes to mind. Then, as the poem begins to take shape, pick and choose those that fit and best bear out the poem's developing direction. Most poets' manuscripts are embroidered in the margins with lists of details, adjectives, whatever. A. E. Housman's list of words for "_____ counties" in "Bredon Hill" (page 107)—*sunny, pleasant, checkered, patterned, painted, colored*—show him accumulating such a range of possibilities.

Descriptive Implication

Particulars may give a poem its richly colored surface, evoking vividly for the reader the subject or the setting in which an action occurs. They may also, implicitly, provide a sort of running commentary on the subject or action—and on the speaker's attitude about either. Consider the selection of detail in this poem by Elizabeth Bishop (1911–1979):

First Death in Nova Scotia

In the cold, cold parlor
my mother laid out Arthur
beneath the chromographs:
Edward, Prince of Wales,
with Princess Alexandra,   5

and King George with Queen Mary.
Below them on the table
stood a stuffed loon
shot and stuffed by Uncle
Arthur, Arthur's father.   10

Since Uncle Arthur fired
a bullet into him,
he hadn't said a word.
He kept his own counsel
on his white, frozen lake,   15
the marble-topped table.
His breast was deep and white,
cold and caressable;
his eyes were red glass,
much to be desired.   20

"Come," said my mother,
"Come and say good-bye
to your little cousin Arthur."
I was lifted up and given
one lily of the valley   25
to put in Arthur's hand.
Arthur's coffin was
a little frosted cake,
and the red-eyed loon eyed it
from his white, frozen lake.   30

Arthur was very small.
He was all white, like a doll
that hadn't been painted yet.
Jack Frost had started to paint him
the way he always painted   35
the Maple Leaf (Forever).
He had just begun on his hair,
a few red strokes, and then
Jack Frost had dropped the brush
and left him white, forever.   40

The gracious royal couples
were warm in red and ermine;
their feet were well wrapped up
in the ladies' ermine trains.

They invited Arthur to be   45
the smallest page at court.
But how could Arthur go,
clutching his tiny lily,
with his eyes shut up so tight
and the roads deep in snow?   50

The poem very selectively presents a child's view of death. Almost nothing outside the "cold, cold parlor" is mentioned, nor anything before or after the one event, seeing little Arthur in his coffin. Only two details of the parlor are referred to, the color lithographs of the royal family and the stuffed loon on its marble-topped table. Although no other furnishings are mentioned, these two are sufficient to suggest the ornate and rather formal nature of the room, as well as something about the household (its patriotism, its family loyalty, its propriety). We accept the poem as autobiographical and assume the speaker to be a little girl.

The loon and the chromographs of the royal family have several aspects in common. Like Arthur himself and his coffin ("a little frosted cake"), both are studies in white and red. The loon's breast and "frozen lake" of marble-topped table are white, and his glass eyes are red. "The gracious royal couples" are "warm in red and ermine" (a white, thick fur)—the only colors noted. Arthur is "white, forever," except for the "few red strokes" of his hair. Very likely it is the red and white of the loon and the chromographs that make the little girl notice them and associate them with her dead cousin. And both are connected with death. "Uncle Arthur, Arthur's father" had killed the loon and had it stuffed. And the ermine of the royal family similarly comes from animals that have been killed to provide decorative fur. These particulars give the poem its icy, rich unity: red and white; warm (royal family) and cold (loon). The funeral reminds the little girl of a birthday, the "little frosted cake" of the coffin.

The particulars suggest beautifully the little girl's incomprehension of what she is witnessing. The loon is not so much dead as silent: "Since Uncle Arthur fired / a bullet into him, / he hadn't said a word." "He kept his own counsel" and only "eyed" little Arthur's coffin. The girl's fantasy that the royal family had "invited Arthur to be / the smallest page at court" is the only way that she can translate her cousin's death into her experience. ("Jack Frost" suggests the dimensions of her experience.) Her mother's well-meaning but too careful " 'Come and say good-bye / to your little cousin Arthur' " invites the fantasy. Although the girl doesn't understand, she is nonetheless aware that the confusion between life (red) and death (white) will resolve itself ominously. "But how could Arthur go, / clutching his tiny lily, / with his eyes shut up so tight / and the roads deep in snow?" (Lily and snow are yet more white.) That question, with which the poem ends, shows how fragile is her defense against the grim truth.

Bishop's handling of the details of "First Death in Nova Scotia" quietly gathers up nuances until they become symbolic. The poem does not *state* its evaluation of the child's experience, but *implies* it in the choice of particulars. The literal reds and whites of loon and royal family symbolize the confusion about life and death in her feelings. Like most effective details, they function in more than one way, on more than one level. As Pound says, "the natural object is always the adequate symbol."

The choice and ordering of the details help reveal the way the narrator feels about the narrative. This is **tone:** the poet's or the speaker's attitude toward the material. Tone may be, for instance, approving, disapproving, pitying, admiring, doubting, ironic. Every element in a poem, including diction, imagery, and rhythm, will contribute to its tone, establishing a mood, conveying the poet's or the speaker's sense of the subject. Robert Frost's tone in "An Old Man's Winter Night" might be described as pitying. E. E. Cummings's tone in "next to of course god america i" is satiric. The tone of a poem may be mixed, as Howard Nemerov's "Learning by Doing" mingles lyrical with satiric or witty.

Here the voice of the poem is, of course, the little girl's. (Behind it we also sense the poet's, selecting, controlling.) The tone is uncomprehending and, finally, questioning. Her uncertainty is suggested by the displacement of her attention from Arthur's corpse to the familiar and so comforting loon and chromographs. The mother must beckon her forward: " 'Come,' said my mother, / 'Come and say good-bye / to your little cousin Arthur.' " In the final lines, the shift from the close-up view of Arthur, eyes shut, "clutching his tiny lily," to the wide-shot of "the roads deep in snow" outside, lets us see her incomprehension from a pitying distance.

Camera Work

One useful way of thinking of **visual detail** is as "camera work": camera angle or location, close-up or distant shot, fade-in or fade-out, panning, montage, and so on. Working with only the black squiggles of words on a page, the poet somehow controls what the reader sees with his or her mind's eye. Bishop first makes us see a white, frozen lake and then the marble-topped table when she says that the stuffed loon

> kept his own counsel
> on his white, frozen lake,
> the marble-topped table.

The two, in effect, become one; lake turns into table. It is, of course, a simple enough comparison and, in reading, happens so fast that we scarcely notice. But we have for a moment had a glimpse of an iced-over lake, something like a superimposition of two shots in a film. The poet no doubt manages such things intuitively, absorbed in the scene in his or her own inner eye, but nonetheless picking angle, distance, focus. Look at Roethke's "My Papa's Waltz" again (page 65), and note how cinematographically it is done. We never glimpse the father's face. We see his *hand* twice, however: close-ups of the hand on the boy's wrist, the battered knuckle; and of the "palm caked hard by dirt." We are also given a close-up of the buckle and the shirt. The camera is *at the boy's eye-level,* sees what he sees; and the man now speaking sees again what he saw as a boy. Note, incidentally, that he says "My right ear scraped a buckle," not the expected reverse: "A buckle scraped my right ear." How perfectly we see that he cannot blame the father for anything!

As another instance of camera work, consider again Shakespeare's quatrain:

That time of year thou mayst in me behold
When yellow leaves, or none, or few, do hang
Upon those boughs which shake against the cold,
Bare ruined choirs, where late the sweet birds sang.

Line 2 shows us first the yellow leaves of fall, then the later absence of leaves. It is a distant shot; we don't see a particular tree, simply yellow leaves in the aggregate. But notice how, as the camera seems to pan from "yellow leaves" to "none," it suddenly stops and moves in for a close-up shot: "or few." So close are we to a few leaves, we are probably seeing a single tree. The sense of loss is intensified, and the desolation of the few surviving leaves is greater than that produced by "none." "Boughs" in line 3 seems a close-up still, but we are now looking *up* into the branches. In line 4 the branches are compared to "Bare ruined choirs"; that is, choirlofts of a ruined and roofless church. For a moment we have the impression of standing inside such a church, looking upward through its rafters (like the branches) at the sky. The film word for the effect might be a "dissolve." It is only momentary, however; and in the last half of line 4 we are looking at the early winter boughs again, but this time with a superimposed shot of the same boughs in summer, with birds in them. The musical association between the songbirds and the choirlofts underlies the shift. Good description is not only a matter of choosing effective details but also of visualizing them effectively, from the right angle and the right distance.

Telling a story always involves the projection of scenes into the reader's or hearer's mind. The poet's narrative methods, as in the thirteenth-century Scottish ballad "Sir Patrick Spence," often approximate the film techniques of dissolve, jump-cut, or superimposition. Notice how the anonymous poet, especially in the syntactical leap of lines 11–12, dissolves one scene into another. What the poet chooses to show—or *not* to show—is illuminating.

Sir Patrick Spence

The king sits in Dumferling toune,
   Drinking the blude-reid wine:
"O whar will I get guid sailor
   To sail this ship of mine?"

Up and spak an eldern knicht°,   *knight* 5
   Sat at the kings richt kne:
"Sir Patrick Spence is the best sailor
   That sails upon the se."

The king has written a braid° letter,   *broad, forthright*
   And signed it wi' his hand,   10
And sent it to Sir Patrick Spence,
   Was walking on the sand.

The first line that Sir Patrick red,
   A loud lauch lauchèd° he;   *laugh, laughed*
The next line that Sir Patrick red,   15
   The teir° blinded his ee.   *tear*

"O wha° is this has don this deid,   *who*
   This ill deid don to me,
To send me out this time o' the yeir,
   To sail upon the se!   20

"Mak haste, mak haste, my mirry men all,
   Our guid schip sails the morne."
"O say na sae°, my master deir,   *not so*
   For I feir a deadlie storme.

"Late late yestreen I saw the new moone,   25
   Wi' the auld° moone in hir arme,   *old*
And I feir, I feir, my deir master,
   That we will cum to harme."

O our Scots nobles wer richt laith°   *loath*
   To weet° their cork-heild schoone°; *wet; cork-heeled shoes* 30
Bot lang owre a'° the play wer playd,   *But long before all*
   Their hats they swam aboone°.   *above them*

O lang, lang may their ladies sit,
  Wi' their fans into their hand,
Or ere° they se Sir Patrick Spence   *before*   35
  Cum sailing to the land.

O lang, lang may the ladies stand,
  Wi' their gold kems° in their hair,   *combs*
Waiting for their ain° deir lords,   *own*
  For they'll se thame na mair.   40

Haf owre°, haf owre to Aberdour,   *halfway over*
  It's fiftie fadom° deip,   *fathom*
And thair lies guid Sir Patrick Spence,
  Wi' the Scots lords at his feit.

The sparks that kindle poems are their particulars. A list of things we see in "Sir Patrick Spence"—blood-red wine / king's right knee / letter signed with his hand / sand / a tear blinding an eye / new moon with the old moon in her arm / cork-heeled shoes / hats swimming / sitting ladies with fans / standing ladies with combs in their hair—provides a curiously moving visual synopsis of the story.

That it is the king's *right* knee attests to the scene's unquestionable reality. That the letter is signed with his *hand* explains why Sir Patrick, though he knows the peril, has no choice but to obey. His contempt for the nobles is suggested by their being loath (far too strong an emotion?) to wet their fancy shoes, perhaps as they went aboard the ship. And their fancy hats swimming above them reminds us both of the nobles' vanity and of their tragedy which is nonetheless moving. The ladies' sitting, then standing, tells the distress occasioned by the wreck . . . which is yet (fans, combs) pitifully inadequate. Focusing on the nobles' deaths (it's *their* hats we see) leaves unmarked and unimagined the doubtless courageous deaths of Sir Patrick and his loyal crew. The last two lines:

And thair lies guid Sir Patrick Spence,
  Wi' the Scots lords at his feit.

strangely treat Sir Patrick, not as he must be (fifty fathoms deep), but as if he were formally laid out for burial, with the lords—arranged like the dog at the knight's feet in the copper plaque on a tomb—at his feet. The poet needn't explain to us, he has simply shown us, what true nobility is.

"Go in fear of abstractions," Pound advises. In too many poems, words like *love, peace, nature, beauty,* or *truth* have the empty, pretentious ring of words in political speeches. Particulars are proof-positive in a way abstractions cannot be. On the other hand, the eighteenth-century critic Samuel Johnson warned the poet not to "count the streaks of the tulip." "Nothing," he said, "can please many, and please long, but just representations of general nature." Whether from particulars or from the merely novel, "the pleasures of sudden wonder are soon exhausted, and the mind can only repose on the stability of truth." Perhaps ours is a more skeptical age or at least an age less certain of the truth, but we are inclined to trust William Carlos Williams's famous dictum, "No ideas but in things." It does not mean *no* ideas; rather, it means ideas arrived at, "universals of general applicability" discovered through particulars, the local.

Universals in particulars. Ideas in things. Not the one nor the other, but the inductive relationship of the two. How would one sort out Robert Herrick's ideas from his things in "Delight in Disorder" without robbing both of their significance? Or Elizabeth Bishop's understanding of the child's experience in "First Death in Nova Scotia" from the objects that exemplify her confusion?

Marianne Moore is the master of mingling abstractions with particulars, to the renewal of both. Observe, in "Critics and Connoisseurs," how carefully she plays particulars and abstractions off each other, distinguishing between the admirable (because unconscious) fastidiousness of the child and the unfortunate (because conscious and self-serving) fastidiousness of the Ming "products," the battleshiplike swan, the foolish ant, and, of course, the critics and connoisseurs whom she addresses.

Critics and Connoisseurs

There is a great amount of poetry in unconscious
    fastidiousness. Certain Ming°   *Chinese dynasty*
        products, imperial floor coverings of coach-
wheel yellow, are well enough in their way but I have seen some-
    thing
            that I like better—a   5
                mere childish attempt to make an imperfectly bal-
                    lasted animal stand up,
            similar determination to make a pup
                eat his meat from the plate.

I remember a swan under the willows in Oxford,   10
    with flamingo-colored, maple-
        leaflike feet. It reconnoitered like a battle-
ship. Disbelief and conscious fastidiousness were
        ingredients in its
            disinclination to move. Finally its hardihood was   15
                not proof against its
           proclivity to more fully appraise such bits
             of food as the stream

bore counter to it; it made away with what I gave it
   to eat. I have seen this swan and   20
     I have seen you; I have seen ambition without
   understanding in a variety of forms. Happening to stand
       by an ant-hill, I have
         seen a fastidious ant carrying a stick north, south,
            east, west, till it turned on   25
         itself, struck out from the flower bed into the lawn,
         and returned to the point

from which it had started. Then abandoning the stick as
   useless and overtaxing its
     jaws with a particle of whitewash—pill-like but   30
   heavy—it again went through the same course of procedure.
         What is
     there in being able
       to say that one has dominated the stream in an attitude of
        self-defense;
       in proving that one has had the experience   35
        of carrying a stick?

Just as the poem distinguishes between two kinds of fastidiousness, conscious and unconscious, so it distinguishes (by showing us) two kinds of conscious fastidiousness: the swan's false and snobbish reserve and the ant's false and pointless activity. Either way it is "ambition without / understanding," which comes as she notes "in a variety of forms." The child's fastidiousness is unconscious, devoted to whatever its object is. The poem's abstractions are thus sharp and useful, not soggy inflations. It is written in 9-line stanzas of approximate syllabics, with lines 1–3 and 8 having always 14, 8, 12, and 12 syllables. The usually slight variations in lines 4–7 and 9—perhaps resulting from revision of an exactly-counted early version—may serve as a formal reminder that there is little point in being too fastidious.

The difference between statement and implication is important. Abstractions *state* a meaning, and particulars may *imply* a meaning. Abstractions also, too easily, overstate, if only by drawing a conclusion and so precluding further consideration. Moore's abstractions very precisely bring the particulars into focus without stopping thought about them. They guide, but do not force, and so leave something for the reader to do. Moore's preference is recorded: "I myself, however, would rather be told too little than too much." Or, as Frost says in "Mending Wall,"

But it's not elves exactly, and I'd rather
He said it for himself.

Clarity

A word on **obscurity**: nobody, I think, is in favor of it. Robert Francis puts it pithily: "It is not difficult to be difficult." If what you are saying is worth saying, nothing can be gained (and everything can be lost) by obscuring it. If what you are saying is not worth saying, no one is going to like you any better for making that fact hard to discover. Obscurity isn't mystery. Clear water, through which the stones on the bottom can be seen in precise detail, is far more mysterious than muddy water. Nor is obscurity the same as **ambiguity.** In the positive sense, ambiguity means that more than one meaning is possible simultaneously; and this can often be enriching, as it is when William Stafford says, in "Traveling through the Dark," "I thought hard for us all." He might mean "for us humans," including even the reader in the group of those concerned. He might also mean "for this little group of man, deer, and fawn." Or he might mean, too, because he has just said that he "could hear the wilderness listen," "the wilderness and the other creatures nearby" or even "all of nature." *And* he might mean, as well, the car with its "lowered parking lights" and its purring engine, which has ironically come to seem almost a living participant in the little red-lit scene. How to take the ambiguous phrase "for us all" is left to the reader. *All* the meanings may be relevant at once, like concentric circles; they are complementary, reenforcing one another. But when such meanings are contradictory—or just point in totally different directions—the result is obscurity. Given several exclusive choices, a reader is like the proverbial ass between two piles of hay. It couldn't make up its mind and so starved to death.

The beginning poet will find that being clear can be a task, for what seems obvious to the poet may be anything but obvious to the reader. I have often watched student poets writhe as class discussions about their poems came to silly conclusions about what they meant. The fault is sometimes the reader's, who isn't paying enough attention and misses a signal. But all too often the poet, in his or her ingenious solitude, has so tangled and hidden the signals in the underbrush that it is no wonder no one sees them. Even trying to be perfectly plain, the poet may, nonetheless, for some odd reason, accidentally end up not being clear.

One of the richnesses of poetry is that, like the circles from a stone dropped in water, its meanings ripple outward. Poems may well mean things the poets didn't intend, along, of course, with those they did intend. This is true so long as those circles of meaning, no matter how far from the poem's center, are concentric: those meanings must complement and not contradict or interfere with the central, literal meanings of the poem. With any poem that works in a personal way, a reader's response will inevitably call up his or her own experience, associations, and feelings. These will never be exactly like the poet's, just as one person can never hope to convey by description the *exact* mental picture of a particular place to another person. (Even pointing out a particular star to someone is hard.) So long as the reader's "poem" doesn't violate the poet's "poem," change its direction or alter its main shape, the transaction is proper. Indeed, it is what any poet hopes for: that a reader will make the poem truly his own or her own.

Visual details—description—are the touches of color that bring an argument to life (Moore's wonderfully accurate "maple- / leaflike feet" of the swan). They make a scene vivid and convincing (the nobles' floating hats in "Sir Patrick Spence"). They can be psychological or dramatic symbols (Bishop's loon). Notice, however, that none, if any, of the poems we have been discussing is wholly or mainly descriptive. Purely descriptive poems, though we are all tempted to write them, are likely to be boring, like slides of someone's trip to Europe. Description needs some dramatic or thematic thrust to carry it. A poem about the yellow iris in the garden can't be as interesting as the real yellow iris in the garden. Pound's advice: "Don't be 'viewy' . . . the painter can describe a landscape much better than you can."

Still, like a photograph of something we hope never to forget, description has its force. As William Carlos Williams says in "Poem,"

> The rose fades
> and is renewed again
> by its seed, naturally
> but where
>
> save in the poem   5
> shall it go
> to suffer no diminution
> of its splendor

QUESTIONS AND SUGGESTIONS

1. After studying a piece of bread or a sliced-open orange for twenty minutes or so, write a description of it. Concentrate on what you *see*, but use smell, touch, and taste, if they help.

2. Write a poem about one of the following (or a similarly dumb thing). Put in a lot of particulars. See what you can make of it.

fried amethysts	*a squirrel's tail*	*hammers*
lion-breath	*hopscotch*	*four oranges*
blue	*counting bricks in a wall*	

3. Compare these poems (one eighteenth-century, one twentieth-century) on a similar subject, a child encountering a lamb. What inferences can be drawn about Starbuck's child?

The Lamb

WILLIAM BLAKE   (1757–1827)

Little Lamb, who made thee?
  Dost thou know who made thee?
Gave thee life, and bid thee feed
By the stream and o'er the mead;
Gave thee clothing of delight,   5
Softest clothing woolly bright;
Gave thee such a tender voice,
Making all the vales rejoice?
  Little Lamb, who made thee?
  Dost thou know who made thee?   10

  Little Lamb, I'll tell thee!
  Little Lamb, I'll tell thee:
He is called by thy name,
For he calls himself a Lamb,
He is meek and he is mild;   15
He became a little child.
I a child and thou a lamb,
We are called by his name.
  Little Lamb, God bless thee!
  Little Lamb, God bless thee!   20

Lamb

GEORGE STARBUCK   (b. 1931)

Lamb, what makes you tick?
You got a wind-up, a Battery-Powered,
A flywheel, a plug-in, or what?
You made out of real Reelfur?
You fall out of the window you bust?   5
You shrink? Turn into a No-No?
Zip open and have pups?

I bet you better than that.
I bet you put out by some other outfit.
I bet you don't do nothin.   10
I bet you somethin to eat.

4. "Curse of the Cat Woman," by Edward Field (b. 1924), draws on an old horror movie for its subject. How would you describe the poem's tone? What phrases or

images let us know the poem is humorous? Is there also, perhaps, a serious overtone?

It sometimes happens
that the woman you meet and fall in love with
is of that strange Transylvanian people
with an affinity for cats.

You take her to a restaurant, say, or a show,   5
on an ordinary date, being attracted
by the glitter in her slitty eyes and her catlike walk,
and afterwards of course you take her in your arms
and she turns into a black panther
and bites you to death.   10

Or perhaps you are saved in the nick of time
and she is tormented by the knowledge of her tendency:
That she daren't hug a man
unless she wants to risk clawing him up.

This puts you both in a difficult position—   15
panting lovers who are prevented from touching
not by bars but by circumstance:
You have terrible fights and say cruel things
for having the hots does not give you a sweet temper.

One night you are walking down a dark street   20
and hear the pad-pad of a panther following you,
but when you turn around there are only shadows,
or perhaps one shadow too many.

You approach, calling, "Who's there?"
and it leaps on you.   25
Luckily you have brought along your sword
and you stab it to death.

And before your eyes it turns into the woman you love,
her breast impaled on your sword,
her mouth dribbling blood saying she loved you   30
but couldn't help her tendency.

So death released her from the curse at last,
and you knew from the angelic smile on her dead face
that in spite of a life the devil owned,
love had won, and heaven pardoned her.   35

5. John Updike's "Dog's Death" tells a little domestic story. How are the necessary parts of the exposition and narrative arranged, ordered for effect? What details keep the tender subject from seeming sentimental? Does the latitude the poet has allowed himself in rhyming (or not rhyming) help to keep the poem from seeming pat?

She must have been kicked unseen or brushed by a car.
Too young to know much, she was beginning to learn
To use the newspapers spread on the kitchen floor
And to win, wetting there, the words, "Good dog! Good dog!"

We thought her shy malaise was a shot reaction.   5
The autopsy disclosed a rupture in her liver.
As we teased her with play, blood was filling her skin
And her heart was learning to lie down forever.

Monday morning, as the children were noisily fed
And sent to school, she crawled beneath the youngest's bed.   10
We found her twisted and limp but still alive.
In the car to the vet's, on my lap, she tried

To bite my hand and died. I stroked her warm fur
And my wife called in a voice imperious with tears.
Though surrounded by love that would have upheld her,   15
Nevertheless she sank and, stiffening, disappeared.

Back home, we found that in the night her frame,
Drawing near to dissolution, had endured the shame
Of diarrhoea and had dragged across the floor
To a newspaper carelessly left there. *Good dog.*   20

6. In "The Philosophy of Composition," Poe argues that "the death, then, of a beautiful woman is, unquestionably, the most poetical topic in the world." Think of several subjects that seem to you likely to make interesting poems. Imagine how you might handle two or three of them. Try to write a poem of the best one.

7. Suppose you were writing a description of the sunken hulk of the luxurious passenger liner *Titanic*, which went down in 1912 after hitting an iceberg in the North Atlantic. What visual details would you focus on or invent? For each, imagine the placement or movement of the camera. Close-up, middle, or distant shots, for example? In what sequence? Carefully arrange a sentence or several sentences to duplicate that effect.

8. One of the pleasures of this poem by Elizabeth Spires (b. 1952) is its topicality. Note also how the poet uses fantasy to extend the ordinary.

At the Bambi Motel

Walls the color of old plums, a "tapestry"
above the bed: 4 dogs playing cards,
smoking cigars. One cheats, aces tucked
in his vest, squints at the schnauzer's
royal flush and sighs. A wall-size mirror   5
doubles the room, doubles the double

bed into something immense, a mattress
for a troupe of acrobats.
Where are we? How did we get here?
And most of all, where's Bambi?   10
I wouldn't, couldn't have dreamed
up this place if I'd read true romance
magazines for a year. In room 12,
someone's having a row with someone
else. *Cow!* he accuses her.   15
Pipsqueak! You call this a honeymoon!
she yells back. Fighting
must have a titillating effect.
Silence for a minute. The pop of a cork.
And then of all things, giggling!   20
I bet somebody's made the front page
of *The National Enquirer* staying here.
What if our room's broken into by mistake?
What if the guy next door is a senator,
the girl Miss Panty Hose of 1968?   25
I chain the door shut, tape the keyhole
under your doubting gaze.
Your eyes glaze over, you begin your
impersonation of a sex maniac
who can't get his clothes undone.   30
Sin makes us blush like innocents
nevertheless . . .
                      I fall asleep
dreaming of Bambi. There's a forest fire!
I must get the dogs out! Intoxicated,
they dive out a window into a snowbank,   35
cards falling out of their clothes.
(Snow? An hour ago it was August!)
Room 12 lends the fire department champagne
to put out the flames. The senator's
distressed—Miss Panty Hose is more   40
undressed than I am. She grabs him
by the nose, makes him say "cheese"
for the photos. Where will we stay now?
The dogs are grateful. One knows
a place down the road, Roxie's.   45
"They treat you real good there," he growls,
"pink lightbulbs and wait till you see
what's on their walls . . ."

The Black Snake   1979

MARY OLIVER   (b. 1935)

When the black snake
flashed onto the morning road,
and the truck could not swerve—
death, that is how it happens.

Now he lies looped and useless   5
as an old bicycle tire.
I stop the car
and carry him into the bushes.

He is as cool and gleaming
as a braided whip, he is as beautiful and quiet   10
as a dead brother.
I leave him under the leaves

and drive on, thinking
about *death:* its suddenness,
its terrible weight,   15
its certain coming. Yet under

reason burns a brighter fire, which the bones
have always preferred.
It is the story of endless good fortune.
It says to oblivion: not me!   20

It is the light at the center of every cell.
It is what sent the snake coiling and flowing forward
happily all spring through the green leaves before
he came to the road.

Van Busbeke Discovers the Tulip, 1550   1967

DEBORAH BLISS

The Dutchman, whistling, paces
past the white mosque, the lapis

lazuli gleaming in its
ceiling. (He's had breakfast,

had time to think fondly of ancient   5
history, of ice-flaked milk

and Dutch buns in his library
looking over Leyden°.)   *city in Holland*

Here in a warmer land,
here in Ancyra°, boys   *Ankara, Turkey* 10

cool the water-skins
in the Paphlagonian° breeze.   *Black Sea province*

RES GESTAE DIVI AUGUSTI°:   *deeds of divine Augustus*
Van Busbeke, bending down

in the marble antechamber,   15
copies the Latin, benignly

nibbling his stylus. He pushes
his spectacles to the bridge

of his nose, sunburnt from the jaunt
up the River Sangarius. And soon   20

he hums absently (like
his daughters' knitting-songs

at home in Holland's watery
spring, by the slow fire).

At noon he discards his gear.   25

Across the muddy bazaars,
the goat pasture, the river,

he and his party, lunch-
bound, discover tulips.

Festival flowers, turbaned,   30
they pass in a green flotilla.

Oh *Proserpina*°—carmine—
Chrysolora°—yellow—

and *Pottebakker*°—white—   *varieties of tulip*
such souvenirs for Holland!   35

Introduction of the Shopping Cart   1982
Oklahoma City, 1937

GERALD COSTANZO   (b. 1945)

There was a man
who collected facts.

After work he rode twenty stories,
let himself in
to cartons filled with index cards   5
and his crucial lists.

Facts reveal useful lives.
He got things right.

The shopping cart invented
by Sylvan Goldman,   10
Oklahoma City, 1937.

When the man passed on
his relatives came.

P. T. Barnum had four daughters.

They searched through his cartons 15
for ten dollar bills.

The sky, which on cloudless
days appears to be azure,
has no true color.

He wasn't eccentric. 20
When they found nothing,
they threw everything
out.

His final fact:
you live and you die. 25

The shopping cart. P. T. Barnum.

The sky.

Photograph of the Girl   1983
SHARON OLDS   (b. 1942)

The girl sits on the hard ground,
the dry pan of Russia, in the drought
of 1921, stunned,
eyes closed, mouth open,
raw hot wind blowing 5
sand in her face. Hunger and puberty are
taking her together. She leans on a sack,
layers of clothes fluttering in the heat,
the new radius of her arm curved.
She cannot be not beautiful, but she is 10
starving. Each day she grows thinner, and her bones
grow longer, porous. The caption says
she is going to starve to death that winter
with millions of others. Deep in her body
the ovaries let out her first eggs, 15
golden as drops of grain.

Names of Horses

DONALD HALL   (b. 1928)

All winter your brute shoulders strained against collars, padding
and steerhide over the ash hames, to haul
sledges of cordwood for drying through spring and summer,
for the Glenwood stove next winter, and for the simmering range.

In April you pulled cartloads of manure to spread on the fields,   5
dark manure of Holsteins, and knobs of your own clustered with oats.
All summer you mowed the grass in meadow and hayfield, the mowing
    machine
clacketing beside you, while the sun walked high in the morning;

and after noon's heat, you pulled a clawed rake through the same acres,
gathering stacks, and dragged the wagon from stack to stack,   10
and the built hayrack back, uphill to the chaffy barn,
three loads of hay a day from standing grass in the morning.

Sundays you trotted the two miles to church with the light load
of a leather quartertop buggy, and grazed in the sound of hymns.
Generation on generation, your neck rubbed the windowsill   15
of the stall, smoothing the wood as the sea smooths glass.

When you were old and lame, when your shoulders hurt bending to graze,
one October the man, who fed you and kept you, and harnessed you every
    morning,
led you through corn stubble to sandy ground above Eagle Pond,
and dug a hole beside you where you stood shuddering in your skin,   20

and lay the shotgun's muzzle in the boneless hollow behind your ear,
and fired the slug into your brain, and felled you into your grave,
shoveling sand to cover you, setting goldenrod upright above you,
where by next summer a dent in the ground made your monument.

For a hundred and fifty years, in the pasture of dead horses,   25
roots of pine trees pushed through the pale curves of your ribs,
yellow blossoms flourished above you in autumn, and in winter
frost heaved your bones in the ground—old toilers, soil makers:

O Roger, Mackerel, Riley, Ned, Nellie, Chester, Lady Ghost.

Poems to Consider   187

Fern Hill

1946

DYLAN THOMAS   (1914–1953)

Now as I was young and easy under the apple boughs
About the lilting house and happy as the grass was green,
    The night above the dingle° starry,   *wooded valley*
        Time let me hail and climb
      Golden in the heydays of his eyes,   5
And honoured among wagons I was prince of the apple towns
And once below a time I lordly had the trees and leaves
        Trail with daisies and barley
    Down the rivers of the windfall light.

And as I was green and carefree, famous among the barns   10
About the happy yard and singing as the farm was home,
      In the sun that is young once only,
        Time let me play and be
      Golden in the mercy of his means,
And green and golden I was huntsman and herdsman, the calves   15
Sang to my horn, the foxes on the hills barked clear and cold,
        And the sabbath rang slowly
      In the pebbles of the holy streams.

All the sun long it was running, it was lovely, the hay
Fields high as the house, the tunes from the chimneys, it was air   20
      And playing, lovely and watery
        And fire green as grass.
      And nightly under the simple stars
As I rode to sleep the owls were bearing the farm away,
All the moon long I heard, blessed among stables, the night-jars°   *birds* 25
      Flying with the ricks°, and the horses   *haystacks*
        Flashing into the dark.

And then to awake, and the farm, like a wanderer white
With the dew, come back, the cock on his shoulder: it was all
      Shining, it was Adam and maiden,   30
        The sky gathered again
      And the sun grew round that very day.
So it must have been after the birth of the simple light
In the first, spinning place, the spellbound horses walking warm
      Out of the whinnying green stable   35
        On to the fields of praise.

And honoured among foxes and pheasants by the gay house
Under the new made clouds and happy as the heart was long,
    In the sun born over and over,
        I ran my heedless ways,   40
    My wishes raced through the house high hay
And nothing I cared, at my sky blue trades, that time allows
In all his tuneful turning so few and such morning songs
    Before the children green and golden
        Follow him out of grace,   45

Nothing I cared, in the lamb white days, that time would take me
Up to the swallow thronged loft by the shadow of my hand,
    In the moon that is always rising,
        Nor that riding to sleep
    I should hear him fly with the high fields   50
And wake to the farm forever fled from the childless land.
Oh as I was young and easy in the mercy of his means,
    Time held me green and dying
    Though I sang in my chains like the sea.

Characters:
Dukes and Dying Ladies,
Pigs and Pedestrians

In every poem there is a voice, a **speaker**—someone who *says* whatever it is. Usually it is the poet. Often, however, it is not. In Emily Dickinson's famous "Because I could not stop for Death," the speaker describing her own death can hardly be the poet. In the same way, the Victorian Englishman Robert Browning was not the Renaissance Italian duke who speaks in "My Last Duchess" (page 198); nor, obviously, is Rita Dove (b. 1952) "The House Slave" who speaks in her poem (page 244). These speakers are **dramatic characters,** or *personae* (singular: **persona**), and the poems in which they appear are **dramatic monologues.**

The poet's freedom to invent or imagine, to create fictional characters and scenes, is of course as great as the novelist or playwright's. The truth of *Othello* or *Huckleberry Finn* is not less for their being imaginative constructs. It is always our own experience of deception and jealousy, of hypocrisy and brotherhood, of pride or valor or love, that makes such works possible for us as writers, and certifies them for us as readers when they are true.

In a sense, every poem is a dramatic monologue, an utterance with an "utterer," a speaker, and an at least implicit circumstance in which the utterance is uttered. For readers who don't know the poet personally, any poem involves the perception of a presented character, real or otherwise. Thus, even the poet writing or trying to write in his or her own voice, is always creating a self, in tone, stance, theme. As in life we show different faces to different people or in different situations (at the beach, in church), so in writing, often without realizing it, we change or adjust the voice we use, presenting ourselves differently; we quite naturally adopt somewhat different *personae*. This process may be deliberate and, when the issues are serious, may even amount to working out one's identity, that is, to self-discovery.

The poem brings its own stage, scenery, and actor. Even in a long didactic poem like Pope's *An Essay on Criticism*, it is likely that the poet is, as lecturers do, using a voice more authoritative than his or her real conversational voice. (Pope was in fact only twenty-three when he donned the magisterial robes for this poem.) A speaker's range of diction, familiarity or formality, choice of images, and so on, create his or her character for the reader. The **tone** of a poem includes, as well as the poet's attitude toward the subject, the poet's (or speaker's) attitude toward himself or herself, and an attitude toward the reader or audience. (A love poem addressed to a "you" is nonetheless meant to be overheard by a reader.)

Because people are interesting, putting people into poems is one of the elementary ways of making poems interesting, whether the poet (or someone very like the poet) is the only character or the poet invents a whole cast, as Shakespeare, Browning, and Frost do. As in fiction, a character may be presented either in the first person or in the third person. The old man in Frost's "An Old Man's Winter Night" is presented in the third person ("he"), much as an omniscient narrator of a novel might present him. The old man is alone, no one else is there; but like an omniscient camera's eye the reader observes him clomping from room to room. Notice that a convention is involved. We don't ask how we or Frost can know what no one is there to observe. The scene is of course imagined. Frost may in fact have known the old man and the house, and be imagining what occurs on such a cold, lonely night. Or he may be projecting: that is, writing about *his own* experience alone in a house on a real night but presenting it as the experience of the dramatically more interesting, isolated old man. We'll never know what in the poem is imagined, what real. But the poem is true because the feeling, we recognize, is true; we know enough of lonely nights, frost on windowpanes, moonlight on snow, and so on, to empathetically suspend disbelief.

The speakers in Bishop's "First Death in Nova Scotia" and Miller Williams's "Ruby Tells All" (page 58), however close to or far from the poets themselves and their actual experiences, are presented in the first person ("I"); that is, they are allowed to present themselves in their "own" words. Notice again, conventions. It doesn't even occur to us to wonder how the poet might have heard or overheard Ruby, and we aren't for a moment tempted to believe that Ruby is capable of recounting her life so succinctly and movingly, much less in blank verse. It is enough that the language doesn't violate the range of what we may guess is her experience: "Then a bird-loud morning late one April . . ."

X. J. Kennedy uses both first and third person in presenting the drunken woman in the next poem. The speaker in the first and last stanzas describes her from the outside and recounts the accompanying action, but she speaks for herself in the main portion of the poem.

In a Prominent Bar in Secaucus One Day

To the tune of "The Old Orange Flute"
or the tune of "Sweet Betsy from Pike"

In a prominent bar in Secaucus° one day
Rose a lady in skunk with a topheavy sway,
Raised a knobby red finger—all turned from their beer—
While with eyes bright as snowcrust she sang high and clear:

"Now who of you'd think from an eyeload of me   5
That I once was a lady as proud as could be?
Oh I'd never sit down by a tumbledown drunk
If it wasn't, my dears, for the high cost of junk.

"All the gents used to swear that the white of my calf
Beat the down of the swan by a length and a half.   10
In the kerchief of linen I caught to my nose
Ah, there never fell snot, but a little gold rose.

"I had seven gold teeth and a toothpick of gold,
My Virginia cheroot was a leaf of it rolled
And I'd light it each time with a thousand in cash—   15
Why the bums used to fight if I flicked them an ash.

"Once the toast of the Biltmore°, the belle of the Taft°,
I would drink bottle beer at the Drake°, never draft,
And dine at the Astor° on Salisbury steak
With a clean tablecloth for each bite I did take.   20

"In a car like the Roxy° I'd roll to the track,   *movie palace*
A steel-guitar trio, a bar in the back,
And the wheels made no noise, they turned over so fast,
Still it took you ten minutes to see me go past.

"When the horses bowed down to me that I might choose,   25
I bet on them all, for I hated to lose.
Now I'm saddled each night for my butter and eggs
And the broken threads race down the backs of my legs.

"Let you hold in mind, girls, that your beauty must pass
Like a lovely white clover that rusts with its grass.   30
Keep your bottoms off barstools and marry you young
Or be left—an old barrel with many a bung.

"For when time takes you out for a spin in his car
You'll be hard-pressed to stop him from going too far
And be left by the roadside, for all your good deeds,   35
Two toadstools for tits and a face full of weeds."

All the house raised a cheer, but the man at the bar
Made a phonecall and up pulled a red patrol car
And she blew us a kiss as they copped her away
From that prominent bar in Secaucus, N.J.   40

1 *Secaucus:* town in the industrial marsh of New Jersey, near New York City. 17,
18, 19 *Biltmore, Taft, Drake, Astor:* once fashionable hotels in New York.

Part of the fun (and of the pathos) in this portrait comes of our recognizing
that, however much truth is mingled with her exaggeration, she was never quite so
much a lady as she believes. Her language tells us about her world: "All the *gents*
used to swear that the white of my calf / *Beat* the down of a swan *by a length and a
half.*" Her ideas of elegance fall painfully short: bottle beer in preference to draft
and, as an instance of fine dining, the humdrum Salisbury steak. In this way the
poet communicates *around* what she is saying so that we perceive her as he wants us
to, not as she perceives herself. The irony on her part is unintentional; the irony on
the poet's part isn't. We end up admiring her less for the reason she gives (that she
was once a grand lady) than for her blarney and her bravery of spirit. Like
Chaucer's not very different Wife of Bath, she is indomitably human.

Even a mythical or historical character, such as the familiar Eve in the
following poem by Linda Pastan (b. 1932), may become freshly exciting if the poet
discovers an aspect no one has thought of. As with particulars, the secret is
noticing.

Mother Eve

Of course she never was a child herself,
waking as she did one morning
full grown and perfect,
with only Adam, another innocent,
to love her and instruct.   5
There was no learning, step by step,
to walk, no bruised elbows or knees—

no small transgressions.
There was only the round, white mound
of the moon rising,   10
which could neither be suckled
nor leaned against.
And perhaps the serpent spoke
in a woman's voice, mothering.
Oh, who can blame her?   15

When she held her own child
in her arms, what did she make
of that new animal? Did she love Cain
too little or too much, looking down
at her now flawed body as if her rib,   20
like Adam's, might be gone?
In the litany of naming that continued
for children instead of plants,
no daughter is mentioned.   *See Genesis, esp.*
But generations later there was Rachel°,   25
all mother herself, who knew   *chapters 29–30, 35.*
that bringing forth a child in pain
is only the start. It is losing them
(and Benjamin so young)
that is the punishment.   30

Negative Capability

Underlying the poet's ability to empathize, to project, imagine, create characters, is what John Keats called "negative capability." (He used the phrase in a letter to his brothers George and Thomas, 21 December 1817.) A "quality . . . which Shakespeare possessed so enormously," it is essentially the capability "of remaining content with half-knowledge" and "annulling self," and so being able to enter other identities. In another letter (to Richard Woodhouse, 27 October 1818), Keats speaks of "the chameleon poet." "A poet," he says, "is the most unpoetical of anything in existence, because he has no Identity—he is continually in for and filling some other body." The empathy includes men and women of course, but also "The Sun,—the Moon,—the Sea . . ." Negative capability comes to a sort of emptying of the self, suspending judgments, so as to imagine others and even the natural from the inside: "if a sparrow come before my window, I take part in its existence and pick about the gravel" (letter to Benjamin Bailey, 22 November 1817). In conversation, according to Woodhouse, Keats even "affirmed that he can conceive of a billiard Ball that it may have a sense of delight from its own roundness, smoothness volubility & the rapidity of its motion"!

Without making Gerald Stern (b. 1925) responsible for my application of Keats's phrase, let me cite his dizzyingly empathetic poem:

Peace in the Near East

While I have been flooding myself with black coffee
and moving slowly from pajamas to underwear to blue corduroys
my birds have been carrying twigs and paper and leaves and straw
back and forth between the box elders and the maples.
—They are building the Aswan Dam out there;   5
they are pulling heavy wheelbarrows up the hillsides;
they are dragging away old temples stone by stone;
they are wiping the sweat from their black bodies.

Ah, soon, soon they will be sitting down
like rich Mamelukes in their summer palaces on the Nile,   10
greeting the Arabian ambassador on the right,
greeting the Russian ambassador on the left,
and finally even the Jew himself, a guest
in his own garden, a holder of strange credentials,
one who is permitted to go through the carrots   15
only with special consent, one who is scolded
if he gets too close to the raspberry bushes,
one who looks with loving eyes at the water
and the light canoes that float down to the locks
for the meeting of princes in their little rubber tents—   20
by the picnic tables and the pump and the neat pile of gravel and the
        naked sycamores;
by the cement spillway that carries a ton of water a minute
under the old generating plant;
by the sandy beach down below where the fishermen sit
on their canvas stools feeding worms to the river—   25
worm after worm to the starving river,
in exchange for the silver life in their tin buckets,
in exchange for silence.

The vision is so comically and seriously complex that it is virtually untraceable. The speaker has been watching birds "carrying twigs and paper and leaves and straw" to build a nest. This painful labor suddenly reminds him of the building of the Aswan Dam in Egypt. It is more than a comparison, however. For what he says is that the *birds* "are building the Aswan Dam out there," in his yard! Quickly he is imagining the dam complete, "the rich Mamelukes in their summer palaces" greeting ambassadors. (*Mamelukes:* members of a ruling military class.) But the speaker is Jewish and troubled by these successes—being one who requires "special consent," he would be (is often) "scolded" by the birds "if he gets too close to the raspberry bushes." It isn't too much to guess* that there is, beyond his garden, a river with canoes, locks, picnic tables, pump, pile of gravel, sycamores, and fishermen (the "princes in their little rubber tents"?)—a river which he similarly confabulates with the Nile. The fishermen are "feeding . . . / worm after worm to the starving river, / in exchange for the silver life in their tin buckets, / in exchange for silence."

Funny, touching, this fantasy mingles his garden and the Near East, the local river and the Nile. In a way that is both bitter and charming, it juxtaposes a variety of examples of greed and property and possession and ill-use. He is at once, in the changing perspectives, possesser ("my birds") and dispossessed. (Perhaps he has also been one of the fishermen, trading lives "to the starving river" for other lives, "for silence.") Politics has never been felt more amusingly, or more ruefully. From the first line, in which he is "*flooding*" himself with coffee, the swirling associations are convincing, links and connections which the mind, set free, might make.

Another householder, another tone:

Suburban

JOHN CIARDI

Yesterday Mrs. Friar phoned. "Mr. Ciardi,
    how do you do?" she said. "I am sorry to say
this isn't exactly a social call. The fact is
    your dog has just deposited—forgive me—
a large repulsive object in my petunias."   5

I thought to ask, "Have you checked the rectal grooving
    for a positive I.D.?" My dog, as it happened,
was in Vermont with my son, who had gone fishing—
    if that's what one does with a girl, two cases of beer,
and a borrowed camper. I guessed I'd get no trout.   10

But why lose out on organic gold for a wise crack?
    "Yes, Mrs. Friar," I said, "I understand."
"Most kind of you," she said. "Not at all," I said.
    I went with a spade. She pointed, looking away.
"I always have loved dogs," she said, "but really!"   15

---

*Book jackets are occasionally useful. The biographical note on the back of *Lucky Life*, in which "Peace in the Near East" appears, mentions that Stern lived, when the poem was written, in Raubsville, Pennsylvania. Raubsville is on the Delaware River.

I scooped it up and bowed. "The animal of it.
    I hope this hasn't upset you, Mrs. Friar."
"Not really," she said, "but really!" I bore the turd
    across the line to my own petunias
and buried it till the glorious resurrection   20

when even these suburbs shall give up their dead.

The poet—"Mr. Ciardi," Mrs. Friar calls him—similarly triangulates a complex
scene. He checks his sarcasm (lines 6–7) and uses only an irony that Mrs. Friar will
safely miss (lines 16–17). He does so, we sense, due to his son's being in Vermont
with a girl, a fact which seems to come into the poem as an aside: as a father he
disapproves but understands. We discount the excuse he offers ("why lose out on
organic gold . . .?"). More likely, it is the common humanity he shares with Mrs.
Friar: wishing somehow the world and others were simpler and less troublesome. He
handles it better than she does, but is also troubled. The "glorious resurrection" of
course is the fresh petunias that will be fueled by the turd. But that idea of burial
and resurrection leads to the shadowy irony of the last, isolated, line: "when even
the suburbs shall give up their dead." In her starchy and life-denying primness Mrs.
Friar in a sense is "dead" already—he has one last ironic poke at her. But the tone is
graver, more pitying than annoyed. The modulation of tone gives the anecdote a
complex, inner drama.

What is funny may have underlying seriousness. That is so, too, of this
dramatic monologue in which Katharyn Machan Aal (b. 1952) empathetically lets
Hazel, a charwoman in a Howard Johnson's, speak for herself. Ironically, we see
the fairy-story allusion that Hazel misses. Notice how the poet uses dialect and line,
controlling the flow and inflections of what Hazel says.

Hazel Tells Laverne

last night
im cleanin out my
howard johnsons ladies room
when all of a sudden
up pops this frog   5
musta come from the sewer
swimmin aroun an tryin ta
climb up the sida the bowl
so i goes ta flushm down
but sohelpmegod he starts talkin   10
bout a golden ball
an how i can be a princess
me a princess
well my mouth drops

all the way to the floor   15
an he says
kiss me just kiss me
once on the nose
well i screams
ya little green pervert   20
an i hitsm with my mop
an has ta flush
the toilet down three times
me
a princess   25

Irony

Irony is saying one thing and meaning another, as when you drop a pile of dishes and someone says, "Beautiful!" With good reason the term has come up in discussing a number of the poems in this chapter. For in poems with a dramatic speaker, irony (in one or another of its various forms) is the poet's way of communicating with the reader *around* what the speaker is himself or herself saying. Irony may deepen and enrich by making the reader aware of things (or aware of them in ways) the speaker doesn't see ("In a Prominent Bar in Secaucus One Day") or perhaps won't admit ("Suburban"). It may even contradict the whole drift of what the speaker is saying. Notice how Robert Browning (1812–1889), who never says a word in his own voice, uses unintentional irony to characterize the villainous Duke of Ferrara (who speaks the whole poem):

My Last Duchess

That's my last duchess painted on the wall,
Looking as if she were alive. I call
That piece a wonder, now: Frà Pandolf's hands
Worked busily a day, and there she stands.
Will't please you sit and look at her? I said   5
"Frà Pandolf" by design, for never read
Strangers like you that pictured countenance,
The depth and passion of its earnest glance,
But to myself they turned (since none puts by
The curtain I have drawn for you, but I)   10
And seemed as they would ask me, if they durst,
How such a glance came there; so, not the first
Are you to turn and ask thus. Sir, 'twas not

Her husband's presence only, called that spot
Of joy into the Duchess' cheek: perhaps   15
Frà Pandolf chanced to say "Her mantle laps
"Over my lady's wrist too much," or "Paint
"Must never hope to reproduce the faint
"Half-flush that dies along her throat": such stuff
Was courtesy, she thought, and cause enough   20
For calling up that spot of joy. She had
A heart—how shall I say?—too soon made glad,
Too easily impressed; she liked whate'er
She looked on, and her looks went everywhere.
Sir, 'twas all one! My favor at her breast,   25
The dropping of the daylight in the West,
The bough of cherries some officious fool
Broke in the orchard for her, the white mule
She rode with round the terrace—all and each
Would draw from her alike the approving speech,   30
Or blush, at least. She thanked men—good! but thanked
Somehow—I know not how—as if she ranked
My gift of a nine-hundred-years-old name
With anybody's gift. Who'd stoop to blame
This sort of trifling? Even had you skill   35
In speech—which I have not—to make your will
Quite clear to such an one, and say, "Just this
"Or that in you disgusts me; here you miss,
"Or there exceed the mark"—and if she let
Herself be lessoned so, nor plainly set   40
Her wits to yours, forsooth, and made excuse,
—E'en then would be some stooping; and I choose
Never to stoop. Oh sir, she smiled, no doubt,
Whene'er I passed her; but who passed without
Much the same smile? This grew; I gave commands;   45
Then all smiles stopped together. There she stands
As if alive. Will't please you rise? We'll meet
The company below, then. I repeat,
The Count your master's known munificence
Is ample warrant that no just pretense   50
Of mine for dowry will be disallowed;
Though his fair daughter's self, as I avowed
At starting, is my object. Nay, we'll go
Together down, sir. Notice Neptune, though,
Taming a sea-horse, thought a rarity,   55
Which Claus of Innsbruck cast in bronze for me!

The Duke is addressing the agent of a Count, whose daughter he wants to marry and make his next Duchess. He is on his best behavior. Nonetheless, we quickly see his domineering ("since none puts by / The curtain I have drawn for you, but I" or "if they durst"); his pride ("My gift of a nine-hundred-years-old name"); his arrogance ("and I choose / Never to stoop"); his greed ("no just pretense / Of mine for dowry"); and, of course, the falseness of his jealousy, for in fact he can say nothing that does not suggest that his last Duchess was young and innocent and charming. The agent is not his equal, but the Duke declines precedence—"Nay, we'll go / Together down, sir"—in a gesture that is meant to appear democratic and in fact appears calculated and false. He unintentionally sums up his unpleasant purpose: "his fair daughter's self, as I avowed / At starting, is my object." *Object.* Like the painting, and like the little Neptune "cast in bronze for me!" The pun is Browning's, of course, speaking around the Duke's monologue since the Duke means only "my aim, my objective."

Another monologue in which the reader is led to perceive more, or differently, than the speaker is "I heard a Fly buzz" by Emily Dickinson (1830–1886):

> I heard a Fly buzz—when I died—
> The Stillness in the Room
> Was like the Stillness in the Air—
> Between the Heaves of Storm—
>
> The Eyes around—had wrung them dry—   5
> And Breaths were gathering firm
> For that last Onset—when the King
> Be witnessed—in the Room—
>
> I willed my Keepsakes—Signed away
> What portion of me be   10
> Assignable—and then it was
> There interposed a Fly—
>
> With Blue—uncertain stumbling Buzz—
> Between the light—and me—
> And then the Windows failed—and then   15
> I could not see to see—

The first three stanzas present a typical deathbed scene. The room is quiet with the ominous silence that sometimes falls between the "Heaves of Storm," an image that suggests the interrupted agonies of the dying speaker. The dashes and the emphatic capital letters give an impression of breathless portentousness, and there is already a curious abstractness about the speaker's perceptions. The relatives and perhaps friends in the room are mentioned impersonally only as "Eyes around" and "Breaths." They and the speaker alike await the moment of death, "when the King

/ Be witnessed—in the Room." Whether the "King" is God or more simply death, the expectation is a large and dramatic one: "King." But no majestic event occurs: only a fly appears, that unpleasant insect drawn to carrion.

The confusion of the speaker's senses is suggested by her application of visual qualities to a sound: "With Blue—uncertain stumbling Buzz." (This is **synesthesia:** the perception, or description, of one sense modality in terms of another, as when we describe a voice as velvety or sweet.) Impossibly for so small a creature, the fly seems to "interpose" "Between the light—and me." In line 15 the speaker, still trying to account for her loss of sight outside herself, blames the "Windows," reporting oddly that they "failed." The final line records the still flickering consciousness inside the already senseless body before it, too, goes out like the speck of afterlight on a television screen: "I could not see to see—" The final dash suggests the simple tailing off of awareness, without resolution. The grand expectation of "the King" has been ironically foreclosed by the merely physical, naturalistic collapse of sense and consciousness. The dying speaker never understood.

Irony comes in as many flavors as ice cream. **Verbal Irony** involves a discrepancy between what is *said* and what is *meant.* To say "Lovely day!" when the weather is awful, for instance. Irony of this sort may range from poking fun to sarcasm. Dick's comment, in a poem by Matthew Prior (1664–1721), is ironic in this way:

A True Maid

No, no; for my virginity,
    When I lose that, says Rose, I'll die;
Behind the elms, last night, cried Dick,
    Rose, were you not extremely sick?

He seems to express sympathy but is really rebuking her, exposing the false piety of her remark. Verbal irony, when it involves understatement, may also be serious and tender, as in X. J. Kennedy's

Little Elegy

for a child who skipped rope

Here lies resting, out of breath,
Out of turns, Elizabeth
Whose quicksilver toes not quite
Cleared the whirring edge of night.

Earth whose circles round us skim,   5
Till they catch the lightest limb,
Shelter now Elizabeth
And for her sake trip up Death.

Saying that she merely "lies resting, out of breath, / Out of turns," meaning that she is dead, is ironic understatement, touching in its restraint and in its gentle reminder of what death does to such youthful vitality.

Instances of irony may also be distinguished by whether it is deliberate or accidental. As in the last example, the speaker may be quite conscious of it. Or, as in "My Last Duchess" or "I heard a Fly buzz," the speaker may be unconscious of the irony. The term **dramatic irony** is used when the speaker or character acts in a certain way because he is unaware of something the reader or audience knows. Hamlet does not kill the King when he is at prayer, lest the King, repentant and thus in a state of grace, go straight to heaven. Hamlet does not know what the audience has been shown: that the King, burdened with guilt because he cannot regret his crime, is unable to pray. It is dramatic irony that gives Aal's "Hazel Tells Laverne" (page 197) its rueful theme of missed opportunities.

When the speaker within the poem is aware of the irony, it can be ex-cruciatingly painful. Notice, in this poem by W. D. Snodgrass (b. 1926), how the speaker's double awareness colors everything. When he says of the kids in lines 1–2 that "they'll stay the night," we understand that he is comparing: *we won't.*

Leaving the Motel

Outside, the last kids holler
Near the pool: they'll stay the night.
Pick up the towels; fold your collar
Out of sight.

Check: is the second bed   5
Unrumpled, as agreed?
Landlords have to think ahead
In case of need,

Too. Keep things straight: don't take
The matches, the wrong keyrings—   10
We've nowhere we could keep a keepsake—
Ashtrays, combs, things

That sooner or later others
Would accidentally find.
Check: take nothing of one another's   15
And leave behind

Your license number only,
Which they won't care to trace;
We've paid. Still, should such things get lonely,
Leave in their vase   20

An aspirin to preserve
Our lilacs, the wayside flowers
We've gathered and must leave to serve
A few more hours;

That's all. We can't tell when   25
We'll come back, can't press claims;
We would no doubt have other rooms then,
Or other names.

He isn't speaking to the other lover, but musing to himself, running a checklist of things to attend to ("is the second bed / Unrumpled, as agreed?")—or perhaps speaking *for* both of them, in the single isolation they ironically share: "Our lilacs." The dismal possibilities for keepsakes, "Ashtrays, combs," measure the situation; and even these, like the motel matches, are off-limits. The flowers will last only "A few more hours," and the putting an aspirin in their water to preserve them a bit, "should such things get lonely," is a sad domestic gesture, more sorrowing than hopeful. They are, we understand, casual lovers, without plans or "claims." The self-directed irony of the last line is savage. Should they come back, he has said in line 27, "We would no doubt have other rooms then." He adds: "Or other names." The very abruptness is a whiplash that tells us he doesn't mean merely that they would sign in under a different false name. The plural "rooms," like the plural "names," also tells. They would "no doubt" be, each, with different lovers. Such irony may well make a reader flinch!

Life itself is often ironic; that is, things turn out in unexpected ways, surprising us by the discrepancy between appearance and reality. Thomas Hardy's "During Wind and Rain" (page 111) or this poem by Edwin Arlington Robinson (1869–1935) exemplify such **situational irony:**

Richard Cory

Whenever Richard Cory went down town,
We people on the pavement looked at him;
He was a gentleman from sole to crown,
Clean favored, and imperially slim.

And he was always quietly arrayed,   5
And he was always human when he talked;
But still he fluttered pulses when he said,
"Good-morning," and he glittered when he walked.

And he was rich—yes, richer than a king—
And admirably schooled in every grace;   10
In fine, we thought that he was everything
To make us wish that we were in his place.

So on we worked, and waited for the light,
And went without the meat, and cursed the bread;
And Richard Cory, one calm summer night,   15
Went home and put a bullet through his head.

Robert Frost's "Home Burial" (page 216), a poem rich in irony, has in it
perhaps as much about the relationship of a man and a woman as any poem in
English does. Like a short story, it presents a complete scene, telling as much about
the couple as we could want to know. There is truth on the husband's side, as there
is truth on the wife's. His accidentally ironic comment on the "little graveyard"
where their dead child is buried—"Not so much larger than a bedroom, is it?"—and
her accidentally ironic overtones as she describes him digging the child's grave—

"I saw you from that very window there,
Making the gravel leap and leap in air,
Leap up, like that, like that, and land so lightly
And roll back down the mound beside the hole.
I thought, Who is that man? I didn't know you.
And I crept down the stairs and up the stairs
To look again, and still your spade kept lifting . . ."

—lead to the inexplicable sexuality at the heart of their quarrel. Randall Jarrell's
essay on the poem in *The Third Book of Criticism*, as fine as commentary can ever
be, shows how Frost has packed every gesture, every word with dramatic significance. Every object in the poem—the stairs, the window, the spade, the mound
and hole of the grave-digging, the door—become symbols to help interpret the
characters and their action and reaction.

Symbols

A **symbol** is something that stands for or represents something else, like the *x*
in an algebraic equation or the stars and stripes in the American flag. In literature a
symbol stands for or represents something, usually thematic and intangible, beyond
the literal. Symbols may be fairly minor and local to a particular poem, like the
loon and royal family in "First Death in Nova Scotia," whose white and red
symbolize all the little girl ambiguously understands of her cousin's death, or like
the short-lived flowers in "Leaving the Motel" that symbolize these lovers' relationship. Symbols may be more general and open-ended, as the highly specific wheelbarrow in William Carlos Williams's "The Red Wheelbarrow" symbolizes labor,
fertility, or even the importance of seeing the world in a certain way. Some things,
from frequent use, carry larger symbolic associations. In Williams's "Poem" ("The
rose fades . . ."), for instance, we understand that he is not talking specifically

about the *rose,* but about all the transitory and beautiful things for which the rose is a traditional symbol, as in Robert Herrick's "Gather ye rosebuds while ye may, / Old time is still a-flying; / And this same flower that smiles today / Tomorrow will be dying," which is addressed "To the Virgins, to Make Much of Time."

The value of symbols lies in their resonance. Because their meaning is not specifically stated, it can spiral out like circles in water; or, like a beam of light, it can illuminate anything that lies in its path, at whatever distance. It may symbolize any number of situations of the same kind. Equally, actions and events may become symbols. Any poem that works, that communicates its excitement, despair, or confusion, does so because it achieves a symbolic resonance. The poet will find symbols aplenty in the material at hand. Things *become* symbolic as he or she works with them, the less self-consciously, the better. Imposing symbols invariably makes them ring false.

Some poems are deliberately, primarily symbolic, like Robert Frost's

The Road Not Taken

Two roads diverged in a yellow wood,
And sorry I could not travel both
And be one traveler, long I stood
And looked down one as far as I could
To where it bent in the undergrowth;   5

Then took the other, as just as fair,
And having perhaps the better claim,
Because it was grassy and wanted wear;
Though as for that the passing there
Had worn them really about the same,   10

And both that morning equally lay
In leaves no step had trodden black.
Oh, I kept the first for another day!
Yet knowing how way leads on to way,
I doubted if I should ever come back.   15

I shall be telling this with a sigh
Somewhere ages and ages hence:
Two roads diverged in a wood, and I—
I took the one less traveled by,
And that has made all the difference.   20

The difference between two paths in a real wood, we understand, isn't likely to be very important. Certainly it would not have the significance the poem claims: "And that has made all the difference." Paths in a wood are pretty much alike, and if the speaker by chance had come upon a pot of gold on this particular walk, he could have told us. In a real wood it is possible to return another day and find little changed.

So we sense at once that "The Road Not Taken" is primarily symbolic. It is a poem about the nature of choice, and the significance claimed ("all the difference") makes clear that it is about some sort of life-choice. The difference comes, the speaker claims, from his having taken "the one less traveled by." The poem seems a simple and proud affirmation.

But Frost is rarely as simple as he seems. Despite the assertion "I took the one less traveled by," the two roads (as lines 6–12 are at some pains to make clear) were virtually indistinguishable: "just as fair," "perhaps the better claim," "really about the same," "equally lay / In leaves no step had trodden black." It certainly wasn't a case of choosing between good and bad: "sorry I could not travel both." A reader may also wonder, since "way leads on to way" in life, how the speaker can know what lay down that other road, or know what difference his choice made. Why does the speaker, in the present of speaking the poem, not just assert the claim in the last two lines, rather than *predicting* that he will do so at a distant future time, "ages and ages hence"? Why that "sigh"? And above all, if the point is the pleasure and advantage of the road taken, why is the poem called "The Road *Not* Taken"? The symbolism is more complicated and interesting than a reader might at first perceive.

Consider how aptly and naturally, and how amusingly, this poem by Katha Pollitt (b. 1949) uses the onion as symbol:

Onion

The smoothness of onions infuriates him
so like the skin of women or their expensive clothes
and the striptease of onions, which is also a disappearing act.
He says he is searching for the ultimate nakedness
but when he finds that thin green seed   5
that negligible sprout of a heart
we could have told him he'd only be disappointed.
Meanwhile the onion has been hacked to bits
and he's weeping in the kitchen most unromantic tears.

Dramatic Material

The variety available to the poet for handling dramatic material is wide. Consider two poems on essentially the same subject, an automobile accident, by Karl Shapiro (b. 1913) and J. D. Reed (b. 1940). In both poems the speaker comes upon the aftermath of an accident at night and reports it vividly. Their themes are, I think, very similar. First:

Auto Wreck

KARL SHAPIRO

Its quick soft silver bell beating, beating,
And down the dark one ruby flare
Pulsing out red light like an artery,
The ambulance at top speed floating down
Past beacons and illuminated clocks 5
Wings in a heavy curve, dips down,
And brakes speed, entering the crowd.
The doors leap open, emptying light;
Stretchers are laid out, the mangled lifted
And stowed into the little hospital. 10
Then the bell, breaking the hush, tolls once,
And the ambulance with its terrible cargo
Rocking, slightly rocking, moves away,
As the doors, an afterthought, are closed.

We are deranged, walking among the cops 15
Who sweep glass and are large and composed.
One is still making notes under the light.
One with a bucket douches ponds of blood
Into the street and gutter.
One hangs lanterns on the wrecks that cling, 20
Empty husks of locusts, to iron poles.

Our throats were tight as tourniquets,
Our feet were bound with splints, but now,
Like convalescents intimate and gauche,
We speak through sickly smiles and warn 25
With the stubborn saw of common sense,
The grim joke and the banal resolution.
The traffic moves around with care,
But we remain, touching a wound
That opens to our richest horror. 30
Already old, the question Who shall die?
Becomes unspoken Who is innocent?

For death in war is done by hands;
Suicide has cause and stillbirth, logic;

And cancer, simple as a flower, blooms.
But this invites the occult mind,
Cancels our physics with a sneer,
And spatters all we knew of denouement
Across the expedient and wicked stones.

The scene is urban. In the first stanza we see the old-fashioned ambulance (with a bell instead of a siren) arrive, take on "its terrible cargo," and depart. Everything is strangely depersonalized. We never see the ambulance's driver or attendants; the machine itself, rather than the people, seems the actor: "The doors leap open . . . are closed." Passives only imply the human actions: "Stretchers are laid out, the mangled lifted / And stowed. . . ." Except for the one word "mangled," nothing is said of the victims. The grisly life-or-death reality seems repressed, suggested only indirectly by images: the ambulance bell is "beating, beating" like a heart, and the ambulance warning-flasher is "Pulsing out red light like an artery." The ambulance seems less to drive than to fly—"floating down," it "Wings in a heavy curve, dips down," which perhaps suggests its angelic function. The hill it descends registers only impressionistically in the "beacons and illuminated clocks" it passes.

In stanza 2 the speaker, one of the crowd of onlookers (for whom he speaks), makes the shock of witnessing the experience explicit: "We are deranged." By contrast, the cops are "large and composed," doing their jobs, apparently impervious to the horror. We learn almost offhandedly that more than one car was involved: "the wrecks that cling, / Empty husks of locusts, to iron poles." In stanza 3 the onlookers' shock is acknowledged in displaced images similar to the "beating, beating" and "red light like an artery" of stanza 1: "Our throats were tight as tourniquets, / Our feet were bound with splints." The onlookers' internalization of what they are seeing is clear. Now, with the worst over, they are "Like convalescents" and begin to speak to one another with the familiarity of survivors: "intimate and gauche." Yet they "remain, touching a wound." The question has become more than the random suddenness of the accidental ("Who shall die?"): it is *why?* Having presented the experience, in stanza 4 the speaker sums up the onlookers' "wound." Other kinds of death have reasons, seem logical; but accidental death "Cancels our physics with a sneer," destroying not only our ideas of cause and effect but also our deepest need for appropriate dramatic conclusion ("denouement"). So cruel is accident that the simply amoral stones must seem "wicked." Shapiro's speaker makes the poem's theme explicit.

Here, for contrast, is J. D. Reed's poem.

The Weather Is Brought to You

It is 64° in Devereaux,
and a volunteer pumper
hoses gas from the expressway.

Troopers with the faces of mandrills
hobnail over crushed metal,   5
using big flashlights like pointers
in a planetarium.

Sprockets dangle in the weeds,
torn radiators gurgle,

and the dead wait under wool blankets,   10
expiring
like tungsten filament
in a hissing, broken headlight.

Reed's speaker, also an onlooker, mainly reports what he sees. Unlike the speaker in "Auto Wreck," he does not describe his feelings; and the poem's theme is never directly stated. The title and first line suggest that he is a driver, listening to his car radio, who comes upon and passes the accident scene slowly. The simple ", / and" of lines 1–2, linking the weather report he has been hearing to the accident scene, suggests how casually and unexpectedly he comes upon it. He sees the fire truck in the highway first, as he approaches; then the wrecks being inspected by the troopers; then, nearer, the sprockets "in the weeds" and the bodies by the side of the highway. The order of the details indicates the succession of the speaker's notice. What he sees is as impressionistic as the first stanza of "Auto Wreck." The verb "hobnail" (of their boots) suggests the unfeeling crudeness of the troopers' job, and the image of their "big flashlights like pointers / in a planetarium" suggests the merely academic precision of their inspection. They seem alien to the human, "with the faces of mandrills," animal and unsympathetic; and presumably the red and blue flashers of the emergency vehicles also give them the colors characteristic of mandrills' faces. Close-ups show the sprockets, which "dangle in the weeds," and then "the dead." Ironically they are covered by "wool blankets," whose warmth is irrelevant.

The report is less factual than it seems. Oddly, the victims are both already "the dead" and "expiring," as if the speaker is unsure. Also oddly, the burning out of the headlight in the last lines—

like tungsten filament
in a hissing, broken headlight

—cannot be part of the scene. This would have occurred much earlier, immediately with the crash and long before the policemen and fire truck arrived. The detail enters the poem as a *comparison* for how the "dead" are "expiring." Even this comparison of the human to the mechanical seems odd, reenforced by the displaced attribution to the "torn" radiators of the throat sound "gurgle." Much of this is no doubt due to the strangeness of suddenly coming upon the scene. But the displacements are not unlike the repression in "Auto Wreck," and the speaker's feelings—surprise, strangeness, and awe at the least—may be inferred.

The poem's title is, of course, an announcer's tag, to be completed with the name of an advertiser. Isolated here, however, it suggests more: the *weather*, not just the weather report, is brought to us by . . .? Accidents, like the weather, are things that simply occur, are imposed on us seemingly by forces of which we can have little comprehension. The comparison of the flashlights to "pointers in a planetarium," in this context, implies more than it might otherwise. The universe is inexplicable; we understand it only indirectly and with difficulty. After two sentence-stanzas, even the breaking of the last sentence into two stanzas may suggest the speaker's discomposure, if not hesitation, in coming to the human center of the accident. That he actively imagines the "hissing, broken headlight" implies that his feelings are anything but passive. The theme of Reed's poem is left unstated, for the reader to gather as he or she repeats the experience in the mind's eye. But the poet has very carefully provided the essential suggestions.

QUESTIONS AND SUGGESTIONS

1. Consider the dramatic implications in these poems. Who is the speaker? What do we know about him? What is the situation in which we imagine the poem was spoken?

a) *The Flea*

JOHN DONNE   (1572–1631)

Mark but this flea, and mark in this
How little that which thou deny'st me is;
It sucked me first, and now sucks thee,
And in this flea our two bloods mingled be;
Thou know'st that this cannot be said   5
A sin, nor shame, nor loss of maidenhead,
  Yet this enjoys before it woo,
  And pampered swells with one blood made of two,
  And this, alas, is more than we would do.

Oh stay, three lives in one flea spare,   10
Where we almost, yea more than, married are.
This flea is you and I, and this

Our marriage bed, and marriage temple is;
Though parents grudge, and you, we're met
And cloistered in these living walls of jet.   15
  Though use° make you apt to kill me,   *habit*
  Let not to that, self-murder added be,
  And sacrilege, three sins in killing three.

Cruel and sudden, hast thou since
Purpled thy nail in blood of innocence?   20
Wherein could this flea guilty be,
Except in that drop which it sucked from thee?
Yet thou triumph'st, and say'st that thou
Find'st not thyself, nor me, the weaker now;
  'Tis true; then learn how false, fears be;   25
  Just so much honor, when thou yield'st to me,
  Will waste, as this flea's death took life from thee.

b) *Carpe Diem°*

JUDSON JEROME   (b. 1927)

Seize (enjoy) the day. Latin tag for poems that advise the enjoyment of present pleasures.

Our daughter has been using my razor. I found
it soapy on the bathroom sink.
Please finish your coffee and come back to bed.
It's later than we think.

c) *Maybe Dats Youwr Pwoblem Too*

JIM HALL   (b. 1947)

All my pwoblems
who knows, maybe evwybody's pwoblems
is due to da fact, due to da awful twuth
dat I am SPIDERMAN.

I know, I know. All da dumb jokes: 5
No flies on you, ha ha,
and da ones about what do I do wit all
doze extwa legs in bed. Well, dat's funny yeah.
But you twy being
SPIDERMAN for a month or two. Go ahead.   10

You get doze cwazy calls fwom da
Gubbener askin you to twap some booglar who's
only twying to wip off color T.V. sets.
Now, what do I cawre about T.V. sets?
But I pull on da suit, da stinkin suit,   15
wit da sucker cups on da fingers,

and get my wopes and wittle bundle of
equipment and den I go flying like cwazy
acwoss da town fwom woof top to woof top.

Till der he is, some poor dumb color T.V. slob   20
and I fall on him and we westle a widdle
until I get him all woped. So big deal.

You tink when you SPIDERMAN
der's sometin big going to happen to you.
Well, I tell you what. It don't happen dat way.   25
Nuttin happens. Cubbener calls, I go.
Bwing him to powice. Gubbener calls again,
like dat over and over.

I tink I twy sometin diffunt. I tink I twy
sometin excitin like wacing cawrs. Sometin to make   30
my heart beat at a difwent wate.
But den you just can't quit being sometin like
SPIDERMAN.
You SPIDERMAN for life. Fowever. I can't even
buin by suit. It won't buin. It's fwame wesistent.   35
So maybe dat's youwr pwoblem too, who knows.
So maybe dat's da whole pwoblem wif evwytin.
Nobody can buin der suits, day all fwame wesistent.
Who knows?

2. Try writing a poem in the voice of one of the following:

a turtle turned on his back by kids

a major league outfielder

a widow

a boy who is proud of a pocket knife he has stolen

Michael Jackson

Count Dracula's housecat

the frog in Aal's "Hazel Tells Laverne" (page 197)

3. Each of these poems presents a woman, speaking in her own voice. Consider the differences in character and presentation that let the poets define the women. If you don't recognize the woman in c, look at Appendix I.

a) *Woman's Work*
   JILL FRESHLEY•

   From the west window
   I can see the men
   gathered around the calf,

strung up for the butchering
like the crucified Christ.   5
Their breath hangs, like hickory smoke,
in the air for a moment,
and I'm glad to be in my kitchen,
warm and smelling of bread.
They make the first cut   10
down his white belly
and warm their hands
in the steam belching out
as the snow beneath them flushes
a sudden and angry red.   15

I turn my head away,
recalling the many chilly mornings
I'd fed that calf, stroked its muzzle
and called it by name.
I take the loaves from the oven   20
and set them to cool,
then sit down to my knitting again.
I remember the year on my birthday
when we went up in the airplane
and I thought how from there   25
the plowed fields resembled an afghan,
all golden like harvested corn,
like the brown when it's planted
and the green when it's grown.

b) *Elda May*

GLENN BROOKE*

Eighty-seven now, or thereabouts, Elda May
lives in the oak cabin she built
back in '23, up in Gunner's Run.
She'd rather carry water the half mile
from the creek than have neighbors.   5

I saw her shoot a buck from her porch.
Blue gingham dress faded as a museum flag,
gray hairs pulled fierce to be straight,
she plinked the eight point in the ear.

Elda May's good with her scattergun, too.   10
Just ask the sheriff, Jack Barnes,
what nearly happened to his toes
when he stepped on her turnip greens.

I asked her once, had she ever taken a beau?
Her eyes dimmed soft, like hickory smoke   15

drifting over the autumn hillsides.
"Maybe once . . . but memory's poor, boy."

Jack claims she shot her beau, too,
but most folks don't believe him.

c) *In 1856 she won second prize in the Bread Division*
at the local Cattle Show . . .

—Ellmann & O'Clair

ALBERT GOLDBARTH   (b. 1948)

The poultry pecks its cages like nightmare
clockworks. They're the universe,
maybe, before man thinks up Sequential Time.
Their skins are a first dream of quill pens. And

so the undulant fields about her today,   5
light wheats, and brooding ryes, are raw
tables: schema of home and safety. This
is a County Fair, and here's a choir of strawberry jams

beneath their paraffin halos, and these
are the showcattle being rubbed between   10
brushed flanks so in pleasure they'll
still for the judges . . . She looks down.

A bee is architecting
air around a flower. The judges are here.
The bee see the bee see the bee. And now   15
they've left, with ahems. And now she's writing

We know, by now—the Word was first
And—after—earth, and grain, and grass—
As world to Him—'tis rising, now,
The making of my Second Place.   20

d) *The Lament of an Old Eskimo Woman*

TIM CALHOUN*

I say to them, my children
That the old ways are gone.

That motor-boat, rifle, down-jacket
have usurped
Eskimo kyak, harpoon and seal.   5

They do not hear me, my children.

When I lift the map
of my face

before white man's reflecting glass
the snow   10
in my being gathers
and I cry
and mourn the lost world of my mother.

4. "I can't put toothbrushes in a poem, I really can't" (Sylvia Plath). Give it a try.

5. With Katha Pollitt's "Onion" in mind, think of several other common objects
and how they might have symbolical force in a poem. Write a poem using the most
interesting one.

6. Write a poem about either your father or your mother, using an anecdote (real
or imagined) that occurs before you were born. Maybe an old photograph will help.

7. Read a biography of a celebrity or historical figure who interests you, looking for
an incident that might make a poem. Even if you don't write the poem, plan how
you might handle it.

POEMS TO CONSIDER

Faintheart in a Railway Train   *1920*

THOMAS HARDY (1840–1928)

At nine in the morning there passed a church,
At ten there passed me by the sea,
At twelve a town of smoke and smirch,
At two a forest of oak and birch,
    And then, on a platform, she: 5

A radiant stranger, who saw not me.
I said, 'Get out to her do I dare?'
But I kept my seat in my search for a plea,
And the wheels moved on. O could it but be
    That I had alighted there!   10

Home Burial   1914

ROBERT FROST   (1874–1963)

He saw her from the bottom of the stairs
Before she saw him. She was starting down,
Looking back over her shoulder at some fear.
She took a doubtful step and then undid it
To raise herself and look again. He spoke   5
Advancing toward her: 'What is it you see
From up there always—for I want to know.'
She turned and sank upon her skirts at that,
And her face changed from terrified to dull.
He said to gain time: 'What is it you see,'   10
Mounting until she cowered under him.
'I will find out now—you must tell me, dear.'
She, in her place, refused him any help
With the least stiffening of her neck and silence.
She let him look, sure that he wouldn't see,   15
Blind creature; and awhile he didn't see.
But at last he murmured. 'Oh,' and again, 'Oh.'

'What is it—what?' she said.

                              'Just that I see.'

'You don't,' she challenged. 'Tell me what it is.'

'The wonder is I didn't see at once.   20
I never noticed it from here before.
I must be wonted to it—that's the reason.
The little graveyard where my people are!
So small the window frames the whole of it.
Not so much larger than a bedroom, is it?   25
There are three stones of slate and one of marble,
Broad-shouldered little slabs there in the sunlight
On the sidehill. We haven't to mind *those*.
But I understand: it is not the stones,
But the child's mound—'

                              'Don't, don't, don't, don't,' she cried.   30

She withdrew shrinking from beneath his arm
That rested on the bannister, and slid downstairs;

And turned on him with such a daunting look,
He said twice over before he knew himself:
'Can't a man speak of his own child he's lost?'   35

'Not you! Oh, where's my hat? Oh, I don't need it!
I must get out of here. I must get air.
I don't know rightly whether any man can.'

'Amy! Don't go to someone else this time.
Listen to me. I won't come down the stairs.'   40
He sat and fixed his chin between his fists.
'There's something I should like to ask you, dear.'

'You don't know how to ask it.'

               'Help me, then.'

Her fingers moved the latch for all reply.

'My words are nearly always an offense.   45
I don't know how to speak of anything
So as to please you. But I might be taught
I should suppose. I can't say I see how.
A man must partly give up being a man
With women-folk. We could have some arrangement   50
By which I'd bind myself to keep hands off
Anything special you're a-mind to name.
Though I don't like such things 'twixt those that love.
Two that don't love can't live together without them.
But two that do can't live together with them.'   55
She moved the latch a little. 'Don't—don't go.
Don't carry it to someone else this time.
Tell me about it if it's something human.
Let me into your grief. I'm not so much
Unlike other folks as your standing there   60
Apart would make me out. Give me my chance.
I do think, though, you overdo it a little.
What was it brought you up to think it the thing
To take your mother-loss of a first child
So inconsolably—in the face of love.   65
You'd think his memory might be satisfied—'

'There you go sneering now!'

'I'm not, I'm not!
You make me angry. I'll come down to you.
God, what a woman! And it's come to this,
A man can't speak of his own child that's dead.'   70

'You can't because you don't know how to speak.
If you had any feelings, you that dug
With your own hand—how could you?—his little grave;
I saw you from that very window there,
Making the gravel leap and leap in air,   75
Leap up, like that, like that, and land so lightly
And roll back down the mound beside the hole.
I thought, Who is that man? I didn't know you.
And I crept down the stairs and up the stairs
To look again, and still your spade kept lifting.   80
Then you came in. I heard your rumbling voice
Out in the kitchen, and I don't know why,
But I went near to see with my own eyes.
You could sit there with the stains on your shoes
Of the fresh earth from your own baby's grave   85
And talk about your everyday concerns.
You had stood the spade up against the wall
Outside there in the entry, for I saw it.'

'I shall laugh the worst laugh I ever laughed.
I'm cursed. God, if I don't believe I'm cursed.'   90

'I can repeat the very words you were saying.
"Three foggy mornings and one rainy day
Will rot the best birch fence a man can build."
Think of it, talk like that at such a time!
What had how long it takes a birch to rot   95
To do with what was in the darkened parlor.
You *couldn't* care! The nearest friends can go
With anyone to death, comes so far short
They might as well not try to go at all.
No, from the time when one is sick to death,   100
One is alone, and he dies more alone.
Friends make pretense of following to the grave,
But before one is in it, their minds are turned
And making the best of their way back to life
And living people, and things they understand.   105
But the world's evil. I won't have grief so
If I can change it. Oh, I won't, I won't!'

'There, you have said it all and you feel better.
You won't go now. You're crying. Close the door.
The heart's gone out of it: why keep it up?   110
Amy! There's someone coming down the road!'

'You—oh, you think the talk is all. I must go—
Somewhere out of this house. How can I make you—'

'If—you—do!' She was opening the door wider.
'Where do you mean to go? First tell me that.   115
I'll follow and bring you back by force. I *will!*—'

To an Athlete Dying Young   1896

A. E. HOUSMAN   (1859–1936)

The time you won your town the race
We chaired you through the market-place;
Man and boy stood cheering by,
And home we brought you shoulder-high.

To-day, the road all runners come,   5
Shoulder-high we bring you home,
And set you at your threshold down,
Townsman of a stiller town.

Smart lad, to slip betimes away
From fields where glory does not stay   10
And early though the laurel grows
It withers quicker than the rose.

Eyes the shady night has shut
Cannot see the record cut,
And silence sounds no worse than cheers   15
After earth has stopped the ears:

Now you will not swell the rout
Of lads that wore their honors out,
Runners whom renown outran
And the name died before the man.   20

So set, before its echoes fade,
The fleet foot on the sill of shade,
And hold to the low lintel up
The still-defended challenge-cup.

And round that early-laurelled head   25
Will flock to gaze the strengthless dead,
And find unwithered on its curls
The garland briefer than a girl's.

Fat   1980

CONRAD HILBERRY (b. 1928)

Wait. What you see is another person
hanging here. I am the girl who jumps
the Hodgman's fence so quick they never see me.
Skipping rope, I always do hot peppers.
But once on the way home I got in a strange   5
car. I screamed and beat on the windows,
but they smiled and held me. They said I could go
when I put on the costume, so I climbed
into it, pulled up the huge legs,
globby with veins, around my skinny shins,   10
pulled on this stomach that flops over itself,
I pushed my arm past the hanging elbow fat
down into the hand and fingers, tight
like a doctor's glove stuffed with vaseline.
I hooked the top behind my neck, with these   15
two bladders bulging over my flat chest.
Then I pulled the rubber mask down over
my head and tucked in the cheek and chin
folds at the neck, hiding the seam. I hate
the smell. When they pushed me out of the car,   20
I slipped and staggered as though the street
was wet with fish oil. You see what this costume is.
If you will undo me, if you will loan me a knife,
I will step out the way I got in.
I will run on home in time for supper.   25

The Bats

BRENDAN GALVIN   (b. 1938)

Somebody said for killing one
you got a five-dollar reward
from Red Farrell the game warden,
because at night they drank cow blood,
dozens of them plastered on the cow   5
like leaves after a rain,
until she dropped.
If they bit you you'd get paralyzed for life,
and they built their nests
in women's hair, secreting goo   10
so you couldn't pull them out
and had to shave it off.
That was how Margaret Smith got bald,
though some said it was wine.
But who ever saw one   15
or could tell a bat from the swifts
they sometimes flew with,
homing on insects those green evenings?
We never climbed the fence of Duffy's orchard
to catch them dog-toothed   20
sucking on his pears,
and the trouble was, as Duffy always said,
that in the dark you couldn't
recognize them for the leaves
and might reach up and get bit.   25
So the first time one of us found one
dead and held it open,
it looked like something crucified
to a busted umbrella,
the ribbed wings like a crackpot would make   30
to try and fly off of a dune.
As if it was made up of parts
of different animals, it had long bird-legs
stuck in lizard wrinkle pants,
and wire feet.   35
It wasn't even black, but brown and furry
with a puppy nose,
and when we threw it at each other
it wouldn't stick on anyone.

Then someone said his father knew somebody   40
who used to hunt between town and the back shore.
Coming home one night he ran across
a bat tree in the woods,
must have been hundreds folded upside down
pealing their single bell-notes through the dark.   45

Tuesday Morning, Loading Pigs   1984

DAVID LEE   (b. 1944)

The worse goddam job of all
sez John pushing a thick slat
in front of the posts
behind the sow in the loading chute
so when she balked and backed up   5
she couldn't turn and get away
I never seen a sow or a hog load easy
some boars will
mebbe it's because they got balls
or something I don't know   10
but I seen them do it
that Brown feller the FFA
he's got this boar he just opens the trailer door
he comes and gets in
course he mebbe knows what   15
he's being loaded up for

it was this Ivie boy back home
the best I ever seen for loading
he wasn't scared of nothing
he'd get right in and shove them up   20
he put sixteen top hogs
in the back of a Studebaker pickup
by hisself I seen it
when he was a boy he opened up
the tank on the tractor   25
smelling gas
made his brains go soft they sed

he failed fifth grade
but it wasn't his fault
he could load up hogs   30

I always had to at home
cause I was the youngest
I sed then it was two things
I wouldn't do when I grown up
warsh no dishes or load up hogs   35
by god they can set in the sink
a month before I'll warsh them
a man's got to have a principle
he can live by is what I say
now you grab her ears and pull   40
I'll push from back here
we'll get that sonofabitch in the truck

Sueños°   1983
                                                                  °Dreams

JAMES REISS (b. 1941)

In my dreams I always speak Spanish.
The cemetery may be in Brooklyn,
and I may be kneeling on a rise
looking out at the skyline of the city,
but I will whisper, *Mira el sol°*.   *Look at the sun* 5

And it is true the late morning
sun will turn that bank of skyscrapers
the color of bleached bone in Sonora,
and all the window washers of Manhattan
will white-out like a TV screen   10

in Venezuela turning to snow.
But the gray face on the headstone photograph
has a nose like my father's,
and his voice had the lilt of the ghettos
of central Europe.   15

So I should kneel lower and say something
in Yiddish about fathers, grandfathers,
the hacked limbs of a family tree
that reaches as high as Manhattan.
I should say, *Grampa, I loved those times*   20

we ran through the underpasses in Central
Park, you with your cane, I with my ice
cream cones, shouting for echoes,
bursting out into sunlight—
if I only knew the language to say it in.   25

Metaphor:
To Keep Cows in

Metaphor is the ever-fresh, magical center of poetry. Aristotle declared that "the greatest thing by far is to be a master of metaphor. It is the one thing that cannot be learned from others; and it is also a sign of genius, since a good metaphor implies an intuitive perception of the similarity in dissimilars." Two millennia later Robert Frost remarked, "There are many other things I have found myself saying about poetry, but the chiefest of these is that it is metaphor, saying one thing and meaning another, saying one thing in terms of another." Inextricably entwined both with the ways in which we think and with the origin and nature of language itself, metaphor seems inexhaustibly complex in theory. Fortunately, just as we needn't know much about human musculature to run, we needn't have a theory of metaphor to use it. Asked "What's a metaphor?" the poet, happy to be the one who causes the trouble (not the one who has to straighten it out), may be inclined to answer with the hoary pun that appears in the chapter's title.

Frost's definition is adequate: *"saying one thing in terms of another."* A **metaphor** is a comparison of whatever is under discussion (the subject, or a part of it) with something that would not normally be a part of that subject. If you say that you are "busy as a bee," the bee enters metaphorically into the statement. Conventionally the subject (or part) being compared is called the **tenor**: the thing to which it is compared, the **vehicle.** Imagine an opera singer being taken in a cart to be burned at the stake—the singer is the important thing, the cart only a means of transportation. The comparison may be explicit or implicit. When it is explicit, or stated, it is called **simile** and is syntactically announced by *like* or *as*. "He is busy *as a bee*" is a simile. The similes are italicized in the following:

The wild tulip, at end of its tube, blows out its great red bell
Like a thin clear bubble of blood

Robert Browning

A twitch, a twitter, an elastic shudder in flight
And serrated wings against the sky,
Like a glove, a black glove, thrown up at the light
And falling back

D. H. Lawrence

I wandered lonely *as a cloud*

William Wordsworth

Similes are also used extensively by Alfred, Lord Tennyson (1809–1892) in

Tears, Idle Tears

Tears, idle tears, I know not what they mean,
Tears from the depth of some divine despair
Rise in the heart, and gather to the eyes,
In looking on the happy autumn-fields,
And thinking of the days that are no more.   5

Fresh *as the first beam glittering on a sail,*
That brings our friends up from the underworld,
Sad *as the last which reddens over one*
That sinks with all we love below the verge;
So sad, so fresh, the days that are no more.   10

Ah, sad and strange *as in dark summer dawns*
The earliest pipe of half-awakened birds
To dying ears, when unto dying eyes
The casement slowly grows a glimmering square;
So sad, so strange, the days that are no more.   15

Dear *as remembered kisses after death,*
And sweet *as those by hopeless fancy feigned*

On lips that are for others; deep as love,
Deep as first love, and wild with all regret;
O Death in Life, the days that are no more!   20

When the comparison is implicit, or unstated, the term *metaphor* itself is used. A metaphor compresses the comparison, asserting or assuming the identity of tenor and vehicle. "The man *is a busy bee*." "The waves *were angry*." "The gun *barked*." "A ship *ploughs* the sea." The compression can often be untangled into a looser form, where the tenor and vehicle are identifiable. "The waves were like a person who is angry." "The gun made a noise like the bark of a dog." "The ship goes through the sea as a plough goes through the soil." The compression of a metaphor, in effect, suppresses an element or elements of the comparison. Richard Wilbur, in "Year's End," speaks of the "death of ferns / Which laid their fragile *cheeks* against the stone / A million years." We understand something like this: "their fragile *fronds, which are as soft as cheeks*." I say "something like" because somewhat different "translations" of the metaphor are possible. Because associations and connotations abound, no two readers respond in exactly the same way. "Cheeks" are human attributes; thus, a personification is involved. The ferns are like dying persons who lay their cheeks "against the stone." The delicacy of ferns might even suggest that they are like dying girls. For the sensitive reader a very ephemeral but significant little dramatic scene may be buried in the seemingly simple metaphor, "cheeks."

The tones and overtones of metaphor give it its power. Exact translation is elusive, and from that, of course, comes the suggestive richness of metaphor, its ability not only to compact and compress but also to express the inexpressible. Metaphors are italicized in the following fragments:

The silver *snarling* trumpets 'gan to chide

John Keats

The *dust* of snow

Robert Frost

Life's *but a walking shadow, a poor player*
That struts and frets his hour upon the stage
And then is heard no more. It is a tale
Told by an idiot, full of sound and fury,
Signifying nothing.

William Shakespeare

Each wight who reads not, and but scans and spells,
Each word-*catcher* that *lives* on syllables,

Ev'n such *small* critics some regard may claim,
Preserved in Milton's or in Shakespeare's name.
Pretty! in amber to observe the forms
Of hairs, or straws, or dirt, or grubs, or worms!
The things, we know, are neither rich nor rare,
But wonder how the devil they got there?

Alexander Pope

Here is a whole poem, by Peter Wild (b. 1940):

Natural Gas

When you push the lever up
the warm gases *leap* through the house.

All night I lie awake
as beside me you lie *buried* in the dark,
listening to the thermostat click on and off,   5

the ghosts of the fierce creatures
starting, stopping, puzzled in the pipes
all the way from Texas.

Metaphor often surprises us into seeing things afresh, as if with new eyes. Qualities in the metaphor focus, in the subject, qualities we might not have noticed or noticed so vividly. The English poet Craig Raine (b. 1944) is a master. Rain, he says, "scores a bull's-eye every time." A beetle on its back struggles "like an orchestra / with Beethoven." Scissors go "through the material / like a swimmer doing crawl." A city seen from the air is "a radio / with its back ripped off." Of a light bulb: "light ripens / the electric pear." A rose grows "on a shark-infested stem." Steel-frame spectacles seem "like a broken bike." The title poem of his first book is a little treasury of metaphorical riddles. (If you don't recognize what "Caxtons" are, check William Caxton in an encyclopedia.)

A Martian Sends a Postcard Home

Caxtons are mechanical birds with many wings
and some are treasured for their markings—

they cause the eyes to melt
or the body to shriek without pain.

I have never seen one fly, but   5
sometimes they perch on the hand.

Mist is when the sky is tired of flight
and rests its soft machine on ground:

then the world is dim and bookish
like engravings under tissue paper.   10

Rain is when the earth is television.
It has the property of making colours darker.

Model T is a room with the lock inside—
a key is turned to free the world

for movement, so quick there is a film   15
to watch for anything missed.

But time is tied to the wrist
or kept in a box, ticking with impatience.

In homes, a haunted apparatus sleeps,
that snores when you pick it up.   20

If the ghost cries, they carry it
to their lips and soothe it to sleep

with sounds. And yet, they wake it up
deliberately, by tickling with a finger.

Only the young are allowed to suffer   25
openly. Adults go to a punishment room

with water but nothing to eat.
They lock the door and suffer the noises

alone. No one is exempt
and everyone's pain has a different smell.   30

At night, when all the colours die,
they hide in pairs

and read about themselves—
in colour, with their eyelids shut.

The Metaphorical Link

Language itself is deeply metaphorical. We speak of the *eye* of a needle, the *face* of a cliff, the *hands* of a clock, the *heel* of a hand, the *branch* of a river, getting down to *brass tacks*, *crab* grass, a check that *bounces*, an election won by a *landslide*, a person's going *haywire*, an idea's *dawning* on us, the years *rolling by*. So familiar are such phrases that we usually don't notice that they are metaphorical; we don't actually think of faces, hands, landslides, the tangly wire used for baling hay, or whatever. Such dead metaphors show a primary way in which language changes to accommodate new possibilities. Confronted with something new, for which there is no word, we thriftily adapt an old word as a comparison, and soon the new meaning seems perfectly literal. The part of a car that covers the engine, for instance, is a *hood*. On early cars, it was in fact rounded and looked very like a hood; but the word survives, although now hoods are flat and look nothing like hoods. (They still cover the engines' *heads*.) Sometimes the perfectly literal becomes metaphorical. Actual trunks were strapped to the back of early automobiles, and the word survives, although now the trunks are built-in and we may forget their likeness to trunks in an attic. Such metaphors continue to be useful even after their sense has evaporated. We say someone is "mad as a hatter" although there aren't many hatters around and although the chemical they used (which, in fact, often made them crazy) is no longer used.

The world itself is wordless, and Adam's giving names to the beasts in Eden is one of the great archetypal human activities. There are still many things, actions, feelings, and relationships for which there are no words, or only specialized or technical words. There are no words for the V of the hand between thumb and forefinger, for a single filament of a spider's web, for the strange green of stormlight, or for the many looks and appearances of the sea's surface. Eskimos have, understandably, more than twenty different words for kinds of snow, while we barely distinguish two or three. Translators often find no precise equivalent in the way that two languages notice or measure out the parts of the world. Feelings are particularly inarticulate and almost always need metaphor to get themselves into language. The general words we have—*love, hate, compassion, awe, anger,* and the like—really express little about specific cases. A man may *love* his wife, his dog, a spring day, pistachio ice cream, and Vermont. To verbalize the exact feeling, he may well need metaphor. "O, my luve's like a red, red rose." Different lovers might say a white rose, a daisy, a zinnia, a violet, or almost anything, even pistachio ice cream. In such cases the poet (or any of us) borrows the vocabulary, the mode of discourse, that belongs to something else and uses it to say whatever there are no words for ("ploughs," "a bee," "dust," "a thin clear bubble of blood").

Richard Wilbur wittily suggests the inescapability of metaphor:

Praise in Summer

Obscurely yet most surely called to praise,
As sometimes summer calls us all, I said
The hills are heavens full of branching ways
Where star-nosed moles fly overhead the dead;
I said the trees are mines in air, I said   5
See how the sparrow burrows in the sky!
And then I wondered why this mad *instead*
Perverts our praise to uncreation, why
Such savor's in this wrenching things awry.
Does sense so stale that it must needs derange   10
The world to know it? To a praiseful eye
Should it not be enough of fresh and strange
That trees grow green, and moles can course in clay,
And sparrows sweep the ceiling of our day?

Even wanting to dispense with metaphor ("this mad *instead*"), the speaker falls back
into it without thinking: "And sparrows *sweep the ceiling of our day.*" Notice that
metaphor is hidden in aviators' or meteorologists' use of the word "ceiling," and
that "sweep" may well not be merely fanciful if the sparrows are snapping up midges
and mosquitoes. The seemingly innocent word "course" is also metaphorical,
recalling its Latin root, meaning "to run." "Course" also means "to hunt," and
moles do that as well. Is "course" here literal or metaphorical, or both? Does "trees
grow green" mean that they grow and are green, or that they produce greenness, as
a farmer might grow a crop? Perhaps they "become" ("grow" in the sense of "turn")
green? Is the compression of "trees grow leaves that are green" a metaphorical
compression? (**Synecdoche** is a type of metaphor in which a part of something
stands for the whole, as when someone speaks of an employee as a "hired hand.")
Where they join, language and the world may take on a magical complexity.

Metaphors work in a bewildering variety of ways (no catalog could be made)
and do a bewildering variety of jobs, sometimes so complexly that no conscious
analysis can follow them. They may illustrate or explain (the heart is like a pump);
emphasize; heighten; communicate information or ideas; carry a tone, feeling, or
attitude. They may even work—Hart Crane's phrase is the **"logic of metaphor"**—
as a mode of discourse, a sort of language of associations, as they do in Dylan
Thomas's "Twenty-Four Years" (page 258) or in "Sir, Say No More" by Trumbull
Stickney (1874–1904):

Sir, say no more,
Within me 'tis as if
The green and climbing eyesight of a cat
Crawled near my mind's poor birds.

The eerie sensation communicates perfectly, though a critic might work all day to untangle the threads the image knots up so simply.

So accustomed are we to metaphor that we hardly notice how fully it serves. In Shakespeare's Sonnet 73 ("That time of year thou mayst in me behold"), for instance, metaphors provide almost the whole effect of the poem, translating emotions into vivid and dramatic particulars about winter trees, choirlofts, twilight, embers. The metaphors virtually stand for or present the emotion. Like literal particulars, metaphors enrich the texture and color of a poem, as well as often being a principal means for evoking the feeling.

For practical purposes, the distinction between simile and metaphor is far less important than their similarity. Syntactically, simile is perhaps simpler, closer to the straightforward, logical uses of language. But the evocative functions of metaphor and simile can be measured properly only by the unique force of specific instances. The oddly popular notion that metaphor is stronger than simile, more forceful or evocative, is not really true. Consider the sonnet by William Wordsworth:

Composed upon Westminster Bridge, September 3, 1802

Earth has not anything to show more fair:
Dull would he be of soul who could pass by
A sight so touching in its majesty:
This City now doth, like a garment, wear
The beauty of the morning; silent, bare,   5
Ships, towers, domes, theatres, and temples lie
Open unto the fields, and to the sky;
All bright and glittering in the smokeless air.
Never did sun more beautifully steep
In his first splendour, valley, rock, or hill;   10
Ne'er saw I, never felt, a calm so deep!
The river glideth at his own sweet will:
Dear God! the very houses seem asleep;
And all that mighty heart is lying still!

This fine panorama of early-morning London offers a rare instance of simile and metaphor doing the same job at the same moment. "Like a garment" in line 4 is a simile, "wear" a metaphor. Unquestionably the simile is stronger, governs the effect more than the metaphor, which a reader notices secondarily, if at all. By being very general, "like a *garment*" makes the personification of the city vague and keeps it from interfering with the brilliant visual details of the literal scene: "silent, bare, / Ships, towers, domes, theatres, and temples lie." The "beauty of the morning" seems diaphanous, filmy—"bare" suggests almost nothing—and so with exquisite tact the simile establishes the personification of the sleeping city as feminine. This is balanced, with equal tact, by the masculine sun and river of the final lines. The sexual overtones, which give the sonnet a curiously moving loveliness, seem hardly more than a faint "overimage" superimposed on the literal scene with the finest delicacy.

The syntactical distinction between simile and metaphor may offer different advantages in practice. But "O, my luve's like a red, red rose" and "O, my luve is a red, red rose" are functionally more alike than different. Look again at Browning's lines:

> The wild tulip, at end of its tube, blows out its great red bell
> Like a thin clear bubble of blood

Again unquestionably, the simile "Like a thin clear bubble of blood" is more startling, more evocative, than either of the metaphors, "tube" for the stem and "great red bell" for the flower. It clearly carries the main, somewhat unpleasant tone of the passage (the speaker is comparing the city and the country to the disadvantage of the latter). The vaguely clinical "tube" (and "bell," which has laboratory overtones) beautifully set up the grimly lovely "Like a thin clear bubble of blood."

In a way, it is surprising that metaphor works at all, much less that it usually works instantly and intuitively. The reader, without analysis, perceives those elements or qualities of tenor and vehicle that are pertinent and ignores those that are irrelevant. Analysis can follow intuition and enumerate the relevant elements or qualities of the comparison. But the sum of the parts of the enumeration, however illuminating, rarely equals the effect of the comparison as a whole. Always, as with the last lines of Wilbur's "Praise in Summer," the nuances and associations of a metaphor go beyond the certainties that analysis, plodding after, can pin down.

Consider the opening image of Robert Burns's familiar "A Red, Red Rose":

> O, my luve's like a red, red rose
> That's newly sprung in June.

We understand this relatively simple metaphor at once, but what has gone into our understanding? What likenesses justify the comparison? How is a woman like and unlike a rose? A list of likenesses would include such qualities as beautiful, fresh, young, natural, and might go on to sweet-smelling, happy or good-natured (since we connect roses with happy occasions), healthy, lively, and so on. There is really no way of being sure that such a listing is complete. Someone might suggest further qualities—passionate, perhaps, because of the intensity of "red, red" and the traditional linking of roses with physical beauty, red with strong feelings.

On the other hand, a list of *unlikenesses*, which we instantly dismiss or ignore, might include such qualities as having thorns (being prickly), being red (a heavy drinker?), being angry (red is the color of wrath), growing out of the ground, reproducing by pollen, and so on. So experienced and expert are we all at handling metaphor that we make such discriminations effortlessly and without articulating them. Context guides our response. If the line were, say, "O, my mother-in-law's like a red, red rose," we might well reorder the qualities we include and exclude in our response.

Richard Wilbur's comparison of a cricket and a hearse is somewhat easier to account for:

Exeunt

> Piecemeal the summer dies;
> At the field's edge a daisy lives alone;
>   A last shawl of burning lies
>   On a gray field-stone.
>
> All cries are thin and terse;   5
> The field has droned the summer's final mass;
>   A cricket like a dwindled hearse
>   Crawls from the dry grass.

Cricket and "dwindled hearse" are both long, dark or black, and shiny. The insect's slow movement ("Crawls") and the solemn speed of a hearse (which might be described as moving at a crawl) correspond. The adjective "dwindled" makes sure that we see the hearse at such a distance or in such reduction that the cricket isn't overshadowed by its mass. Miniaturization suggests fragility. The hearse's associations with death appropriately color the late-summer slow pace of the cricket, whose normal sprightliness and agility are past, and imply its impending death with the coming of cold weather. Differences are muted (size, by "dwindled") or ignored (legs or wheels, for example). Compared to the hearse, the cricket symbolizes and suggestively pictures the "death" of the summer.

Pattern and Motif

Often metaphors function locally; that is, they have no particular connection to other metaphors or other parts of the poem, as in X. J. Kennedy's "In a Prominent Bar in Secaucus One Day,"

> In the kerchief of linen I caught to my nose
> Ah, there never fell snot, but *a little gold rose.*

Or, later,

Now I'm *saddled* each night for my butter and eggs
And *the broken threads race* down the backs of my legs.

"Gold rose," "saddled," and "broken threads" are essentially separate images. Metaphors often, however, work in patterns or interactions, as with Browning's "tube" and "thin clear bubble of blood" or, more generally, the male and female personifications in Wordsworth's sonnet about London. In Kennedy's poem, for example, the snot—little gold rose image does form a secondary pattern with other flower/plant images:

Let you hold in mind, girls, that your beauty must pass
Like a lovely white clover that rusts with its grass

and

And be left by the roadside, for all your good deeds,
Two toadstools for tits and a face *full of weeds.*

The connection is minimal, but the sequence—gold rose, rusting clover, toadstools, weeds—provides a motif of the poem's theme. (**Motif:** a pattern of recurrent, unifying images or phrases.) Similarly, the various racing references and images form a motif that reveals the woman's experience and character.

In Wilbur's "Exeunt," however, the metaphors make a very tight pattern. In line 1 the metaphorical "the summer dies" links to the metaphorical "hearse" in line 7. In line 2 "lives alone" begins the personification of the flower. That "daisy" is also a feminine name hints further at the personification. The metaphorical "shawl of burning" (late summer sun, or perhaps fallen leaves) in line 3 fits this developing image of an elderly woman, as does the literal "gray" in line 4. The last occasion of the full hum of the summer field is described metaphorically in line 6 as a "final mass," presumably a funeral mass, after which the cricket-hearse appears. Each metaphor is appropriate where it appears; but together, all suggest a comparison to the death of an old woman—a deftly implied little tale that parallels, and evokes feelings for, the literal end of summer. The poem's title, "Exeunt," the plural Latin word used in stage directions for the departure of several characters from the stage, suggests that the dramatic implications of the poem are more than accidental.

Such unifying links, patterns, or motifs between and among the metaphors in a poem must, in part, be conscious on the poet's part. But it is probably a matter more of recognizing and developing possibilities than of cold-bloodedly inventing or imposing them. A poem of mine, for example, began with a visual comparison of the sun to a dandelion (color, shape, glowing spokes). The moon's likeness to another sort of flower followed readily, and this developing pattern called for a metaphor for stars, which in turn suggested the rhyme in the fourth line. The changeable moon's occasional likeness to a scythe fits the pattern:

In the Field Forever

Sun's a roaring dandelion, hour by hour.
Sometimes the moon's a scythe, sometimes a silver flower.
But the stars! all night long the stars are clover,
Over, and over, and over!

Often, as here, the poet need only perceive the potential pattern in the material.

When metaphors dominate or organize a passage or even a whole poem, they are called **extended metaphors** or **conceits.** Secondary metaphors spring from a first, controlling metaphor, as does the varied car imagery in Ted Kooser's "Looking for You, Barbara" (page 249). In this poem by Mary Oliver, the extended metaphor controlling the whole is a comparison of music to a brother "Who has arrived from a long journey," whose reassuring presence makes the flux and danger of the world—"the maelstrom / Lashing"—seem, for the moment, tamed.

Music at Night

Especially at night
It is the best kind of company—

A brother whose dark happiness fills the room,
Who has arrived from a long journey,

Who stands with his back to the windows   5
Beyond which the branches full of leaves

Are not trees only, but the maelstrom
Lashing, attentive and held in thrall

By the brawn in the rippling octaves,
And the teeth in the smile of the strings.   10

So compelling is the fantasy of the metaphor that it is impossible to say whether the trees outside the windows are part of the metaphorical description of the brother or part of the literal scene. The real and the imagined weave into one picture.

The "distance" between the tenor and the vehicle of a metaphor, or between the tones usually associated with them, controls the effect. "A rose is like a carnation" narrows the gap too closely, and the emotional or intellectual spark is faint and uninteresting. "A rose is like a locomotive" opens the gap too wide, and no spark gets across; we have no idea what qualities of rose and locomotive are being compared. In general, the greater the distance between tenor and vehicle, the greater is our surprise and pleasure, but only if the comparison seems just, accurate, congruent, not merely a wild stab. Burns's "O, my luve's like a red, red rose" seems straightforward because girls and roses are traditionally associated. But X. J. Kennedy's " 'Ah, there never fell snot, but a little gold rose' " is shocking, because our feelings about boogers, roses, and gold are worlds apart. The metaphor succeeds (delights us) when we realize how right, after all, the comparison is. In context, a reminder of the speaker's pitiful pretentiousness, it is humorously in character.

John Donne, in "A Valediction: Forbidding Mourning" (page 249), presents the calm parting of true lovers (one of whom is going on a journey) in terms of metaphors from religion, geology, astronomy, and metallurgy. He compares their parting to the unworried death of virtuous men, to the unharmful movements of the heavens ("trepidation of the spheres") in contrast to earthquakes, and to the fineness of gold leaf which, though hammered to "airy thinness," never breaks. The poem's final image is yet more startling: the lovers are likened to a pair of drawing compasses! The whole world seems ransacked and brought to bear, to center, on these lovers, whose parting comes to seem as momentous as the metaphors that express it.

Emily Dickinson's poem "A Route of Evanescence" similarly delights us when we realize what it is about and how evocative its comparisons are. In the first four lines we see something moving rapidly—a wheel, colors (cochineal is a brilliant red dye)—but it is so fast ("Rush") that we cannot identify it.

> A Route of Evanescence
> With a revolving Wheel—
> A Resonance of Emerald—
> A Rush of Cochineal—
> And every Blossom on the Bush   5
> Adjusts its tumbled Head—
> The mail from Tunis°, probably,   *North African city*
> An easy Morning's Ride—

The mystery clears in lines 5–6 when we gather that, whatever it is, it has to do with disturbing the flowers on a bush—a hummingbird! The mere glimpse of its colors and fan-shape in lines 1–4 evokes the bird's quick and jerky flight ("Resonance," "Rush"). The personification of the blossoms as "tumbled heads" prepares for the metaphorical guess in lines 7–8: "The mail from Tunis, probably." The exaggeration, "An easy Morning's Ride," offhandedly insists on the hummingbird's speed in flight and points to the exotic quality of an ordinary back yard that enjoys such colors as emerald and cochineal. If we remember that many of our bird-neighbors winter in Florida or South America (if not North Africa), the metaphor hardly seems farfetched. If we also remember that the hummingbird picks up and delivers pollen from flower to flower—that population of "tumbled Head[s]"—the comparison with the "mail" seems less than outrageous. Even the pun mail/male may not be irrelevant, so we may guess why the news so "tumble[s] Head[s]"! The poem's dazzling metaphors lead not only to a vivid action picture of the humming-bird but also to a fresh experience of how strange and colorful the merely everyday truly is.

Mixed Metaphor

Metaphors may go wrong in several ways; when this happens, they are usually called **mixed metaphors.** The trouble sometimes comes from not shielding the comparison from qualities that are irrelevant or unintentionally off-key. "Her eyes are lakes, along whose edge a velvet green of scum sparkles with insects like a jeweler's tray," for instance, is a blunder. Too many things are happening at once; and though the jeweler's tray is a lively image, the reader is all too likely to be misdirected into responding to the scum around the eyes. Or the trouble comes when elements of a metaphor are not congruent with one another, as in "The feather of smoke above the cabin slowly flapped its wings and disappeared across the winter sky." A feather doesn't have wings, and we can't imagine the flapping of what does not exist. Eliminating the individual feather and making the first part of the image less distinct, however, might make it work: "The feathery smoke above the cabin slowly flapped its wings and disappeared across the winter sky."

In "It Dropped so low—in my Regard" Emily Dickinson insists on having a metaphor two ways and very nearly, if not completely, spoils a poem:

> It dropped so low—in my Regard—
> I heard it hit the Ground—
> And go to pieces on the Stones
> At bottom of my Mind—
>
> Yet blamed the Fate that flung it—*less*   5
> Than I denounced Myself,
> For entertaining Plated Wares
> Upon my Silver Shelf—

"It" is apparently some idea, illusion, or bit of wishful thinking, which is revealed to be false. In stanza 1 it is compared to something fragile, breakable, like glassware: "And go to pieces on the Stones." But in stanza 2 it is compared to merely "Plated Wares": silver plate rather than sterling silver. Such metal can't fall and break, "go to pieces"; rather, it bends or dents. The poem is left with its central metaphor irreconcilably divided against itself.

Metaphor is predominantly visual. The range, however, is from the sharp and colorful, through a variety of the less distinct, to essentially nonvisual images. Muted, vague, shadowy, partial shots (to return to the film analogy) are possible;

soft superimpositions, close-ups, momentary flashes to a different scene. We do, and we do not, *see* something breaking in the first stanza of "It Dropped so low—in my Regard." The difference between "feather of smoke" and "feathery smoke" is largely one of making the image less distinct. Consider Shakespeare's Sonnet 30:

> When to the sessions of sweet silent thought
> I summon up remembrance of things past,
> I sigh the lack of many a thing I sought,
> And with old woes new wail my dear times' waste:
> Then can I drown an eye, unused to flow,   5
> For precious friends hid in death's dateless night,
> And weep afresh love's long since cancelled woe,
> And moan the expense of many a vanished sight:
> Then can I grieve at grievances foregone,
> And heavily from woe to woe tell o'er   10
> The sad account of fore-bemoaned moan,
> Which I new pay as if not paid before.
>> But if the while I think on thee, dear friend,
>> All losses are restored and sorrows end.

Muted in puns, the main pattern of images is a series of legal and quasi-legal terms: "sessions," "summon," "dateless," "cancelled," "expense," "grievances," "account," "pay," "losses," "restored," which together suggest a court proceeding over some financial matter. Only the *tone* comes through, however: a certain judicial solemnity, an irrecoverable loss, some technical injustice, which the miraculous appearance of the "dear friend" overturns. This shadowy story exists more as a quality of the sonnet's diction than as metaphor, and yet it is the sum of a number of passing comparisons. We see no courtroom and, so delicately is it written, are hardly aware of the source of the metaphors.

Metaphorical Implication

Even simple metaphors may work with an almost inexhaustible subtlety and often do much more than either poet or reader may be aware. Consider two poems, two girls, two pairs of metaphors in "A Red, Red Rose" by Robert Burns (1759–1796) and "She Dwelt Among the Untrodden Ways" by Wordsworth. First, the Burns:

> O, my luve's like a red, red rose
> That's newly sprung in June.
> O, my luve's like the melodie
> That's sweetly played in tune.

As fair art thou, my bonnie lass,   5
So deep in luve am I;
And I will luve thee still, my dear,
Till a'° the seas gang° dry.   *all; go*

Till a' the seas gang dry, my dear,
And the rocks melt wi' the sun;   10
And I will luve thee still, my dear,
While the sands o' life shall run.

And fare thee weel, my only luve,
And fare thee weel a while!
And I will come again, my luve,   15
Though it were ten thousand mile!

Focus on the two metaphors in the first stanza. Read the four lines over and over until you can say them with your eyes shut. Relax. Let the associations be visual. Experience them instead of thinking about them.

The metaphors—rose, melody—tell us a good deal about the speaker's affection for, and pleasure in, the girl. They also tell us, I think, more about the girl herself than we realize. We have mentioned such qualities as beautiful, fresh, young, natural, and perhaps sweet-smelling, happy or good-natured, healthy, lively, and maybe passionate. The metaphor of the "melodie" in lines 3–4 might reenforce some of these and incline us to add having a musical voice or being in harmony with herself and her environment. Let me ask you some questions about her, however, which may at first seem silly. Don't try to answer them by thinking, but just see whether an answer comes to you. If one doesn't, don't worry about it. Go from question to question slowly and don't bear down on any of them. Every reader's responses will differ a little because we are going beyond what is really demonstrable to the deep resonances of the images. Most readers, though, will agree on many of the responses. Hard to define though it may be, there will be something like a consensus. Look for what you see just beyond the edge of your field of vision, for what you know just beyond the edge of your knowledge.

> *Is the girl a city girl or a country girl?*
> *Is she an indoor girl or an outdoor girl?*
> *Is she an introvert or an extrovert? quiet or fun-loving? shy or fond of company?*
> *What is her complexion? the color of her hair? Is she slight or robust?*
> *Does she like dancing?*
> *Where is the melody played? indoors or outdoors? by whom? with what instruments?*

This testing of the impressions we carry away from the metaphors is imprecise, and there is surely nothing provable about them; yet we can begin to trace them from things in the poem. Although the two images—rose, melody—are separate, there are perhaps interactions between them. Having visualized the rose outdoors, we may well, lacking anything to prevent it, imagine the melody as played outdoors. The word "melodie" itself suggests that the music is not very sophisticated, so that something like chamber music is unlikely. That it is noteworthy that the melody is "played in tune" (hardly remarkable for accomplished or professional musicians) suggests amateur players. Something about lines 1–2, probably "newly sprung in June," suggests naturalness of growth, like a wild rose, or may at least shield out the impression of a very formal garden or one deliberately cultivated. "Sweetly" and "newly sprung" imply youth and innocence, and they temper somewhat the passionate color of the "red, red rose," so that an impression of the sexuality of the girl is registered but not made much of. The pun in "sprung" perhaps suggests physicality, vigor, liveliness. "Red, red" may suggest rosiness of cheek; not a pale, indoor girl, she is used to the outdoors and sunshine and physical exercise. Is she likely of a darker complexion, dark-haired? The music implies other people, a gathering, doubtless a happy one; and one at which the girl, like the melody, is not far from the center of attention. She is gregarious, then, active, popular, easy in company, and not shy.

Music outdoors, amateur musicians, a fiddle perhaps. Roses. A sociable occasion. A lively, beautiful girl, a "bonnie lass," fond of company. A *country dance?*

Such are the resonances of Burns's metaphors. The "rightness" he probably felt when he wrote these lines (like the "rightness" we feel when we read them) almost certainly derives from a quick, intuitive apprehension of just such accumulating associations and nearly undetectable nuances.

Turn now to Wordsworth's poem: another country girl, another pair of images.

She dwelt among the untrodden ways
    Beside the springs of Dove,
A maid whom there were none to praise
    And very few to love:

A violet by a mossy stone   5
    Half hidden from the eye!
—Fair as a star, when only one
    Is shining in the sky.

She lived unknown, and few could know
    When Lucy ceased to be;   10
But she is in her grave, and, oh,
    The difference to me!

Wordsworth tells us, apart from the two metaphors in stanza 2, a good deal more about Lucy than Burns tells about his lass. But the resonance of the metaphors is no less fascinating. Lucy's beauty is of a very different kind. In contrast to a rose, the violet offers quite other qualities: pale, delicate, quiet, shy, very young, fragile, and, in context, sickly. The moss implies shade, trees, moisture, perhaps a moist spot not far from a stream. We don't see these things, of course, but have a sense of them outside the frame of the picture. The camera is in for a close-up shot, for we see the violet clearly. The moss also implies that the stone is imbedded, not movable. The stone's mass and hardness emphasize, by contrast, the violet's smallness and fragility. Its immobility and mossy age emphasize the violet's sensitivity; its permanence, the violet's youth and transience. The stone is very like (and it would not be irrelevant if we are reminded of) a gravestone. ("Her grave" is in fact mentioned in stanza 3.) The stone also, doubtless, symbolizes the harsh, isolating, and indifferent circumstances of her life. The syntax is ambiguous; we can't conclude whether the violet hides itself or the stone hides it. If she is shy and withdrawn, it is perhaps not altogether by choice.

Another ambiguity links the images of violet and star. Is the violet "Fair as a star"? or is it Lucy, directly, who is "Fair as a star"? It matters little, since the comparison necessarily involves all three, but the ambiguity has the effect of relating violet and star more directly than the images in Burns's first stanza are related. The star is presumably the evening star, at twilight, when it is for a brief time the "only one" before the gathering dark lets other stars be seen. The soft, dusk color of the sky may be pale and violet. And both violet and star are shapes radiating from a center. The fragility of the evening's first star, as it first becomes visible, parallels the delicacy and half-hiddenness of the violet. The transition from violet to star is flawless.

The star adds other qualities to the emotional portrayal of Lucy in these metaphors. Bright, sharp, fine, its beauty is permanent and enduring, though it will soon be "lost" among the many bright stars of the night sky. It is, also, as the violet was not, publicly visible. The transition from violet to star, from close-up to long shot, is itself an image of Lucy's death, her disappearance from earth and reappearance in heaven. So, the poem implies, Lucy's unknown beauty in life was transformed in death to a kind of perfection and permanence. The two couplets seem irreversible, as are Burns's couplets. (Try it.)

Here, at its subtlest, metaphor turns into symbol. The natural object suffices. Things become meanings. Naming creates a world. As John Crowe Ransom noted: "The image cannot be dispossessed of a primordial freshness, which idea can never claim. An idea is derivative and tamed. The image is in the natural or wild state, and it has to be discovered there, not put there, obeying its own law and none of ours."

QUESTIONS AND SUGGESTIONS

1. Make up as many metaphors or similes as you can for a common object (street light, fire plug, telephone pole, dandelion leaves, floor lamp, shoe, cat's eyes, end of a leaf's stem where it connected to its twig, stars, or others). Use the best one in a poem.

2. A metaphor or simile has been omitted from these passages. What comparisons would you choose? (The originals are in Appendix I.)

    a) Raspberries _____, redly in their leaves   [verb]

    b) [of a country funeral procession going up a hill road]

        Four cars like _____
        behind the hearse, old Chevies and a Ford,
        they fluttered up where the land rose out of view

    c) A black fly flew slowly up,
        droning, _____-ing the halves of the air

    d) In a week or two, forsythia
        will shower its peaceful _____
        all over the towns.

    e) The clarinet, a dark tube
        _____ in silver

    f) Big as _____,
        two white launches between water and sky
        march down the bay.

    g) The green creek whirled by a boat's wash
        into _____

    h) Dreams are the soul's _____

3. Study the elements of Pound's "In a Station of the Metro" (page 135). Can you decide whether it is day or night outside the subway station? Clear or rainy? What are the people in the station wearing?

4. In this poem by Rita Dove (b. 1952), notice the similes and metaphors. How are they suitable for the presumably historical speaker? In what ways do they "color" the poem's literal details?

The House Slave

The first horn lifts its arm over the dew-lit grass
and in the slave quarters there is a rustling—
children are bundled into aprons, cornbread

and water gourds grabbed, a salt pork breakfast taken.
I watch them driven into the vague before-dawn   5
while their mistress sleeps like an ivory toothpick

and Massa dreams of asses, rum and slave-funk.
I cannot fall asleep again. At the second horn,
the whip curls across the backs of the laggards—

sometimes my sister's voice, unmistaken, among them.   10
"Oh! pray," she cries. "Oh! pray!" Those days
I lie on my cot, shivering in the early heat,

and as the fields unfold to whiteness,
and they spill like bees among the fat flowers,
I weep. It is not yet daylight.   15

5. Each of these poems is centered in its metaphors. As far as possible, itemize the elements that go into each comparison. Don't quit too soon!

a) *"Taking the Hands"*

ROBERT BLY (b. 1926)

Taking the hands of someone you love,
You see they are delicate cages . . .
Tiny birds are singing
In the secluded prairies
And in the deep valleys of the hand.   5

b) *On Being Served Apples*

BONNIE JACOBSON·

Apples in a deep blue dish
   are the shadows of nuns
Apples in a basket
   are warm red moons on Indian women
Apples in a white bowl   5
   are virgins waiting in snow
Beware of apples on an orange plate:
   they are the anger of wives

c) *Watermelons*

CHARLES SIMIC (b. 1938)

Green Buddhas
On the fruit stand.
We eat the smile
And spit out the teeth.

d) *Waking from Sleep*

ROBERT BLY

Inside the veins there are navies setting forth,
Tiny explosions at the water lines,
And seagulls weaving in the wind of the salty blood.

It is the morning. The country has slept the whole winter.
Window seats were covered with fur skins, the yard was full   5
Of stiff dogs, and hands that clumsily held heavy books.

Now we wake, and rise from bed, and eat breakfast!—
Shouts rise from the harbor of the blood,
Mist, and masts rising, the knock of wooden tackle in the sunlight.

Now we sing, and do tiny dances on the kitchen floor.   10
Our whole body is like a harbor at dawn;
We know that our master has left us for the day.

e) *Outfielder*

STEPHEN DUNN (b. 1939)

So this is excellence: movement
toward the barely possible—
the puma's dream
of running down a hummingbird
on a grassy plain.

f) *Brief Song*

ELTON GLASER (b. 1945)

When love carries us
to this altitude
of lean air, our heads
clear, our hearts
open like parachutes.

g) *The Release*

JOSEPH BRUCHAC   (b. 1942)

At sunset
the shadows of all the trees
break free and go running
across the edge of the world.

h) *Top Model Gives Interview*

JOHN FREDERICK NIMS   (b. 1914)

Fine thigh, fine breasts, fine brow. Thoughts mean and canned.
Poor little she-ape at the Steinway grand.

6. Consider the similes in this poem by Lord Byron. (Sennacherib was a powerful
king of Assyria, 702–680 B.C. See *Isaiah*, chapters 36–37.) Look back at "Very Like
a Whale," page 114; is Nash unfair?

The Destruction of Sennacherib

The Assyrian came down like the wolf on the fold,
And his cohorts were gleaming in purple and gold;
And the sheen of their spears was like stars on the sea,
When the blue wave rolls nightly on deep Galilee.

Like the leaves of the forest when summer is green,   5
That host with their banners at sunset were seen:
Like the leaves of the forest when autumn hath blown,
That host on the morrow lay withered and strown.

For the Angel of Death spread his wings on the blast,
And breathed in the face of the foe as he passed;   10
And the eyes of the sleepers waxed deadly and chill,
And their hearts but once heaved—and for ever grew still!

And there lay the steed with his nostril all wide,
But through it there rolled not the breath of his pride;
And the foam of his gasping lay white on the turf,   15
And cold as the spray of the rock-beating surf.

And there lay the rider distorted and pale,
With the dew on his brow, and the rust on his mail;
And the tents were all silent, the banners alone,
The lances unlifted, the trumpet unblown.   20

And the widows of Ashur are loud in their wail,
And the idols are broke in the temple of Baal;
And the might of the Gentile, unsmote by the sword,
Hath melted like snow in the glance of the Lord!

7. Choose two quite dissimilar things (e.g., *rose* and *snot, book* and *orchard, stone* and *father, car radio* and *cat's face, sunset* and *home run, housefly* and *computer*). In what ways are they nonetheless similar? How might they be compared in a poem? Try a few lines of verse using the comparison.

8. In this fine poem by Robert Francis, how is the comparison of the woman to "an old apple" visually accurate? Tonally suggestive? See if you can decide whether line 8 is literal or metaphorical. Given the poem's subject, what is the effect of the *a a a a* rhyme scheme?

Cadence

Puckered like an old apple she lies abed,
Saying nothing and hearing nothing said,
Not seeing the birthday flowers by her head
To comfort her. She is not comforted.

The room is warm, too warm, but there is chill   5
Over her eyes and over her tired will.
Her hair is frost in the valley, snow on the hill.
Night is falling and the wind is still.

POEMS TO CONSIDER

Sonnet 130   1609

WILLIAM SHAKESPEARE (1564–1616)

My mistress' eyes are nothing like the sun;
Coral is far more red than her lips' red;
If snow be white, why then her breasts are dun;
If hairs be wires, black wires grow on her head.
I have seen roses damasked, red and white,   5
But no such roses see I in her cheeks;
And in some perfumes is there more delight
Than in the breath that from my mistress reeks.
I love to hear her speak, yet well I know
That music hath a far more pleasing sound;   10
I grant I never saw a goddess go;

My mistress, when she walks, treads on the ground:
  And yet, by heaven, I think my love as rare
  As any she belied with false compare.

Icicles   1978

MARK IRWIN*

Slender beards of light
hang from the railing.

My son shows me
their array of sizes:

one oddly shaped,   5
its queer curve,

a clear walrus tooth,
illumined, tinseled.

We watch crystal cones
against blue sky;   10

suddenly some break loose:
an echo of piano notes.

The sun argues
ice to liquid.

Tiny buds of water,   15
pendent on dropper tips,

push to pear shapes:
prisms that shiver silver

in a slight wind
before falling.   20

Look, he says laughing,
a pinocchio nose,

and grabs one
in his tiny hand,

touching the clear carrot,   25
cold to his lips.

Looking for You, Barbara   1976

TED KOOSER (b. 1939)

I have been out looking for you,
Barbara, and as I drove around,
the steering wheel turned through my hands
like a clock. The moon
rolled over the rooftops and was gone.   5

I was dead tired; in my arms
they were rolling the tires inside;
in my legs they were locking the pumps.
Yet what was in me for you
flapped as red in my veins   10
as banners strung over a car lot.

Then I came home and got drunk.
Where were you? 2 A.M.
is full of slim manikins
waving their furs from black windows.   15
My bed goes once more around the block,
and my heart keeps on honking its horn.

A Valediction: Forbidding Mourning   1633

JOHN DONNE (1572–1631)

As virtuous men pass mildly away,
    And whisper to their souls to go,

Whilst some of their sad friends do say
    The breath goes now, and some say, No;

So let us melt, and make no noise,   5
    No tear-floods, nor sigh-tempests move,
'Twere profanation of our joys
    To tell the laity our love.

Moving of th' earth° brings harms and fears,   *earthquakes*
    Men reckon what it did and meant;   10
But trepidation of the spheres°,   *irregular movements in the heavens*
    Though greater far, is innocent.

Dull sublunary° lovers' love   *below the moon; hence,*
    (Whose soul is sense) cannot admit   *subject to change*
Absence, because it doth remove   15
    Those things which elemented° it.   *composed*

But we by a love so much refined
    That our selves know not what it is,
Inter-assured of the mind,
    Care less, eyes, lips, and hands to miss.   20

Our two souls therefore, which are one,
    Though I must go, endure not yet
A breach, but an expansion,
    Like gold to airy thinness beat.

If they be two, they are two so   25
    As stiff twin compasses are two;
Thy soul, the fixed foot, makes no show
    To move, but doth, if th' other do.

And though it in the center sit,
    Yet when the other far doth roam,   30
It leans and hearkens after it,
    And grows erect, as that comes home.

Such wilt thou be to me, who must
    Like th' other foot, obliquely run;
Thy firmness makes my circle just,   35
    And makes me end where I begun.

Reading Plato

JORIE GRAHAM   (b. 1951)

This is the story
    of a beautiful
lie, what slips
    through my fingers,
your fingers. It's winter,   5
    it's far

in the lifespan
    of man.
Bareheaded, in a soiled
    shirt,
speechless, my friend   10
    is making

lures, his hobby. Flies
    so small
he works with tweezers and   15
    a magnifying glass.
They must be
    so believable

they're true—feelers,
    antennae,   20
quick and frantic
    as something
drowning. His heart
    beats wildly

in his hands. It is   25
    blinding
and who will forgive him
    in his tiny
garden? He makes them
    out of hair,   30

deer hair, because it's hollow
    and floats.

Past death, past sight,
    this is
his good idea, what drives   35
    the silly days

together. Better than memory. Better
    than love.
Then they are done, a hook
    under each pair   40
of wings, and it's Spring,
    and the men

wade out into the riverbed
    at dawn. Above,
the stars still connect-up   45
    their hungry animals.
Soon they'll be satisfied
    and go. Meanwhile

upriver, downriver, imagine, quick
    in the air,   50
in flesh, in a blue
    swarm of
flies, our knowledge of
    the graceful

deer skips easily across   55
    the surface.
Dismembered, remembered,
    it's finally
alive. Imagine
    the body   60

they were all once
    a part of,
these men along the lush
    green banks
trying to slip in   65
    and pass

for the natural world.

19 Lake Street

CHASE TWICHELL (b. 1950)

At last the maples
throw off their soft red buds,
and the neighbors emerge
to scrape the lawns.
New mothers wheel their offspring   5
up and down over the curbs,
absorbed by the awkwardness.
And which of all the elements
is the strangest?
The little spirits struggling   10
in their yellow blankets,
the huge trees falling to pieces?
The dismantled, oily parts
of a machine laid out on rags
like a metal picnic?   15
A curtain shivers. Someone is watching
the tulips enlarge in the gardens.
They force their closed,
still colorless flowers
up out of the bare dirt.   20

9

Beyond the Rational:
Burglars and Housedogs

All the arts, poetry among them, are magical. For there is always something that cannot be controled or contrived, something beyond the artist's own powers. Labor at it as he or she may, the best is always what just "comes," what is unpredictable and unexpected. "No surprise for the writer," Robert Frost says, "no surprise for the reader."

The Greeks explained the magic by positing the **Muses,** nine goddesses, the daughters of Zeus and Mnemosyne, whose aid and inspiration poets and musicians invoked. Calliope, Enterpe, Erato, and Polyhymnia were the muses of epic, lyric, love, and sacred poetry. Often the muses were fickle and difficult to please—we hear, even today, the phrase "courting the muse." The Christian and Renaissance explanation was similar: **inspiration** (from Latin, "to be breathed into"). The divine wind blows where it will. The Romantic explanation was **genius,** some freak of nature or of soul. Today the explanation given would probably be the **subconscious,** a bubbling up from the nonrational parts of the mind.

Whether the source be seen as outside or within the poet, these are all explanations that do not explain. "Creative man," C. G. Jung says, "is a riddle that we may try to answer in various ways, but always in vain." The power remains unexpected and mysterious. Randall Jarrell likens it to being struck by lightning. The poet may stand on high ground in a thunderstorm, but nothing guarantees that he or she will be struck. (The public, though, fancies poets who look as if they had been struck often.)

The arts, in their origins, were primitive and no doubt occult. Stone Age humans drew, on the walls of their caves, the beasts they hunted in order to gain some mysterious, ceremonial mastery over them. The oldest poems were the charms, spells, incantations, curses, and prayers that accompanied the magical rites of preliterate cultures. Their function was to ward off evil or cure a toothache or invoke the gods. In *The Origin of Consciousness in the Breakdown of the Bicameral Mind* (1976), Julian Jaynes argues that poetry was originally the "divine knowledge" or "divine hallucinations" of primitive man before the dawn of individual consciousness. "The god-side of our ancient mentality . . . usually, or perhaps always, spoke in verse. . . . Poetry then," he adds, "was the language of the gods."

Children are the most accessible primitives we have, and the old word magic still functions among them. "King's X"—though no modern child has the faintest inkling of its meaning—establishes a truce. "Sticks and stones may break my bones / But words don't hurt a bit" remains a magical incantation against insult. Name magic, primitive man's reluctance to have his name known lest it be used in spells against him, still continues as in "Puddentane, / Ask me again and I'll tell you the same." Children even use poetry as a form of government. "Eenee, meenee, mynee, moe. . . ." Remember? Or "One potato, two potato, three potato, four. . . ." Such charms are part of an oral subculture that children pass along from generation to generation because, like all preliterate peoples, children delight in words, find them powerful, and fear them.

Though we don't admit it, adults aren't much different. There are certain words that everybody knows but can't use in public (and that I can't write here); they are taboo. We use magical words in court and in church and when we quarrel. Toilet walls, like walls of ancient caves, are covered with drawings and runes and rhymes, as Edward Field reports in a poem called "Graffiti":

. . . that whole wall, the size of a school blackboard,
figured over as it was like an oriental temple,
the work of a people, a folk artifact,
the record of lifetimes of secret desires,
the forbidden and real history of man.

Like graffiti, dirty jokes are an ineradicable, subliterary folk art. Not necessarily funnier than clean jokes, they are a way of handling subjects otherwise too hot to handle—to pass on taboo information or to find out things we are too serious about to discuss openly. Safe behind the defensive leer of jokes we can communicate boldly about what we most fear and most desire. Something like this is happening when we avoid the words for dying by using **euphemism,** that is, evasive circumlocutions like "pass on" or (again hiding behind a superior leer) "kick the bucket."

Like those primitive genres, graffiti and dirty jokes, poetry too deals with "hot" subjects. Love and death are its themes. The poem that matters begins always where we are most vulnerable, where we care the most; and it comes, as Richmond Lattimore says in "Verse," "Of some oyster's-irritant, some cinder promoting / iris and spangle." Like whistling in the dark, or talking to yourself, poetry has to do with what troubles us. For the poet, writing is often a process of self-discovery.

A good poem, read again and again over the years, seems magically fresh, saying more each time than we recall, showing itself to us in ever new lights. Passing centuries often do not dim this mysteriously self-renewing energy. We are not mistaken in believing that such poetry comes from, and keeps us in touch with, a fundamental power deep within the human psyche, where dark rivers from time-beyond-memory carve the stone. The sound, "the musical qualities of verse," which T. S. Eliot (1888–1965) calls the **"auditory imagination,"** may be one source of this power. It is, he says,

> the feeling for syllable and rhythm, penetrating far below the conscious levels of thought and feeling, invigorating every word; sinking to the most primitive and forgotten, returning to the origin and bringing something back, seeking the beginning and the end. It works through meanings, certainly, or not without meanings in the ordinary sense, and fuses the old and obliterated and the trite, the current, and the new and surprising, the most ancient and the most civilised mentality.

The age-old forms of language itself, its glacial mass and electrical suddenness, are molds from which every new thought and discovery must take their shapes in our consciouness.

Another source of the inexhaustible energy may be images, literal or metaphorical, which reach beneath consciousness to some magical comprehension deep in our personal and racial memories. Freudian symbols and Jungian arche-types, magic talismans, superstitions, and dreams seem outcroppings of this sub-terranean granite of the human experience.

Poets need not, perhaps should not, concern themselves too directly with these issues. It is enough that the energy exists and that they may, when they are writing well, tap it—as we flip an electric light switch without thinking of the fossils, eons old, the trees and animals that drew energy from the sun, then dissolved into the black lakes and frozen black rivers, from which we in turn draw through dynamos and copper wires light into the lamp on the desk. Certain kinds of poems, however, particularly in the twentieth century, have depended on this ancient, subliminal power in new ways, especially by suppressing the ordinary conscious working of the mind so that the profound effects of language and images may be more direct. Eliot describes the assumptions:

> The chief use of the "meaning" of a poem, in the ordinary sense, may be (for here again I am speaking of some kinds of poetry and not all) to satisfy one habit of the reader, to keep his mind diverted and quiet, while the poem does its work upon him: much as the imaginary burglar is always provided with a bit of nice meat for

the house-dog. This is a normal situation of which I approve. But the minds of all poets do not work that way; some of them, assuming that there are other minds like their own, become impatient of this "meaning" which seems superfluous, and perceive possibilities of intensity through its elimination.

Eliot's *The Waste Land* is an extreme example of such a poem, in which the "habits" of narrative or argument (in the sense of sequential thinking) have been suppressed in favor of a succession of characters, voices, scenes, fragments of scenes, images, quotations, allusions, snippets.

It seems true enough that we are not merely or exclusively rational creatures, that we often think and feel by leaps and intuitions, and that the subterranean or subconscious levels of our being—that part of the mind that is awake and dreaming even when we sleep—cannot be ignored. Rational control is sometimes dangerous repression. On the other hand, we *are* also rational, conscious beings. Order, as much as impulse, is part of our nature. Shaking down sensations and impressions into some logical or narrative form often has great value.

The danger of what may be loosely called the nonrational in poetry—whether in whole poems or in parts—is obscurity. Giving up or going beyond conscious order, the poet must assume that other sensibilities are enough like his or her own to respond to or follow the kind of irrational "order" it is establishing. If the poet errs in this assumption or fails somehow to accomplish what he or she thinks is being done, the incomprehensible poetry resulting will be private in the worst sense; that is, only the poet will understand it. The risk will often be worth taking, but the poet should get the best advice he or she can. ("Well, my friend said it makes sense to him," is not enough.) Later, if not sooner, a good reader's conscious mind will want to satisfy itself about the kind of experience the poem is. We must feel convinced of its "rightness." This is perhaps what Wallace Stevens meant when he remarked, "Poetry must resist the intelligence almost successfully."

"Logic of Metaphor"

Metaphor itself, even at its simplest, always touches the nonrational. "The clock has hands" will seem, depending on how we look at it, either plain everyday sense or somewhat frighteningly surreal. Metaphor compares, and common sense or reason quickly justifies it. We perceive the likenesses, the grounds of the comparison—or enough of them—and so assimilate the metaphor as a perfectly comprehensible part of whatever sort of sense the poem is making. When the comparison is extended beyond the ready likenesses, however, or when metaphors multiply one on the other, they may begin to make a kind of sense of their own. For Dylan Thomas, for instance, metaphor sometimes seemed almost a language in itself. The resulting poems, though comprehensible, seem more nonrational than rational in method. Here is Thomas's description of his process:

I make one image—though "make" is not the word; I let, perhaps, an image be "made" emotionally in me and then apply to it what intellectual and critical forces I possess; let it breed another, let that image contradict the first, make the third image, bred out of the other two together, a fourth contradictory image, and let them all, within my imposed formal limits, conflict. Each image holds within it the seed of its own destruction, and my dialectical method, as I understand it, is a constant building up and breaking down of the images that comes out of the central seed, which is itself destructive and constructive at the same time. . . . Out of the inevitable conflict of images—inevitable, because of the creative, recreative, destructive and contradictory nature of the motivating centre, the womb of war—I try to make that momentary peace which is a poem.

Thomas is describing a self-breeding series of **associations**—one image suggesting another in memory or imagination—with the images, in their sequence, replacing rational or discursive ways of saying something. The poet's "intellectual and critical forces," notice, are not suspended, but work only beneath the poem's metaphorical surface to control and direct it. When the method fails and the poet has not arranged the images so that a reader's responses follow them naturally, the result is impenetrable obscurity. When it succeeds, it produces poems of great compressive power, like this poem by Dylan Thomas:

Twenty-Four Years

Twenty-four years remind the tears of my eyes.
(Bury the dead for fear that they walk to the grave in labour.)
In the groin of the natural doorway I crouched like a tailor
Sewing a shroud for a journey
By the light of the meat-eating sun.   5
Dressed to die, the sensual strut begun,
With my red veins full of money,
In the final direction of the elementary town
I advance for as long as forever is.

This is a birthday poem, and in line 1 the speaker refers to the reminiscences such an occasion may initiate. But they are not happy memories ("tears"), and in the parenthetical line 2 he dismisses such losses, perhaps the loss of persons he loved ("the dead"). Several things are happening at once in the line, but they can be sorted out. The reason for putting aside the reminiscences is to prevent that sadness from troubling "the dead," from making their deaths a "labour." Perhaps by "the dead" he means only "our dead selves, the selves we were in the past." The line might be paraphrased, if so: "Forget the past and its sadness lest it make those who are aging and dying, that is, walking to the grave, suffer needlessly." The "walk to the grave," of course, becomes the poem's central image: life as a journey "In the final direction of the elementary town," which is apparently death (elementary in the sense of simple, reduced-to-elements). "Labour" is chosen as the image for distress because it suggests hardship but also because it suggests the pain of childbirth.

Line 3 describes the child in the womb, in the fetal position ("crouched like a tailor"). Thomas reverses the clearer "In the natural doorway of the groin," making it "In the groin of the natural doorway," in order to recall the architectural sense of "groin" (the curved line or edge formed by the intersection of two vaults or arches), a term frequently used of church architecture and so adding a religious overtone. "Labour" in line 2 makes the image of the tailor crouched over his sewing appropriate; it also suggests that the fetus in some sense shared in the "labour" of his own birth. The "shroud" he sews is perhaps his skin, or more generally the awareness of death (which birth necessarily implies). Hence, in line 6, when the poem returns to the present tense, he is "Dressed to die." The sun is "meat-eating" in its strength and symbolizes the natural forces, time or decay, to which life in the flesh is subject.

Nonetheless, in the poem's last four lines, the feeling is the buoyant one of youth. The journey is a "sensual strut"; and "my red veins full of money" images the excitement of having life and vigor to spend. Death as "the elementary town" seems no longer particularly frightening. "Town" suggests life, a community; and for the moment, only the "direction" is "final." The bravery of the last line ("I advance") is muted somewhat by the paradox of "for as long as forever is," which implies that "forever" has in fact a limited duration—for the speaker it may be only as long as his life is. The poem's loose pattern of linking rhymes—labour-tailor-jour-, journey-money, mon-sun-begun-town—is framed by eyes-is and seems as circular, open, as the poem's theme.

Thomas's language of metaphor—little in the poem is literal—is essentially traditional (life is a journey), but the force of its jostling images seems more primitive. The landscape is biological. The self is alone. Even the social convention of money seems detached from its everyday uses. The difference I am pointing to may be seen by comparing Thomas's compound metaphors with Shakespeare's compound metaphors in Macbeth:

To-morrow, and to-morrow, and to-morrow
Creeps in this petty pace from day to day
To the last syllable of recorded time;
And all our yesterdays have lighted fools
The way to dusty death. Out, out, brief candle!   5
Life's but a walking shadow, a poor player
That struts and frets his hour upon the stage
And then is heard no more. It is a tale
Told by an idiot, full of sound and fury,
Signifying nothing.   10

For all his isolating guilt, Macbeth seems a man talking to men and women; he is a member of a social fabric which, though stretched, does not tear. By contrast, Thomas's poem seems barbaric, private, dreamlike.

Surreality

Influenced by psychology, our usual analogy for the nonrational in twentieth-century poetry is the dream. A French movement of the 1920s, **Surrealism,** has given us a word that sums up the artistic applications of the unconscious: **surreal.** The unconscious, free-associative, nonrational modes of thought (intuition, feeling, fantasy, imagination) put us in touch with a *surreality*, literally, a *super*reality. It includes both the inner and the outer world, dream and reality, the flux of sensations or feelings and the hard, daylight facts of experience. In theory the rational is not so much dismissed as transcended, or absorbed.

The term *surreal* has been used so widely and so loosely that it means little more than, in some positive sense, nonrational; in any event, the poet is less interested in definitions than in the fresh possibilities for handling experience or feeling in poems. Consider this poem by Mark Strand:

Eating Poetry

Ink runs from the corners of my mouth.
There is no happiness like mine.
I have been eating poetry.

The librarian does not believe what she sees.
Her eyes are sad   5
and she walks with her hands in her dress.

The poems are gone.
The light is dim.
The dogs are on the basement stairs and coming up.

Their eyeballs roll,   10
their blond legs burn like brush.
The poor librarian begins to stamp her feet and weep.

She does not understand.
When I get on my knees and lick her hand,
she screams.   15

I am a new man.
I snarl at her and bark.
I romp with joy in the bookish dark.

Almost without thinking, the reader knows what is happening. The speaker has been delightedly reading poems in a library—"eating" them, that is, literally taking them into himself as one ingests food, turning them into his own substance. They make him happy. The librarian, by contrast, is a figure of disapproval, sad, uncomprehending, repressed ("her hands in her dress"). Having been "eaten," the poems are "gone." But the dogs—the feelings or meanings freed by the poems—"are on the basement stairs and coming up," presumably from the *sub*conscious. They are emotional, excited, beautiful. The librarian is angry and frustrated by their rowdy intrusion. Trying to appease her, the speaker tries to communicate his joy and fellow feeling, to make her understand. Freed himself, doglike happy with released feelings, he only scares her: "When I get on my knees and lick her hand, / she screams." He snarls and barks and romps with joy: "I am a new man." The poem affirms the transforming power of poems.

The poem is clearly a metaphorical fantasy. The point is not what literally occurred between the speaker and the librarian—probably nothing much, perhaps no more than his sensing or imagining her disapproval—but the feeling of the experience. The individual happiness of reading poems is somehow at odds with the impersonal, overdisciplined effect of a library. The poem's dreamlike, arbitrary fantasy (why dogs?) will not bother the reader for whom it is simply "right."

The nonrational poem can register that edge of consciousness where the mind plays tricks on us. The leaves, stems, and flowers of a curtain suddenly seem to be faces—one, then another, and so on. At a concert we suddenly find ourselves fantasizing that we are the conductor or the soprano anxious about the moment when we shall begin to sing. In a strange room we suddenly have the feeling that we have been there before—*déjà vu*. In this poem by Charles Simic (b. 1938) the speaker is taking a nap with a woman he loves. It is after lunch, and the "lazy rustle" of leaves has made them sleepy. For no particular reason, or for no reason in the poem at least, the speaker finds himself imagining a prisoner, who is imagining them.

The Prisoner

He is thinking of us.
These leaves, their lazy rustle
That made us sleepy after lunch
So we had to lie down.

He considers my hand on her breast,   5
Her closed eyelids, her moist lips

Against my forehead, and the shadows of trees
Hovering on the ceiling.

It's been so long. He has trouble
Deciding what else is there.   10
And all along the suspicion
That we do not exist.

The imaginary prisoner is perhaps the dozy speaker's awareness of his good fortune—lunch, summery trees, a woman he loves, which, for a prisoner, would be
something like paradise—and his awareness of the precariousness of such happiness. In stanza 1 the lovers are "us," "we." But in stanza 2, possibly as she has drifted
off to sleep, it becomes "my hand on her breast," not on "your breast." The lovers
have drifted apart into separate consciousnesses, and in his unease and isolation,
the half-awake speaker responds to his own immediate experience at a distance, in
the perspective of the imaginary prisoner: "He considers my hand on her breast, /
Her closed eyelids. . . ."

In stanza 3 the speaker almost becomes the prisoner: "It's been so long" is the
prisoner's awareness, duplicating in some way the speaker's own deep disbelief in
his happiness. As he slips toward sleep, the speaker's loosening sense of his
surroundings becomes the prisoner's difficulty in imagining the background of his
fantasy of the lovers: "He has trouble / Deciding what else is there." And the
speaker's inner distrust of his reality becomes the imaginary prisoner's suspicion of
his imaginary lovers: "And all along the suspicion / That we do not exist." The
communal "we" reappears in the last line only to negate its reality: "That we do not
exist."

The prisoner, we realize, has been all along a projection of the speaker
himself, of some deep fear or self-doubt that will not allow him to accept his real
experience for what it is. Isolated in his own consciousness and in his own history,
he is "The Prisoner" of the title. In the dim, unguarded moments between his
wakefulness and sleep, we know the truth about him and, in some measure, about
ourselves.

The strangeness in the commonplace, or the strangeness in us sometimes as we
observe the commonplace, makes the world more mysterious. Looking into a
shoe-repair shop window at night, the poet may begin to be aware of the strange
travels and history that bring the shoes to this place (W. S. Merwin, "Shoe
Repairs," page 274). Looking at an iris, the poet may see the dark curve of the
anther as tracks, as a train driving "deep into the damp heart of its stem." And he
may then recall a train journey he took as a boy with his grandmother and (perhaps
from a film or who knows where) the image of a boy on a French railway platform
holding an iris and "waving goodbye to a grandmother"—until reality is lost in the
connections the mind makes (David St. John, "Iris," page 282). Imagining what it
must be like inside a stone, "cool and quiet / Even though a cow steps on it

full weight," the poet remembers that "sparks fly out / When two stones are rubbed" and thinks that "perhaps it is not dark inside after all; / Perhaps there is a moon shining" (Charles Simic, "Stone," page 24). The poet may find in old "Chevrolet wheels . . . / Lying on their backs in the cindery dirt," in "shredded inner tubes abandoned on the shoulders of thruways," in "curly steel shavings . . . on garage benches," and in the "roads in South Dakota that feel around in the darkness . . .," personifications of his despair about the America of the Vietnam War years (Robert Bly, "Come with Me," page 280). Like talking to ourselves, such a fantasy may express the deepest and most serious feeling; we reveal ourselves in daydreams no less than in sleeping dreams.

Nonsense and Serious Nonsense

When the fantasy goes beyond our ability to rationalize it, to explain its symbolical equivalence, it becomes nonsense, as in nursery rhymes or the tra-la-la's of song. This need not mean that nonsense-poems have no meaning or significance, only that we can't specify or point to it with much confidence. Nonsense, of course, may often just be pleasurable in itself, for instance, in the happy non sequiturs of this quatrain by the nineteenth-century primitive, William McGonagall (1830–1902):

The Hen it is a noble beast,
The Cow is more forlorner
Standing in the rain
With a leg at every corner.

But in the Age of Freud, who knows what hidden feelings (rebellious or sexual) find their expression when we hear "the cow jumped over the moon" or "the dish ran away with the spoon"?

A familiar example, by Lewis Carroll (1832–1898):

Jabberwocky

'Twas brillig, and the slithy toves
　　Did gyre and gimble in the wabe;
All mimsy were the borogoves,
　　And the mome raths outgrabe.

"Beware the Jabberwock, my son! 　　　　　　　　　　　　5
　　The jaws that bite, the claws that catch!
Beware the Jubjub bird, and shun
　　The frumious Bandersnatch!"

He took his vorpal sword in hand:
    Long time the manxome foe he sought—   10
So rested he by the Tumtum tree,
    And stood awhile in thought.

And as in uffish thought he stood,
    The Jabberwock, with eyes of flame,
Came whiffling through the tulgey wood,   15
    And burbled as it came!

One, two! One, two! And through and through
    The vorpal blade went snicker-snack!
He left it dead, and with its head
    He went galumphing back.   20

"And hast thou slain the Jabberwock?
    Come to my arms, my beamish boy!
O frabjous day! Callooh! Callay!"
    He chortled in his joy.

'Twas brillig, and the slithy toves   25
    Did gyre and gimble in the wabe;
All mimsy were the borogoves,
    And the mome raths outgrabe.

Whatever it is, this is not the recognizable world in which we live. Humpty Dumpty's explanation, "Well, 'slithy' means 'lithe and slimy' . . . there are two meanings packed up in one word," doesn't get us very far. Nor does Carroll's explanation of "frumious" as combining "fuming" and "furious." Even if it were possible to satisfactorily explain all the strange, made-up words, we wouldn't be likely to bother, preferring to leave them unsolved and wonderful. *That* is precisely why we like the poem. The story is clear enough: a boy slays the dreaded Jabberwock. It is unquestionably archetypal, like David and Goliath. (**Archetype:** a symbol of very general or mythical familiarity.) It doesn't matter much whether we know who the "beamish boy" is, nor what evil fellow the Jabberwock is, nor why the boy searches out the Jabberwock rather than the Jubjub bird or the "frumious Bandersnatch." Neither are we much worried that the Jubjub and Bandersnatch survive. It's rather pleasant and scary to know that there are still some evil fellows out there for another day. John Ciardi's suggestion that "Jabberwocky" is a satire of the pompous bugaboos "of a great deal of Victorian morality and social pretense" is a good one. But the happy nonsense survives its explanations with some irreducible meaning of its own.

    Kenneth Koch (b. 1925) is the author of this zany contemporary nonsense:

You Were Wearing

You were wearing your Edgar Allan Poe printed cotton blouse.
In each divided up square of the blouse was a picture of Edgar Allan Poe.
Your hair was blonde and you were cute. You asked me, "Do most boys
    think that most girls are bad?"
I smelled the mould of your seaside resort hotel bedroom on your hair
    held in place by a John Greenleaf Whittier clip.
"No," I said, "it's girls who think that boys are bad." Then we read
    Snowbound together   5
And ran around in an attic, so that a little of the blue enamel was scraped
    off my George Washington, Father of His Country, shoes.

Mother was walking in the living room, her Strauss Waltzes comb in her
    hair.
We waited for a time and then joined her, only to be served tea in cups
    painted with pictures of Herman Melville
As well as with illustrations from his book *Moby Dick* and from his
    novella, *Benito Cereno.*
Father came in wearing his Dick Tracy necktie: "How about a drink,
    everyone?"   10
I said, "Let's go outside a while." Then we went onto the porch and sat
    on the Abraham Lincoln swing.
You sat on the eyes, mouth, and beard part, and I sat on the knees.
In the yard across the street we saw a snowman holding a garbage can lid
    smashed into a likeness of the mad English king, George the Third.

We almost recognize this as a scene from the world we live in, but things keep
going wrong with that perception. There are (or were) sweatshirts with the likeness
of Beethoven on them, but the rest? "Edgar Allan Poe printed cotton blouse,"
"John Greenleaf Whittier" hair-clip, "George Washington, Father of His Country,
shoes," and "Abraham Lincoln" porch swing? People don't sit on porch swings
when there are snowmen.

    The poem's oddness resists the reader's intelligence fairly successfully. The
unseasonal porch swing and the speaker's morbid as well as unseasonal smelling
"the mould of your seaside resort hotel bedroom on your hair," have a peculiar,
disconnected quality. He and the girl run around "in *an* attic," not in *the* attic as we
might expect. It is all rather dreamlike. We may guess that the poem is a satire on a
certain kind of culturally pretentious family, or on American culture itself (with its
repressive notion of sexuality). But it might as easily be praising the variety (*Moby
Dick* and the comic strip's Dick Tracy) and inimitable independence of American
culture—hence, the battered garbage can lid that looks like George the Third. The
poem seems, to borrow Eliot's phrase, "not without meanings in the ordinary

sense," but it nonetheless evades them, returning the reader to its amusing and enigmatic surface. The touch is high Buster Keaton.

The power of language allows the juxtaposition of all sorts of things, from the palpably untrue to the delectably outrageous. "He awoke in the morning, the early sunlight filtering through the locust, and saw a pterodactyl perched on the roof of his neighbor's house." "A dandelion grew out of Mary's ear. It was very pretty but it kept scratching her." "The Jabberwock, with eyes of flame, came whiffling through the tulgey wood." The parts of language are interchangeable. Strung together in predictable ways, they make recognizable sense: "The blue jay flew up to the tree." Strung together in unusual, surprising ways, they make non-sense: "The tree flew up to the blue jay." The habit of language gives such non-sense at least a momentary credibility; it sounds as if it might be true, until we test it. When, for whatever reason, we find we *like* it, such non-sense becomes nonsense. Like the nonsense of dreams, recombining the stuff of our real experience in crazy ways, it may be somehow significant.

Nonsense may be serious as well as comic. This poem by John Ashbery (b. 1927), for example. ("Lacustrine" means "of or pertaining to a lake; living or occurring on or in lakes, as various animals and plants; formed at the bottom or along the shore of lakes, as geological strata.")

These Lacustrine Cities

These lacustrine cities grew out of loathing
Into something forgetful, although angry with history.
They are the product of an idea: that man is horrible, for instance,
Though this is only one example.

They emerged until a tower   5
Controlled the sky, and with artifice dipped back
Into the past for swans and tapering branches,
Burning, until all that hate was transformed into useless love.

Then you are left with an idea of yourself
And the feeling of ascending emptiness of the afternoon   10
Which must be charged to the embarrassment of others
Who fly by you like beacons.

The night is a sentinel.
Much of your time has been occupied by creative games
Until now, but we have all-inclusive plans for you.   15
We had thought, for instance, of sending you to the middle of the desert,

To a violent sea, or of having the closeness of the others be air
To you, pressing you back into a startled dream

As sea-breezes greet a child's face.
But the past is already here, and you are nursing some private project.   20

The worst is not over, yet I know
You will be happy here. Because of the logic
Of your situation, which is something no climate can outsmart.
Tender and insouciant by turns, you see

You have built a mountain of something,   25
Thoughtfully pouring all your energy into this single monument,
Whose wind is desire starching a petal,
Whose disappointment broke into a rainbow of tears.

This sounds as if it makes sense. The sentences go on as if confident they are say-ing something. The tone is clear and logical: "for instance, / Though this is only one example." Flickers of recognition or familiarity keep the reader going forward. But who the apparently trapped "you" is and who the controlling, apparently malevolent "we" are, or what and where "These lacustrine cities" are, cannot be inferred from the poem. Like a dream, the closed system of the poem makes its own kind of sense, if it makes sense at all. Elsewhere, in a poem called "What Is Poetry," Ashbery speaks of "Trying to avoid / Ideas, as in this poem." As Paul Carroll notes in a fine essay on Ashbery's "Leaving the Atocha Station" (in *The Poem in Its Skin,* Big Table, 1968), "multiple combinations of words and images (islands of significance) continually form, dissolve, and reform." The invitation is, Carroll argues, for the reader to become a poet "helping to create" the poem.

Such poems are analogous to abstract art—words and images, even whole sentences, used for their tone and color rather than for their representation. Or they are analogous to music. Ashbery has said:

> I feel I could express myself best in music. What I like about music is its ability of being convincing, of carrying an argument through successfully to the finish, though the terms of this argument remain unknown quantities. What remains is the structure, the architecture of the argument, scene or story. I would like to do this in poetry.

Often, in such poems, we intuit the intended feeling easily enough but, being unsure of the literal circumstances that cause the feeling, we must remain unsure of its appropriateness. In William Carlos Williams's wonderful "Great Mullen," for instance, we overhear a lively quarrel in a meadow. The antagonists seem to be a mullen (or mullein, a weed of the figwort family), a drop of dew on a blade of grass, and a cricket. But it is impossible to tell exactly which speaker says what.

Great Mullen

One leaves his leaves at home
being a mullen and sends up a lighthouse
to peer from: I will have my way,
yellow—A mast with a lantern, ten
fifty, a hundred, smaller and smaller   5
as they grow more—Liar, liar, liar!
You come from her! I can smell djer-kiss
on your clothes. Ha, ha! you come to me,
you—I am a point of dew on a grass-stem.
Why are you sending heat down on me   10
from your lantern?—You are cowdung, a
dead stick with the bark off. She is
squirting on us both. She has had her
hand on you!—well?—She has defiled
ME.—Your leaves are dull, thick   15
and hairy.—Every hair on my body will
hold you off from me. You are a
dungcake, birdlime on a fencerail.—
I love you, straight, yellow
finger of God pointing to—her!   20
Liar, broken weed, dungcake, you have—
I am a cricket waving his antennae
and you are high, grey and straight. Ha!

The dashes, which suggest interruptions, and the frequent uncertainty about
who is speaking, convey the agitation of the quarrel. In the first lines the mullen
seems to be speaking, defending its uprightness by describing its tall stalk and
bubbling of yellow flowers. The sea imagery ("lighthouse," "A mast with a lantern") and the mullen's arch tone in referring to itself ("One leaves his leaves at
home / being a mullen") show the aloofness the mullen feels—or pretends to
feel—toward the common meadow and its other inhabitants.

Most of the rest of the poem is spoken by the other voices, the drop of dew and
the cricket. "Liar, liar, liar!" says the drop of dew. Far from being lofty and pure,
these voices insist, the mullen is earthbound and impure. Its light falls not on the
vastness of the sea, but on "a point of dew on a grass-stem." And it is not light, but
heat, that the mullen sheds: "Why are you sending heat down on me / from your
lantern?" The other voices emphasize, not the mullen's stalk and flowers, but the
rosette of flat, homely, woolly leaves at its base, which are likened to a pat of
"cowdung" and, later, to "dungcake, birdlime on a fencerail." The insults and
mockery of the other voices reprove the mullen's pretentiousness and recall it to its
base, earthy origin. It is, after all, a weed.

But who is the "She" referred to in the accusations? "You come from her! I can smell djer-kiss / on your clothes." "She has had her / hand on you!—well?—She has defiled / ME." In the context of the meadow she might well be the earth herself, from which the mullen, with its tall stalk and sea imagery, has been trying to dissociate itself. The stalk, of course, points both away from and down to its earthy origins:

> I love you, straight, yellow
> finger of God pointing to—her!

The other voice expresses, in addition to fiercely ironic reproof ("pointing to—her!"), its affection for the wayward mullen ("I love you").

More, nonetheless, seems involved in the scene than analysis accounts for. The characterization of the mullen as masculine gives the accusations a tone of anger at a sexual betrayal: "You come from her! I can smell djer-kiss / on your clothes." It helps to know that, as Williams explained, " 'djer-kiss' was when I wrote the poem, the name of a very popular perfume with which ladies used to scent their lingerie." A feeling of infidelity and jealousy permeates the poem, but analysis can take the matter no further than that. The poem remains a poem about a quarrel in a meadow, comic and, in some untraceable way, also very much more than comic. What it all stands for we might guess, but could never be certain of were it not for the poet's having told us, much later:

> It is a poem which technically I treasure as among one of my best though most unusual. . . . The dialogue is correctly assumed to be between a young poet and his wife, with whom he is deeply in love but to whom he has been unfaithful—in the way a man and woman in the modern world often are. The reference to ejecta, "birdlime" etc., is disgust with himself—but he will not evade speaking of it. God be my witness!

From the enigmatic playfulness of nursery rhymes to the abstract formalism of "These Lacustrine Cities" or the encoded seriousness of "Great Mullen," poetry has always been in some deep way nonrational. The subliminal powers of rhythm and image are as ancient as language itself; the poet-shaman, a traditional figure. But after Freud, the woods of fantasy and the Alps of dream seem neither more nor less than parts of the everyday world in which we live.

A Note on Humor

As William Hazlitt noted in 1819, "Man is the only animal that laughs and weeps; for he is the only animal that is struck with the difference between what things are, and what they ought to be . . . To explain the nature of laughter and tears, is to account for the condition of human life."

We properly give greater weight to the tears—what is serious, solemn, sublime—than to what is funny. This is an ancient bias, which led Aristotle to give precedence to tragedy over comedy. Tragedy imitates noble actions, while comedy dramatizes the ludicrous and foolish. Comedy aims at representing men as worse, tragedy as better than in actual life. Yet laughter has its part. More than just the cleansing laughter that rebukes folly, we know the laughters of innocent mirth and pleasure, of relief, of reconciliation. The marriages at the end of A Midsummer Night's Dream are not perfect and permanent in the way that the deaths at the end of King Lear or Antigone are, but they are better models of the fallability and the ever-renewed going-on of our real lives.

In poetry, this natural bias toward the serious became, in the last century, almost an unnatural exclusion of the comic. That great Victorian, Matthew Arnold, claiming for poetry only the loftiest truth of "high seriousness," clubbed even the generous and humane Chaucer and ended by declaring that "Dryden and Pope are not classics of our poetry, they are classics of our prose." In Arnold's wake, in 1867, the English poet Frederick Locker-Lampson distinguished between "poetry" and, coining the phrase, "light verse." He saw it as "another kind of poetry . . . which, in its more restricted form, has somewhat the same relation to the poetry of lofty imagination and deep feeling, that the Dresden China Shepherds and Shepherdesses of the last century bear to the sculpture of Donatello and Michael Angelo." Though Locker-Lampson meant the term *light verse* as praise of sorts, his distinction has turned into a villainous Mr. Hyde, dividing poetry (seriousness) from mere light verse (humor). In cahoots with the twentieth-century Dracula of obsessive and intellectual criticism (which essentially holds that no ordinary reader can really read a poem, novel, or play on his or her own), Locker-Lampson's distinction has been devastating. Laughter and light-heartedness have virtually been dismissed from among the emotions proper to literature. Poetry, struggling on as *heavy* verse, has lost touch with the general reader. And light verse—after several great generations of its own: from Edward Lear, C. S. Calverley, Lewis Carroll, and W. S. Gilbert in England to Robert W. Service, Don Marquis, Dorothy Parker, Phyllis McGinley, Cole Porter, and Ogden Nash in America—has fallen into the shadows: isolated, trivialized. There's not a shred, not a line of Ogden Nash in the 1456 pages of that giant tombstone, The Norton Anthology of Modern Poetry.

As long as there is laughter and as long as there is verse, of course, someone will always be bringing the two together. A comic tradition that includes Chaucer, Shakespeare, Pope, and Byron isn't about to vanish. Poets have gone on being funny from time to time, as the reader of this book will have observed. But it may be useful to nudge the beginning poet: it is all right to be, on occasion, droll, amusing, merry, witty, jocular, ribald, satiric, or boisterous. All poems, thank goodness, can't be Hamlet or "Ode to a Nightingale." As Pound's Propertius asks (page 407), "But for something to read in normal circumstances? / For a few pages brought down from the forked hill unsullied?" When you are in love, write love poems. When you grieve, write poems of sorrow. When you are feeling silly and notice a good pun, write

A River Rhyme

WILLIAM COLE   (b. 1919)

It was floodtime on the Seine:
Flotsam, jetsam, garbage, then
Five cats clinging to a plank—
Un, deux, trois cats sank!

Or:

The Owl

ROBERT N. FEINSTEIN   (b. 1915)

Though I don't wish to seem too fanatical,
I consider the owl ungrammatical.
"To-whit, to-who" he sits and keens;
"To-whit, to-*whom*" is what he means.

(**Pun:** using a word so as to suggest two quite incongruous meanings or applications at once. Example: telling a condemned man at the gibbet that he'll get the *hang* of it.)

In general, comedy depends upon perceiving some incongruity or disproportion (man in top hat slips on banana peel). It may involve, say, the taking literally of something that is meant figuratively, as in this parody of an Elizabethan sonnet by Wendy Cope (b. 1945). (Strugnell is a fictitious poet; Sir Philip Sidney, of course, was the Elizabethan sonneteer.)

Strugnell's Bargain

My true love hath my heart and I have hers:
We swapped last Tuesday and we felt elated
But now, whenever one of us refers
To "my heart," things get rather complicated.
Just now, when she complained "My heart is racing,"   5
"You mean *my* heart is racing," I replied.
"That's what I said." "You mean the heart replacing
Your heart my love." "Oh piss off, Jake!" she cried.
I ask you, do you think Sir Philip Sidney

Got spoken to like that? And I suspect   10
If I threw in my liver and a kidney
She'd still address me with as scant respect.
Therefore do I revoke my opening line:
My love can keep her heart and I'll have mine.

The joke, equally, may be on the reader or hearer, who is momentarily conned into misunderstanding, as in this dry little poem by Edward Willey (b. 1933):

Family Eccentric

Marie is bald and doesn't
give a damn. To prove it
she often spits in public
and hates to wear a hat.

I hope she changes   5
for the better before
she learns to talk.

Or the pleasure may be largely formal, as often with limericks, with Broadway show tunes, or with clerihews. Named for its inventor, Edmund Clerihew Bentley (1875–1956), the **clerihew** is a comic form of four lines of irregular length, of which the first line is (or ends with) the name of a famous person or historical character. The rhyme scheme is *a a b b*, and the fun is rhyming on the proper name—and somehow making a pertinent comment on the personage. Here are several:

Zane Grey
Struck pay
Dirt and
Quicksand.

Paul Curry Steele   (b. 1928)

Leach, Alexander Archibald
has long been called
more elegant-
ly, Cary Grant.

Anonymous

St. Jerome
abandoned brush and comb

and bread and jam and everything nice.
He did it on divine advice.

Vonna Adrian   (b. 1906)

The range of humor is very wide, from verbal wit (like puns) to the comedy of character (Chaucer's Wife of Bath, Shakespeare's Falstaff, Katharyn Machan Aal's "Hazel Tells Laverne," page 197). What's funny may mingle with the lyrical, as in Howard Nemerov's "Learning by Doing" (page 85), or may be in its own way grim and serious enough, as in this meditation by William Trowbridge (b. 1941):

Enter Dark Stranger

In "Shane," when Jack Palance first appears,
a stray cur takes one look and slinks away
on tiptoes, able, we understand, to recognize
something truly dark. So it seems when we
appear, crunching through the woods. A robin   5
cocks her head, then hops off,
ready to fly like hell and leave us the worm.
A chipmunk, peering out from his hole beneath
a maple root, crash dives when he hears
our step. The alarm sounds everywhere. Squirrels,   10
finches, butterflies flee for their lives. Imagine
a snail picking up the hems of his shell
and hauling ass for cover. He's studied carnivores,
seen the menu, noticed the escargots.

But forget Palance, who would have murdered Alabama   15
just for fun. Think of Karloff's monster,
full of lonely love but too hideous
to bear; or Kong, bereft with Fay Wray
shrieking in his hand: the flies buzz our heads
like angry biplanes, and the ants hoist pitchforks   20
to march on our ankles as we watch the burgher's daughter
bob downstream in a ring of daisies.

With its often cartoony diction (the chipmunk that "crash dives," that snail in the colloquial phrase "picking up the hems of his shell / and hauling ass for cover"), this is a wonderfully comic vision of the human, seeing us among the creatures like the movies' Frankenstein or King Kong. But it is also a sad and pitying vision. The comic distortion of reality is not in the poem, we recognize, but in our usual sense of human benevolence and well-being—as we gnaw and trample our way through the creation.

If literature is a mirror in which we may see ourselves, the comic is no more dispensable than the sublime or the tragic.

QUESTIONS AND SUGGESTIONS

1. Imagine that you are a blade of grass, a house, a daisy by an alley, a brick in a sidewalk, a mountain, or a basketball. What might it *feel* like (specific sensations like the touch of air, ground, a hand)? What has its experience been? What might it be aware of? Write a poem in the first person, pretending to be that object.

2. Write down a column of arbitrary rhyme words. Fill in the poem with images and sentences, saying anything at all that pops into your head. Don't try to make sense, but make it sound good. *Now* read it over and over aloud, think about it. Does it make any sense? Does it have anything to do with whatever else you have been thinking and feeling?

3. In this poem how does W. S. Merwin deftly prepare the reader for the poem's leap from the picture of the nighttime shoe repair shop (stanzas 1–2) to the image of it as an "Ark" into which "in another life" we will step down (stanza 3)? Do such initially surprising phrases as "scheduled deaths," "couples," "eyes of masks / from a culture lost forever," and "Ark," seem ultimately justified? (Recall, for instance, that the lace-holes of shoes are called "eyes.") How does the poem's lack of punctuation affect its tone? its theme?

Shoe Repairs

Long after the scheduled deaths of animals
their skins made up into couples
have arrived here
empty
from many turnings   5
between the ways of men
and men

In a side street
by brown walls over a small light
the infinite routes   10
which they follow a little way
come together

to wait in rows in twos
soles
eyes of masks   15
from a culture lost forever

We will know the smell
in another life
stepping down
barefoot into this Ark   20
seeing it lit up but empty
the destined racks
done with the saved pairs
that went out to die each alone

4. In both of these poems, the speakers make statements which seem at first to be enigmatic, but which turn out to have reasonably clear symbolic meaning. In "The Trapper," does the comparison to "the size of a very small boy" suggest an interpretation? Or, in "Encounter," the image of grass "whispering of its native land"? Using one or the other of these poems as a model, create a character for whom a trade or a landscape provides the elements of a fantasy.

a) *The Trapper*

PETER KLAPPERT   (b. 1942)

I am digging a pit
deeper than I will need.

Already
on the other side of this mountain
something is crying in a small hoarse voice.   5

It is breaking its teeth on my teeth.

Some shy animal is taking its paw
apart in the darkness.
Some poor animal is looking through its bones.

When I grab at my lungs they contract   10
like an old leather bellows.

Something the size of a very small boy
is kicking against that trap.

b) *Encounter*

RICHARD SHELTON   (b. 1933)

In some small flatland town
a stranger waits for me to arrive by train

and when I step down not knowing
where I am or why I have come
I will recognize him and give him my hand   5
He will fold my pain like a newspaper
and tuck it under his arm
He will take charge of everything

He will open a car door
I will get in and he will drive   10
expertly down Main Street out of town
toward open country where the sky
is half the world

As night comes on
we will hear grass beside the road   15
whispering of its native land
and when the stars bear down like music
I will begin to understand how things
that have never happened before
can happen again   20

5. Is this a poem or a graffito?

Born a virgin.
Died a virgin.
Laid in her grave.

6. What different attitudes toward war do you find in these poems? What strategies
have the poets used to present their themes?

a) *To Lucasta, Going to the Wars*

RICHARD LOVELACE   (1618–1657)

Tell me not, sweet, I am unkind,
      That from the nunnery
Of thy chaste breast and quiet mind
      To war and arms I fly.

True, a new mistress now I chase,   5
      The first foe in the field;
And with a stronger faith embrace
      A sword, a horse, a shield.

Yet this inconstancy is such
      As you too shall adore;   10
I could not love thee, dear, so much,
      Loved I not honour more.

b) *Thematic*

JOHN CIARDI (1916–1986)

Estrid the Conqueror raised seven red-handed
sons, all lopped in the Conquest, and he bloodlet
too pale to recruit such captains again.

It was a famous grief and long in the practice
of ethnic tragedians, though Estrid ruled   5
less than a six month's rage, the throne

gone to an idiot nephew whose reign ground on
through so dull a peace, three generations of poet
tick-tocked time without recording his name.

So much for the great emotions. All art knows   10
frenzy matters, of course. Yet one may ask:
whose? to whom? in which of the lost kingdoms?

c) *Waiting for the Barbarians*

CONSTANTINE CAVAFIS (1863–1933)

Translated from the Greek by Richmond Lattimore

Why are we all assembled and waiting in the market place?

It is the barbarians; they will be here today.

Why is there nothing being done in the senate house?
Why are the senators in session but are not passing laws?

Because the barbarians are coming today.   5
Why should the senators make laws any more?
The barbarians will make the laws when they get here.

Why has our emperor got up so early
and sits there at the biggest gate of the city
high on his throne, in state, and with his crown on?   10

Because the barbarians are coming today
and the emperor is waiting to receive them

and their general. And he has even made ready
a parchment to present them, and thereon
he has written many names and many titles.   15

Why have our two consuls and our praetors
come out today in their red embroidered togas?
Why have they put on their bracelets with all those amethysts

and rings shining with the glitter of emeralds?
Why will they carry their precious staves today   20
which are decorated with figures of gold and silver?

Because the barbarians are coming today
and things like that impress the barbarians.

Why do our good orators not put in any appearance
and make public speeches and do what they generally do?   25

Because the barbarians are coming today
and they get bored with eloquent public speeches.

Why is everybody beginning to be so uneasy?
Why so disordered? (See how grave all the faces
have become!) Why do the streets and squares empty so quickly,   30
and they are all anxiously going home to their houses?

Because it is night, and the barbarians have not got here,
and some people have come in from the frontier
and say that there aren't any more barbarians.

What are we going to do now without the barbarians?   35
In a way, those people, they were a solution.

7. Write a silly nonsense poem. Coin a few words, and see if a reader can guess
what they mean.

8. Try a clerihew or two. Or a limerick.

POEMS TO CONSIDER

from *A Midsummer-Night's Dream (V, i)*   1600

WILLIAM SHAKESPEARE (1564–1616)

Lovers and madmen have such seething brains,
Such shaping fantasies, that apprehend
More than cool reason ever comprehends.
The lunatic, the lover, and the poet
Are of imagination all compact.   5
One sees more devils than vast hell can hold;
That is, the madman. The lover, all as frantic,
Sees Helen's beauty in a brow of Egypt.
The poet's eye, in a fine frenzy rolling,

Doth glance from heaven to earth, from earth to heaven;   10
And as imagination bodies forth
The forms of things unknown, the poet's pen
Turns them to shapes and gives to airy nothing
A local habitation and a name.
Such tricks hath strong imagination,   15
That, if it would but apprehend some joy,
It comprehends some bringer of that joy;
Or in the night, imagining some fear,
How easy is a bush supposed a bear!

from *Song of the Exposition*   *1871*

WALT WHITMAN (1819–1892)

Come, Muse, migrate from Greece and Ionia,
Cross out please those immensely overpaid accounts,
That matter of Troy and Achilles' wrath, and Aeneas', Odysseus' wanderings,
Placard "Removed" and "To Let" on the rocks of your snowy Parnassus,
Repeat at Jerusalem, place the notice high on Jaffa's° gate and on Mount
    Moriah°,   5
The same on the walls of your German, French and Spanish castles, and
    Italian collections,
For know a better, fresher, busier sphere, a wide, untried, domain awaits,
    demands you.

Responsive to our summons,
Or rather to her long-nursed inclination,
Joined with an irresistible, natural gravitation,   10
She comes! I hear the rustling of her gown,
I scent the odor of her breath's delicious fragrance,
I mark her step divine, her curious eyes a-turning, rolling,
Upon this very scene.

I say I see, my friends, if you do not, the illustrious émigré, (having it is true in
    her day, although the same, changed, journeyed considerable,)   15
Making directly for this rendezvous, vigorously clearing a path for herself,
    striding through the confusion,
By thud of machinery, and shrill steam-whistle undismayed,

Bluffed not a bit by drain-pipe, gasometers, artificial fertilizers,
Smiling and pleased with palpable intent to stay,
She's here, installed amid the kitchen ware!   20

5 *Jaffa, Mount Moriah:* places mentioned in the Old Testament. Moriah was the mountain on which Abraham was commanded to sacrifice Isaac.

Come with Me   1964

ROBERT BLY *(b. 1926)*

Come with me into those things that have felt this despair for so long—
Those removed Chevrolet wheels that howl with a terrible loneliness,
Lying on their backs in the cindery dirt, like men drunk, and naked,
Staggering off down a hill at night to drown at last in the pond.
Those shredded inner tubes abandoned on the shoulders of thruways,   5
Black and collapsed bodies, that tried and burst,
And were left behind;
And the curly steel shavings, scattered about on garage benches,
Sometimes still warm, gritty when we hold them,
Who have given up, and blame everything on the government,   10
And those roads in South Dakota that feel around in the darkness . . .

Poem   1950

FRANK O'HARA *(1926–1966)*

The eager note on my door said "Call me,
call when you get in!" so I quickly threw
a few tangerines into my overnight bag,
straightened my eyelids and shoulders, and

headed straight for the door. It was autumn   5
by the time I got around the corner, oh all

unwilling to be either pertinent or bemused, but
the leaves were brighter than grass on the sidewalk!

Funny, I thought, that the lights are on this late
and the hall door open; still up at this hour, a   10
champion jai-alai player like himself? Oh fie!
for shame! What a host, so zealous! And he was

there in the hall, flat on a sheet of blood that
ran down the stairs. I did appreciate it. There are few
hosts who so thoroughly prepare to greet a guest   15
only casually invited, and that several months ago.

Blood Hour   1985

CAROL MUSKE (b. 1945)

The long grass blows flat
as I pass through it, dreaming,
with my taller brother and the .22.
He is teaching me how to handle a rifle.

Early sunset rakes across our path: 5
three burning clouds, the great
chieftains, rise above us.

When I look through the sight
I see the door opening miles away
across the plains, a woman setting   10
an old cradle out on her porch.

My brother puts his arm around
my shoulders from behind, his head
cocked next to mine—adjusting
the arm's cantilever, adjusting   15
as much as he can, the crooked line of fire

that I will see, in reverse,
from the next second forward:

from the cradle to the burning island
on which we stand—
from the dead bullet to the barrel
and back into the live shell chamber.

20

Iris

1976

DAVID ST. JOHN (b. 1949)

There is a train inside this iris:

You think I'm crazy, & like to say boyish
& outrageous things. No, there is

A train inside this iris.

It's a child's finger bearded in black banners.   5
A single window like a child's nail,

A darkened porthole lit by the white, angular face

Of an old woman, or perhaps the boy beside her in the stuffy,
Hot compartment. Her hair is silver, & sweeps

Back off her forehead, onto her cold & bruised shoulders.   10

The prairies fail along Chicago. Past the five
Lakes. Into the black woods of her New York; & as I bend

Close above the iris, I see the train

Drive deep into the damp heart of its stem, & the gravel
Of the garden path   15

Cracks under my feet as I walk this long corridor

Of elms, arched
Like the ceiling of a French railway pier where a boy

With pale curls holding

A fresh iris is waving goodbye to a grandmother, gazing   20
A long time

Into the flower, as if he were looking some great

Distance, or down an empty garden path & he believes a man
Is walking toward him, working

Dull shears in one hand; & now believe me: The train   25

Is gone. The old woman is dead, & the boy. The iris curls,
On its stalk, in the shade

Of those elms: Where something like the icy & bitter fragrance

In the wake of a woman who's just swept past you on her way
Home   30

& you remain.

A Band of Poets Desert
from the Red Army, Forever   1977

TIM CALHOUN

All day our horses ran away with us.
Suddenly the edge vanished.
Stars emerged in the heavens,
Halving themselves infinitely
To make new night flowers.   5

As we galloped near the river without color,
Our minds let go of the reins.
A few individual men
Were lost permanently.
We did not mourn the passing there.   10

By dawn an absolute candle
Gilded the tiny mushroom towns silver,
And smeared gold behind my eyes.
I could not distinguish my comrades
From the one anothers of my being.   15

Clearly the war was over now.
Though a cannon toiled in the distance
And church bells thudded in their rims,
All this behind us became forgotten country.
For what we discovered is never lost.   20

As She Has Been Taught   1983

MEKEEL McBRIDE   (b. 1950)

The building, a tall one, is on fire again.
On the twenty-first floor, she,
dressed in smoky silks,
settles in to watch.
Below, she can see enameled firetrucks   5
roaring down streets
no wider than the ruler on her desk.

She wonders how they think they'll stop the fire
with their tiny hoses
and matchstick ladders.   10
Watching her building shadowed on the next
she sees the roof's on fire,
the silhouette of it
fanned into flames

that almost look   15
like dancers
twining topsy-turvy in a dark field.
She feels safe, feels warm
in the celluloid flames that are,
after all, only the red silks   20
her sleeping mind has wrapped around her.

But the rescue squad
of volunteer pharmacists,
and paper-pale priests
kicks down the door, helps her   25
through the iridescent halls
into blackened streets
where she is blanketed
by the ladies auxiliary.

Even though the alarm   30
has been silenced, they slip her
into the colorless cradle of amnesia
while her lover, his arms scalded
by a great bouquet of crimson roses,
wanders dully   35
through the water-ruined rooms.

The Gift of the Magi   1982

PETER MEINKE   (b. 1932)

The angel of the Lord sang low
and shucked his golden slippers off
and stretched his wings as if to show
their starlit shadow on the wall
and did the old soft shoe, yeah,   5
did the buck and wing.

The Magi put their arms around
each other, then with chorus-line
precision and enormous zest
they kicked for Jesus onetwothree   10
high as any Christmas tree
and Caspar was the best.

And Melchior told a story that
had Joseph sighing in the hay
while holy Mary rolled her eyes   15
and Jesus smiling where He lay
as if He understood, Lord,
knew the joke was good.

But Balthazar began to weep
foreseeing all the scenes to come: 20
the Child upon a darker stage
the star, their spotlight, stuttering out—
then shook his head, smiled, and sang
louder than before.

There was no dignity that night: 25
the shepherds slapped their sheepish knees
and tasted too much of the grape
that solaces our sober earth
O blessèd be our mirth, hey!
Blessèd be our mirth!   30

Programming Down on the Farm   1985

MICHAEL SPENCE (b. 1952)

As all those with computers know,
Input-output is called I/O.
But farmers using these machines
See special letters on their screens.
So when they list a chicken fence
To "Egg Insurance and Expense,"
Into what file would it go?
Of course to EIE I/O.

Grading

1984

JOHN RIDLAND   (b. 1933)

"Grading's no problem. An experienced teacher can grade anything."
AN EXPERIENCED TEACHER

He grades the cat on being cat
(straight A), the grapefruit on juiciness
(B+) and sweetness (B), his wife
on sleeping soundly (last night, D
–); he grades the morning (C   5
+, *be more definite*), the dog
for coming quickly when it's called
(A–, *good dog, good dog*), for
fetching the paper (*Fetch it!*—F).
In broad daylight he grades the moon   10
last night at midnight, *Well defined,*
clear, and complete (pure A, pure A);
his breakfast lunch and dinner (Pass);
his shoes (Unsatisfactory);
of course he grades the morning paper   15
(low C for content, C for form);
the window (B, maybe B–,
try to be more imaginative).

He grades the way he drives to school
(B+ *woops*, D), the radio—   20
rather, its choice of music (A
+, for Segovia's guitar
followed by Goodman's clarinet),
the fat opossum in the road
(plain D for *dead*), the old man trudging   25
in red sweatsuit and jogging shoes
(Not Pass), the parking lot (OK),
colleagues for cordiality
(A, B, C, D, none of the above)
and courage in the line of duty   30
(withheld: cf. the Privacy Act).
He's graded God (*You should do better*
than this, with Your Advantages.
Try to improve by putting more

of Yourself into it, C–);
and *homo sapiens* (*barely passing,*
YOU ARE IN TROUBLE!);

                    and himself
(Delivery, B: Coherence, C;
Organization, D; Good will,
A! A!), and grades his grading (C,
inflated, whimsical), his life
(B+ *as far as it goes, keep going*),
tomorrow and tomorrow and
tomorrow (*Where's your outline?* C,
no, Incomplete. *Please see me soon.*)

III

Process:
Making the Poem Happen

Starting a Poem:
Wind, Sail, and Rigging

Ancient and new mingle in poetry. The road on which the beginning poet stands, if he or she looks back, disappears into the past, where it once wound across the dusty savannah, through Ice-Age mountains. W. S. Merwin (b. 1927) recalls the lost beginning of every art:

Memory of Spring

The first composer
could hear only what he could write

Civilizations have risen and fallen. But the arts, even though the works and sometimes the artists' names are forgotten, have been passed along from living hand to living hand. Writing about the greatest of the Greek sculptors, Praxiteles, whose famous statue of Aphrodite has been lost, Robert Francis sums up the succession:

Aphrodite as History

Though the marble is ancient
It is only an ancient

Copy and though the lost
Original was still more ancient
Still it was not Praxiteles   5
Only a follower of Praxiteles
And Praxiteles was not first.

Stone falls from stone. Paint flakes. Languages alter or disappear. "We write in
sand," Edmund Waller wrote in the seventeenth century; "our language grows /
And, like the tide, our work o'erflows." Even the great and sophisticated Chaucer
grows irretrievably quaint, and Shakespeare must begin to be read with the
magnifying glass of history.

Yet happily, because old poems fade, we always need new poems. The human
truth, however durable, must always be reimagined and made fresh. The poet lives
"in a spring still not written of." "All things fall and are built again," William
Butler Yeats says in "Lapis Lazuli" (page 322); "those that build them again are
gay."

Tradition is the long handle that gives force to the blow of the new, sharp
head of the axe. The beginning poet will do well to heed Pound's counsel: "Make it
new." Without change, art stagnates. Yet, as T. S. Eliot points out in "Tradition
and the Individual Talent," the poet "is not likely to know what is to be done,
unless he lives in what is not merely the present, but the present moment of the
past, unless he is conscious, not of what is dead, but of what is already living." John
Dryden (1631–1700) has suggested the fate of those rash poets who

Puffed with vain pride, presume they understand,
And boldly take the trumpet in their hand. . . .
With impudence the laurel they invade,
Resolved to like the monsters they have made.
Virgil, compared to them, is flat and dry;   5
And Homer understood not poetry.

Imitation, Masters, Models, and So Forth

We only want to write a poem in the first place because we have read a poem
that truly takes us. The poem we write will inevitably be (or at least try to be) like
that poem. What else can it be? The poet's notions of what poetry is, of what
poems can do, come from the poems she or he knows and admires. For the poet, *all*
poems are about poetry—its range, its limits, it potentialities. The undisguised
admiration "*I can do that*" is the seed from which every poet sprouts and grows.

If the beginning poet could be given only one word of advice, it would unquestionably be: *Read.* Nothing that anyone knows or can tell you about poetry will be as useful as what you discover, firsthand, yourself. The more poems you know of all kinds, old and new, fashionable and unfashionable, the more possibilities open for your own writing. And don't read only what everyone else is reading. Try the dusty corners, the odd nooks. Browse. Sniff out.

What you are looking for are the poems—the poets—that blow you away, the poems and poets on your wavelength. Find one. Find another. Buy the books with your lunch money. These poems will be your models, after which you will willy-nilly fashion your own poems. These poets who speak to you will be your "masters." A poet's secrets are hidden in the open, in the poems, and it isn't necessary to clean her brushes or cook his dinner to apprentice yourself to the best poets writing.

Far from being a problem, **imitation** is the only and inescapable route toward becoming a poet. As a student, you may write Donne poems, Yeats poems, Frost poems, Roethke poems, and any number of other poets' poems. Every role you like, you will try out, not always consciously. As you discover and absorb admiration after admiration, the influences begin to neutralize each other and naturally disappear. The poems you write will begin to be in your own voice, not in Ginsberg's or Plath's or Wilbur's. The greater danger is not in being too much influenced but in being too little influenced—fixing early or fanatically on a single master and clinging to that one voice, or finding the whole truth in one cranky theory or another. Beware especially of theories: it is *poems* you want.

There is, after all, no disgrace in having learned something from somebody. You needn't reinvent the wheel.

And don't worry about "finding your own voice." That will, like puberty, just happen. No one really knows what her or his actual voice sounds like—we are all surprised by a tape recorder. The conscious effort, too early, to develop an "individual voice" is likely to result only in strain, staginess, and mannerism. If Buffon's famous dictum is correct, *"Le style c'est l'homme même"*—"Style is the man himself"—then its converse is reassuringly true: "The man himself is his style." There is no point in trying to fake it. Like fingerprints, you'll have it. When poets no longer sound like anyone else, they sound like themselves.

"Le style c'est l'homme même." If the poet is a beery and blustery fellow, then his style will be and should be beery and blustery. If the poet is a dark and depressive woman, then her style will be and should be dark and depressive. The poet who is neither, however, should be wary of finding himself or herself with someone else's hangover or in somebody else's hairshirt. Don't strike poses. Liars have to keep track of more than one version of everything. Be natural.

Even deliberate imitation can be a good exercise. Attempting to write a poem in the style of a poet you admire (or despise!) will focus any number of technical qualities: diction, imagery, rhythm, and so on. (What, after all, makes Yeats *sound* like Yeats, or Stevens *sound* like Stevens?) A variation is attempting to *re*write a particular poem. Read a poem you like but don't know well, perhaps three or four times, without trying to commit it to memory. Then, after an hour, try to reproduce it. In his teens, Benjamin Franklin trained his prose style in this way, using essays in the *Spectator* as models. As he reports in *The Autobiography*, "By comparing my work afterwards with the original, I discovered many faults and amended them." It was also exhilarating, "for I sometimes had the pleasure of fancying that, in certain particulars of small import, I had been lucky enough to improve the method of the language, and this encouraged me to think I might possibly in time come to be a tolerable English writer."

Strictly, **parody** is the exaggerated imitation of a work of art. Following the mannerisms of style (like Whitman's catalogs or Dickinson's breathless dashes) and of subject (like Frost's country matters), the parodist pokes fun at (and sometimes holes in) the original, as Anthony Hecht's "The Dover Bitch" skewers Matthew Arnold's "Dover Beach" (pp. 314–315). More loosely, parody can be a starting point for a quite differently amusing poem. For example, this by James Camp (b. 1923):

After the Philharmonic

Two paths diverged in a well-known park,
One well-lit, the other—dark.
And since I did not wish to die,
I took the one more travelled by.

Or this by Gene Fehler (b. 1940):

If Richard Lovelace Became a Free Agent

Tell me not, fans, I am unkind
    For saying my good-bye
And leaving your kind cheers behind
    While I to new fans fly.

Now, I will leave without a trace
    And choose a rival's field;
For I have viewed the market place
    And seen what it can yield.

Though my disloyalty is such
    That all you fans abhor,
It's not that I don't love you much:
    I just love money more.

Stirrings

Writing a poem is an exciting and chancy business. It is, as A. E. Housman said, "either easy or impossible." When the magic happens, it is easy. Usually it is both at once. Ideas well up, words appear, images offer themselves, and the poem begins to materialize on the page. But not the whole poem, perfect, complete. Only a shadowy version appears at first: fragments, phrases, an unfinished rhythm—and a luminous sense of the poem-to-be. What Dylan Thomas calls the poet's "craft or sullen art" must finish the job. Edgar Degas's comment is perhaps also true of a poem: "A painting . . . requires as much cunning, rascality, and viciousness as the perpetration of a crime."

Craft isn't just cold-blooded carpentry, though good carpentry is part of it. It is the ability to keep the poem moving, to tease or coax more of the poem out of the shadows, to hold onto the wave-length from which the flickering signals are coming. It is something like the skill with which a good fisherman plays a fish, knowing when to reel in, when to give slack, in order finally to bring it to the boat. All poets must learn, as best they can, from their own experience, how to court their muse, how to draw from the mysterious source, whatever it is, deep within themselves. Poets tend to be as superstitious as baseball players, with little rituals, recipes, and tricks: a favorite pen, a preferred place, a lucky time of day or night. Silence or jazz. Pencil or typewriter. Walking or at the desk. Coffee or chartreuse.

Explanations probably do not matter so long as the poet gets on with writing the poems. Poems come, or don't; are good, or not. In practice X. J. Kennedy's punningly titled poem is good advice:

Ars Poetica

The goose that laid the golden egg
Died looking up its crotch
To find out how its sphincter worked.

Would you lay well? Don't watch.

The poet's technical experience, technical readiness, is like a finely tuned radio apparatus that is activated by the message, whenever it comes and wherever it comes from.

It is impossible to say just when, how, or why the first stirrings of a poem appear. Noticing, keeping antennae out, listening for that first transmission, *wanting* to write a poem, are all part of it. An experience that doesn't at the time seem the least bit like a poem may begin, later, to produce one—like watching a friend tie fishing flies, or seeing a painting in a museum. Like the novelist, the poet is, in this sense, always on duty. As James Thurber noted, "I never quite know when I'm not writing. Sometimes my wife comes up to me at a party and says, 'Dammit, Thurber, stop writing.' " It's a habit, this turning experience into words, trying it out.

One way to train the habit is to keep a notebook. Many poets do, jotting down ideas, observations, images, phrases, bits from reading, and so on. Gerard Manley Hopkins meticulously recorded things he saw and occasionally even made drawings; years later, a phrase or bit of description would appear in a poem. Making notes sharpens the poet's attention and, whether or not the notes are referred to later, tends to imprint something on the memory. As Frost says, though, "The impressions most useful to my purpose seem always to be those I was unaware of and so made no note of at the time." Poets who don't keep a proper notebook nonetheless accumulate bits and pieces of poems on scraps of paper or the backs of envelopes. The probable fate of such poetic impulses is a few sputterings and then nothing. Most poets have file boxes of leftover, half-written poems. Few come to life again, but Thomas Hardy sometimes wrote poems forty years after the fact, using "old notes."

Anything can be the start of a poem: something noticed, something read, a scene, a dream, a memory, an image, two words rubbing together into a phrase. Realizing that it is, or might be, the beginning of a poem is the first step. The second is letting the associations flow, following the drift, freeing the currents of the idea or feeling. There may seem about it a kind of inevitability, as if the poem had been gathering unnoticed for years. "Swimmer in the Rain" (page 121), for instance, drew on memories going back to my boyhood, physical sensations I hadn't consciously thought of in more than twenty years. Wordsworth notes that poetry

> takes its origin from emotion recollected in tranquillity; the emotion is contemplated till, by a species of re-action, the tranquillity gradually disappears, and an emotion, kindred to that which was before the subject of contemplation, is gradually produced, and does itself actually exist in the mind. In this mood successful composition generally begins.

The stronger and more confusing the emotion, perhaps, the longer the subconscious gestation necessary for it to begin to organize itself into a poem.

One of the things a poet learns is how to "play" a poem, how not to force it, how to hold off from trying to write it until *it* is ready. Richard Wilbur reports that he waited fourteen years, occasionally jotting down a phrase "that might belong to a poem," before he started to write "The Mind-Reader"; he took another three years to finish the poem. Asked how long he was likely to work on a poem, he said, "Long enough." In forcing a poem, trying to write it too soon, the poet is likely to make a hash of it—which may explain many of those broken poems in the file box. Trying to write in the heat of an emotion, rather than recollecting it later in tranquillity, after the subconscious has had a chance to work, is all too likely to produce posturing, self-pity, overstatement, or sentimentality—those spoilers of genuine feeling. It is like trying to sing while someone is pounding on your finger with a hammer; if it can be done, it won't be done well.

Whatever it is, wherever it originates, the poem always begins with a *given*, in which the poet is aware of the possibility of a poem. Walking and driving, fairly boring activities that leave the mind free to wander, are ways of looking for those gifts. So, too, are the trancelike states of listening to music, drifting off to sleep, and insomnia. The poet is, in Freud's phrase, a "professional daydreamer." The conscious mind relaxes its control; thoughts, images, and memories drift in and out of consciousness—and suddenly sometimes, as if glimpsed in peripheral vision, there is the beginning of a poem. Prolonging that state, drawing as much as possible of the poem into words, is the aim. Wordsworth "wrote" all 159 lines of "Tintern Abbey" in his head, on a four- or five-day walking tour. "Not a line of it was altered, and not any part of it written down till I reached Bristol." In the fourth book of *The Prelude*, recalling a favorite dog, Wordsworth describes how he composed poems during idle walking and talking to himself:

Among the favourites whom it pleased me well
To see again, was one by ancient right
Our inmate, a rough terrier of the hills;
By birth and call of nature pre-ordained
To hunt the badger and unearth the fox   5
Among the impervious crags, but having been
From youth our own adopted, he had passed
Into a gentler service. And when first
The boyish spirit flagged, and day by day
Along my veins I kindled with the stir,   10
The fermentation, and the vernal heat
Of poesy, affecting private shades
Like a sick Lover, then this dog was used
To watch me, an attendant and a friend,
Obsequious to my steps early and late,   15
Though often of such dilatory walk
Tired, and uneasy at the halts I made.
A hundred times when, roving high and low,
I have been harassed with the toil of verse,
Much pains and little progress, and at once   20
Some lovely Image in the song rose up
Full-formed, like Venus rising from the sea;
Then have I darted forwards to let loose
My hand upon his back with stormy joy,
Caressing him again and yet again.   25
And when at evening on the public way
I sauntered, like a river murmuring
And talking to itself when all things else

Are still, the creature trotted on before;
Such was his custom; but whene'er he met   30
A passenger approaching, he would turn
To give me timely notice, and straightway,
Grateful for that admonishment, I hushed
My voice, composed my gait, and, with the air
And mien of one whose thoughts are free, advanced   35
To give and take a greeting that might save
My name from piteous rumours, such as wait
On men suspected to be crazed in brain.

A charming picture, the poet spared the embarrassment of being caught talking to himself by his faithful terrier!

What William Stafford calls "**random writing**"—free associating, just putting anything down, however nonsequential or silly, like talking to oneself on paper— may also work to discover the beginning of a poem. Here, for instance, is a poem of his:

Ask Me

Some time when the river is ice ask me
mistakes I have made. Ask me whether
what I have done is my life. Others
have come in their slow way into
my thought, and some have tried to help   5
or to hurt—ask me what difference
their strongest love or hate has made.

I will listen to what you say.
You and I can turn and look
at the silent river and wait. We know   10
the current is there, hidden; and there
are comings and goings from miles away
that hold the stillness exactly before us.
What the river says, that is what I say.

Of "Ask Me," Stafford reports:

My poem started from amid random writing I was doing in my usual morning attempts to scare up something by putting anything down that came to mind. I was at a country place; it was early morning; I was all alone, and feeling that way—in a pleasant way, with a fire in the Franklin stove, the dark outside. It was winter, and I guess the cold made me launch in the way I did, "Some time when the river is ice . . ."

Like the less mechanical wool-gathering of walking or driving or falling to sleep, random writing is a valuable tactic, especially when the poet is stuck and not writing, when he or she is waiting (in Nemerov's phrase) "for what would come next to come next," or when he or she has an assignment due.

Keeping the poem moving, finishing it, is the harder part of the process. Even when the inspiration holds, when the wind is in the sail (the image is Ben Jonson's), more is required than luck or following an impulse. Just as the quality of sail and rigging is important, so is the quality of the training and equipment the poet can bring to bear: the ability to handle the craft, to tack and steer a course, and to take advantage of the wind so as to arrive somewhere rather than merely to be blown this way and that. It is too late, in a gale, to learn. Being lucky is often knowing *how* to be lucky. Like the good tennis player or the expert sailor, the poet uses accumulated experience in every new situation without being aware that he or she is doing so. Choosing words, images, rhythm, line division for best effect, and whether or not to rhyme may be an intuitional process but is also a result of training. Skill is experience brought to bear on the present.

Even in that rare case when a whole poem simply comes without any conscious effort on the poet's part—the most famous case is Samuel Taylor Coleridge's "Kubla Khan"—it can do so only for the trained sensibility. Here is Coleridge's account:

> In the summer of the year 1797, the Author, then in ill health, had retired to a lonely farm-house between Porlock and Linton, on the Exmoor confines of Somerset and Devonshire. In consequence of a slight indisposition, an anodyne had been prescribed, from the effects of which he fell asleep in his chair at the moment that he was reading the following sentence, or words of the same substance, in "Purchas's Pilgrimage": "Here the Khan Kubla commanded a palace to be built, and a stately garden thereunto. And thus ten miles of fertile ground were inclosed within a wall." The Author continued for about three hours in a profound sleep, at least of the external senses, during which time he has the most vivid confidence, that he could not have composed less than from two to three hundred lines; if that indeed can be called composition in which all the images rose up before him as *things*, with a parallel production of the correspondent expressions, without any sensation or consciousness of effort. On awaking he appeared to himself to have a distinct recollection of the whole, and taking his pen, ink, and paper, instantly and eagerly wrote down the lines that are here preserved. At this moment he was unfortunately called out by a person from Porlock, and detained by him above an hour, and on his return to his room, found, to his no small surprise and mortification, that though he still retained some vague and dim recollection of the general purport of the vision, yet, with the exception of some eight or ten scattered lines and images, all the rest had passed away like the images on the surface of a stream into which a stone has been cast, but, alas! without the after restoration of the latter.

In *The Road to Xanadu* John Livingston Lowes has traced, with fine psychological insight, the sources of the poem's content in Coleridge's reading and experience.

The poet's imagination was assimilating and sorting and combining its materials without any apparent intervention by his conscious mind. His technical skills were also, necessarily, at work, rhyming, metering, dividing lines. For a person not a poet the same dream or vision might have been equally marvelous, but it would not have produced a *poem*.

When inspiration is up, when the poem is coming, when the wind is in the sail, the poet must go with it. "And the secret of it all is," Walt Whitman reported,

> to write in the gush, the throb, the flood, of the moment—to put things down without deliberation—without worrying about their style—without waiting for a fit time and place. . . . You want to catch its first spirit—to tally its truth. By writing at the instant the very heartbeat of life is caught.

Put down everything, however odd. The scrawl and chaos of many a poet's manuscripts result from the haste of following out an impulse, of trying to keep up with the speed of the muse. As Ben Jonson notes in his "commonplace book" *Timber, or Discoveries* (1640–41):

> If we have a fair gale of wind, I forbid not the steering out of our sail, so the favor of the gale deceive us not. For all that we invent doth please us in the conception of birth, else we would never set it down. But the safest is to return to our judgment, and handle over again those things the easiness of which might make them justly suspected.

The warning is fitting. Put everything down, but *judge* it later. Not everything the muse dictates or the poet writes is valuable. Much may be wasteful, corny, sloppy, or worse. Many of the unfinished poems in the file box are just embarrassing, pompous or silly, and it is easy in retrospect to see why they disintegrated in the effort to finish them.

The last act in the writing of any poem is always a critical one: the judgment that it is finished. Everything should be there that needs to be, but no more than is needed. And whatever it is, it must seem worth saying.

"The Principle of Decision"

In truth, every creative act in the process of writing the poem, every word, image, or line-break, is also a critical act. Every possibility that comes to mind for what might come next in the poem must be approved or tossed aside. The approval or rejection may be tentative; often parallel possibilities may, for a time, be held in mind, bracketed in the body of the poem or jotted down in the margin. It may help to list possible words for a spot in the poem somewhere in the vicinity. Is the rose to be, for example,

red	incarnadine	blood-red
crimson	fluffy	sunset
scarlet	red, red	leafy

or any number of thousands of other possibilities? The intention here seems to be color, but "fluffy" and "leafy" show other temptations. Early on, every choice is likely to be tentative, especially when the poet is unsure of the poem's direction. At this stage the writing will properly be trial-and-error blundering. The standard against which possibilities may be tested can hardly be more than a vague or shadowy idea of the poem. But as the tentative choices begin to accumulate, as the idea of the poem clarifies, as the poem in effect materializes on the page, more and more it imposes its own demands and necessities. The direction revealing itself, the poet begins to rule out alternate routes, and choices become more decisive. The writing of even a few lines may be a mingling of a hundred creative and critical acts in rapid, almost invisible succession. Inspiration and evaluation work together like two hands trying to untangle a snarl of fishing line. "Style," Susan Sontag has noted, "is the principle of decision in a work of art, the signature of the artist's will."

Fairly soon the poet must make a commitment to form. Again it may be a tentative commitment, with the first formal decisions provisional, but a commitment nonetheless. Sometimes the poet will have a preconception about the form he or she wants to use, as Pope habitually turned to rhymed and end-stopped pentameter couplets. Sometimes, when the poet is more open, the very first line written (which need not be the first line of the poem) will *feel* like a line that fits the coming poem. Sometimes the initial jottings will be more notelike and the poem will seem, for a while, more like a random assortment of jigsaw puzzle pieces. Early on, in any event, the poet will be looking to discover what sort of form the poem will develop. Length of line? Free verse? Meter? Rhyme? Stanza? Among the possibilities that begin to arise, the poet will be trying to sort out the ones he or she wants. A thin poem? A fat poem? Solid or skeletony? Tight? Loose? Long? Short? Both the sound and the look of the poem, like its real subject and direction and tone, may be open for a time. Gradually, as the first shadowy choices are made, the commitment increases; and the tentative formal qualities of the poem become, themselves, standards by which to measure fresh possibilities, blanks into which newly arriving inspirations must be fitted. Some poems reveal their formal qualities clearly and definitely. More often, the poet has little but instinct to go on.

Every small choice is, of course, important, and each narrows the possibilities that follow. The most crucial one is probably **line.** The poet's sense of line—what makes a line, how much a line can hold or how little it can manage with, the balance or imbalance of a line, the weight or lightness of a line—may be his or her most valuable piece of equipment, the compass or gyroscope. In action, this sense may seem an instinct, but it will have been learned in the reading and writing of many lines. Working in a fixed meter is perhaps the best training in line because trying to fit a flexible content to a rigid pattern requires great dexterity. In meter the poet is constantly testing how much a given line can carry before it begins to feel crowded and clogged, or how little before it begins to feel empty and thin. When a poet smooths into lines of something like the same weight a content that tends to bunch and spread accordion-like, she or he develops a keen sense of line and of the use of run-ons and end-stops. The best free verse may well be written by poets who, like William Carlos Williams, have done an apprenticeship in pentameter.

William Stafford's "Ask Me" (page 298) was written in three drafts. A comparison of the first draft with the finished poem shows Stafford's skill in handling lines and in discovering the line-breaks in the nearly seamless material. Here is the first draft:

> Some time when the river is ice, ask me
> the mistakes, ask me whether what I have
> done is my life. Others have come
> in their slow way into the thoughts. And
> some have tried to help or to hurt. 5
> Ask me what differences their strongest efforts
> have made. You and I can then turn
> and look at the silent river and wait.
> We will know the current is there,
> hidden, and there are comings and goings 10
> miles away that hold the stillness
> exactly before us. If the river says anything,
> whatever it says is my answer.

Major changes in substance are few: "the mistakes" in line 2 is to become "mistakes I have made," which is clarifying and emphatic (though "my mistakes" would have been clear enough; "their strongest efforts / have made" in lines 6–7 is to become "their strongest love or hate has made," replacing a flat phrase with a sharp one and underlining the ironic leveling of the effect of "help" or "hurt." The sentence "I will listen to what you say" will be added, focusing the imagined dramatic dialogue and sharpening the sense that what the speaker would say is different from what the "you" might say about such things. The merely conditional "If the river says anything, / whatever it says is my answer" becomes the ambiguously definite "What the river says, that is what I say," which is both tighter and more highly charged.

All these alterations strengthen the poem, as do a number of smaller changes: making a separate sentence of the second "ask me" in line 2, making a continuing sentence of the "And/some have tried" and of the third "ask me" in lines 4–6, for instance, or using the more dramatic dash in line 6 of the final version. Simultaneously, Stafford is almost completely relining the poem. Only the first line remains the same and keeps its line-break. These changes, along with breaking the poem into two equal stanzas (questions and response), also strengthen it. Both verbal and rhythmic changes are being made at the same time, each making room for or requiring the other. Asked about the principles of technique he consciously used, Stafford replied:

> My impulse is to say that I had no principles of technique at all in mind. As I look back over the first draft, I do realize, though, that I was getting satisfaction out of syncopating along in the sentences; that is, I find some pleasure in just opening and closing sentences—starting and then holding before myself a feeling that the measure and flow of utterance will lend itself to an easy forwarding of what I am saying.

He added:

> My lines are generally just about equal; where a line breaks, though, means something to me, and some of the juggling was meant to preserve how definite the slash [run-on] line is in such changeover sequences as me/mistakes, have/done, and/some, etc.

The syncopation, this laying of sentences across the line-ends, occurs in both draft and final version. In the final version, however, it has taken on a structural quality. The invitations to "ask me" flow through the first seven lines, all of which are run-on except the seventh; thus, the falling momentum comes to rest only, and properly, with the end-stopped line 7. In the first draft line 5 is end-stopped, and the end of the poem's thematic first half falls indecisively in the middle of a line. By contrast, the rhythmic management in the final version is superb.

The poem turns on line 8, which is properly end-stopped and establishes the speaker's balance in the face of what the imaginary interlocutor would say. The lines then run-on through line 13, which is end-stopped to prepare for the decisive final statement, now complete and taut in its own line. In the draft, by contrast, the end-stopping of "and look at the silent river and wait" seems a false pause; and the line-and-a-half of the final statement seems rhythmically somewhat open-ended as well as substantially conditional. Flow and stasis, movement and poise are not only a central part of the poem's theme but also its essential rhythmic quality. The equal stanzas suggest, structurally, both the tension and the poise in the poem's feeling.

Interestingly, "Ask Me" seems to be free verse. The lines are "generally just about equal." But most of the lines approximate iambic tetrameter. Several, like line 7 ("their strongest love or hate has made"), are exactly metrical. In an intermediate version, the poem's last line would have been very strongly metrical as well: "What the river says is what I say." Stafford's final alteration of the line to "What the river says, that is what I say," though still approximately countable as tetrameter, hardens the rhythm away from the temptingly pat iambs—*and* suggests, dramatically, that the speaker's final poise is not smooth nor too easy. "Ask Me" is, in its unintentional nearness to a metrical norm, a perfect example of a poet's unerring instinct for the handling of line.

Determining the line and form may unlock the rest of a poem, allowing it to spread and fill like water into a design. What follows is my entire first draft of "Swimmer in the Rain" (p. 121). Having got this far, I bogged down, and the rest of the page is covered with doodles.

No one but <u>him</u> to see

the rain begin—fine <u>scrim</u>

far down the <u>bay</u>, ~~like~~ smoke,

smoking and hissing its <u>way</u>

toward, ~~and then~~{up the creek

where he ~~drifted~~swam, waited

a suit clad <u>in</u>

supple, ~~green~~ glass

to his neck.

The minor tinkerings on this first draft are not so important as the accidental rhymes ("him-scrim," "bay-way") that I noticed and underlined; they provided the new start on the second draft. The rhymes suggested, in order to set up the "him" rhyme, switching from a three-beat line to a two-beat line. The second draft, after a fitful try, dropped the rhyming; but with the two-beat line established, the poem *flowed* out onto the pages, reaching fifty-two lines in an hour or so. Here, slightly simplified, is the first part of the second draft:

No one but him

to see/ seeing the rain

, ~~like~~ smoke,

start/ ~~begin,~~ a scrim ∧

far down the bay,

in a line

~~and~~ advances ~~till~~∧

————————————— between two grays

Till ∧ the salt-grass rustles

and the ~~marsh~~ creek's mirror

in which he stood--

cold, ~~gr~~ and supple/

to his neck, like clothing--

ripple/ begins to dimple.

Several alternative words are noted (with slashes) in the left margin. Other changes are made by crossing out and inserting. The rhyme peters out after the first few lines, though "rustles-supple-dimple" keeps the possibility open. It was obvious, as the poem grew longer, that rhyming such short lines would be obtrusive. To avoid repeating "begin" (it appears in the last line of the passage), I scratched it out in line 3 and let "start" stand. This change made room for the insertion of "like smoke," a detail from the first draft that had been crowded out in the two-beat lines. I then scratched "like," making lines 3–4 read: "start, a scrim, smoke / far down the bay." In further drafts the smoke image moves, and "scrim" returns to the end of line 3. The rhymes in lines 1–4 remain, a hint of initial formality that, dissolved by the pace of events, perhaps mirrors the accelerating and overcoming sensation of the rain. The poem ends with the same line with which it began. As with the reappearance of the clothing image in the last lines, the poem just turned out that way—I certainly didn't have any rationalizations in mind.

The crucial decision, which in effect released the poem, was the choice of the two-beat line. On the first draft I was stuck because the three-beat lines were simply too *horizontal*—too slow, too paced for the excitement, the fast-changing movement, the multiplicity of the rain. The verticality, the speed of the two-beat lines were the *poem's* choice, something I learned from the developing poem, not something I imposed on it. The norm is iambic; but in lines so short, simple substitutions produce a varied, shifting rhythm without seeming uncontrolled or loose:

> Thĕ dróps | bóunce úp,
>
> líttlĕ | fóuntăins
>
> áll ă|róund hĭm,
>
> swíft, mó|mĕntá|rў—
>
> ĕverў dróp | tóssed báck
>
> ĭn áir | ătóp
>
> ĭts tí|nў cól|ŭmn—

That quick, two-beat rhythmic pattern and the quick, balancing, piling-up, syntactical elaborations of the multiplying images, I believe, were the necessary technical discoveries.

Talking to Oneself

Talking to oneself, *literally*, like Wordsworth on the footpath with his terrier, may be a help in keeping the poem going. Say it over aloud, as far as it has gone. As the look of a poem matters, so does its sound; and the poet will keep testing its sound in his or her ear. Both the awkward and the good things will become more obvious with repetition. Saying the poem over from the beginning will improve the continuity of the rhythm as well as of the sense. Sometimes, when the poem is stuck, this going back provides the momentum for getting across the hard spot. Ben Jonson (1573?–1637) advises:

> Repeat often what we have formerly written; which besides that it helps the consequence, and makes the juncture better, it quickens the heat of imagination, that often cools in the time of setting down, and gives it new strength, as if it grew lustier by the going back. As we see in the contention of leaping, they jump farthest that fetch their race longest; or, as in throwing a dart or javelin, we force back our arms to make our loose the stronger.

Enjoying the sound of his or her own voice, sculpting, relishing, caressing the unfinished poem is part of the job, one of the tools.

Talking to oneself is, however, more than a useful tactic. In a larger sense, it is a revealing analogy for the very process of writing poetry.

We usually talk to ourselves (I do, at least) when we are upset. If what is upsetting is a complex and doubtful choice or problem—like whether to take a job in a distant city—the talking takes the form of "If I do this, then. . . . But. . . . Or. . . . Then. . . ." The verbalization is a sort of fantasized planning, working through (in the psychological phrase) a series of interlocking contingencies, balancing ambiguous losses and gains. Like think-tank game playing, the fantasy is a way of trying to project and evaluate the uncertain. The ramifying choices and connections of a poem, like "Swimmer in the Rain" or Jorie Graham's "Reading Plato" (page 251), are a similar testing and probing. The poet doesn't know where the poem will end (unlike, say, the writer of an editorial); and literally talking it through to himself or herself, verbalizing, trying out the unfocussed possibilities may be the method of writing. From a given, a nub, the poem discovers its own course. As Frost puts it, "Like a piece of ice on a hot stove the poem must ride on its own melting. A poem may be worked over once it is in being, but may not be worried into being."

Often, more significantly, talking to oneself is highly emotional, charged. Upset by an injustice, rejection, or unexpected flout—by an infuriating parent or bureaucrat, an unfaithful friend or lover—we go away by ourselves, talking *to* that person. The talking takes the form of a speech we might have made or still might make. Angry and hurt just where we are most vulnerable, we rehearse the speech over and over—going back to the beginning to quicken the heat of the imagination, as Ben Jonson says—until we have just the sharp, cutting, stinging "logic" the frustration calls for. The fantasy needn't result in a real speech of course; usually doesn't in fact. What we are doing, mostly, is working out the exact edge or shape of the feeling, focussing and refocussing until it seems satisfactorily defined, "out there." The problem may not be solved, but the feeling is resolved. Usually relieved and purged, we can more or less go on with our lives.

When the nub of a poem is an upsetting, strong emotion—grief, for instance, or an inexplicable elation—the poem is talking to oneself exactly in this sense. We are working out, discovering the feeling. Writing a poem is less *stating* a fixed position (like the editorial writer) than it is *exploring, projecting,* and *discovering.* The things worth finding out, of course, are always those we don't already know. The poem is a catharsis, an objectifying of the emotion and its circumstances, putting it somehow "out there" in the poem. As Frost adds, a poem's "most precious quality will remain its having run itself and carried away the poet with it . . . It can never lose its sense of a meaning that once unfolded by surprise as it went."

Our feelings are all genuine, since we have them. But many of them are not "true" feelings; that is, feelings we can accept, affirm, live with. For example, rage at an old lady driving twenty miles per hour in a thirty-five mile zone when we are in a hurry is not a "true" feeling. Nor is envy of a friend who has come into some good fortune. Nor is self-pity. We have these feelings, but we don't approve them or act on them. Often, we don't know what we feel, or have contradictory feelings. As with a delicately balanced mobile, it would be easy in a different mood to feel compassionate toward the old lady in the car.

Sorting out the multiplicity of our feelings, understanding them, editing them, coming to terms with them (whether in action or in art) is as much a moral process as it is an aesthetic one. How we do this is related to what kind of person we choose to be. For the poet, as later for the right reader, the poem (in Frost's words) "ends in a clarification of life—not necessarily a great clarification, such as sects and cults are founded on, but in a momentary stay against confusion."

The danger to the poet in relying on what we may call "false" feelings is **sentimentality:** feelings in excess of, unjustified by, their specific cause. Who hasn't stood alone, late on a rainy night, looking out the window at a deserted street; then, feeling desolate, written a poem about the dark tragedy of everything? In the morning, however, with the sun out and the birds chittering, these gloomy pronouncements seem silly and empty. Self-pity is emotionally like taking a bath in warm syrup—"poor me"—and can be destructive when we let ourselves believe it. Hamlet is credible when he says suicidally, in context, "To be or not to be: that is the question"; a beaming undergraduate, girlfriend on his arm, is not.

The exploring and weighing of feelings is, in part, what Wordsworth meant in saying that poetry "takes its origin from emotion recollected in tranquillity."

All good poetry is the spontaneous overflow of powerful feelings: and though this be true, poems to which any value can be attached were never produced on any variety of subjects but by a man who, being possessed of more than usual organic sensibility, had also thought long and deeply. For our continued influxes of feeling are modified and directed by our thoughts, which are indeed the representatives of all our past feelings.

Among the "busted" poems in the file box, some the poet just lost interest in. Some the poet couldn't bring off technically. And more than the poet would like to admit simply melted away because the feeling, sappy, soppy, soupy, couldn't bear the weight of attention that a good poem demands. Like many of the feelings we are testing when we talk to ourselves, they are embarrassing when we look back on them, "false" to the steadied center of our beings.

As Pound notes, "In depicting the motions of the 'human heart' the durability of the writing depends on the exactitude. It is the thing that is true and stays true that keeps fresh for the new reader."

Close kin to sentimentality, **overstatement** is to the ideas of a poem what sentimentality is to feelings. Like the used-car salesman's hard sell, overstatement, claiming too much, asserting something beyond what seems justified, makes a reader uncomfortable, then resistant. One fraction of an ounce over and the scale tips. **Understatement,** on the other hand, is always safe, and its calm usually carries a reassuring air of conviction. Your best reader won't miss anything. Consider a poem by Philip Larkin (1922–1985).

Talking in Bed

Talking in bed ought to be easiest,
Lying together there goes back so far,
An emblem of two people being honest.

Yet more and more time passes silently.
Outside, the wind's incomplete unrest   5
Builds and disperses clouds about the sky,

And dark towns heap up on the horizon.
None of this cares for us. Nothing shows why
At this unique distance from isolation

It becomes still more difficult to find   10
Words at once true and kind,
Or not untrue and not unkind.

How quietly, carefully, Larkin picks his words. The couple's mutual loss is subtle. It is only "more difficult to find / Words at once true and kind." The couple is still at a "unique distance from isolation"—still together, still close. "Or not untrue and not unkind" is still not "untrue and unkind." Yet the implication of the last line is that words "untrue and unkind" would be all too easy to find. Moreover, the sense that the malaise is progressive, accumulating, is unmistakable ("more and more time passes silently"), although the poem refuses to predict or to draw the conclusions of its evidence. The speaker's feeling comes through indirectly in the image of "the wind's incomplete unrest." Like the wind's, his unrest, his uneasiness remains "incomplete." If the reader senses that, like the clouds, marriages are built and dispersed by unrest, it is the reader's conclusion. "Nothing shows why" is the simple assertion on which the poem's painful awareness turns.

Overstatement may have dramatic uses, as in George Herbert's "The Collar" (page 118) where the speaker's sentimental exaggerations characterize his unstable state of mind:

> I struck the board and cried, "No more;
>   I will abroad!
> What? shall I ever sigh and pine?"

Bold, deliberate overstatement—**hyperbole**—can be effective in the appropriate context. We are familiar with everyday hyperbole like "I'd give my right arm for a piece of that pie." We know that the statement isn't to be taken literally. This sort of understood overstatement appears in Dylan Thomas's "Fern Hill" (page 188)—"I was prince of the apple towns"—or in this poem by John Donne (1573–1631), in which the morning sun is shining in on another pair of lovers in bed:

The Sun Rising

Busy old fool, unruly sun,	
Why dost thou thus,	
Through windows and through curtains call on us?	
Must to thy motions lovers' seasons run?	
Saucy pedantic wretch, go chide	5
Late school boys and sour prentices°,	*apprentices*
Go tell court huntsmen that the king will ride,	
Call country ants to harvest offices;	
Love, all alike, no season knows nor clime,	
Nor hours, days, months, which are the rags of time.	10
Thy beams, so reverend and strong	
Why shouldst thou think?	
I could eclipse and cloud them with a wink,	
But that I would not lose her sight so long;	
If her eyes have not blinded thine,	15
Look, and tomorrow late tell me,	
Whether both th' Indias of spice and mine	
Be where thou leftst them, or lie here with me.	
Ask for those kings whom thou saw'st yesterday,	
And thou shalt hear, All here in one bed lay.	20

She's all states, and all princes, I,
 Nothing else is.
Princes do put play us; compared to this,
All honor's mimic, all wealth alchemy.
  Thou, sun, art half as happy as we,   25
   In that the world's contracted thus;
  Thine age asks ease, and since thy duties be
  To warm the world, that's done in warming us.
Shine here to us, and thou art everywhere;
This bed thy center is, these walls, thy sphere.   30

Angry at being disturbed by the morning light, the speaker tells the sun to go wake others instead: schoolboys, apprentices, the king's huntsmen, farmers. Stanzas 2 and 3 are almost nothing but hyperbole. The speaker could "eclipse and cloud" the sun (by closing his eyes), unless the beauty of the woman's eyes has already blinded the sun. He asserts that the "Indias of spice and mine" are in fact here, in the person of the woman; and all kings in himself. "She's all states, and all princes, I, / Nothing else is." The lovers are, he says, in fact the whole world, their bed the center of the sun's orbit. The deliberate exaggeration is playful but not unserious; the self-absorbed lovers are a world in themselves.

Tacking

As a sailor tacks to take advantage of the wind at an angle, several tricks may help the poet keep the poem going in the process of writing. One is simply to be very delicate about the moment he or she first commits a line to paper. Poems begin in the head, and often they will continue to develop there, in the relatively free-floating mixture of thought. Putting something on paper tends to fix it; and there is a time, early on, when the shoots of a poem are still too frail for transplanting. Words that feel full and grand in the mind sometimes look skinny and naked on paper. All that blankness can be intimidating, swallowing up the small handful of words that try to break the silence. To change the metaphor every poet must carefully select the moment to jerk the line and try to set the hook.

On the other hand, at a certain point in the process of writing, seeing the poem becomes important. The lines in the poet's head will inevitably feel somewhat different on paper, and that difference can prompt fresh ideas and directions. The appearance of a poem on the page is part of its total effect. Early enough for the poem not to have "jelled" too much, it is a good idea to use a typewriter. Because we are accustomed to reading poems in print, the poet will see much more clearly how the poem *looks* in a typewriter's approximation of print. Lines will be longer or shorter than the poet imagined, for instance, and the poem thinner or chubbier or more graceful.

The beginning poet will want to experiment with using typewriter, pencil, and pen; with different colors of ink; with script or printing; with lined or unlined paper; with single sheets, tablets, and notebooks. Such things may not be important, or they may. Poems have been written by night-light on an army footlocker after lights-out, and in worse places. But the poet is entitled to prefer working at a desk or (like Frost) with a lapboard in an easy chair. Ernest Hemingway liked to stand at a dresser on which his typewriter sat.

Writing out the poem *in prose*—that is, sketching it or outlining it—is a device some poets, including Yeats, have found useful, particularly for organizing argumentative or longer poems. When a poet is stuck, this may be a way of getting distance and perspective.

Frequently a single inspiration will result in a tangle of possibilities, which may in fact become several poems. A poem might well go in a variety of directions, or have in it the potential for making any number of points. The poet may need to untwine some of these, putting them aside before the poem at hand can proceed coherently. Walter Savage Landor advises:

In every poem train the leading shoot;
Break off the suckers. Thought erases thought,
As numerous sheep erase each other's print
When spongy moss they press or sterile sand.
Blades thickly sown want nutriment and droop,
Although the seed be sound and rich the soil;
Thus healthy-born ideas, bedded close,
By dreaming fondness perish overlain.

To "train the leading shoot," then, will occasionally help the poet who arrives at an impasse. The trouble may be that two or more intentions, ideas, feelings, images, approaches, or even whole poems have grown and twisted on a single stem, and none can really flourish without being separated from the others. The mixed image of china and silver in Emily Dickinson's "It Dropped So Low—In My Regard" (page 238) is an example of how such inconsistent elements can find their way into a poem. The same thing can happen with ideas. "Purple passages" are especially good at concealing this kind of problem. Show the poem to a critical friend. He or she may accidentally stumble on the key. Or walk around the block and then look at the poem again.

Be clear, especially in the ambiguous and shadowy early stages of a poem. The stronger the wind in the sail, the greater the need for alert seamanship. As Quintilian observed, "One should not aim at being possible to understand, but at being impossible to misunderstand." Clarity, like a strong light, will often show the way. The poet who doesn't bother to straighten things out for himself or herself can't hope that the reader will care to do any better later. "Technique," Pound said, "is the test of sincerity."

QUESTIONS AND SUGGESTIONS

1. Try "random writing." Put a first phrase down; then keep going.

2. On a long walk or drive, keep trying to turn things you see into words—and see if you don't find a poem. In this one, note, the church was observed; the rest (lines 17–26), imagined or called up from other experiences.

Salvation

PAMELA AZUSENIS·

Driving past a red brick church
on a back road
in a rocky, hunger-stricken stretch
of Pennsylvania at dusk,
at the moment   5
the red neon cross clicks on
and faltering
blinks
with twisted tubes below spelling
"Jesus Saves."   10
Against the cold black hills
the buzzing sign hangs
in desperate conviction
with distant, dimly lit houses
buried in tree covered blackness   15
like misplaced stars.
Inside them the people emulate their saviour
carefully saving
mismatched buttons and bits of twine
for corporeal repairs,   20
and old Sears catalogues
and wrinkled trading stamps
for their children
on the approaching Christmas,
taking care to insure   25
the only redemption in this land.

3. Here is a poem of mine with several words or images omitted. In the context, what words or images would *you* insert if it were your poem? Compare your suggestions with the original in Appendix I. What gains or losses do you see?

In a Spring Still Not Written Of

This morning
with a class of girls outdoors, I saw
how frail poems are
in a world   with flowers,   *participle or adjective*
in which, overhead,   5
the great elms
—green, and tall—
stood   leaves in their arms.   *participle*

The girls listened equally
to my drone, reading, and to the bees'   10
ricocheting
among them for the   on the bone.   *noun*
or gazed off at a distant mower's
              of green   *noun*
and clover, flashing,   15
threshing in the new,   sunlight.   *adjective*

And all the while, dwindling,
tinier, the voices—Yeats, Marvell, Donne—
sank drowning
in a spring still not written of,   20
as only the sky
clear above the brick bell-tower
—blue, and white—
was shifting toward the hour.

Calm, indifferent, cross-legged   25
or on elbows half-lying in the grass—
how should the great dead
tell them of dying?
They will come to time for poems at last,
when they have found they are no more   30
the beautiful and young
all poems are for.

4. Here are the title and first line or lines of several poems. Choose one that is intriguing and write the poem this beginning suggests to you. (The poems are in Appendix I.)

a) *The Opening*

    Down its length the rifle barrel

b) *The Passionate Shepherd to His Love*

> Come live with me and be my love,
> And we will all the pleasures prove

c) *The Lark and the Emperor*

> Strangle the Lark.
> Place its pink tongue under glass

d) *Feeding Prisoners*

> The weeds give up suddenly after a small struggle

5. "The Dover Bitch" (1959) by Anthony Hecht (b. 1923) parodies the famous Victorian poem "Dover Beach," written about 1851 by Matthew Arnold (1822–1888). Is Hecht's point insightful? fair? Does Arnold's poem nonetheless survive the comment? Is there a poet or poem you wish to parody?

Dover Beach

The sea is calm tonight.
The tide is full, the moon lies fair
Upon the straits;—on the French coast the light
Gleams and is gone; the cliffs of England stand,
Glimmering and vast, out in the tranquil bay. 5
Come to the window, sweet is the night-air!
Only, from the long line of spray
Where the sea meets the moon-blanched land,
Listen! you hear the grating roar
Of pebbles which the waves draw back, and fling, 10
At their return, up the high strand,
Begin, and cease, and then again begin,
With tremulous cadence slow, and bring
The eternal note of sadness in.

Sophocles long ago 15
Heard it on the Aegean, and it brought
Into his mind the turbid ebb and flow
Of human misery; we
Find also in the sound a thought,
Hearing it by this distant northern sea. 20

The Sea of Faith
Was once, too, at the full, and round earth's shore
Lay like the folds of a bright girdle furled.
But now I only hear
Its melancholy, long, withdrawing roar, 25

Retreating, to the breath
Of the night-wind, down the vast edges drear
And naked shingles° of the world.   *gravel beaches*

Ah, love, let us be true
To one another! for the world, which seems   30
To lie before us like a land of dreams,
So various, so beautiful, so new,
Hath really neither joy, nor love, nor light,
Nor certitude, nor peace, nor help for pain;
And we are here as on a darkling plain   35
Swept with confused alarms of struggle and flight,
Where ignorant armies clash by night.

The Dover Bitch

(A Criticism of Life)

So there stood Matthew Arnold and this girl
With the cliffs of England crumbling away behind them,
And he said to her, "Try to be true to me,
And I'll do the same for you, for things are bad
All over, etc., etc."   5
Well now, I knew this girl. It's true she had read
Sophocles in a fairly good translation
And caught that bitter allusion to the sea,
But all the time he was talking she had in mind
The notion of what his whiskers would feel like   10
On the back of her neck. She told me later on
That after a while she got to looking out
At the lights across the channel, and really felt sad,
Thinking of all the wine and enormous beds
And blandishments in French and the perfumes.   15
And then she really got angry. To have been brought
All the way down from London, and then be addressed
As a sort of mournful cosmic last resort
Is really tough on a girl, and she was pretty.
Anyway, she watched him pace the room   20
And finger his watch-chain and seem to sweat a bit,
And then she said one or two unprintable things.
But you mustn't judge her by that. What I mean to say is,
She's really all right. I still see her once in a while
And she always treats me right. We have a drink   25
And I give her a good time, and perhaps it's a year
Before I see her again, but there she is,
Running to fat, but dependable as they come.
And sometimes I bring her a bottle of *Nuit d'Amour*.

6. The last two lines of "The Eagle" by Alfred, Lord Tennyson have been omitted below. Observing the meter and rhyme scheme established in the first stanza, complete the poem. What do the tone and metaphors in lines 1–4 call for in the completion? When you check the whole poem in Appendix I, judge how well Tennyson's last two lines carry out the potential in 1–4.

The Eagle

He clasps the crag with crooked hands;
Close to the sun in lonely lands,
Ringed with the azure world, he stands.

The wrinkled sea beneath him crawls;

_____

_____

7. Here is a "group" poem written by a class of fifth-graders. Using the blackboard as a "mind," they put in all the "snake" words and images they could think of and then, making up the simplest of stories, filled in *a b c b* quatrains. How'd they do?

The Snake

Suddenly it flickered at my feet
    As I walked in the garden,
And just as suddenly I felt
    It make my breathing harden.

It might have been a cord or chain   5
    Left lying after play,
It seemed as still as a pole,
    And didn't move away.

But I knew that it was something else,
    Something not to step on,   10
Colorful and creepy and slimy
    And cool, like a live weapon.

Like a tiny pitchfork, quick as lightning,
    Its tongue sparked from its socket.
It looked as thin and slim and hissing   15
    And mean as a countdown rocket.

Its eyes glowed like a switchboard
    That showed the systems were on.
He scared me—and I scared him,
    For suddenly he was gone.   20

8. Get up two hours before you usually do—best if it's not light out yet. Find a comfortable vantage-point (window, back steps, bus-stop bench) and make sen-

tences for everything you observe. Metaphors are welcome ("The first light, blue as a gas flame . . .").

POEMS TO CONSIDER

Fable   1847

RALPH WALDO EMERSON   (1803–1882)

The mountain and the squirrel
Had a quarrel;
And the former called the latter "little Prig."
Bun replied,
"You are doubtless very big;   5
But all sorts of things and weather
Must be taken in together
To make up a year
And a sphere.
And I think it no disgrace   10
To occupy my place.
If I'm not so large as you,
You are not so small as I,
And not half so spry.
I'll not deny you make   15
A very pretty squirrel track;
Talents differ: all is well and wisely put;
If I cannot carry forests on my back,
Neither can you crack a nut."

Browsers   1983

MICHAEL FINLEY   (b. 1950)

He flipped through the magazines
in the periodical room.

The Cadillac, he thought to himself,
is definitely the
Rolls-Royce of automobiles.   5

She sauntered through the stacks,
fingertips dusting
the tops of rows.
The things I don't know,
she shook her head sadly,   10
could fill a book.

They stand back to back
in the checkout line,
shifting their weights
from one foot to the next,   15

like two ships passing
in broad daylight.

First Love   *1985*

MICHAEL WATERS   (b. 1949)

So what if you're living in Jersey
with a man who works for the phone company.
Your life must be miserable—
a name lost in a row of mailboxes

studding the loud, gravel drive,   5
your husband shaking the whole trailer
when he grunts onto you each night,
his workshirts souring in one corner.

So what if none of this is true
and your daughters grow lovely on lawns,   10
if your husband steps off the 5:14
asking, "Can we do nothing this evening?"

I imagine the fireplace, the flokati rug,
the cat sighing on her silk pillow.

So what if I live just across the river   15
and speak to the immigrant shopkeepers

or to no one, so what if I chain
my dog to a hydrant for hours, so what
if I buy a single pork chop for dinner.
So what if this life flows on, if I read   20

a passage in some Russian novella
and think of you, if I go to the table
to write this poem, but have nothing to say
except *so what, so what, so what?*

To Paint a Water Lily   1959

TED HUGHES (b. 1930)

A green level of lily leaves
Roofs the pond's chamber and paves

The flies' furious arena: study
These, the two minds of this lady.

First observe the air's dragonfly   5
That eats meat, that bullets by

Or stands in space to take aim;
Others as dangerous comb the hum

Under the trees. There are battle-shouts
And death-cries everywhere hereabouts   10

But inaudible, so the eyes praise
To see the colours of these flies

Rainbow their arcs, spark, or settle
Cooling like beads of molten metal

Through the spectrum. Think what worse   15
Is the pond-bed's matter of course;

Prehistoric bedragonned times
Crawl that darkness with Latin names,

Have evolved no improvements there,
Jaws for heads, the set stare,   20

Ignorant of age as of hour—
Now paint the long-necked lily-flower

Which, deep in both worlds, can be still
As a painting, trembling hardly at all

Though the dragonfly alight,   25
Whatever horror nudge her root.

Make Big Money at Home! Write Poems in Spare Time!   1962

HOWARD NEMEROV (b. 1920)

Oliver wanted to write about reality.
He sat before a wooden table,
He poised his wooden pencil
Above his pad of wooden paper,
And attempted to think about agony   5
And history, and the meaning of history,
And all stuff like that there.

Suddenly this wooden thought got in his head:
A Tree. That's all, no more than that,
Just one tree, not even a note   10
As to whether it was deciduous
Or evergreen, or even where it stood.
Still, because it came unbidden,
It was inspiration, and had to be dealt with.

Oliver hoped that this particular tree   15
Would turn out to be fashionable,
The axle of the universe, maybe,

Or some other mythologically
Respectable tree-contraption
With dryads, or having to do   20
With the knowledge of Good and Evil, and the Fall.

"A Tree," he wrote down with his wooden pencil
Upon his pad of wooden paper
Supported by the wooden table.
And while he sat there waiting   25
For what would come next to come next,
The whole wooden house began to become
Silent, particularly silent, sinisterly so.

Poem for a Future Academic   1984

JAY MEEK   (b. 1937)

I've loved having words to live with,
and in twenty-five years

it'll be the twenty-fifth anniversary
of the words to this poem.

Don't look in it for hidden meanings.   5
What I've written

is what I meant,
and I meant to hide nothing from you.

When students write their hard poems,
be generous with them,   10

but do not call them creative writers.
I think they are poets.

Myself, I never wanted to be a poet—
I write what I write.

And I hope you will like what I write   15
without feeling my work

gives you an importance
you haven't already found in yourself.

If some day you teach my simple lyric,
do not call me   20

by my given name,
and do not leave my name on the board.

I've loved the chance I had at life.
Twenty-five years!

O, if you can make my life your living,   25
I hope you eat well.

Do not hate the poets of your own time.
Tell your students I said hello.

Lapis Lazuli   1939

WILLIAM BUTLER YEATS   (1865–1939)

I have heard that hysterical women say
They are sick of the palette and fiddle-bow,
Of poets that are always gay,
For everybody knows or else should know
That if nothing drastic is done   5
Aeroplane and Zeppelin will come out,
Pitch like King Billy bomb-balls in
Until the town lie beaten flat°.

All perform their tragic play,
There struts Hamlet, there is Lear,   10
That's Ophelia, that Cordelia;
Yet they, should the last scene be there,
The great stage curtain about to drop,
If worthy their prominent part in the play,

8 The English King William III, whose cannon won the Battle of Boyne in Ireland in
1690.

Do not break up their lines to weep.   15
They know that Hamlet and Lear are gay;
Gaiety transfiguring all that dread.
All men have aimed at, found and lost;
Black out; Heaven blazing into the head:
Tragedy wrought to its uttermost.   20
Though Hamlet rambles and Lear rages,
And all the drop-scenes drop at once
Upon a hundred thousand stages,
It cannot grow by an inch or an ounce.

On their own feet they came, or on shipboard,   25
Camelback, horseback, ass-back, mule-back,
Old civilizations put to the sword.
Then they and their wisdom went to rack:
No handiwork of Callimachus°,   *Greek sculptor, 5th* C. B.C.
Who handled marble as if it were bronze,   30
Made draperies that seemed to rise
When sea-wind swept the corner, stands;
His long lamp-chimney shaped like the stem
Of a slender palm, stood but a day;
All things fall and are built again,   35
And those that build them again are gay.

Two Chinamen, behind them a third,
Are carved in lapis lazuli°,   *a deep-blue*
Over them flies a long-legged bird,   *semiprecious stone*
A symbol of longevity;
The third, doubtless a serving-man,   40
Carries a musical instrument.
Every discoloration of the stone,
Every accidental crack or dent,
Seems a water-course or an avalanche,   45
Or lofty slope where it still snows
Though doubtless plum or cherry-branch
Sweetens the little half-way house
Those Chinamen climb towards, and I
Delight to imagine them seated there;   50
There, on the mountain and the sky,
On all the tragic scene they stare.
One asks for mournful melodies;
Accomplished fingers begin to play.
Their eyes mid many wrinkles, their eyes,   55
Their ancient, glittering eyes, are gay.

Revising (I):
Both Ends of the Pencil

Craft completes magic; technique carries out inspiration. Sometimes poets claim otherwise, pretending that making poems is all too arcane and mysterious a process to be explicable. But as Edmund Waller (1606–1687) put it wittily:

Poets lose half the praise they should have got,
Could it be known what they discreetly blot.

His contemporary, John Dryden, translating Boileau's *L'Art Poétique* (1674), offered this advice:

Gently make haste, of labor not afraid;
A hundred times consider what you've said:
Polish, repolish, every color lay,
And sometimes add, but oftener take away.
'Tis not enough, when swarming faults are writ,
That here and there are scattered sparks of wit.

Technique is knowing how to use, to focus, to deploy what comes magically. As every creative act calls for a critical one, an evaluation, so it also requires a technical act: shaping, placing, incorporating. Inspiration and technique are like the two legs of a long-distance runner. As each inspiration shows technique how to do the next thing, technique opens the way for the next inspiration.

The secret of writing is rewriting. As W. H. Auden notes, "Literary composition in the twentieth century A.D. is pretty much what it was in the twentieth century B.C.: nearly everything has still to be done by hand." Rewriting is exploring, trying out. The poet uses both ends of the pencil. Luckily, unlike the sculptor or the painter, the poet can go back to earlier versions if he or she makes a mistake. A typical way is to scratch out and add, scratch out and add, scribbling alternatives in the margin, until the sheet is embroidered with corrections—and then to recopy the best version that can be sorted out of it. Then the poet goes on scratching out and adding on that draft. There are 175 work-sheets for a poem by E. E. Cummings ("rosetree, rosetree"), and Donald Hall reports that "The Town of Hill" (page 348) went through fifty or sixty drafts; "three years of intensive work, with lots and lots of changes." The poem's deceptive simplicity is a result of labor, fusing Hall's boyhood memories of the town that was later abandoned and flooded to make a lake, with his present vision of the underwater town. Like simplicity, spontaneity and naturalness are usually the result of hard work. Easy writing tends to produce hard reading; hard writing, to produce easy reading. As one beginning poet, Sharon Lillevig, observed:

Effortless

The fluid
dancer sweats.

Leaps and Carpentry

This chapter will look at a number of poets' actual revisions, as examples of the creative process, of the lucky leaps and the careful carpentry. Consider first this poem of Richard Wilbur's.

Love Calls Us to the Things of This World

The eyes open to a cry of pulleys,
And spirited from sleep, the astounded soul
Hangs for a moment bodiless and simple
As false dawn.
                    Outside the open window
The morning air is all awash with angels.   5

Some are in bed-sheets, some are in blouses,
Some are in smocks: but truly there they are.
Now they are rising together in calm swells
Of halcyon feeling, filling whatever they wear
With the deep joy of their impersonal breathing;   10

Now they are flying in place, conveying
The terrible speed of their omnipresence, moving
And staying like white water; and now of a sudden
They swoon down into so rapt a quiet
That nobody seems to be there.
                     The soul shrinks   15

From all that it is about to remember,
From the punctual rape of every blessed day,
And cries,
        "Oh, let there be nothing on earth but laundry,
Nothing but rosy hands in the rising steam
And clear dances done in the sight of heaven."   20

Yet, as the sun acknowledges
With a warm look the world's hunks and colors,
The soul descends once more in bitter love
To accept the waking body, saying now
In a changed voice as the man yawns and rises,   25

"Bring them down from their ruddy gallows;
Let there be clean linen for the backs of thieves;
Let lovers go fresh and sweet to be undone,
And the heaviest nuns walk in a pure floating
Of dark habits,
            keeping their difficult balance."   30

This is a superb, passionate poem. The sight of laundry being drawn into the morning air between two buildings becomes first a vision of wished-for angelic purity; and then, with accepting insight, of the mingled purity and impurity of the human condition. Seeing the pieces of laundry billowing in the breeze, the waking person momentarily mistakes them for angels. Not fully awake, he is an "astounded soul," "for a moment bodiless and simple." He "shrinks" from facing the dirtying reality of the world. As if answering the "cry of pulleys," the soul "cries":

"Oh, let there be nothing on earth but laundry,
Nothing but rosy hands in the rising steam
And clear dances done in the sight of heaven."

But in stanza 5, reminded by the sun's "warm look," "The soul descends once more in bitter love / To accept the waking body"—its own inescapable attachment to dirtying reality—and, in the last stanza, to accept the dirtying world itself. The wish for purity is replaced by compassion for the ambiguities and precariousness of the human condition.

The poem's trajectory is psychological, dramatic; its theme, deeply Christian, though not in a doctrinal way; its title, from Saint Augustine. The initial mistaking of laundry for angels seems natural enough for the half-awakened consciousness; the whimsicality of the mistake is recognized soon enough, as the breeze slackens: "nobody seems to be there." But the universal desire for purity, the wish to avoid the inevitable sullying of "every blessèd day," is, however accidentally raised and fancifully expressed, real and in no way whimsical. The colloquial emphatic "blessèd" accidentally carries on the religious imagery. The poem's always useful puns ("spirited from sleep," "awash with angels," "The soul shrinks") culminate in the nuns' "dark habits." Even "the heaviest" (most tempted and worldly) of them, nonetheless, walk "in a pure floating," "keeping their difficult balance," *in* but not *of* the world. With the somewhat biblical word "linen," the "ruddy gallows" suggests the crucifixion, and the "thieves" the two thieves on crosses on either side of Christ. Christ, the poem subtly reminds us, also descended in love into the world and the flesh. The soul's two speeches are, of course, prayers, recognizing that, although the world is often less ideal than we might wish, we must nonetheless live in it and love it.

Richard Wilbur has generously published the first six drafts of the poem's opening lines. In them it is possible to follow the developing poem as it searches for both its language and its form.

DRAFT 1

My eyes came open to the squeak of pulleys
My spirit, shocked from the brothel of itself

Lack of punctuation after the first line suggests that this draft is notational, trying out possibilities for opening the poem. The lines are iambic pentameter, and we can guess that the poet has been mulling them over in his head until they have taken on a distinct metrical shape before trying them on paper. The oddity in the lines is the image "brothel." Sleep, the withdrawal of the soul from the body, is seen very forcefully as a sort of self-indulgence on the soul's part. The implicit rebuke, which will be softened in the final poem to an awareness of the soul's natural but mistaken repugnance for the "things of this world," shows that the thematic direction of the poem is already given. The paradox (or confusion) of a fleshly image for the soul's self-indulgence is striking. That the poet distrusts "brothel," however, is clear from the second draft, where the image is altered.

My eyes came open to the shriek of pulleys,
And the soul, spirited from its proper wallow,
Hung in the air as bodiless and hollow

In place of the literal but uninteresting "squeak" of pulleys, the poet tries "shriek," which personifies them. The fairly straightforward "shocked" is replaced by the pun "spirited"—in the sense of something's being carried away mysteriously or secretly. Punctuated, the lines begin to be a sentence. Whichever word came first, a rhyme has suggested itself: "wallow-hollow," and so a further formal possibility has been engaged. In the third draft, perhaps foreseeing trouble in rhyming "pulleys," the poet reverses the word order and replaces "shriek" with "cry."

DRAFT 3

My eyes came open to the pulleys' cry.
The soul, spirited from its proper wallow,
Hung in the air as bodiless and hollow
As light that frothed upon the wall opposing;
But what most caught my eyes at their unclosing
Was two gray ropes that yanked across the sky.
One after one into the window frame
. . . the hosts of laundry came

Propelled, no doubt, by a desire to get on with it, and apparently released by the possibility of rhyming, the poem makes a spurt forward. Without the negative connotations of "shriek" (and its too attention-getting personification), "cry" seems right, meaning ambiguously both to call out in grief or suffering, and to announce. While "pulleys' cry" is awkward, it sets up the very usable rhyme of "sky"—which the poet may not yet know how he will use but which provides an easy target for a subsequent line. Again, whichever came first, the rhyme-pairs "opposing-unclosing" and "frame-came" allow the draft to move forward to the completion of its exposition and what sounds like the end of a stanza. The dots in line 8 indicate a blank the poet leaves to be filled later.

Rhyming has got the poem this far. But the poet is plainly unsatisfied, as the unfinished and unpunctuated line 8 shows. In the fourth draft *all* the rhyme-words except "cry" disappear from the poem, and "cry" moves back to a less clumsy place in its line. The causes, if not the order, of the poet's dissatisfactions can be guessed. "Wallow" muted somewhat the comparison of the soul's weakness to fleshliness, but the confusion is still there, along with an unfortunate animal connotation. Because "hollow" suggests the vacant interior of something solid, it isn't really accurate for the soul. Saying "the wall opposing," to set up the rhyme, is rather stagy—the normal phrase would be "the opposite wall." Saying "at their unclosing" is mere padding. Lines 5–6 seem inaccurate or, at least, a needless digression, for the laundry, not the "two gray ropes," is surely what "most caught my eyes." I suspect it caused the poet some pain to give up the nice detail of the ropes, and especially the word "yanked," which is the first word in the poem to strike naturally and unaffectedly the colloquial tone that the final version values in "awash," "shrinks," "blessèd," "hunks," and "ruddy" (an English colloquialism meaning reddish, and suggesting "bloody"). The window "frame" distracts from what is seen through the window, and line 7 as a whole is open to the misreading of coming *into* the room through the window. "One by one" also limits the view of the laundry and, if allowed to stand, would preclude the panoramic view in the final version's second and third stanzas.

DRAFT 4

The eyes open to a cry of pulleys,
And the soul, so suddenly spirited from sleep,
Hangs in the air as bodiless and simple
As morning sunlight frothing on the floor,
While just outside the window
The air is solid with a dance of angels.

Freedom from rhyme now permits the poem to do in six lines what it had done in eight, and the first line has reached its final form. In line 2 the soul is now spirited merely from "sleep" instead of brothel or wallow. "Hollow" is replaced with the apt "simple" ("bodiless and simple"); that is, simply itself, uncomplicated, in its own nature. But "simple" also means ignorant or foolish, as in "simple-minded"; and the pun looks forward to the poem's ultimate judgment on the soul's natural but foolish desire to avoid the dirtying world. Lines 5–6 of this draft focus quickly and unceremoniously on the laundry/angels. The house-cleaning between the third and fourth drafts sweeps away "the hosts of laundry," which was obviously an attempt to sneak up on the word "angels." The fourth draft is direct: "The air is solid with a dance of angels." The explanatory "laundry" is dropped. The bed-sheets, blouses, smocks of the second stanza will make the exposition perfectly clear; and the first stanza can end without apology on the startling appearance of "angels."

The tightening of this draft includes the tentative dropping of iambic pentameter. For the moment the lines will be left not only without rhymes but also free to determine their own length. The possibility is a stanza of lines of differing lengths, such as the poet has used in other poems. If the indentations indicate equal line-length (as they conventionally do), the poet is reading lines 1 and 5 as three feet, line 2 as five feet, and lines 3–4 and 6 as four feet. He is counting loosely, I think, waiting to see how things fall out before being more decisive. For instance, line 1 might be scanned: "The éyes | ópen | tŏ a crý | ŏf púl|lĕys"—four feet. But, apparently, the poet is scanning it as three feet: "Thĕ eyes óp|ĕn tŏ ă cry | ŏf púl|lĕys" This line and the efficient line 5 ("While just outside the window") are the main beneficiaries of dropping the pentameter requirement.

Suggested by this metrical concession (or suggesting it), one of the major changes in the poem occurs: the shift from past to present tense, with a consequent increase in immediacy, appropriate to the Keatsian impressionism of the poem. "Hangs" now looks forward to the "ruddy gallows" of the last stanza, as "hung" could not. The other major change is from the first to the third person: "My eyes" become only "The eyes," opening the way to "the man yawns and rises" in stanza 5. The soul, rather than a first-person speaker, becomes the poem's protagonist. This change provides an important, measuring distance between the voice of the poem and the soul, whose fantasies and recognitions make up the central action. Having this central action occur entirely within the soul, at some remove from the man, who seems almost unaware of this drama, avoids any thorny questions about the relationship of body, mind, and soul—or who/what corrects the soul's mistaken wish for untainted purity. The poem's psychology is, thus, allegorized, simplified. The initial punitive tone toward the soul ("brothel") disappears, and it is the soul itself that, recognizing its understandable desire to disentangle itself from them, "descends in bitter love / To accept the waking body" and the world. The soul's deflection from its true compassion is only momentary, occurring in those few instants of waking before "the man yawns and rises." In the next draft the poet underlines this revision by altering line 3 from "hangs in the air as bodiless and simple" to "Hangs for a moment bodiless and simple." Everything—vision of laundry as angels, the two prayers—in a moment; and the soul's momentary error is not sinful lapse but a *simple* foolishness which it corrects quickly. (This change from first to third person was already implicit in the second draft's "My eyes . . . *the* soul," but it took two further drafts to respond to the cue.) Significant advance as the fourth draft is, the stanza is not finished.

DRAFT 5

The eyes open to a cry of pulleys,
And spirited from sleep, the astounded soul
Hangs for a moment bodiless and simple
As dawn light in the moment of its breaking:
        Outside the open window
The air is crowded with a

The unnecessary "so suddenly" in line 2 vanishes (being spirited away is always sudden to the victim); and its space in the line is given to "astounded," which conveys the dramatic excitement one would feel at perceiving angels outside the bedroom window. It also, of course, prepares the way for making allowances for the soul's momentary error. With "for a moment" substituted in line 3, the poem's first three lines are complete. Line 4 gets rid of the "frothed" and "frothing" of the third and fourth drafts. The idea of froth's bubbly airiness, whether on "wall opposing" or on the floor, may picture flickery early sunlight; but the connotations are so negative—foam, frothing at the mouth—that the possibility is discarded. The floor seems as irrelevant and digressive as the wall opposing had been. Line 5 is sharpened: the rather empty "While just" is dropped and the window is made "open," which conveys the immediacy of the angels, as if they might indeed enter the room. Picking up the "open" (verb) of line 1, "the open window" (adjective) here makes the vision doubly close and surprising. In line 6 the poet discards the too static and dense adjective "solid"—"The air is solid with a dance of angels"—in favor of the plainer but more active "crowded." But, before he can add either "dance of angels" or "host of angels," the pending possibilities, the draft breaks off.

The most decisive thing the poet does in the fifth draft is to firm the meter. The four lines that begin with the left margin are iambic pentameter, which is to become again the norm of the poem; the half indentation of line 1 indicates that it is now being scanned as tetrameter, the full indentation of line 5 that it is now being scanned as trimeter.

DRAFT 6

The eyes open to a cry of pulleys,
And spirited from sleep, the astounded soul
Hangs for a moment bodiless and simple
As false dawn.
    Outside the open window,
The air is leaping with a rout of angels.
    Some are in bedsheets, some are in dresses,
        it does not seem to matter

The weakest line in the fifth draft was line 4: "As dawn light in the moment of its breaking." "in the moment" is niggling and lamely repeats "for a moment" in line 3; "of its breaking" is essentially empty. At a stroke in that sixth draft, the poet drops those phrases and alters "As dawn light" to "As false dawn"—period. The economy is complete. False dawn, the early light before sunrise, is itself "bodiless and simple," a vague, incomplete stage, eerie and somehow nonphysical. Like the soul's fanciful vision and its wish for utter and untested purity, it is "false dawn"; the soul's truer prayer is saved, like the sun's "warm look" itself, for the fifth and sixth stanzas. As the progression from false dawn to sunrise is natural, so, by implication, is the soul's from false prayer to true.

The other troublesome line in the fifth draft is line 6: "The air is crowded with a"—which is left unfinished. As "solid" was too heavy and static, so "crowded" is too flat. In the sixth draft the poet tries again for liveliness and surprise: "The air is leaping with a rout of angels." "Rout," which suggests unruliness, suitably describes the free-blowing laundry and adds the unexpected pleasure of imagining a boisterous and disorderly crowd of angels. Heavenly fun, the word implies, needn't be dull. But the word is hardly serious enough for the variety of angelic attitudes and meanings that are to follow in stanzas 2 and 3 ("calm swells of halcyon feeling," "the terrible speed of their omnipresence," for example). And "The air is leaping" seems dyslexic, though perfectly clear. Presumably on the next try, the poet hits the mark of the line exactly: "The morning air is all awash with angels," with its vividly descriptive and explanatory pun.

Presumably, too, in the final draft, the next two lines are properly put forward to stanza 2. (Why the poet alters "dresses" to "blouses" in the first line of stanza 2 is a puzzle the reader may consider.) With the poet's recognition that the two short lines, 4 and 5, together make a single pentameter line, the essential form of the poem's first stanza is set: one line of tetrameter, five of pentameter. Problems in maintaining that pattern in subsequent stanzas might have sent the poet back to rework stanza 1, but didn't. The decision whether to print "As false dawn. Outside the open window" as a continuous line or a dropped-line was presumably deferred. It was made only when other stanzas showed places where a dropped-line could be effective, especially in stanza 3 ("That nobody seems to be there. / The soul shrinks") and stanza 6 ("Of dark habits, / keeping their difficult balance"), where the dropped-line, along with the metrical irregularities, beautifully illustrates the precariousness in the line's meaning. Not incidentally, the drafts show the poet writing with practiced ease in metered lines, deftly using the trochaic "open" in line 1 for its surprise and positioning (after the first draft) the word "hangs" at the beginning of its line.

The poem is developing in several ways simultaneously. Its main idea, at first fuzzy and uncertain, clarifies with each successive draft. As the details of the scene are considered, then accepted or dropped, the visual impression sharpens. The diction becomes exact; tone and nuance focus with precision. And, by no means least important, after several trials the form settles into a pattern that is appropriate and comfortable. From so sure and carefully modulated a beginning, the poet can continue with confidence.

Trial-and-Error

Similar trial-and-error appears in four successive versions of three lines of "Hyperion" by John Keats (1795–1821). The crux is the image in lines 8–9. Here is the entire opening passage of the poem, with the first of Keats's four versions in italics:

Deep in the shady sadness of a vale
Far sunken from the healthy breath of morn,
Far from the fiery noon, and eve's one star,
Sat gray-haired Saturn°, quiet as a stone,   *an ancient Titan*
Still as the silence round about his lair;   5
Forest on forest hung about his head
Like cloud on cloud. *No stir of air was there,*
Not so much life as what an eagle's wing
Would spread upon a field of green eared corn,
But where the dead leaf fell, there did it rest.   10
A stream went voiceless by, still deadened more
By reason of his fallen divinity
Spreading a shade: the Naiad 'mid her reeds
Pressed her cold finger closer to her lips.

It is a melancholy scene. Saturn sits motionless in the silent, shading forest. The first phrase of the passage is exactly descriptive with its static internal off-rhyme: "stir-air-there." The trouble that Keats senses is in the image for this stillness in the next two lines. From his next version we can see what particularly bothered him. The clumsy and unnecessary "what" was obviously used merely to keep the meter. An easy solution would have been to remove the word in favor of an adjective describing the eagle. He might then have written: "Not so much life as a young eagle's wing." But Keats was also unsatisfied with the eagle. Probably he sensed that it was too positive and vigorous an image of power to be appropriate to the "fallen divinity" he was depicting. In the second version of the lines he exchanges the eagle for the tonally more relevant vulture.

> No stir of air was there,
> Not so much life as a young vulture's wing
> Would spread upon a field of green eared corn

The image that Keats intends is apparently of a large, powerful bird of prey circling high in the sky, probably gliding rather than flapping; and the point is that its wing causes absolutely *no motion* in the field of easily swayed grain far below. (In British usage *corn* indicates wheat or some other edible grain, not American corn.) Perhaps Keats has in mind the shadow of the bird's wing passing over, but not moving, the limber stalks. The vulture might suit the picture of Saturn in his vale, and even its youth might provide a useful contrast to Saturn's age and weakness.

As the third version reveals, however, Keats discards the entire image. Possibly, carrion or no, the youthful, powerful bird spoils the unvarying tone of the mournful passage. Certainly, the "field of green eared corn"—sunny, spacious, and vital—does not fit the enclosed, "shady" forest scene of defeated Saturn. Interesting though the image is in itself, it seems a wrong choice.

So, in the third version, dropping the bird image altogether, Keats tries again:

> No stir of air was there,
> Not so much life as on a summer's day
> Robs not at all the dandelion's fleece

The substitution of the untended weed for the "green eared corn" strikes the right note; and the light, easily dislodged, white-tufted seeds of the dandelion provide a good measure for the absolute stillness of air as well as, in their color and implicit ruin, a vivid parallel to the "gray-haired," ruined Titan. The image has a literal rightness and consistent, useful overtones. The double negatives, "Not . . . not . . .," may feel awkward at first, but they follow "No stir of air was there" with an emphatic absoluteness. Even the awkwardness seems, rhythmically, to mirror the uselessness of the utterly still air with its inability to dislodge even a seed. For some months Keats let the lines stand so.

Several problems must have bothered him into another, final, revision. Possibly the very choice of the lowly, common, near-comic dandelion came to seem inappropriate to a poem on a classical subject. More significantly, Keats must have recognized that "fleece," though visually accurate and fluffy enough for a head of dandelion seeds, is a poor image in the context. For one thing, fleece is really quite oily and rather heavy. For another, a fleece is not easily robbed (it would require taking the sheep whole or at least clipping him). Pieces of wool might be snagged from a fleece, but not by the wind—and ease of dislodgement is essential to the image. In any event, robbing a bit of wool from a fleece makes no sense. One other aspect of the image may have concerned Keats: the picture he has given is of a single dandelion, close-up. Having the camera farther away, so as to suggest the extent of the breezelessness, seems to have been a consideration in the revision Keats made:

> No stir of air was there,
> Not so much life as on a summer's day
> Robs not one light seed from the feathered grass

As the psychologist Rudolf Arnheim comments in *Poets at Work*, "The precision of the botanist suggested by practical language ('dandelion') is given up in favor of a description which omits the identifications of the plant but specifies the expressive perceptual features of weight and movement." Like the dead leaf in the next line, the identity of the "seed from the feathered grass" is left abstract, generic. Visually, nothing is allowed to compete with the main pictorial presentation of Saturn. The rhythm of the revised line is masterful: "Robs not one light seed from the feathered grass." The five utterly even, accented syllables at the beginning of the line suggest an evenly light, precarious balance without movement. After this, the slightly enhanced speed of "from the feathered grass" seems to pass like the looked-for, but nonexistent, breath of air. Not the least of Keats's mastery is using spondees to convey an impression of lightness! Trying and erring, waiting for the right touch, the poet carefully works beyond the initial impulse.

William Butler Yeats also approached the process of rewriting seriously:

The friends that have it I do wrong
Whenever I remake a song,
Should know what issue is at stake:
It is myself that I remake.

He sometimes rewrote, years later, poems that had already been published in a book. (W. H. Auden and Marianne Moore also continued to revise earlier poems throughout their careers.) Here, for example, as Yeats published it in 1892, is

The Sorrow of Love

The quarrel of the sparrows in the eaves,
   The full round moon and the star-laden sky,
And the loud song of the ever-singing leaves
   Had hid away earth's old and weary cry.

And then you came with those red mournful lips,   5
   And with you came the whole of the world's tears,
And all the sorrows of her labouring ships,
   And all burden of her myriad years.

And now the sparrows warring in the eaves,
   The crumbling moon, the white stars in the sky,   10
And the loud chanting of the unquiet leaves,
   Are shaken with earth's old and weary cry.

     Grave, languorous, and lovely, "The Sorrow of Love" shows the effect on the speaker of the woman "with those red mournful lips." Before her, he was unaware of "earth's old and weary cry"; and sparrows, moon, stars, and leaves had seemed only themselves. The quarreling sparrows keep this picture from seeming overpretty. After the woman, all these things of the world are, for him, "shaken with earth's old and weary cry." The positive images become now negative: "the full round moon" decays and is "crumbling," "the ever-singing leaves" are now "unquiet." Even the sparrows' quarreling is worse, "warring."

     With "those red mournful lips," the woman herself seems already to have suffered "the sorrow of love" and to bring with her, from the speaker's point of view, "the whole of the world's tears." Presumably because she rejects him, she is his induction into the "sorrow of love." It isn't quite clear what the "labouring ships" have to do with the sorrow of love, but like the sparrows, moon, stars, and leaves, they reflect the speaker's feelings about everything after the sad and beautiful woman.

When Yeats revised the poem in 1925, although only one of the rhyme-words is altered ("years" to "peers"), the poem is transformed:

The brawling of a sparrow in the eaves,
The brilliant moon and all the milky sky,
And all that famous harmony of leaves,
Had blotted out man's image and his cry.

A girl arose that had red mournful lips   5
And seemed the greatness of the world in tears,
Doomed like Odysseus and the labouring ships
And proud as Priam murdered with his peers;

Arose, and on the instant clamorous eaves,
A climbing moon upon an empty sky,   10
And all that lamentation of the leaves,
Could but compose man's image and his cry.

In discussing the 1892 version, I have used the word "woman." Although it does not appear in the text and there is nothing directly indicative of age, it seems more accurate to the history implied by her sorrowful experience of love than the word "girl" might. One of the major changes in the 1925 version, then, is the description of her as a "girl," which, at a single touch, increases the poem's pathos: so much sorrow in one so young is profoundly moving. Another major change is the depersonalization of the relationship in the poem. With the use of the third person—"girl" instead of "you"—the speaker's relationship to her (having been rejected or whatever) becomes irrelevant. In the later version, only his experience of her sorrow causes his darkened attitude. The poem loses much less in this playing down of the personal than it gains in poignancy. That gain is intensified by a third major change, in which "earth's old and weary cry" becomes "man's image and his cry." At best, the sorrow of love could have been associated only vaguely with the personified "earth." Dropping this rather weak elegance, Yeats accurately focuses the poem's tragic vision on the human. The natural details of sparrow, moon, stars, leaves (which, after all, exist apart from the human) seemed in stanza 1 to be sufficiently absorbing in themselves. After the girl has appeared, in stanza 3, their clamor, emptiness, and "lamentation" are felt by the speaker to express his feeling. The fourth major change, in lines 7–8, makes powerful use of the ships, which in the first version were a fuzzy image:

Doomed like Odysseus and the labouring ships
And proud as Priam murdered with his peers

Both epics of Homer, *Odyssey* and *Iliad,* are called into evidence. Though Odysseus and Priam are mentioned, and though these comparisons characterize the doomed, proud girl, the effect is also to imply a comparison to the two heroic women of these epics, the beautiful and doomed Helen and the proud and faithful Penelope. The "labouring ships" suggest Agamemnon's fleet as much as Odysseus's hard travels. The image of the "murdered" Priam, last king of Troy, encompasses the destruction of Troy. Thus, in their allusive fashion, these two lines gather into Yeats's poem the whole of the heroic and amorous weight of *Iliad* and *Odyssey*. The poem's claim that the sorrow of love centers "man's image and his cry" thus gathers a convincing historical density.

The "And . . . And . . . And . . ." construction of the first version is replaced by more muscular syntax. Details in the first version that were somewhat misty or romantic, like "the ever-singing leaves," are hardened and sharpened. The plural quarreling and warring sparrows—which might now distract from the distinction between the natural and the human and offer a competing miniature to the vision of the Trojan War—become only a single brawling and clamorous sparrow. Yeats here accepts a small loss in order to clarify the shape of the whole poem, as perhaps he also does in letting go the image of the "crumbling" moon.

The reduction of the number of words in the poem makes it seem cleaner and more direct; compare the effect of "The full round moon and the star-laden sky" with the effect of "The brilliant moon and all the milky sky"; or the elimination of the redundant "song" and "singing" in line 3. Dropping the somewhat fussy indentation of lines increases the poem's directness visually. The sound of the final version is everywhere more resonant. Consider the alliteration of the last two lines of the two versions:

And the loud chanting of the unquiet leaves,
    Are shaken with earth's old and weary cry

and

And all that lamentation of the leaves,
    Could but compose man's image and his cry.

The diction in general becomes more dramatic: "you came" in the first version becomes the powerful "A girl arose" in the final version; and the dramatic repetition of "Arose" at the beginning of the third stanza gives a dynamic impetus to the poem's climax, which the flat "And now" did not. Though it may be a subjective response, "arose" and "red mournful lips" also seem somehow to exchange colors in a subtle resonance.

"The Sorrow of Love" is a case of masterful rewriting. The not very clearly incorporated ships in the 1892 version show that only in the final version did Yeats accomplish what he had intended more than thirty years earlier. Yeats perhaps assumed in 1892 that the Homeric allusion was sufficiently clear.

Testing

One of a poet's most difficult jobs is assessing whether the words on the page, which seem right, will convey to a reader a feeling or impression identical to his or her own. If I describe for you the house in which my family lived when I was five years old, for instance, I have in my mind a picture of it, indeed, a whole set of pictures. I can close my eyes and see it. But when I describe it to you, do the words call up exactly the same picture? Obviously, they cannot. If I have chosen the right words, the significant details, the best that can be hoped is that you will visualize a house much *like* the house I am describing, on a street much like the street, and so on. Unless I am describing a building you have also seen (the Empire State Building, say) there is no way we can have identical images in our minds. (Films made from novels we like often disappoint because they rarely reproduce things as we imagined them.)

As writers, we deal at best in impressions of visual scenes, people, ideas, or feelings. The poet's words will always call up, for her or him, the precise scene or feeling. But the poet must consider accurately the effect the words will have on a reader, if they are to evoke in the reader something sufficiently like.

Poets tend to become almost insatiable testers and tinkerers. The old saw has it that no poet ever finishes a poem but merely abandons it. With good reason the poet learns to put a new poem away in a drawer for a time, then to have another look. What may seem a stroke of genius at midnight in the first flush of composition may appear quite otherwise in the morning or the following week. In this, poets are like manic depressives—up, down, up—about what they are doing. Because the poem that seems great today can seem dumb tomorrow and wonderful again the day after, poets need friends, other members of a writing class, and eventually editors. What may be obvious to someone else, though not to the poet, may very well start him or her going again on the poem, or provide the clue to patching a thin spot or avoiding a clunker.

Friends are handy but are sometimes too well-meaning. Praise is always nice, but the poet wants (or should want in that heart of hearts) the unvarnished truth. Dryden's seventeenth-century advice still fits:

> . . . to yourself be critic most severe.
> Fantastic wits their darling follies love;
> But find you faithful friends that will reprove,
> That on your works may look with careful eyes,
> And of your faults be zealous enemies: 5
> Lay by an author's pride and vanity,
> And from a friend a flatterer descry,
> Who seems to like, but means not what he says:

Embrace true counsel, but suspect false praise.
A sycophant will every thing admire;   10
Each verse, each sentence sets his soul on fire:
All is divine! there's not a word amiss!
He shakes with joy, and weeps with tenderness;
He overpowers you with his mighty praise.
Truth never moves in those impetuous ways;   15
A faithful friend is careful of your fame,
And freely will your heedless errors blame;
He cannot pardon a neglected line. . . .
No fool can want a sot to praise his rhymes.
The flattest work has ever in the court   20
Met with some zealous ass for its support;
And in all times a forward scribbling fop
Has found some greater fool to cry him up.

Find those, as Pope says, "Who to a friend his faults can freely show."

It must also be said that poets have spoiled good poems by one revision too
many, as Keats did in this stanza from his ballad "La Belle Dame Sans Merci." He
altered the wonderfully particular and so mysterious

> She took me to her elfin grot,
>   And there she wept and sighed full sore,
> And there I shut her wild wild eyes
>   With kisses four . . .

to the lame

> She took me to her elfin grot,
>   And there she gazed and sighed deep,
> And there I shut her wild sad eyes—
>   So kissed to sleep.

An alert editor (John Frederick Nims, who was then editing *Poetry*) saved one
of James Wright's finest poems from a disastrous revision. Here is the poem in its
final version, which, except for the changing of the title from the original "The
Blessing," is the poem Wright submitted and Nims accepted in 1960:

A Blessing

Just off the highway to Rochester, Minnesota,
Twilight bounds softly forth on the grass.

And the eyes of those two Indian ponies
Darken with kindness.
They have come gladly out of the willows   5
To welcome my friend and me.
We step over the barbed wire into the pasture
Where they have been grazing all day, alone.
They ripple tensely, they can hardly contain their happiness
That we have come.   10
They bow shyly as wet swans. They love each other.
There is no loneliness like theirs.
At home once more,
They begin munching the young tufts of spring in the darkness.
I would like to hold the slenderer one in my arms,   15
For she has walked over to me
And nuzzled my left hand.
She is black and white,
Her mane falls wild on her forehead,
And the light breeze moves me to caress her long ear   20
That is delicate as the skin over a girl's wrist.
Suddenly I realize
That if I stepped out of my body I would break
Into blossom.

Before the poem could be published, however, Wright sent this revised
version:

Just Off the Highway to Rochester, Minnesota

Twilight bounds softly out on the grass.
They have come gladly out of the willows
To welcome my friend and me.
We step over the barbed wire into the pasture
Where they have been grazing all day, alone.   5
And the eyes of those two Indian ponies
Darken.
I would like to hold the slenderer one in my arms,
For she has walked over to me
And nuzzled my left hand.   10
She is black and white,
Her mane falls wild on her forehead.
At home once more,
They begin munching the young tufts of spring in the darkness.

I think   15
That if I stepped out of my body I would break
Into blossom.

Wisely, Nims insisted on the original version and Wright agreed, changing only the title from "The Blessing" to "A Blessing" when the poem appeared in *The Branch Will Not Break* in 1963.

The revision is weaker in every particular. The main excisions (lines 9–12 and 20–21) not only flatten the description by removing two of the ponies' significant actions ("ripple tensely," "bow shyly"), but also omit the speaker's understanding of their eagerness in greeting the human visitors. Their "loneliness," moreover, is complex, for they also "love each other." They are sharing their own mutual affection, intimacy, with the visitors. The speaker understands this because he and his "friend" have come forward, presumably, in the same spirit. That the ponies "can hardly contain their happiness" prepares for the speaker's realization that his emotion, too, cannot be contained: "if I stepped out of my body I would break / Into blossom."

The ponies' sharing their love for each other with the visitors explains the speaker's curiously sexual, romantic response ("I would like to hold the slenderer one in my arms"). The revision also omits his caressing response, which completes the exchange of shared intimacies between the animals and the persons, and omits the simile ("delicate as the skin over a girl's wrist") that embodies and makes real the human half of this exchange.

In smaller ways, too, the revision is weaker. The delay in specifying "ponies" makes the opening exposition clumsily ambiguous. Omitting "with kindness" allows "Darken" to seem negative or even threatening. Moving "At home once more, / They begin munching the young tufts of spring in the darkness" down to precede the final three lines makes this action seem the culmination of the anecdote—whereas, in the original, it is this gesture of acceptance that draws from the speaker his longing "to hold the slenderer one in my arms." And the flatly rational "I think" loses the tone of surprise and excitement in "Suddenly I realize . . ."

Wright's one, later revision—from "The Blessing" to "A Blessing"—is a fine stroke, however. As Kevin Stein notes, this small change opens up the anecdote and lets Wright imply that such a transcendent moment "is more than an isolated occurrence, and, indeed, is likely to happen again."

The risks of spoiling a poem make the process of revising exciting, and are, of course, less perilous than not revising at all. Happily, unlike the painter or sculptor, the poet can easily rescue an earlier draft if he or she has begun to mess up the poem. Either way, "A hundred times consider what you've said."

QUESTIONS AND SUGGESTIONS

1. Here are Yeats's initial sketches of the poem "After Long Silence" (page 353) and a number of lines and alternatives from advancing drafts. Study them, noting the poem's growth, and compare them with the final version.

    a) Recording a visit to Olivia Shakespear in October 1929 as a proposed "Subject":

> Your hair is white
> My hair is white
> Come let us talk of love
> What other theme do we know
> When we were young
> We were in love with one another
> And then were ignorant.

    b) Notes:

> 1) Your other lovers being dead and gone
> 2) Those other lovers being dead and gone
>
> friendly light
> hair is white
>
> 1) Upon the sole theme of art and song
> 2) Upon the supreme theme of art and song
> 3) Upon that theme so fitting for the aged; young
>   We loved each other and were ignorant
>
> Once more I have kissed your hand and it is right
> All other lovers being estranged or dead
>
> The heavy curtains drawn—the candle light
> Waging a doubtful battle with the shade
>
> 1) We call our wisdom up and descant
> 2) We call upon wisdom and descant
>   Upon the supreme theme of art and song
>   Decrepitude increases wisdom—young
>   We loved each other and were ignorant
>
> The candle hidden by its friendly shade
> The curtain drawn on the unfriendly night
> That we descant and yet again descant
> Upon the supreme theme of art and song

1) The friendly lamp light hidden by its shade
2) Unfriendly lamp light hidden by its shade

1) And shutters clipped upon the deepening night
2) Those curtains drawn upon the deepening night

That we descant and yet again descant
Upon the supreme theme of art and song—
Bodily decrepitude is wisdom—young

Once more I have kissed your hand and it is right
All other lovers being estranged or dead
Unfriendly lamplight hidden by its shade
The curtains drawn upon the deepening night—

2. Here are drafts and revisions of lines by William Wordsworth and Rupert Brooke (1887–1915), and of a poem by Robert Frost. Consider why the poets made the changes and whether they involve gains or losses.

a) from Wordsworth's *The Prelude*:

> Magnificent
> The morning was, in memorable pomp,
> More glorious than I ever had beheld.
> The sea was laughing at a distance; all
> The solid mountains were as bright as clouds.

> Magnificent
> The morning rose, in memorable pomp,
> Glorious as e'er I had beheld—in front
> The sea lay laughing at a distance; near,
> The solid mountains shone, bright as the clouds.

b) from Wordsworth's "The Green Linnet":

> The May is come again:—how sweet
> To sit upon my orchard-seat!
> And birds and flowers once more to greet,
>   My last year's friends together:
> My thoughts they all by turns employ;
> A whispering leaf is now my joy,
> And then a bird will be the toy
>   That doth my fancy tether.

> Beneath these fruit-tree boughs that shed
> Their snow-white blossoms on my head,
> With brightest sunshine round me spread
>   Of spring's unclouded weather,

In this sequestered nook how sweet
To sit upon my orchard-seat!
And birds and flowers once more to greet,
    My last year's friends together.

c) from Rupert Brooke's "The Soldier":

If I should die think of me
That in some corner of a foreign field
Something of England lies.

If I should die, think only this of me:
That there's some corner of a foreign field
That is forever England. There shall be
In that rich earth a richer dust concealed

d) Robert Frost:

In White   1912

A dented spider like a snowdrop white
On a white Heal-all, holding up a moth
Like a white piece of lifeless satin cloth—
Saw ever curious eye so strange a sight?
Portent in little, assorted death and blight   5
Like the ingredients of a witches' broth?
The beady spider, the flower like a froth,
And the moth carried like a paper kite.

What had that flower to do with being white,
The blue Brunella every child's delight?   10
What brought the kindred spider to that height?
(Make we no thesis of the miller's° plight.)   *miller-moth*
What but design of darkness and of night?
Design, design! Do I use the word aright?

Design   1936

I found a dimpled spider, fat and white,
On a white heal-all, holding up a moth
Like a white piece of rigid satin cloth—
Assorted characters of death and blight
Mixed ready to begin the morning right,   5
Like the ingredients of a witches' broth—
A snow-drop spider, a flower like a froth,
And dead wings carried like a paper kite.

What had that flower to do with being white,
The wayside blue and innocent heal-all?   10
What brought the kindred spider to that height,
Then steered the white moth thither in the night?
What but design of darkness to appall?—
If design govern in a thing so small.

3. Choose a completed but somehow still unsatisfactory poem of your own, and
have another try at revising it. Read it aloud several times. Does anything make
you wince—something you'd be embarrassed to show? (Maybe that's where the
trouble is.) Try taking out one or two words (the least effective) or, if the poem is
metered, a foot out of each line; does that open it up? Look back through the drafts
for a lost word, image, or detail that might start the poem moving again. Type it
over, varying the stanzas or breaking it into stanzas.

4. Write a deliberate imitation of a poet as a way of exploring his or her technique.
What qualities of subject, form, diction, and so on, are most telling? Here is a
student's imitation of Alexander Pope. Compare it to the passages by Pope on pages
83 and 404. Is it a fair likeness?

Essay on Pope

The poet's proper study is his kind,
Both to instruct, and to inspire the mind;
Nor least of all the rhyming breed is Pope,
Who springs eternal in the muses' scope.
In Homer first he found the poet's chart,   5
The rules of Nature are the rules of Art;
And whither Homer went, went Pope in stride,
Both followed Nature, and avoided Pride.
His meters danced the dainty minuet,
The partners, speech and accent, finely met,   10
Or swiftly stomped along the printed ways
With steps as thund'rous as his scorn, or praise.
He taught the lowly urchin couplet skill
To use the common tongue, yet not speak ill,
To preach philosophy, or sing a strain   15
Of sylvan song, or curse in Horace' vein;
And drilled his eager pupil in the rules
Of poise, precision, grace. O best of schools:
A poet skilled in craft, oft filled with fire,
None better to instruct, or to inspire!   20

5. Here are three *very* tempting, deft, or powerful poems by students. What
suggestions for revising would you offer, if any? As much as possible, consider the

potential in each poem's subject as well as the poet's apparent intention. Be specific. Be helpful.

a) *Without the Ditch*

WILLIAM VAUGHAN*

A reconcilement of remotest mind
needs more than wind to gather death from gestures,
death from time, your death as steady an impression
as a stabbed horse screaming opera in a storm.

The flowing gules, the horse-blood of a storm   5
pulmonary to the wind, darkening like war,
seen in visored, chilling rain,
the zig-zagged, hand-cranked blackness of before.

A membrane-webbed surcease of too-soft snow
rhymed with the world's dead fur, untenanted.   10
One fatal star descried but warily
to hint in ophthalmic shovel-fulls of light

how clouds fight up some crippled swan
and with tall hands pull down the conquered sky.
What is our life without the sudden pillow,   15
our death without the ditch, in which to die?

b) *Naked Fifty-Eight-Year-Old Women*

STEVE MILLER*

He knows the second cousin of the stepson
    of the professor who wrote my physics text.
He knows the precise formula for the chemical
    in my popsicle that makes it taste like cherry
    instead of grape.   5
He knows the intricate mating habits
    of the little black bugs that make their home
    among the roots of my favorite spider plant.
He knows the favorite ice cream of the granddaughter
    of the aged woman who painted the fluorescent numbers 10
    on my desk-top alarm clock.
He knows the name of the beagle that belongs to the girl
    who stomped on the grapes that went into the wine
    that I drank last night.
He knows many things, but he doesn't know that,   15
    sometimes, the mind, like most fifty-eight-year-old
    women, should not be exposed.

c) *Lovers in the Health Science Library*

STACEY MOODY˙

Your warm strong fingers carefully graze my shoulders
The action potentials travel down the fibers
From the receptor cells just under the skin
Through the peripheral nerve and the plexus
Ascending the anterior spinal thalamic tract   5
Summating in the thalamus
Creating awareness of the warmth
Between you and me.

6. Recall an encounter with a wasp, spider, beetle, praying mantis, snail, or the like. Look the creature up in a good encyclopedia or natural history text, if possible one with color photographs. Might there be a poem in it?

POEMS TO CONSIDER

from *The Task*   1785

WILLIAM COWPER   (1731–1800)

    There is a pleasure in poetic pains
Which only poets know. The shifts and turns,
Th' expedients and inventions, multiform,
To which the mind resorts, in chase of terms
Though apt, yet coy, and difficult to win—   5
T'arrest the fleeting images that fill
The mirror of the mind, and hold them fast,
And force them sit till he has pencil'd off
A faithful likeness of the forms he views;
Then to dispose his copies with such art,   10
That each may find its most propitious light,
And shine by situation, hardly less
Than by the labour and the skill it cost;
Are occupations of the poet's mind
So pleasing, and that steal away the thought   15
With such address from themes of sad import,

That, lost in his own musings, happy man!
He feels th' anxieties of life, denied
Their wonted entertainment, all retire.
Such joys has he that sings. But ah! not such,   20
Or seldom such, the hearers of his song.
Fastidious, or else listless, or perhaps
Aware of nothing arduous in a task
They never undertook, they little note
His dangers or escapes, and haply find   25
There least amusement where he found the most.

The Town of Hill   1971

DONALD HALL   (b. 1928)

Back of the dam, under a
flat pad

of water, church
bells ring

in the ears of lilies,   5
a child's swing

curls in the current
of a yard, horned

pout sleep
in a green   10

mailbox, and
a boy walks

from a screened
porch beneath

the man-shaped   15
leaves of an oak

down the street looking
at the town

of Hill that water
covered forty

years ago,
and the screen

door shuts
under dream water.

Miracle Mile

1984

for Gerald Stern

ED OCHESTER   (b. 1939)

Why weep?
I am going to drive past Elby's Big Boy
and back, I am going to park beneath
the statue of Big Boy with his checkered pants
and his greasy cowlick like Reagan's,
I am going to admire his rosy cheeks
rounded as buttocks, and walk in to order
the minced veal parmesan. I am going to eat
garlic bread until the rich oil
runs down my jowls
and wipe my hands on dozens of paper napkins
insubstantial as dreams. I am going to think Cafe Brulot
as I drink a Coke and tip ten percent.
I am going to drive
past Cappelman's Discount Clothes
whistling Vivaldi and honk at the girls.
I am going to circle Our Lady of Perpetual Misery
lit by floodlights and the crowd queuing up
at the Red Lobster to gobble Surf 'N Turf
and drive past what may be a rapist humble
as Uriah Heep leaning against a Honda
in the outer dark of the parking lot at Sears.
I am going to walk into the Monroeville Mall
where George Romero shot *Night of the Living Dead*
and admire the heavy ironware in Horne's,
the electric woks and the microwaves,

the Dazey food strippers, the juice extractors
with automatic pulp ejectors,
the Wear-ever popcorn poppers,
toaster ovens without end   30
and the kids walking the Walkman
around the Mall in a *paseo*
and shoplifting small goods—
a bra transparent as our prayers—
or palming packs of rubbers with the couple   35
on the package silhouetted by the setting sun.
I am going to admire the toucan in the Mall's aviary,
his beak the shape of a giant Brazil nut,
and be fitted for Harris tweed
at Hughes & Hatcher, where the cretinous salemen   40
bob and slaver over my big roll of bills.
I'm going to chuckle at the basset hound
smoking a pipe in the Hushpuppy display—
she looks like a friend—and I am going to buy
chocolate pretzels at the Bavarian Haus.   45
I am going to drive past the Sheraton
more beautiful than any building in Japan.
I am going to follow the rumble and stink
of the garbage trucks into the dawn
and think of Camus, how he said he knew   50
with a certainty that our work is nothing
but the long journey to recover
through the detours of art
the two or three simple
great images which first   55
gained access to our hearts.

The Saint and the Lady   1979

MICHAEL HEFFERNAN   (b. 1942)

The holy Serenus was a gardener
who used to love to caress his eggplants
and plump zucchini with a prayer like this
to God the Father: Lord of rind and seed,
think on Thy son, Serenus, in his need.   5

There was a tree that overarched his garden
and on it a sign that read: NO WOMEN—
HERMIT. But one day a lady wandered through
on her way home (after her lover went
his own way home through the bushes) and espied   10

Serenus gazing up at her from his hoe,
saying in his thin, brittle voice: Woman,
for shame. It is not meet for you to be here.
My garden is a holy place for God
and me, and womankind should not be found here.   15

Quite angry, she ran off and told her husband,
who was a fat and lethal governor,
so the blameless Serenus was dragged away
to have his head cut off by some soldiers.
He was styled a martyr on account of this.   20

Man in the Attic   1980

CONRAD HILBERRY   (b. 1928)

He hoists himself into the attic and crawls
toward the eaves where he knows the leak must be.
He hears the rain rush up the roof, then down
and over the edge. He has a plan. He will catch

the water in a cake pan before it seeps   5
into the bedroom ceiling. Already the plaster
swells to an enormous sore and drips
sometimes with yellow matter. On his belly

now he pushes the pan ahead of him,
scraping his head on a nail. Feeling back   10
into the dark for the wet place, he finds
splinters, crumbs of plaster, and a soft fur

of dirt. In the acute angle of the eaves,
the boards are warped and vaguely damp,

but there is no drip, nothing you could catch   15
in a pan. Further and further back: nothing.

When he thinks of himself wedged in under the slope
of his own attic, impaled on roofing nails—
a grown man stretched out on his belly
contriving to catch rain in a cake pan—   20

he almost cries. Below, he knows, his wife
watches the swollen ceiling drain on their bed.

Ye Who Have Toiled   1863

WALTER SAVAGE LANDOR   (1775–1864)

Ye who have toiled uphill to reach the haunt
Of other men who lived in other days,
Whether the ruins of a citadel
Raised on the summit by Pelasgic° hands,
Or chamber of the distaff and the song . . .   5
Ye will not tell what treasure there ye found,
But I will.
            Ye found there the viper laid
Full-length, flat-headed, on a sunny slab,
Nor loth to hiss at ye while crawling down.
Ye saw the owl flap the loose ivy leaves   10
And, hooting, shake the berries on your heads.
   Now, was it worth your while to mount so high
Merely to say ye did it, and to ask
If those about ye ever did the like?
Believe me, O my friends, 'twere better far   15
To stretch your limbs along the level sand
As they do, where small children scoop the drift,
Thinking it must be gold, where curlews soar
And scales drop glistening from the prey above.

4 *Pelasgic:* the Pelasgians, a prehistoric people who inhabited Greece before the Hel-
lenes. Some of their crudely hewn stonework survives.

Up-Hill

1861

CHRISTINA ROSSETTI   (1830–1894)

Does the road wind up-hill all the way?
    Yes, to the very end.
Will the day's journey take the whole long day?
    From morn to night, my friend.

But is there for the night a resting-place?   5
    A roof for when the slow dark hours begin.
May not the darkness hide it from my face?
    You cannot miss that inn.

Shall I meet other wayfarers at night?
    Those who have gone before.   10
Then must I knock, or call when just in sight?
    They will not keep you standing at that door.

Shall I find comfort, travel-sore and weak?
    Of labour you shall find the sum.
Will there be beds for me and all who seek?   15
    Yea, beds for all who come.

After Long Silence

1933

WILLIAM BUTLER YEATS   (1865–1939)

Speech after long silence; it is right,
All other lovers being estranged or dead,
Unfriendly lamplight hid under its shade,
The curtains drawn upon unfriendly night,
That we descant and yet again descant   5
Upon the supreme theme of Art and Song:
Bodily decrepitude is wisdom; young
We loved each other and were ignorant.

12

Revising (II):
Seven-Eighths of the Iceberg

Revising is most of what a poet can actively *do*. Since few poems will arrive from the muse complete, in the clear (as cryptologists put it) and unscrambled, the beginning poet will do well to look over the shoulder of as many poets as may be observed in the act of revising. The job is painful enough when it is one's own poem that is being tinkered at and (one hopes!) improved. Doubly or trebly painful to follow in detail what other poets have done. Yet, like baseball, poetry is a game of inches or half-inches; and no true beginner will begrudge hours spent meticulously and happily watching Darryl Strawberry or Cal Ripkin or Richard Wilbur or Marianne Moore at work.

Tightening and shaping, two operations that are continuous in rewriting, are the focus of this chapter.

Tightening

A good rule of thumb is that a poem (or any writing) should be only as long as is necessary to do its job. There is leeway, of course, but as Shakespeare put it, "It is better to be brief than tedious." Writing is linear: it takes time to read words. Any idea expressed in a hundred words that could have been said fully in fifty must be *less intense* because it is spread over a longer reading time. Redundancies, vague or empty epithets, and rhetorical roundabouts cause, second by second in the reading, a loss in impact; they inevitably lower interest and blur focus. Unnecessary words clutter, confuse, and distract. In his funny and very practical essay on "Fenimore Cooper's Literary Offenses"—in the form of "mock" lectures to the Veterinary College of Arizona—Mark Twain (Samuel L. Clemens, 1835–1910) shows how several inflated passages from Cooper's novels might have been advantageously tightened. One he reduces from three hundred twenty words to two hundred twenty, without loss in content. Another he reduces from eighty words to forty. Although Twain is discussing prose, his account is pertinent.

> In studying Cooper you will find it profitable to study him in detail—word by word, sentence by sentence. For every sentence of his is interesting. Interesting because of its make-up; its peculiar make-up, its original make-up. Let us examine a sentence or two, and see. Here is a passage from Chapter XI of *The Last of the Mohicans*, one of the most famous and most admired of Cooper's books:
>
>> Notwithstanding the swiftness of their flight, one of the Indians had found an opportunity to strike a straggling fawn with an arrow, and had borne the more preferable fragments of the victim, patiently on his shoulders, to the stopping-place. Without any aid from the science of cookery, he was immediately employed, in common with his fellows, in gorging himself with this digestible sustenance. Magua alone sat apart, without participating in the revolting meal, and apparently buried in the deepest thought.
>
> This little paragraph is full of matter for reflection and inquiry. The remark about the swiftness of the flight was unnecessary, as it was merely put in to forestall the possible objection of some overparticular reader that the Indian couldn't have found the needed "opportunity" while fleeing swiftly. The reader would not have made that objection. He would care nothing about having that small matter explained and justified. But that is Cooper's way; frequently he will explain and justify little things that do not need it and then make up for this by as frequently failing to explain important ones that do need it. . . .
>
> No, the remark about the swiftness of their flight was not necessary; neither was the one which said that the Indian found an opportunity; neither was the one which said he *struck* the fawn; neither was the one which explained that it was a "straggling" fawn; neither was the one which said the striking was done with an arrow; neither was the one which said the Indian bore the "fragments"; nor the remark that they were preferable fragments; nor the remark that they were *more* preferable fragments; nor the explanation that they were fragments of the "victim"; nor the overparticular explanation that specifies the Indian's "shoulders" as the part of him that supported the fragments; nor the statement that the Indian bore the fragments patiently. None of those details has any value. We

don't care what the Indian struck the fawn with; we don't care whether it was a straggling fawn or an unstraggling one; we don't care which fragments the Indian saved; we don't care why he saved the "more" preferable ones when the merely preferable ones would have amounted to just the same thing and couldn't have been told from the more preferable ones by anybody, dead or alive; we don't care whether the Indian carried them on his shoulders or in his handkerchief; and finally, we don't care whether he carried them patiently or struck for higher pay and shorter hours. We are indifferent to that Indian and all his affairs.

There was only one fact in that long sentence that was worth stating, and it could have been squeezed into these few words—and with advantage to the narrative, too: "During the flight one of the Indians had killed a fawn and he brought it into camp."

You will notice that "During the flight one of the Indians had killed a fawn and he brought it into camp," is more straightforward and businesslike, and less mincing and smirky, than it is to say, "Notwithstanding the swiftness of their flight, one of the Indians had found an opportunity to strike a straggling fawn with an arrow, and had borne the more preferable fragments of the victim, patiently on his shoulders, to the stopping-place." You will notice that the form "During the flight one of the Indians had killed a fawn and he brought it into camp" holds up its chin and moves to the front with the steady stride of a grenadier, whereas the form "Notwithstanding the swiftness of their flight, one of the Indians had found an opportunity to strike a straggling fawn with an arrow, and had borne the more preferable fragments of the victim, patiently on his shoulders, to the stopping-place" simpers along with an airy, complacent, monkey-with-a-parasol gait which is not suited to the transportation of raw meat.

I beg to remind you that an author's way of setting forth a matter is called his Style, and that an author's style is a main part of his equipment for business. The style of some authors has variety in it, but Cooper's style is remarkable for the absence of this feature. Cooper's style is always grand and stately and noble. Style may be likened to an army, the author to its general, the book to the campaign. Some authors proportion an attacking force to the strength or weakness, the importance or unimportance, of the object to be attacked; but Cooper doesn't. It doesn't make any difference to Cooper whether the object of attack is a hundred thousand men or a cow; he hurls his entire force against it. He comes thundering down with all his battalions at his back, cavalry in the van, artillery on the flanks, infantry massed in the middle, forty bands braying, a thousand banners streaming in the wind; and whether the object be an army or a cow you will see him come marching sublimely in, at the end of the engagement, bearing the more preferable fragments of the victim patiently on his shoulders, to the stopping-place. Cooper's style is grand, awful, beautiful; but it is sacred to Cooper, it is his very own, and no student of the Veterinary College of Arizona will be allowed to filch it from him.

In one of his chapters Cooper throws an ungentle slur at one Gamut because he is not exact enough in his choice of words. But Cooper has that failing himself. If the Indian had "struck" the fawn with a brick, or with a club, or with his fist, no one could find fault with the word used. And one cannot find much fault when he strikes it with an arrow; still it sounds affected, and it might have been a little better to lean to simplicity and say he shot it with an arrow.

"Fragments" is well enough, perhaps, when one is speaking of the parts of a dismembered deer, yet it hasn't just exactly the right sound—and sound is something; in fact sound is a good deal. It makes the difference between good music and poor music, and it can sometimes make the difference between good literature and indifferent literature. "Fragments" sounds all right when we are talking about the wreckage of a breakable thing that has been smashed; it also sounds all right when applied to cat's meat; but when we use it to describe large hunks and chunks like the fore- and hindquarters of a fawn, it grates upon the fastidious ear.

"Without any aid from the science of cookery, he was immediately employed, in common with his fellows, in gorging himself with this digestible sustenance."

This was a mere statistic; just a mere cold, colorless statistic; yet you see Cooper has made a chromo out of it. To use another figure, he has clothed a humble statistic in flowing, voluminous and costly raiment, whereas both good taste and economy suggest that he ought to have saved these splendors for a king, and dressed the humble statistic in a simple breech-clout. Cooper spent twenty-four words here on a thing not really worth more than eight. We will reduce the statistic to its proper proportions and state it in this way:

"He and the others ate the meat raw."

"Digestible sustenance" is a handsome phrase, but it was out of place there, because we do not know these Indians or care for them; and so it cannot interest us to know whether the meat was going to agree with them or not. Details which do not assist a story are better left out.

"Magua alone sat apart, without participating in the revolting meal" is a statement which we understand, but that is our merit, not Cooper's. Cooper is not clear. He does not say who it is that is revolted by the meal. It is really Cooper himself, but there is nothing in the statement to indicate that it isn't Magua. Magua is an Indian and likes raw meat.

The word "alone" could have been left out and space saved. It has no value where it is.

Here is Mark Twain's reduction of the passage, cut by 50 percent!

During the flight one of the Indians had killed a fawn and he brought it into camp. He and the others ate the meat raw. Magua sat apart, without participating in the meal, and apparently buried in the deepest thought.

Poetry is especially an art of compression. That does not mean that all poems should be epigrams; nor that, at the expense of clarity or good manners, a poem should be clogged, crammed, or written in telegramese. But the poet should follow William Strunk's rule not to use two words when one will do and must continually weigh the effect of every word she or he uses. Padding a line to keep the form, instead of finding a necessary detail, results in slackness. Richard Wilbur could have padded the first lines of the stanzas in "Love Calls Us to the Things of This World" to make five feet—"The eyes come open to a cry of pulleys," for example—but he chose the shorter, precise "The eyes open to a cry of pulleys."

Reconciling form and content isn't always easy. Where they are irreconcilable, there is no doubt that a poet should ease the formal demands. But the effort to meet the requirements of a tentative form often leads the poet to discover possible words, ideas, images he or she would not otherwise have considered. Form *tests* content. A possibly helpful tactic for the poet writing in meter is to try at some late stage to shorten every line by one foot. Sometimes this test leads to wrenching or distortion and only confirms the lines as written, but sometimes a word comes out of a line easily, revealing a soft spot in the poem. When a word doesn't matter much to the poem, the poet should find one that does.

In poetry every word should be doing more than one job. Its sound, as well as its sense, matters. Moreover, the feeling of mysterious depth in a good poem frequently comes from the implicit, from nuances and connotations, as in Burns's "red, red rose" and "melodie." Everything need not be *said*. Ernest Hemingway's counsel is pertinent:

> If a writer of prose knows enough about what he is writing about, he may omit things that he knows and the reader, if the writer is writing truly enough, will have a feeling of these things as strongly as though the writer had stated them. The dignity of movement of an iceberg is due to only one-eighth of it being above water.

Hemingway says elsewhere that this is a kind of writing "with nothing that will go bad afterwards." What is *not* there—the implicit, the merely intimated, the nuance—will have its effect.

Tighten, then. Consider this draft by a student, D. A. Fantauzzi:

Moorings

A collection of white, yellow, red
hulks of sailboats—
bugs with wings
folded down their backs,
tucked out of the wind,
sitting still.

Through the heart
a tall pin
sticks each to the blue-green mat.

Sharply observed, the poem presents a colorful scene. Still, a good instinct would test the poem. Here is the text again, with possible excisions shown by brackets:

[A collection of] white, yellow, red
[hulks of] sailboats—
bugs with wings
folded down their backs,
[tucked out of the wind,]
[sitting still.]

[Through the heart]
a tall pin
sticks each to the blue-green mat.

The plural "sailboats" might be sufficient without "A collection of." Though the comparison between sailboats and a display of pinned insects makes the word relevant, it has little force where it is, before the comparison is indicated. In line 2 "hulks of" seems unnecessary and misleading. "Hulks" both feels too large and clumsy for sailboats *and* suggests abandoned or battered vessels. The comparison of sails to wings is precise (both are means of propulsion by air) and necessary; the sails are literally "folded down their backs," as might also be the case of insects' wings. "Tucked out of the wind" seems needlessly explanatory, and the action seems too volitional because in the comparison the insects are obviously dead. Line 6 seems wasted as well as somewhat inaccurate. "Sitting" seems too flat and motionless for sailboats on open water, especially if there is wind; and it applies poorly to the lifeless, impaled insects. The feeling of "Through the heart" is right, but since neither sailboats nor insects have hearts, the line seems imprecise, almost a cliché.

Each of these potential deletions raises a question the poet should consider. How necessary is this word, or detail, to the poem I am trying to write? Here is the poem as it might be arranged, with the cuts made:

White, yellow, red sailboats—
bugs with wings
folded down their backs.

A tall pin
sticks each to the blue-green mat.

Perhaps the unbalanced, low, flat shapes of the poem suggest the folded-down sails. Perhaps, at this stage, some other phrase or detail or other order will occur to the poet. Might the word "collection" go somehow into stanza 2? Might "away from the wind"—a slight alteration of "tucked out of the wind"—make a good final line and recover some of the pathos of "Through the heart"? How would that affect the rhythm? Asking and answering such questions is the process of writing a poem.

The poet's revision adds a detail—"in rows"—that both helps the picture and reenforces the comparison. He decided to keep the phrase "A collection of," which sets up the comparison and prevents a reader's imagining the sailboats as dispersed.

A collection of white, yellow, red
sailboats—bugs with wings
folded down their backs,
in rows.

A tall pin
sticks each to the blue-green mat.

Slackness (wasted words, wasted motions) goes against Anton Chekhov's belief, expressed in a letter to Maxim Gorki, that "when a person expends the least possible movement on a certain act, that is grace." A remark of Ezra Pound's in 1914 is tongue-in-cheek but not without point: "A Chinaman said long ago that if a man can't say what he has to say in twelve lines he had better keep quiet." Not all poems should be short, of course, nor as short as Pound's "In a Station of the Metro" (page 135), which from a thirty-five line draft became a two-line poem! But every poem should be as short as it can be.

Our century's most remarkable excision occurs in Marianne Moore's famous and often anthologized "Poetry," which was first published in 1921. Moore tinkered with this poem from time to time over the years. This is its most familiar version (1935):

Poetry

I, too, dislike it: there are things that are important beyond all this fiddle.
    Reading it, however, with a perfect contempt for it, one discovers in
    it after all, a place for the genuine.
        Hands that can grasp, eyes
        that can dilate, hair that can rise   5
            if it must, these things are important not because a

high-sounding interpretation can be put upon them but because they are
    useful. When they become so derivative as to become unintelligible,
    the same thing may be said for all of us, that we
        do not admire what   10
        we cannot understand: the bat
            holding on upside down or in quest of something to

eat, elephants pushing, a wild horse taking a roll, a tireless wolf under
    a tree, the immovable critic twitching his skin like a horse that feels a
    flea, the base-
    ball fan, the statistician—   15
        nor is it valid
            to discriminate against 'business documents and

school-books'; all these phenomena are important. One must make a
   distinction
   however: when dragged into prominence by half poets, the result is not
   poetry,
   nor till the poets among us can be   20
   'literalists of
   the imagination'—above
       insolence and triviality and can present

for inspection, 'imaginary gardens with real toads in them', shall we have
   it. In the meantime, if you demand on the one hand,   25
   the raw material of poetry in
   all its rawness and
   that which is on the other hand
       genuine, you are interested in poetry.

In 1967, almost a half century after the poem was written, she revised it for her
Complete Poems. This is her final version:

I, too, dislike it.
   Reading it, however, with a perfect contempt for it, one discovers in
   it, after all, a place for the genuine.

Everything, *everything,* after the first two sentences has been deleted!—all the
marvelous details and the endlessly quoted statement of the ideal in poetry,
" 'imaginary gardens with real toads in them.' " Moore's admirers were dumb-
founded. The 1935 text was printed in one of the notes at the back of *Complete
Poems,* perhaps because, as T. S. Eliot said of the famous notes to "The Waste
Land," anyone who bought the book and found the poem missing "would demand
his money back." But Moore was absolute. The *entire* "Author's Note" at the
beginning of *Complete Poems* asserted unremittingly: "Omissions are not accidents."
   Critical opinion at present holds that this astonishing revision was a mistake,
and editors of anthologies have continued to reprint the familiar version of
"Poetry." Fond as we may be of that version, however, disagreeing with any poetic
judgment of Marianne Moore's, especially one that she took fifty years to reach,
must be rash. And it seems important, for the beginning poet as well as for Moore's
most devoted fans, to take pains to understand her long-deliberated revision. We
need not doubt that it was as much a sacrifice for her as it seems for us. That she felt
impelled to make it, nonetheless, argues for the seriousness of her reasons.
   In both reading and teaching the 1935 version of the poem, I have often felt a
fuzziness at its center. I always assumed that the poem was right and that my feeling
was somehow in error. Now, Moore's unforgiving omission makes the question
pertinent. The extraordinary catalog of the bat, elephants, wild horse, wolf, critic,

baseball fan, and statistician, along with " 'business documents and / school-books,' " is clearly offered as examples of the "genuine." They are the "things that are important" for which there is in poetry "a place." When they are "dragged into prominence by half poets"—misused in some way—"the result is not poetry." As the 1924 version of the poem makes plain, the misuse occurs in making them "unintelligible." Here is that version, entire:

> I too, dislike it:
> there are things that are important
> beyond all this fiddle.
> The bat, upside down; the elephant pushing,
> the tireless wolf under a tree,   5
> the base-ball fan, the statistician—
> "business documents and schoolbooks"—
> these phenomena are pleasing,
> but when they have been fashioned
> into that which is unknowable,   10
> we are not entertained.
> It may be said of all of us
> that we do not admire what we cannot
> understand;
> enigmas are not poetry.   15

In the critically favored 1935 version, the unintelligibility is said to result from these things having become "derivative" (line 9). Subject matter, handled from poem to fashionable poem with decreasing reference to plain reality, might be said to become "derivative" and so "unintelligible"—poetic stage property like the rose or spring. But the catalog given hardly supports such an interpretation: the bat, elephants, wild horse, and so on, are hardly instances of overused and, thus, derivatively handled subject matter. Just what "half poets" she refers to as having "dragged into prominence" these things, or how, is totally unclear.

The 1935 version, which is only slightly altered from the original 1921 version, seems fatally ambiguous. The pronoun "they" in "When they become so derivative as to become unintelligible" plainly refers, not to the catalog that will shortly follow, but *back* to the "Hands that can grasp, eyes that can dilate, hair that can rise / if it must" of the preceding stanza. A sensible reading of the catalog makes it a list of examples of what "we / do not admire" because "we cannot understand." The oddities in the catalog—the bat's "holding on upside down," the elephants' "pushing," the wild horse's "taking a roll," and especially the "immovable" critic's "twitching his skin like a horse that feels / a flea"—obviously embody this satiric intention, making the catalog not a list of the "genuine" but of the "unintelligible."

In his *Marianne Moore*, published in 1964 (Moore may have seen it before making her final revision of the poem in 1967), Bernard F. Engel innocently assumes yet another reading of the catalog, seeing it as referring to the "all of us" who "do not admire what we cannot understand." He writes: "The 'us' is delightfully and pointedly represented as creatures engaged in a variety of activities"! Engel tries to recenter his reading by adding, "All of 'us' are possible subjects; even the business and schoolroom documents sometimes excluded from the canon of literary material may be used for poetry." Implausible as such an interpretation may seem, it underlines some central ambiguity in the poem, which Engel is trying to straddle. The two catalogs that begin with "Hands that can grasp" and "the bat" are only roughly parallel and seem imperfectly, confusingly related.

The original 1921 version differs in only a few words from the familiar 1935 version. Clearly, Moore was unhappy with the original version when she exchanged it for the simplified 1924 version, whose weakness in turn led her to replace it in 1935 with a version only slightly modified from the original. Whatever had bothered her about that version obviously still bothered her in 1967 when she struck out all of it except the first three lines. The excision followed a longstanding dissatisfaction with the poem. Unless there is material not yet published, we can only guess at the dissatisfaction, but it was clearly neither sudden nor impulsive.

Donald Hall's acute questions—"What poetry is she referring to? All poetry? Some particular kind?"—seem to me as relevant to the 1935 version as to the 1967; and one might add, "What half poets?" The questions are easier to answer for the 1967 version: yes, all poetry, any poetry. Fiddle though it all is, "one discovers in / it, after all, a place for the genuine." And that, Moore seems to be telling us in 1967, is that.

If we miss the catalog with its delicious exemplifications, we may remember that there are wonderful examples all around, on every page of the *Complete Poems*. If we miss the incisive conclusion,

> In the meantime, if you demand on the one hand,
> the raw material of poetry in
>   all its rawness and
>   that which is on the other hand
>   genuine, you are interested in poetry.

at least we need not worry over the poem's indecisive pronouns: "I," "one," "we," and finally "you." If we miss the righteous condemnation of those unspecified "half poets," whose poems have already vanished, we may come to prefer Marianne Moore's final fairness to them in letting the matter drop. If we miss the splendid phrase, "imaginary gardens with real toads in them," we may recall that we still have it, along with her unquenchable passion for precision and her unqualified witness on behalf of tightening. It is a tough league to play in. "Omissions," she says, "are not accidents."

Shaping

The other essential operation in composition is **shaping.** As the words of a poem come, they must be displayed in lines. Sometimes the earliest verbalization carries with it an intuitive sense of how the poem might be broken into lines, but often the earliest phrases are accompanied by no particular feeling of lineation. They may even be a scattering of disconnected phrases with no certainty even as to which should come first. One of the poet's tasks as the poem develops is opting for some possible form, however tentative, which can be tested and altered as draft leads to draft. Meter? Rhyme? Free verse? Longer lines? Stanzas? The initial preference may be habitual, and often comes from a deeply ingrained and successfully practiced feeling—as Williams instinctively worked in very short lines, or Whitman in very long lines. But a given poem may call for a different sort of form. For instance, in "Yachts" William Carlos Williams elected to work in much longer lines than was his custom: "Today no race. Then the wind comes again. The yachts / move, jockeying for a start, the signal is set . . ." Both the tentative choice of form and the experimental sculpting or fitting of further parts to the poem are shaping. Once a poem begins in one way, in short free verse lines, say, it is usually better for the rest of it to follow in that way—not to change into long lines, for instance, toward the end. Every poem should be formally a whole. A poem *can* mix forms, especially a longer, sectioned poem; but unless there is a clear thematic reason, such mixed-form poems may seem merely half-baked.

In writing stanzaic poems, whether in free verse or in meter, the poet should repeat the established pattern in subsequent stanzas and use it fully so that there is no falling off or slackening. Consider A. E. Housman's:

I Hoed and Trenched and Weeded

I hoed and trenched and weeded,
  And took the flowers to fair;
I brought them home unheeded;
  The hue was not the wear.

So up and down I sow them   5
  For lads like me to find,
When I shall lie below them,
  A dead man out of mind.

Some seed the birds devour,
  And some the season mars,   10
But here and there will flower
  The solitary stars,

And fields will yearly bear them
    As light-leaved spring comes on,
And luckless lads will wear them
    When I am dead and gone.

15

Of its composition, Housman commented: "Two of the stanzas, I do not say which, came into my head, just as they are printed. . . . A third stanza came with a little coaxing after tea. One more was needed, but it did not come: I had to turn to and compose it myself, and that was a laborious business. I wrote it thirteen times, and it was more than a twelvemonth before I got it right." Poems don't always unwind from the top. Robert Lowell recalls that his well-known "Skunk Hour" was "written backwards," the last two stanzas first, then the next-to-last two, and finally the first four in reverse order. It is sometimes useful to scribble out with scanning marks the base meter of a stanza to be written, or to show the holes in a passage that are left to be filled when the inspiration carries the poem further:

The boys met by the bridge, and climbed

beneath it where the gray owls were:

⏑ ´ ⏑ ´ ⏑ ´ the nest

in which, in feathers more like fur,

two little owls . . .

Such marks hold open the passage and let the poet see clearly where something is missing.

    Working in free verse is little different. Lack of a firm rubric allows more freedom, but that makes choices among various possibilities more arbitrary and, for a careful poet, uncertain. Thus, the whole poem is likely to remain in suspension longer in free verse. Line-breaks may want a lot of testing; the poet needs to juggle run-on and end-stopped lines for variety and rhythm. If a stanza pattern has appeared, fitting further material into it becomes a measuring and shaping of that material. Good free verse has a tight surface tension on which the poet's seemingly trivial vacillations and tinkerings with line or word-placement work like the delicate feet of a water-strider on water.

    So far, in these chapters about rewriting, we have been examining fair copies or transcriptions from poets' manuscripts, not actual working manuscripts with their scribbles and scrawls, scratchings out and interlinings, arrows, notations, jottings, marginal lists, and even phone numbers, doodles, or coffee stains. For the poet's own use, often set down in haste, actual manuscripts are usually a mess and often indecipherable. The seven worksheets of "The Girl Writing Her English

Paper," however, are fairly legible; and the facsimiles reproduced here will illustrate some of the twists and turns I took in rewriting this poem.

WORKSHEET 1

The first draft of the poem is an unusually complete version. The first five and one-half lines, along with several other phrases, had been composed in my head; as I wrote, most of the rest of the draft came cleanly. The four-line first sentence set a tentative stanza pattern, into which everything that followed fell readily. The only gap was line 3 of the second stanza, which I left to be filled in, sensing that the details of the girl's mess would finish the stanza and could be sorted out later. (Line 4 of that stanza immediately got too long, so I noted, with a slash, details that I would probably push back up to fill line 3.) I made a false start on stanza 4, "wondering at," but quickly scratched it out and the stanza wrote itself straightforwardly. At this stage the poem felt metrical, and without paying much attention I let the lines fall out roughly four, five, or six feet. Like the four-line stanzas, it seemed to want to happen.

The inserted image of "petals" filled out line 2 of stanza 2, and I arrowed "Open books, notebooks," etc., down to line 3. Other tinkerings suggested exchanging the vague "pretty" for the further detail of "in blond jeans" in line 1, replacing the clinical "inspects" with the gesture "bends to" or "bending to," and shortening the very long next-to-last line. I wasn't sure whether to leave the lover *in* the scene, and tried "somewhere" and the less direct "thinking of" instead of "watching." Wanting to see what the poem looked like, so revised, I copied it on worksheet 2. (Since the appearance of a poem on the page is important, I always single-space. Double-spacing would allow more room to work, but I want to see the shape of the poem as it would appear in print.)

A Girl Writing ~~Her~~ a Paper for her English Class

in (blond) jeans
She curls, sprawls on one [pretty] hip
and elbows on the floor before the fire
in ~~a~~ the fire-lit, lamp-lit, light-sodden room
while all dark circles around outside.

The wreckage of her labor—elegant as Eden—
—like petals dropped in the storm
surrounds her, open books, notebooks, sheets, {penciling
>^<   }(notes,)
                                               loose
a cup, cigarets /the little tobacco farm (house, pond),
                                          drift of smoke.

                    and writes a
                                             word
She bites a nail, scratches (& unscratches) a ~~line~~,
a (frail) watch (silver) on her wrist, her hair
like a shaken waterfall hiding her face
              bends to   text
as she ~~inspects~~ } the ~~poem~~. Her lover waits/
bending to

          wondering at
somewhere second to a poem; watches, pretending to read,
        thinking of   had
but watching her. So fine an attention   ^ done.
                       a   lost
To what ~~another~~ man (dead centuries) [lost sleep
                                          To make.]
If all the lights were out, starlight would come in.
)v
                              the

The poem "stuck" here for some time. I studied this version on at least four occasions over several days (there are indications of three different pens and a pencil). Only two verbal changes are suggested ("breakage" for "wreckage" in line 5, "sun-woven" for "shaken" in line 11), but neither is accepted. In line 8 "*tobacco farm*" is wrong, since the point is not a farm that grows tobacco; and I arrowed "tobacco" over to modify and explain the "smoke-string." By "house" I meant the girl's book, by "pond" the clear-glass ashtray; obviously the image is awkwardly handled. Mainly, I felt, the poem was puffy, mushy, in need of tightening. With pencil lines I tried crossing out one line in each stanza: the overly rhetorical "in the fire-lit, lamp-lit, light-sodden room" in stanza 1; the whole line with the farm image in stanza 2; the rather prosy "She bites a nail, scratches (and unscratches) a word" in stanza 3; and the first halves of the first two lines in stanza 4. At another time I tried underlining in ink the parts of the poem that seemed important; I then copied them out in longhand at the bottom of the page. The result, without stanzas at all, felt dull.

At a third time, with another pen, I also underlined the sentence "So fine an attention . . ." and added the suggestion for another image—"The stars still nailed into the sky"—at the bottom of the sheet. (I did nothing further with the image, probably because it seemed static and emphasized the stars' distance rather than their closeness.) In considering ways of tightening the poem, the crucial decision was to abandon the fairly heavy stanzas and the possibility of meter, both of which made the poem feel stuffy and more literary than it wanted to be.

Going on to worksheet 3, I left behind the melodramatically ominous "while all dark circles around outside" (my feelings about the girl and the scene were mainly cheerful), the needlessly specific details about her watch and hair, and the lover. *In* the scene he was a distraction and his rather self-pitying jealousy of being "second to a poem" seemed falsely dramatic, and "somewhere," he wasn't usable because he could at most be guessing about her at work. I wanted to concentrate on the picture of the girl, absorbed in a poem.

A GIRL WRITING A PAPER FOR HER ENGLISH CLASS

She curls in blond jeans, sprawls on one hip
[and elbows on the floor] before the fire
~~in the fire-lit, lamp-lit, light-sodden room~~
while all dark circles around outside.

breakage?   The wreckage of her labor—elegant as Eden—
surrounds her like petals dropped in a storm—
open books, notebooks, a cup, sheets, pencilings,
~~the little tobacco farm (smoke-string, house, pond).~~

~~She bites a nail, scratches (and unscratches) a word,~~   : ?
a silver watch frail on her wrist, her hair
sun-woven   like a shaken waterfall hiding her face
bending to the text. Her lover waits

~~somewhere, second to a poem;~~ pretending to read,
~~but thinking of her.~~ So fine an attention
to what a man dead centuries had done.
If all the lights were out, the starlight would come in.

In jeans, - ~~sprawling~~ on one hip
(before the fire)
The wreckage of her labor-elegant as Eden,
as petals dropped in a storm :
open books, notebooks, cup, sheets, pencilings,
the little farm (tobacco, smoke-string, house, and pond).
If all the lights were out, the starlight would come in.

The stars still nailed into the sky

Having tested the possibility of metered stanzas, however loosely, I could now test the possibilities of free (more exactly, *freed*) verse. There are now stanzas of one, three, four, three, and two lines. After looking at stanzaless free verse at the bottom of worksheet 2, I wanted the greater sharpness and distinctness of a poem in stanzas.

The chief advance in this draft is the relatively clean sorting out of the farm image. House and pond have vanished. The smoke is now rising, literally, from the ashtray. The "fields" have been added, appropriately, next to "papers," whose rectangular shapes make the comparison clear. And the fields have suggested (drawing on the Latin *versus*, meaning both furrows and lines) the phrase "the poem's furrows," which brings the comparison to a focus. Although neither fields nor furrows appear in the earlier versions of the image, I believe I was half-aware of where the farm image was headed.

The untidy "open books, notebooks, a cup, sheets, pencilings" has become succinctly only "books, notebooks, papers" and of course "ashtray." With the lover out of the way, the poem can now draw its moral directly, addressing the reader:

Consider the fine attention she gives
to words of a man long dead.

An alternative, typed in the margin, "Reflect, you who do not write poems," awkwardly identified the speaker as a poet, though not the author of the poem about which the girl is so absorbedly writing. The flatness of the moral as stated called up the livelier insertion: "you lunkheads who don't write poems."

In the one-line stanza 1, "on one hip" is first struck out and then rescued to follow "lying." Perhaps because a one-line stanza seemed to stop the flow of the poem almost before it had started, a slash indicates a proposed line break before "by the fire." Stanza 2 is tightened by exchanging "as" for "or" and deleting the comma after "Eden." Stanza 3 is tightened by the excision of the empty "It is" and the needless "She follows." Thus, stanza 2 can lead directly into stanza 3, and the period is crossed out and a dash, then a colon (too formal), and then a dash again is inserted. Also for flow, a period in stanza 4 is deleted in favor of a comma. There is one other noteworthy change: the clumsier nine-word title is replaced by a six-word version.

THE GIRL WRITING HER ENGLISH PAPER

is in jeans, ~~on one hip~~ *lying* by the fire.

The wreckage of her labor, elegant as Eden,
or ~~as~~ petals from a tree,
surrounds her / ≠ / –

~~It is~~ a little farm ≠ , *smoke*
~~smoke~~ rises *ing* from the ashtray / ,
books, notebooks, papers, fields / ;
~~She follows~~ the poem's furrows.

Consider, ~~I~~f the lights went out,
there would be stars overhead / ,
t ~~T~~he starlight would come in.
        you lunkheads who don't write poems)
Consider, the fine attention she gives   Reflect,
to words of a man long dead.   you who do
                                              not write
                                              poems

Typing this draft, I noticed that three of the five stanzas now had three lines. The first two lines of stanza 3 could easily be combined into a single line, giving it three lines as well. The stanza shape—long, shorter, and still shorter lines—was already there in stanza 2 and almost there in stanzas 4 and 5; and, with the combining of lines 1 and 2, there in stanza 3. Changes in stanzas 4 and 5 were made both to clarify the substance and to bring out the stanza shape. The first preachy "Consider" in stanza 4 is dropped, the proper subjunctive "were to go out" inserted for "went out," and the sense of surprise increased with "suddenly." After considering moving "she gives" to the next line, I struck it out and (a poor change) made the line read: "this fine, slow attention." Either way, it is a weak line and will be much improved in the typing of worksheet 5.

The only stanza not essentially conforming to the shape, stanza 1, is the focus of major tinkering. The copulative "is" gives way to the more active "lies" as main verb, and three additional details are considered: pencil to lip, slimness, blondness. "Slim" is considered, then rejected as the least useful of the three. The draft's last intention is:

lies on one hip by the fire,
in jeans, pencil to her lip.
She's very blond.

In the retyping on worksheet 5, however, the adjective "still" is added to line 1, the "pencil" turns into a "pen," and "She's" reduced to "is"—all in the interests of stanza-shape. (And the elements in line 2 will be reversed.)

THE GIRL WRITING HER ENGLISH PAPER

~~is~~ (in jeans,) ~~lying~~ *lies* on one hip ——————, *pencil to her lip.*
by the fire., /\ ~~she's slim, and very~~ *she's very blond.*

The wreckage of her labor, elegant as Eden
or petals from a tree,
surrounds her—

a little farm, smoke
rising from the ashtray, }
book$, notebooks, papers, fields;
and the poem's furrows.

I
~~Consider,~~ if the lights ~~went~~ *were to go* out, *suddenly,*
there would be stars overhead,
~~the~~ starlight would come in.

Consider, you lunkheads who don't write poems,
This ~~the~~ fine attention ~~she gives~~
to words / of a man, long dead.
, slow

The poem is nearing its final form. Stanza 1 seems messy, a not very rhythmic-al collection of fragmentary details. Since the title is now treated as part of the poem's opening sentence and is the right length, the idea of counting it as the first line of stanza 1 came easily. Brackets indicate deletion of the less important details, and "blond" is arrowed up to precede "in jeans." Problem solved.

Stanza 5 remains troublesome. The slangy brusqueness of "lunkheads" was clearly out of tone with the rest of the poem. People who don't write poems aren't necessarily lunkheads. Trying out two more polite versions of the line, I chose the less assertive: "Consider, if you don't believe in poems." In copying this draft, I had stumbled on a much improved version of the second line: "how pensively she attends," with its accidental pun on "pen"; and the only problem seemed to be that the last line was not shorter. Dropping the unnecessary "to" made it fit, albeit barely.

THE GIRL WRITING HER ENGLISH PAPER

lies on one hip by the fire, [still,]   } ϱ ll?
[pen to cheek,] in jeans/ .
[is very] blond,   Is blond

The wreckage of her labor, elegant as Eden
or petals from a tree,
surrounds her—

a little farm, smoke rising from the ashtray,
book, notebooks, papers, fields;
the poem's furrows.

If the lights were to go out suddenly,
stars would be overhead,
starlight come in.   if you
                                     all you who don't believe
                                              in poems,
Consider, you lunkheads who don't write poems,/
how pensively she attends
to words of a man long dead.

I made two tiny alterations—substituting the indefinite for the definite article in line 8 and avoiding the repetition of the word "star" in line 11—and the poem seemed finished. In this version it was accepted and printed.

THE GIRL WRITING HER ENGLISH PAPER

lies on one hip by the fire,
blond, in jeans.

The wreckage of her labor, elegant as Eden
or petals from a tree,
surrounds her—

a little farm, smoke rising from the ashtray,
book, notebooks, papers, fields;
_a_ ~~the~~ poem's furrows.

If the lights were to go out suddenly,
stars would be overhead,
their ~~star~~light come in.

Consider, if you don't believe in poems,
how pensively she attends
words of a man long dead.

Reading the poem to an audience a year later, I found myself wishing that the last stanza wasn't there. The point was not to club anybody for not liking poetry, but to express my awe and astonishment at a girl's utter absorption in a poem. With her lover long gone from the poem, it hardly mattered that the poet might be "long dead." I realized that I could trust the stanza about the starlight. So real was her concentration that the factual room with its firelight and lamplight might simply vanish and the reality of the poem and of her culturing labor would continue to exist, a little farm under real stars. In her role as reader she completes the poem. I also saw why mentioning Eden in the poem had seemed important. The labor of reading poems, like the labor of writing poems, is an allusion to Yeats's "Adam's Curse" (page 88): "It's certain there is no fine thing / Since Adam's fall but needs much labouring."

So I dropped the last stanza. The poem was as short as Pound's Chinese had said a poem should be—and, I thought again, finished. Several years passed. The poem was in a collection, *Swimmer in the Rain* (1979), and in the first edition of this textbook (1982).

But a vague dissatisfaction with the last line persisted. I didn't know what the problem was until—again reading the poem to an audience, in Kansas—the *right* line suddenly came to me. I had been aware, I think, that "their light come in" wasn't really necessary, only emphasizing what line 11 already does: "stars would be overhead." But stopping there would leave the rhythm unfinished, and the stanza pattern uncompleted.

In the instant before I said the line, I knew how it should really go—and changed it. At once the weakness of "their light come in" was also plain. It left the *room* vaguely in place, with the starlight coming in an unmentioned window, rather than simply overhead. Instead of implying such a limit, the new line extends mysteriously the little world of the farm. I hesitated over whether it should be "wood" or "woods," and "still and dark" or "dark and still." But the line as it first appeared was the line toward which the poem had been heading, in spite of me, from the beginning.

lies on one hip by the fire,
blond, in jeans.

The wreckage of her labor, elegant as Eden
or petals from a tree,
surrounds her—

a little farm, smoke rising from the ashtray,
book, notebooks, papers, fields;
a poem's furrows.

If the lights were to go out suddenly,
stars would be overhead,
~~their light come in.~~

the edge of the wood (still and dark).
?

FINAL (?) VERSION

The Girl Writing Her English Paper

lies on one hip by the fire,
blond, in jeans.

The wreckage of her labor, elegant as Eden
or petals from a tree,
surrounds her—

a little farm, smoke rising from the ashtray,
book, notebooks, papers, fields;
a poem's furrows.

If the lights were to go out suddenly,
stars would be overhead,
the edge of the wood still and dark.

QUESTIONS AND SUGGESTIONS

1. If Ezra Pound was correct in saying that poetry should be at least as well written as prose, Ernest Hemingway revising Ernest Hemingway is worth study. As a war correspondent in 1922, Hemingway cabled the first version to the Toronto *Daily Star*. The second version appeared as a vignette in his collection of stories, *In Our Time*, in 1925. Compare the two versions.

a) In a never-ending, staggering march the Christian population of Eastern Thrace is jamming the roads towards Macedonia. The main column crossing the Maritza River at Adrianople is twenty miles long. Twenty miles of carts drawn by cows, bullocks and muddy-flanked water buffalo, with exhausted, staggering men, women and children, blankets over their heads, walking blindly in the rain beside their worldly goods.

This main stream is being swelled from all the back country. They don't know where they are going. They left their farms, villages and ripe, brown fields and joined the main stream of refugees when they heard the Turk was coming. Now they can only keep their places in the ghastly procession while mud-splashed Greek cavalry herd them along like cow-punchers driving steers.

It is a silent procession. Nobody even grunts. It is all they can do to keep moving. Their brilliant peasant costumes are soaked and draggled. Chickens dangle by their feet from the carts. Calves nuzzle at the draught cattle wherever a jam halts the stream. An old man marches bent under a young pig, a scythe and a gun, with a chicken tied to his scythe. A husband spreads a blanket over a woman in labor in one of the carts to keep off the driving rain. She is the only person making a sound. Her little daughter looks at her in horror and begins to cry. And the procession keeps moving

b) Minarets stuck up in the rain out of Adrianople across the mud flats. The carts were jammed for thirty miles along the Karagatch road. Water buffalo and cattle were hauling carts through the mud. No end and no beginning. Just carts loaded with everything they owned. The old men and women, soaked through, walked along keeping the cattle moving. The Maritza was running yellow almost up to the bridge. Carts were jammed solid on the bridge with camels bobbing along through them. Greek cavalry herded along the procession. Women and kids were in the carts crouched with mattresses, mirrors, sewing machines, bundles. There was a woman having a kid with a young girl holding a blanket over her and crying. Scared sick looking at it. It rained all through the evacuation.

2. Here is the first draft of a poem called "In One Place." If it were your poem, how would you revise it? (The poet's final version appears in Appendix I.)

In One Place

The tree grows in one place.

A seed goes down, and something
holds up two or three leaves
the first year.

       Then the spindling
goes on climbing, branching,
up, up, up,

       until birds
live in it and no one can
remember it wasn't there.

The tree stands always here.

3. Consider these two versions of a poem by D. H. Lawrence (1885–1930), called "The Piano" in the early version, "Piano" in the later. What effects do the omissions have in the much shorter version, in which the speaker's experience is significantly reinterpreted? How is the poem's theme changed? How does the sharpening of the focus on the two women clarify the sexuality of the speaker's inner conflict?

a) Somewhere beneath that piano's superb sleek black
   Must hide my mother's piano, little and brown, with the back
   That stood close to the wall, and the front's faded silk both torn,
   And the keys with little hollows, that my mother's fingers had worn.

   Softly, in the shadows, a woman is singing to me   5
   Quietly, through the years I have crept back to see
   A child sitting under the piano, in the boom of the shaking strings
   Pressing the little poised feet of the mother who smiles as she sings.

   The full throated woman has chosen a winning, living song
   And surely the heart that is in me must belong   10
   To the old Sunday evenings, when darkness wandered outside
   And hymns gleamed on our warm lips, as we watched mother's fingers glide.

   Or this is my sister at home in the old front room
   Singing love's first surprised gladness, alone in the gloom.
   She will start when she sees me, and blushing, spread out her hands   15
   To cover my mouth's raillery, till I'm bound in her shame's heartspun bands.

   A woman is singing me a wild Hungarian air
   And her arms, and her bosom, and the whole of her soul is bare,

And the great black piano is clamouring as my mother's never could clamour
And my mother's tunes are devoured of this music's ravaging glamour.   20

b) Softly, in the dusk, a woman is singing to me;
   Taking me back down the vista of years, till I see
   A child sitting under the piano, in the boom of the tingling strings
   And pressing the small, poised feet of a mother who smiles as she sings.

   In spite of myself, the insidious mastery of song   5
   Betrays me back, till the heart of me weeps to belong
   To the old Sunday evenings at home, with winter outside
   And hymns in the cosy parlour, the tinkling piano our guide.

   So now it is vain for the singer to burst into clamour
   With the great black piano appassionato. The glamour   10
   Of childish days is upon me, my manhood is cast
   Down in the flood of remembrance, I weep like a child for the past.

4. This poem by Edward Thomas (1878–1917) opens with the simple "Yes." of
memory. Something—in a newspaper, a conversation?—recalls the name of a rural
station at which a train the speaker was riding once mysteriously stopped. The
event had no significance and has been long forgotten. But remembered, it seems
poignant. Why? How has the poet structured the scene to emphasize the sense of
loss? In what way does the rhyme in stanza 4, on secondary accents (Glós-tér-shùr),
help provide an appropriate music?

Adlestrop

Yes. I remember Adlestrop—
The name, because one afternoon
Of heat the express-train drew up there
Unwontedly. It was late June.

The steam hissed. Someone cleared his throat.   5
No one left and no one came
On the bare platform. What I saw
Was Adlestrop—only the name

And willows, willow-herb, and grass,
And meadowsweet, and haycocks dry,   10
No whit less still and lonely fair
Than the high cloudlets in the sky.

And for that minute a blackbird sang
Close by, and round him, mistier,
Farther and farther, all the birds   15
Of Oxfordshire and Gloucestershire.

5. Here, printed as prose (with normal prose punctuation added), is William Carlos Williams's poem "Young Woman at a Window." Try out several ways of lining it as verse. Compare your best version with the original—and six other student versions—in Appendix I.

> She sits with tears on her cheek, her cheek on her hand, the child in her lap, his nosed pressed to the glass.

6. After reading Pound's "The Bath Tub" (page 384), think of *symbolic* uses to which other common, household objects or mechanisms might be put—a dripping faucet, a burnt-out lightbulb, a dead-bolt lock on a door, clothes tumbling in a front-loading washer, and such. Think of a serious *and* a comic meaning for each.

7. Imagine a poem, *using an archeologist's eye*, about a drive-in movie in the daytime, a marina in winter, a supermarket or department store after hours, a set of tennis courts in snow, a graveyard of old boxcars, or the like. Forget what you know. What might the place seem to an alien? What uses might be guessed? (E.g.: A drive-in—a field of metal flowers or idols? A department store—some sort of museum or temple?)

POEMS TO CONSIDER

Lion & Honeycomb   1962

HOWARD NEMEROV (b. 1920)

He didn't want to do it with skill,
He'd had enough of skill. If he never saw
Another villanelle, it would be too soon;
And the same went for sonnets. If it had been
Hard work learning to rime, it would be much   5
Harder learning not to. The time came
He had to ask himself, what did he want?
What did he want when he began
That idiot fiddling with the sounds of things.

He asked himself, poor moron, because he had   10
Nobody else to ask. The others went right on
Talking about form, talking about myth
And the (so help us) need for a modern idiom;
The verseballs among them kept counting syllables.

So there he was, this forty-year-old teen-ager   15
Dreaming preposterous mergers and divisions
Of vowels like water, consonants like rock
(While everybody kept discussing values
And the need for values), for words that would
Enter the silence and be there as a light.   20
So much coffee and so many cigarettes
Gone down the drain, gone up in smoke,
Just for the sake of getting something right
Once in a while, something that could stand
On its own flat feet to keep out windy time   25
And the worm, something that might simply be,
Not as the monument in the smoky rain
Grimly endures, but that would be
Only a moment's inviolable presence,
The moment before disaster, before the storm,   30
In its peculiar silence, an integer
Fixed in the middle of the fall of things,
Perfected and casual as to a child's eye
Soap bubbles are, and skipping stones.

It Fell on a Summer's Day   1601

THOMAS CAMPION   (1567–1620)

It fell on a summer's day
While sweet Bessie sleeping lay
In her bower, on her bed,
Light with curtains shadowèd,
Jamey came; she him spies,   5
Opening half her heavy eyes.

Jamey stole in through the door;
She lay slumbering as before.
Softly to her he drew near;
She heard him, yet would not° hear.   *pretended not to*   10
Bessie vowed not to speak;
He resolved that dump° to break.   *reverie*

First a soft kiss he doth take;
She lay still, and would not wake.
Then his hands learned to woo;   15
She dreamt not what he would do,
But still slept, while he smiled
To see love by sleep beguiled.

Jamey then began to play;
Bessie as one buried lay,   20
Gladly still through this sleight
Deceived in her own deceit.
And since this trance begun
She sleeps every afternoon.

Titanic   1983

DAVID R. SLAVITT (b. 1935)

Who does not love the *Titanic?*
If they sold passage tomorrow for that same crossing,
who would not buy?

To go down . . . We all go down, mostly
alone. But with crowds of people, friends, servants,   5
well fed, with music, with lights! Ah!

And the world, shocked, mourns, as it ought to do
and almost never does. There will be the books and movies
to remind our grandchildren who we were
and how we died, and give them a good cry.   10

Not so bad, after all. The cold
water is anaesthetic and very quick.
The cries on all sides must be a comfort.

We all go: only a few, first-class.

The Bath Tub

1916

EZRA POUND (1885–1972)

As a bathtub lined with white porcelain,
When the hot water gives out or goes tepid,
So is the slow cooling of our chivalrous passion,
O my much praised but-not-altogether-satisfactory
    lady.

The Mill Back Home

1978

VERN RUTSALA (b. 1934)

Logs drowse in the pond
Dreaming of their heroes
Alligator and crocodile

I Learn I'm 96% Water

1976

ALBERT GOLDBARTH (b. 1948)

and stare out over the edge of this little
dinghy I've named The 4 Percent. Such
a large sea . . .! Such a tiny

motor: this spermtail whipping like crazy . . .!
"The sailor *is* the sea." How   5
Zen! I float in my floating.
The body bobs in its life.

Sentimental Poem   1978
for Woody

MARGE PIERCY (b. 1936)

You are such a good cook.
I am such a good cook.
If we get involved
we'll both get fat.
Then nobody else will have us.   5
We'll be stuck, two
mounds of wet dough
baking high and fine
in the bed's slow oven.

Heartbreak in Tuktoyaktuk   1986

LOUIS PHILLIPS (b. 1942)

The longest Inuvialuktun word that linguists have identified is a bit of a jawbreaker. It is "tuktusiuriagatigitqingnapin'ngitkiptin'nga." Translation: "You'll never go caribou hunting with me again."

CHRISTOPHER WREN IN *THE NEW YORK TIMES* (JULY 9, 1985)

How many times has it been sd, in jest:
Tuktusiuriagatigitqingnapin'ngitkiptin'nga?
But when you turned to me & sd:
Tuktusiuriagatigitqingnapin'ngitkiptin'nga,
There was no laughter on your lips.   5
I sd. "Huh? Could you repeat that slowly?"

But, of course, you couldn't,
& so we have continued our hunt for caribou,
Tho, of course, it isn't quite the same
Ever since you tried to say to me   10
Tuktusiuriagatigitqingnapin'ngitkiptin'nga.

Digging to China   1986

DON WELCH   (b. 1932)

You're digging to China, but you stop when Louis Homer yells.
He says Mr. Quist's cocker spaniel's having pups.
In the garage where everyone can see them, he yells.
They comes out slick as spit, he yells.

Louis is right. There are six black ones   5
and one brown one. The black ones get licked up first.
The brown one is never licked all over and it's smaller.
After Louis wonders aloud if he should pick it up,

you suggest a weenie roast.
Yes, he says, you get the weenies, I'll get the matches,   10
meet me behind Bullock's at the haystack
and don't forget the sticks, he says.

Louis has his weenie on end to end.
You have yours stuck through the middle.
Louis has a bigger knot on the end of his weenie.   15
It doesn't take yours as long to ooze.

You blow on yours. Louis eats his hot.
The haystack is on fire. It's running up the curtains
of its sides the way fire does when a movie saloon's ablaze
and John Wayne has just socked a villain   20

who has just hit John with a chair.
And the firetruck's longer than Eddie Dubonny's garbage truck.
It says Gothenburg Fire Dept. in snaky gold letters on the door,
and its hoses suddenly jump tight.

The whole lot is black.   25
Your mother tells a fireman she should take a stick to you.
Louis says you set the fire, he got the weenies.
You say Louis set the fire and you got the weenies.

Louis's mom runs home to check her weenies.
Your mom says wait till your dad gets home.   30
Your dad has this hair brush with raised Gothic initials
(years later you'll say he only used it when he felt medieval).

But when he finally hits your butt, red characters issue from your mouth,
and in the middle of it all you know he's saying
you can't go out anymore that night,   35
and so you're lying there, thinking of that liar Louis,

and you know it's late because somebody's turned the locusts off
and your pillow's dry, and then you're dreaming.
You're dreaming the hole you dug to China's slowly closing,
when suddenly, Jolene Booker, the neighbor girl is there,   40

and her mouth's wide open, and she's yelling, but there's no sound in the
    dream.
Her mouth's just a hole under a little blonde moustache,
a hole lined with cutworms, and way back there there's a pink nail,
hanging like a lantern in a Chinese basement.

13

Oddments:
From the Green Cloth Bag

When I was an undergraduate, an elderly and thoroughly eccentric professor allegedly composed his lectures in the following manner. As he thought of ideas he might use, he wrote them on scraps of paper that he stuffed into a green cloth bag hanging from the right arm of his wooden study chair. When the time came to prepare the lecture, he would sit naked in the chair, draw the bits of paper out of the bag, study them, and put those he wanted for the lecture into a second green cloth bag hanging from the left arm of the chair. This he took to the classroom, emptied onto the lectern, and, from the notes thus assembled, discoursed with his customary aplomb.

Such, roughly, is the method by which the notes that make up this chapter have been brought together. Last, where it belongs, is the practical *business* of being a poet.

"Professional Poet"

One of the great pleasures is Robert Francis's book of tiny essays, *The Satirical Rogue on Poetry*. Here, entire, is his essay "Professional Poet":

Someone the other day called me a professional poet to my face.

"Don't call me that," I cried. "Don't call anybody that. As well talk about a professional friend."

"Oh!" he said.

"Or a professional lover."

"Oh!"

Cap. and Punc.

Trivial matters, **capitalization** and **punctuation.** Once upon a time the convention was that every line began with a capital letter. Now the poet has a choice. Poets may follow that convention, or, like Cummings, write entirely in lower case (or anything in between). My own rule is to capitalize exactly as I would in prose—first word in a sentence, proper nouns, and so on. The trouble with anything too far from the norm, unless one has a very good reason, is that it may seem self-conscious and pretentious.

The same goes for the norms of punctuation. Like every other part of a poem, its commas and semicolons and dashes and periods are important. They help control the flow of the poem for the eye and guide the pauses and emphases of the voice. A lowly comma may, as in Creeley's "I Know a Man" (page 40), play a crucial part in the poem's meaning.

Poems may be written without punctuation, however, for special effect—as in W. S. Merwin's "Shoe Repairs" (page 274), where the voice seems more of inner meditation or thought than of speech. The poet using such a convention, however, must control, with line-breaks, spacing, and especially careful syntax, the flow of the poem so that a reader doesn't become uncertain or confused and stumble over the ideas or rhythm. Merwin's control in "For the Anniversary of My Death" is perfect; and the meaning properly flows out into silence.

For the Anniversary of My Death

Every year without knowing it I have passed the day
When the last fires will wave to me
And the silence will set out
Tireless traveller
Like the beam of a lightless star   5

Then I will no longer
Find myself in life as in a strange garment
Surprised at the earth
And the love of one woman

And the shamelessness of men
As today writing after three days of rain
Hearing the wren sing and the falling cease
And bowing not knowing to what

Interestingly, Merwin has varied his conventions slightly from book to book. In *The Lice* (1967), from which "For the Anniversary of My Death" is taken, he capitalizes the first letter of each line. In *The Carrier of Ladders* (1970), he capitalizes only the first letter of each stanza, as in "Shoe Repairs," or—the practice in subsequent books—only the first letter of the opening line of each poem. But he maintains, throughout, the convention of the capital for the first person singular pronoun, "I," no doubt to avoid the self-consciousness that the lower case, "i," would convey.

Cummings's eccentric and delightful use of capital letters and punctuation is well known ("Me up at does," page 7, or "chanson innocente," page 143) and almost always has a thematic point. In "chanson innocente," for instance, only two words are capitalized: "in *Just-* / spring" and "balloon*Man*." Both provide emphasis in the phrases in which they appear (just *barely* spring). But if the reader has taken the poem's hint, in "goat-footed," that the balloon-seller is a sort of Pan (the lecherous goat-footed god), the two capitalized words may be reassuring: he is "Just-Man." Cummings is a hard act to follow, however, and his nose-thumbling tricks usually seem secondhand in another poet's hands.

The Law of Distraction

The "Law of Distraction" says that, in a poem, any stylistic feature that draws attention to *itself* and so away from the subject and feeling, is risky. Even though it allows a reader to be distracted for only the tiniest flicker of a second, a flashy word, an odd (or missing) comma, an ambiguous bit of syntax, an accidental misspelling, or the like, risks a dangerous, albeit subliminal, loss of full attention. Don't leave clamps inside the patient.

Bad Poems, Finicky Ways, and Excellence

William Stafford has remarked: "Writing is a reckless encounter with whatever comes along . . . A writer must write bad poems, as they come, amongst the better—and not scorn the 'bad' ones. Finicky ways can dry up the sources." True. Poets can only write the next poem they have to write. There isn't much for it except trying always to write well.

It is, though, the good poems the poet wants, the one that shines like an emerald lost in a bowl of peas.

How good, not how many, is the criterion. There are plenty of poems fair-to-middling. The poem population swells enormously each year, in more than 700 little magazines, in literally thousands of books and chapbooks. Poets & Writers' A *Directory of American Poets and Fiction Writers* (1985–1986) lists 4,341 published, publishing poets. And creative writing classes are full. Even counting the poems being written would be like counting a waterfall.

Excellence, however, isn't democratic.

Poetic Fashions

Ignore them. Go on doing what you are doing. Or, if that is impossible, go as hard as you can in the opposite direction, away from what is fashionable. When in doubt, ask yourself what Andrew Marvell would have thought of it, or Marianne Moore, or whichever poet you believe in.

On Reading Criticism

Criticism is just talk about poetry (or whatever). Good criticism is just good talk about poetry, and that has value. Pound was probably too fierce: "Pay no attention to the criticism of men who have never themselves written a notable work." A good critic himself, C. S. Lewis was at once fairer and fiercer: "It is always better to read Chaucer again than to read the critics."

Critics who write about criticism die and go to Yale.

The Function of Poetry

"Poetry is indispensable," said the French poet Jean Cocteau, "—if I only knew what for." And in his elegy "In Memory of W. B. Yeats," W. H. Auden says in passing that "poetry makes nothing happen."

Wallace Stevens, however, in a fine essay "The Noble Rider and the Sound of Words," argues that (along with other artists) the poet's "role is to help people live their lives." Reality is always imagined. No reality, no view of reality, even the bleakest, is not in fact imagined, for we can only know the world through the mind. So, discussing nobility, he ends:

But as a wave is a force and not the water of which it is composed, which is never the same, so nobility is a force and not the manifestations of which it is composed, which are never the same . . . It is not an artifice that the mind has added to human nature. The mind has added nothing to human nature. It is a violence from within that protects us from a violence without. It is the imagination pressing back against the pressure of reality. It seems, in the last analysis, to have something to do with our self-preservation; and that, no doubt, is why the expression of it, the sound of its words, helps us to live our lives.

Different as William Carlos Williams's poems are from Stevens's, his vision is the same. "The birth of the imagination," he says in the prologue to *Kora in Hell*, "is like waking from a nightmare." In *Spring and All* he asserts:

To refine, to clarify, to intensify that eternal moment in which we alone live there is but a single force—the imagination . . . an actual force comparable to electricity or steam, it is not a plaything but a power that has been used from the first to raise the understanding.

Confronted by the vastness and apparent intractability of reality, "not knowing which way to turn," the individual cannot escape "crushing humiliation" unless able to somehow "raise himself to some approximate co-extension with the universe." "This," Williams declares, "is possible by aid of the imagination." The world—its cats, roses, plums, men, and women—gets its value from works of art, which "stand between man and nature as saints once stood between man and the sky." As an afternoon in the Metropolitan Museum of Art looking at paintings like Brueghel's *The Corn Harvest*, Vermeer's *Young Woman with a Water Jug*, Pieter De Hooch's *Scene in a Courtyard*, and Frans Hals's *The Merry Company* can make the faces in the Fifth Avenue bus, afterward, seem beautiful Dutch faces, so all the arts have to do with the way we see the world, other people, and ourselves. It is not hyperbole when Williams writes, in "Asphodel, That Greeny Flower":

My heart rouses
         thinking to bring you news
                  of something
that concerns you
         and concerns many men. Look at   5
                  what passes for the new.
You will not find it there but in
         despised poems.
                  It is difficult
to get the news from poems   10
         yet men die miserably every day
                  for lack

of what is found there.

<pre>
          Hear me out
                  for I too am concerned   15
and every man
          who wants to die at peace in his bed
                  besides.
</pre>

In "Defense of Poetry," Robert Francis states flatly: "I would say that a poem worth defending needs no defense and a poem needing defense is not worth defending. I would say it is not our business to defend poetry but the business of poetry to defend us."

"The Indecipherable Poem"

Robert Francis again:

I have no love for the indecipherable poem, but for the indecipherable poet I have often a warm friendly feeling. He is usually a bright chap, perhaps brilliant, a good talker, someone worth knowing and worth watching. He is also often a college undergraduate majoring in English and in love with writing.

In his literature and writing courses it is taken for granted that the significant poets are the difficult ones. So, what less can an undergraduate poet do than be difficult himself?

Difficulty, of course, is not the only virtue of great poets. They give us passion, vision, originality. None of these the undergraduate poet probably has, but he *can* be difficult. He can be as difficult as he wants to be. He can be as difficult as anybody else. He need only give the words he uses a private set of meanings. It is not difficult to be difficult.

What I mean is, a poem that is very difficult to read may not have been at all difficult to write.

One poem sufficiently difficult can keep a creative writing class busy a whole hour. If its young author feels pleased with himself, can we blame him? He is human. He has produced something as difficult as anything by Ezra Pound. Why shouldn't he be pleased?

If he wants to, he can let his classmates pick away at his poem indefinitely and never set them straight. If his teacher ventures to criticize a phrase or a line, the author can say that the passage is exactly as he wants it. Is it awkward? Well, he intended it to be awkward since awkwardness was needed at that point. This would be clear, he murmurs, to anyone who understood the poem.

Nobody can touch him. Nobody at all. He is safe. In an ever-threatening world full of old perils and new, such security is to be envied. To be able to sit tight and pretty on top of your poem, impregnable like a little castle perched on a steep rock.

Drugs, Drink, Luck, Work, and the Great Moment

Forget about trying to write when your best friend wouldn't trust you to drive. The roads on Parnassus are steep. Get high on what you are writing. "Nothing goes by luck in composition," Thoreau said. "It allows of no tricks." Charles Baudelaire defined inspiration as "working every day." "Then," as Robert Lowell notes, "the great moment comes when there's enough resolution of your technical equipment, your way of constructing things, and what you can make a poem out of, to hit something you really want to say. You may not know you have it to say."

Allusions

Explain whatever is necessary, in the poem. Avoid referring to things or people no one will remember in a year or so, like senators.

Rules

Break any of the rules when you have to.

A Hand in the Back of the Room

The owner of the hand in the back always wants to know: "How does one become a poet?" The answer is that it is almost always an accident. Liking poems turns into writing poems, and somewhere along the way the beginner shows them to friends, a teacher, the other members of a writing class; and if they are encouraging, he or she takes a chance and sends some of them off to the editor of a magazine. Probably the editor sends them back because it is likely that they aren't really very good—yet. Perhaps the beginner publishes a few in the school or college literary magazine. He or she reads more poems and writes more poems. And sometimes—only sometimes—despite all the discouragements. . . .

Is it excellence or fame or wealth or some even less reputable motive that drives them? Or simply the fascination of words, images, ideas? Poets might well be hard-put to say themselves. Maybe Eudora Welty's reply to a student's asking "Why do you write?" is best. She replied, "Because I am good at it."

Don't be embarrassed to be a beginner. Had there been creative writing classes in the sixteenth century, who knows, the hand in the back of the room might have belonged to a sophomore named Will Shakespeare.

Getting Organized

Keep the drafts of a poem. With the papers clipped together, latest version on top, you can add any correspondence (like an editor's letter of acceptance) to the pile, along with the printed version when it comes along. A complete record of the poem will always be in one place. Some poets date the drafts.

As time goes on and poems multiply, a system of manila folders will keep them straight: a folder labeled NEW POEMS for poems currently being written, a folder labeled POEMS OUT for poems that are finished and out to magazines, and a folder labeled PUBLISHED POEMS. Perhaps, also, a folder labeled OLD POEM MSS, for busted poems that no longer seem likely to work. (Typing-paper boxes make good storage and can be kept on a shelf out of the way.) Some such system will let you keep the decks clear for action.

A heavy clamp binder is also useful for an up-to-date set of good, finished poems. (Make an extra carbon or Xerox copy when you send poems out to magazines.) This binder is handy for carrying to poetry readings and also provides a loose draft of the book you are working toward.

Submitting to Magazines

When should a beginning poet start sending poems out to magazines? As soon as she or he has three or four good, finished poems. It costs very little and is exciting. A poet with several groups of poems in the mail can look forward with suspense to the letter carrier. Sending poems out may also be a stimulus to finishing poems. Horace's classical advice—to wait nine years before publishing—might keep the poet from making a mistake (and of course, nothing will come of sending out sloppy, unfinished poems), but learning from mistakes may be more useful in the long run than trying not to make them.

The probability, of course, is rejection. Even a very good poet will soon have enough rejection slips to wallpaper his or her study. *Don't be discouraged.* Poems may be rejected for a hundred reasons that have nothing to do with their quality. The magazine is currently overstocked (most magazines are); it gets more good poems than it can possibly use (most magazines do); it has just accepted another poem about octopuses and doesn't want to publish anything similar; or the editor just had a phone call from her husband about their child's orthodontist's bill. Have a look at the rejected poems; if they still look pretty sound to you, put them in another envelope and ship them off again to another magazine. Robert Francis looks at rejections this way, in an essay called "Weighed in the Balance":

"I didn't feel settled quite firmly enough on a choice among these poems," writes the editor of *Poetry.*

An appropriate statement, surely. Honest. Also tactful. I have no complaint.

I am entirely reconciled. Indeed, I am more reconciled than an editor might suppose possible. If there is the least doubt in the editorial mind of the worthiness or suitability of my poem, I much prefer he send it back. I don't want to squeak by. I don't want to creep into the fold.

Perhaps it is pride, but I prefer not to have a poem accepted for any other reason than love. Having known love, now and then, I cannot be content with anything less. Now and again an editor has loved a poem of mine before it was in print, and a reader has loved it afterwards. On such love, on the memory of it, I can live for a while.

Perhaps it is pride, perhaps it is conceit, but I can't keep out of mind the possibility that the poem the editor rejects may have turned the tables on him. While he was judging the poem, the poem may have quietly been judging him. In the eyes of eternity it may be the editor and not the little poem that was weighed in the balance and found wanting.

Editors *do* read poems submitted to them, and they *do* buy poems from unknown poets. Sooner or later, a rejection slip will carry a little scribbled note: "Sorry" or "Fine work" or "Liked 'Apples.' " Sooner or later, there will appear a letter of acceptance and perhaps a small check. (Checks for poems are usually small checks.)

To which magazines should you submit poems? Each poet makes and keeps revising a personal list. The rule of thumb is to stick to magazines you have seen and know. If you like the poems in a magazine, odds are, you and the editor are on approximately the same wavelength. If you don't much like the poems in a magazine, probably you are wasting stamps. Both *The Writer* and *Writer's Digest* print a useful list of "poetry markets" in one issue each year. Writer's Digest Books publishes *Poet's Market* by Judson Jerome; the 1986 issue, 374 pages, lists some 1,300 periodicals and presses that print poems, specifying the kind of poetry each wants, what they pay, and how to submit manuscripts. Dustbooks publishes *Directory of Poetry Publishers* (which lists more than a thousand book and magazine publishers) as well as the fatter *International Directory of Little Magazines and Small Presses*. Poets & Writers' *Coda* prints announcements from editors wanting poems. All of these are treasuries of information about magazines' needs or peculiarities. If you can't find a magazine in your library, write for a sample copy (enclosing the single copy price).

Start at the top. If *The New Yorker* or *Atlantic* or *Poetry* is where you wish to be published, by all means send poems there first. Then send them to the other magazines on your list, in descending order of your preference. How long your list is, how quickly it slopes to magazines of modest prestige, depends on your patience, your conviction, and perhaps your supply of postage money. When you bump into a new magazine you like, add it to your list. When a magazine takes six months to reply or sends the manuscript back misfolded or with a shoe-print, delete it. Magazines that pay should be high on the list. (Samuel Johnson: "Sir, no man but a blockhead ever wrote except for money.")

Never send the same poems to two magazines at the same time. If your poems are lousy, the practice will work like a charm—they will all come back. But if there is a good poem among them, sooner or later both editors will accept the same poem and you'll have made a good start on a bad reputation. The proper response to editorial slowness is to take the magazine off your list. In general, a month is prompt; two months, reasonable. After three months, I'd send the editor a postcard wondering whether the poems have been lost in the mail and, if they still happen to be on his or her desk, asking for their return.

The mechanics of submitting are simple. Type each poem cleanly, single-space, in the center of a sheet of regular 8 1/2 × 11-inch bond paper. Put your name and address near the upper left corner. If a poem requires more than one page, a heading near the top right corner of the second (and each subsequent) page shows your name, short title, and page number.

A dumb convention, which you can ignore, is accompanying the manuscripts with a cover letter stating that the enclosed poems are being submitted for publication and that the editor's earnest consideration will be gratefully appreciated, and so forth. That's obvious. So never mind, unless there really is something out of the way that needs explaining. And don't nudge, shove, or elbow, as by saying your poems have just been taken by *This Review* or *That Quarterly.* Let the poems speak for themselves, neatly typed (use a fresh ribbon), carefully proofread, one to a page.

Three or four poems in a group are about right, maybe up to seven or eight. Fold the sheets together, like a business letter, and use regular business-size envelopes. (Manila envelopes, which let the poems go flat, cost more, are niftier, and make no difference. If you use a manila envelope, don't enclose a regular-size envelope for the poems' return, expecting the editor to fold them for you. He or she will just be annoyed.) Address the editor by name if you know it, or simply "Poetry Editor."

Always make carbon copies or Xerox copies, which may be useful later for checking and which can be clipped to the drafts.

Always enclose a self-addressed, stamped envelope (SASE) or, if the manuscript is going abroad, International Reply Coupons (available at any post office). Fold the return envelope and tuck it in with the poems.

Keep a log of submissions. With a giant paperclip, clip together copies of the poems (with drafts) in each group, along with a 5 × 8-inch card. As the group goes and comes, enter on the card the date sent and the magazine, then the date returned and any acceptance or comment. A small notebook will do as well. Dates and other particulars of publication should also be recorded, which may help keep track of copyrights when the time comes to gather a book manuscript.

If anyone wants money to publish or consider your poems, duck.

By and large, publishers lose money on poetry. That's their problem—as it's the poets' problem that they, too, lose money writing the poems (not to mention sleep, etc.). Nonetheless, poets should be grateful to publishers (and to the un- or underpaid editors); and a proper way to express that gratitude is by buying the good books and subscribing to the good magazines. So by all means vote with your bucks. But vote your conscience. Don't pay bribes.

Copyright

A significant provision of the new copyright law (Title 17, USC), which went into effect on 1 January 1978, extends copyright protection of a work to the author's lifetime plus fifty years. That protection begins with the creation of the work, so the penciled poem on your desk is included. An author *may* register unpublished work (Form TX, one copy of the work, and a $10 fee), but there is no need to go to this trouble. The publisher of any reputable periodical or book will register the work on publication. Even though the registration is made in the publisher's or magazine's name, the copyright belongs to the author—*unless there is a written agreement to the contrary.* In the absence of such a written agreement, a magazine acquires only the right to initial publication in one of its issues. The author retains copyright and full control. So don't sign anything, except a check. If in doubt, consult someone who knows about such things.

One small complication. Although registration by the author (as distinct from, and in addition to, registration by the publishers of magazines or books) is not necessary for a work to be protected by copyright, such registration, it appears, *is* necessary for the author to bring suit for copyright infringement. Section 408: "such registration is not a condition for copyright protection." *But* Section 411: "no action for infringement of the copyright in any work shall be instituted until registration of the copyright claim has been made." To be safe, the writer apparently must register works himself or herself, preferably within three months of publication and absolutely within one year of publication. Form TX (along with a $10 fee and two copies of the periodical or book) for a single poem. Several poems in one or in several periodicals can be registered as a group: Form GR/CP (in addition to the TX's and along with a single $10 fee and two complete copies of each periodical). Whether all this is worth it, is anybody's guess. If you think you might want to sue somebody for stealing your poems, write for full information and forms to the Copyright Office, Library of Congress, Washington, D.C. 20559.

Book publication is always by contract (written agreement) which gives the publisher control of the copyright, even when the publisher registers it in the author's name. Book contracts are normally standard and fair. But ask someone who knows before you sign one.

The permission and fee for reprinting your poems in anthologies, when they are from a book in print, will be handled by your publisher, usually to your advantage. Before poems are collected in a book and again after copyright has reverted, the author must handle these permissions and set the fees. Something like two or three dollars a line is average, but there are variables like the size of the edition, the anthology's price, the likelihood of profitability (which is why your publisher's Permissions Department knows how to handle this advantageously). If anything, err a trifle on what may seem to you the high side in setting fees; the anthologist can always ask you to lower them. You should specify the form the acknowledgment is to take, usually just "Copyright 1986 by Jane Doe," and, if the poem has appeared in a magazine, something like "First printed in *The Other Journal.*"

Book Publication

Ideally, the beginning poet makes a reputation in magazines and, as poems and prestige accumulate, arrives at a chapbook or book. Almost the only sure thing is that you won't wake up the next morning to find yourself famous.

Readings

Oddly, poets are likely to earn more from giving readings of their poems in schools or colleges than from actual publication. However small, an audience offers a lively chance to test new poems and provides what publication cannot—an immediate and personal response. Well-known poets command fees of two thousand dollars or more, but fees of a hundred or so (plus expenses) are common. Beginning poets will do well to accept whatever invitations to read come along, usually for free, at their own schools or at public libraries, bookstores, coffeehouses, and sometimes prisons.

Poets develop their own styles in giving readings, and you will probably have plenty of examples from which to form your own. Listening to poems, especially poems that aren't familiar, takes a lot of concentration; so read slowly and allow an audience to relax between poems, by chatting informally about them. Find out from your host how long you are expected to read and stay within that limit. As a rule, underselling works better than overselling, although a little showmanship helps.

Don't be disappointed when, at your first reading, the audience turns out to be four people (or maybe five, if you count the janitor who stops in the doorway to listen). The fewer they are, the rarer—and so deserving of your best. As Robert Francis says about something else, "Very well. Very well, indeed. But when were rubies and diamonds sold by the peck?"

Money

One of the freedoms of the poet, since in our society at least poetry doesn't make money, is to do as he or she wishes. Little magazines usually pay in copies—two copies; others pay a dollar or two per line. A poem that may last as long as the English language, an immortal masterpiece, might bring twenty-five dollars. The few commercial magazines that still publish poetry do better, but not by much. Given the modest sale of books of poems, the average book earns only several hundred dollars—if that. A lucky poem can earn several hundred dollars from anthologies over the years. And there may be, too, occasional prizes and grants—several hundred dollars here, maybe several thousand dollars there. These days the National Endowment for the Arts and the various state arts councils are usually the tooth fairy. But, as Ezra Pound's notorious Mr. Nixon (no, not *that* notorious Mr. Nixon) advised the young writer:

> . . . give up verse, my boy,
> There's nothing in it.

Still, there is the freedom. And there is the art of poetry, in which the least of us may for a time be a companion of Geoffrey Chaucer and John Milton and Alexander Pope and William Yeats. Every poet may share the hope of the Roman poet Sextus Propertius (died 15 B.C.), in Ezra Pound's elegant translation "Homage to Sextus Propertius," that he may write a few pages that will not "go to rack ruin beneath the thud of the years."

There is the money, too. If not a living, still something. A tidy sum is a tidy sum, and payment at all for doing what one loves is a good wage. You need not, at any rate, be modest about expecting or accepting modest payments; nor about claiming, when tax time comes around, the modest privileges of your "small business."

For so, if you have any income to speak of, the Internal Revenue Service must regard you, albeit with suspicion. The proper form is Form C of the 1040: "Profit (or Loss) from Business or Professions (Sole Proprietorships)." Armed with it you may deduct or depreciate your books and your typewriter and your desk. On it you may deduct your expenses, the paper and envelopes and paperclips and manila folders and postage and the like, as well as your mileage and motel bill and tolls when you travel to give readings. You may deduct your copyright fees, anything you pay a typist, long-distance calls about readings or publishing a book, and sometimes even a portion of your rent and utilities. You may even claim, on capital expenses like a typewriter or desk, the 10% Investment Tax Credit (Form 3468). For you are, willy-nilly, a business every bit as much as IBM and General Motors. ("What is good for the poet is good for the country," you may freely declare.)

A good tax accountant (also deductible) can quickly show you the ins and outs, and how to keep the simple records necessary. A little spiral notebook suffices, along with the habit of asking for receipts at the post office or stationery store and yet one more manila folder to stuff the receipts into. Profits (or losses) may be carried over to the appropriate line on Form 1040 and added to (or deducted from) the rest of your income. A fair general rule is, use writing expenses to offset writing income and don't push. The IRS can also decide that writing is a hobby.

The poet's aim may be, like Frost's in "Two Tramps in Mud Time," to join vocation and avocation—"As my two eyes make one in sight." But few poets earn a living by poetry. Williams was a doctor, Stevens was an attorney for an insurance firm, and Frost himself did a lot of teaching. The money, like the honors, if they come, is likely to come too late to do the poet much good. Get a job.

A Last Word

Ben Jonson advised the poet, wisely, "to live merrily, and to trust to good verses."

QUESTIONS AND SUGGESTIONS

1. In the library browse among the poetry in magazines like *Poetry, Atlantic, Hudson Review, The Nation, Antaeus, Poetry Northwest, Poetry Now, Cutbank, Southern Review, Ploughshares, Open Places, Field, American Poetry Review, Black Warrior Review, North American Review, New Republic, Three Rivers Poetry Journal, Iowa Review, Ohio Review, Georgia Review, Carolina Quarterly, Nimrod, Prairie Schooner, Epoch, Hanging Loose, New Letters, Tar River Poetry, Southern Poetry Review,* or (criticism) *Parnassus.*

2. Buy a book of poems.

3. Here are six accomplished poems by students. If you were an editorial assistant for a poetry magazine, would you recommend any for publication? Consider carefully your reaction to each poem. (See Appendix I.)

a) *Miner*

JEANNE FRANK*

Home from the nightshift,
he watches the snow
as it blows and drifts
at the back doorstep,
and curses it to hell.   5
His workclothes smell
of sweat and the breath
of engines, as he takes
his shovel, shoulders it,
and goes out, tarnishing   10
the moonlight; miner
in a field of diamonds.

b) *The Invention of the Snowman*

MARK IRWIN*

Somewhere beyond the bounds of sleep,
my bones undressed, rising from their flesh
to become this selfless, falling dust.

It was then that I wanted ears
with which to hear the familiar cries   5
of those children building me.

And of course, I had no eyes—
only this unfailing bandage of light,
the snow sewing its colorless view.

But worst of all, this thirst to be living—   10
to understand those small, clumsy hands
making the same careless mistakes as gods.

c) *Pandora's Dressing Table*

BONNIE JACOBSON*

The sea was a blue flower
Lolling on a reedy stem
Pandora fingered a moment,
Satisfied her eyes were bluer.

Mark, the moon was a white bee   5
In the blue flower withering
And the earth was an amber earring
On Pandora's dressing table.

Reason was her bumbling suitor
Stung daft by the waning moon.   10
Pandora reaching for her rouge
Is wind, whittling dry bee and flower.

d) *The Divers*

JOHN STUPP*

They descend like stones,
leaving air to mark passage.
Once underwater, they
exchange glances, unzip
skin to reveal: 5
gills, small fins. At night
they sleep with
girls in the village, who will
awake, impaled on
secret hooks. Now, in the morning   10
they sit grinning
on the docks. This is the photograph
I took of them. Click.

e) *Forgive And Forget*

KATHERINE KINSEY*

Straightening things on my desk,
I find a book of matches,
Matches you pressed on me, though I don't smoke,
Leaving a restaurant after dinner—

After dinner, after our first argument,   5
Our pairing still unmeasured and unmanaged,
After the first relieved forgiving of wrongs
Still imperfectly imagined.

I put the matches in the top drawer,
A drawer I seldom open, and   10
Saw unmailed invitations to a party never held
In a time now almost forgotten.

The next time I open the drawer,
Will I know where the matches came from?

f) *Prayer*

WILLIAM R. JOHNSON*

I like to believe
through the white hospital walls
you can feel the crops rising.

If I could leave Ohio I would tell you how
everything outside your window in Iowa is ripe   5
how women and barley sway the same way,
how bicycling airless roads
you can pull off to a cool wetness
under thick stalks of corn. You can drink deep
from your water bottle and listen as the leaves breathe,   10
each grain another sun.

I would listen
to your dry throat breathing like hands
husking through a long field.

4. Look back at Gavin Ewart's "Sonnet: The Last Things" (page 147). Did you notice that the poem is unrhymed and not written in iambic pentameter? In what ways *does* it follow the conventions of the form?

5. Write a poem about writing poems. Use metaphors and particulars to make it colorful. What's it like? Like planning, planting, tending, and harvesting a garden? Like manufacturing a machine tool? Perhaps focus on some detail of the process of writing (the padding sheet you use to protect the platen of your typewriter, or the miles of words stored in the tiny cylinder of a pencil lead).

6. Prepare and send out a group of poems to the first magazine on your list.

POEMS TO CONSIDER

from *An Essay on Criticism*   1711

ALEXANDER POPE

'Tis hard to say, if greater want of skill
Appear in writing or in judging ill;
But, of the two, less dangerous is the offense
To tire our patience, than mislead our sense.
Some few in that, but numbers err in this,   5
Ten censure wrong, for one who writes amiss;
A fool might once himself alone expose,
Now one in verse makes many more in prose.
  'Tis with our judgments as our watches, none

Go just alike, yet each believes his own.   10
In poets as true genius is but rare,
True taste as seldom is the critic's share;
Both must alike from Heaven derive their light,
These born to judge, as well as those to write.
Let such teach others who themselves excel,   15
And censure freely who have written well.
Authors are partial to their wit, 'tis true,
But are not critics to their judgment too?

Poets   1969

X. J. KENNEDY

These people are . . . quenched. I mean the natives.
        D. H. LAWRENCE, LETTER OF AUGUST 14, 1923 FROM DOVER, N.J.

Le vierge, le vivace, et le bel aujourd'hui . . .

   What were they like as schoolboys? Long on themes
And short of wind, perpetually outclassed,
Breaking their glasses, always chosen last
   When everyone was sorted out in teams,

   Moody, a little dull, the kind that squirmed   5
At hurt cats, shrank from touching cracked-up birds,
With all but plain girls at a loss for words,
   Having to ask to have their fishhooks wormed,

   Snuffers of candles every priest thought nice,
Quenchers of their own wicks, their eyes turned down   10
And smoldering. In Dover, my home town,
   No winter passed but we had swans in ice,

   Birds of their quill: so beautiful, so dumb,
They'd let a window glaze about their feet,
Not seeing through their dreams till time to eat.   15
   A fireman with a blowtorch had to come

Thaw the dopes loose. Sun-silvered, plumes aflap,
Weren't they grand, though?—not that you'd notice it,
Crawling along a ladder, getting bit,
 Numb to the bone, enduring all their crap.   20

The Perfect Suicide   *1977*

ROGER PFINGSTON (b. 1940)

In his despair he made a poem
with a gun in it. He shot himself
again and again until he got it right.

Stepping Out of Poetry   *1977*

GERALD STERN (b. 1925)

What would you give for one of the old yellow streetcars
rocking toward you again through the thick snow?

What would you give for the feeling of joy as you climbed
up the three iron steps and took your place by the cold window?

Oh, what would you give to pick up your stack of books   5
and walk down the icy path in front of the library?

What would you give for your dream
to be as clear and simple as it was then
in the dark afternoons, at the old scarred tables?

Seven Wealthy Towns

ANONYMOUS

Seven wealthy towns contend for Homer dead
Through which the living Homer begged his bread.

from *Homage to Sextus Propertius*°   1917

EZRA POUND

Shades of Callimachus°, Coan ghosts of Philetas°
It is in your grove I would walk,
I who come first from the clear font
Bringing the Grecian orgies into Italy,
      and the dance into Italy.   5
Who hath taught you so subtle a measure,
     in what hall have you heard it;
What foot beat out your time-bar,
    what water has mellowed your whistles?

Out-weariers of Apollo° will, as we know, continue their Martian° generali-
  ties,   10
   We have kept our erasers in order.
A new-fangled chariot follows the flower-hung horses;
A young Muse with young loves clustered about her
   ascends with me into the æther, . . .
And there is no high-road to the Muses.   15

Annalists will continue to record Roman reputations,
Celebrities from the Trans-Caucasus will belaud Roman celebrities
And expound the distentions of Empire,
But for something to read in normal circumstances?
For a few pages brought down from the forked hill° unsullied?   20
I ask a wreath which will not crush my head.
     And there is no hurry about it;
I shall have, doubtless, a boom after my funeral,
Seeing that long standing increases all things
      regardless of quality.   25

And who would have known the towers
                 pulled down by a deal-wood horse°;   *the Trojan horse*
Or of Achilles° withstaying waters by Simois°
Or of Hector° spattering wheel-rims,
Or of Polydmantus°, by Scamander°, and Helenus° and Deiphoibos°?   30
Their door-yards would scarcely know them, or Paris°.
Small talk O Ilion°, and O Troad°
                 twice taken by Oetian gods°,   *of Mount Oeta*
If Homer had not stated your case!

And I also among the later nephews of this city   35
                 shall have my dog's day,
With no stone upon my contemptible sepulchre;
My vote coming from the temple of Phoebus° in Lycia°, at Patara°,
And in the mean time my songs will travel,
And the devirginated young ladies will enjoy them   40
                 when they have got over the strangeness,
For Orpheus° tamed the wild beasts—
                 and held up the Threician river;
And Citharaon° shook up the rocks by Thebes
            and danced them into a bulwark at his pleasure,   45
And you, O Polyphemus°? Did harsh Galatea almost
Turn to your dripping horses, because of a tune, under Aetna?
We must look into the matter.
Bacchus and Apollo in favour of it,
There will be a crowd of young women doing homage to my palaver,   50
Though my house is not propped up by Taenarian° columns from Laconia
      (associated with Neptune° and Cerberus°),
Though it is not stretched upon gilded beams;
My orchards do not lie level and wide
                 as the forests of Phaecia,
                 the luxurious and Ionian,   55
Nor are my caverns stuffed stiff with a Marcian° vintage,
My cellar does not date from Numa Pompilius°,
Nor bristle with wine jars,
Nor is it equipped with a frigidaire patent;
Yet the companions of the Muses   60
                 will keep their collective nose in my books,
And weary with historical data, they will turn to my dance tune.

Happy who are mentioned in my pamphlets,
         the songs shall be a fine tomb-stone over their beauty.
           But against this?   65

Neither expensive pyramids scraping the stars in their route,
Nor houses modelled upon that of Jove in East Elis°,   *temple of Zeus,*
Nor the monumental effigies of Mausolus°,   *in Greece*
                    are a complete elucidation of death.

Flame burns, rain sinks into the cracks   70
And they all go to rack ruin beneath the thud of the years.
Stands genius a deathless adornment,
                    a name not to be worn out with the years.

Sextus Propertius: Roman poet (died 15 B.C.); *Homage to Sextus Propertius:* free translation (or adaptation) of a number of Propertius's elegies.   1 *Callimachus, Philetas:*
Greek poets of the 3rd and 4th centuries B.C.   10 *Apollo:* Greek sun-god, patron of
all the arts; *Martian:* warlike (of Mars, god of war).   20 *forked hill:* Parnassus, two-
peaked mountain of the Muses.   28–31 *Achilles:* Greek hero of the Trojan war; *Hec-
tor, Polydmantus, Helenus, Deiphoibos, Paris:* Trojans; *Simois, Scamander:* rivers of
Troy.   32 *Ilion:* the citadel; *Troad:* the state.   38 *Phoebus:* Apollo; *Lycia, Patara:*
places in Asia Minor.   42 *Orpheus:* poet who tamed beasts and held back rivers by
playing his lyre.   44 *Citharaon:* Amphion (of Mount Citharaon), who raised the
walls of the city of Thebes with his music.   46 *Polyphemus:* cyclops who loved and
was rejected by the sea-nymph Galatea.   51 *Taenarian:* marble from quarry at Tae-
narus, in Greece; *Neptune:* Roman sea-god; *Cerberus:* three-headed dog guarding the en-
trance to Hades. 56–57 *Marcian (Ancus Marcius), Numa Pompilius:* legendary kings of
early Rome.   68 *Mausolus:* king buried in a grand tomb; hence, the word
mausoleum.

Selecting a Reader   1974

TED KOOSER   (b. 1939)

First, I would have her be beautiful,
and walking carefully up on my poetry
at the loneliest moment of an afternoon,
her hair still damp at the neck
from washing it. She should be wearing   5
a raincoat, an old one, dirty
from not having money enough for the cleaners.
She will take out her glasses, and there
in the bookstore, she will thumb

over my poems, then put the book back   10
up on its shelf. She will say to herself,
"For that kind of money, I can get
my raincoat cleaned." And she will.

Craft Lost in Texas   1982

PETER KLAPPERT (b. 1942)

The poet and all
six passengers of
a small poetry reading
were lost late last night
when they went into a dive   5
outside of Houston.

My Muse   1985

JAMES LAUGHLIN (b. 1914)

My muse keeps irregular hours
Her name is Anthea which is a flower in Greece
It's obvious that she doesn't sit by her phone waiting for my calls
Don't call me, she says, I'll call you
And she calls at the most inconvenient hours, like 3 A.M. in the middle of the
    night   5
That seems to be a favorite time for her
Like when she might be getting home from a night on the town with some
    other poet
Naturally she doesn't tell me anything about him but I have my suspicions
If it turned out to be Howard Moss I would shoot her
But that really isn't likely because . . . well I won't say it . . . de mortuis in
    cerebro arteque nihil nisi bonum   10
She calls in the middle of the night a lot, it's like the old long distance
    operator before Ma Bell computerized

One ring then a little wait then three rings, I can always tell it's her
Anyway who else is going to call in the middle of the night
Unless it's Gregory Corso when he's been drinking
The last time Gregory called it was to ask me if I would leave him my teeth in
    my will   15
So she calls about 3 A.M. usually, my muse does
I have to keep a pencil and yellow pad handy to be ready for her
And sometimes she talks so fast I can't get it all down before she hangs up
It's inconvenient
But I'm loyal, we've been together, if you can call it that, for a long time   20
I suppose there are a lot of unemployed muses around on Helikon these days
    but I'm loyal, call me Philemon but she sure isn't Baucis
After she's called and I've written down her message I'm all keyed up and
    usually have to take half a valium to get back to sleep
I wish she would keep store hours
I wish I could call her and not have to wait for her to call me
But you know how muses are   25
I guess that's why old poets always had invocations to their muses at the start
    of their long poems
They were apple polishing, trying to keep their muse in line to get better
    service.

APPENDIX 1

Notes to the Questions
and Suggestions

Chapter 1

1. a) *For a Lady I Know*

COUNTEE CULLEN   (1903–1946)

She even thinks that up in heaven
Her class lies late and snores,
While poor black cherubs rise at seven
To do celestial chores.

b) *Potatoes*

GERALD COSTANZO   (b. 1945)

Grandpa said potatoes
reminded him of school.

Potatoes and school.
He said he'd wake nearly

freezing, kindle a fire
and throw two potatoes

5

on. Going to school
he carried them to

warm his hands. To
warm his feet he ran.   10

He said by noontime
those potatoes almost

froze, said he ate a lot
of cold potatoes for lunch.

Chapter 3

1. a) *Epigram: Of Treason*

   Trĕasŏn | dŏth nĕv|er prŏs|pĕr, what's | thĕ reas|ŏn?
   For if | it pros|pĕr, nŏne | dare call | ĭt treas|ŏn.

   b) *Death of the Day*

   My pĭc|turĕs black|ĕn 'in | their frames
      As night | cŏmes ŏn,
   Ănd youth|fŭl maids | ănd wrink|lĕd dames
      Ăre now | all ŏne.
   Death ŏf | thĕ day! | ă stern|er Death
      Dĭd worse | bĕfore;
   Thĕ fair|ĕst form, | thĕ sweet|ĕst breath,
      Ăway | hĕ bore.

   c) *Tribute*

   What thĕ | bee knows
   Tastĕs ĭn | thĕ hon|ey
   Sweet | ănd sun|ny.
   Ŏ wise | bee. Ŏ rose.

   d) *First Sight*

   Lambs | thăt learn | tŏ walk | ĭn snow
   Whĕn | their bleat|ĭng clouds | thĕ air

Meet | a vast | unwel|come, know
Noth|ing but | a sun|less glare.
New|ly stumb|ling to | and fro
All | they find, | outside | the fold,
Is | a wretch|ed width | of cold.
'As | they wait | beside | the ewe,
Her fleec|es wet|ly caked, | there lies
Hid|den round | them, wait|ing too,
Earth's | immeas|urable | surprise.
They could | not grasp | it if | they knew,
What | so soon | will wake | and grow
Ut|terly | unlike | the snow.

2. Version of the Lewis Thomas passage:

Afield, a single ant of any kind
Cannot be said to have much on his mind;

Indeed, it would be hard by rights to call
His neurons, few, loose-strung, a mind at all,

Or say he had a thought half-way complete.
He is more like a ganglion with feet.

Circling a moth that's dead, four ants—or ten—
Will seem more like a real idea then,

Fumbling and shoving, Hill-ward, bit by bit,
As if by blind chance slowly moving it.

But only when you watch, in crowded dance
Around their Hill, a thousand massing ants

As black and purposeful as scribbling ink,
Do you first see the whole beast, see it think,

Plan, calculate—a live computer's bits
Of dark intelligence, its crawling wits.

5. *The Garden Seat*

Its former green is blue and thin,
And its once firm legs sink in and in;
Soon it will break down unaware,
Soon it will break down unaware.

At night when reddest flowers are black   5
Those who once sat thereon come back;
Quite a row of them sitting there,
Quite a row of them sitting there.

With them the seat does not break down,
Nor winter freeze them, nor floods drown,   10
For they are as light as upper air,
They are as light as upper air!

Chapter 4

1. Housman tried "sunny," "pleasant," "checkered," "patterned," and "painted" before he hit on the word he finally chose: "colored." Why do you think he preferred "colored" to the other adjectives? Consider the qualities of the scene each suggests.

2. Possible rhymes might include:

circle = *work'll*
stop-sign = *drop mine*
rhinoceros = If ever, outside a zoo,
                     You meet a rhinoceros
                     And you *cross her, fuss*
                     Is exactly what she'll do.

Anonymous

evergreen = *never seen*
broccoli = Look at the *clock! Oh, me!*
pelican = Ogden Nash used "belly can" and "hell he can."
umbrella = The rain it raineth every day,
                     upon the just and unjust *fella,*
                  but more upon the just, because
                     the unjust hath the just's umbrella.

Anonymous

4. *The Fourth of July*

HOWARD NEMEROV   (b. 1920)

Because I am drunk, this Independence Night,
I watch the fireworks from far away,
From a high hill, across the moony green
Of lakes and other hills to the town harbor,

Where stately illuminations are flung aloft,   5
One light shattering in a hundred lights
Minute by minute. The reason I am crying,
Aside from only being country drunk,
That is, may be that I have just remembered
The sparklers, rockets, roman candles, and   10
So on, we used to be allowed to buy
When I was a boy, and set off by ourselves
At some peril to life and property.
Our freedom to abuse our freedom thus
Has since, I understand, been remedied   15
By legislation. Now the authorities
Arrange a perfectly safe public display
To be watched at a distance; and now also
The contribution of all the taxpayers
Together makes a more spectacular   20
Result than any could achieve alone
(A few pale pinwheels, or a firecracker
Fused at the dog's tail). It is, indeed, splendid:
Showers of roses in the sky, fountains
Of emeralds, and those profusely scattered zircons   25
Falling and falling, flowering as they fall
And followed distantly by a noise of thunder.
My eyes are half-afloat in happy tears.
God bless our Nation on a night like this,
And bless the careful and secure officials   30
Who celebrate our independence now.

6. There is a big, old wooden box,
       Without a thing inside.
   It therefore needs, and has, no locks.
       The top is open wide.

   Here is a big, old wooden box
       Which needs, and has, no locks.
   Because it holds nothing inside,
       Its top is opened wide.

   The top is open wide;
       There are no locks.
   For nothing's kept inside
       This wooden box.

Chapter 7

3. The speaker in "In 1856 she . . ." is Emily Dickinson.

Chapter 8

2. a) Raspberries *splash,* redly in their leaves
   b) Four cars like a *kite's tail* / behind the hearse
   c) droning, *unzipping* the halves of the air
   d) will shower its peaceful *rockets* / all over the towns
   e) The clarinet, a dark tube / *tallowed* in silver
   f) Big as *wedding cakes,* / two white launches
   g) whirled by a boat's wash / into *Queen Anne's lace*
   h) Dreams are the soul's *home movies*

Chapter 10

3. The original words in "In a Spring Still Not Written Of" are: "burning up" in line 4, "carrying" in line 8, "blossom" in line 12, "astronomies" in line 14, and "untarnished" in line 16.

4. a) *The Opening*

   DANIEL TOWNER   (b. 1952)

   Down its length the rifle barrel
   is generosity: the smoothness
   of steel, the long spiral

   down the hole. Try to imagine the gun
   without love—impossible.   5
   Every report is a sad speech.

   I say to you there can be no beauty
   greater than that of the cool flower-stem
   opening softly, each day, against the forehead.

   b) *The Passionate Shepherd to His Love*

   CHRISTOPHER MARLOWE   (1564–1593)

   Come live with me and be my love,
   And we will all the pleasures prove
   That valleys, groves, hills, and fields,
   Woods, or steepy mountain yields.

   And we will sit upon the rocks,   5
   Seeing the shepherds feed their flocks
   By shallow rivers, to whose falls
   Melodious birds sing madrigals.

And I will make thee beds of roses
And a thousand fragrant posies,   10
A cap of flowers and a kirtle°   *skirt*
Embroidered all with leaves of myrtle;

A gown made of the finest wool
Which from our pretty lambs we pull;
Fair lined slippers for the cold,   15
With buckles of the purest gold;

A belt of straw and ivy buds,
With coral clasps and amber studs.
And if these pleasures may thee move,
Come live with me and be my love.   20

The shepherd swains° shall dance and sing   *lads*
For thy delight each May morning.
If these delights thy mind may move,
Then live with me and be my love.

c) *The Lark and the Emperor*

W. M. ABERG (b. 1957)

Strangle the Lark.
Place its pink tongue under glass.
Weave the feathers into a coat.
The Hungarians
will build violins from the bones.   5
Pour cinnamon and honey
into the electric fountain.
When you hear the lock turn,
pull the switch.
It will be the Emperor.   10

d) *Feeding Prisoners*

GERALD STERN (b. 1925)

The weeds give up suddenly after a small struggle
and fall into your hands like German prisoners.
Suddenly you are surrounded by a whole division of undressed men
who are looking to you for wisdom and shelter.
Now you have to grow food again.   5
You have to put stakes in the ground
to mark the boundaries
and tie little rags
to the invisible wires.
You have to start moving the rusted tanks out   10
and stack the oil drums up behind the latrines.

You have to think up a plan for getting out food and water.
Suddenly you are back again in a crowded city
full of corruption and loneliness
after your quick and easy victory.   15

6. *The Eagle*

ALFRED, LORD TENNYSON   (b. 1809–1892)

He clasps the crag with crooked hands;
Close to the sun in lonely lands,
Ringed with the azure world, he stands.

The wrinkled sea beneath him crawls;
He watches from his mountain walls,   5
And like a thunderbolt he falls.

Chapter 12

2. *In One Place*

ROBERT WALLACE   (b. 1932)

        —something
holds up two or three leaves
the first year,

                and climbs
and branches, summer   5
by summer,

        till birds
in it don't remember
it wasn't there.

5. Which of these versions is closest to yours? Before you go on to the transcript of
the class discussion that follows, see if you can determine which version is the
Williams poem:

a) She sits with tears
        on her cheek,
   Her cheek
        on her hand,
   The child
        in her lap,
   His nose
        pressed to the glass.

b) She sits with tears
on her cheek,
her cheek
on her hand,
the child
in her lap,
his nose
pressed to the glass.

c) She sits with tears on her cheek,
her cheek on her hand,
the child in her lap,
his nose pressed to the glass.

d) She sits with
tears on

her cheek
her cheek on

her hand
the child

in her lap
his nose

pressed
to the glass

e) She sits with tears
On her cheek her cheek
On her hand the child
In her lap his nose
Pressed to the glass.

f) she sits
with tears on her cheek,

her cheek on her hand, the child

in her lap
his nose pressed to the glass

g) She sits with tears
on her cheek
her cheek on her hand
the child in her lap, his nose
pressed to the glass.

A student opened the discussion by saying that she liked version *c*, which seemed clearest and easiest to follow. True, but it was also, several others thought, pretty plain. Line-breaks coincided with the punctuation, so the lines merely repeated the phrase-units of the prose. Well, said the first girl, *e* just seemed confusing.

Everyone agreed. If all the lines of *c* were end-stopped, all the lines of *e* were run-on; and the middle three lines of *e* seemed to force parts of two phrases together into units that made no sense and somehow kept competing with the literal meaning: "On her hand the child," for instance. Someone said the omission of commas added to the confused impression. Someone else felt that the line-capitals were intrusive, overly formal; the lowercase first letters in all the other versions except *a* seemed easier, more natural.

Several students rose to the defense of *a*. It wasn't confusing, and the alternating indented lines gave it a distinctive look on the page. It seemed more vivid, as well as being clear, because the shorter lines with single short phrases emphasized things more. The interrelationship of the ideas was emphasized by the parallel prepositional phrases of lines 2, 4, 6, 8. Awfully mechanical? someone asked. Putting "pressed" in line 8 along with the prepositional phrase made a good variation, it was suggested, and kept the "found" pattern from being dull. Each pair of lines in *a*, someone saw, included exactly the phrase-units of *c*'s four lines. Version *a* was better, because the mixture of end-stopped and run-on lines gave variety to the flow.

The discussion took a new turn when someone noticed that the *lines* of *a* and *b* were identical, except for the capitalization and indentation. The class divided about equally, many preferring the more formal presentation of *a*, many preferring the more natural presentation of *b*. No one thought line-capitals would enhance *b*, but even *a*'s defenders thought that lower case at the beginnings of lines 3, 5, 7 would "soften" that version's impression in a useful way.

Why, I wondered, did the poem want softening? What's really going on in it?

It's a picture of a woman crying. Just something the poet saw.

Did he know the woman?

No. He just saw her.

Why is she crying? Did the poet know why?

Everyone agreed that he didn't know the reason, but it seemed obvious that she was crying because she was separated from her husband or lover. Perhaps he was dead. Her despondency seemed settled, resigned (cheek on hand). And the importance of the child, on whom half the poem focuses, suggested he was a burden. He was too young to share her grief, but his looking out the window might imply the departure of the father. Like at a bus-station window, someone said.

Even if the poet couldn't know why she was crying, he had to know where he saw her, I said. Why doesn't he tell us?

Presumably the particular place doesn't matter, the class agreed. The important part was the woman and her grief, which was timeless and not dependent on the particular circumstances. If the child in her lap was close enough to press his nose against the window, someone suggested, *she* was very close to it, too. A bus window? Her defeated longing was universal. The fact that the poem—and the poet—notice her and pass on reenforces the painfulness of her isolation. There is nothing to be done.

What about versions *d* and *f?*

The stanzas, especially in *f*, someone said, make the versions look more like notes. There isn't even a period at the end of *f*. And no capital letters at all, even to begin the sentence. Version *d* begins with a capital, but there's no punctuation whatever. The omission of the period in both versions makes the event seem unfinished; the woman's life, her grief, go on outside the frame of the poem. In *f* commas are used after "on her cheek" and "on her hand," a girl said, but not after "in her lap," so that the slightly stronger pull of the run-on—"in her lap / his nose pressed to the glass"—makes it seem more *pressed* to the glass. That's the impression I get, she said. I don't know.

Isn't using punctuation and then not using it, I asked, pretty inconsistent?

No one wanted to say it was consistent, but several frowns showed the class was unhappy about where I seemed to be heading.

No, I said, I like the version. What I was really after was the poet's *reason* for using punctuation and then not using it. The first two and a half lines seem fairly normal. They are end-stopped (the break after "she sits" occurs at a strong phrase-unit) and have commas. But the last two and a half lines are run-on, dividing the phrase "the child // in her lap" not just over lines but over stanzas; and there's no punctuation at all after the comma in line 3.

The poem speeds up, the girl said, seems more confusing.

And maybe that suggests that the woman's grief focuses on the child—he's what concerns and worries her, what makes her loss unmanageable? The poem could have put the child in earlier in the description and ended with the tears? Ending with the child makes his presence the most telling detail? His nose to the window suggests having come up against a barrier.

They can look through—the window is like the future. They can look through, but can't go through.

Is *f* the real poem? someone else asked.

It's very effective, I said. I like the way it both finds a pattern in the material (the short, then long lines of stanzas 1 and 3) and then varies from that pattern so it doesn't seem rigid. Stanza 2 is one line, not two. And the syntactical units in stanzas 1 and 3 fit differently, aren't parallel like the rather mechanical prepositional phrases in lines 2, 4, 6, 8 of version *a*. So *f* seems both formal and informal at once. It's not just a random jotting. It's considered. But it's also not rigid, and lets the subject's emotion come through in its rhythm and form.

So *f*'s the poem?

I shook my head.

d then?

Yes, I said, after a look at my watch. It's *d*. What about *d?*

The couplets make it seem very rigid, someone said. Except for the last, all the stanzas are run-on. It seems forced, very *harsh* somehow.

The run-ons are especially strong, another student pointed out. Not just between a noun and a prepositional phrase, as in *f* ("the child // in her lap"), but between the preposition and its noun, as in "with / tears" or "her cheek on // her hand." It's all very agitated.

As if, I said, it mirrored the woman's agitation? The prepositional phrases about the child ("in her lap" and "to the glass") aren't broken by run-ons.

Yes, another student said. It has a feeling of confusion, like version *e*.

But unlike *e* it's not really confusing. After the first line at least, every line has only one important word in it.

All nouns, I said: "tears" in line 2, "cheek" in 3, "cheek" in 4, "hand" in 5, and so on. That gives the version a static quality. It seems fixed *and,* in the run-ons, agitated. Rigid in its couplets *and* confusing in the way the sentence fits over them.

You mean like the woman?

I nodded. Pattern and confusion. Do you think so? Try reading it aloud for us.

He read the poem carefully, giving each line its identity but not really pausing anywhere.

The most important word is "pressed," someone said. All the lines but that have two or three syllables. So "pressed," in a line by itself, stands out.

The word's not even necessary, someone else said. Saying "his nose to the glass" would be sufficient.

I still like *f,* a girl said.

The bell rang, of course.

Chapter 13

3. All six poems have been published.

APPENDIX II

Select Bibliography

A. For Reference

In addition to a good dictionary:

Norman Lewis, ed., *Roget's New Pocket Thesaurus in Dictionary Form*, rev. ed., Berkley, 1977.

Alex Preminger, ed., *Princeton Encyclopedia of Poetry and Poetics*, Princeton University Press, 1965.

Lewis Turco, *The New Book of Forms*, University Press of New England, 1986.

Clement Wood, *The Complete Rhyming Dictionary*, rev. ed., Doubleday, 1936.

B. Anthologies

Kingsley Amis, ed., *The New Oxford Book of English Light Verse*, Oxford University Press, 1978.

Donald M. Allen, ed., *The New American Poetry*, Grove Press, 1960.

William S. Baring-Gould, ed., *The Lure of the Limerick,* Crown, 1967.

Willis Barnstone, ed., *Modern European Poets,* Bantam, 1966.

Michael Benedikt, ed., *The Poetry of Surrealism,* Little, Brown, 1974.

Stephen Berg and Robert Mezey, eds., *The New Naked Poetry,* Bobbs-Merrill, 1976.

Hayden Carruth, ed., *The Voice That Is Great Within Us,* Bantam, 1970.

Philip Dacey and David Jauss, eds., *Strong Measures: Contemporary American Poetry in Traditional Forms,* Harper & Row, 1986.

Richard Ellmann and Robert O'Clair, eds., *The Norton Anthology of Modern Poetry,* Norton, 1973.

Paul Engle and Joseph Langland, eds., *Poet's Choice,* Dial, 1962.

Gavin Ewart, ed., The *Penguin Book of Light Verse,* Penguin Books, 1980.

Edward Field, ed., *A Geography of Poets,* Bantam, 1979.

Donald Hall, Robert Pack, and Louis Simpson, eds., *New Poets of England and America,* Meridian, 1957.

Donald Hall and Robert Pack, eds., *New Poets of England and America,* Second Selection, 1962.

Daniel Halpern, ed., *The American Poetry Anthology,* Avon, 1975.

William Harmon, ed., *The Oxford Book of American Light Verse,* Oxford University Press, 1979.

William Heyen, ed., *American Poets in 1976,* Bobbs-Merrill, 1976.

Donald Junkins, ed., *The Contemporary World Poets,* Harcourt, Brace Jovanovich, 1976.

Philip Larkin, ed., *The Oxford Book of Twentieth Century English Verse,* Oxford University Press, 1973.

Ron Padgett and David Shapiro, eds., *An Anthology of New York Poets,* Random House, 1970.

Robert Payne, ed., *The White Pony: An Anthology of Chinese Poetry,* John Day, 1947.

A. Poulin, Jr., ed., *Contemporary American Poetry,* 4th ed., Houghton Mifflin, 1985.

Dudley Randall, ed., *The Black Poets,* Bantam, 1971.

Mark Strand, ed., *The Contemporary American Poets,* World, 1969.

Robert Wallace, ed., *Light Year '84,* Bits Press, 1983.

Robert Wallace, ed., *Light Year '85,* Bits Press, 1984.

Robert Wallace, ed., *Light Year '86,* Bits Press, 1985.

Robert Wallace, ed., *Light Year '87,* Bits Press, 1986.

Miller Williams, ed., *Contemporary Poetry in America,* Random House, 1973.

Oscar Williams, ed., *A Little Treasury of Modern Poetry,* 3rd ed., Scribner's, 1970.

Oscar Williams, ed., *The Silver Treasury of Light Verse,* New American Library, 1957.

C. On Poetry, Writing Poetry, and Poets

Donald M. Allen and Warren Tallman, eds., *The Poetics of the New American Poetry,* Grove Press, 1973.

W. H. Auden, *The Dyer's Hand and Other Essays*, Random House, 1962.

Elaine Berry, *Robert Frost on Writing*, Rutgers University Press, 1973.

Robert Bly, *Talking All Morning*, University of Michigan Press, 1980.

Robert Boyers, ed., *Contemporary Poetry in America*, Schocken Books, 1974.

Paul Carroll, *The Poem in Its Skin*, Big Table, 1968.

Malcolm Cowley, ed., *Writers at Work* (Second Series), Viking, 1963.

Robert Francis, *Pot Shots at Poetry*, University of Michigan Press, 1980.

Robert Francis, *The Satirical Rogue on Poetry*, University of Massachusetts Press, 1968.

Stuart Friebert and David Young, eds., *A Field Guide to Contemporary Poetry and Poetics*, Longman, 1980.

Paul Fussell, *Poetic Meter and Poetic Form*, rev. ed., Random House, 1979.

George Garrett, ed., *The Writer's Voice*, Morrow, 1973.

Walker Gibson, ed., *Poems in the Making*, Houghton Mifflin, 1963.

Harvey Gross, ed., *The Structure of Verse*, new edition, Ecco, 1979.

Donald Hall, ed., *Claims for Poetry*, University of Michigan Press, 1982.

Donald Hall, *Goatfoot Milktongue Twinbird*, University of Michigan Press. 1978.

Charles O. Hartman, *Free Verse: an Essay on Prosody*, Princeton University Press, 1980.

Robert Hass, *Twentieth Century Pleasures*, Ecco Press, 1984.

John Hollander, *Rhyme's Reason: A Guide to English Verse*, Yale University Press, 1981.

John Hollander, *Vision and Resonance: Two Senses of Poetic Form*, Oxford University Press, 1975.

Humphrey House, ed., *Notebooks and Papers of Gerard Manley Hopkins*, Oxford University Press, 1937.

David Ignatow, *Open Between Us*, University of Michigan Press, 1980.

Paul B. Janeczko, ed., *Poetspeak: In Their Work, About Their Work*, Bradbury Press, 1983.

Randall Jarrell, *Poetry and the Age*, Knopf, 1953.

Randall Jarrell, *The Third Book of Criticism*, Farrar, Straus & Giroux, 1969.

Judson Jerome, *On Being a Poet*, Writer's Digest Books, 1984.

Donald Justice, *Platonic Scripts*, University of Michigan Press, 1984.

Galway Kinnell, *Walking Down the Stairs*, University of Michigan Press, 1978.

Maxine Kumin, *To Make a Prairie*, University of Michigan Press, 1979.

David Lehman, ed., *Ecstatic Occasions, Expedient Forms*, Macmillan, 1986.

Howard Nemerov, *Figures of Thought*, Godine, 1978.

Howard Nemerov, ed., *Poets on Poetry*, Basic Books, 1966.

John Frederick Nims, *A Local Habitation: Essays on Poetry*, University of Michigan Press, 1985.

Charles Norman, ed., *Poets on Poetry*, Free Press, 1962.

Anthony Ostroff, ed., *The Contemporary Poet as Artist and Critic*, Little, Brown, 1964.

George Plimpton, ed., *Writers at Work* (Third Series), Viking, 1967.

George Plimpton, ed., *Writers at Work* (Fourth Series), Viking, 1976.

Ezra Pound, *ABC of Reading*, New Directions, 1934.

Rainer Maria Rilke, *Letters to a Young Poet*, trans. M. D. Herter Norton, Norton, 1934.

James Scully, ed., *Modern Poetics*, McGraw-Hill, 1965.

Karl Shapiro, *In Defense of Ignorance*, Random House, 1960.

Louis Simpson, *A Company of Poets*, University of Michigan Press, 1981.

Louis Simpson, *A Revolution in Taste*, Macmillan, 1978.

W. D. Snodgrass, *In Radical Pursuit*, Harper & Row, 1974.

William Stafford, *Writing the Australian Crawl*, University of Michigan Press, 1978.

Lewis Turco, *Visions and Revisions: Of American Poetry*, University of Arkansas Press, 1986.

Alberta T. Turner, ed., *50 Contemporary Poets: The Creative Process*, Longman, 1977.

Alberta T. Turner, ed., *45 Contemporary Poems: The Creative Process*, Longman, 1985.

Alberta T. Turner, ed., *Poets Teaching*, Longman, 1980.

David Wagoner, ed., *Straw for the Fire: From the Notebooks of Theodore Roethke*, Doubleday, 1972.

Barry Wallenstein, *Visions and Revisions*, Crowell, 1971.

Miller Williams, *Patterns of Poetry*, Louisiana State University Press, 1986.

James Wright, *Collected Prose*, University of Michigan Press, 1983.

INDEX OF AUTHORS AND TITLES

by permission of the University of Massachusetts Press. "Excellence," "Glass," and "Aphrodite as History." From *Robert Francis: Collected Poems, 1936–1976*. Copyright © 1976 by Robert Francis. Reprinted by permission. "Pitcher." From *The Orb Weaver*. Copyright © 1948, 1960 by Robert Francis. Reprinted by permission of Wesleyan University Press.

Frank, Jeanne, "Miner." Copyright © 1977 by Jeanne Frank. Reprinted by permission.

Freshley, Jill, "Woman's Work." Copyright © 1981 by Jill Freshley. Reprinted by permission.

Frost, Robert, "Dust of Snow," "An Old Man's Winter Night," "Provide, Provide," "Stopping by Woods on a Snowy Evening," "Home Burial," "The Road Not Taken," and "Design." From *The Poetry of Robert Frost*, edited by Edward Connery Lathem. Copyright © 1969 by Holt, Rinehart and Winston; copyright © 1958 by Robert Frost; copyright © 1967 by Lesley Frost Ballantine. Reprinted by permission of Henry Holt and Company. "In White." From *The Dimensions of Robert Frost* by Reginald L. Cook. Copyright © 1958 by Reginald L. Cook. Reprinted by permission of Henry Holt and Company.

Gallagher, Tess, "Kidnaper." From *Instructions to the Double* by Tess Gallagher. Copyright © 1976 by Tess Gallagher. Reprinted by permission of Graywolf Press.

Galvin, Brendan, "The Bats." From *No Time for Good Reasons* by Brendan Galvin. Copyright © 1974 by Brendan Galvin. Reprinted by permission of the University of Pittsburgh Press.

German, Brad, "Working Men." Copyright © 1982 by Brad German. Used by permission.

Gildner, Gary, "The Girl in the Red Convertible." From *Digging for Indians* by Gary Gildner. Copyright © 1971 by Gary Gildner. Reprinted by permission of the University of Pittsburgh Press.

Glaser, Elton, "Brief Song." Copyright © 1975 by Elton Glaser. Reprinted by permission.

Glück, Louise, "The Racer's Widow." Copyright © 1968 by Louise Glück. Reprinted by permission.

Goldbarth, Albert, "I Learn I'm 96% Water." Copyright © 1976 by Albert Goldbarth. "In 1856 she . . . ." Copyright © 1980 by Albert Goldbarth. Reprinted by permission.

Graham, Jorie, "Reading Plato." From *Erosion*. Copyright © 1983 by Princeton University Press. Reprinted by permission of Princeton University Press.

Hall, Donald, "The Town of Hill." From *The Town of Hill* by Donald Hall. Copyright © 1971 by David R. Godine. Reprinted by permission of David R. Godine, Publisher, Inc. "Names of Horses." From *Kicking the Leaves* by Donald Hall. Copyright © 1978 by Donald Hall. Reprinted by permission of the author.

Hall, Jim, "Maybe Dats Youwr Pwoblem Too." From *The Mating Reflex*. Copyright © 1980 by Jim Hall. Reprinted by permission of Carnegie-Mellon University Press.

Hecht, Anthony, "The Dover Bitch." From *The Hard Hours* by Anthony Hecht. Copyright © 1967 by Anthony Hecht. Reprinted with the permission of Atheneum Publishers.

Heffernan, Michael, "The Saint and the Lady." From *The Cry of Oliver Hardy* by Michael Heffernan. Copyright © 1979 by Michael Heffernan. Reprinted by permission of the University of Georgia Press and the author.

Heinrich, Sheila, "disappearances." Copyright © 1975 by Sheila Heinrich. Reprinted by permission.

Hemingway, Ernest, vignette from *In Our Time* by Ernest Hemingway. Copyright © 1958 by Ernest Hemingway. Reprinted with the permission of Charles Scribner's Sons. October 20, 1922 *Toronto Star* dispatch from *By-Line: Ernest Hemingway, Selected Articles and Dispatches of Four Decades*, edited by William White. Copyright © 1967 by By-Line Ernest Hemingway, Inc. Reprinted with the permission of Charles Scribner's Sons.

Hilberry, Conrad, "Storm Window," "Fat," "Man in the Attic," and "The Vanishing Horseman." Copyright © 1980 by Conrad Hilberry. Reprinted by permission.

Hollander, John, "Eskimo Pie." From *Types of Shape* by John Hollander. Copyright © 1969 by John Hollander. Reprinted with the permission of Atheneum Publishers.

Hopkins, Gerard Manley, "Hurrahing in August" and "Pied Beauty." From *Poems of Gerard Manley Hopkins*. Copyright © 1948 by Oxford University Press. Reprinted by permission.

Housman, A. E., "Bredon Hill," "Loveliest of Trees," and "I Hoed and Trenched and Weeded." From *The Collected Poems of A. E. Housman*. Copyright © 1965 by Holt, Rinehart and Winston; copyright © 1968 by Robert E. Symons. Reprinted by permission. "In the Morning, In the Morning." From *The Collected Poems of A. E. Houseman*. Copyright © 1922 by Holt, Rinehart and Winston; copyright © 1950 by Barclays Bank, Ltd. Reprinted by permission of Holt, Rinehart and Winston, Publishers; The Society of Authors as the literary representatives of the Estate of A. E. Housman; and Jonathan Cape, Ltd., Publishers.

Hughes, Ted, "To Paint a Water Lily." From *Lupercal* by Ted Hughes. Copyright © 1959 by Ted Hughes. Reprinted by permission of Harper & Row, Publishers, Inc., and Faber and Faber, Ltd.

Irwin, Mark, "Icicles." Copyright © 1978 by Mark Irwin. Reprinted by permission. "The Invention of the Snowman." From *Shenandoah: The Washington and Lee University Review*. Copyright © 1980 by Washington and Lee University. Reprinted with the permission of the Editor.

Jacobson, Bonnie, "Pandora's Dressing Table." Copyright © 1977 by Bonnie Jacobson. "On Being Served Apples." Copyright © 1980 by Bonnie Jacobson. Reprinted by permission.

Jerome, Judson, "Carpe Diem." Copyright © 1986 by Judson Jerome. Reprinted by permission.

Johnson, William R., "Onset." First appeared in *Hiram Poetry Review*. Copyright © 1984 by William R. Johnson. "Prayer." First appeared in *Antioch Review*. Copyright © 1985 by William R. Johnson. Both reprinted by permission of the author.

Kennedy, X. J., "Little Elegy," "First Confession," "In a Prominent Bar in Secaucus One Day," "Poets," and "Ars Poetica." From *Cross Ties* by X. J. Kennedy. Copyright © 1985 by X. J. Kennedy. Reprinted by permission of the University of Georgia Press and the author.

Kinsey, Katherine, "Forgive and Forget." Copyright © 1981 by Katherine Kinsey. Reprinted by permission.

Pastan, Linda, "Jump Cabling." First appeared in *Light Year '85.* Copyright © 1984 by Linda Pastan. "Mother Eve." First appeared in *The Georgia Review.* Copyright © 1985 by Linda Pastan. Reprinted by permission.

Patchen, Kenneth, "The Murder of Two Young Men by a Kid Wearing Lemon-colored Gloves." From *Collected Poems of Kenneth Patchen.* Copyright © 1945 by Kenneth Patchen. Reprinted by permission of New Directions.

Pfingston, Roger, "The Perfect Suicide." Copyright © 1977 by Roger Pfingston. Reprinted by permission.

Phillips, Louis, "Heartbreak in Tuktoyaktuk." Copyright © 1986 by Louis Phillips. Reprinted by permission.

Piercy, Marge, "Sentimental Poem." Copyright © 1978 by Marge Piercy. Reprinted by permission.

Pollitt, Katha, "Onion." From *Antarctic Traveller* by Katha Pollitt. Copyright © 1977 by Katha Pollitt. Reprinted by permission of Alfred A. Knopf, Inc.

Pound, Ezra, "In a Station of the Metro," "The Garden," "Homage to Sextus Propertius" (Section I), "The Three Poets," "The Bath Tub," and lines from "The Return." From *Personae* by Ezra Pound. Copyright © 1926 by Ezra Pound. Lines from "Canto II." From *The Cantos* by Ezra Pound. Copyright © 1934 by Ezra Pound. Reprinted by permission of New Directions.

Raine, Craig, "A Martian Sends a Postcard Home." From *A Martian Sends a Postcard Home* by Craig Raine. Copyright © 1979 by Craig Raine. Reprinted by permission of Oxford University Press.

Raschke, Suzanne, "Move into the Wheat." Copyright © 1981 by Suzanne Raschke. Reprinted by permission.

Reed, J. D., "The Weather Is Brought to You." From *Expressways* by J. D. Reed. Copyright © 1969 by J. D. Reed. Reprinted by permission of Simon & Schuster, Inc.

Reiss, James, "Sueños." From *Express* by James Reiss. Copyright © 1983 by James Reiss. Reprinted by permission of the University of Pittsburgh Press.

Ridland, John, "Grading." Copyright © 1984 by John Ridland. Reprinted by permission.

Riley, Tom, "The Battle of Muldoon's." Copyright © 1985 by Tom Riley. Reprinted by permission.

Robinson, Edwin Arlington, "Richard Cory." From *The Children of the Night* by Edwin Arlington Robinson. Copyright © 1897 under the Berne Convention. Reprinted with the permission of Charles Scribner's Sons.

Roethke, Theodore, "My Papa's Waltz." Copyright © 1942 by Hearst Magazine, Inc. "I Knew a Woman." Copyright © 1954 by Theodore Roethke. Both from *The Collected Poems of Theodore Roethke.* Reprinted by permission of Doubleday & Company, Inc.

Rose, Jan M. W., "Spider." Copyright © 1977 by Jan M. W. Rose. Reprinted by permission.

Rosenberger, F. C., "Birthday Quatrain to a Beautiful Lady." First appeared in *Poet Lore.* Copyright © 1979 by F. C. Rosenberger. Reprinted by permission.

Rutsala, Vern, "The Mill Back Home." From *Walking Home from the Icehouse* by Vern Rutsala. Copyright © 1978 by Vern Rutsala. Reprinted by permission of Carnegie-Mellon University Press and the author.

St. John, David, "Iris." From *Hush* by David St. John. Copyright © 1976 by David St. John. Reprinted by permission of Houghton Mifflin Company.

Shapiro, Karl, "Auto Wreck." From *Collected Poems: 1940–1978* by Karl Shapiro. Copyright © 1970 by Karl Shapiro. Reprinted by permission of Random House, Inc.

Shelton, Richard, "Encounter." From *The Bus to Veracruz* by Richard Shelton. Copyright © 1978 by Richard Shelton. Reprinted by permission of the University of Pittsburgh Press.

Simic, Charles, "The Prisoner." From *Charon's Cosmology* by Charles Simic. Copyright © 1977 by Charles Simic. Reprinted by permission of George Braziller, Inc. "Stone." From *Dismantling the Silence* by Charles Simic. Copyright © 1971 by Charles Simic. Reprinted by permission of George Braziller, Inc. "Watermelons." From *Return to a Place Lit by a Glass of Milk* by Charles Simic. Copyright © 1974 by Charles Simic. Reprinted by permission of George Braziller, Inc.

Slavitt, David R., "Titanic." From *Big Nose* by David R. Slavitt. Copyright © 1983 by David R. Slavitt. Reprinted by permission of Louisiana State University Press.

Slack, Frances T., "I think the needle is stuck." Copyright © 1982 by Frances T. Slack. Used by permission.

Smith, Arthur, "Extra Innings." From *Elegy on Independence Day* by Arthur Smith. Copyright © 1985 by Arthur Smith. Reprinted by permission of the University of Pittsburgh Press.

Snodgrass, W. D., "Leaving the Motel." From *After Experience* by W. D. Snodgrass. Copyright © 1968 by W. D. Snodgrass. Reprinted by permission of the author.

Spacks, Barry, "In the Fields." Copyright © 1978 by Barry Spacks. Reprinted by permission.

Spence, Michael, "Programming Down on the Farm." Copyright © 1985 by Michael Spence. Reprinted by permission.

Spires, Elizabeth, "At the Bambi Motel." First appeared in *Poetry.* Copyright © 1979 by Elizabeth Spires. Reprinted by permission.

Stafford, William, "Traveling Through the Dark." From *Stories that Could Be True* by William Stafford. Copyright © 1960 by William Stafford. Reprinted by permission of Harper & Row, Publishers, Inc. "Ask Me." From *50 Contemporary Poets,* edited by Alberta T. Turner. Copyright © 1977 by Longman, Inc. Reprinted by permission.

Starbuck, George, "Lamb." From "Translations from the English" in *White Paper: Poems* by George Starbuck. Copyright © 1965 by George Starbuck. Reprinted by permission of Little, Brown and Company in association with the Atlantic Monthly Press.

Steele, Paul Curry, "Clerihew." From *Anse on Island Creek and Other Poems* by Paul Curry Steele. Copyright © 1976 by Paul Curry Steele. Reprinted by permission of Mountain State Press and the author.

Stern, Gerald, "Peace in the Near East," "Feeding Prisoners," and "Stepping Out of Poetry." From *Lucky Life* by Gerald Stern. Copyright © 1977 by Gerald Stern. Reprinted by permission.

Stevens, Wallace, "The Idea of Order at Key West" and "A Rabbit as King of the Ghosts." From *The Collected*

Macs

FOR

DUMMIES

A Wiley Brand

12TH EDITION

by Edward C. Baig

Personal Technology columnist for *USA TODAY*

Macs For Dummies®, 12th Edition

Published by
John Wiley & Sons, Inc.
111 River Street
Hoboken, NJ 07030-5774
www.wiley.com

Copyright © 2013 by John Wiley & Sons, Inc., Indianapolis, Indiana

Published by John Wiley & Sons, Inc., Indianapolis, Indiana

Published simultaneously in Canada

For general information on our other products and services, please contact our Customer Care Department within the U.S. at 877-762-2974, outside the U.S. at 317-572-3993, or fax 317-572-4002.

For technical support, please visit www.wiley.com/techsupport.

Wiley also publishes its books in a variety of electronic formats. Some content that appears in print may not be available in electronic books.

Library of Congress Control Number: 2013932113

ISBN: 978-1-118-51719-2 (pbk); ISBN 978-1-118-51725-3 (ebk); ISBN 978-1-118-65039-4 (ebk); ISBN 978-1-118-65041-7 (ebk)

Manufactured in the United States of America

10   9   8   7   6   5   4   3

About the Author

Edward C. Baig writes the weekly Personal Technology column in *USA TODAY* and makes regular appearances on USA TODAY video podcasts. He is also the coauthor of *iPhone For Dummies; iPad For Dummies,* 5th Edition; and *iPad mini For Dummies* (all published by John Wiley & Sons, Inc.).

Before joining *USA TODAY* as a columnist and reporter in 1999, Ed spent six years at *Business Week,* where he wrote and edited stories about consumer tech, personal finance, collectibles, travel, and wine tasting. He received the Medill School of Journalism 1999 Financial Writers and Editors Award for his contributions to the "*Business Week* Investor Guide to Online Investing." That came after a three-year stint at *U.S. News & World Report,* where Ed was the lead tech writer for the News You Can Use section but also dabbled in numerous other topics. Ed fondly remembers putting together features on baseball card investing, karaoke machines, and the odd things people collect, including Pez dispensers, vintage radios, and magic memorabilia.

Ed began his journalistic career at *Fortune,* gaining the best training imaginable during his early years as a fact checker, and as a contributor helping with the Fortune 500 project, *Fortune* magazine's annual list of the 500 largest U.S. corporations. Through the dozen years he worked at the magazine, Ed covered leisure-time industries, penned features on the lucrative dating market and the effect of religion on corporate managers, and was heavily involved in the magazine's Most Admired Companies project. Ed also started up *Fortune*'s Products to Watch column, a venue for low- and high-tech items.

Ed has been passionate about gadgets and technology since buying his first reel-to-reel tape recorder and shortwave radio as a boy. He has also purchased 8-track cartridge players (still in the attic somewhere) and the Magnavox Odyssey video game console, not quite the Xbox of its time. These days, when he's not spending time with his family or at the keyboard of his myriad computers, Ed can be found rooting for the New York Giants and New York Mets, listening to music of all types, and watching movies.

He has a B.A. in political science from York College and an M.B.A. from Adelphi University.

Dedication

This book is dedicated to my remarkable and gorgeous children: daughter Sydney, who at a very early age became fascinated with the iTunes Visualizer, and son Sammy, who cannot resist pounding (quite literally) on the keyboard. This book is also dedicated to my beautiful wife Janie, who takes on more than any other human being I know, with grace, passion, and love, and to my canine "daughter" Sadie who believes that everyone who rings the doorbell must be visiting her. It is also dedicated to my late dog Eddie, who always reminded me through his barks that it is I who lived and worked in *his* house, not the other way around. Finally it is dedicated to my mom Lucy, for the values you instilled in me and are starting to instill in your grandchildren and great-grandchildren. I love you all.

Author's Acknowledgments

No book like this is ever written in isolation, and I've received wonderful support from lots of people. Let me start by again thanking my agent, Matt Wagner, for turning me into a *For Dummies* author.

At Wiley, I'd like to thank Vice President and Publisher Andy Cummings, Sr. Acquisitions Editor Bob Woerner, Project Editor Paul Levesque, Project Editor (on previous editions) Susan Pink, Copy Editor John Edwards, and Technical Editor Dennis Cohen, who each makes me look good — your services are simply invaluable. Lots of other folks at Wiley do amazing work behind the scenes. I don't know all your names, but please know you have my utmost respect and appreciation.

I also couldn't pull this off without considerable help through this and other editions of this book from many people at Apple. So special thanks to Katie Cotton, Steve Dowling, Natalie Kerris, Bill Evans, Keri Walker, Teresa Brewer, Greg (Joz) Joswiak, Trudy Muller, Tom Neumayr, Janette Barrios, Jennifer Hakes, Colin Smith, Amy Bessette, Amy Barney, Monica Sarker, Christine Monaghan, Kirk Paulsen, David Moody, and others in Cupertino. Apologies if I've left your name off this list.

Thanks, too, to Jim Henderson, Geri Tucker, Nancy Blair, Jefferson Graham, and other work colleagues and friends for your backing and for putting *USA TODAY*'s stamp of approval behind this project.

Last but certainly not least, to all my friends and family members who not only encouraged me to write this book but also forgave me for my disappearing acts when deadlines loomed. I've run out of excuses.

Publisher's Acknowledgments

We're proud of this book; please send us your comments at http://dummies.custhelp.com. For other comments, please contact our Customer Care Department within the U.S. at 877-762-2974, outside the U.S. at 317-572-3993, or fax 317-572-4002.

Some of the people who helped bring this book to market include the following:

Acquisitions and Editorial

Senior Project Editor: Paul Levesque

Acquisitions Editor: Bob Woerner

Copy Editor: John Edwards

Technical Editor: Dennis Cohen

Editorial Manager: Leah Michael

Editorial Assistant: Annie Sullivan

Sr. Editorial Assistant: Cherie Case

Composition Services

Project Coordinator: Sheree Montgomery

Layout and Graphics: Amy Hassos

Proofreaders: Jessica Kramer, Toni Settle

Indexer: BIM Indexing & Proofreading Services

Publishing and Editorial for Technology Dummies

　　Richard Swadley, Vice President and Executive Group Publisher

　　Andy Cummings, Vice President and Publisher

　　Mary Bednarek, Executive Acquisitions Director

　　Mary C. Corder, Editorial Director

Publishing for Consumer Dummies

　　Kathleen Nebenhaus, Vice President and Executive Publisher

Composition Services

　　Debbie Stailey, Director of Composition Services

Contents at a Glance

Table of Contents

Chapter 10: Delivering the Goods on E-Mail 175

Introduction

· ·

*W*hat an amazing time to get to know the Mac. For years, these elegantly designed computers have been a model of simplicity and virus-free stability. But that's never stopped Apple from making these machines even harder to resist by applying stunning changes.

Consider Apple's seismic embrace of Intel a few years ago. It means you, Mr. or Ms. Computer Buyer, can have your cake and eat it too. (I love a good cliché when I need it.) You can benefit from what remains the best marriage in personal computing (the blessed union between Mac hardware and Mac software), but you no longer have to ditch the Microsoft Windows–based software you currently use out of habit, due to business obligations, or because you don't know any better.

Indeed, this book is partially targeted at Windows vets who are at least thinking about defecting to the Mac. It is also squarely aimed at people who are new to computers — and the Internet — period. And though this is primarily a book for beginners, I trust that people who have already dabbled with computers in general and Macs in particular will find it useful.

About This Book

A word about the *For Dummies* franchise I'm proud to be a part of: These books are built around the idea that all of us feel like dopes whenever we tackle something new, especially when the subject at hand (technology) reeks with a jargon-y stench.

I happen to know that you don't have a dummy bone in your body, and the publishers at Wiley know it too. *Au contraire.* (How dumb can you be if you speak French?) If anything, you've already demonstrated smarts by purchasing this book. You're ready to plunge in to the best computing environment I know of.

Because you're so intelligent, you're probably wondering "who is this guy asking me for 400 pages or so of my time?" Go ahead and read my bio, which appears just before the Table of Contents.

What you won't find in the bio is this: I'm a relative latecomer to the Mac. I grew up on MS-DOS computing and then migrated like most of the rest of the world to Windows. I still use Windows machines every day.

But I've long since become a devoted Mac convert, and I use my various Apples every day too. (No snide remarks, please; I find time for other pursuits.)

Conventions Used in This Book

Anyone who has skimmed the pages of this or other *For Dummies* books knows that they're not exactly *War and Peace.* Come to think of it, it's too bad Tolstoy got to that name first. It would make a great title when the definitive account of the Apple-Intel alliance is written.

Macs For Dummies makes generous use of numbered and bulleted lists, and screen grabs are captured, by the way, using a handy little freebie Mac utility (invaluable to writers of books like this) called *Grab.* See, you haven't even escaped the introduction, and I threw in your first Mac lesson, just like that.

You'll also note several sidebars in the book, containing material that's not part of the required syllabus (well, nothing is really required). I hope that you'll read them anyway. Some sidebars are technical in nature, and some provide a little historical perspective.

How This Book Is Organized

The beauty of the *For Dummies* format is that you can jump around and read any section you want. You are not obliged to follow a linear structure. Need to solve a problem? Head straight to the troubleshooting section (see Chapter 20) and do not pass Go. Want to find new music to listen to while pounding away on the computer? Meet me in Chapter 14.

An organizing principle *is* at work here. This edition of *Macs For Dummies* is split into a half-dozen parts. If you're new to computing, you might want to digest this book from start to finish.

Part 1: Getting Started with Macs

In Part I, I lay out the groundwork for your Mac education, from turning the machine on to navigating the Mac desktop. You are introduced to ports and connectors, the dock, freebie programs, and the various Macs models.

Part II: Mac Daily Dealings

If Part I was mainly for seminars and lectures, Part II is where you get to do lab work. You find out how to process words and print and how to start taming the OS X operating system.

Part III: Rocketing into Cyberspace

Part III covers all things Internet. You find out how to get connected, conduct online research, shop, and send e-mail. I also introduce Time Machine, the slickest and easiest computer backup anywhere, and iCloud, Apple's online hangout for storing stuff, keeping things in sync, and even helping you locate a missing computer.

Part IV: Getting an iLife

In Part IV, you really move into the fun stuff — the programs that may have driven you to purchase a Mac in the first place: iTunes, iPhoto, iMovie, and GarageBand.

Part V: The Creepy Geeky Section

Part V is the part of this computer book that you might imagine is most, well, like a computer book. Don't worry, you can read the chapters in this section without being branded a nerd. In any event, it's chock-full of practical information on networking and diagnosing problems.

Part VI: The Part of Tens

Listmania is a *For Dummies* trademark. Check out Part VI for ten dashboard widgets plus ten more nifty things a Mac can do, from playing chess to telling a joke.

Icons Used in This Book

Sprinkled in the margins of these pages are little pictures, or icons. I could have easily mentioned icons in the earlier "Conventions Used in This Book" section, because icons are *For Dummies* conventions too, not to mention essential ingredients in today's computers. I use the following four of them throughout this book.

A Remember icon means that a point of *emphasis* is here. So along with remembering your spouse's birthday and where you put the house keys, you might want to retain some of this stuff.

I present the Tip icon when a shortcut or recommendation might make the task at hand faster or simpler.

Some percentage of *For Dummies* readers will get so hooked on computing that they will become the geeks of tomorrow. These are the people who will welcome the presence of these pointy-faced little icons. Others among you would rather swallow turpentine than read an overly technical passage. You can safely ignore this material. (Still, won't you be the least bit curious about what it is you might be missing?)

This icon is my way of saying pay heed to this passage and proceed gingerly, lest you wreak the kind of havoc that can cause real and possibly permanent damage to your computer and (by extension) your wallet.

Where to Go from Here

I've made every effort to get things right and present them in a coherent manner. But if I've erred in any way, confused you, made you mad, whatever, drop me an e-mail at baigdummies@gmail.com. I truly welcome your comments and suggestions, and I'll do my best to respond to reasonable queries in a timely fashion. Mac people aren't shy about voicing their opinions. Oh, and because all writers have fragile egos, feel free to send *complimentary* e-mails my way too.

At the time I wrote this book, I covered every Mac model available and the latest versions of Mac OS X and iLife. Apple occasionally slips in a new Mac model or a new version of OS X or iLife between book editions. If you've bought a new Mac that's not covered in the book, or if your version of Mac OS X or iLife looks or behaves a little differently, be sure to check out the book's companion website for updates on the latest releases from Apple (www.dummies.com/go/MacsFD12eupdates).

Above all, I hope you have fun reading the book, and more importantly, I hope you have a grand old time with your Mac. Thanks for buying the book.

Part I

In this part . . .

- Get to know the lay of the Mac landscape by familiarizing yourself with the tools of the Mac trade.

- Find out how to do the Mac basics — like turning on your Mac, working with the mouse and keyboard, and running applications.

- See how to get around the Mac desktop and how to navigate the folder structure on your hard drive.

- Check out the many Macs to choose from when looking to fulfill your computing needs.

- Visit www.dummies.com for great Dummies content online.

Chapter 1

Adventuring into the Mac World

. . . .

. . . .

*F*orgive me for getting too personal right off the bat, but next to your spouse or significant other, is there anyone or anything you touch more often than a computer keyboard? Or gaze at more intensely than a monitor?

If this is your initial dalliance with a Macintosh, you're probably already smitten — and quite possibly at the start of a lifelong affair.

Despite its good looks, the Mac is much more than a trophy computer. You can admire the machine for flaunting intelligent design, versatility, and toughness. A Mac can take care of itself. As of this writing, the Mac has avoided the scourge of viruses that plague PCs based on Microsoft Windows. Apple's darlings are a lot more stable too, so they crash and burn less often.

Mac-Spectacular Computing

You shouldn't be alarmed that far fewer people own Macs compared with PCs. That's like saying fewer people drive Ferraris than drive Chevys. Strength in numbers is overrated — and even at that, the trend toward Apple's computers is in plus territory.

Besides, as a new member of the Mac community, consider the company you are about to keep. Mac owners tend to belong to the cool crowd: artists, designers, performers, and (can't resist this one) writers.

Sure, these same people can be smug at times. I've had Mac mavens go ballistic on me for penning *positive* reviews that were not flattering enough. Or for even daring to suggest that Macs aren't always perfect. The machines come pretty darn close, though, so you're in for a treat if you're new to the Mac. It has been suggested that most Windows users go to their computers to complete the task at hand and be done with it. The Mac owner also gets things done, of course. The difference is that using machines branded with the Apple logo tend to be a labor of love. Moreover, with Intel chips inside Macs, Apple's computer can double as a pretty darn effective Windows machine.

Checking out shapes and sizes

Apple has a tremendous advantage over the companies promoting Windows PCs because it is the single entity responsible for producing not only the computer itself but also the important software that choreographs the way the system behaves. Everything is simpatico.

This situation is in stark contrast to the ways of the PC world. Companies such as Dell and Hewlett-Packard manufacture hardware. Microsoft produces the Windows software that fuels the machines. Sure, these companies maintain close ties, but they just don't share Apple's blood relationships.

You'll find a variety of Macintoshes meant to sit on top of your desk, thus the term *desktop computer.* These are discussed in greater detail in Chapter 4. Just know for now that the main examples of the breed are the iMac, the Mac mini, and the Mac Pro.

Mac *laptops,* so named because they rest on your lap and are portable, are the MacBook Pro and the Twiggy-thin MacBook Air. (You remember the 1960s svelte supermodel Twiggy, right?) They are often referred to as *notebook computers* or just plain *notebooks.* As with spiral notebooks, they can fit into a briefcase or backpack.

Matching a Mac to your needs

Haven't settled on which Mac to buy? This book provides assistance. Cheap advice: If you can eyeball the computers in person, by all means do so. Apple operates nearly 400 retail stores worldwide, mostly in North America. You also find retail outlets in the United Kingdom, Italy, China, France, Spain, Germany, Japan, and elsewhere. Trolling through these high-tech candy stores is a delight. Of course, you can also buy Macs on the Internet or in traditional brick-and-mortar computer and electronics stores, including Best Buy.

Just be prepared to part with some loot. Although the gap between the cost of PCs and Macs is narrowing, you will typically pay more for a Mac versus a comparable unit on the PC side.

(Uh oh! The Mac diehards are boiling at that remark: I can practically see their heads exploding as they rant: "There is no such thing as a *comparable* Windows machine.")

Selecting handy peripherals

As you might imagine, a full range of peripherals complement the Mac. Although much of what you create in *bits* and *bytes,* to put it in computer-speak, stays in that electronic form, at some point, you're probably going to want to print your work — on old-fashioned paper, no less. Fortunately, a number of excellent printers work with Macs. I provide details in Chapter 8.

You may also choose a *scanner,* which in some respects is the opposite of a printer. That's because you start with an image already in paper form and then scan, or translate, it into a form that your computer can understand and display. Okay, so you can also scan from slides or microfiche, but you get my point.

Some machines combine printing and scanning functions, often with copier and fax capabilities as well. These are called *multifunction,* or *all-in-one,* devices.

Communicating with Your Mac

The Mac isn't at all standoffish like some human objects of affection. It's friendly and approachable. In the following sections, I tell you how.

It's a GUI

Every mainstream computer in operation today employs what's called a *graphical user interface,* or GUI. The Mac's GUI is arguably the most inviting of all. It consists of colorful objects or pictures on your screen, plus windows and menus (for more, see Chapter 3). You interact with these using a computer *mouse* or other *pointing device* to tell your machine and its various programs how to behave. The latest Macs also incorporate *multitouch gestures* that control actions on the screen — your fingers glide across a touchpad on Mac laptops or the Magic Trackpad accessory that you can purchase to use with a desktop. You can also use gestures on the surface of the Magic Mouse. Either approach sure beats typing instructions as arcane commands or taking a crash course in programming. For that matter, Mountain Lion lets you use voice commands and dictation as well.

With great tools for you

Given the Mac's versatility, I've often thought it would make a terrific product to peddle on one of those late-night infomercials. "It slices, it dices. Why it even does more than a Ginsu Knife or Popeil Pocket Fisherman!"

Indeed, have you ever paused to consider what a computer is anyhow? Consider a few of a computer's most primitive (albeit handy) functions. A Mac can

- Tell time
- Display family portraits
- Solve arithmetic problems
- Play movies
- Let you chat with friends

I dare say that you didn't surrender a grand or two for a simple clock, photo album, calculator, media player, or telephone. But it's sure nice having all those capabilities in one place, and as that announcer on TV might bark, "That's not all folks."

I can't possibly rattle off all the nifty things a Mac can do in one section (besides, I encourage you to read the rest of the book). But whether you bought or intend to buy a Mac for work, play, or more likely some combination of the two, some little birdie tells me that the contents of the Mac's tool chest will surpass your expectations.

And output, too

I'm confident that you'll spend many pleasurable hours in front of your computer. At the end of the day, though, you're going to want to show other people how productive and clever you've been. So whether you produce legal briefs, spiffy newsletters for the PTA, or music CDs for your summer house's beach bash, the Mac will make you proud.

Living the iLife

All the latest Macs are loaded with a terrific suite of software programs called *iLife* to help you master the digital lifestyle you are about to become accustomed to. (On some older systems, you can purchase the upgraded iLife suite of programs.) I dig deeper into the various iLife components throughout Part IV. Here's a sneak preview:

- **iTunes:** Apple's popular program for buying and listening to music, and buying or renting movies and TV shows. It's available free on all Macs, and though it is also found on Windows computers, it is technically a member of the iLife family.

- **iPhoto:** The great photographer Ansel Adams would have had a field day with iPhoto. This software lets you organize and share your best pictures in myriad ways, including placing them in calendars or in coffee table books. You can even find pictures by where you took them and who is in them.

- **iMovie:** Can an Academy Award be far behind? iMovie is all about applying cinematic effects to turn your video into a piece of high-minded art that would make Martin Scorsese proud. Who knows, maybe Apple will find work for you at Disney or Pixar.

- **GarageBand:** Did somebody mention groupies? GarageBand lets you make music using virtual software instruments. The latest version also helps you create online radio shows, or podcasts.

Reaching Outside the Box

The modern computing experience extends well beyond the inner workings of the physical contraption on your desk. Computing is more about what occurs in the magical kingdom of cyberspace, better known as the Internet.

Getting online

In Chapter 9, you discover all there is to know about finding your way to the Internet and the many paths you can take when you get there. The Mac comes with the software you need to get started (and the circuitry required) to connect online through fast broadband methods. If you get a hand-me-down Mac, it might still dial up the Internet through a conventional phone line — but by now we won't be spending much time on such ancient communication methods. Such models are increasingly scarce.

Hanging in the iClouds

So much of what we do on computers nowadays happens online, or as it is frequently referenced, in the cloud. Apple's online service is appropriately called iCloud, and it's a place to manage photos, music, documents, contacts, calendars, and more, and to keep all this data synchronized not only across all the Macs you might own, but also across other devices too, including Apple's own iPhone smartphone, and iPad tablet computer. Read Chapter 12 for more details on the iCloud service.

Networking with or without wires

Ask a few people to explain what networking is all about, and they'll probably utter something about trying to meet and cozy up to influential people who might help them advance their careers or social lives.

A Mac can help with such things, too, but that's not the kind of networking I have in mind. Computer networks are about having two or more machines communicate with one another to share files, pictures, music, and most importantly, a connection to various online outposts. Even on a Mac, this networking business can get kind of geeky, though Apple does as good a job as anyone in helping to simplify the process. You can network by connecting certain cords and cables. The preferred method is to do so without wires. Networking is explained in Chapter 18.

Staying Safe and Trouble-Free

As noted, the Mac has historically been able to avoid the nasty viruses and other malevolent programs that give Windows owners the creeps. In the nastiest scenarios, those Windows machines (or certain programs) are shut down, and personal information is surreptitiously lifted. In this day and age, not even Mac owners should let their guard down. (And remember, in some instances, the Mac can double as a Windows machine.) Chapter 13 offers counsel on avoiding online dangers.

No matter how much care and feeding went into producing these beautiful computers, when all is said and done, we are talking about physical contraptions filled with circuits and silicon. Machines break, or at the very least, get cranky. So drop by Chapter 20, where I outline common troubleshooting steps you can take to ensure that you and your computer develop your relationship gracefully. It's the high-tech alternative to couples counseling.

Chapter 2

The Nuts and Bolts of Your Mac

In This Chapter

▶ Turning on the computer and getting set up

▶ Taming the mouse

▶ Keying in on the keyboard

▶ Saving your work

▶ Mastering memory

▶ Finding common ports and connectors

*H*ave you taken the plunge and purchased a Mac? If so, you've made a fabulous decision.

I bet you're dying to get started. You may even have begun without reading these initial instructions. Fine with me. No offense taken. The Mac is intuitive, after all, and the title on this cover notwithstanding, you're no dummy. I know, because you had the good sense to buy a Macintosh — and this book. Besides, what would it say about Apple's product designers if they couldn't make you understand how to turn on the computer?

If you didn't jump the gun, that's cool too. That's why your humble servant, um, author, is here.

Turning On and Tuning In Your Mac

To borrow a line from a famous musical, "Let's start at the very beginning, a very good place to start . . ." In the *Do-Re-Mi*'s of Macintosh computing, plugging the computer in the wall is a very good place to start. It doesn't get a whole lot more complicated from there.

Finding the On button

Take a second to locate the round On, or power, button. Where it resides depends on the Mac model you purchased, but finding it shouldn't be too taxing. I'll even give away the secret on recently issued models. On the latest iMac, the On button is on the lower-left back panel of the monitor (when you are facing the monitor). On Mac laptops, the button is at the upper-right corner of the keyboard.

Go ahead and press the On button now. Explosive things are about to happen. Not those kinds of explosives; it's just that igniting your first session on the Mac makes you *da bomb* (translation: old-time slang for awesome or cool).

To let you know that all is peachy (or should I say Apple-y?), you hear a musical chime while the Apple logo briefly shows up on the screen in front of a gray background. A spinning gear appears just below the Apple logo.

Getting credentials

Powering up a new Mac for the first time may make you feel like you're entering the United Nations. After the Apple logo disappears, a lengthy interrogation process commences.

You are kindly instructed to pledge allegiance to a particular language. Deutsch als Standardsprache verwenden and Gebruik Nederlands als hoofdtaal are among the 30 choices in a list box. If you don't know what either of these means, you should probably make another choice. As you move up or down the list, you may hear an audible voice explaining how to set up your Mac. For example, "To use English as the main language, press the Return key" is what most people will hear initially, because English is the top choice in the list. But as you highlight alternate options, you'll hear instructions in other languages.

Make your selection by pressing Return or by clicking with the mouse (see details later in this chapter).

Next, you get to tell your nosy computer your country or region. Because I chose English, the countries shown are the United States, Canada, United Kingdom, Australia, New Zealand, and Ireland. You can select the Show All check box to display dozens of other countries. You don't need to whip out a passport. But you need to click Continue to move on. Select the Show All check box to see all the possible country options.

I clicked the United States and then clicked the on-screen Continue button (a right-pointing arrow inside a circle), but you can obviously select whichever language and/or nation is appropriate for your living situation.

From there, you get to select a keyboard layout. U.S. and Canadian English are the choices if you stuck with the English language. Again, you can choose Show All for additional choices.

As the cross examination goes on, you get to select any available *Wi-Fi,* or wireless Internet, service to use. You may have to enter a network password. If you don't connect to the Internet wirelessly or for the moment lack an Internet connection, click the Other Network Options button (a circle with right- and left-pointed arrows). That's where you can choose a wired Ethernet connection, assuming that your Mac is so equipped and that you have an available Ethernet cable. Or you can indicate that you do not have an available Internet connection. (For more on networking, I direct you to Chapter 18).

You're presented with the option to transfer network settings, user accounts, documents, applications, files, e-mail, and various preferences from another computer to this one. The process once typically involved connecting a *FireWire* cable, which you discover more about later in this chapter. But you have other options.

With the introduction a few years ago of the MacBook Air notebook, Apple upgraded its software so that you could migrate from another Mac wirelessly over a computer network. The reason: Air models and most Macs introduced since then lack the FireWire option. The computers do have a variety of other ports that I also discuss later in this chapter.

You may also be presented with the option to transfer information from another *partition* on this Mac. That's a geeky term I'll skip for now.

And you can migrate from another Mac *volume* using OS X's Time Machine feature. Read Chapter 13 to find out how to go back in time.

If this is your maiden voyage on the *SS Macintosh,* the previous choices are unimportant. Instead, select the Not Now option and click Continue. (Don't worry; you can always transfer settings later using the Mac's Migration Assistant.)

As the interrogation drill continues, you next get to decide whether to enable Location Services. Through the wonders of technology, the Mac can determine your approximate location, which can help you find nearby places to eat or shop or assist you in getting from one place to another.

Location Services work with a variety of apps or programs, including Twitter, Reminders, Safari, and more. You have lots of reasons why enabling the feature can be a good thing. But if knowing your location wigs you out from a privacy perspective, Apple understands and gives you the chance here to opt out. But if you're okay with the concept (as your humble author is), select the Enable Location Services on This Mac check box and click Continue.

The next step is to provide your Apple ID, the credentials that let you buy songs in the iTunes Store, download apps in the Mac App Store, use iCloud, and more. You can use different Apple IDs for each of these. Chances are you already have an Apple ID if you own an iPhone or iPad. But if you don't have an Apple ID yet, creating one is free and easy. Apple does ask for your birthday and year that you were born, which it says it will use to retrieve your password if you ever forget it (though that hardly seems all that secure). Type your first and last name, and choose the e-mail address that you want to use for your Apple ID — either a current address or a new free iCloud address. In choosing a new Apple ID, enter a password and choose a security question to help you retrieve that password later — perhaps the first record album you ever owned or the first celebrity you ever met. And no, Apple won't ask for your Social Security number or driver's license information.

Before your setup is complete, you must read the terms and conditions required to use your Mac and all matters of legalese pertaining to OS X, iCloud, Game Center, Privacy, and more. You just knew the attorneys had to get their two cents in somewhere, right?

Assuming that you said yes to an already existing iCloud account, the Mac will provide the option to update your contacts, calendars, reminders, and bookmarks. You can also check off the e-mail addresses at which others can contact you via Messages (chat and instant messaging) and FaceTime (video calling), topics to be addressed in Chapter 11.

You also get to turn on a feature in iCloud called Find My Mac, which as its name suggests, is a way for you to find a computer you may have inadvertently left in a taxi or that, heaven forbid, was stolen. (You'll have to turn on Location Services for Find My Mac to function.) Read more about this potential life, um, Mac-saver in Chapter 12.

Read the next section to find out about creating your computer account.

Creating an identity

You're almost ready to begin touring the computer, but not quite. An important step remains. You must choose an identity, or a *user account,* to tell the Mac that you are the Grand Poobah of this particular computer. As this almighty administrator, you and you alone can subsequently add accounts for other members of your family or workplace, each with a password that keeps them from snooping into one another's computing workspace (see Chapter 5).

Type the full name of the account holder (for example, *Cookie Monster),* the account name (*Cookie*), the password (*chocolatechip* or, better yet, something that's harder to guess), and the password again to verify it. You can select an option to allow your Apple ID to reset this user password (another reason why picking an Apple ID is a good idea). And you can require the password when logging in. You are also asked to type a password hint (*yummy flavor*) as a gentle reminder should you ever forget your password. Failing to remember things may not happen to you, but it sure happens to me.

There are workarounds for resetting a password, but you hope it doesn't come to that. And if your Mac didn't come with a Restore disk — and the most recent Macs ditch the optical drive— you'll need a second computer that has such a drive to reset the administrative account password.

You are also asked to choose or take an account picture, but obviously can only take such a picture if your Mac is equipped with a camera. If you're camera-shy, choose one of the few dozen images Apple supplies.

Clocking in

Because it probably already seems like day is turning into night, this is as appropriate a time as any to, well, select your time zone by clicking near where you live on the world map that appears. If you're connected to the Internet, the computer can determine the date and time automatically.

Registering your Mac

When all is said and done, the nice folks at Apple would also like you to register your Mac. Letting Apple know who you are gives the company the opportunity to flood you with promotional e-mails. But you can register and opt out of the promotional e-mails. Or you can skip registering altogether, but you would then be ineligible for short-duration telephone support.

Making acquaintances

Depending on how you set things up, you may see a *welcome screen* listing all the people on the computer with a user account, each with a personal mug shot or other graphical thumbnail next to his or her name. Click the name or picture next to your thumbnail. You're asked to enter your password (assuming that you have one). Type it properly, and you are transported to the main working area, or *desktop*.

The desktop I am referring to here is the *interface* that you see on the computer display, not to be confused with a desktop-type machine.

Shutting down

I began this chapter with a noble discussion of how to turn on the Mac. (Humor me if you didn't think the discussion was even remotely noble.) So even though you barely have your feet wet, I'm going to tell you how to turn off the dang thing. Don't you just hate people who not only give away the ending (it's the butler) but also tell you to do something and then tell you why you shouldn't have done it?

Okay. Ready? Sayonara time.

Using the arrow-shaped *cursor,* which you control with your mouse or track-pad, stab the small logo found at the upper-left corner of the screen. Click once, and a drop-down menu appears. Move the cursor down until the Shut Down entry is highlighted. You know a command or an entry is highlighted because a blue strip appears over its name.

Pressing Enter on the keyboard or clicking Shut Down brings up what's called a *dialog* (see Figure 2-1). I'm no shrink, but it's obvious based on the question the computer asks inside this box that it suffers from separation anxiety. "Are you *sure* you want to shut down your computer now?"

Figure 2-1: Are you sure you want to shut down?

Are you sure you want to shut down your computer now?

If you do nothing, the computer will shut down automatically in 54 seconds.

☐ Reopen windows when logging back in

Cancel | Shut Down

Do nothing, and the machine will indeed turn itself off. On machines that ran previous Mac operating systems — Snow Leopard and Leopard, for example — you had two minutes to change your mind. On the computers running more recent versions of OS X, Lion and the current iteration Mountain Lion, you have up to a minute. If you want to say "so long" immediately, click the Shut Down button. If you hold down the Option key when choosing Shut Down, this dialog is bypassed.

Having second thoughts? Click Cancel.

Giving your Mac a nap

Apart from guilt, why not shut down? The main reason is that you can let the computer catch a few *Z*s without turning it off. A sleeping Mac consumes far less energy than one that's in a conscious state. Mac's don't snore, but you know they're alive because of a dim blinking light. As it turns out, your machine is a light sleeper. You can wake it up right away by pressing any key on the keyboard. Best of all, whatever you happened to be working on is just where you left it. That's also the case when you restart a Mac running Lion or Mountain Lion that you've completely shut down, as all your open apps and documents get restored on restart by default.

If you're going to leave the Mac on for an extended period of time, make sure that it's plugged in to a surge protector that can protect the machine from lightning. More expensive surge protectors have backup batteries.

You can make a Mac laptop go to sleep immediately by shutting its cover. Lift the cover to wake it up. To make a desktop machine go to sleep, click the Sleep command on the menu — you know, that menu at the upper-left corner of the screen bearing the logo.

As part of Mountain Lion, some Mac notebooks (those with built-in flash storage) can exploit a feature known as Power Nap. Though you may think your Mac is in dreamland, it still periodically updates Mail, Contacts, Calendar, Reminders, Notes, Photo Stream, Find My Mac, and an iCloud feature known as Documents in the Cloud. Don't worry if you don't know what all these features are — I get to them throughout the book. Just take comfort in the fact that your Mac may be sleeping, but it's not sleeping on the job.

Mousing around the Interface

By now you're catching on to the idea that this computing business requires a lot more clicking than Dorothy had to do to get back to Kansas. She used ruby slippers. You get to use a mouse or (increasingly) a trackpad.

A computer mouse is generally less frightening than that other kind of critter. In keeping with this *Wizard of Oz* comparison, not even the Cowardly Lion would be scared of it. And though your high-tech rodent can get finicky at times, you're unlikely to set traps to bring about its demise.

Older mice connect to the computer through cords. The mice included with Macs sold in the last several years are wireless. Not every Mac is sold with a mouse, however. Laptops come with trackpads. On a Mac mini, you have to supply your own mouse (and monitor for that matter). In each case, mice are called *pointing devices* because — brace yourself for this advanced concept — they're devices that sort of point. (You can also use what are called *trackballs,* though Apple doesn't ship them. They're available from companies such as Kensington and Logitech and they have relatively small but devoted followers. There is also a market for pen devices or styluses, made by companies such as Wacom.

I'll explain. You roll the mouse across a flat surface (typically your desk or perhaps a specialized mouse pad). As you do so, a cursor, or an insertion point, on the screen miraculously apes the movement of your hand gliding the mouse. (Note to self: The mixed metaphor police, a.k.a. my editor, must love the mention of a mouse and a monkey in the same breath.) If the mouse loses touch with the surface of your desk, the cursor will no longer move.

When you place the cursor precisely where you want it, you're ready for the clicking part. Place your index finger on the upper-left portion of the mouse, press down quickly, and let go. You'll hear a clicking sound, and in some cases, your entire body will tingle with satisfaction. You have mastered the fine art of clicking.

Don't get too cocky. Now try *double-clicking,* an action often required to get something accomplished. You're pretty much repeating the preceding exercise, only now you're clicking twice in rapid succession while keeping the cursor in the same location. It may take a little practice, but you'll get it.

Left- and right-clicking

If you've been using a Windows, UNIX, or Linux computer, you're accustomed to working with a mouse that has two or more buttons. More times than not, you click or double-click using the upper-left button. That's where the remarkably unoriginal name of *left-clicking* comes from. Left-clicking usually serves the purpose of selecting things on the screen. By contrast, the opposite action, *right-clicking,* brings up a menu of shortcut commands. Apple also calls right-clicking *secondary* clicking.

Until recently, the typical Apple mouse had just one button, the functional equivalent of the left button on a Windows mouse. (Apple used to sell a programmable critter branded Mighty Mouse that behaved like a multibutton mouse.) Having just one button on a Mac is less of a big deal than you might think. That's because you can effectively right-click, or bring up a shortcut menu, with a one-button Mac mouse anyway. To accomplish this great feat, press Control on the keyboard while you click.

Apple eventually retired the Mighty Mouse in favor of the multitouch Magic Mouse and the Magic Trackpad. The former comes standard with Mac desktops; the latter is an option. (See the upcoming section "Touchy-feely computing.")

Pointing and clicking on a laptop

You can attach a regular mouse to any Mac laptop, but it is not always convenient to use one when you're on a 767 or working in tight quarters.

Fortunately, as I've already mentioned, Mac portables have something called a trackpad, a smooth area just below the keyboard. You glide your finger on the trackpad to choreograph the movement of the cursor. On older Mac notebooks, the button just below the trackpad handles clicking chores. On more recent models, you can mimic a click by tapping on the surface of the trackpad itself.

What a drag

The mouse is responsible for at least one other important bit of business: *dragging.* Position the cursor on top of the symbol or icon you want to drag. Then hold down the mouse button and roll the mouse across your desk. As you do so, the icon moves to a new location on the screen.

Touchy-feely computing

If you use any of the Mac's distant cousins — the iPad, iPhone, or iPod touch — your fingers get a good workout because these devices have *multitouch* displays that are responsive to finger *gestures.* You already know how cool it is to spread your fingers and then pinch them together to zoom in and out of photos and web pages, among other gestures.

Macs of recent vintage are touchy too, but only in a good way. You can employ various gestures on MacBook Pro and MacBook Air laptops with silky smooth glass trackpads. For instance, you can swipe your fingers to flip through pictures and do such tricks as rotate images. But Apple doesn't confine touch computing to its portable computers. Both the Magic Mouse and a $69 accessory called Magic Trackpad let you bring touch gestures to Mac desktops. Magic Trackpad, and for that matter some Apple mice, take advantage of *Bluetooth* wireless technology, a topic addressed further in Chapter 18.

Knowing What's Handy about the Keyboard

As with any computer — or an old-fashioned typewriter for that matter — the Mac keyboard is laid out in *QWERTY* style, meaning that the top row of letters starts with *Q, W, E, R, T,* and *Y.* But a computer keyboard also contains a bunch of specialized keys that the inventors of the typewriter wouldn't have dreamed of.

Finding the major functions

The top row of the Mac keyboard carries a bunch of keys with the letter *F* followed by a number. From left to right, you go from F1, F2, F3, all the way (in some cases) to F16. These are your loyal *function keys,* and their particular marching orders vary among Mac models. Depending on your setup, pressing certain F keys has no effect at all.

The F9, F10, F11, and F12 keys on older Macs relate to a feature called *Exposé,* since folded into the *Mission Control* feature, which I explain in Chapter 5. And F8 used to launch a feature called *Spaces,* also now part of Mission Control. On newer keyboards and laptops, and with the most recent operating system, F3 is reserved for Mission Control, and F4 is for another feature addressed in Chapter 5 called *Dashboard.* Meanwhile, F7, F8, and F9 are media keys for such functions as rewinding, playing, pausing, and fast-forwarding music, movies, and slideshows. F10 is for muting the sound.

On Mac laptops, the F1 and F2 keys can raise or lower the brightness of your screen. Those functions are performed by the F14 and F15 keys on other types of Macs. And just to keep your fingers on their, um, toes, be aware that some exceptions exist.

Those various F keys may be difficult to spot at first on a laptop. They have teeny-tiny labels and share keys. It's a good thing that some function keys also have little pictures that help explain their purpose. You'll have to press the fn key at the same time you press a function key to make it, well, function as a function key. Otherwise, such keys will perform their other duties.

The keys you use every day

Quick quiz: Guess which keys you use most often? Too easy. The keys you use every day are the ones representing vowels and other letters with low point values in *Scrabble.*

Naturally, these aren't the only keys that work overtime. The spacebar, comma, and period are darn busy. If you're into hyperbole, the exclamation mark key puts in an honest day's effort, too. Don't let me shortchange Shift or Return. And I know you accountants in the crowd spend a lot of time hammering away at all those number keys.

More keys to success

You'll find these other keys extremely useful, but remember, not all keyboards look the same or have each and every key mentioned here:

✔ **esc:** The great Escape key. The equivalent of clicking Cancel in a dialog.

✔ ◆ ◆)) ◀ **:** These keys raise, lower, or mute the volume of the computer's speakers, though in laptops, certain function keys perform these duties.

✔ ▲ **:** No doubt this is James Bond's favorite key. Press it, and one of two things is supposed to happen. On some Macs, a CD or DVD loaded inside the guts of the computer spits out of a hidden slot. On the Mac Pro, the tray holding the disc slides out.

✔ **Delete, delete:** You are not reading double. Some Mac keyboards have two delete keys, each with a different assignment. Regular delete is your Backspace key. Press it, and it erases the character directly to the left of the cursor. The second delete key, which sometimes appears as Del and sometimes as delete accompanied by an *x* inside a small pentagon, is the forward delete key. It wipes out the character to the right of the cursor. Confusingly, on some laptops, as well as Apple's aluminum keyboard, you can purge the letter to the right of the cursor by pressing fn and delete at the same time.

✔ **Home, End:** The jumpiest keys you will come across. Press Home and you may be instantly vaulted to the top of the document or web page window in which you are working. Press End and you often plunge to the bottom, depending on the application. You won't see Home or End on all Mac keyboards.

✔ **Page Up, Page Down:** A keyboard alternative for moving up or down one huge gulp or screenful at a time. Again, you won't see these keys on all keyboards. If you don't see them, press the fn key with the up- or down-arrow key.

✔ **Option:** Pressing Option (labeled Alt Option on some keyboards) while you press another key generates symbols or accents such as an umlaut. You can't possibly recall them all, though over time, you'll learn the key combinations for symbols you regularly call upon. For example, press Option and 2 for ™, Option and V for √, and Option and R for ®. Feel free to play around with other combinations.

✔ **Control:** The Control key and the mouse click make a powerful combination. Control-clicking yields pop-up *contextual menus* that only make sense in the moment. For example, Control-clicking a term in the Microsoft Word word processing program displays a menu that lets you find a synonym for that word, among other options. Because finding a synonym doesn't make a lot of sense when you Control-click a picture in iPhoto (see Chapter 15), the action opens up different possibilities, including editing, rotating, and duplicating an image.

✔ ⌘**:** Pressing the cloverleaf key while you press another keyboard character creates keyboard shortcuts, a subject worthy of its own topic (see the next section).

Taking a shortcut

If you hold the mouse in high regard, you may want to give the little fellow time off now and then. That's the beauty of keyboard shortcuts. When you simultaneously press ⌘ and a given key, stuff happens. You just have to remember which combination of keys to use under which circumstances.

To understand how such shortcuts work, consider the popular act of copying material from one program and reproducing it in another. You are about to practice *copy-and-paste* surgery.

I present two ways to do this. One method leaves pretty much everything up to your mouse. The other, while still using the mouse a little, mainly exploits keyboard shortcuts.

The first option follows:

1. **Use the mouse to highlight, or select, the passage you want to copy.**

2. **On the menu bar at the top of the screen, choose Edit⇨Copy.**

3. **Move the mouse and click to place your mouse at the point where you want to paste the text.**

4. **Choose EditPaste.**

   The copied material magically appears at its new destination.

Here is the keyboard shortcut method:

1. **Highlight the text you want to copy.**

2. **Hold down the ⌘ key while you press the C key.**

   The result is the same as if you had clicked Edit and Copy.

3. **Move the mouse and click to place the mouse at the point where you want to paste.**

4. **Press ⌘ and the V key.**

   You just pasted the text.

Many clickable menu items have keyboard equivalents. These shortcuts are displayed in the various menus to the right of their associated commands, as shown in Figure 2-2. Note that some keyboard shortcuts shown in the menu appear dimmed. That's because the commands can't be used at this particular point. And some shortcuts require both the ⌘ key and one or more additional modifier keys, as in Shift+⌘+N to select New Folder.

You can modify keyboard shortcuts in System Preferences. Open System PreferencesKeyboardKeyboard Shortcuts. Double-click the shortcut you wish to change, and hold down the new keys.

Keyboard shortcuts

New Finder Window	⌘N
New Folder	⇧⌘N
New Folder with Selection	^⌘N
New Smart Folder	⌥⌘N
New Burn Folder	
Open	⌘O
Open With	▶
Print	⌘P
Close Window	⌘W
Get Info	⌘I
Compress	
Duplicate	⌘D
Make Alias	⌘L
Quick Look "All My Files"	⌘Y
Open Enclosing Folder	⌘R
Add to Sidebar	⌘T
Move to Trash	⌘⌫
Eject	⌘E
Burn "Desktop" to Disc...	
Find	⌘F
Label:	
× ▫ ▫ ▫ ▫ ▫ ▫ ▫	

Figure 2-2:
To use a keyboard shortcut or not to? That is the question.

Storing Stuff on the Hard Drive or SSD

You keep lots of things on a computer. Software you've added. Photos, songs, movies. Your graduate thesis comparing Lady Gaga's appeal to Madonna's popularity. Apple left a lot of stuff behind, too, mainly the files and programs that make your Mac special.

The bottom line: Computers are a lot like houses. The longer you stick around, the more clutter you accumulate. And despite your best rainy day intentions, you almost never seem to get rid of the junk.

Besides, you have plenty of treasures worth holding on to, and you need a place to store them. The great storage closet on your computer is called the *hard drive,* and just as with a physical closet, the bigger it is the better. You may even choose to add a second or third hard drive. You can almost always take advantage of the extra storage. Plus, you can use an additional hard drive to *back up,* or keep a copy of, your most precious digital keepsakes. For that matter, an additional hard drive is required for Time Machine — a feature well worth exploring, as you discover later.

Indeed, I cannot ram into your heads hard enough the following point: However you choose to do so, back up, back up, back up.

A hard drive is not the only form of storage on the Mac. On some models, you can substitute or add a *solid-state drive,* or *SSD.* Advantages: SSDs have no moving parts, making them more durable than a hard drive in a laptop you cart around, and such drives are faster than their hard drive counterparts, so they're useful on desktops as well. Chief downside: SSDs don't yet offer near the storage capacities of most hard drives because they're way more expensive.

When you order a Mac that has both a hard drive and an SSD, Apple will preload applications and Mac OS X itself on the SSD. The hard drive is best reserved for your documents, pictures, and other files.

On recent iMacs, Apple offered an option called a Fusion Drive, which combines the benefits of both: greater storage through a traditional hard drive, and the speed of an SSD. Apple loads the operating system in flash, plus all the apps, pictures and other data you call upon most frequently. It's all managed automatically in the background — to you, it appears as if there's only one drive on the system. Apple claims up to 3½ times faster performance over a regular hard drive, but be aware that Fusion Drive, at the time of this writing, added $250 to the price of the computer, so it isn't cheap.

Memory Essentials, or RAM On

Not sure whether you caught my not-so-subtle use of the word *ram* in the preceding section. That's to get you thinking about the other kind of *RAM.* It stands for *random access memory* or, mercifully, just *memory* for short. (I can't help but think that accessing my own memory is random, which may explain why I can recall things from the third grade but not from yesterday.) Just as you want as capacious a hard drive as possible, you also want to load as much RAM into your system as you can possibly afford.

Here's why. The hard drive is the place for your long-term storage requirements. RAM is *temporary storage,* and having lots of RAM on hand helps when you open several programs at once and work with large documents. You may be editing videos, listening to music, and crunching numbers, all while pausing your work to defend the planet by deep-sixing evil aliens in some computer game. Dude, you are doing some serious high-tech juggling, otherwise known as *multitasking.* Multitaskers guzzle up RAM.

Geeks refer to the amount of memory and hard drive space you have in terms of *bits* and *bytes.* The itsy-bitsy *bit* (short for binary digit) is the tiniest unit of information handled by a computer. Eight bits make up a *byte,* and a byte typically represents a letter, a punctuation mark, or a digit on your screen. I know. That's an awful lot to chew, um, byte on.

You'll see measurements in *kilobytes,* or KB (actually 1,024 bytes), *megabytes,* or MB (1,048,576 bytes), and *gigabytes,* or GB (1,073,741,824 bytes). Perspective: At the time of this writing, the least expensive iMac comes with a 1-*terabyte* (TB) hard drive and 8GB RAM.

At the other extreme, the souped-up Mac Pro computer can handle up to 8 *terabytes* (TB) of internal storage and up to 64GB RAM. A terabyte is 1,024 gigabytes.

Locating the Common Ports and Connectors

Industry-standard jacks, holes, and connectors on the back or side of your Mac (depending on whether you have a desktop or laptop and which model) may look funky. You may think you can't live without (most of) them until, that is, you discover, otherwise. Because over the years, Apple has a way of changing the standard ports and connectors. Either way, think of these connectors as your bridge to the gaggle of devices and peripherals that want to have a relationship with your computer. (See Figure 2-3.)

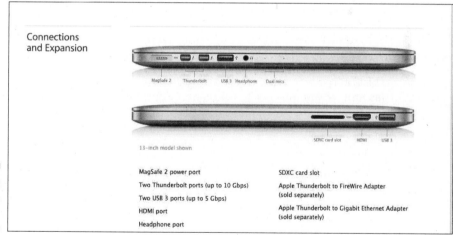

Figure 2-3:
Hook me up, Scotty.

Peripherally speaking: USB versus FireWire

Ralph Kramden never drove a *Universal Serial Bus.* But you will take the USB route quite often. That's because USB (pronounced "you-S-bee") connects printers, scanners, digital cameras, webcams, iPods, joysticks, speakers, keychain disk drives, piano keyboards, and even your mouse and computer keyboard to your desktop or laptop.

The state of the art for USB ports on modern Macs is USB 3.0. Older Macs have slower USB 1.1 or USB 2.0 ports.

Plugging in a USB device is as simple as, well, plugging it in (though some-times you have to load software first). You can often remove USB devices from the computer without causing harm by merely pulling the cable or device out of the jack.

Sometimes, however, the Mac prefers that you let it know before pulling out the cable or device. For example, to remove an iPod connected by USB — also referred to as *unmounting* the device — your Mac typically wants you to click a tiny icon in the iTunes software source list, next to the name you've assigned to the portable music player. Failure to click the icon can cause unpleasant consequences. (For complete details on iTunes, refer to Chapter 14.)

USB generally works like a charm. But like most things in life, you occasionally find drawbacks. For one, given all the devices that love USB, you may run out of available ports. In that case, you can buy a USB *expansion hub.* If you do so, I recommend a hub that you can plug in to an electrical outlet.

Many USB devices don't require any kind of electrical outlet because they draw power from the Mac itself. You can recharge an iPod, for example, by plugging it into a Mac's USB port. But some USB ports — typically those that reside on the keyboard — are relative weaklings. They work fine with low-power devices such as your mouse but may not with, say, a power-thirsty digital camera. If you plug a USB device into a port in the keyboard and it doesn't work, try plugging it into a USB port directly on the back or side of the computer.

FireWire is the friendly name coined by Apple for a connector that Sony calls iLink and that is also known by the unfortunate descriptor IEEE 1394. (I won't bore you with an explanation except to say that it's the reason why engineers are engineers and not marketers.) FireWire is a speedy connector that's often used with digital camcorders. But it also connects external hard drives and older iPods.

FireWire comes in two flavors: the older *FireWire 400* specification and its faster cousin, *FireWire 800*. Only certain Macs can handle the speedier guy — and if you have an older FireWire cable, you'll need an adapter to plug it into a FireWire 800 port. And as mentioned earlier in this chapter, the MacBook Air doesn't have a FireWire port. Nor does the MacBook laptop. Nor does the latest MacBook Pro. And nor does the latest iMac. How come? Read on.

Introducing Thunderbolt

I just told you that Apple has a way of changing the ports and connectors on its computers, along the way completely doing away with some. Apple sometimes does this to popularize a new standard, even before too many devices that can connect to this particular new port are even available.

Such is the deal with Thunderbolt. This versatile port is Apple's zippiest ever, letting you shovel data to and from peripherals up to 20 times faster than with USB 2.0 and up to 12 times faster than FireWire 800. If your Mac is so equipped — and only the latest machines are outfitted with the port — you can connect a Thunderbolt-capable high-resolution display or certain storage devices. At the time of this writing, Thunderbolt, um, hadn't yet taken the public by storm (sorry, couldn't resist again). But figure it is only a matter of time before more Thunderbolt options appear.

Two of a kind: The phone jack and Ethernet

Now that we've entered the speedy broadband era, dialup modems are yesterday's news, which is why Apple long ago ditched them as standard issue on newer Macs. If you get a hand-me-down Mac, it may have a phone jack that is identical to the wall outlet where you plug in a regular phone. You connect a phone line to this jack to take advantage of a dialup modem to connect to the Internet (Chapter 9). Well, "take advantage" may not be the best way to put it anymore. For the extreme situation where dialup is your only option, you can purchase a USB dialup modem online.

The end of the cable that plugs in to an *Ethernet* jack looks just like a phone jack on steroids. Ethernet's main purpose in life is to provide a fast outlet to the Internet or your office computer network. The latest Macs that have any type of Ethernet have Gigabit Ethernet ports because of their zippy speeds.

Jacks of all trades

The appearance of the following connectors varies by machine:

- ✔ **MagSafe power port:** This clever connector is used to plug in and power up your Mac, with a magnet ensuring that the power cord stays connected. A variation of this connector, called MagSafe 2, appears on newer machines. Alas, it is incompatible with the original, at least without an optional adapter.

- ✔ **Mini DisplayPort (or Video out):** This port (found on Mac Pro currently), connects a Mac to an external monitor or projector for, say, giving classroom presentations. You can buy adapters for connecting to systems that use *DVI* or *VGA* connectors. On other current Mac models, the capability is via the Thunderbolt port through an adapter.

- ✔ **Audio in and Audio out:** These two are separate ports for connecting microphones and external speakers or headphones. You can use headphones, of course, to play games or take in tunes, without bothering your next-door neighbor or cubby mate.

- ✔ **Lock:** Found on laptops and the Mac mini, this tiny hole is where you fit in a Kensington Security lock cable. With one end securely attached to the computer, you loop a Kensington cable around the leg of a heavy desk or other immovable object. The hope is that you'll prevent a thief from walking off with your notebook. The laptop cable is similar to a bicycle lock and cable that you wrap around the bicycle wheel and a pole to help stymie a thief.

- ✔ **SD card slot:** Secure Digital (SD) memory cards are used with many popular digital cameras. When you have pictures or videos stored on such cards, you can easily transfer them to a Mac with an SD card slot, which appears on recent Macs. You will see some of these slots referred to as an SDXC, with the XC signifying extended capacity.

- ✔ **HDMI:** With a cable connected to HDMI (shorthand for *High-Definition Multimedia Interface*), you can hook up certain models to a high-definition television.

- ✔ **ExpressCard slot:** The ExpressCard slot (for adding memory card readers or TV tuners) had started to replace the PC Card slot you find on older Mac notebooks. But then Apple ended up nixing this slot as well. You'll still see it on some older models, which is why I am listing it here.

Making the right connections on your computer, as in life, can take you a long way.

Chapter 3

Getting to the Core of the Apple

· ·

· ·

lthough I'm sure he never used a personal computer a day in his life, the wise Chinese philosopher Confucius could have had the Mac in mind when he said, "If you enjoy what you do, you'll never work another day in your life." People surely enjoy their Macs, even when they *are* doing work on the machine. Before you can totally whoop it up, however, it's helpful to get down a few more basics. That way you'll better appreciate why this particular Apple is so yummy.

Navigating the Mac Desktop

All roads lead to and depart from the computer's *desktop,* a confusing name if ever there was one. In this context, I do not mean the physical hardware that might sit on top of, say, a mahogany desktop. Rather, the computer desktop is the desktop that takes over the whole of your computer screen. On a PC, this element is known as the Windows desktop. On a Macintosh, it is the Mac desktop or (as an homage to the machine's operating system) the OS X desktop.

Time and time again, we will come upon an important part of your desktop called *Finder,* which is a place to organize and sometimes search through the files and folders of your Mac. Finder may serve as a launchpad for all that you do on your computer.

Have a peek at Figure 3-1, which shows a typical Mac desktop layout. In the past, the default background was blue. In recent iterations of OS X, the starry default desktop is called Aurora. If you're not feeling celestial, you can alter that background and make other cosmetic changes. (See Chapter 5.) The time is displayed near the upper-right corner of the screen, and a trash can is at the lower right. Look around and you'll see other funky-looking graphical *icons* on the screen.

Let me try this comparison. A Major League ballpark always has foul lines, bases 90 feet apart, and a pitcher's rubber 60 feet and 6 inches from home plate. These are standard rules to be followed. But outfield dimensions and seating capacities vary dramatically. So do dugouts, bullpens, and stadium architecture.

Certain conventions apply to the Mac desktop too; then you can deviate from those conventions. So in the end, everyone's Mac desktop will look different. For now, I address some of the main conventions.

Figure 3-1:
The typical
Mac
desktop.

Clicking the Menu Bar

See the narrow strip extending across the entire top of the desktop screen? Yes, the one with the little picture of an apple at the extreme left side, and words such as File, Edit, and View to its right. This is your *menu bar,* so named because clicking the apple — or any of the words or icons in the strip — brings up a *menu,* or list, of commands. (Sorry, it's not that kind of menu. You can't order tapas.)

Single-click the apple, and a menu pops up with some important functions. Readers of Chapter 2 are already familiar with the Sleep and Shut Down commands. You will also find Software Update, System Preferences, Force Quit, and other commands that I revisit throughout this book. Suffice it to say, the ![apple] menu is so relevant that it is available from any application you're working in.

Now click the top item under the ![apple] menu, About This Mac. The *window* that appears lets you know the version of the Mac OS X operating system software you're running (see Chapter 6); the kind of *processor,* or main chip, that the system is operating on; and the amount of on-board memory.

Click More Info in the same window, and you can choose to click the System Report button or the Software Update button. Click the former to summon the *System Profiler.* Among other things, you can find your machine's serial number, darn useful information if you're ever captured by the enemy. I trust that you already know your name and rank. (According to the Geneva Conventions, that's all you need to reveal to Microsoft.)

Most of the rest of the stuff in the System Profiler, frankly, is a lot of technical mumbo-jumbo presented in list form. However, some information is worth knowing, including your system power settings and the connected printers.

Clicking Software Update instead has the same effect as tapping Software Update from the ![apple] menu. That is, you'll be transported to the Mac App Store where you'll be notified of any programs on your computer that have updates.

Understanding Icons, Folders, and Windows

You've already been introduced to *icons,* the cutesy pictures that miraculously cause things to happen when you click or double-click them. The beauty of graphical computing is that you need not give a moment's thought to the heavy machinations taking place under the hood after you click an icon.

Try clicking the icon near the lower-left corner of the screen that is a square with a face inside. It's on the *dock,* an area of the screen that I address later in this chapter. The icon you've just clicked summons Finder. A window containing more icons appears. These represent the various software applications loaded on your hard drive or SSD, plus *folders* stuffed with files and documents.

Now try this one out for size: See whether you can locate your *home folder.* Giveaway hint: It's the one with a picture of a house and your name. Click the home folder, and examine the *subfolders* in the adjacent window, ones for the documents you have created, plus movies, music, pictures, and more.

Windows dressing

The mere mention of windows may make some of you skittish. It might conjure up thoughts about a certain vision of computing propagated by that really rich fellow hanging out in the Seattle outskirts. But I'm not speaking of Microsoft or Bill Gates. The windows under discussion here start with a lowercase "dubya."

There's nothing small about these windows' capabilities. Just as opening windows in your house can let in fresh air, opening and closing Mac windows can do so too, at least metaphorically.

Of course, the windows on the Mac can do a heck of a lot more than your typical windows at home, unless you live with Willy Wonka. These windows can be stretched, dragged to a new locale on the desktop, and laid one on top of another. To help you understand these windows, check out Figure 3-2.

A stunning view

The Mac graciously lets you peek at information from four main perspectives. Open the View menu in the menu bar and choose to view the contents as icons, in a list, in columns, or with Cover Flow.

Back and forth buttons – Move to the previous or next window

Close – Click the red gumdrop button to close the window

Minimize – Click the yellow circle to send window into hiding

Zoom – Click this green button to make your entire window grow

View – Four buttons to change the perspective to icon, list, column, or Cover Flov

Sort by Name, Kind, Application, Date, Size, Label

Search box – Search terms to find relevant items

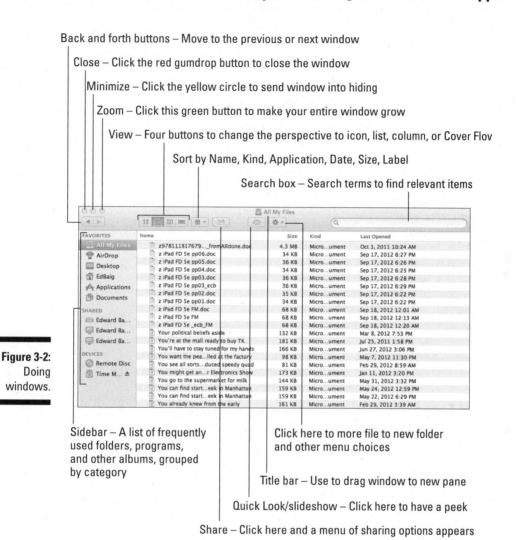

Figure 3-2:
Doing
windows.

Sidebar – A list of frequently used folders, programs, and other albums, grouped by category

Click here to more file to new folder and other menu choices

Title bar – Use to drag window to new pane

Quick Look/slideshow – Click here to have a peek

Share – Click here and a menu of sharing options appears

Alternatively, click the appropriate View button in the toolbar at the top of the Finder window, as shown in Figure 3-3, and choose Icons, List, Columns, or Cover Flow. Can't, um, view those View buttons? I'll zoom in for a close-up of these views.

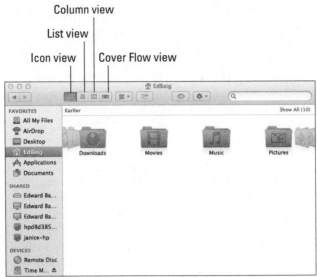

Column view

List view

Icon view

Cover Flow view

Figure 3-3:
An icon view of the home folder.

By icon

In the example shown in Figure 3-3, I explored the home folder window through what's known as the *Icon view* because the windows are populated by those pretty little pictures. You know the Music subfolder by its icon of a musical note. And you know the Movies subfolder by the small picture of a strip of film.

If you're in a playful mood, when you're back in the desktop or Finder (or have nothing better to do), you can change the size of the icons by choosing View➪Show View Options and dragging the Icon size slider from left to right. Okay, so a more practical reason for changing the size of the icons is that they may be too small for you to see. Or maybe it's just the opposite, and you have such keen vision that you don't want to take up computing real estate with icons that are too large.

Drag the Grid spacing slider to change the distance between icons.

By accessing View Options on the View menu, you can also alter the position of an icon label (by clicking the Bottom or Right option). You can change the color of the window background or use one of your own images as the background. You can also arrange the order of icons by the date they were modified, date they were created, size, kind, or label. Select the Show Item Info check box to display how many items are in the various folders. You can also select check boxes to make sure that you always open Finder in the Icon view or are always able to browse in this view. Or choose Snap to Grid to make icons obediently align themselves in rows and columns.

By list

Look on the View menu, and note the check mark next to the As Icons item. Now click the As List item, and the check mark moves there. The icons shrink dramatically, and the subfolders appear, well, as a list. Thus, you are living in *List View* land, as shown in Figure 3-4. A lot more info is displayed in this view, including the date and time a file was modified, its size, and the type of file (such as application or folder). And by clicking a column heading, you can sort the list anyway you see fit.

Suppose that you're looking for a file in your Documents folder. You can't remember the name of the file, but you can remember the month and day you last worked on it. Click the Date Modified heading, and subfolders and files are now listed chronologically, oldest or newest first, depending on the direction of the tiny triangle next to the heading. Click the Date Modified heading again to change the order from most recent to oldest or vice versa.

If size matters (and doesn't it always?), click the Size heading to display the list from the biggest file size to the smallest or smallest to biggest. Again, clicking the little triangle changes the order.

If you would rather organize the list by type of file (such as plain text or folder), click the Kind column heading to clump together like-minded entries.

Click a heading to sort.

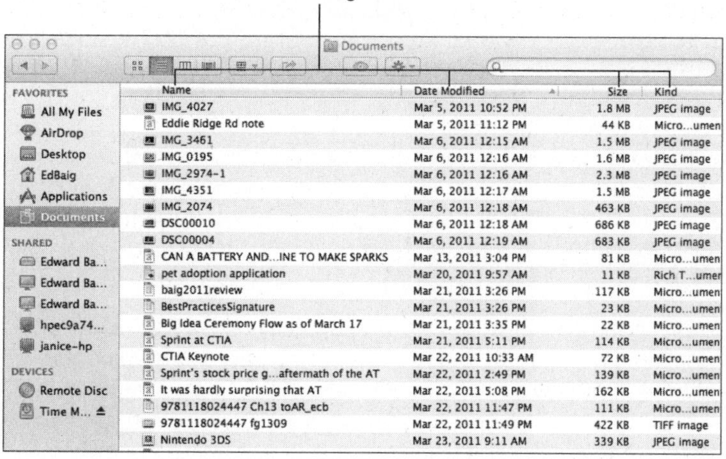

Figure 3-4: The List view.

By columns

Next, choose View⇨As Columns. Again, the check mark moves, altering your perspective. Several vertical panes appear inside one large window. These smaller windows within windows show a progression.

At the far left is a pane called the *sidebar,* a regular hangout for your network, hard drive, home folder, applications, documents, movies, and more.

Now suppose that the home folder is highlighted in the sidebar. The pane to its immediate right displays its contents. Highlight an item in that pane, and the column to its immediate right reveals its contents. Each time you highlight an entry in a particular pane, a new pane appears to its right.

You can resize a column pane by positioning the mouse pointer onto the line between columns. The arrow becomes a cross. Then drag the line in either direction, as shown in Figure 3-5. To resize all the columns simultaneously, press the Option key while dragging. You can expand the entire window by dragging it at the lower right.

By Cover Flow

If you're old enough to have owned a record collection, you likely remember rummaging through album covers to find one you wanted to play. Heck, some of you did the same with CD jewel cases. That's the principle behind Cover Flow, the three-dimensional album art feature that Apple introduced a while back in iTunes.

Figure 3-5:
When in Rome, try the Column view.

Cover Flow is pretty nifty. To access Cover Flow, click the Cover Flow icon on the Finder toolbar or choose View⇨As Cover Flow.

By dragging the slider shown in Figure 3-6, you can flip through high-resolution previews of documents, images, Adobe PDF files, and more, just as you can flip through those album covers in iTunes.

What's more, you can skip past the first page in multipage PDF documents or slides in a presentation created with Apple's own Keynote program. To do so, move the mouse over the Cover Flow image and click the arrows that appear.

Try playing a movie from Cover Flow by clicking the arrow that appears. Here's how. Click Movies in the sidebar, and then drag the slider until the movie you want to watch shows up. Click once on the still image from the movie in question so that a circle with an arrow appears. Click the circle to start playing. The inside arrow turns into two horizontal lines when you mouse over the movie that is playing; click the circle again to pause the movie. Without knowing it, you've just had your first quick look at Quick Look, as the next section elaborates.

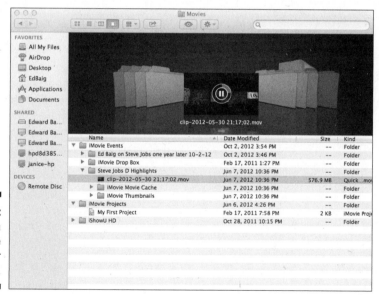

Figure 3-6:
Watching a movie inside the Cover Flow view.

Have a Quick Look

Indeed, Apple gives the Mac faithful yet another clever way to peek at the contents of files on the computer — without having to launch the applications that created those files.

More than living up to its moniker, Quick Look lets you look at a file as a pretty decent-sized thumbnail or even full-screen. And Quick Look might also be called Quick Listen because you can even play music. Indeed, the feature works with all sorts of files — PDFs, spreadsheets, Microsoft Word documents, movies, and more — because Quick Look plug-ins for many other formats are available on the Internet.

Here's how to invoke QuickLook:

1. **Highlight a file in Finder.**

2. **Click the Quick Look button (labeled in Figure 3-2) on the toolbar or press the spacebar on the keyboard.**

   The file jumps out at you in a window. To display the file full-screen, click the button shown in Figure 3-7 that looks like two diagonal arrows pointing in opposite directions.

3. **If you're looking at a picture and want to add it to your iPhoto image library, click the Add to iPhoto button.**

4. **If you decide to open the file you are previewing inside its associated program, click the Open With button in the upper-right corner of the screen. The Mac will suggest the program with which to open it — Preview, Microsoft Word, and so on.**

   To exit Quick Look, click the *x* in the circle or press the spacebar again.

You can preview multiple images in Quick Look. Just highlight more than one file and click the Quick Look toolbar button or press the spacebar. You can then use the Forward or Back arrow to manually navigate through the files. Or, click Play to preview the files in a slideshow. Finally, you can click the Index Sheet button — visible only if you've selected more than one file at a time — to peek at documents in a grid. The button resembles a rectangle with four small squares in it. A good way to find all your photos in one place is to click All My Files in Finder, sort them by Kind, and start sifting through all those that are picture-type files, typically (but not always) JPEG images.

Throughout OS X Mountain Lion, Apple added a Share button and so-called Share Sheets that, well, make it simpler to share digital files with other folks. So it goes in Quick Look. If you click the Share button, you can whisk the file off in an e-mail, share it in an instant message (through Messages), or share it with another nearby Mac through AirDrop. You can also post it to Twitter, Facebook, or Flickr.

Figure 3-7:
Quick, take
a look at my
picture.

Click to add to iPhoto   Click to close

Click to exit full screen

What's Up, Dock?

Your eyes can't help but be drawn to the colorful, reflective, three-dimensional bar at the bottom of the screen, shown in Figure 3-8. This is your *dock*, and it may comfort those familiar with Microsoft's way of designing a computer interface to think of the dock as a rough cross between the Windows taskbar and the Start menu. In my humble opinion, it's more attractive than the Windows taskbar. More fun too. Drag a window near the bottom of the screen and you'll sort of see the window's reflection illuminate that part of the dock.

Figure 3-8:
Docking
your icons.

Try single-clicking a non-running icon in the dock. The little picture bobs up and down like a school kid desperate to get the teacher's attention so that he can safely make it to the bathroom.

What you'll find on the dock

The dock is divided by a faint vertical line into two parts. To the left of the line are programs and other tools. To the right are any open files and folders, plus a collection of expandable folders or icons called Stacks, of which I'll have more to say later in this chapter. You'll also find the trash can. Keep in mind that the mere act of single-clicking a dock icon launches a program or another activity. When you mouse over a dock icon, the title of the appropriate application, document, or folder appears.

Through the years, Apple has made several refinements to the dock. On newer Macs, the following icons appear by default on the left side of the dock (the order in which they appear is, for the most part, up to you):

- ✔ **Finder:** With a goofy face on top of a square, the Finder icon looks like it belongs in a *SpongeBob SquarePants* cartoon. Single-clicking here brings up the main Finder window I discuss earlier in this chapter.

- ✔ **Launchpad:** As its name suggests, the Launchpad is a launching pad for all the apps on your system, each represented by a colorful icon. It bears a striking resemblance to the home screens on those iOS devices such as the iPad or iPhone. Use the trackpad, if your computer has one, to swipe from one Launchpad screenful of icons to another.

- ✔ **Mission Control:** Nope, it's not a place for NASA engineers (though I suspect many of those guys and gals own Macs). In Mission Control, you can get a bird's-eye view of everything that's open on your Mac. You can summon Mission Control from the dock, or by using an upward three-finger swipe on a trackpad or a double tap (not double-click) with a Magic Mouse. (For more on Mission Control, check out Chapter 5.)

- ✔ **Safari:** This icon represents Apple's fine web browser (see Chapter 9).

- ✔ **Mail:** Yes, Apple has a built-in e-mail program, and a good one (see Chapter 10).

- **Contacts:** Formally named Address Book, this application is the place for phone numbers, e-mail addresses, and other contact information (more later in this chapter).

- **Calendar:** Once known as iCal, this is your Mac's excellent built-in calendar (more later in this chapter).

- **Reminders:** Are you forgetful? Let this handy app remind you what's on your list of to-dos or in your Calendar with an alert that is attached.

- **Notes:** Your convenient repository for quick jottings.

- **Messages:** Once known as iChat, this application is Apple's answer to instant messaging/text messaging (see Chapter 11).

- **FaceTime:** The magic of video calling. That's FaceTime.

- **Photo Booth:** Go here to take your account picture or goofy images.

- **iPhoto:** The shoebox for storing, sharing, touching up, and applying special effects to digital images (see Chapter 15).

- **iTunes:** Everyone knows Apple's renowned musical jukebox, long ago expanded to movies and TV shows, too (see Chapter 14).

- **App Store:** Apple's online emporium for purchasing Mac apps from Apple (including any new versions of OS X) and programs from outside software publishers. You get system updates and updates to programs here too. Apps for your Mac run the gamut of course, and are segregated into business, entertainment, news, social networking, utilities, and several other categories.

- **System Preferences:** You can have it your way (see Chapter 5).

In addition, you may see these dock icons, depending upon the age of your Mac, and what you choose to dock on the dock:

- **Dashboard:** The round gauge is the front end for clever little applications called widgets (see Chapters 6 and 21 for more information).

- **Game Center:** The place for fun and games. Sign in with your Apple ID and keep tabs on your game apps, scores, and the old and new friends you choose to play with.

- **iMovie:** This is the place to edit videos (see Chapter 16).

- **GarageBand:** This is where you can launch your musical career (see Chapter 17).

- **Time Machine:** A clever backup feature lets you restore lost files by going back in time to find them (see Chapter 13).

And these appear on the right bank:

- **Stacks:** These are collections of icons to keep your desktop organized and tidy. In OS X Mountain Lion, Apple supplies a premade Stacks for downloads.

- **Trash:** Hey, even computer garbage has to go somewhere (see Chapter 7).

Loading up the dock

Adding favorite items to the dock is as simple as dragging and dropping them there. Of course, the more icons that get dropped in the dock, the more congested the joint gets. Even icons deserve breathing room. To remove items, just drag them slightly outside the dock and wait for the little white poof cloud to appear. When it does, release the mouse button, and your icon has been safely removed. Don't worry — the application itself remains on the Mac.

You can alternately remove a dock icon by dragging it to the trash can.

Still another method: If you have an old-fashion two-button mouse, right-click it (or press Control on the keyboard at the same time you click). You see an option for Options. Choose Remove from Dock as one of those options.

Here's another neat stunt:

1. **Open the menu.**

2. **Choose Dock⇨Turn Magnification On.**

   Now, as your cursor runs over the icons, the little pictures blow up like bubble gum.

If you're into resizing dock icons, choose Dock⇨Dock Preferences. Make sure that the Magnification box is selected and drag the Magnification slider from left (Min) to right (Max), depending on your fancy. A separate slider lets you alter the dock size.

You can also alter the size of the dock itself by clicking the line separating the programs and Stacks, and dragging it to the left or right.

And speaking of that dividing line, you can call up a menu of all dock-related commands by right-clicking or Control-clicking the line.

Docking the dock

The first time you notice the dock, it appears at the bottom of your screen. Apple doesn't make you keep it there. The dock can move to the left or right flank of the screen, depending, I suppose, on your political persuasion.

Again, choose the Dock command from the menu. Choose either Position on Left or Position on Right. Pardon the pun, but your dock is now dockside.

If you find that the dock is getting in the way no matter where you put it, you can make it disappear, at least until you need it again. Choose ⌘⇨Dock⇨Turn Hiding On.

When Hiding is on, drag the cursor to the bottom (or sides) of the screen where the dock would have otherwise been visible. It magically glides into view. The dock retreats to its cave when you glide the cursor away. If you find you miss the dock after all, repeat the previous steps, but now choose Turn Hiding Off.

A minimizing effect

The dock isn't the only thing you'd like to nudge out of the way from time to time. Sometimes entire windows take up too much screen real estate or cover up other windows you want to see. You can close the objectionable window altogether, but that is sometimes a Draconian maneuver, especially if you intend to work in the window again a moment or so later.

You can minimize the window instead. Move the mouse to the upper-left corner of your open window and find the tiny yellow droplet flanked by tiny red and green droplets. (That is, they're red, yellow, and green by default.) I'd show you a picture, but this book is in black and white. In any case, if you single-click the yellow circle in the upper-left corner of a window, the entire thing shrivels up and lands safely on the right side of the dock (assuming that you've stuck with Minimize using a Genie effect in dock preferences; the alternative is to Minimize using a Scale effect).

To restore the window to its full and (presumably) upright position, single-click its newly created dock icon.

Be careful not to click the tiny red circle instead. That closes the window instead of minimizing it.

Clicking the green circle maximizes the window to its full potential and clicking it again returns it to the previous size. If one of the circles appears with no color, it means that particular function is currently unavailable.

Stockpiling Stacks

I have myriad stacks of paper in my office. And in theory anyway, all the papers in one stack are related to all the other papers in the same stack.

This same organizing principle applies to a handy feature called Stacks. *Stacks* are simply a collection of files organized by theme, and they do wonders for all you clutterholics in the crowd, of which, alas, I am one. You'll find Stacks to the right of the divider on the dock.

As already noted, Apple has already put together a useful premade Stack for all the stuff you may download — such as saved Mail attachments, file transfers through Messages, and files captured from the Internet with the Safari browser. In the past, Apple also provided Stacks for applications and for documents, but no longer does so. But it's no biggie because — as you'll see — it's a breeze to create your own Stacks.

I'm fond of the Downloads Stack in particular, which bobs up and down to let you know a new arrival is there. Before the introduction of the Stacks feature, downloaded files had a tendency to mess up your desktop.

The icon for the Downloads Stack takes the form of the most recent item you've downloaded — a PowerPoint presentation, Audible audio file, or whatever it happens to be.

Opening Stacks

To view the contents of a Stack, click the Stacks icon. It immediately opens in one of three ways:

✔ Icons for the files, along with their names, fan out in an arc (see Figure 3-9).

   The most recent file is at the bottom of the fan.

✔ Files and names appear as a grid (see Figure 3-10). You can scroll through the items in Grid view.

✔ Stacks can also appear in a list.

Figure 3-9:
Fanning out
your files.

Figure 3-10:
You can
blow up
your Stack
in more than
one way.

A cool special effect: Hold down the Shift key when you click a Stack, and it opens in slow motion, as a fan or a grid. If you already had a Stack open when you Shift-click another Stack, you can watch one collapse slowly while the other opens.

You can dictate whether Stacks spring out as a fan, grid, or list. Right-click or Control-click the Stacks icon in the dock to instantly bring up the Stack's *contextual menu,* as shown in Figure 3-11. Or hold down the left mouse button for just a second until the menu appears. From the menu, choose Fan, Grid, List, or Automatic (essentially letting the Mac choose for you) to give the Stack your marching orders. You'll notice a few other choices in this contextual menu. For example, you can sort the Stacks icons by name, date added, date modified, date created, or kind of file.

You can summon a contextual menu for all your other dock items, making it a snap to remove the item from the dock, open the program in question when you log in, or show it in Finder.

Adding Stacks

You can turn any folder in your arsenal into a Stack by dragging it from Finder or the desktop to the right of the dock's dashed line and to the left of the trash can. It's as easy as that.

Figure 3-11: A menu to control Stacks.

Quitting time

It's 5 p.m. (or in my world, hours later), so it's quitting time. Here's how to punch out of a specific application. Just to the right of the menu, you see the name of the program you're currently working in. Suppose that it's Safari. Single-click the Safari name and choose Quit Safari from the drop-down menu. Or if you had been working in, say, Word, you'd choose Quit Word from the drop-down menu. Here's a quickie keyboard alternative: Press ⌘+Q to instantly quit the program you're using or, in the case of an application such as Microsoft Word, get a chance to save the file before quitting. One more way to quit: Right-click (or Control-click) an application icon in the dock and choose Quit from the contextual menu.

Getting off work was never so easy.

A Gaggle of Freebie Programs

A major fringe benefit of Mac ownership is all the nifty software you get gratis. Many of these freebie programs, notably those that are part of iLife, are such a big deal that they deserve entire chapters unto themselves.

In the following sections, I discuss programs of smaller stature. I'm not demeaning them; in fact, a number of these *bundled* programs are quite handy to have around.

You'll find some of the programs I am about to mention in the Applications stack in the dock, assuming that you have such a collection. But another good place to look is the *Applications folder,* accessible in a number of ways, as indicated here:

- ✔ Click Applications in the sidebar.
- ✔ Choose Go⇨Applications.
- ✔ Press the keyboard shortcut Shift+⌘+A.
- ✔ And again, if you have an Applications stack, click it to see what's inside.

Staying organized

Not all of us have the luxury of hiring an assistant to keep our life in some semblance of order or just to provide a jolt of caffeine when we need it. I sure don't (sigh).

Regrettably, a Mac still can't make coffee. But it is reassuring that the computer can simplify other administrative chores. Here's how.

Contacts

You just met an attractive stranger on the way to the Apple store, right? Contacts, accessed through the Applications folder or by clicking its dock icon, is a handy repository for addresses, phone numbers, and e-mail addresses. You can also add a picture and note about the person ("awfully cute; owns a Mac").

After opening the program, here's how to add a Contacts entry:

1. **Click the + sign (shown in Figure 3-12).**

   You can alternatively open Contacts and choose File⇨New Card.

2. Type the person's first and last names, company, phone number, and other information in the appropriate fields.

Press the Tab key to move from one field to the next. You can skip fields if you don't have information and add others as need be. For example, to add space for a new mobile phone number entry, click the + next to the field name.

3. Close Contacts.

TIP

If someone sends you a virtual address card (known as a *vCard*), just drag it into the Contacts window. If you already have an entry for the person, you'll have the option to blend the new data with the old.

You can instantly display a map to a person's house in your Contacts. Here's how:

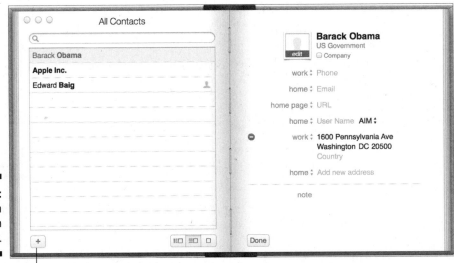

Figure 3-12:
Adding an entry in Contacts.

Click here to add a contact

1. Hold down the Control key while clicking an address.

2. Click Show Address in Google Maps in the contextual menu.

Safari opens, displaying a Google Map page of the address.

3. Click to get directions or search for a nearby pizza shop or other destination.

As you might imagine, Contacts has close ties to a bunch of other Mac applications that I discuss later in this book, most notably Mail and Messages. You can also synchronize contacts with other computers using your iCloud account, a topic I describe in Chapter 12. If you have a Yahoo! address book, you can synchronize that too. And you can synchronize your Contacts with an account that uses a Microsoft Exchange server.

If you set up accounts with Facebook or Twitter by visiting System Preferences (Chapter 11), profile information from those accounts will be automatically populated in Contacts.

Creating Smart Groups

Now suppose a whole bunch of people in your Contacts have something in common. Maybe you all play softball on weekends. (That's a good thing. Break away. Have fun. Limber up. Your computer will be waiting for you when you get back.) A *Smart Group* is a terrific way to manage information in Contacts on all your teammates.

The key is to add a descriptive word that lumps you all together in the Notes field. Something, like, voila, softball. So whenever a new contact comes along and you type the word *softball,* he or she will become part of your Smart Group.

To create a Smart Group from scratch, follow these steps:

1. **Choose File⇨New Smart Group.**

2. **In the Smart Group Name field, type a name for your group.**

   I typed **Weekend athletes**.

3. **Click the + and specify the group criteria using the pop-up menus, as shown in Figure 3-13.**

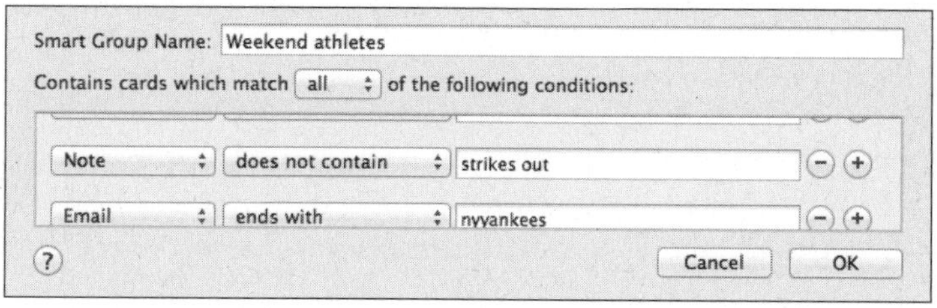

Figure 3-13:
Creating
a Smart
Group.

Smart Group Name: Weekend athletes

Contains cards which match [all ⬍] of the following conditions:

| Note ⬍ | does not contain ⬍ | strikes out | ⊖ ⊕ |
| Email ⬍ | ends with ⬍ | nyyankees | ⊖ ⊕ |

⑦   Cancel   OK

Calendar

It's swell that all your friends want to join the team. But good luck figuring out a time when everybody can play.

For assistance, consult the Mac's personal calendar application, newly renamed Calendar from iCal. It lets you share your calendar with people on the same computer or "publish" a calendar over the Internet to share with others, perhaps by subscribing to iCloud. The program can help you find a convenient time that everyone can meet.

The app also lets you subscribe to public calendars over the Internet (movie openings, religious holidays, and so on). As you might imagine, it can also show the birthdays of folks residing in your Contacts, including birthdays populated by making a connection to the vastly popular social network, Facebook.

You can use Calendar to track different activities for family members or to track the different phases of your own life (meetings at work, Boy Scout troop meetings for your son, and so on). And you can send meeting invitations to people in and out of your workplace — Calendar is tightly integrated with the Mac's Mail program (see Chapter 10).

Reminders

If you need a reminder of all the things you have to do — finish writing a *For Dummies* chapter, for example — the Reminders app lets you display to-do lists (sorted by list or a date on your calendar). Check out Figure 3-14 for one of the Reminders views. Through iCloud, Reminders can be pushed to all your compatible devices: other Macs, iPhone, iPad, iPod touch, or a PC. You can receive notifications of reminders through Notification Center (covered later in this chapter). You can move from one Reminders list to another by swiping from left to right or right to left on a trackpad. In a clever twist, if your Mac knows your current location or knows where you're headed, it can remind you of something when you get to your specified destination, or remind you to leave your current whereabouts.

Stickies

Walk around your office, and I'll lay odds that some of your colleagues have yellow Post-it notes attached to their computer monitors. You too, huh? They're a great way to make your supervisor think you're really busy.

The Mac provides an electronic version of Post-its called *Stickies.* Just like the gluey paper kind, electronic notes let you jot down those quickie shopping lists, phone numbers, and to-dos.

Figure 3-14:
Remind
me of all
the things I
have to do.

But virtual Sticky Notes have it all over their paper counterparts. Consider these stunts:

- ✔ You can resize Sticky Notes by dragging the handle on the note's lower-right corner.

- ✔ You can import text or graphics, alter fonts and font sizes, and change colors.

- ✔ You can check the spelling of words in the note.

- ✔ You can create translucent Sticky Notes to see what's behind them.

- ✔ You can delete a note without crumpling it or crossing out its contents.

- ✔ You won't clutter up your good-looking Macintosh computer. (You have to concoct another scheme to convince your boss how hard you're working.)

Creating a new Sticky doesn't count as work. After opening the app, choose File⇨New Note. Then start scribbling, um, typing.

Notes

Stickies aren't the only kind of notes on your Mac. Through OS X, Apple added a Notes app that is similar to the app found on iOS devices such as the iPad or iPhone. The Notes app serves a similar purpose as Stickies and makes the latter redundant. In Notes, you can jot down quick musings, enter the amounts you spent on groceries, add frequent flier numbers — you name it. You can organize notes in folders, search across all of them, display them full-screen, drag in photos or attachments, pin them to your desktop (just like a Sticky), and push them to your other devices through iCloud. By clicking the Action button at the bottom of a line — the Action button resembles an arrow trying to break out of a rectangle — you can share a note via e-mail or Messages. If you double-click a note name in the column of note headings (see Figure 3-15), you can open a note in its own window to keep on your desktop, even after you close the Notes app.

My advice: Take note of Notes — I think you'll end up using this handy app a lot.

Notification Center

Apple provides a neat way to deliver unobtrusive system-wide notifications and alerts in the upper-right corner of your screen. It's Notification Center, a convenient feature borrowed from iOS. In Notification Center, as shown in Figure 3-16, you can receive e-mail alerts and peek at Calendar appointments, Reminders, Facebook notifications, and more. And notifications can come from third-party apps.

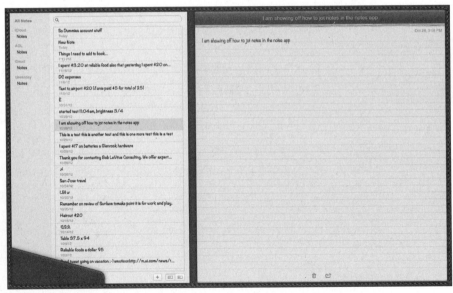

Figure 3-15:
Take Notes.

You have a few ways to manage the notifications that you receive, which may come in the form of banners that turn up in the upper-right corner of the screen and then go away after five seconds. Or, they may appear as alerts that stay visible until you actively dismiss them.

You can see all your missed notifications in Notification Center by clicking the Notification Center icon in the upper-right corner of the screen. Alternatively, take two fingers to the right edge of your trackpad and swipe to the left.

Inside Notification Center, you can post an update to Facebook or send a tweet in Twitter. You can also temporarily turn off alerts and banners. A switch at the top does just that. Alerts and banners are brought back the next day, unless you again turn the switch off.

To make further decisions about which apps can notify you and how, visit System Preferences.

Tooling around for a reference

A lot of what people do on a computer is look things up, mainly through Internet search engines (see Chapter 9) and other online tools (see Chapter 11). Help is closer at hand — in the Applications folder.

Figure 3-16:
Notification
Center
keeps you
informed.

Dictionary

Finding the meaning of words or phrases is as simple as typing them in a search box. Finding the meaning of life is something else altogether. The Mac supplies versions of the *New Oxford American Dictionary* and *Oxford American Writer's Thesaurus.* You can consult an Apple Dictionary to look up terms you can't find in this book. You can also visit the popular Wikipedia online encyclopedia or transfer English words to Japanese or vice versa. The computer can even read a dictionary entry out loud.

TextEdit

TextEdit is a freebie word processor. Although it offers nowhere near the flexibility of an industrial-strength word processor such as Microsoft Word (see Chapters 7) or Apple's own Pages, it's no slouch. You can create short-cuts for phrases you use all the time. You can make tables and lists and apply a bunch of formatting tricks. And it can accommodate Word documents (if someone sends you one).

Calculator

Hey, if all of us could do math in our heads, we wouldn't need a calculator. The Mac supplies not one but three on-screen calculators: Basic, Scientific, and Programmer. Choose the one you need from the calculator's View menu.

The Basic calculator is for people like me who find the need to perform simple arithmetic here and there. You can use the numeric keypad on your keyboard, if it has one, or use the mouse to click the calculator's keypad.

The Scientific version adds square root, sin, cos, and other keys whose mere thought causes me to break out in hives. (Don't count on seeing me as a future author of *Math For Dummies*.)

The Mac calculator is capable of tricks that blow away even the fanciest pocket calculator, such as going online to fetch the latest currency exchange rates. You can also do quick conversions, such as going from Celsius to Fahrenheit.

And, you can pick the number of decimal places up to 15 digits. Any math nerds in the crowd?

QuickTime in the nick of time

QuickTime X, Apple's on-board multimedia player, comes to the rescue when you want to watch a movie (but not a DVD), play sounds, or display pictures. QuickTime typically pops up as needed. QuickTime X lets you trim and edit videos, among other features.

Preview

Preview is a versatile program that lets you view graphics files and faxes, see screen captures, convert graphic file formats (for example, from TIFF to JPEG), and handle PDFs with panache. (PDF is shorthand for Adobe's *Portable Document Format.*) Preview typically loads automatically as needed. For example, if you double-click a PDF file that someone sent you, Preview is probably the program that lets you read it. You can use Preview also to rotate, resize, and crop images in one of the many file types it recognizes.

In Preview, it's also easier to select text that falls into a single column of a document, rather than having it wrap around to select text in multiple columns.

Further improvements to Preview came with Mountain Lion. You can access PDF documents and images from anywhere via the iCloud feature known as Documents in the Cloud. And you can easily share things in Preview by tapping a Share button that lets you drop documents in Messages, AirDrop, or Mail.

Chapter 4

Here a Mac, There a Mac, Everywhere a Mac Mac

hich of the following describes you?

✔ Based on what you already know (or gleaned from this book), you are on the righteous path toward purchasing a Macintosh computer. *The challenge now is figuring out which model makes the most sense.*

✔ You already own a Mac and are looking to add a second or even third machine to your arsenal. *The challenge now is figuring out which model makes the most sense.*

✔ You received this book as a gift and have no intention of buying any computer. *The challenge now is explaining to the person who gave it to you why no model makes sense (without hurting his or her feelings).*

Regrettably, I can't help anyone in the third group. Feel free to tag along anyway.

Intel's Inside?

The computer industry creates strange bedfellows sometimes, maybe none stranger than the blissful 2005 union between Apple and Intel. To veteran Mac diehards, placing Intel *processors,* or chips, inside their beloved computers was a scandal analogous to an intimate liaison between George Jetson and Wilma Flintstone.

Intel was the enemy, after all. Its processors belonged inside Windows' computers, not Apple's, hence the derided (from a Mac point of view) moniker Wintel. Suffice it to say, Apple's head honcho at the time, Steve Jobs, blew a few minds when he broke the news that the company was jilting long-fancied *PowerPC G4* and *G5* processors produced by IBM and Motorola and going with chips made by Intel. In a relatively short time, Apple overhauled its entire hardware lineup with Intel chips.

Some seven years (as of this writing) after their shocking union, Intel and Apple appear to have a stable marriage. But rumors about Apple always fly, and because Apple designs its own chips for its iPhone and iPad, perhaps its chips designs will eventually become a major part of the Mac.

So what is a processor anyway? Put simply, it is the brains behind your computer.

Two chips are better than one

Most Macs reborn with Intel processors actually have at least two chips engineered on a single slab of silicon. The dual-core chips (found on some models as this book was being prepared) boast twice the computational horsepower of a more traditional single-chip design. The idea is that the two chips can team up and share resources as needed but also conserve power if one of the core chips is not needed for a particular function. But why stop there? As this book was being written, the trend was moving toward *quad-core* chips and, in the case of Mac Pros, even more robust processors, with up to 12 power cores.

But are you giving up something to get something?

The burning issue for Mac loyalists was whether the presence of Intel would somehow mess things up. The answer turned out to be a resounding no. Intel-based machines still looked like Macs, quacked like Macs, and behaved like Macs.

Big Mac or Little Mac? The Laptop-versus-Desktop Decision

Desktop? Laptop? Or notebook? Okay, that was a bit of a trick question because people use *notebook* and *laptop* to refer to the same thing. So it's really desktop versus laptop/notebook.

 I'm obliged to at least raise the notion of purchasing a tablet instead of a notebook/laptop because, as coauthor of *iPad For Dummies*, 5th Edition (published by John Wiley & Sons, Inc.), I think Apple's slate should be part of the conversation of what to buy. For now, though, I'll leave the debate for another time and stick to which Mac makes more sense for you.

As always, the choice comes down to lifestyle, economics, and what you do for a living. If you burn lots of frequent-flier miles, chances are you'll gravitate to a laptop. If you tend to be home- or office-bound, a desktop might be more suitable.

I'll give each side its due. Here are the reasons for buying a Mac desktop:

- ✔ You generally get more computing bang for the buck.
- ✔ It has more generous storage, a bigger display, and more connectors.
- ✔ Upgrading it is easier.
- ✔ You won't slow anyone down checking in at airport security.
- ✔ The machine looks cool in your home or office.

And here's why you would want to buy a Mac laptop:

- ✔ It's light and portable.
- ✔ It's appealing if you work or live in cramped quarters.
- ✔ It runs off battery or AC power.
- ✔ You can impress your seatmate on an airplane.

If a Desktop Is Your Poison

Buying an Apple desktop computer does not mean that you have to start rearranging the furniture or buying new furniture. Sure, Mac desktops generally take up more space than Mac notebooks. But the machines are no larger than they have to be and are so handsome that you'll want to show them off.

iMac

As shown in Figure 4-1, the *iMac* is the most elegantly designed desktop computer on the planet.

Now that I've said that, let me mention a proviso: The iMac is the most elegantly designed desktop computer on the day that I write this. By the time this book gets to you, the gang inside the company's Cupertino, California, headquarters may well have one-upped themselves.

Now that *that* lawyerly comment is out of the way, it's back to the captivating charmer at hand. The innards of the all-in-one system — Intel Core i5 or i7 processor, memory, hard drive (and/or solid-state drive), and more — are concealed inside a beautiful and remarkably thin 5-mm flat-screen monitor. You can't help but wonder where the rest of the computer is, especially if you're accustomed to seeing a more traditional tower-type PC design. Apple sells iMacs with 21.5-inch monitors (measured diagonally) or whopping 27-inch monitors, each an LED-backlit display with cinematic widescreen *aspect ratios.* The machine is covered in glass, and comes with a wireless mouse and keyboard.

You can outfit the iMac with up to a 3-terabyte hard drive or up to 768GB of flash storage. And the new iMac unveils a new storage option — the Fusion Drive — which combines a hard drive with flash storage. The drive determines which apps and files you use most often and keeps those in the faster flash portion.

With the latest iMac, Apple is moving away from the Super Drive (CD/DVD) player that was once standard on the iMac. When you placed a CD or DVD in the slot on the iMac's right side, it got sucked inside the machine like a dollar in a vending machine's bill changer. Because you are encouraged to buy most software these days online, notably through the Mac App Store, physical discs are not as prevalent as they once were. Still, if you have a lot of CDs and/or DVDs lying around, you can purchase an optional external USB SuperDrive for $79.

The small peephole at the top of the monitor covers a built-in high-definition *FaceTime* video camera, used for FaceTime video calls as well as for pictures you take in Photo Booth

iMacs used to come with a white Bic lighter–sized Apple remote used to control music, videos, and other media through Apple's alternative full-screen *Front Row* software interface, but the media center–type software application was discontinued when OS X Lion appeared in the summer of 2011. You can still buy an Apple Remote, now gray and taller than the original, as an optional $19 accessory.

Figure 4-1:
The elegant
iMac.

Courtesy of Apple

Mac mini

Is the *Mac mini* shown in Figure 4-2 really a desktop? After all, Mac mini is easily mistaken for a bread box or a coaster on steroids. But the petite 1.4-inch-tall, 7.7-inch-square aluminum contraption is indeed Apple's crazy (and cozy) notion of what a "budget" desktop computer is all about. At 2.7 pounds, Mac mini is portable, but not in the same sense as a notebook you would fly with cross-country. (Carting this computer from room to room is more like it.)

Models cost $599 or $799 as of this writing (or $999 for a mini equipped with Apple's OS X Server), but keep in mind that this is a BYOB computer — as in bring your own keyboard, mouse, and monitor. (The assumption is that you have these already, but if not, Apple will happily sell them to you.) Given its size and price, Mac mini might make an ideal second or third computer and is a perfect dorm room companion.

Figure 4-2:
Mini-me's
favorite
Macintosh.

Courtesy of Apple

Because Mac mini has HDMI (High-Definition Multimedia Interface), you can also hook it up to a big-screen TV or take advantage of a superior speaker system. And Mac mini includes the smarts to play back music or videos stored on other computers in your house, including Windows systems.

A Fusion Drive (1TB hard drive combined with 128GB flash) is an option here as well.

Mac Pro: A Mac with muscle

The muscular Mac Pro — it's capable of up to 12 cores of processing power through the Intel Xeon — is a preferred system for graphics designers, video production professionals, scientists, music producers, developers, and so on. If you're not one of those folks, scram. Then again, it's awfully hard not to be seduced by the machine's powerful graphics and storage options.

Going Mobile

You don't have to be a traditional road warrior to crave a notebook these days. You might just need something to schlep from lecture hall to lecture hall, your home to your office, or maybe just from the basement to the bedroom. And some computers are worth having (such as the MacBook Air, described shortly) just because they are so darn sexy.

In choosing any laptop, take into account its *traveling weight*. Besides the weight of the machine itself, consider the heft of the AC power cord and possibly a spare battery (though Macs of recent vintage don't let you replace the battery yourself).

One of the first decisions you have to make is how big a screen you want. Bigger displays are nice, of course, but they weigh and cost more. And you may be sacrificing some battery life. Hmm, are you getting the sense that this battery business is a big deal? It can be, which is why I offer tips, at the end of the chapter, on how to stay juiced.

As part of its migration to Intel processors, Apple retired two longtime members of its laptop lineup in 2006, the ivory white iBook (popular with students) and the silver PowerBook. The MacBook was later put out to pasture as well, leaving just the MacBook Air and MacBook Pro on the mobile roster.

MacBook Pro

Apple's top-of-the-line *MacBook Pro* notebook, boasting a beautiful Retina display, is shown in Figure 4-3. It comes in 13- and 15-inch versions, with a base model starting at $1,699 as of this writing, on up to $2,799 or more depending how you configure it. You can get a MacBook Pro without the glorious Retina display for $1,199 on up; it too comes in 13- and 15-inch configurations. Constructed from a solid slab of aluminum, MacBook Pros are fast and boast souped-up NVIDIA graphics (great for 3-D games and videos) and long-lasting batteries.

MacBook Pro did relinquish some features found on old PowerBooks and old MacBook Pros. Yes, it ditched the optical disc drive, though that is still available as an external accessory. And the hard drive went by way of all flash storage. The latest models, though, are the first notebooks to come with a pair of Thunderbolt ports, Apple's speedy new connector. USB 3.0 connectors are also included on the MacBook Pro and Air models, as is an HDMI port on the Pro.

A FireWire port is no longer available, so you'll need an optional adapter if that connector is still important to you. Ambient sensors that can illuminate the keyboard when the cabin lights are dimmed on an airplane are included. If that doesn't create a mood and show the cute passenger in 12C how resourceful you are, nothing will. You can also use the glass multitouch trackpad and navigate using some of the finger gestures mentioned later in this chapter.

MacBook Air

It's hard to imagine how thin and light MacBook Airs are without seeing them and picking them up. They are dream computers to take on the road. Pictures — even the ones in Figure 4-4 — do not do them justice. As with the MacBook Pros, the machines are crafted from a single slab of aluminum. The smaller models have 11.6-inch displays, weigh just 2.4 pounds, and measure just 0.68 inches at the rear, before tapering down to a mere 0.11 inches at their thinnest point in the front. They cost $999 or $1,099 in their base configurations.

Figure 4-3:
A handsome 15-inch MacBook Pro with Retina display.

Larger 13.3-inch-display models also measure 0.68 inches in the rear and a hair over a tenth of an inch thick at the front. And despite the larger screen size, the machines aren't a whole lot heavier (2.96 pounds). They cost $1,199 and $1,499 in their base configurations.

Apple has still managed to include full-size backlit keyboards, multitouch track-pads, and battery life (for wireless web surfing) of up to 5 or 7 hours depending on the model. Too bad the battery is sealed and not easily replaced.

The Airs use all-flash storage in lieu of hard drives, and because flash is expensive, storage is cramped: 64GB or 128GB on 11.6-inch base models or 128GB or 256GB on 13.3-inch versions. You can go as high as 512GB of flash storage.

Keep in mind that any Lilliputian computer exacts compromises. So it goes with Air. You'll find no integrated CD/DVD drive,. and you'll find just a pair of USB 3.0 ports and no Ethernet connector. Apple has added Thunderbolt ports to the latest models, and the new MagSafe 2 power port connector. The larger MacBook Air includes an SD card slot. The machines also come with 4GB of RAM (upgradeable at the time of purchase to 8GB).

Figure 4-4:
Floating on MacBook Air.

Taming the Trackpad

In Chapter 2, I introduce the trackpad, the smooth rectangular finger-licking surface below the keyboard that's your laptop's answer to using a mouse. On the latest Mac laptops, the entire trackpad is a clickable button.

You can still use a regular mouse with a laptop, of course, and may prefer to do so if you're at your regular desk. If you're sitting in coach instead, the mouse is an unwelcome critter, especially to the passenger sitting next to you. Don't be surprised if he or she calls an exterminator (or at least the flight attendant).

The best place to train a trackpad is in Trackpad preferences. Choose ⇨ System Preferences⇨Trackpad. As shown in Figure 4-5, you have numerous options for making things happen with one, two, three, and even four fingers, by selecting the appropriate check boxes.

Figure 4-5: The key to taming your trackpad on different laptops.

A handy little video window helps you figure out what to do.

Many multitouch gestures were borrowed from the Mac's famous corporate cousin, the iPhone. You can zoom in on a web page in Safari or a photo in iPhoto by *pinching*, or placing your thumb and forefinger together on the trackpad and then pulling them apart. And with the *swipe* gesture, you can navigate web pages with three fingers by dragging from right to left to page forward, and left to right to retreat.

Here are a few more options:

- Drag the Tracking Speed slider to change how fast the pointer moves, and drag the Double-Click Speed slider to set how fast *you* have to double-click.

- You can use one finger tap to click — or one finger for a secondary click in either the lower-right corner of the trackpad or the lower-left corner.

- You can show the desktop by spreading your thumb and three fingers.

- You can rotate using two fingers.

Keeping Your Notebook Juiced

Although Apple has dramatically improved the battery life across all its notebooks, sooner or later, your battery will lose its charge, especially if Murphy (the fellow behind that nasty law) has any say in the manner. And you can be sure that you will be chargeless at precisely the worst possible moment. Like when your professor is prepping you for a final exam. Or you are about to discover whodunit while watching a movie on an overseas flight. I hasten to point out that watching a flick will drain your battery a lot faster than working on a spreadsheet.

You may routinely keep the computer plugged in to recharge the battery. Still, Apple recommends pulling the plug periodically to keep the juices flowing. If you didn't plan on using the computer for six months or more (and why the heck not?), on older Mac laptops, you could remove the battery and store it with about a 50-percent charge. You couldn't always resuscitate a fully discharged battery that had been kept on the sidelines too long.

OK, maybe it's time to spill the bad news. Sealed batteries mean no more do-it-yourself. You are a prisoner to the Apple battery replacement service.

Rechargeable batteries have a finite number of charging cycles, so even with the best feed and caring, they have to be replaced eventually. It will be evident when it's time to put the battery out to pasture because it will no longer hold a charge for very long. Remember to give it an environmentally correct burial.

However, don't give up the fight just yet. You can take steps to boost your battery's longevity. Your computer is smart about conservation. When plugged in, it feels free to let loose. That means the hard drive (if there is one) will spin around to its heart's content, and the display can be turned up to maximum brightness settings.

You can tell a Mac how to behave when it is unplugged:

- ✔ **Dim the screen.** Your laptop battery likes nothing better than mood lighting. Press F1 on the keyboard to turn down the brightness.

- ✔ **Open *Energy Saver*** (see Figure 4-6) by clicking the battery gauge on the menu bar and then selecting open Energy Saver Preferences. (Alternatively, choose ⌘⇨System Preferences and click Energy Saver.) You have options to put the hard drives to sleep when possible (a swell idea), to slightly dim the display when using a battery (equally swell idea), or to automatically reduce brightness before the display goes to sleep. You'll notice other options in Energy Saver, including a slider to put the computer to sleep when it's not used for a certain period, plus a slider to put the display to sleep after the machine is inactive. If you click Schedule, you can determine when the computer starts or wakes up or goes to sleep.

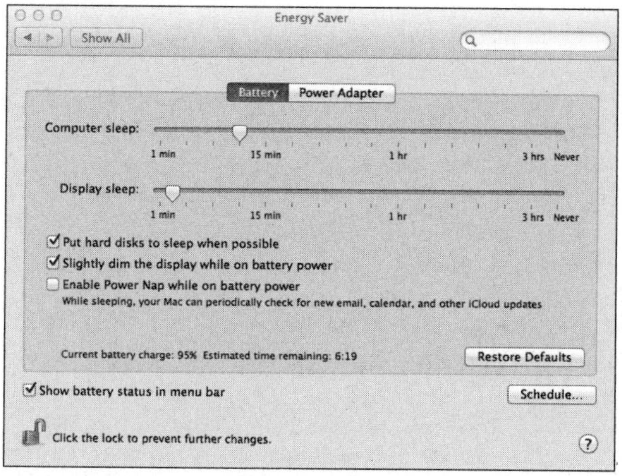

Figure 4-6:
Mac con-
servation.
Inside
Energy
Saver.

- ✔ **Shut down the *AirPort* wireless networking feature** (see Chapter 18) if you're not surfing the Internet, sending and receiving e-mail, or sharing files over the network. AirPort hogs power. And you shouldn't be using it anyway if you're traveling on an airplane that doesn't offer Wi-Fi.

- ✔ Likewise, **turn off the wireless settings for Bluetooth** if you're on a plane or if you just want to save some juice.

After all, given all your aspirations with your computer, the last thing you want is to run out of power.

Part II
Mac Daily Dealings

Check out the article "Eyeing Your Printer Needs" (and more) online at www.
dummies.com/extras/macs.

In this part . . .

- ✔ Find out how to you can customize your Mac to better fit your needs.

- ✔ See what's new in Mountain Lion, the brand new version of the Mac OS X operating system.

- ✔ Explore how to create and edit documents using TextEdit, the built-in word processor for OS X.

- ✔ Check out the article "Eyeing Your Printer Needs" (and more) online at www.dummies.com/extras/macs.

Chapter 5

Making the Mac Your Own

You adore your family and friends to death but have to admit that they get under your skin from time to time. They know how to push your buttons, and you sure know how to push theirs. People are fussy about certain things, and that includes you (and me).

So it goes with your Macintosh. The presumption is that you and your Mac are going to cohabit well into the future. Still, it can't hurt to get off on the right foot and set up the machine so that it matches your preferences and expectations, and not some programmer's at Apple. The software you load on your system differs from the programs your best buddies install on their computers. You tolerate dozens of icons on the Mac desktop; they prefer a less cluttered screen. You choose a blown-up picture of Homer Simpson for your desktop background; your pals go with a screen-size poster of Jessica Simpson.

Establishing User Accounts

As much as the computer staring you in the face is your very own Mac, chances are you'll be sharing it with someone else: your spouse and kids, perhaps, if not your students and coworkers. I know you generously thought about buying each of them a computer. But then your little one needs braces, you've been eyeing a new set of golf clubs and, the truth is, your largesse has limits. So you'll be sharing the computer, all right, at least for a while. The challenge now is avoiding chaos and all-out civil war.

The Mac helps keep the peace by giving everyone his or her own user account, which is a separate area to hang out in that is password protected to prevent intrusions. (The folks at Apple can't do much to avert fights over *when* people use the computer — though moms and dads have some control over when junior gets to use the machine.)

Ranking user accounts

In Chapter 2, I explain how you create your own user account as part of the initial computer setup. But not all user accounts are created equal, and yours is extra special. That's because as the owner of the machine, you're the head honcho, the Big Cheese, or in the bureaucracy of your computer, the *administrator.*

Being the Big Cheese doesn't earn you an expense account or a plush corner office with a view of the lakefront. It does, however, carry executive privileges. You get to lord over not only who else can use the machine but who, if anyone, gets the same administrative rights you have.

 Think long and hard before you grant anyone else these dictatorial powers. Only an administrator can muck around with system settings such as Date & Time and Energy Saver. And only an administrator can effectively hire and fire, by creating or eliminating other user accounts. Naturally, an administrator can also install software.

Here's a quick look at the hierarchy of accounts:

- ✓ **Administrator:** As outlined previously, you have almighty powers, at least when it comes to your computer.

- ✓ **Standard:** You can't mess with other people's accounts. But you pretty much have free reign when it comes to your own account. That means you can install software, alter the look of your desktop, and so on.

- ✓ **Managed with Parental Controls:** Consider this Mom's and Dad's Revenge. The kids may get away with murder around the house, but they can't get away with murder on the Mac.

- ✓ **Sharing Only:** This type of account is a limited account for sharing files remotely across a network.

- ✓ **Group:** By creating a group account, you can share files with the members of said group. It's really a type of account comprised of one or more accounts.

- ✓ **Guest:** Willing to let the babysitter play with your Mac after putting the little ones to bed? A guest account lets her log in without a password (though you can still restrict her activities through parental controls). You can allow guests to connect to shared folders on the system. Or not. And the beauty of one of these accounts is that after a guest has logged out, traces of her stay are removed, right down to the temporary home folder created for her visit.

Creating new accounts

So now that you know about the different types of user accounts, I'll discuss more about setting up one. To create a new account for one of your coworkers, say, follow these steps:

1. **Choose ⌘⇨System Preferences, and then click the Users & Groups icon in the System section.**

   Alternatively, you can click your username in the upper-right corner of the screen, mouse down to Users & Groups Preferences, and then click that item, or you can get to System Preferences through its dock icon.

   It's worth remembering how you get to System Preferences because you'll be spending a lot of time there in this chapter. The Users & Groups window that appears is shown in Figure 5-1.

Figure 5-1: Change account preferences here.

2. **If the Password tab isn't highlighted, click it.**

3. **Click the + in the lower-left corner (right there below the list of names).**

   If the + appears dimmed, you have to click the padlock at the bottom of the screen and enter your username and password to proceed. (You'll encounter this padlock throughout System Preferences and must click it and enter an administrative password before being allowed to make changes.)

4. In the screen shown in Figure 5-2, do the following:

    a. On the New Account pop-up menu, choose one of the account designations listed in the preceding section [such as Administrator, Standard, or (as shown here) Managed with Parental Controls].

    b. Enter a full name, an account name, a password, the password verification, and (if you choose) a password hint in the blank fields shown.

    For help in choosing a password, click the key next to the password field. Of course, you may want to give a coworker or other person sharing an account the ability to enter his or her own password and username.

    c. Click Create User.

    You are brought back to the Users & Groups window.

Unless you have a good reason to do otherwise, deselect the Allow User to Administer This Computer check box (refer to Figure 5-1). You also have the option to allow one of your other users to set his own Apple ID and to reset his password using Apple ID. If automatic login is turned on in your computer, you'll have the option to turn it off. (You may leave the remaining steps to the new account holder — letting him or her choose an identifying picture, for example.)

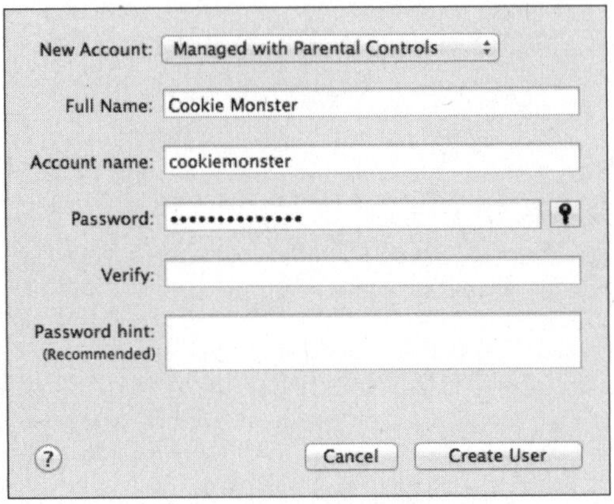

Figure 5-2:
Add a new account here.

New Account:	Managed with Parental Controls ⬍
Full Name:	Cookie Monster
Account name:	cookiemonster
Password:	•••••••••••• 🔑
Verify:	
Password hint: (Recommended)	

?   Cancel   Create User

5. Click the Picture thumbnail.

It will either show your mug or a picture of an object, a butterfly say or tennis ball. You are brought to the screen outlined in the next step.

6. Select the small image that will be displayed next to the username when the account holder logs on to the computer.

You can click the archery target, piano keyboard, gingerbread cookie, luscious lips, or other goofy iconic images presented in the Users & Groups window. But account holders may well want to choose one of their own images. To do so, follow these steps:

a. Click Camera from the list shown after you clicked the Picture thumbnail in the Users & Groups window.

This launches the FaceTime camera on the front of your Mac. You see what the camera sees in a small window.

b. Click the camera icon that shows up just under the window of your own face after launching the FaceTime camera

After a three-two-one countdown, your mug (or the other account holder's mug) is captured. If satisfied with the result, click Done, and that image will serve as the account picture. If not satisfied, click Cancel to reshoot.

c. You can also click Recents from the list on the side of the Users & Groups window to, well, see any of the recent images that either you shot or that Apple supplies that might make a suitable account picture.

Check out the next section for another, more enjoyable way to create an account picture.

Entering the Photo Booth

Remember when you and your high school sweetheart slipped into one of those coin-operated photo booths at the five-and-dime? Or maybe it was your mom or dad's high school sweetheart. Don't worry, I'm not telling what went on behind that curtain. You or your parent probably confiscated the evidence years ago, a strip with all those silly poses.

Silly poses are back in vogue. Apple is supplying its own photo booth of sorts as a built-in software feature on Macs with integrated iSight or renamed FaceTime cameras. You can produce an acceptable account picture to use when, say, you're exchanging instant messages (see Chapter 11).

Apple's Photo Booth and the photo booth of yesteryear — and today, because you'll still see them around — have some major differences. For starters, you don't have to surrender any loose change with Apple's version. What's more, you don't have to hide behind a curtain (which is kind of too bad), though you'll see a picture of a curtain in the Photo Booth icon. And that old-fashioned photo booth can't match Apple's other stunts — making movie clips or having your mug appear in front of a *moving* roller coaster or other fluid backdrop.

Taking a Photo Booth picture

Open Photo Booth by clicking its name in the Applications folder, clicking its dock icon or clicking its Launchpad icon. You can snap an image right away by merely clicking the red oblong shutter button below the large video screen that serves as a viewfinder, as shown in Figure 5-3.

Upon doing so, a three-two-one countdown ticks off. On zero, the display flashes, and your portrait is captured. But consider your other options. Take a gander at the three little icons at the lower-left corner of the screen, and the dial just below them. (The dial only appears when you open Photo Booth in full-screen mode.) If you click the leftmost icon or roll the dial with your trackpad to the left, and then click the shutter button, Photo Booth will take four successive snapshots in a row, right after the three-two-one countdown. The just-captured images appear in a single "four-up" snapshot, showing, well, your four poses. You have activated *burst mode*.

Figure 5-3:
It's a snap.
The main
Photo Booth
view.

Click to take a movie clip   Shutter button   Click to enter
the Special
Effects menu

Click to take a still picture

Click to take four quick pictures

Clicking (or dialing) the icon in the middle sticks with the one-shot approach, while making use of the icon on the right puts Photo Booth in video mode. After the countdown, the computer starts making a little video, complete with audio. You have to click the shutter button again (now labeled Stop) to cease recording. A red digital counter reminds you that you are still shooting.

You can remove any of the still images or videos you've captured in Photo Booth by clicking a thumbnail of those images and clicking the circled X that appears on the upper-left-hand corner of the thumbnail.

Applying special effects

So far I've told you how to capture straightforward images (assuming that you didn't stick your tongue out). Now the real fun begins. You can summon your inner mad scientist and apply a series of warping effects.

Click the Effects button. A Brady Bunch–like grid appears, with each square revealing a different effect — some silly, some creepy, just like the screen shown in Figure 5-4. Click the arrows adjacent to the Effects button to check out another set of effects.

Click a square to preview the potential effect in a much larger window, and ultimately choose that one or another effect. Click Effects and then the middle of this tic-tac-toe grid to revert to the normal view.

You can make it look as though the picture was taken with a thermal camera or an X-ray or drawn with a colored pencil. You can turn the image into pop art worthy of Warhol or make it glow radioactively. You can apply a chipmunk effect, or a lovestruck image in which red hearts are seen floating around your head. And you can place yourself in a mirror image reminiscent of the Doublemint gum twins.

Click the arrows on the screen to display a new set of effects. When you click some effects (such as bulge, squeeze, or twirl), you see a slider that you can use with the mouse to tweak the level of distortion.

Admiring and sharing Photo Booth photos

The pictures and movies that you make in Photo Booth turn up at the bottom of the Photo Booth program in an on-screen photo strip. To admire the image, just click the corresponding thumbnail.

Figure 5-4:
How
goofy (or
creepy) can
you get?
Applying
effects
in Photo
Booth.

You also have several options for sharing the picture or movie with others. By choosing the appropriate button, you can make it your account picture or buddy picture (for use as a *buddy icon)* in Messages. You can also drop the image into a message, e-mail the picture through the Mac's Mail application, or send it to your iPhoto picture library. You can use it on Facebook, Twitter, or Flickr. Or make it available to a nearby Mac through AirDrop. Still another option is to drag it to your desktop.

You can also export the thumbnail by selecting it, choosing File from the Photo Booth menu, and then selecting Export. That way, you can use the image file in a third-party application or web-based e-mail client.

Using Parental Controls: When Father (or Mother) Knows Best

Suppose one of the new accounts you create is for your impressionable off-spring, Cookie Monster. As a responsible parent, you want to set limits to keep him out of trouble. And as a responsible Mac owner, you want to keep him from unwittingly (or otherwise) inflicting damage on the computer.

It's time to apply *parental controls.* Presumably, you already set up Cookie Monster as a managed account with parental controls. If not, choose the proper user account — Cookie Monster in this example — and click to select the Enable Parental Controls check box in the Users & Groups window in System Preferences. When you do so, Cookie Monster's account goes from being a regular standard account to a managed account, with you as the manager. You have quite a bit of say about what your youngster can and cannot get away with.

In the Users & Groups window, click Open Parental Controls. Alternatively, click Parental Controls in System Preferences. Either way, you'll end up in the same place. In the Parental Controls window, shown in Figure 5-5, select Cookie Monster's name in the list on the left. Now, protective parent, you can do lots of things.

Figure 5-5:
Parental controls may protect your kid and your computer.

Here I dive in to the five tabs at the top of the window:

- ✔ **Apps:** Parents can select the Use Simple Finder check box to provide Cookie Monster with the most restricted barebones desktop. Only three folders reside in the Simple Finder version of the dock (My Applications, Documents, and Shared), plus the trash can. Meanwhile, the only applications your kid gets to see are those you've designated by selecting the Limit Applications check box. In this Apps view, you can also choose whether the little guy can take advantage of App Store apps, and if you say yes, restrict those apps by age rating. As an administrator, you can also choose whether the child can modify the dock. (Dock modification is categorically disallowed in Simple Finder.)

- **Web:** By selecting this tab, you allow unrestricted access to websites or limit access. If you click Customize, you can list your own approved sites, as well as those you don't deem kosher. You can also restrict web access so that all Cookie Monster supposedly gets to see are clean sites. Apple will make the decision on your behalf if you select the Try to Limit Access to Adult Website Automatically check box. You can view sites that meet Apple's approval, and if you agree, click Allow Access to Only These Websites. Discovery Kids, Disney, PBS Kids, National Geographic – Kids, Scholastic.com, and Smithsonian Institution are among the sites that made Apple's list. Meanwhile, I know you trust your kid. All the same, you want to ensure his safety by getting a good handle on his online behavior. Click the Logs button to find out which websites your child visited, which he tried to visit but were blocked, which applications he used, and who in Messages he chatted with. You can summon logs for one day, one week, one month, three months, six months, or one year. Or you can subpoena all the records. You can group logs by date or by website, contact, or app. The option to click Logs also appears under the Apps and People tabs.

- **People:** By selecting the Limit Mail or Limit Messages checkboxes or both, you get to approve who Cookie Monster can exchange e-mails and hold chats with through instant messages. You can also receive an e-mail permission request should Cookie Monster attempt to communicate with someone who isn't on the A-OK list. Within this tab, you can also allow junior to join Game Center multiplayer games and add new friends in Game Center. Or not.

- **Time Limits:** It's not only a matter of who Cookie Monster would like to interact with or what programs he wants to play around with — it's also a matter of when you let him do so. By dragging the sliders shown in Figure 5-6, you can establish weekday and weekend time restrictions. In other words, you can prevent access to the Mac when it's time for him to go beddy-bye, choosing different times on school nights and weekends. Cookie Monster will get a fair warning shortly before shutdown time so that he can save his work. He'll also get the opportunity to plead for more time.

- **Other:** You can do lots of other things to try and keep your child safe and sound. In this catchall area, you can disable the use of Dictation, hide profanity in Dictionary, prevent the kid from changing printer settings, limit CD or DVD burning, and prevent him from changing his password.

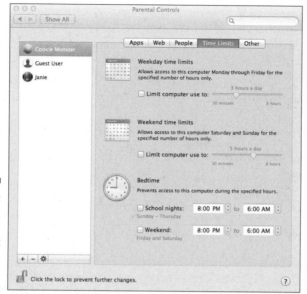

Figure 5-6:
Time's up:
Placing
stringent
limits on
junior.

The Lowdown on Logging In

You can create user accounts for any and all family members or visitors who will be using a particular Mac. And you can control how they log in. In this section, I describe how.

In System Preferences, choose Users & Groups and then click Login Options at the bottom of the left pane, under the list of all the account holders on your system. If need be, click the padlock and enter a username and administrative password. After you're in, you'll see the window shown in Figure 5-7.

To automatically log in a particular user (likely yourself), select the Automatic Login option and choose the appropriate person from the pop-up menu. You'll have to enter a password.

If the computer is set to automatically log you in, any user who restarts the Mac in your absence will have access to your account.

If, at login, you'd like to see a Login screen with a roster of people alongside pictures for their respective accounts, select the section's List of Users radio button. If you'd prefer that each account holder be forced to type his or her own username and password in the appropriate boxes on the Login screen to log in, select the section's Name and Password radio button. This is the most secure method of keeping interlopers at bay.

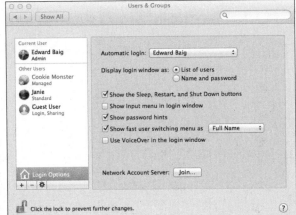

Figure 5-7:
Choosing
login
options.

Either way, press Enter (or Return) or click after entering the password to actually log in. If you type the wrong password, the password text box wobbles as if having a momentary seizure. Type it wrong a few more times, and any password hints you previously entered appear (provided that you chose that option under Login Options).

And logging out

Say that you are ready to call it quits for the day but don't want to shut down the machine. At the same time, you don't want to leave your account open for anyone with prying eyes. *Baig's Law: Just because your family, friends, and coworkers are upstanding citizens doesn't mean they won't eavesdrop.* The way to shut down without really shutting down is to choose ⇨Log Out.

Pulling a fast one

Now consider another all-too-common scenario. You're in the middle of working when — how to put this delicately? — last night's pasta exacts revenge. Nature calls. As you get up to leave, your spouse comes running in, saying, *"Honey, can I quickly check my e-mail?"* You could log out to let her do so, but because you are going to be right back, you figure there has to be a better way. The better way is called *fast user switching*. To take advantage of the feature, you must have previously selected the Show Fast User Switching Menu As check box in the Login Options window. You can display this menu as a name, a short name, or an icon.

Then, to let your spouse (or any other user) butt in, click your username in the upper-right corner of the screen. A list of all account holders appears. The person can then click his or her name and type a password. Like a revolving door, your entire desktop spins out of the way while the other user's desktop spins in. When you return moments later, you repeat this procedure by choosing your name and entering your password. Your desktop twirls back into view, right where you left off.

Letting Someone Go

Sometimes being the boss really does mean being the bad guy. The Mac equivalent of terminating someone is to delete the person's user account from the system. In the Users & Groups window, click the padlock (it's at the lower left of the window) to permit changes. Then select the name of the person getting the pink slip. Click the – button under the list of names.

A dialog presents a few choices: Clicking OK wipes the account from the system but you get to check off whether to save the person's home folder in a disk image (in an appropriately labeled Deleted Users folder), leave his or her home folder where it was in the Users folder, or delete the home folder altogether. The latter is reserved for users who were particularly naughty (and you don't need their files).

Changing Appearances

Now that you're past the unpleasant act of whacking someone from the system, you can get back in touch with your kinder, gentler side — the part of you solely occupied with making the Mac look pretty.

Altering buttons and the desktop

Are you not too keen on the look of the buttons, menus, and windows currently residing on your Mac? Is the wallpaper that Apple's interior designers put behind your desktop attractive enough but not to your taste? You can rip it down and start anew.

Choose System Preferences and then click General. This is where you can alter the menus and the color of those buttons, and apply other cosmetic touches. You can decide, for example, whether to show scroll bars or determine the behavior that occurs when you close documents and windows.

One of the items to consider is to select the Use LCD Font Smoothing When Available check box. Font smoothing reduces jagged edges for some fonts.

Then move on to the Desktop & Screen Saver screen in System Preferences to really start putting your stamp on the place. Make sure that the Desktop tab is highlighted, as shown in Figure 5-8. Click one of the design categories in the list on the left (Nature, Plants, and so on). Various design swatches appear on the right. Best of all, unlike the swatches a salesperson might show you in a home decorating store, you can see what a finished remodeling job here will look like. All you have to do is click.

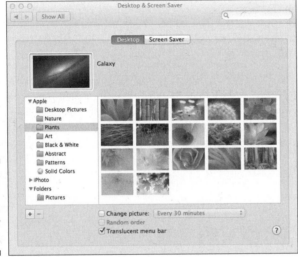

Figure 5-8:
Become
your own
interior
decorator.

The design categories on the left include listings for pictures, albums, and events from your iPhoto library (see Chapter 15). Clicking these options lets you choose one of your own images for the desktop background. Apple's designer collection has nothing over masterpieces that include your gorgeous child.

Choosing a screen saver

Screen savers are so named because they were created to save your screen from a ghostly phenomenon known as burn-in. Whenever the same fixed image was shown on a screen over long periods of time, a dim specter from that image would be permanently etched onto the display. Burn-in isn't much of an issue anymore due to the growing prevalence of LCD and LED displays, but the screen saver moniker survived. Today the value of the screen saver is strictly cosmetic, in the same way that you may choose a vanity license plate or a ring tone for your cell phone.

In the Desktop & Screen Saver pane of System Preferences, click the Screen Saver tab. (Not there? Choose System Preferences and then click Desktop & Screen Saver.)

Click one of the screen savers in the box on the left, as shown in Figure 5-9, choosing such effects as shifting tiles or sliding panels. You can eyeball screen savers in the small preview area to the right and pick the source of the pictures by clicking a drop-down dialog under the preview area. Images from National Geographic are particularly stunning, but I also recommend Cosmos or Nature Patterns. And you can choose slideshows from your own pictures as screen savers, using various special effects including one modeled after the work of documentary filmmaker Ken Burns. When you choose a slideshow, you then get to select the pictures folder to use as the source of that slideshow. Click the drop-down box in the preview area to make that selection. Click the Shuffle Slide Order check box to make the pictures appear in random order.

If you want to know what words such as *soporific* or *flume* mean, choose the Word of the Day screen saver. It's not as pretty as some other options, but at least it'll boost your vocabulary.

Love music? Consider Apple's iTunes Artwork screen saver, shown in Figure 5-10. This handsome grid of 40 album covers from your iTunes music library is constantly changing; every three seconds, one of the 40 album cover pictures is swapped for another picture.

Figure 5-9:
Beautifying your display with a screen saver.

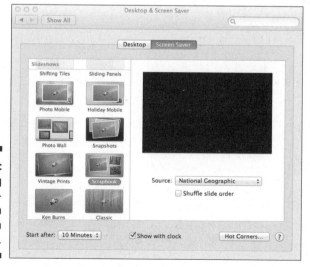

Figure 5-10:
This iTunes
Artwork
screen
saver is off
the charts.

If you want to display the time with your chosen screen saver, select the Show with Clock check box.

After choosing a screen saver (or again having Apple choose one for you randomly), choose a time for the screen saver to kick in from the Start After drop-down list. Your choices here range from 1 minute to 1 hour (or Never, which kind of renders the whole idea of a screen saver beside the point).

Tidying Up with Mission Control

You're so frantically busy that your papers end up strewn every which way, empty coffee cups litter your desk, and boxes pile on top of boxes. Worse, you can't lay your hands on the precise thing you need the very moment when you need it. Sound familiar? Psychiatrists have a technical name for this kind of disorder. It is called being a slob. (Takes one to know one.)

Things can get untidy on the Mac desktop, too, especially as you juggle several projects at once. At any given time, you may have opened System Preferences, Dictionary, Calendar, an e-mail program, numerous word processing documents, and then some. Windows lay on top of windows. Chaos abounds. You have fallen into the dark abyss that is multitasking.

Apple has the perfect tonic for MDLS (Messy Desktop Layered Syndrome), shown in Figure 5-11. The antidote is *Mission Control,* and it is as close as your F3 key on current Apple keyboards (and F9 or fn+F9 on older keyboards). Mission Control essentially merges features that were introduced by Apple in earlier versions of OS X. One was called Exposé, and it lives on within Mission Control. The other is called Spaces. Mission Control provides a unified view of everything on your system: Dashboard, any open desktops, full-screen applications that are open, plus other apps that are open.

Go ahead and press F3 now. Each previously open but obstructed window emerges from its hiding place, like crooks finally willing to give themselves up after a lengthy standoff. All the windows are proportionately (and simultaneously) downsized so that you can temporarily see them all at once, as shown in Figure 5-12.

You have several other ways to summon Mission Control. You can swipe up with three fingers on a trackpad. You can click the Mission Control icon in the dock. You can click the Mission control icon in Launchpad. Or you can double-tap (but not double-click) a Magic Mouse.

Under Mountain Lion, open windows in Mission Control view are neatly arranged in a grid with the title of the window below each one. At the upper-left portion of the Mission Control screen, you'll see a thumbnail window representing Dashboard, a repository for handy widgets that reveal the time, the weather, and other information. (This is the case anyway if you have selected the Show Dashboard as a Space option in the Mission Control section of System Preferences.) I'll have more to say about Dashboard in the next chapter.

Figure 5-11:
A cluttered desktop before putting Mission Control to work.

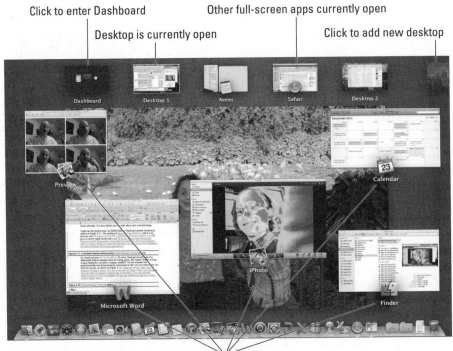

Click to enter Dashboard

Other full-screen apps currently open

Desktop is currently open

Click to add new desktop

Other open apps
(non-full screen)

Figure 5-12:
Mission
Control in
action.

To the right of Dashboard on the top row is a thumbnail with a white border around it. That's the desktop that you're currently working in. Adjacent to that desktop window are windows for any open full-screen apps that you have going at the moment. (The *full-screen* feature enables the app in question to take over the entire screen; you know you can go full-screen when you see a Full Screen icon in the upper right corner of an app window, identifiable as a slanting line with arrows on either end.)

Now while you're in Mission Control, move the cursor all the way to the upper-right corner of the screen. A partially obscured desktop thumbnail slides into view from the right side. It has + on it. Click the + to open a new desktop, which appears as a mini-representation inside Mission Control of that new desktop. You can drag an application window or icon to move it to the new space. You must leave Mission Control to see the "real" full-screen desktop.

If in Dock preferences you've specified that the Dock should appear on the right side of the screen rather than the bottom, then the mini-representation to open a new desktop appears from the left side of the screen rather than the right side.

This begs the question of why you'd want a new desktop in the first place. The answer is simple: You may want to keep only those programs and windows related to a distinct pastime in one dedicated location. Prior to OS X Lion (and Mountain Lion), Apple handled this in Spaces, which lets you display only the stuff required to tackle the projects at hand. Spaces is now part of Mission Control too.

So maybe you're an e-mailin', web-surfin' kind of dude. Maybe you're putting together a family scrapbook. And maybe you're writing a *For Dummies* book in your spare time. Either way, you may want desktops or spaces dedicated to those vocations.

To remove an extra desktop after your assignment is complete, roll your cursor over the Desktop thumbnail in Mission Control until a circled X appears. Click the X to make the desktop go away.

Below this top row of thumbnails are all the application windows that you are using at the moment (not those that you were using in full-screen mode).

If you move the cursor over one of the visible windows, you see a blue border framing the window. To bring that window front and center while leaving the other Mission Control windows as they are for the moment, press the spacebar on your keyboard. Alternatively, point to the window you want to bring to the front (to work on) and do one of the following: click inside the window or press either F9 or F3, depending on your keyboard.

Mission Control is good for a few other stunts, and these are the default keys to make them happen:

- ✔ **F10 (or Ctrl+F3 on the newer keyboards):** Opens all the windows in the application you're currently using. If you're working on a document in TextEdit, for instance, any other open documents in the program will also be brought to the front lines.

- ✔ **F11 (or ⌘+F3 on the new keyboard):** Hides all windows so that you can admire the stunning photograph you chose for your desktop.

If you have something against F9, F10, and F11 (or other keys you're using for Exposé), open System Preferences, choose Mission Control, and assign alternative keys. And if you have something against keys in general, you can arrange to have the Mac do its thing by moving the cursor to one of the four so called Hot Corners of the screen. For example, you can make Mission Control appear by moving the cursor to one of the designated corners. Other options on the drop-down Hot Corners menu let you summon application windows, your desktop, Dashboard, Notification Center, or Launchpad. You can also start or disable a screen saver from a Hot Corner. Or put the display to sleep from one.

You can designate your Hot Corner choices (assuming that you want to take advantage of the feature) from within the Desktop & Screen Saver screen of System preferences.

Take a gander at some of your other Mission Control options within System Preferences. You can select check boxes to show Dashboard as a space, to automatically rearrange spaces based on most recent use, to switch to a space with open windows for a given application, and to group windows by application.

When you're done with Mission Control, swipe three fingers down on the trackpad or double-tap the Magic Mouse. You can also click the desktop that you want to go to or one of the windows representing the application you want to work on.

Sitting Dockside

If you've been with me from the beginning, you know that the dock provides one-click access to the most called-upon applications, folders, and files on your Mac. And Exposé, now essentially folded into Mission Control, is a complementary system for making sure that you can quickly and easily get to the one app or file you need among all those you already have open. As part of the older Snow Leopard version of OS X, Apple figured out how to combine these functions in a feature then called Dock Exposé.

Here's how it worked. Say you've opened several web page windows through the Safari browser. Click and hold on the Safari icon in the dock, and all open windows attached to the app appear on the computer desktop lined up in neat rows. Select a window by clicking it or hover over it with your mouse and press the spacebar to make the window larger and easier to read. Clicking and holding on any other dock application works the same way; the windows belonging to the app are unshuffled and spread out like so many solitaire cards on your desktop.

In Mountain Lion, the behavior changed some: Now when you click and hold on the dock icon, a menu appears. Click Show All Windows to reveal the open windows.

Launching Launchpad

If you have an iPhone or iPad, the iOS-inspired Launchpad app launcher on your Mac will look awfully familiar — a screen decorated by colorful icons, as shown in Figure 5-13. Click an icon to launch the underlying program. If you have lots of programs on your system, you soon end up with multiple

Launchpad screens — the max number of icons displayed on any single Launchpad screens is 35.

To move from one Launchpad screen to another, just swipe with two fingers in either direction. Or, use your mouse to click a dot below all the icons, each one signifying one of your Launchpad screens.

You can find a single app if it's not immediately visible on the screen by typing its name in the search box provided at the top of each Launchpad page. As you type letters in this search box, Launchpad reduces the number of icons shown to only those that might make a match.

You can also organize icons into folders by simply dragging one on top of another. The idea is that you'd put all related icons in the same folder — one for your photography-related programs, say, and another for music. (See Figure 5-14 for an example.) As you do, Apple takes a stab at what it thinks the folder name should be, but don't fret if you're not happy with the given title. Click the title inside the folder and choose an alternative name more to your liking.

Launchpad Search field

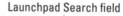

Figure 5-13: Launchpad is a jumping-off point for your apps.

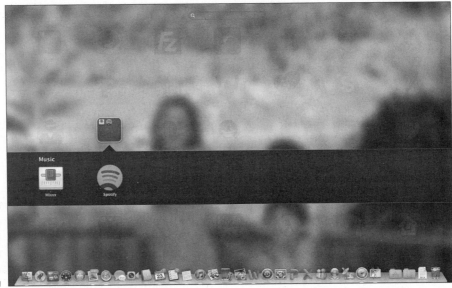

Figure 5-14:
Dragging
music apps
into a folder.

System Preferences: Choosing Priorities

You may be wondering what's left. I've already dug inside System Preferences
to alter the desktop and screen saver, establish parental controls, muck
around with Mission Control, and then some. But as Figure 5-15 shows, you
can still do a lot more. I explore some of these options now and some later in
other chapters.

Figure 5-15:
Doing it my
way through
System
Preferences.

Getting in sync with date and time

You established the date, time, and time zone when you set up the Mac initially (in Chapter 2). In System Preferences, you can change the appearance of the clock from a digital readout to an analog face with hands. If you choose a digital clock, you can flash the time separators — or not. You can display the time with seconds, use a 24-hour clock, or both. You can even have the Mac announce the time on the hour, the half hour, or the quarter hour and customize the voice you hear. Or, you can remove the date and time from the menu bar at the top of the screen. Finally, you can choose the time zone or let the Mac set the time zone automatically using your current location.

Displays

If you are hunky-dory with what your display looks like, feel free to ignore this section. Read on if you are the least bit curious about *resolution* and what changing it will do to your screen. Resolution is a measure of sharpness and is expressed by tiny picture elements, or *pixels*. *Pixels* is such a nice-sounding word that I always thought it would make a terrific name for a breakfast cereal, something like new Kellogg's *Sugar-Coated Pixels.* But I digress.

Apple really does try to make this stuff simple. So you'll see a setting by default that is meant to be best suited for your computer. For example, on the MacBook Pro with the Retina display, the default that is already checked off is the resolution that Apple has determined is "Best for Retina Display." If you deselect that check box and choose "Scaled" instead, you see other options for showing off larger text or a setting that shrinks everything so that you have more space on the screen.

By contrast, on a MacBook Air without the Retina display, you can leave the default "Best for Built-in Display" option selected. But if you go with "Scaled" again, you see resolution choices written out as 1440 x 900, 1280 x 800, 1152 x 720, 1024 x 768, and so on. The first number refers to the number of pixels horizontally, and the second number is the number of pixels vertically. Higher numbers reflect higher resolution, meaning that the picture is sharper and you can fit more things on the screen. At lower resolutions, the images may be larger but fuzzier, though this depends on your monitor. The resolution options you see in System Preferences vary according to the Mac you have. Lower resolutions also *refresh,* or update, more quickly, though you'll be hard-pressed to see this with most modern monitors. As it happens, the refresh rate doesn't mean boo on iMacs or laptops with LCD or flat-panel displays.

You can also calibrate the color that a Mac displays. Best advice: Play around with these settings if you must. More often than not, you can leave well enough alone.

Sound

Ever wonder what the *Basso* sound is? Or *Sosumi* or *Tink?* I'd play them for you if this was an enhanced e-book, but because it isn't, check out these and other sound effects in System Preferences. You'll hear one of them whenever the Mac wants to issue an alert. Sound Preferences is also the place to adjust speaker balance, microphone settings, and pretty much anything else having to do with what you hear on the Mac.

Software update

Your Mac may be a machine, but it still has organic traits. And Apple hasn't forgotten about you just because you've already purchased one of its prized computers. From time to time, the company will issue new releases of certain programs to add features it won't make you pay for, to *patch* or fix bugs or to thwart security threats. For a full log, click Installed Updates.

You can have the Mac check for automatic software updates, including system data files and security updates. If you choose, the Mac will fetch important updates in the background and bother you only when the program update is ready to be installed. Software Update is accessible also directly from the menu.

Apple now makes system and third-party software updates available through the Mac App Store. In Software Update preferences, you can select an option to automatically download apps purchased on other Macs, according to the Apple ID account you use to sign in to the App Store. Through Notification Center, you will be notified when a system update is available.

Accessibility

Some physically challenged users may require special help controlling the Mac. Choose Accessibility under System Preferences, and click the option that you need assistance with under headings Seeing, Hearing, and Interacting. (Some of the options are visible in Figure 5-16.)

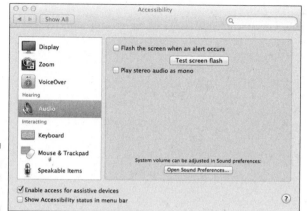

Figure 5-16:
Accessibility
preferences.

Among the options, you can arrange to

✔ Turn on the built-in screen reader, VoiceOver, to hear descriptions of what's on your display. And by opening the VoiceOver utility, you can change the default voice.

✔ Enhance the contrast or alter the display from black on white to white on black.

✔ Flash the screen when an alert sound occurs.

✔ Zoom in on the screen to make everything appear larger. Or enlarge the size of the pointer if you have trouble seeing the mouse cursor.

✔ Use a Slow Keys function to put a delay between when a key is pressed and when the result of that key press is accepted. Or, if you can't easily press several keys at once, use Sticky Keys to press groups of modifier keys (Shift, ⌘, Option, and Control) in a sequence.

Your computer can recognize most Braille displays the moment you plug them in. Mac OS X systems even can recognize wireless Bluetooth displays in Braille.

You can call upon an Accessibility pane no matter what you are doing on your Mac. On the keyboard, press ⌘+Option+F5 to summon this helpful toolkit or to get to the aforementioned Accessibility preferences.

The Mac may share a nickname with a certain McDonald's hamburger. But it's actually an old Burger King slogan that is most apt when describing your computer. As this chapter has shown, you can "have it your way."

Chapter 6

Apple's Feline Fetish

· ·

· ·

The late Apple cofounder and CEO Steve Jobs was apparently fond of big cats. Before Apple unleashed Mountain Lion, previous versions of Mac OS X software carried such *purr-fect* monikers as Cheetah, Puma, Jaguar, Panther, Tiger, Leopard, Snow Leopard, and Lion. (Apple used the code words Cheetah and Puma internally.) It was unclear as this book went to press, which cat Apple was breeding inside its Cupertino, California, cages. A Lynx perhaps?

As strong a release as it is, the name OS X just doesn't have the bite that Mountain Lion or any of the other giant kitty nicknames command. However, X (for ten) is the most celebrated use of roman numerals this side of the Super Bowl.

Mountain Lion actually represents OS X version 10.8. Apple used to update its operating system every 18 months to two years, give or take. The company now plans to bring out a new iteration of its operating system software more on a yearly basis, typically with a boatload of new features and identified by an increased decimal point. Apple says OS X version 10.8 Mountain Lion piled more than 200 new features onto its predecessor version 10.7 Lion. I never counted.

During the year, Apple will make interim tweaks to its operating system. You will know because the OS takes on an extra decimal digit. At the time of this writing, Apple was up to OS X version 10.8.2 (pronounced "ten dot eight dot two"). I wonder how many features must be added before Apple changes the designation to OS XI.

To check out the version of Mac software running on your system, choose About This Mac. Choose Software Update to see whether the OS (and, for that matter, other programs) are up to date. And with Mountain Lion, Apple delivers updates through the Mac App Store. It's also the only supported way to upgrade the very operating system, should you still own a Mac running Lion or some prior version of OS X.

The cost of a Mountain Lion upgrade is $19.99, and you will need a Mac that meets the minimum requirements. That's an iMac dating to the middle of 2007 or newer, a Mac mini from early 2009 or newer, a MacBook from late 2008 or newer, a MacBook Air from late 2008 or newer, a Mac Pro from early 2008 or newer or an Xserve from early 2009 or newer. You would also need to have been running Lion to upgrade to Mountain Lion.

How Many Features? Let Me Count the Ways

As noted, Apple added more than 200 features to the Mac OS in Mountain Lion, on top of the hundreds it added previously in Lion, in Snow Leopard and so on. Mountain Lion brought OS X a bit closer to iOS, the operating system at the core of Apple's iPhone and iPad. Indeed, some of the features found in Mountain Lion — Reminders, Notes, Messages, Notification Center, Game Center, among them — made their first appearance in iOS. And Mountain Lion was Apple's first OS X release since unveiling iCloud, the subject of Chapter 12.

I've already discussed some of these features already, and I will get around to other enhancements throughout the book. And though not the focus of this book, let me mention that Apple aimed many new features at Chinese users, with improved text input for Simplified and Traditional Chinese, and support for Sina Weibo, a popular microblogging service in China.

Disclaimer: I'm not trying to demean any of these enhancements. These obviously provide great value to someone, just not your average U.S. consumer. (Danish spell checker, anyone?) Feel free to skip ahead.

Searching with Spotlight

Part of what makes OS X so powerful is *Spotlight,* the marvelous desktop search utility that debuted with Tiger and improved with subsequent versions of OS X. Search is a big deal. A computer isn't much good if you can't easily lay your hands on the documents, pictures, e-mail messages, and programs you need at any particular moment. When most people think about searching on a computer, they probably have Google, Yahoo!, Bing, or some other Internet search engine in mind. Internet search is of course a big deal too, and I spend some time discussing it in Chapter 9.

The searching I have in mind here, however, involves the contents of your own system. Over time, Mac users accumulate thousands of photos, songs, school reports, work projects, contacts, calendar entries — you name it. Spotlight helps you locate them in a blink. It starts spitting out search results before you finish typing.

What's even better is that Spotlight can uncover material in documents and files. That's incredibly useful if you haven't the foggiest idea what you named a file.

You can use Spotlight by following these steps:

1. **Click the magnifying glass icon in the upper-right corner of the menu bar.**

   Or press ⌘ and the spacebar simultaneously. (Select the check box under Spotlight in System Preferences if the shortcut doesn't work.) The Spotlight search box appears.

2. **Enter the word or phrase you want to search for.**

   The instant you type the first letter, a window shows up with what Spotlight considers the most likely search matches. The search is immediately refined as you type extra keystrokes, as shown in Figure 6-1.

Say you're planning a tropical vacation and remember that your cousin Gilligan e-mailed you a while back raving about the beach at some deserted Pacific island. You can open the Mac Mail program and dig for the missive from the dozens that Gilligan sent you. (Evidently, he had a lot of time on his hands.) But it's far simpler and faster to type Gilligan's name in Spotlight.

Or maybe you want to give Gilligan a quick buzz. Without Spotlight, you would probably open your Contacts to find your cousin's phone number. The faster way is to type **Gilligan** in Spotlight and then click his name next to Contacts in the results window. Contacts opens, displaying Gilligan's contact page.

Rummaging through your stuff

Spotlight is built in to the very fabric of the operating system. Quietly behind the scenes, Spotlight indexes, or catalogs, most files on the computer so that you can access them in a moment's notice. The index is seamlessly updated each time you add, move, modify, copy, or delete a file.

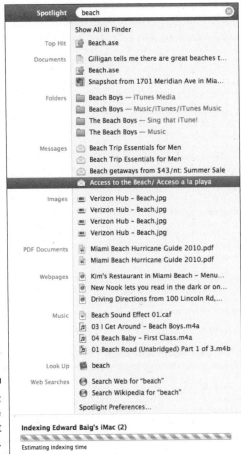

Figure 6-1:
The
Spotlight
search box.

Moreover, Spotlight automatically rummages through *metadata,* the informa-tion about your data. Digital photographs, for example, typically capture the following metadata: the camera model used to snap the image, the date, the aperture and exposure settings, whether a flash was used, and so on. For example, if a friend e-mails you pictures taken with a Sony camera, you can quickly find those images — as opposed to, say, the pictures you took with your own Canon — by entering the search term *Sony.*

Spotlight is one confident sucker. It boldly takes a stab at what it thinks is the *top hit,* or search result you have in mind. The top hit in Figure 6-1 is an Adobe Swatch Exchange file called Beach.ase, not necessarily what I was looking for. So Spotlight's track record is pretty good but not perfect. If it guesses right, click the Top Hit entry or press Return or Enter. That will launch the appli-cation in question, open a particular file, or display the appropriate folder in Finder. As is often the case, you'll find a shortcut. Press ⌘ and Return to launch the top hit.

Spotlight is arguably the zippiest way to launch an application. Just start typing its name into the Spotlight search field, and it should show up as the top hit after only a few letters (and sometimes a single keystroke). Press Return to launch the program.

As you roll the cursor over the Spotlight list, a Quick Look window appears to the left of the list, showing the photo, e-mail, or whatever file is the object of your search.

Of course, as noted previously, Spotlight isn't always going to get the top hit right, so it also displays what it considers to be the next 20 or so most likely matches. Results are segregated into categories (Applications, Documents, Folders, PDF Documents, Music, Messages, Images, Movies, Bookmarks, and so on). Again, just click an item to launch or open it.

Click at the bottom of the list to search the web for your chosen topic (beach, in this case) or the Wikipedia online encyclopedia.

Some searches yield more than 20 or so possible outcomes — often a heck of a lot more. That's what Show All in Finder (refer to Figure 6-1) is all about. Clicking Show All in Finder doesn't, in fact, show you everything. Most of the time, your screen wouldn't be nearly big enough. Instead, Show All opens a separate Finder window like the one shown in Figure 6-2. And as you are about to see, it is a pretty powerful window indeed.

If you get a flood of results and aren't sure which is the one you're looking for, Spotlight provides a good spot to use the Quick Look feature. (See Chapter 3.) Just click the Quick Look icon and, well, have a quick look at the sorted files until you find the proper one.

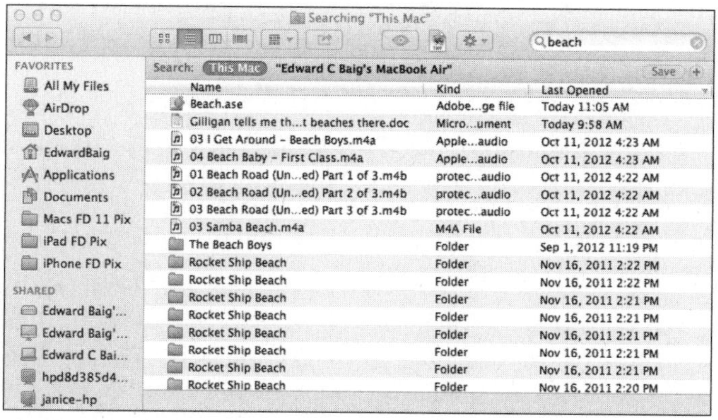

Figure 6-2: Spotlighting the Spotlight results in a Finder window.

You can't search every internal file with Spotlight or, for that matter, display them through Quick Look — at least not without a software add-on called a *plug-in*. Bento and FileMaker databases and InDesign and Quark documents are among the files that are in this category.

Intelligent searching

You can customize search results in numerous ways by telling Spotlight where to search and by telling it, in precise detail, the criteria to use in that search.

Look over here

I'll start with where to look. If the contents you're searching for reside on the Mac before your very eyes (as opposed to another on your network), make sure that the Search: This Mac button (refer to Figure 6-2) is the one you choose.

The button to its immediate right changes depending upon what you have highlighted and what you are searching. In Figure 6-2, you see All My Files (refer to Figure 6-2), also found under Favorites in the navigation tree to the left. Choosing either option tells Spotlight to look nowhere else but in that folder (and its subfolders).

Sometimes, the next button shows any other computer on your network for which you have sharing rights. In Figure 6-2, my MacBook Air is visible even though the Finder window shown resides on my iMac.

The Shared option will not appear if no other Mac is on your network with file sharing turned on. Indeed, you'll have to set up the computers so that they're in a sharing mood (see Chapter 18 for more).

Search this, not that

Now that Spotlight knows where to set its sights, it's time to tell it what exactly you are looking for. Do you want Spotlight to search for an item by its filename? Or do you want it to hunt for nuggets buried somewhere deep inside those files? Remember that in searching for something, you don't necessarily want to cast too wide a net.

The best way to narrow results is to enter as specific a search term as possible right off the bat. As you plan your vacation, typing **beach** will probably summon the e-mail message Gilligan sent you. But because Spotlight will find *all* files or programs that match that text, results may also include PowerPoint presentations with a beach theme, pictures of your family by the seashore, and songs on your hard drives sung by the Beach Boys. Typing **Gilligan** and **beach** together will help you fine-tune your search.

If you know the type of item you're looking for, such as Gilligan's e-mail as opposed to his picture, you can filter the search in another way. Enter the search term followed by *kind,* a colon, and the file type you are looking for, as in

```
Gilligan kind:email
```

If you want to search for a presentation someone sent you on the world's best seaside resorts but can't remember whether the presentation was created in AppleWorks (a discontinued Apple office-type suite prior to iWork), Keynote, or PowerPoint, try

```
seaside resort kind:presentations
```

And if you want to search only for presentations opened in the past week, type

```
seaside resort kind:presentations date:last week
```

To search for an application such as Microsoft Word, type

```
Word kind:application
```

To search Gilligan's contact information, type

```
Gilligan kind:contacts
```

To search for music, type

```
Beach Boys kind:music
```

To search for pictures at the beach, type

```
Beach kind:images
```

And so on. The kind keywords all date back to OS X Tiger, when Spotlight was introduced. Such keywords were expanded since, so you can now use a label such as author, as in author:baig, or width, as in width:768-1024.

Here are a few other advanced Spotlight techniques:

✔ **Boolean query:** You can enter a search phrase using AND, NOT, or OR (in caps as shown) within parentheses. So you can type **(Mary Ann OR Ginger) NOT Mrs. Howell** to bring up references to either of the first two castaways but not the millionaire's wife. You can substitute a hyphen (-) for NOT, as in *vacation - island* to indicate that you don't want to see any trip pictures from your tropical adventures.

- **Dates:** By entering **kind:message created 3/11/12**, you can search for an e-mail you sent on March 11 wishing a pal a happy birthday. You can also enter a range of dates as in **kind:images date 3/11/12 - 3/15/12**.

- **Quotes and phrases:** By placing quotation marks around a particular phrase, Spotlight will search for that exact phrase. If looking for a song with *Blue Sky* in it, put quotes around the phrase (as in *"Blue Sky"*) to have Spotlight look for that precise match. Otherwise, Spotlight will search for anything with the words *blue* and *sky* in it.

- **Look Up:** In Chapter 3, I introduce Dictionary as one of the freebie programs that come on a Mac. Thanks to Spotlight, you can get to the word you want the meaning of in a hurry. Type the word you have in mind in the Spotlight search field, and along with all the other results, Spotlight will give you a Look Up option. Click Look Up and Spotlight will take you to Dictionary.

- **Calculator:** Spotlight will solve a math problem for you without you having to summon the Calculator program. Just type the problem or math equation in the search box, and Spotlight will serve up the result. For example, to divide 654 by 7, all you need to do is type in **654/7**, and Spotlight will provide the answer (93.428571429).

- **Web history:** Spotlight follows you around the web — sort of. That is, it indexes the names of sites you've recently visited. Just enter a search query that relates to a site you want to return to.

Searching your way

As the boss, you can specify which categories will appear in Spotlight search results. To do so, open Spotlight Preferences by clicking at the bottom of the Spotlight results window or from the main System Preferences window. With the Search Results tab selected, you can select or deselect the types of items you want Spotlight to search, as shown in Figure 6-3. You can also drag the categories in the order in which you want results to appear.

If you click the Privacy tab, you can prevent Spotlight from searching particular locations. Click the Add button (+) or drag folders or disks into the Privacy pane to let Spotlight know that these are off-limits. Spotlight will remove any associated files from the index and prevent you from searching items in the directory in question.

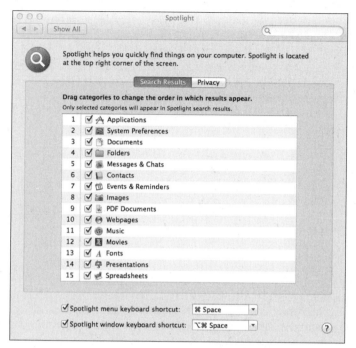

Smart Folders

When you go to all the trouble of selecting specific attributes for your search query, you may want to revisit the search in the future — incorporating the latest information, of course. And that's why the Finder's Spotlight window has the handy Save button that you read about in the previous section. And there's an important wrinkle to that Save button that is worth expanding upon.

Traditionally, the files on your computer are organized by their location on your disk. *Smart Folders* change the organizing principle based on the search criteria you've chosen. These folders don't give a hoot where the actual files that match your search criteria reside on the machine. Those stay put in their original location. You are, in effect, working on *aliases*, or shortcuts, of those files. (See the next chapter for more on aliases.)

What's more, behind the scenes, Smart Folders are constantly on the prowl for new items that match your search criteria. In other words, they're updated in real time.

To create a Smart Folder, click that Save button in the Finder window and your Smart Folder from here on will get updated as need be in real time. (The Save button is shown in the upper right in Figure 6-2.) Alternatively, in the Finder, choose File⇨New Smart Folder to create a new Smart Folder. A box pops up asking you to specify a name and destination for your newly created

Smart Folder, as shown in Figure 6-4. If you want, select the Add to Sidebar check box to easily find the Smart Folder you just created.

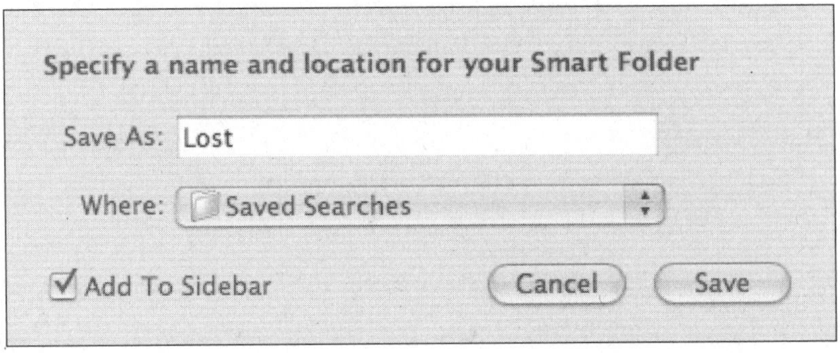

Specify a name and location for your Smart Folder

Save As: Lost

Figure 6-4:
Here's
the Smart
Folder win-
dow.

Where: Saved Searches

☑ Add To Sidebar   (Cancel)   (Save)

Figure 6-4:
Here's
the Smart
Folder win-
dow.

A premade Smart Folder already exists in the sidebar labeled Documents. But you may want to create a simple Smart Folder containing all the documents you've worked on in the past seven days. Give it an original name. Oh, I dunno, something like *What a Hellish Week!* In any case, all your recent stuff is easily at your disposal. Your older documents will pass new arrivals on their way out.

Fiddling with Dashboard Widgets

Apart from prowling the virtual corridors of cyberspace or interacting with Apple's iLife programs, most of your face time on a Mac will find you engaged with some full-blown (and often pricey) software application — even if you take advantage of a relatively narrow set of features.

The wordsmiths among you couldn't subsist without Microsoft Word or some other industrial-strength word processor. You graphic artists live and breathe Adobe Photoshop. But personal computing isn't always about doctoring photos or penning the great American novel (or a *For Dummies* book). Sometimes all you want is a quick snippet of information — the temperature, a stock quote, or a phone number.

That's what a gaggle of mini-applications known as *widgets* are all about. Indeed, these lightweight programs generally serve a useful and singular purpose: from letting you track an overnight package to finding out whether your favorite team covered the spread. Frankly, you can perform many of these tasks through the web or other programs on your desktop. But few do it with the convenience and flair of widgets.

Fronted by large colorful icons, widgets come at you en masse when you summon *Dashboard.* This translucent screen, shown in Figure 6-5, lies on top of your desktop. Nothing underneath is disturbed.

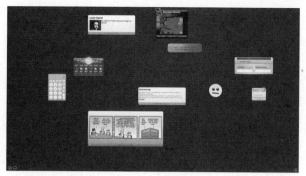

Figure 6-5:
Widgets
star in the
Dashboard
collection.

To open Dashboard, swipe with three or four fingers to the right on the trackpad or click the Dashboard icon in the dock if the icon is there. Or you can press the F12 key on older keyboards or F4 on newer Apple keyboards. Pressing the key again closes Dashboard. You can exit also by clicking the right-pointing arrow inside a circle at the lower-right corner of the screen.

To get you started, Apple supplies a collection of basic widgets (Calculator, Clock, Calendar, Weather). Thousands more widgets, many of great interest, are available online. You can embark on a widget hunt at `www.apple.com/downloads/dashboard`. Another way to get there is to right-click (or Control-click) the Dashboard icon in the dock and click More Widgets.

When you call up Dashboard, only the widgets you previously used and haven't closed appear on the screen, right where you left them. The rest in your collection are hanging out behind the scenes. Click the + button in the lower-left corner of the screen to access them on a display similar to what is shown in Figure 6-6. If you want to enlist one of these backstage widgets, just click its icon, and it makes it onto the grand Dashboard. You can also drag one widget on top of another to place them into a folder, just as you were able to do in the Launchpad feature described in Chapter 5.

Figure 6-6:
Widget-
mania after
clicking
the +.

While on this screen, you'll notice the More Widgets button at the lower left, leading you again to a page on Apple's website where you can find some more cool widgets.

If you want to move any of your widgets backstage again, click the dash inside a circle. An X button will appear on all the widgets. Click the X on the widget you want to usher out of the way.

The great majority of downloadable widgets are gratis. A few are available as *shareware,* meaning that you can try them before paying. Whether you fork over the loot is up to your conscience, but unless you think the program is worthless, its creator should be rewarded for his or her efforts.

Some widgets are extensions to other programs on your computer, such as the ones that display data from Calendar or your Contacts or bring up blank Sticky Notes. But most widgets grab feeds off the Internet, so you need an online connection. Widgets in this category might tell you what's on the tube tonight or deliver a surfing report (on waves, dude, not cyberspace).

Chapter 7
Handling All That Busy Work

- -

In This Chapter

▶ Preparing your documents

▶ Selecting text

▶ Dragging, dropping, cutting, and pasting

▶ Revealing fonts

▶ Formatting documents

▶ Dictating text

▶ Saving your work

▶ Making revisions

▶ Taking out the trash

▶ Understanding aliases

- -

*I*n professional football, the skill position players — quarterback, running backs, and wide receivers — get a disproportionate amount of the glory when a team wins and assume most of the blame when they fall on their collective fannies. But any halfway-competent field general will tell you that those in the trenches typically determine the outcome.

Sure, you want to draw up a razzamatazz game plan for your Mac. Probably something involving stupendous graphics and spine-tingling special effects. A high-tech flea-flicker, to keep it in the gridiron vernacular.

After all, you bought the computer with the intention of becoming the next Mozart, Picasso, or at the very least Steve Jobs. (*What, you expected Peyton or Eli Manning?*)

But for this one itty-bitty chapter, I am asking you to keep your expectations in check. You have to make first downs before you make touchdowns. Forget heaving Hail Marys down the field. You're better off grinding out yardage the tough way.

In coach-speak, the mission of the moment is to master the computing equivalent of blocking and tackling: basic word processing and the other fundamentals required to get you through your daily routine.

Practice these now. You can pour the Gatorade on my head later.

Form and Function: The Essentials of Word Processing

I'm old enough to recall life before word processors. (Hey, it wasn't *that* long ago.)

I can't possibly begin to fathom how we survived in the days before every last one of us had access to word processors and computers on our respective desks.

Pardon the interruption, but I'm not thrilled with the preceding sentence. Kind of wordy and repetitious. Permit me to get right to the point.

I can't imagine how any of us got along without word processors.

Thanks, much more concise.

The purpose of this mini-editing exercise is to illustrate the splendor of word processing. Had I produced these sentences on a typewriter instead of a computer, changing even a few words would hardly seem worth it. I would have to use correction fluid to erase my previous comments and type over them. If things got really messy, or if I wanted to take my writing in a different direction, I'd end up yanking the sheet of paper from the typewriter in disgust and begin pecking away anew on a blank page.

Word processing lets you substitute words at will, move entire blocks of text around with panache, and display characters in various typefaces or using specific fonts. You won't even take a productivity hit swapping typewriter ribbons (or swapping out balls with different fonts) in the middle of a project, though, as the next chapter reveals, you will at some point have to replace the ink in your printer.

Before running out to buy Microsoft Word (or another industrial-strength and expensive) word processing program for your Mac — and I'm not suggesting you don't — it's my obligation to point out that Apple includes a respectable word processor with OS X. The program is *TextEdit,* and it calls the Applications folder home. TextEdit will be our classroom for much of this chapter.

Creating a Document

The first order of business in using TextEdit (or pretty much any word processor) is to create a new *document.* There's really not much to it. It's about as easy as opening the program itself. The moment you do so, a window with a large blank area on which to type appears, as Figure 7-1 shows.

Figure 7-1:
In the beginning was a blank page.

Have a look around the window. There at the top, you see *Untitled* because no one at Apple is presumptuous enough to come up with a name for your yet-to-be-produced manuscript. I get around to naming (and saving) your stuff later. In my experience, it helps to write first and add a title later, though, um, scholars may disagree.

Notice the blinking vertical line at the upper-left edge of the screen, just below the ruler. That line, called the *insertion point,* might as well be tapping out Morse code for "start typing here."

Indeed, friends, you have come to the most challenging point in the entire word processing experience, and believe me it has nothing to do with the software. The burden is on you to produce clever, witty, and inventive prose, lest all that blank space go to waste.

Okay, get it? At the blinking insertion point, type with abandon. Something original like

> It was a dark and stormy night

If you type like I do, you may have accidentally produced

> It was a drk and stormy nihgt

Fortunately, your amiable word processor has your best interests at heart. See the dotted red line below *drk* and *nihgt* in Figure 7-2? That's TextEdit's not-so-subtle way of flagging a likely typo. This presumes that you've left the default Check Spelling as You Type activated in TextEdit Preferences. That seems like a safe presumption because you're at the beginning of this exercise. (You can also have TextEdit automatically correct your spelling mistakes by checking off that option in Preferences, but for the moment, I'll stick to the default.)

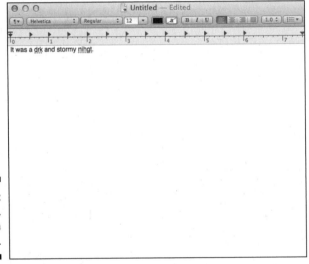

Figure 7-2:
Oops,
I made a
mistake.

You can address these snafus in several ways. You can use the computer's Delete key to wipe out all the letters to the left of the insertion point. After the misspelled word has been quietly sent to Siberia, you can type over the space more carefully. All traces of your sloppiness disappear.

Delete is a wonderfully handy key. I'd recommend using it to eliminate a single word such as *nihgt*. But in our little case study, we have to repair *drk* too. And using Delete to erase *drk* means sacrificing *and* and *stormy* as well. Kind of overkill if you ask me.

Back to football. It's time to call an audible. A few quick options:

- ✔ Use the left-facing arrow key (found on the lower-right side of the keyboard) to move the insertion point to the spot just to the right of the word you want to deep-six. No characters are eliminated when you move the insertion point that way. Only when the insertion point is where it ought to be do you again hire your reliable keyboard hit-man, Delete.

- ✔ Eschew the keyboard and click with the mouse to reach this same spot to the right of the misspelled word. Then press Delete.

- ✔ Of course you need not delete anything. You can merely place the insertion point after the *d* and type an *a*.

Now try this helpful remedy. Right-click (or Control-click) anywhere on the misspelled word. A list appears with suggestions, as shown in Figure 7-3. Single-click the correct word, and voila, it instantly replaces the mistake. Be careful in this example not to choose *dork*.

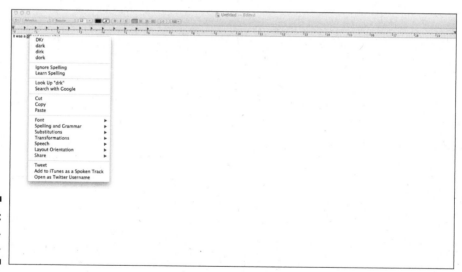

Figure 7-3:
I'm no dork.
I fixed it.

Selecting Text in a Document

You can try another experiment. Double-click a word. See what happens. It's as if you ran a light-blue marker across the word. You've *highlighted,* or *selected,* this word so that it can be deleted, moved, or changed.

Many times, you'll want to select more than a single word. Perhaps a complete sentence. Or a paragraph. Or several paragraphs. Here's how to highlight a block of text to delete it:

1. **Using the mouse, point to the block in question.**

2. **Press and hold down the left mouse button and drag the cursor (which bears a slight resemblance to the Seattle Space Needle) across the entire section you want to highlight.**

   The direction in which you drag the mouse affects what gets highlighted. If you drag horizontally, a single line is selected. Dragging vertically selects an entire block. You can highlight text also by holding down Shift and using the arrow keys.

3. **Release the mouse button when you reach the end of the passage that you want highlighted, as shown with *Once upon a time* in Figure 7-4.**

4. **To immediately wipe out the selected text, press Delete.**

   Alternatively, start typing. Your old material is exorcised upon your very first keystroke and replaced with the new characters you type.

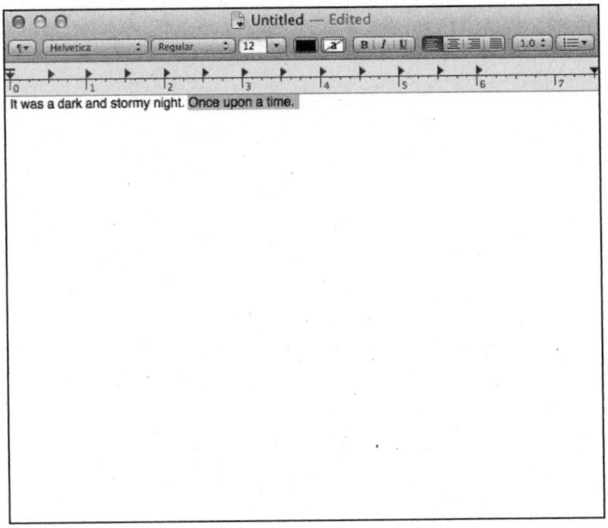

Figure 7-4:
Highlighting
text.

To jump to a specific line of text, choose Edit⇨Find⇨Select Line. Then enter its line number and click Select. Or to jump ahead, say, five lines, add the + symbol, as in +5. To jump backward five lines, enter –5 instead. In both instances, click Select.

To select several pages of text at once, single-click at the beginning portion of the material you want to select, and then scroll to the very bottom. While holding down the Shift key, click again. Everything between clicks is highlighted.

Now suppose you were overzealous and selected too much text. Or maybe you released the mouse button a bit too soon so that not enough of the passage you have in mind was highlighted. Just click once with your mouse to deselect the selected area and try again.

Another screwup. This time, you annihilated text that upon further review you want to keep. Fortunately, the Mac lets you perform a do-over. Choose Edit⇨Undo Typing. The text is miraculously revived. Variations of this lifesaving Undo command can be found in most of the Mac programs you encounter. So before losing sleep over some silly thing you did on the computer, visit the Edit menu and check out your Undo options.

Dragging and Dropping

In Chapter 3, I discuss *dragging and dropping* to move icons to the dock. In this chapter, you drag an entire block of text to a new location and leave it there.

Select a passage in one of the ways mentioned in the preceding section. Now, anywhere on the highlighted area, click and hold down the mouse button. Roll the mouse across a flat surface to drag the text to its new destination. Release the mouse button to drop off the text. And if you hold down the Option key, you can drag a copy, which allows you to duplicate a passage without having to cut and paste (see next section).

The preceding paragraph presupposes that you're using a mouse. Using a trackpad to select or highlight text takes a different skill: Press and hold down against the surface of the trackpad with your index finger. Then, without lifting your index finger, drag your middle finger along the surface to select the material you have in mind. At that point, you can release your fingers.

You are not restricted to dragging and dropping text in the program you're working in. For example, you can lift text completely out of TextEdit and place it into Word, Sticky Notes, or Pages, Apple's own word processing program for (among other things) producing spiffy newsletters and brochures.

Alternatively, if you know you'll want to use a text block in another program at some point in the future — you just don't know when — drop it directly onto the Mac desktop (see Figure 7-5) and call upon it whenever necessary.

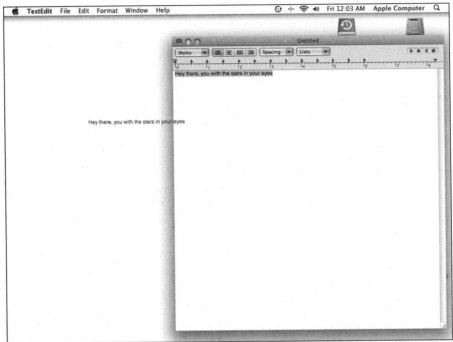

Figure 7-5:
Dropping
text on the
desktop.

Text copied to the desktop is shown as an icon and named from text in the beginning of the selection you copied. Moving text in this manner to an external program or the desktop constitutes a Copy command, not a Move command, so the lifted text remains in the original source.

Cutting and Pasting

In the preceding section, you selected material from one location and moved a copy to another location. By contrast, cutting and pasting lifts material from one spot and moves it elsewhere without leaving anything behind. (In the typewriter era, you literally cut out passages of paper with scissors and pasted them onto new documents.)

After selecting your source material, choose Edit⇨Cut (or press the keyboard alternative ⌘+X). To paste to a new location, first navigate there, click the spot and then choose Edit⇨Paste (or press ⌘+V). If you want to match the style of the text you're moving, click Paste and Match Style instead.

The Cut command is easily confused with the Copy command (⌘+C). As the name suggests, the latter copies selected text that can be pasted somewhere else. Cut clips text out of its original spot.

The very last thing you copied or cut is temporarily sheltered on the clipboard. It remains there until it's replaced by newer material that you copy or cut.

If you can't remember what you last placed on the clipboard, open Finder and choose Edit➪Show Clipboard.

Changing the Font

When typewriters were in vogue, you were usually pretty much limited to the typeface of the machine. Computers being computers, you can alter the appearance of individual characters and complete words effortlessly. I'll start with something simple.

In TextEdit, take a gander at the tiny B, I, and U buttons on the toolbar above the ruler. They stand for Bold, Italic, and Underline. (You see these same choices on the Font submenu, found under the Format menu within TextEdit.) Try these now. Click the I, and highlighted text becomes *text*. Now try B for Bold. Highlighted text becomes **text**. Now try U for Underline. Highlighted text becomes <u>text</u>.

I recommend using keyboard shortcuts in this instance. Just before typing a word, try pressing ⌘+I for *italics* or ⌘+B for **bold**. When you want to revert to normal type, just press those respective keyboard combinations again.

Making words bold or italic is the tip of the proverbial iceberg. You may want to experiment with other choices under the Font menu. You can make text take on a faint tint (Outlined). You can change the kerning (spacing), ligatures (the stroke that joins adjacent letters, according to the Dictionary on the Mac), baselines, or character shape.

For a more dramatic statement, you might dress up documents with different *fonts,* or typefaces.

Open the Format menu and choose Font➪Show Fonts. The window in Figure 7-6 appears. You can change the typeface of any highlighted text by clicking a font listed in the pane labeled Family. Choices carry names such as Arial, Baghdad, Chalkboard, Courier, Desdemona, Helvetica, Papyrus, Stencil, and Times New Roman.

Unless you wrote your graduate thesis on *fontomology* (don't bother looking up the word; it's my invention), no one on the *For Dummies* faculty expects you to have a clue about what any of the aforementioned fonts look like. I sure don't. Cheating is okay. Peek at your document to see how highlighted words in the text change after clicking different font choices.

As usual, another way to view different fonts is available. In the lower-left corner of the Fonts window, click the icon that looks like a gear or cog. Choose Show Preview from the menu that appears. You'll be able to inspect various font families and typefaces in the preview pane that appears above your selection. To revert to the status quo, click the gear icon again and then choose Hide Preview from the menu that appears. (See Figure 7-7.)

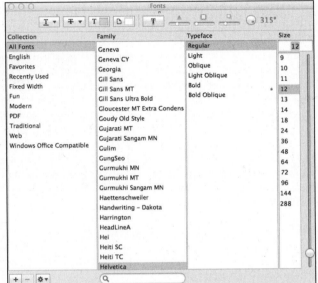

Figure 7-6:
A fonts
funhouse.

You can also preview the type size of your chosen font, as measured by a standard unit called points. In general, 1 inch has 72 points.

Revealing the Font Book

You likely have more than a hundred fonts on your computer, if not a lot more. Some were supplied with TextEdit. Some arrived with other word processing programs. You may have even gone on a font hunt and added more yourself from the Internet. At the end of the day, you may need help managing and organizing them.

Previewing your font

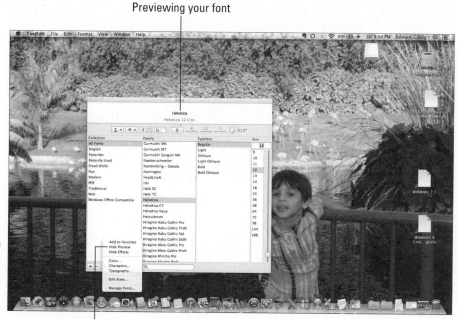

Figure 7-7:
Previewing
your fonts.

Hide/show font preview

That's the purpose behind an OS X program called *Font Book,* found in the
Applications folder. It's shown in Figure 7-8. Think of Font Book as a gallery to
show off all your finest fonts. Indeed, fonts here can be grouped into *font collections,* shown in the left panel. Choices here include English, Fixed Width,
Fun, Modern, PDF, Traditional, and Web. The Traditional collection, for example, assembles classic fonts with names such as Baskerville, Copperplate,
and Didot.

You can create your own font collections by choosing File➪New Collection
and typing a name for the collection. Then just drag fonts from the Font
column into your new collection.

By clicking a name in the Font column, you can sample what your font of
choice looks like in the pane on the right. Drag the slider (labeled in Figure 7-8)
to the right of that pane to adjust the type size of the fonts you're sampling.

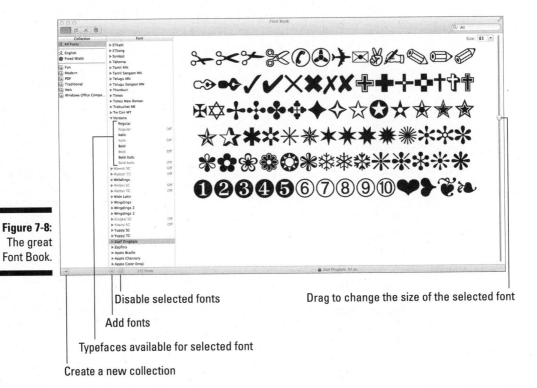

Figure 7-8:
The great
Font Book.

Disable selected fonts

Add fonts

Typefaces available for selected font

Create a new collection

Drag to change the size of the selected font

If you happen to be in Finder, another nifty way to preview fonts is through Quick Look. You'll see the entire uppercase and lowercase alphabet (plus numerals 0 through 9) in the font you've selected.

If you're like most mortals, you'll use a small set of fonts in your lifetime, although the more adventurous among you may find yourself adopting fonts with funky names such as Ayuthaya or Zapf Dingbats. (See the nearby "All in the fonts" sidebar.)

You can disable the fonts you rarely or never use by clicking the little box with the check mark under the Font list (labeled in Figure 7-8). The word *Off* appears next to the font's newly dimmed name. If you change your mind, choose Edit⇨Enable *font you disabled*. Don't worry if you come across an application that requests a disabled font. OS X will open the font on your behalf and shut it down when you close the program.

If you want to add fonts to the machine, click the + button under the same column and browse to the font's location on your computer. You can also open new fonts you've downloaded or purchased with the Font Book application by simply double-clicking them.

All in the fonts

Admit it, you're curious about the genealogy behind the font named Zapf Dingbats. Me, too. For that matter, you may be wondering about the roots of other fonts on the system. Hey, it's your computer; you have a right to know. On the Preview menu, select Show Preview (or press the keyboard shortcut ⌘+I), and the Font Book window reveals all, including the full name of a font, the languages in which it is used, and any copyright and trademark information. Best I can tell, Zapf Dingbats was not created by Archie Bunker.

When a yellow triangle appears next to a name in the Font list, duplicates of that font family are installed. To eliminate doubles, select the font in question and choose Edit⇨Look for Enabled Duplicates. Copies not in use are automatically deactivated.

Changing colors

Too often we get bogged down in the black and white of things. But the Mac is about jazzing things up, with pizzazz and color. And so it goes inside TextEdit, making your documents sing with different hues.

Select the text you want to add a dash of color to and choose Format⇨Font⇨Show Colors. Alternatively, use the keyboard shortcut Shift+⌘+C. Or click the _color well_ on the toolbar and click Show Colors.

A Colors window appears inside your document, fronted by a circle with different hues inside of it. Click anywhere in the circle to go with your preferred color. At the top of the Colors window, you also see small icons. Click one of them to move from the color circle view to a gray scale slider, or to a color palette, spectrum, or crayon view. When you click any of the various color choices, you see a bar in the window with the color that you have just selected. You will also see your chosen color reflected in the color well. If you click the color well, a grid with more color options appears. Click a color inside that window to make a new color selection.

Printing fonts

You can also preview a font family (or families) in the Font Book by printing them. You can display these fonts in three ways, depending on which of the three Report Type options you select from a pop-up menu. The menu appears after you choose File⇨Print. (If you don't see the menu, click the triangle next to the Printer pop-up menu.)

✔ **Catalog:** Numbers and letters in the sample fonts are printed alphabetically (in uppercase and lowercase). Drag the Sample Size slider to alter the size of the sample text.

✔ **Repertoire:** Prints a grid of all the font glyphs or special symbols. This time you can drag a Glyph Size slider.

✔ **Waterfall:** The Niagara Falls of font printing. An entire font alphabet is printed in increasingly larger font sizes until no more room exists on the printed page. You can choose the sample sizes of the text.

Formatting Your Document

Fancy fonts aren't the only way to doll up a document. You have important decisions to make about proper margins, paragraph indentations, and text tabs. And you must determine whether lines of text should be single- or double-spaced (or some other, such as one-and-a-half). Hey, it's still a lot easier than using a typewriter.

Okay, we're back in our TextEdit classroom. Set your margins and tab stops by dragging the tiny triangles along the ruler.

Just above the ruler, almost all the way to the right side, is a pop-up menu with a number in it, showing 1.0 by default. This is the Line and Paragraph Spacing pop-up menu. Leaving it at 1.0 separates the lines in the way you are reading them in this paragraph, in other words, single-spaced.

If I go with 2.0, the line jumps down to here, and the next line

jumps down to here. Yep, that's double-spaced.

You can also pick spacing intervals in between.

The control freaks among you (you know who you are) may want to click Show More under the Spacing menu. It displays the dialog shown in Figure 7-9. Now you can precisely determine the height of your line, the way the paragraphs are spaced (that is, the distance from the bottom of a paragraph to the top of the first line in the paragraph below), and other parameters, according to the points system.

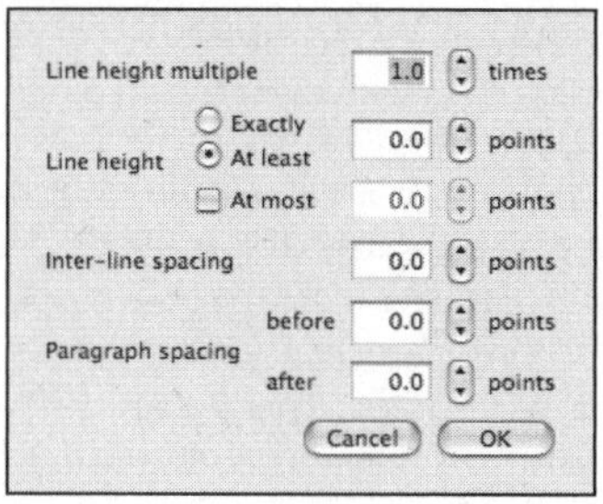
Line height multiple
1.0
times
Line height
Exactly
At least
At most
0.0
points
0.0
points
Inter-line spacing
0.0
points
Paragraph spacing
before
0.0
points
after
0.0
points
Cancel
OK

Figure 7-9: When it has to look just like this.

Here are other tricks that make TextEdit a capable writing companion:

- **Aligning paragraphs:** After clicking anywhere in a paragraph, choose Format⇨Text and choose an alignment (Left, Center, Justify, or Right). Play around with these choices to determine what looks best. You can also click the corresponding alignment buttons above the ruler.
- **Writing from right to left:** I suppose this one's useful for writing in Hebrew or Arabic. Choose Format⇨Text⇨Writing Direction and then click Right to Left. Click again to go back the other way, or choose Edit⇨Undo Set Writing Direction.
- **Locating text:** You can use the Find command on the Edit menu to uncover multiple occurrences of specific words and phrases and replace them individually or collectively.
- **Producing lists:** Sometimes the best way to get your message across is in list form. Kind of like what I'm doing here. By clicking the Lists drop-down menu — it's all the way to the right above the ruler — you can present a list with bullets, numbers, Roman numerals, uppercase or lowercase letters, and more, as shown in Figure 7-10. Click Show More for more options. As an alternative, you can also summon the list by clicking Format⇨List. Keep clicking the choices until you find the one that makes the most sense.

None
1. 2. 3.
1) 2) 3)
A. B. C.
a. b. c.
a) b) c)
I. II. III.
i. ii. iii.
Show More...

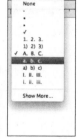

Figure 7-10: Formatting a list.

- ✔ **Creating tables:** Then again, you may want to emphasize important points using a table or chart. Choose Format⇨Table. In the window that appears (see Figure 7-11), you can select the number of rows and columns you need for your table. You can select a color background for each cell by clicking the Cell Background drop-down list and choosing Color Fill, and then choosing a hue from the palette that appears when you click the rectangle to the right. You can drag the borders of a row or a column to alter its dimensions. You can also merge or split table cells by selecting the appropriate cells and then clicking the Merge Cells or Split Cells button.

- ✔ **Using smart quotes:** Publishers sometimes try to fancy up books by using curly quotation marks rather than straight ones. Somehow curly is smarter than straight. Whatever. To use smart quotes in the document you're working on, choose TextEdit⇨Edit⇨Substitutions⇨Smart Quotes. To use curly quotes in all docs, choose TextEdit Preferences, click New Document, and select the Smart Quotes check box. If you've already selected smart quotes but want to go with straight quotes inside a document you're working on, press Ctrl and apostrophe (for a single quotation mark) or Ctrl+Shift+apostrophe for a double quotation mark.

- ✔ **Converting to smart dashes:** You can automatically convert double hyphens (–) into em dashes (—) as you type. Choose TextEdit⇨Edit⇨ Substitutions⇨Smart Dashes. Head to TextEdit Preferences to use smart dashes in all your written masterpieces. Pressing Opt + hyphen on the keyboard gives you an en dash.

- ✔ **Using smart links:** You can set it up so that anytime you type an Internet address (see Chapter 9) in a document, it acts as a link or jumping point to take you to that web page. Choose TextEdit⇨Substitutions⇨Smart Links to use a smart link in the document you are working on. Or visit TextEdit Preferences, click New Document, and select the Smart Links check box to make this feature permanent.

Figure 7-11:
Creating a
table.

✔ **Making transformations:** You can decide after the fact to make text uppercase or lowercase or to capitalize the first letter of every word that makes up a passage. After selecting the text you want to transform in this manner, choose TextEdit⇨Transformations and then choose Make Upper Case, Make Lower Case, or Capitalize.

✔ **Start speaking:** Your loquacious Mac can read text aloud. Select what you want read to you, choose TextEdit⇨Edit⇨Speech, and then choose Start Speaking. To end the filibuster, click Stop Speaking.

✔ **Substituting symbols and text:** You can type **(r)** to summon ® or type **(c)** to produce ©, but you can also build similar shortcuts on your own: perhaps (PC) for *Personal & Confidential* or (FYI) for *For Your Information*. I created one for my byline so that when I type **(ECB)**, I get *Edward C Baig* instead. Such shortcuts go beyond TextEdit; they also work in the Mail, Messages, and Safari applications. To see which shortcuts Apple has created on your behalf — or to configure your own shortcuts — choose System Preferences⇨Language & Text⇨Text. Add a check mark to your choices in the Symbol and Text Substitutions list. (Apple has already selected some of these by default.) Or click the + to add your own shortcuts.

✔ **Conversing with Calendar:** TextEdit automatically detects dates and times when you move a pointer over them in a document. And when it does, a pop-up menu appears, allowing you to create a new event in the Mac's Calendar program (see Chapter 3) or to show the date in question in Calendar. TextEdit can recognize a specific date and time such as March 11 or 5 p.m., but it can also figure out the meaning of text such as *next Tuesday* or *tomorrow*. To turn on date and time recognition for the document you're working in, choose Edit⇨Substitutions⇨Data Detectors. To do it for all documents, select the option in TextEdit Preferences.

✔ **Conversing with Contacts:** Data detection also works with contacts and addresses. When you hover over an address in a TextEdit document, the pop-up menu that appears lets you create or add the address to your Contacts, display a Google map of the location (inside Safari, which opens), or show the address in blown-up text. Simply make sure that data detection is turned on (see the preceding bullet for instructions). Now aren't you impressed by all that your freebie Mac word processor can do?

You can even do more with TextEdit. If you're using a trackpad, try this neat trick: Pinch or unpinch (as I like to call it) to zoom in or out of the characters on the screen.

Saying What's on Your Mind

In Mountain Lion, you can speak wherever you might otherwise type, be it inside TextEdit or in numerous other apps. To turn on this *Dictation* feature, press the function (fn) key on your keyboard twice or choose Start Dictation from the Edit menu. Dictation isn't always perfect, but in a relatively noise-free environment, you should do just fine.

When you dictate, your words are recorded and sent to Apple where everything gets converted into text (hopefully with minimal errors). But other information is also sent to Apple, including your first name, nickname, and contacts. The idea is to help Apple understand what you meant to say, thus improving the accuracy. If you find this troubling, you can turn off Dictation. In System Preferences, click Dictation & Speech and click Off in the Dictation section. Apple will delete your user data and any recent stuff that you recorded.

As noted in Chapter 5, you can also restrict access to Dictation in Parental Controls.

Saving Your Work

You've worked so darn hard making your document read well and look nice that I'd hate to see all your efforts go to waste. And yet in the cruel world of computers, that's precisely what could happen if you don't take a second to *save* your file. And a second is all it takes to save a file — but you can lose everything just as fast.

Stable as it is, the Mac is a machine, for goodness sakes, and not immune to power failures or human foibles. Odd as it may seem, even tech authors pound a calamitous combination of keys from time to time.

All the work you've done so far exists in an ethereal kind of way, as part of *temporary* memory. (See Chapter 2.) Don't let the fact that you can see something on your computer monitor fool you. If you shut down your computer, or it unexpectedly crashes (it's been known to happen even on Macs), any unsaved material will reside nowhere but in another type of memory. Your own.

So where exactly do you save your work? Why on the *Save sheet,* of course. (See Figure 7-12.) It slides into view from the top of your document when you press the keyboard combo ⌘+S or choose File➪Save.

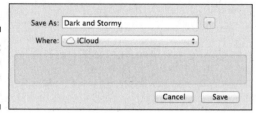

Figure 7-12:
Everyone
needs a file
saver.

Remember way back in the beginning of this chapter when I mentioned that Apple wouldn't dare name a file for you (except to give it the temporary moniker *Untitled*)? Well, this is your big chance to call the file something special by filling in a title where it says Save As. Go ahead and name it, I dunno, *Dark and Stormy*.

When you click the Save button, the contents of Dark and Stormy are assigned to a permanent home on your Mac's hard or solid-state drive, at least until you're ready to work on the document again.

But there's more. You get to choose in which folder to stash the file. In Figure 7-12, you see the default option to save the file to iCloud Apple's online service. Doing so lets you access the document from any computer connected to the Internet. Of course, you need an iCloud account for this option. For more on iCloud, read Chapter 12.

If you'd rather keep the file closer to home, you can save it to your Documents folder or any other folder on your computer. You can choose among several other possible destinations, as becomes clear when you click the arrows in the Where field, revealing various drop-down options. You can stuff your manuscript in any existing folder or subfolder in the sidebar or create one from scratch by clicking the New Folder button and giving the folder a name.

Confession time: I've been holding back. When you christened your opus Dark and Stormy, little did you know that you were actually giving it a slightly longer name: *Dark and Stormy.rtf.* The little suffix, or *extension,* stands for *Rich Text Format,* one of the file format types the Mac makes nice with. You could have saved the file in various Microsoft Word formats instead (such as the *doc* or *docx* extension). Or you could have chosen *HTML,* the language of the web. (See Chapter 9.) Apple doesn't want to bog you down with all this, so you won't routinely see these extensions.

OS X in all its wisdom provides a safety net for saving. In other words, you can now save TextEdit documents automatically.

But if you click on the title name of a document in the title bar, you see various drop-down menu choices: Rename, Move To, Duplicate, Lock, and Revert To. If you choose Rename, for example, you can save a document under a new name.

The Rename, Move To, Duplicate, and Lock options are self-explanatory. That is, you can give the title a new name, move the file to another folder or destination, duplicate or make a copy of it, or lock it to prevent you or anyone else from making inadvertent changes.

Choosing Revert To lets you browse the last-opened version of the file in question or to browse all versions of the file (which summons all the earlier iterations of the file, presented in an interface similar to the Time Machine feature that I address in Chapter 13).

Even with autosave protections, it's a good idea to save and save often as you work on documents. You just never know what will happen.

Making Revisions

Dark and Stormy is safe and sound on your hard drive, on your SSD, or in the iCloud. But after downing a few chill pills overnight, you have a brand-new outlook on life in the morning. You're past your brooding period. You want to rework your inspiration's central theme and give it a new name too, *Bright and Sunny.*

Back to TextEdit you go. As mentioned previously, to rename a document, merely click on its title in the title bar of the document and choose Rename from the drop-down menu choices. The title gets highlighted in blue, indicating that you can type a new name over the old one to change it. Simple, right?

Still you have other options. In TextEdit, choose File⇨Open. A window lists all your documents — those in iCloud as well as those on your Mac. Scroll down in the folder where you last saved your document. Click its name to highlight the document, and click again on the name to make a change. Take these step by step because if you double-click instead, you will open the document.

Because your document is only as permanent as the last time you saved it, remember to save it early and often as you make revisions, even taking into account the fact that some autosaving magic is at work in the background. Besides, TextEdit is not the only program in which you'll want to save your work, so I figured it's a good idea to get you into the habit because you never know when disaster might intervene. Along the way, you can rename your bestseller as I told you by clicking the title inside the new document and by typing a new name where the old name was. You'll still have the previous version under the old name.

You can also rename a file by selecting it (from a Finder window or the desktop) and pressing Enter. Type the new name and press Enter again.

As always, your Mac tries to assist you in these matters. The computer makes the assumption that if you worked on a document yesterday or the day before, you might want to take another stab at it today. And to prevent you, Oh Prolific One, from having to strain too hard digging for a document you may want to edit, choose File⇨Open Recent. Your freshest files will turn up in the list. Just click the name of the document you want to revisit.

Perhaps the fastest way to find a file you want to revise is to use the Spotlight tool. Choose Spotlight by single-clicking its icon at the upper-right corner of the screen and type the name of the manuscript that requires your attention.

It goes without saying that making revisions goes a lot further than just typing a new name for the document. So go crazy, tackle the project with abandon. Make up down or down up. As I said before, what was Dark and Stormy yesterday is Bright and Sunny today.

Taking Out the Trash

Like much else in life, documents, if not entire folders, inevitably outlive their usefulness. The material grows stale. It takes on a virtual stench. It claims storage space you could put to better use.

Yes, it's time to take out the trash.

Use the mouse to drag the document's icon above the trash can on the dock. Release the mouse button when the trash can turns black.

As usual, you have a keyboard alternative, ⌘+Delete. Or you can choose File⇨Move to Trash.

You'll know you have stuff in the trash because the icon shows crumpled paper. And just like your real-life trash bin, you'll want to empty it from time to time, lest your neighbors complain.

To do so, choose Empty Trash on the Finder menu or press ⌘+Shift+Delete. A warning will pop up (see Figure 7-13), reminding you that after your trash is gone, it's gone for good. (Even then, you may be able to get it back by purchasing data recovery software or hiring an expert.)

Figure 7-13:
Think before
trashing.

If you're absolutely, positively certain that you want to get rid of the contents of your trash — and paranoid about industrial spies recovering the docs — choose Secure Empty Trash from the Finder menu instead of the regular Empty Trash command.

Never Mind: Retrieving What You've Tossed

It's pretty easy to pull something out of the trash, provided that you didn't take that last Draconian measure and select Empty Trash. It's less smelly or embarrassing than sticking your hands in a real trash bin. Click the trash icon on the dock to peek at its contents. If you find something worth saving after all, drag it back onto the desktop or into the folder where it used to reside.

Making an Alias

You can create an *alias* of a file to serve as a shortcut for finding it, no matter where it's buried on your Mac. To understand what an alias is, it helps to understand what it's not. It's not a full duplicate of a file. (If you want to create a full duplicate, press ⌘+Shift+D or choose File⇨Duplicate.)

Instead, you are effectively copying the file's icon, not the file itself, meaning that you are barely using any disk space. Clicking an alias icon summons the original file no matter where it's hanging out on the computer — even if you've renamed the file.

Why create an alias in the first place? Perhaps you're not sure where to place a file that you can easily justify putting in any number of folders. For instance, if you have a document titled Seven Dwarfs, it may belong in a folder for Snow White, one for Bashful, one for Doc, and so on. Because the Mac lets you create multiple aliases, you can effectively place the file in each of those folders (even though you and I know it really resides in only one place).

To create an alias, highlight the original icon and press ⌘+L or choose File⇨ Make Alias. You can also drag an icon out of its file window or to another location inside the window while you hold down the Option and ⌘ keys.

As you can see in Figure 7-14, the alias looks like a clone of the original icon, except the *alias* suffix is added to its name and a tiny arrow appears in the lower-left corner of the icon. Clicking either icon — the original or the clone — brings up the same file.

Figure 7-14:
In this
example,
the alias
icon sits to
the right of
the original
file.

If you want to find the location of the original file, highlight the alias icon and choose File⇨Show Original.

To get rid of an alias, drag it to the trash. Doing so does not delete the original file.

If you had separately deleted the original file, however, the alias can't bring it back.

Chapter 8

Printing and Faxing

- -

- -

Computers are supposed to bring relief to pack rats. The idea that you can store documents and files in their electronic state on your hard drive or SSD, or on iCloud — thus reducing physical clutter — has widespread appeal. A few trees may breathe a sigh of relief too.

There's been a lot of buzz over the years surrounding the potential for a paperless society. Perhaps pulp industry executives, who have seen paper production decline of late, are beginning to lose sleep over the possibility.

But paper isn't going away anytime soon. Fact is, you want to pick up something tangible for your own edification and convenience. And you want hard copies to show people. It's better to hand Grandma printed pictures of the newborn rather than pull out a computer (or other gizmo) to show off your latest bundle of joy. What's more, even in the age of e-mail and electronic filings, you still usually print documents and reports for employers, teachers, financial institutions, and (sigh) the Internal Revenue Service.

Which reminds me: Despite wonderful advances in state-of-the-art printers, the counterfeiters among you will find no helpful hints in this chapter about printing money.

Choosing a Printer

What are those state-of-the-art printers? So kind of you to ask. Today's printers generally fall into two main camps: *inkjet* or *laser,* with the differences coming down to how ink makes its way onto a page. (Yes, you can find other variations, especially for photo printing — *dye sublimation* or *dye sub,* anyone?) Printers vary by speed, features, resolution (sharpness), quality of the output, and price.

Popular models are produced by Brother, Canon, Epson, Hewlett-Packard, Lexmark, and Samsung, but you can buy printers from a host of competitors.

Believe it or not, you can still find an el-cheapo, hand-me-down *daisy-wheel* or *dot-matrix* printer on eBay and elsewhere (and some manufacturers still make new ones too that work with modern Macs). But these so-called *impact printers* are most definitely *not* the state-of-the-art that I have in mind, and the assumption here is that you aren't using such a printer.

Inkjets

Inkjet printers consist of nozzles that squirt droplets of ink onto a sheet of paper. Models may be equipped with a single black cartridge and a single color cartridge. Or they may contain several color cartridges.

Where's that magenta cartridge when I need it?

Most of you, I suspect, will end up with an inkjet printer. They are the least expensive to buy, with some rock-bottom models costing as little as $29.99.

Bargains aren't always what they seem, however. The *cost of ownership* of inkjet printers can be exorbitant. You must replace pricey ($30 or so) ink cartridges on a routine basis, more often if you spit out lots of photographs of your pet kitten, Fluffy. So an inkjet printer's cost per page tends to be considerably higher than that of its laser cousins.

Having said that, inkjets are generally the most flexible bet for consumers, especially if you demonstrate shutterbug tendencies. Besides using standard-size 8½-by-11-inch paper, some inkjet models can produce fine-looking, 4-by-6-inch color snapshots on glossy photographic paper. (Photo paper, I'm obligated to point out, is expensive.)

Granted, black text produced on an inkjet won't look nearly as crisp as the text produced by a laser, though it can be quite decent just the same. Under certain conditions, some inks bleed or smudge. But for the most part, the quality of inkjets is perfectly acceptable for producing, say, family newsletters or brochures for your burgeoning catering business. And if you stick to better-quality paper, what you print might even rival consumer laser printers (see the next section).

Lasers

It's somewhat remarkable that a focused laser beam can produce such excellent-quality graphics. Then again, if lasers can correct nearsightedness and be used to perform other medical miracles, perhaps printing isn't such a major deal after all.

Laser printers use a combination of heat, toner, and static electricity to produce superb images on paper. Such printers, especially color models, used to fetch thousands of dollars. To be sure, you'll still find prices for some models in the stratosphere. But entry-level color lasers now cost less than $100 in many cases.

However affordable they have become in recent years, lasers still command a premium over inkjets. But they are far more economical over the long term. Toner cartridges are relatively cheap and don't need to be replaced very often. A highly efficient laser may cost a couple of cents per page to operate, a small fraction of what an inkjet costs to run.

Lasers remain a staple in corporate offices. Businesses appreciate the photocopier-like output and the fact that lasers can handle high-volume printing loads at blistering speeds. The machines typically offer more paper handling options as well. On the other hand, they consume far more electricity than most inkjets, making them less "green."

All-in-ones

Printers print, of course. But if your Mac is the centerpiece of a home office, you probably have other chores in mind. Copying and scanning, for instance. And faxing, too. An *all-in-one* model, otherwise known as a *multifunction* printer, can provide some combination of these tasks. Most multifunction workhorses in home offices are inkjet based.

It's cheaper to buy a single multifunction device than several stand-alone devices. That lone machine takes up less space, too.

If your fax, copier, or scanner goes on the fritz, you may also have to live without a printer while the multifunction unit is under repair.

Connecting and Activating a Printer

Almost all printers compatible with OS X — and that includes most printers sold today — connect to your Mac through the *Universal Serial Bus (USB)* port you became acquainted with in Chapter 2. So much for unretiring the printer in the attic that connects through what's called a *parallel* port.

You'll almost certainly leave the store considerably poorer than you would have first imagined, even with a bargain printer. You gotta buy stacks of paper, extra ink because the starter cartridges included with your printer may not last long, and likely a USB cable.

The good news is that not all printers require a cord. Again, some are compatible with Wi-Fi or Bluetooth.

Ready, Set, Print

You have ink. You have paper. You have a USB cable or wireless. You are antsy. Time's a wasting. I sense impatience. I'll jump to the task at hand.

Plug the printer into an AC wall jack. If you're not exploiting a wireless connection, plug the USB cable into the USB port on the Mac and make sure that it's connected snugly to the printer itself. Turn on your printer. The thing is warmed and ready for action. OS X big-heartedly assembled most of the software *drivers* required to communicate with modern printers. Chances are that yours is one of them. You still may want to install the software that came with the printer. OS X makes sure that your printer driver is as fresh as can be by periodically checking for updates; these show up in Software Updates or the Mac App Store. If for some reason your printer falls through the cracks with regard to updates, visit the printer manufacturer's website.

Configuring wireless or wired (through Ethernet) networked printers is a tad more complicated. For now, I'll assume that you've connected a USB printer. Open the Mac's trusted word processor, TextEdit. Then follow these steps:

1. **Open the document you want to print.**

2. **Choose File⇨Print, or press the keyboard shortcut ⌘+P.**

   Even though we're doing this exercise in TextEdit, you'll find the Print command on the File menu across your Mac software library. The ⌘+P shortcut works across the board too. The Print dialog shown in Figure 8-1 appears, though what you actually see may vary depending on the program you are printing from and the printer you are calling on.

3. **Click the Printer pop-up menu and select your printer, if available.**

   The printer you want to use must be turned on, of course.

4. **If your printer is not listed in the Printer pop-up menu:**

   a. **Select the pop-up menu's Add Printer item.**

      The Add dialog (essentially an add printer setup window) opens.

   b. **If your printer appears in the list, click to select it (if it's not already selected). Click Add and you're golden. Continue with Step 5.**

   c. **If your printer isn't listed, click the printer connection type icon at the top and make the appropriate selection.**

      Choices include Default, Fax (if choosing a fax machine), IP (an Internet printer), and Windows. When you make your choice, the Mac will search for any available printers.

   d. **Highlight the printer you want to use, and then click Add.**

      You can alternatively click the Use pop-up menu and then choose Select Printer Software to find a specific model, if available.

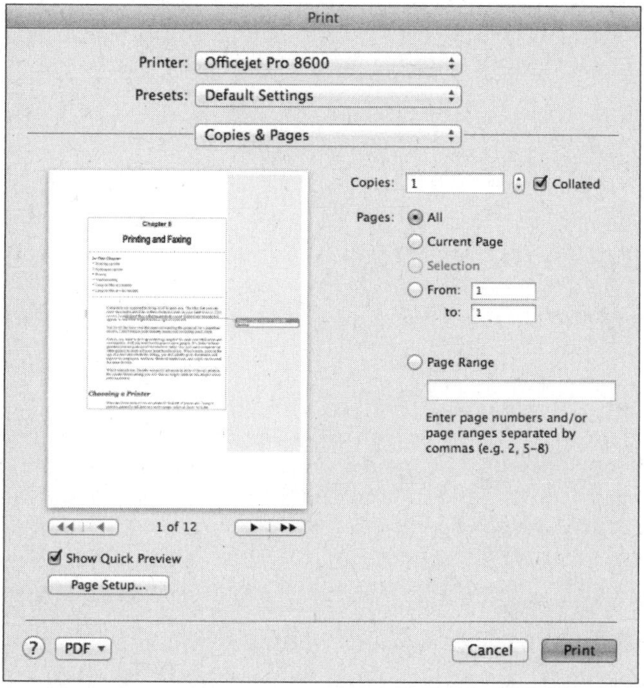

Figure 8-1:
Fit to print?

5. **Choose from the bevy of options in the Print dialog — too numerous to show in one figure.**

   Select which pages to print. (All is the default, but you can give any range by tabbing from one From box to the other.) Click where indicated to select the paper size and print orientation, which you can examine in a quick preview of the document you want to print. You get to select the number of copies you need and whether you want the pages to be collated. You can decide whether to print a header and footer. And you can choose whether to save your document in the Adobe PDF format (along with other PDF options).

   Note that this print dialog differs a bit from program to program. In the Safari browser, for instance, you can choose whether to print backgrounds, an option that doesn't appear in the TextEdit dialog. In TextEdit, one of the choices lets you rewrap the contents to fit the page. You may have to click Show Details to see some of these additional options.

6. **When you're satisfied with your selections, click Print.**

   If all goes according to plan, your printer will oblige.

Even if the Mac instantly recognizes your printer, I recommend loading any Mac installation discs that came with the printer. Why bother? Your printer is already printing stuff. The answer is that the disc might supply you with extra fonts (see Chapter 7) as well as useful software updates.

It wouldn't hurt to also visit the printer manufacturer's website to see whether updated printer drivers are available.

Printing it your way

The Mac gives you a lot of control over how your printer will behave and how your printouts will look.

You may have noticed another pop-up menu in the Print dialog just below the orientation icons that TextEdit is displaying. If you click that menu, a gaggle of other choices present themselves, some of which are shown in Figure 8-2 and as (partially) detailed in the bullet list that follows. Clicking an item calls up a sheet where you can specify the settings you want. (Some listed options are specific to your printer or the application in use, and the menu for these may appear in different places in the dialog for different programs.)

✔ **Layout:** You can select the number of "pages" that will get printed on a single sheet of paper, and determine the way those pages will be laid out. You can choose a page border (Single Thin Line, Double Hairline, and so on). And you can turn two-sided printing on or off, provided that your printer can handle such a task.

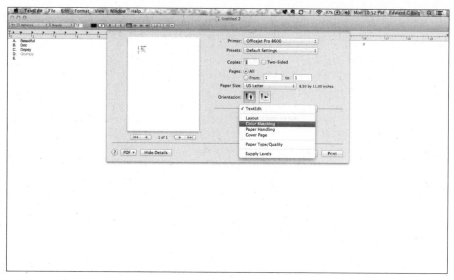

Figure 8-2:
Choosing a
print layout.

✔ **Paper Handling:** You can choose to print only odd- or even-numbered pages or to print pages in reverse order. You can also scale a page so that it fits a legal- or letter-sized sheet, an envelope, or a variety of other paper sizes.

✔ **Color Matching:** Choose this setting to select ColorSync Profiles (from Apple and others). Thus you can match the color on the screen to the color you are printing.

✔ **Cover Page:** Pretend you work for the CIA. Then print a cover sheet stating that everything else you're printing is classified, confidential, or top secret. (Yeah, like they're not going to look.)

✔ **Paper Type/Quality:** This clues the printer in on the type of paper you loaded (inkjet, transparency film, greeting card, brochure, and so on). You also get to choose the print quality. A fast draft uses less ink than printing in the spiffiest, or best, quality. If your printer has more than one tray (for example, a main tray and a photo tray), you can also choose the source of the paper to use. Under the Advanced Print options, you can adjust the volume of ink that is used.

✔ **Borderless Printing:** Tell your printer to print without borders. Or not.

✔ **Real Life Digital Photography:** If you're printing pictures, you can tweak a number of settings. Choices include automatically removing red-eye, enhancing the contrast of pictures, or filling in the dark areas of photographs.

✔ **Supply Levels:** Your Mac can report which ink cartridges may need to be replaced soon and whether the paper tray needs to be filled.

This seems like as good a time as any to see what other print options await you in System Preferences, found per usual on the menu. In the Hardware section of System Preferences, click the Print & Scan icon. You can select the Share This Printer on the Network check box if you're willing to share the printer with other computers in your house or office. You'll also find the following:

- ✓ **Print Queue:** Click the Open Print Queue button to check the status of any current printing jobs, among other things.

- ✓ **Options & Supplies:** You can make sure that you have the current printer driver and check to see whether you have an ample supply of all your inks. If you're low on, say, cyan, you'll get a Low Ink indicator. You can even order from the Apple Store, if it happens to stock the ink you seek.

- ✓ **Printer Utility:** You can open this potentially important setting within System Settings by again clicking the Print & Scan icon, and then clicking Options & Supplies (see the preceding bullet). Click the Utility tab and then click the Open Printer Utility button. The printer utility provides useful data on the connected printer. For example, on the HP printer connected to my Mac, I'm able to clean the print heads, align the print cartridges, and calibrate colors from the Printer Utility.

Previewing your print

Before you waste ink and paper on an ill-advised print job, you probably want to be sure that your documents meet your lofty standards. That means the margins and spacing look spiffy, and you have a clean layout with no *widows* or *orphans*. That's publishing-speak for a lonely word or two on a line of text all to itself.

As you've already seen, the Mac lets you sneak a peek in the small preview window that appears in the TextEdit (and other program's) Print dialog.

If you're satisfied with the preview, go ahead and click Print. If not, go back and apply the necessary changes to your documents.

One more nice thing about printing on your Mac: The various programs you work in might offer you lots more custom printing options. For example, you can print a CD jewel case insert in iTunes (see Chapter 14) or a pocket address book or envelopes in Calendar.

When Printers Stop Printing

As sure a thing as you'll get in computing is that sooner or later (but probably sooner), your printer will let you down. I've already hinted at why.

Running out of ink or toner

Ink is perishable. Especially with an inkjet printer. The symptoms will be obvious. The characters on a page get lighter and lighter each time you print, to the point where they become barely legible. The software that came with your printer may give you an estimate on how much ink you have left each time you print. And once again, you can also check supply levels (on some printers anyway) by clicking the Options & Supplies button in the Print & Scan section of System Preferences, and then clicking Supply Levels. You can also click Supply Levels in the Print dialog.

Running out of paper

Unless you make a habit of peeking at your printer's paper tray, you won't get a fair warning when your paper supply is exhausted. Of course, the rule of thumb is that you will run out of paper the hour before an important term paper is due (or legal brief or journalism deadline; feel free to insert your own catastrophe).

Wherever you buy your ink and paper, I recommend having a spare set around. And do keep a close eye on your ink levels.

Sometimes a printer stops working for no apparent reason. In the Print Queue, try clicking Resume or Resume Printer. If all else fails, turn off and restart your printer.

Hooking Up a Scanner

As with printers, connecting a *scanner* is no big deal. It usually hooks up through USB, although FireWire models are in the marketplace as well, and once more, you have a variety of wireless options. More than likely, you may gain a scanner as part of a multifunction, or all-in-one, device.

Scanners are kind of antiprinters because you already have a printed image that you want to reproduce on your computer screen, such as receipts, newspaper clippings, or photo slides and negatives. Stand-alone scanners may cost less than $50, though you pay a lot more as you add features.

If you click Scanner in the Print Queue, you can tinker with the software provided by your scanner manufacturer. The software may let you remove dust or scratches from an image and restore faded colors.

Your scanner can also team up with an on-board Apple program called Image Capture, found in the Application folder. After launching Image Capture, select your scanner from the list on the left side of the Image Capture window and choose whether you have a document-feeding scanner or a flatbed or transparency-type scanner.

If you're using Lion (or an older version of OS X) select the Detect Separate Images from the Auto selection pop-up menu check box to store each scanned item in its own file and straighten crooked items.

You can also choose whether to store scanned images in a folder (Pictures, Desktop, Documents) or have a separate application on the Mac (such as Preview, iPhoto, or Mail) handle the postscanning chores. And you can choose the format for your scan (JPEG, TIFF, PNG, JPEG 2000, GIF, BMP, PDF). For more advanced scanning options — color restoration or image correction, for example — click Show Details and apply your changes. If you already see a screen with more detailed options, click Hide Details to truncate the window.

When everything is to your liking, click Scan to fire up the scanner. Image Capture works with scanners that have OS X software drivers, as well as some TWAIN-compatible models.

If your computer has Snow Leopard or a later version of OS X, you can scan, view, and make corrections of scanned images in the Preview application. From Preview's File menu, choose Import from Scanner to get started.

Turning the Mac into a fax machine

If your Mac has a built-in, dialup fax modem, which is less and less likely, you don't need a dedicated fax machine. (Apple hasn't included a dialup modem in any Intel-based Macs.) Just connect a telephone cord to the Mac's modem jack and you're all set. As I've pointed out, however, the dialup modem is no longer standard on the latest Macs; it's about a $49 USB add-on, and as of this writing incompatible with Lion and Mountain Lion.

Sending a fax

If you have a fax modem, you'll appreciate the convenience of computer faxing. You don't have to print a document and go to the trouble of feeding it into a dedicated fax machine. Instead, you dispatch faxes directly from any program with printing capabilities. Follow these steps:

1. **Open the document you want to fax.**

2. **Chose File⇨Print.**

3. **Click the PDF button in the lower-left corner of the Print dialog and then choose Fax PDF from the pop-up menu.**

   A sheet such as the one shown in Figure 8-3 appears.

4. **In the To field, type the fax number of the person to whom you want to send the fax, including a 1 and the area code.**

   If necessary to access an outside line, add a dialing prefix such as 9 in the box marked as such.

5. **In the Modem box, select Fax Modem (or whatever) as the means for dispatching your fax.**

   In Figure 8-3, it's the box that shows Fax Information.

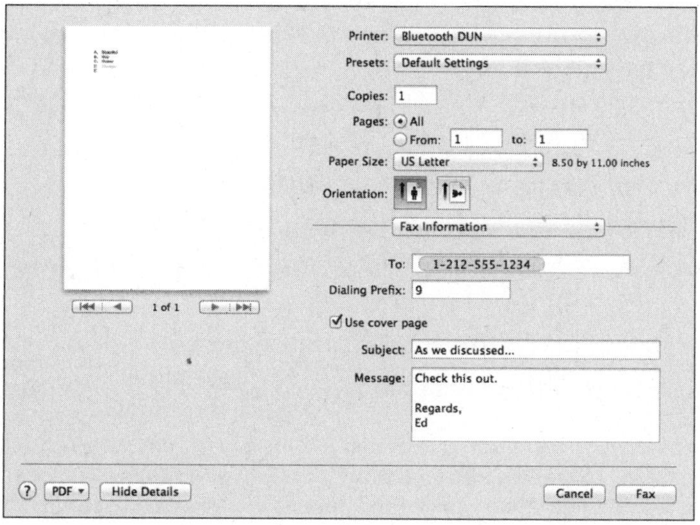

Figure 8-3:
Fill in the necessary fields to send a fax.

6. **If you want to send a cover page, select the Use Cover Page check box and type a subject line and brief message.**

7. **If you click the pop-up menu that says Fax Information, you can choose other options to schedule the delivery of your fax or alter the layout.**

8. **Use the preview window to review the fax before sending it.**

9. **Click the Fax button.**

   You should hear that awful, grinding faxing sound. It's the best evidence that your fax is on its merry way.

Receiving a fax

It makes sense that if a Mac can send a fax, it can receive one too. Make sure that you have an available phone line and that your computer is awake. A Mac in Sleep mode cannot receive a fax. Then follow these steps:

1. **From System Preferences, choose Print & Scan and then click the Open Fax Queue button. If you see Open Print Queue instead, you haven't selected a fax machine in the panel on the left. Clicking a fax choice transforms the Open Print Queue button to Open Fax Queue.**

2. **If your fax number is not shown, enter it.**

3. **Click Receive Options and then select the Receive Faxes on This Computer check box.**

4. **Designate the number of rings before the fax is answered.**

   Make sure that the computer gets to pick up before an answering machine connected to the same phone line.

5. **Choose how you want the incoming fax to be treated:**

   • Save the fax as a PDF file in the Shared Faxes folder that Apple suggests, or save it to another folder

   • Send the fax to a specific e-mail address

   • Automatically print the fax

You can accept an incoming fax even if you haven't bothered to set up the system to receive faxes automatically. Go to System Preferences and choose Print & Scan, and when your fax machine is highlighted in the list to the left of the window, select the Show Fax Status in Menu Bar check box. When the phone rings, click the Fax Status icon on the menu bar and choose Answer Now. If you want, you can also share your fax on the network.

Part III
Rocketing into Cyberspace

In this part . . .

✔ Take your Mac on a spin of the Internet.

✔ Master the minutia of reading, writing, and sending e-mail.

✔ See what chat rooms, instant messenger services, social networking, and online shopping malls have to offer.

✔ Enter the 21st century by setting up residency in the Cloud with the help of iCloud.

✔ Find out how to keep your Mac safe and secure.

✔ Check out the article "Making Sure Your Mac Plays Nice with Microsoft Exchange" (and more) online at `www.dummies.com/extras/macs`.

Chapter 9

Stairway to the Internet

· ·

In This Chapter

▶ Deciding how to connect

▶ Comparing features from ISPs

▶ Browsing with Safari

▶ Finding Top Sites

▶ Discovering a web of online riches

· ·

*R*emember what life was like prior to the middle half of the 1990s? Before this nebulous thing called the Internet changed only *everything?*

Way back in the Dark Ages, people routinely set foot in record stores to buy music. Students went to the library to do research. Folks paid bills with checks and read newspapers on, gosh, paper. They even picked up the telephone to gab with friends.

How passé.

Nowadays, such transactions and exchanges take place gazillions of times a second on the Internet. Cyberspace has become the place to shop, meet your soul mate, and conduct business. It is also a virtual playground for the kids.

You can fetch, or *download,* computer software, movies, and all kinds of other goodies. You may even get the stuff for free. Let your guard down, however, and you can also lose your shirt. (You really have to question how you won the Sri Lankan lottery when you never bought a ticket.)

Nobody in the early days of the Internet could have envisioned such a future. What eventually morphed into the Net, or "the cloud" as it is commonly referred to nowadays, was invented by the nerds of their day: 1960s Defense Department scientists. They constructed — in the interest of national security — the mother of all computer networks.

Hundreds of thousands of computers would be interconnected with hundreds of thousands more. The friendly face of cyberspace — what became the *World Wide Web,* or *web* for short — was still decades away.

Has this somehow passed you by? Forget about fretting if you haven't boarded the cybershuttle just yet. Getting up to speed on the Internet isn't as daunting as you may think. You can enjoy a perfectly rewarding online experience through your Mac without ever deciphering the Net's most puzzling terms, everything from *domain names* to *file transfer protocols*. And you certainly don't have to stay up late cramming for any final exams.

But the Internet is not for people who cherish siestas either. It's as addictive as nicotine. Expect a warning from the surgeon general any day now: Spending time online is hazardous to your sleep cycle.

Feeling brave? Want to take the online plunge anyhow? The rest of this chapter will clue you in on how best to proceed.

Dialing In

Let the games begin. At home, you can find your way online in two main ways, and both involve getting chummy with an important piece of computer circuitry, the *modem*. I address *dialup* modems here and *broadband* modems in the next section.

Dialup is the simplest and cheapest scheme. It's nearly as brainless as making a phone call. Wait a second; it *is* making a phone call. When the modem works its magic, it dials the Internet over a regular phone line as if you were calling your mother. The difference is that no one at the other end will make you feel guilty for not visiting often enough. With any luck, you won't get a busy signal, either.

Dialup used to merit a longer discussion, but such modems are yesterday's news. Apple hasn't sold a Mac with an internal modem since the Intel switchover. If you do have an older model with an internal modem, you only need to locate the phone jack on the back or side of the computer. A little phone icon lets you know you've arrived at the right place. If you haven't embraced broadband yet, you can buy an optional dialup modem that connects to a USB port on the machine. Either way, connect one end of a standard phone cord into the modem jack and the other end into the wall jack where your telephone was connected.

Taking the Broadband Express

If the traditional dialup modem is the local, broadband is the express. Who can blame you for wanting to take the fast train? You'll pay more for a ticket — prices vary, but $30 a month is fairly typical. The positive spin is that you won't need a second phone line. Besides, the broadband express is almost always worth it. After you've experienced a fast hookup, you'll have a difficult time giving it up.

DSL, cable . . .

Broadband service comes in several flavors nowadays. Depending on where you live, you may have a choice of all, some, or none of the various alternatives. All broadband types have dedicated modems that reside outside the computer. In some (but not all) cases, a technician will come to your house (generally for a fee) and connect a broadband modem to the service you have selected. The options are

- **Cable modem:** Sometimes the fastest of the broadband choices — at least if you don't have access to FIOS (see below) — and the one that may well make the most sense if you already subscribe to cable TV. The reason is that your cable company is likely to cut you a small break on the monthly fee (especially if you also opt for phone and TV service through it). The connection involves hooking up the cable TV cord to the modem.

- **DSL:** As with dialup, DSL, which stands for digital subscriber line, works over existing telephone lines. But a big difference compared to dialup is that you can prowl the Internet and make or receive phone calls at the same time. And DSL, like a cable modem, is leagues faster than a dialup modem though usually slower than cable. As with cable, deals can be had if you take on service from the same company that supplies your regular phone service.

- **FIOS:** In this speedy fiber-optic broadband network offered by Verizon, hair-thin strands of glass fiber and laser-generated light pulses transmit data. Verizon was expanding its FIOS network at the time of this writing, but its availability remains somewhat limited.

- **Cellular broadband:** Several emerging wireless technologies can speedily access the Internet when you are out and about with a Mac laptop. And they work through high-speed cellular networks. Zippy wireless broadband inroads were made a few years ago by Verizon and Sprint with a geeky-sounding technology known as *EV-DO (Evolution-Data Optimized* or *Evolution-Data only,* depending who you ask). These are *3G,* or third-generation, wireless networks. Faster *LTE (Long-Term Evolution)* and other *4G* or fourth-generation-type wireless cellular networks have been emerging, too. You may be able to plug in optional cellular modems to exploit these networks, or use a wireless model such as MiFi, made by Novatel Wireless. You typically have to commit to a data plan, often for two years, to take advantage of the portable modems. Data plans might run you about $60 a month. Coverage can be spotty, though, and depending on the strength of the wireless signal, this option might come closer to dialup in terms of speed than to other broadband alternatives.

✓ **Satellite:** A satellite might be your only alternative to dialup if you live in the boondocks. You get the Internet signal the same way you receive satellite TV: through a dish or an antenna mounted on or near your house. If you go the satellite route, make sure that your modem can send, or *upload,* information as well as receive, or *download,* it. Upload speeds are typically much pokier than download speeds, and satellite service in general is sluggish compared to other broadband choices, with the possible exception of cellular. (Of course, uploading and downloading are components of all modem types.) Satellite also commands higher up-front costs than cable or DSL because you have to shell out for the dish and other components.

Always on, always connected

In the dialup world, you make your call, wait for a connection to be established, grab what you are looking for on the Net, and say adios. Heaven forbid you forget something. Each time you want to go back online, you have to repeat this drill. This amounts to too many phone calls, too many hassles.

Broadband generally has fewer hang-ups. The experience is far more liberating because you have a persistent, always-on connection, at least as long as the Mac itself is turned on and your modem doesn't punk out. You won't have to compete with your teenagers for access to the only phone in the house. Web pages get updated. E-mails and instant messages usually arrive in a blink. And you can share your Internet connection with other computers in the house. (See Chapter 18.)

Let Me In

This whole Internet business has one more essential piece: deciding on the outfit that will let you past the Net's front gate. That company is called an *Internet service provider,* or *ISP* for short. You'll invariably have to slip this gatekeeper a few bucks each month, though sometimes paying annually lowers the price of admission. Many ISPs, such as AOL, AT&T, Charter, Comcast, Cox, EarthLink, MSN, and Verizon, are large, well-known enterprises. But tiny unfamiliar companies may also serve the bill.

As always, you'll find exceptions: You may not have to shop for an ISP if your employer provides the Internet gratis. Students often get complimentary access on college campuses, though the costs are likely buried in tuition.

If you signed up for broadband, chances are you've already met your ISP because it's the cable or phone company that set you up. But if you're playing one company off against another, here are key points to consider:

- **Service:** An ISP's reputation is the whole enchilada. Seek companies that do a lot of handholding, from *Getting Started* pamphlets to toll-free technical-support phone numbers. If they do provide toll-free support, give the number a try before you sign up. Look elsewhere if it takes forever for a live person to answer your call.

- **Fees:** Membership fees vary, and companies often run promotions. Compare rate options if you live in a town with multiple broadband choices. Choose a plan in which you are given unlimited access or a generous chunk of hours. Metered pricing in which you are billed hourly isn't smart for anyone but the most disciplined user who seldom expects to go online. Fortunately, such plans are rare.

- **Local number:** This is an important consideration for dialup customers. If possible, choose a plan where you can dial the Net without incurring long-distance charges. If you travel a lot, it's also helpful to have a choice of local numbers in the city or cities you most often frequent.

- **E-mail:** Just for being a customer, some ISPs give you one or more e-mail accounts. More is obviously better if you intend on sharing the computer with family members. Also ask whether the ISP provides tools for cutting down on spam. I have more to say on this topic in Chapter 10.

- **Family protection:** If you have kids, find out whether the ISP offers parental controls or takes other steps to help protect the little ones in cyberspace. Of course, excellent parental controls are built in to OS X.

Going on a Safari

It is virtually impossible to ignore the web. Practically everyone you come across is caught up in the web in one way or another. On a typical day, you might hear how "little Johnny built this amazing web page at school." How your best friend researched symptoms on the web before heading to the doctor. And how you can save a bundle booking your vacation online. Web addresses are plastered on billboards, business cards, and the cover of books like this one.

Just browsing

Technologists have an uncanny knack for making simple things hard. They could ask you to make a phone call over the Internet. But if they told you instead to make a *VoIP,* or *Voice over Internet Protocol,* call, they'd pretend to be really smart. So it is unbelievably refreshing to discover that to browse or surf the web, you need a piece of software that is called, um, a *web browser.* Okay, so they might have called it a web surfer.

Because you had the good sense to purchase a Mac, you are blessed with one of the best browsers in the business. It's aptly named *Safari* because much of what you do in cyberspace is an expedition into the wild, unless your revisionist take on this has to do with the Beach Boys hit *Surfin Safari* (See Figure 9-1.)

Learning to tame Safari means getting fluent with the concept of a web address, or what those aforementioned technologists dub a *URL (Uniform Resource Locator).* I told you, these guys can't seem to help themselves.

and end with a suffix, typically `.com` (pronounced "dot com"), `.edu`, `.gov`, `.net`, or `.org`. What you type in between is often an excellent indicator of where you will end up on the web. So typing **www.usatoday.com** takes you to the nation's largest newspaper. Typing **www.espn.com** leads to a popular sports destination. And so on. You enter the URL into the *Smart Search field* at the top of the browser window (labeled in Figure 9-1). As a web page loads, a blue bar fills the address field to let you know that the page is coming.

Just because of the way things are, web addresses usually begin with `www`.

Financial institutions and other companies sometimes begin a web address with `https://` instead of `http://`. This indicates that encryption is used to make communication to or from the site more secure (in theory anyway).

Smart addressing

Safari was up to version 6.02 at the time this book was going to press. The crash-resistant web browser is intelligent about recognizing addresses. When you start entering an address in the Smart Search field, Safari takes a stab at what it deems is the most likely match, presented at the top of the window shown in Figure 9-2 as the Top Hit. A single click takes you there. But this smart-addressing feature goes a step further by also listing other possible outcomes, culled from your Bookmarks and History, topics you read about later in this chapter.

Previous page

Next page

Show Bookmarks

iCloud tab

Share

Smart Search

Show Downloads button

Reload page

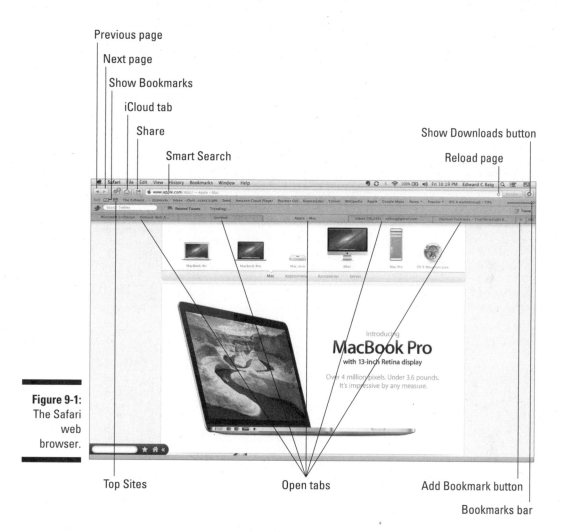

Figure 9-1:
The Safari
web
browser.

Top Sites

Open tabs

Add Bookmark button

Bookmarks bar

What's more, starting with Safari 6, you enter Google search queries in the same unified Smart Search field where you enter a web address. I get to more about search in a few pages.

Clicking links

Web surfing would be tedious if you had to type an address each time you wanted to go from one site to another. Fortunately, the bright minds who invented Safari and other browsers agree.

Figure 9-2:
More often
than not,
the Smart
Search field
gets you
where you
need to go.

On the Safari *toolbar,* you'll typically see a series of buttons or icons to the left of the address box where you entered the URL. The buttons you see and the order in which they appear vary, depending on how you customize the browser (refer to Figure 9-1 for a look at some of these buttons). To make the toolbar disappear, choose View⇨Hide Toolbar. To make it reappear, choose View⇨Show Toolbar.

The left- and right-facing arrow buttons function as the Back and Forward buttons, respectively. So clicking the left arrow transports you back to the last page you were looking at before the page that is currently displayed. Click the right, or Forward, button to advance to a page you have already looked at but backed up from.

Click the toolbar icon that looks like a house, and you go to your starting base, or *home page.* But you won't see it by default as on earlier versions of Safari unless you choose to add it to the toolbar. To do just that (or add other missing icons), choose View⇨Customize Toolbar and drag your favorite items onto the toolbar. If you prefer, drag the default set of icons onto the toolbar.

Home is the site that greets you each time you fire up the browser for the first time. It's no coincidence that Apple chose one of its own web pages as the default Safari starting point. That way, it can promote the company and try to sell you stuff. As you might imagine, home pages are valuable pieces of screen real estate to marketers. Everyone from AOL to Google to Yahoo! would love for you to choose its *portal* as your start page. Fortunately, changing Safari's home page is simple. Choose Preferences from the Safari menu, click the General tab, and then type the web address of your page of choice in the Homepage field, as shown in Figure 9-3.

You'll notice that some text on various web pages is underlined in blue (or some other color). That means it's a *link*. As you move the mouse pointer over a link, the pointer icon changes from an arrow to a pointing finger. Clicking a link takes you to another page (or another location on the same page) without having to type any other instructions.

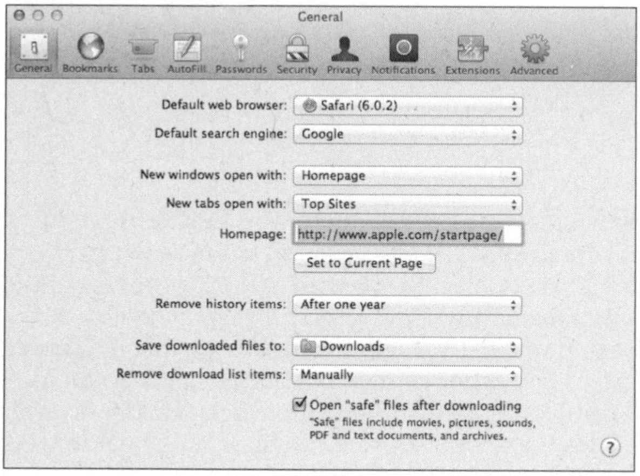

Figure 9-3:
You can change the home page in Safari preferences.

Some links are genuinely useful. If you are reading about the New England Patriots game, you may want to click a link that would lead to, say, quarterback Tom Brady's career statistics. But be wary of other links that are merely come-ons for advertisements.

Using bookmarks

Odds are that you'll rapidly get hooked on a bevy of juicy web pages that become so irresistible you'll keep coming back for more. I won't ask, so you need not tell. Of course it's downright silly to have to remember and type the destination's web address each time you return. Create a *bookmark* instead (known as a *favorite* in Microsoft parlance). The easiest way to add a bookmark is to click the Share button on the toolbar (refer to Figure 9-1). Alternatively, choose the Add Bookmark item on Safari's Bookmarks menu or press the keyboard shortcut ⌘+D. If a + icon is showing on the toolbar, adding a bookmark that way is another option.

You can also add bookmarks for multiple tabs or open pages. On the Bookmarks menu, click Add Bookmarks for These X Tabs, with X representing the number of open tabs or web pages. I'll have more to say about tabs later in this chapter, too.

When you use one of the above methods to add a bookmark, a dialog appears, as shown in Figure 9-4, asking you to type a name for the bookmark you have in mind and to choose a place to keep it for handy reference later.

Figure 9-4:
Where to
book your
bookmarks.

You'll want to return to some sites so often that they deserve VIP status. Reserve a spot for them in Safari's Bookmarks marquee, otherwise known as the *bookmarks bar*. It is situated below the browser's toolbar (and labeled in Figure 9-1). The bookmarks bar is selected on your behalf by default when the dialog pops up asking where to place the bookmark you've just created. Click the drop-down list to find other places to land the new bookmark — you can stash bookmarks into folders, essentially menus of bookmarks segregated by whichever categories make sense. But if the bookmarks bar is indeed your chosen destination, you have an expeditious alternative to placing your new bookmark on the bar: Drag the little icon to the left of the address in the Smart Search field directly onto the bookmarks bar to place it in the precise spot on the bar where you want it.

Clicking the Show All Bookmarks icon lets you manage all your bookmarks.

As alluded to above, you can group bookmarks in menu folders called Collections, as shown in Figure 9-5. If you decide to bookmark the Internet Movie Database home page, for example, you may decide to place it in a Collections folder called Entertainment. Whenever you want to pay a return visit to the site, you open the Entertainment folder and click the bookmark.

Despite your best organizational skills, your list of bookmarks and Collections may become so, well, overbooked that it becomes far less functional. I practically guarantee that you will tire of at least some of the sites now cluttering up your bookmarks closet. To delete a bookmark, highlight its name, click the Edit menu at the top of the screen, and then choose Cut. If you change your mind, choose Edit⇨Undo Remove Bookmark.

If all that seems like too much work, highlight an unwanted bookmark and press the Delete button on your keyboard.

Figure 9-5:
Where to
manage
bookmarks.

Employing the tools of the trade in Safari

Safari is capable of other neat tricks. I describe some of them in the following sections.

Pop-up blocker

Tolerating web advertising is the price we pay for all the rich web resources at our disposal. The problem is some ads induce agita. The most offensive are *pop-ups,* those hiccupping nightmarish little windows that make you think you woke up in the middle of the Las Vegas strip. Pop-ups have the audacity to get between you and the web page you are attempting to read. Turning on the pop-up blocker can shield you from such pollutants. Choose Safari Preferences⇨Security and select the Block Pop-up Windows check box. Once in a great while, a pop-up is worth viewing; to turn off the pop-up blocker, simply repeat this exercise.

From this Security section in Safari preferences, you can also enable or disable *plug-ins, Java,* and *JavaScript,* which have been associated with some security vulnerabilities such as installing diabolical malware. But keep in mind that plug-ins are used by Safari to sometimes show off or play music, pictures, and video, that Java provides animations and certain other interactive features on web pages, and that JavaScript technology enables buttons, online forms, and other web pages to do their thing. Be aware that disabling any of these options may make the web pages you frequent misbehave.

Find

Now suppose that you want to find all mentions of a particular term or phrase on the web page you are looking at. Choose Edit⇨Find from the main menu or press ⌘+F. Type the word you want to find, and Safari highlights all occurrences of the text. Apple's not leaving anything to chance; the rest of the page is dimmed so that you can more easily make out those highlighted words. The number of matches is also displayed, as are arrows that let you go to the next or previous occurrence of the word. In Figure 9-6, I did a find for all mentions of the word *Spurs* in this ESPN news article on the San Antonio NBA franchise.

Figure 9-6: Spurring on a Find query.

SnapBack

Sometimes you get carried away surfing, either while searching Google or just browsing the web. In other words, you move from page to page to page to page. Before you know it, you're in never-never-web land. You can certainly keep clicking the Back button until you return to your starting point. Prior to Safari 6, Apple provided an orange SnapBack icon that appeared in the right side of the then-separate address field and Google search box, letting you return to square one without those excess clicks. The icon is gone, but you can still take advantage of the SnapBack feature by pressing the keyboard combination ⌘+option+S.

Filling out forms and passwords

Safari can remember your name, address, passwords, and other information. So when you start typing a few characters in a web form or other field, the browser can finish entering the text for you, provided that it finds a match in its database. From the Safari menu, choose Preferences⇨AutoFill and select the items you want Safari to use (such as info from your Contacts card). If several choices match the first several letters you type in a form, a menu appears. Press the arrow keys to select the item you have in mind and then press Enter. After the Mountain Lion upgrade, Safari started offering to automatically fill in your web passwords, provided that you were authenticated by entering your system password. To take advantage of this option, make sure that the User Names and Passwords check box is selected in the AutoFill section of Safari Preferences.

Tabbed browsing

Say you want to peek at several web pages in a single browser window instead of having to open separate windows for each "open" page. Welcome to the high art of *tabbed browsing*. Visit Preferences on the Safari menu and then click Tabs. The window shown in Figure 9-7 appears. Place check marks next to each of the settings you want.

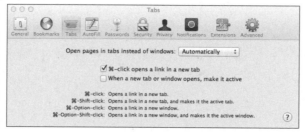

Figure 9-7: Keeping tabs. The tabbed browsing window.

Now, each time you ⌘-click, you open a link in a new tab instead of a window. To toggle from one open web page to another, just click its tab. The tabs appear just under the bookmarks bar. If you press Shift+⌘-click, you can open a new tab and make it the active tab.

To open a new tabbed window, choose File⇨New Tab or press ⌘+T.

To rearrange the way tabs appear, just drag them in any order.

Tab view

If you have a trackpad, you can take advantage of a neat Mountain Lion stunt called Tab view, roughly similar to how you view tabs in Safari on the iPhone. (This also works with the surface of the Magic Mouse.) When you pinch in to zoom, your open tabs line up one next to another, as shown in Figure 9-8. Swipe with two fingers to the left or right to move from one live tab to another, or use the left- and right-arrow keys on your keyboard. You can also click one of the bullets below the tabs to jump to a specific page.

Click the tab itself to leave Tab view and bring the web page represented by the tab to the forefront.

iCloud Tabs

As you probably suspect, Mac owners are fans of Apple in general. So, they may well own other Apple products like the iPhone smartphone, iPad tablet, or iPod touch media player. If these same folks are also members of iCloud and all those Apple playthings are registered, people can take advantage of another feature introduced on the Mac in Safari 6. The feature is iCloud Tabs, and its purpose is straightforward. If you were browsing Safari on one of your other iCloud devices — including, of course, any other Macs you happen to own — you can see the last web pages you visited on those devices when browsing Safari on the machine you're currently using. And that means you can pick up right where you left off.

Swipe to go from open tab to another

Figure 9-8:
Pinch in to
see your live
web pages.

Click a bullet to jump to that tab.

The iPhone, iPad, or iPod touch must be running iOS 6 or later.

Click the iCloud icon labeled in Figure 9-1 to summon the menu shown in Figure 9-9. The beauty of iCloud Tabs is that you can view the pages on those other devices even if Safari is turned off or the device itself is out of action. The exception to the rule is if you turned on the Private Browsing feature that you read about later in this chapter.

Benefiting from History

Say that you failed to bookmark a site and now days later decide to return. Only you can't remember what the darn place was called or the convoluted path that brought you there. Become a history major. Safari logs every web page you open and keeps the record for a week or so. So you can consult the History menu to view a list of all the sites you visited on a particular day during the week. Choose History⇨Show All History or choose Bookmarks⇨Show All Bookmarks and then click History under Collections to view a more complete historical record. You can even search for a site you visited by typing a keyword in the Spotlight search field.

Figure 9-9: iCloud Tabs lets you pick up browsing where you left off on another Apple device.

Top Sites

As you gathered from this history discussion, Safari is watching you. It records how often you head to favorite websites. It knows when you last visited. But don't worry; it's all to your benefit. And with the Top Sites feature that Apple introduced as part of Safari 4, it's even easier to return to your favorite online landing spots. In the Top Sites view, the sites you frequent the most are laid out beautifully as thumbnails that appear on the wall shown in Figure 9-10. With customary panache, Apple has arranged it so that the thumbnails at the bottom of the Top Sites wall reflect off the shiny surface.

If a site has been recently updated, a star will appear in the upper-right corner of its representative thumbnail. As you mouse over a thumbnail, the name and URL are shown at the bottom of the screen. Click any thumbnail to display the site full-screen.

To return to this Top Sites view after you've departed, click the Top Sites button (labeled in Figure 9-1).

As you might imagine, the thumbnails shown in the Top Sites view change as your browsing habits change. But you can also customize the Top Sites page and choose the number of sites that are displayed at any one time. Click the Edit button at the lower left of Figure 9-10 and then the Small, Medium, or Large button that appears at the lower right, as shown in Figure 9-11. If you want to "pin" a site so that it always remains in the Top Sites view, click the pin at the upper left of the thumbnail. Alternatively, click the X if you want to remove the site from Top Sites.

And now back to studying History. You can get to History from Top Sites by clicking the History button at the top of the screen. The sites you've been to are shown off in Cover Flow, a feature that debuted in iTunes (see Chapter 14). Cover Flow lets you glance at the text and graphics on recently visited sites the same way you might look at album covers. (In the most recent version of iTunes that was out when this book was published, Apple removed the Cover Flow feature.)

Figure 9-10:
The crème de la crème: Finding your way through Top Sites.

Figure 9-11:
Customizing
Top Sites.

If you begin typing into the search field from the Search History page, you'll see those results in Cover Flow. You can flip through web pages to find the site you have in mind by dragging the slider along the bottom of the screen.

As I mentioned, you can browse through History by merely typing a few characters in Safari's Smart Search field, since the Smart Search field searches bookmarks and history along with the Web

If you're wigged out by this Internet trail, you can always click Clear History to wipe the slate clean. Or, choose the General tab under Safari Preferences and indicate whether you want to remove all traces of History after one day, one week, two weeks, one month, or one year — or to handle the job manually.

Sharing what you read

As part of Safari 6, Apple placed a new Share button inside many apps. And so it goes in Safari. Sharing favorite web pages is as easy as clicking that Share button. Check out Figure 9-12 to see your menu options. I've already discussed bookmarks, and I'll get to the Reading List option shortly.

But note the other ways that you can share the page you are reading: You can e-mail the web page, share it as an instant message, or post it to Twitter or the popular Facebook social network.

Figure 9-12: Summoning your sharing options.

Figure 9-13 shows the *Share sheet* for Facebook. You have some room to type (or dictate) a message indicating the reason you are sharing this web thingy in the first place. Click the Friends list to determine which of your Facebook pals get to see the attached link and your message. At your discretion, click Add Location to share where you are (or more to the point, where your Mac is) when sending the page.

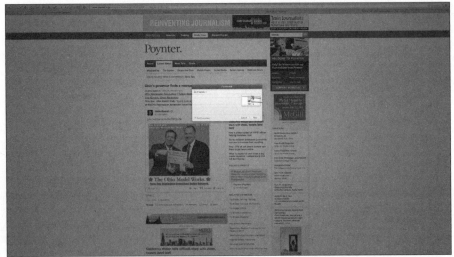

Figure 9-13: Sharing a page on Facebook.

Clutter-free reading

Articles you read online are all too frequently surrounded by advertisements, banners, menu bars, and other potential distractions. What would it be like to read web pages without the excess visual noise? Stop wondering. The Reader feature can place you in a temporary ideal reading environment. Most of, if not all, the clutter is stripped away.

To make that happen, click the Reader button to the right edge of the Smart Search field to transform a story like the *USA TODAY* article shown in the left side of Figure 9-14 to the way it appears on the right. Use the trackpad or mouse to scroll up or down the length of the article.

To e-mail an article from Safari Reader, click the envelope icon in the heads-up display that appears when you roll your mouse over the story. You can also enlarge or decrease the size of the text by clicking the corresponding magnifying glass icons. Click the printer icon to print the article you are reading.

The Reader button only appears when Safari detects an actual article.

Offline reading

Though it may be filled with countless riches, the web doesn't do you much good if you lack a connection to the Internet. But now you can catch up on your reading even without that connection. It's accomplished by saving web pages to the offline reading list. Click the aforementioned Share button, and click Add to Reading List. Safari saves all the pages of the article you are reading, not just the single page you happen to be viewing when you click the Add to Reading List option.

The Reading List may be terrific, for, well, offline reading. But it's also a convenient way to store articles that you want to keep around.

Figure 9-14: Read a web article with clutter or without.

When you're ready to read the article — again, with or without an active Internet connection — click the Reading List icon to the left of the bookmarks bar. The icon resembles a pair of reading glasses. Scroll up or down the list that appears (shown in Figure 9-15) and click the article you want to read. To remove an article after you've read it, roll the mouse over the story and click the X that appears inside a small circle.

Click Clear All to clear the entire offline reading list. Click Unread to just list the articles that you haven't gotten to yet. Click the Reading List icon again to make the list disappear altogether. Click Add Page as another way to add a page to the Reading List, specifically the page adjacent to the list.

Private Browsing

Hey, maybe you do have something to hide. Perhaps you're surfing in an Internet cafe. Or just possibly you're being paranoid. Whatever. Turn on a hush-hush Safari feature called *Private Browsing* by choosing Safari⇨Private Browsing from the main menu. Now Safari won't add the web pages you've visited to the History menu (though you can still use the Back and Forward buttons to return to sites you've been to). When Private Browsing is turned on, AutoFill is turned off, searches are not added to the pop-up menu in the Google search box, and web *cookie* preferences are also deep-sixed. I explain cookie files later in this chapter.

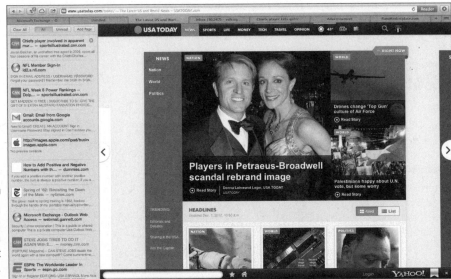

Figure 9-15: Reading without an Internet connection.

Do not track me

While on the subject of privacy, you can ask a website not to track you by clicking this option in the Privacy section of Safari preferences. As of this writing, Do Not Track was an emerging privacy standard supported by Apple.

Web clipping

In Chapter 6, I introduce you to dashboard widgets, those handy little apps for looking up phone numbers or getting sports scores. Coming up in Chapter 21, I list ten of my favorite widgets.

So why are we talking about widgets here? Because Safari lets you create your own, by clipping out a section of a favorite web page. The beauty is that you are giving birth to a live widget that gets refreshed whenever the under-lying web page is updated. In Safari, navigate to the web page you want to transform into a dashboard widget; then click the Open in Dashboard button. The button is not visible by default (and not labeled in Figure 9-1). You can make it appear by choosing Customize Toolbar on Safari's View menu. The icon shows scissors inside a broken-up rectangle.

When you click the button, the screen dims, except for a resizable white rectangle that appears, as shown in Figure 9-16. The rectangle automatically wraps around various portions on the page that seem like a natural section you may want to clip. You can reposition this rectangle so that another sec-tion gets highlighted. And if Apple still doesn't highlight the portions you have in mind, click inside the rectangle to bring up handles that appear on its edges. Drag these with your mouse until the rectangle is expanded to encom-pass the complete section you want to snip out for your widget.

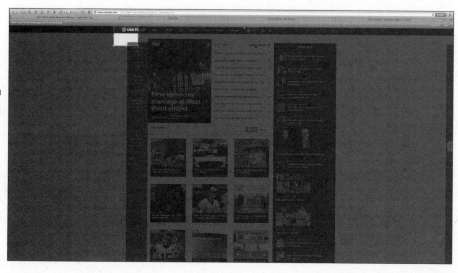

Figure 9-16: Drag the rectangle over the portion of the web page that you want to clip into a widget.

When you're satisfied, click Add, which appears in the upper-right corner of the web screen that you are clipping. The dashboard appears with your newly created widget. You can apply cosmetic changes to the widget by clicking the small *i* button in its lower-right corner. (The "i" only appears when you roll your mouse over the widget; upon doing so, the widget flips around, and you'll see a screen such as the one shown in Figure 9-17.) Your first chore (if you so choose) is to select a new border for your widget by clicking one of the small pictures representing a themed edge.

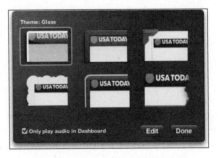

Figure 9-17:
Customize
your widget
by clicking
the i.

Click Edit. You now have the ability to change the size of the widget, revealing more content, or to drag its content to a new place.

Sometimes a widget plays sounds. If you want sound to play only when you've summoned Dashboard, select the Only Play Audio in Dashboard check box.

Make a web picture your desktop picture

Ever come across a stunning picture on the web that you wish you could make your own? Go right ahead. Right-click the picture in question and choose Use Image as Desktop Picture from the menu that appears.

If you choose a low-resolution image, it will look lousy blown up as your desktop background.

Using an Alternative Browser

Safari is swell, but it's not the only game in town. Eventually, you'll stumble upon a website that doesn't make nice with the Apple browser. That's likely because the site was programmed to work solely with the Grand Poobah among browsers, Microsoft's Internet Explorer, or was optimized for another popular browser, Mozilla's Firefox. Hey, no one ever said life was fair (see the nearby "Putting up with Internet Explorer" sidebar).

Putting up with Internet Explorer

For years, Microsoft adopted a kind of *laissez-faire* approach when it came to revving up its famed web browser. It generally left tabbed browsing and other innovations to others. Such is the complacency that sets in when you've bagged a monopolistic share of the market. Still, the venerable browser comes in handy at times, especially if Safari has difficulty communicating with a particular web page you're trying to view (which, frankly, is less and less a problem). If someone gives you an old enough Mac, you may find Internet Explorer in the Applications folder. But not only is IE not on newer systems, Microsoft doesn't even want you to use its browser on a Mac. (The exception is if you run Windows on your Mac, which I discuss in Chapter 19.) In the middle of 2003, the word out of Microsoft's Redmond, Washington, headquarters was that the company was halting all development on IE for the Mac. Then a few years later, Microsoft said it would no longer offer tech support for the Mac version of IE and indicated it also wouldn't provide security or performance updates. The message was practically deafening: Go book a Safari.

Other fine browsers abound. I'm partial to Mozilla's speedy Firefox, which among many niceties preserves and restores your tabs and windows should the browser unexpectedly shut down. Google's Chrome browser is also now available for the Mac. You may also want to check iCab, OmniWeb, and Opera at their respective websites. Another interesting "social browser" to try is RockMelt.

The Skinny on Search Engines

In Chapter 6, I focus on the wonders of searching your Mac through Spotlight. But what about searching all these plum pickings on the Internet while avoiding all that is rotten? An Internet search engine is the best place to begin. These useful tools scan web pages to find links based on instances of the search terms you enter. Most folks start with Google.

Google this

Anyone who is anyone — and that might as well include you — uses Google. Google has become so popular that it's often treated as a verb, as in, I Googled something. It is also why Google's founders have become richer than Croesus.

Haven't the foggiest idea who Croesus was? Just Google the name, and you'll soon discover how this sixth-century Lydian monarch managed to amass a fortune without launching an IPO.

The slowpoke way to Google something is to visit `www.google.com`. Type your search query — *Croesus,* in this example — and click the Google Search button. Safari, however, provides a faster alternative. Just enter your query in the Smart Search box you've been using by now to type in web addresses. Figure 9-18 shows the results of the Croesus search.

Either way, Google will rapidly spit back a list of findings, or *hits,* containing links to web pages. That would be all there is to it, except you'll probably have to help Google narrow things down a tad. The Croesus example yields more than a million hits, more than you bargained for.

Enter an even broader search term such as *rockets,* and Google responds with something on the order of 80-plus million hits. I don't know about you, but I have time to pore through only half of them. What's more, as smart as Google is, it has no way of knowing whether you mean the flying machine that soars into outer space, the basketball franchise that plays in Houston, or even the hamburger chain Johnny Rockets.

The obvious takeaway: The more descriptive you are the better. Two or three search terms almost always work better than one.

You can assist Google in several ways. Putting quotation marks around your search term narrows the returns because the browser thinks you're searching for that exact phrase. This technique works wonders with song or book titles.

Figure 9-18:
A rich
search in
Google.

Here's a sampling of other nifty Google tricks:

- ✔ **Solve arithmetic:** Enter a math problem, such as **63/7.8 =**, and Google supplies the answer (8.07692308).

- ✔ **Provide the forecast:** By adding *weather* next to a city name or postal ZIP Code, you can peek at the current temperature, wind, and humidity and get a quick weather snapshot of the days ahead.

- ✔ **Do a reverse phone lookup:** Type an area code and a phone number, and Google will reveal whose number it is (if listed).

- ✔ **Convert currency:** Want to determine how many dollars there are to the euro? Type, for example, **250 us dollars in euros**.

Bing and Yahoo!

Google is the search engine of choice for many people, but other fine alternatives are available. I'm particularly keen on Bing from Microsoft. Bing puts you in a lovely frame of mind just through the scenic images that decorate its initial search page.

Meanwhile, you always have Yahoo!, kind of the granddaddy of the search business. Moreover, when you go to Yahoo!, at www.yahoo.com, you'll be taken to its web portal, where you can do a lot more than search. *Portals* are launching pads for a gaggle of goodies, including news and entertainment links, stock quotes, games, and e-mail.

And in case you asked, Ask is another search engine that's worth paying a visit. Living up to its name, Ask enables you to ask a variety of questions. An example: *Which US capital is accessible only by boat or plane?* The answer is Juneau, Alaska.

The Davids to the search Goliaths

You may want to do a Google search on search engines because so many smaller specialized ones pop up all the time. (I suppose the creators of these sites want entrée into the same country clubs as the Google guys.) Search companies may narrowly focus on news, health, videos, travel, local goings-on, politics, or shopping. And some, such as Dogpile (www.dogpile.com), merely aggregate or compile results from other leading search engines into one.

You can jump ahead to Chapter 11 to explore more of what you can do on the Internet with Safari (and other browsers). But first, why not join me for a tour of e-mail on your Mac?

Chapter 10

Delivering the Goods on E-Mail

· ·

In This Chapter

▶ Setting up e-mail accounts

▶ Digging in to Exchange

▶ Composing messages

▶ Receiving messages

▶ Dealing with attachments

▶ Handling junk mail

▶ Getting tutored on Smart Mailboxes

▶ Taking note of Notes and Reminders

· ·

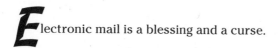lectronic mail is a blessing and a curse.

Why you can't live without e-mail: Messages typically reach the person to whom they're addressed in a few seconds as compared with a few days for *snail mail.* (That's the pejorative label geeks have tattooed on regular postal mail.) You won't waste time licking envelopes either.

Why e-mail drives you batty: It won't take long before you're likely buried under an avalanche of messages, much of it junk mail, or *spam.*

Not that any mail system is perfect. You can only imagine the snide comments heard in the day of the Pony Express: *Love that I got my tax refund and Sears catalog, but the stench on that steed . . .*

If you're an e-mail tyro, you discover the basics in this chapter. But even those who have been sending electronic missives for years might be able to collect a useful nugget or two.

Understanding E-Mail

In broad terms, *e-mail* is the exchange of messages over a communications network, typically the Internet but also a network within an organization.

To use e-mail, you need an e-mail account. These are traditionally offered by employers, schools, or Internet service providers (ISPs) such as AOL, AT&T, Comcast, EarthLink, or MSN. You also need e-mail software to send, receive, and organize these messages. Fortunately, Apple includes such an application with OS X, and there can't be any doubt about what the program does. It's aptly named Mail.

To access Mail, single-click the icon that looks like a stamp on the dock. If for some reason the icon isn't there, choose Mail inside the Applications folder.

The Worldwide E-Mail Exchange

Before telling you how to set up e-mail accounts to work with the Mac's Mail program, know that you can continue to send and read mail in such applications as Microsoft Outlook (Microsoft Entourage in older versions of Office for the Mac). What's more, if you've been sending and receiving e-mail on other computers through web accounts such as Google's Gmail, Microsoft's Hotmail or Outlook, or Yahoo! Mail, you can continue right along on the Mac. AOL, the outfit that popularized the phrase "You've got mail!" works too. Ditto for just about any other e-mail account you may come across.

Having one or more web-based e-mail accounts is nice. You get the tremendous advantage of being able to access mail from any Internet browser (on a Mac, PC, or Linux machine or smartphone or tablet). Plus, popular web e-mail accounts are free and loaded with gobs of storage.

Setting Up a New E-Mail Account

Sending and reading e-mail through the Mac's Mail program is a breeze, after you set the thing up. And Mail setup has gotten ever simpler through various versions of OS X. I've listed several steps in this section, but if you're setting up such mainstream accounts as AOL, Comcast, Gmail, Verizon, or Yahoo!, among others, you need not go beyond the second step:

1. **Open Mail by clicking the Mail icon (it looks like a stamp) on the dock or by double-clicking Mail in the Applications folder.**

First-timers are greeted with a Welcome to Mail window. Later, you see the Add Account window. If you're a member of Apple's iCloud service (see Chapter 12), Mail automatically established an account for you using information you provided in setting up your Mac or from the iCloud pane of System Preferences. If not, proceed as follows.

2. **If you are not a member of iCloud and want to set up a mainstream e-mail account automatically, or want to set up a new account in addition to iCloud:**

   • If you have one of the popular e-mail accounts (such as AOL, Comcast, Gmail, Verizon, or Yahoo!), merely enter your full name (if not already there), current e-mail address, and password in the Add Account window and then click Continue. When Apple sees an e-mail address from a provider it is familiar with, you can click Create and are pretty much finished.

   • If you enter an e-mail address that is unfamiliar to Apple, you'll still enter your full name, e-mail address, and password. Only now the Create button is labeled Continue, and the setup process must go on. Click Continue, and then go to Step 3.

3. **Fill in the general information required in the next screen.**

   You're transported to an Incoming Mail Server window. Fill in the following fields: an Account Type (POP, IMAP, Exchange, or Exchange IMAP) from the menu, optional Description, Incoming Mail Server, User Name, and Password. You can also place check marks next to Contacts and Calendars, if you'd also like to set up those. Check with your ISP if you're not sure how to fill in the information.

   The incoming mail server is where your messages are retrieved.

4. **Click Continue.**

   If you provided the proper credentials, you're good to go on, though you may be asked some security-related questions related to using *Secure Sockets Layer,* or *SSL.* If this is a work account, ask one of the company's information technology specialists, assuming that you have one, to help. If Mail can't verify the account, Apple serves up a warning that you may be putting confidential information at risk.

5. **If requested, add information about your outgoing server, which goes by the name of SMTP.**

   I won't keep you in the dark: SMTP stands for Simple Mail Transfer Protocol. POP, by the way, is short for Post Office Protocol, and IMAP stands for Internet Mail Access Protocol or Internet Message Access Protocol. Again, check with your ISP if you need help on how to fill in the information.

6. **Click Continue to bring up an account summary. If satisfied, click Create to complete the Mail setup process.**

At certain points during the preceding steps, the Mail program tests the information you provide to make sure that the settings are correct. If you run into snags along the way, click the question mark button in the Mail dialog for help. Setting up additional mail accounts involves repeating these steps. Begin by choosing File⇨Add Account in Mail.

Before You Click Send

Sending e-mail is really a snap. With the Mail program open, choose File⇨New Message, press the keyboard alternative ⌘+N, or click the New Mail icon on the Mail toolbar — the one that shows what appears to be a writing instrument inside a square. (Again, if Mail isn't open, click the stamp icon on the dock.) A window like the one shown in Figure 10-1 appears.

Click to send the message   These folks are copied but can't see who else is copied

The main recipient of your message   Show stationary

Click to attach a file   These folks are copied   Message subject

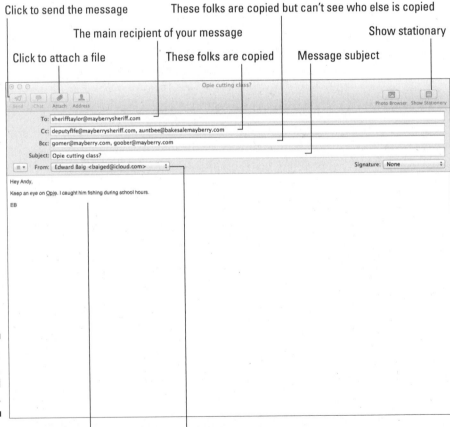

Figure 10-1:
How to send
an e-mail
message.

The main body of the message   The account you are sending from

Addressing your missive

With the New Message window on your screen, you're ready to begin the process of communicating through e-mail with another human being.

In the To box, *carefully* type the recipient's e-mail address. If you type even a single letter, number, or symbol incorrectly, your message will not be deliverable (you should get a bounce-back notification) or, worse, will be dispatched to the wrong person.

As you start banging out an e-mail address, the Mac tries to be helpful. It fills in the name and address of the person it thinks you are trying to reach (culled from your Contacts). Don't worry if the wrong name shows up at first. Keep typing until either Apple guesses correctly or until you have manually entered the full address.

If you are sending mail to more than one recipient, separate the addresses with a comma.

If you want to send mail to folks who are not the primary addressees of your letter, type the addresses for these people (again separated by commas if you have more than one) in the Cc, or *carbon copy,* box.

You have an even easier way to add an e-mail address, provided that your recipient already resides in your Contacts. In the New Message window, click the Address button. Then in your Contacts, just double-click the name of the person who you want to send mail to, and the Mail program takes care of the rest. The real names of these Contacts people appear in the To box (or Cc box); you won't see their actual e-mail address. For example, you'd see the name Tony Soprano rather than boss@sopranos.com. Have no fear; under the hood, Apple is making all the proper arrangements to send your message to the rightful recipient.

You may want to keep the recipients' list confidential. (The Feds need not know where Tony's mail goes.) You can do so in two ways:

- ✔ You can send mail to a group in your Contacts (see Chapter 3) just by typing the group name in the To field. Mail then automatically routes mail to each member's e-mail address. To keep those addresses private, choose Mail⇨Preferences and select Composing. Make sure that the When Sending to a Group, Show All Member Addresses check box is *not* selected.

- ✔ To keep the addresses of recipients who are not members of the same group private, click the little drop-down arrow to the left of the Account box in the New Message window. Choose Bcc Address Field. Bcc stands for *blind carbon copy.* Everyone included in the list will get the message, but they won't have a clue who else you sent it to in the Bcc list.

Composing messages

Keep a few things in mind before pounding out a message. Although optional, it's good e-mail etiquette to type a title, or subject, for your e-mail. (See the "E-mail etiquette" sidebar, later in this chapter.) In fact, some people get right to the point and blurt out everything they have to say in the Subject line (for example, *Lunch is on at noon*).

To write your message, just start typing in the large area provided below the address, Subject, and From (whichever e-mail account) lines. You can also paste passages (or pictures) cut or copied from another program.

The standard formatting tools found with your word processor are on hand. You can make words **bold** or *italic* and add spice to the letters through fancy fonts. On the Format menu, click Show Fonts to display different typefaces. (As an alternative, press ⌘+T.)

On the Format menu, click Show Colors to alter the hues of your individual characters. (As an alternative, press Shift+⌘+C.) Both the Fonts window and the color wheel are shown in Figure 10-2.

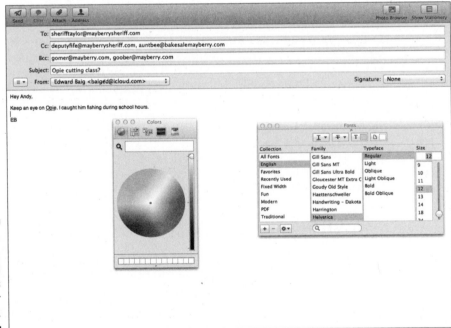

Figure 10-2:
Changing
fonts and
colors
in your
e-mails.

Choosing stationery

It's nice that you just dressed up an outgoing message with fancy fonts and different colors. But there's dressing up e-mail and then there's *dressing* up e-mail. And the OS X crowd can apply just the right visual tonic to outgoing messages.

Apple provides nearly three-dozen spiffy stationery templates as part of OS X, covering most major occasions and organized by category. These include birthday parties, baby announcements, and thank-you notes. Click the Show Stationery button at the upper-right corner of the compose window (refer to Figure 10-1) to check out the possibilities. Clicking one gives you a preview of what your message will look like.

Although many stationery templates include lovely pictures, Apple doesn't expect you to use them in your mailings. These are merely premade drop zones for adding your own pictures. Click the Photo Browser button at the upper-right corner of the New Message window and drag a picture from iPhoto, Aperture, or some other location into the picture placeholder on the template. Double-clicking this new photo lets you pan and zoom the image, letting you place the image just so.

You need not accept Apple's wording in any of these templates either. If you're wishing a Happy Birthday to Janie instead of Jessica, just single-click the area with text and make the substitution. Your words stay true to the design.

Find a stationery pattern you really like? Drag it into the Favorites area to build a custom collection.

Because Mail templates conform to *HTML* (the language of the web), most people receiving your e-mail will be able to view the stationery you intended. It doesn't matter whether they're on a PC or Mac. Mail also lets you use your own custom designs as templates.

Saving drafts

You're almost there. But what if you're waiting to insert an updated sales figure into a message? Or you decide it wouldn't be a bad idea to let off some steam before submitting your resignation (via the cold harsh world of e-mail, no less)? Click the red gumball button at the upper-left corner of the Mail message. A window appears with options to Save, Don't Save, or Cancel. Click Save to save the message as a draft — and do whatever it takes to calm down. When you're ready to resume working on the message, demanding a raise instead, choose Mailbox⇨Go to Favorite Mailbox and click Drafts. Or press ⌘+3.

Attaching files

You can attach a payload to your e-mail. *Attachments* are typically word processing documents, but they can be any type of file: pictures, music, spreadsheets, videos, and more.

To send a file with your e-mail, click the Attach button. In the window that appears, select the file you have in mind from the appropriate folder on your hard drive.

Given the market dominance of that *other* operating system, it's a fair bet that you're sending attachments to a Windows user. Windows is particular about the files it can read. It wants to see the *file extension,* such as .doc (see Chapter 7). Because Apple wants to make nice with the rest of the computing public, all you need to do is select the Send Windows Friendly Attachments check box before sending an attachment to a PC pal. It's in the aforementioned attachments window that appears.

Windows users may receive two attachments when you send mail from a Mac. (And you *coulda* sworn you sent a single file.) One reads `TheNameoftheFileISent` and the other `.__TheNameoftheFileISent`. Your recipients can safely ignore the latter.

You should clue recipients in ahead of time when you're planning on sending them large files, particularly high-resolution images and video. And by all means, refer to the attachment in the message you send. Why?

- ✔ Many Windows viruses are spread through e-mail attachments. Although you know the files are harmless, your Windows pals may be understandably skittish about opening a file without a clear explanation of what you're sending.

- ✔ Sending oversized attachments can slow down or even clog your recipient's e-mail inbox. It can take him or her forever to download these files. Moreover, ISPs may impose restrictions on the amount of e-mail storage that users can have in their inboxes or in the size of a file that can be transported. The company you work for may enforce its own limits. In fact, some employers prevent staffers from sending messages (or replying to yours) until they've freed up space in their inboxes. If the attachment is too big, Mail will list the size in red and (if known) let you know what the actual limit is. Mail won't send the message.

To get past an ISP's size restrictions, Mail gives you the option to resize images. Click the tiny pop-up menu near the upper-right corner of the New Message window, which shows up along with the image you are sending. You can send an image at its actual file size or shrink it to a smaller size. Medium and Large are other options. The menu appears in Figure 10-3. If your largest files reside on an accessible web page, your best bet may be to send a link to folks you are allowing to download those files. You can also share photos and other sizable files in a cloud-based storage locker through the likes of Dropbox, Box, Google Drive, Windows Live SkyDrive, and SugarSync, among other services. If you regularly share photos with a person, consider taking advantage of the Shared Photo Streams feature that I discuss in Chapter 15.

Spell checking

There's a certain informality to e-mail. Rather than type a sentence that says, "How are you?" you might instead type "How r u?" But not always.

Spelling counts (or ought to) when you are corresponding with potential employers or, for that matter, the person currently responsible for your paycheck. I know you won't want to be reprimanded if you send e-mail with misspellings to your seventh-grade English teacher.

Fortunately, Apple provides assistance to the spelling-challenged among us. A spell checker is a basic feature — just don't put all your faith in it. You may have correctly spelled a word you inadvertently used (*through* instead of *threw*, say).

To access the e-mail spell checker, choose Mail➪Preferences and then click Composing. On the Check Spelling pop-up menu, choose As I Type, When I Click Send, or Never.

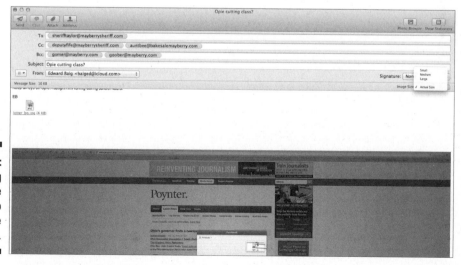

Figure 10-3:
Changing the size of a photo before e-mailing it.

E-mail etiquette

If Emily Post were alive today, she would surely draw up a list of acceptable practices for handling e-mails. In her absence, permit me to school you on e-mail decorum. I've already mentioned a few proper conventions: It helps to add a title or subject line to your e-mail and warn people if you're going to send large attachments. In some instances, you'll also want to use Bcc to protect the anonymity of the other people receiving your messages.

Here are some other conventions. DON'T SHOUT BY USING ALL CAPITAL LETTERS. Typing in lowercase letters like these is much more civilized. And you will avoid someone SHOUTING BACK and deliberately insulting, or *flaming,* you.

Do not forward e-mail chain letters. They will not bring you or your comrades vast riches. Or good luck. On the contrary, chain letters have been proven to cause people to stick needles in voodoo dolls representing the person who passed on the chain letter.

If replying to an e-mail, include the original *thread* by clicking *Reply* rather than composing a new message from scratch. If the original thread does not automatically show up, highlight the pertinent passages of (or all) the incoming message you want to respond to. When you click Reply, the original text will be there. Tailor your reply so that the responses are above or below the original queries.

Keep *emoticons,* such as :) (a smiley face), and text shortcuts, such as LOL (laughing out loud) and IMHO (in my humble opinion), to a minimum. You can use these more often when sending instant messages, as I elaborate in the next chapter.

In general, keep messages short and sweet. Some people get hundreds of e-mails a day. If you want your message to be among those that are read, don't compose an e-mail that is the text equivalent of a filibuster.

Take care to ensure that the message is going to the right place. Nothing's worse than mistakenly sending a message that says "Jack is a jerk" to Jack. For that matter, think long and hard before sending the "Jack is a jerk" memo to Jill. E-mails have a life of their own. They can be intentionally or accidentally forwarded to others. Maybe Jill is on Jack's side. (They've been spotted together fetching a pail of water, you know.) Maybe she thinks *you* are the jerk.

Along this line, remember that e-mails lack the verbal or visual cues of other forms of communication. Maybe you were kidding all along about Jack being a jerk. But will Jack know you are merely pulling his chain? To make sure that he does know, this is one instance where it is perfectly acceptable to use a smiley face.

In general, ask yourself how you'd feel receiving the same message. And don't assume that messages will remain private. (Calling General Petraeus!) Think before sending *anything* in an e-mail that you'd be reluctant to say or see in public.

Ignore these suggestions at your own peril. Somewhere Emily Post is watching.

Assuming that you ignored that last option, the Mail program will underline in red what it thinks are misspelled words, just as TextEdit and other word processors do. Right-click the suspect word and click the properly spelled word from the list of suggested replacements.

If your spell checker keeps tripping over a word that is in fact typed correctly (your company name, for instance), you can add it to the spell checker dictionary. Control-click the word and select Learn Spelling from the pop-up list. Your Mac should never make the same mistake again.

Signing off with a signature

You can personalize Mail with a *signature* plastered at the bottom of every outgoing message. Along with your name, a signature might include your snail mail address, phone numbers, iMessage account name (see the next chapter), and a pithy slogan.

To add your e-mail John Hancock, choose Mail⇨Preferences. Click the Signatures tab, and then click the Add (+) button. You can accept or type over the default signature that Apple suggests and choose whether to match the font already used in the message. You can assign different signatures to different e-mail accounts.

Managing the Flood of Incoming Mail

The flip side of sending e-mail is sifting through the mess of messages that may come your way. You can spend hours trying to get through an e-mail inbox, depending on your line of work.

The little red badge on the Mail icon on the dock indicates the number of unread messages demanding your attention.

New e-mails arrive as a matter of course through the Internet. You can click the Get Mail button on the Mail toolbar to hasten the process, as shown in my little tour of the Mail program in Figure 10-4. As an alternative, select Get New Mail on the Mailbox menu and then specify which mail account from which you want to receive missives. Or, click Get All New Mail or press the keyboard combination Shift+⌘+N. The message tally in the badge next to each Mail account rises until all the messages in the new load have been received.

If you click the Get Mail button and nothing happens, make sure that your account isn't offline (the account name appears dimmed). To remedy the situation, choose Mailbox⇨Take All Accounts Online.

If that too fails to alleviate the problem, choose Window⇨Connection Doctor. Your Mac will verify that you're connected to the Internet and examine each e-mail account to make sure that it's properly configured.

Messages with a blue dot haven't been read

Click drop-down menu to sort by Attachments, Date, Flags,
From, Size, Subject, To, Unread, Ascending or Descending

Get mail

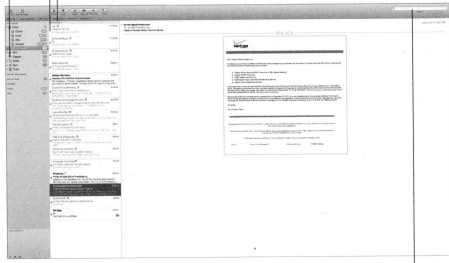

Figure 10-4:
The drill
on reading
e-mail.

Search messages

Single-click an incoming message to read it in the large pane adjacent to the
list of incoming messages. Or double-click a given message to read it in its
own window.

Choosing what to read

I'm no censor. I'd never tell you what you should or shouldn't read — online
or off. So know that I have only your best interests at heart when I urge you
to maintain a healthy dose of skepticism when it comes to tackling your
inbox.

As you pore through said inbox, you'll probably notice mail from companies,
online clubs, or websites that you might have expressed an interest in at one
time or another. You might have subscribed to e-mail newsletters on subjects ranging from ornithology to orthodontics. Most of the mail you get from
these outfits is presumably A-OK with you.

I'll take it as a given that you're going to read all the e-mails you get from colleagues, friends, and family. Well, maybe over time, you'll come to ignore mail from Uncle Harry and Aunt Martha, especially if they insist on sending you lame joke lists. If your mother is now using e-mail to hassle you about how you still aren't married, you have permission to ignore those, too.

That leaves e-mail from just about everyone else, and it likely falls into one of three buckets. These categories fit most people's definition of junk mail, or *spam:*

- ✔ **They're trying to sell you something.** It might be Viagra or Xanax. It might be a (supposedly) cheap mortgage. It might be a small-cap growth stock. It might be a Rolex. It probably means trouble.

- ✔ **They're trying to scam you.** You have to ask yourself, why me? Of all the deserving people on the planet, how is that you have been chosen by a private international banking firm to collect a small fortune left by a rich eccentric? Or the secret funds hidden by a deposed Third World diplomat? This too will probably get you in a pickle. (In Chapter 13, I discuss a special type of scam known as *phishing.*)

- ✔ **They're sending you pornography.** It's out there. In a major way.

Replying to messages

A chunk of the mail that you receive presumably warrants some kind of response. To answer an e-mail with an e-mail of your own, click the Reply (left-pointing) arrow button on the toolbar. Or look inside the message, and roll your mouse over the line that borders the header information with the main body of the message so that Mail controls appear. Click the Reply (left-pointing) arrow. Under both scenarios, an already addressed Reply message window appears, just waiting for you to type or dictate a response. After you've done so, whisk it along like any other e-mail message.

If you want to respond to everyone who was part of the original message, click Reply All (double-left-pointing arrow) instead of Reply.

Organizing Mail by conversation

Mail lets you view messages by conversation with an attractive interface that conceals the repetitive text that would otherwise be visible in a string of separate messages. You know that the feature is turned on when a check mark appears next to Organize by Conversation on the View menu.

When the Conversation feature is on, any of the missives that you receive that relate to an ongoing e-mail exchange with the person (or persons) shows a number that indicates just how many of those messages are in this particular conversation, or *thread*. You'll see examples in Figure 10-5. Click the conversation to see the entire thread in the window to the right of the message list.

You can add a Conversations icon to the Mail toolbar to toggle back and forth between Conversation view and a view in which all the messages are expanded.

VIP Mail

Some mail, obviously, is too important to ignore. So important, in fact, that these senders are given a special status. You have very important people in your life, so it goes without saying that you have very important senders whose messages are not to be missed. Only you know who these folks are — if not your boss, then perhaps prospective clients and/or customers. I'm figuring that most of you will include your spouse, your kids, your parents, and maybe other members of your family.

In its infinite wisdom, Apple lets you turn these very important people into VIP Mail senders. You can choose up to 100 VIPs, in fact, and the process for awarding them this special designation is simple. In a Mail message, look for the star to the left of the person's name. Click the star, and that person is in your exclusive Mail circle. Alternatively, in a Mail message, place the cursor to the right of a sender's name, click the downward-facing arrow, and select Add to VIPs. Or right-click a sender's name and choose Add to VIPs.

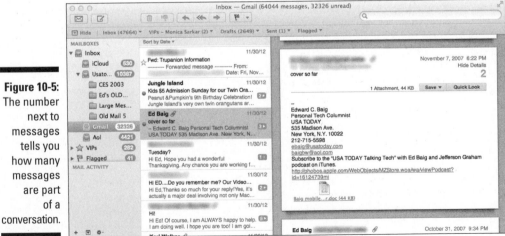

Figure 10-5:
The number next to messages tells you how many messages are part of a conversation.

From now on, or at least until you no longer consider the person worthy of the VIP designation, all mail from these folks lands in a special VIP Mail folder in the navigation pane. (Refer to Figure 10-4.) Mail also adds a mailbox for each VIP on the Favorites bar so that you can look at all your VIPs individually or collectively. It's a great way to keep track of all the mail you've received from your supervisor, lest you forget some crucial task that he or she has asked you to complete.

To remove the VIP designation, after your supervisor has moved on, say, click the star a second time.

You can share iCloud Contacts who are VIPs on one Mac with your other Macs running Mountain Lion. Your iCloud VIPs turn up on the Mail apps on your iOS devices as well.

Opening mail from strangers

What was it your parents taught you about not talking to strangers? That's generally sound advice with e-mail too. As I hinted at in the preceding section, cyberspace has a lot of misfits, creeps, and (I knew I'd have to throw in this phrase somewhere in the book) bad apples. They're up to no good. Because I don't want to cast aspersions on every unknown person who sends you e-mail, go with your gut. Common sense applies.

Even messages that arrive from people you know may not be completely clean, since sometimes Mail accounts are hijacked by the bad guys. Though you can't always tell for sure, if something appears to be amiss when you receive a message from a supposed pal, proceed with caution.

You can learn a lot from the subject line. If it refers to someone you know or what you do, I don't see the harm in opening the message.

If the greeting is generic — *Dear Wells Fargo Customer; Get Out of Debt Now* — I'd be a lot more cautious. Ditto if you don't see a subject line or if you see gross misspellings.

If a sender turns out to be a decent business prospect or your new best friend, you can always add him or her to your Contacts by choosing one of the following alternatives:

- ✔ Choose Message⇨Add Sender to Contacts.
- ✔ Right-click a sender's name or address in the From line of a message and select Add to Contacts. (If you have a one-button mouse, the alternative is Control-click.)

A few other handy shortcuts appear when you right-click a sender's name. As mentioned previously, you can add that person to the VIP list, copy the address, or send him or her a new mail message.

Junking the junk

If senders turn out to be bad news, you can sully their reputation — at least on your own computer. Throw their mail into the junk pile. It's easy: Just click Junk on the Message toolbar.

Marking messages happens to be your way of training the Mail program in what you consider to be spam. Mail flags potentially objectionable messages by highlighting them with a brown tinge. Click Not Junk in the message if the junk label is inappropriate.

You can direct Mail on how to handle the junk. Choose Mail⇨Preferences and then click the Junk Mail tab. The screen shown in Figure 10-6 appears.

By default, the Mail program leaves junk mail in your inbox so that you get to be the final arbiter. If you want OS X to segregate suspect mail into its own mailbox, click the Move It to the Junk Mailbox option.

As a matter of course, Mail exempts certain messages from spam filtering. This includes mail from senders who are in your Contacts, as well as senders who already received mail from you. Messages that use your full name are also exempt. In the Junk Mail section of Mail Preferences, remove the check mark next to any Mail preferences you want to change.

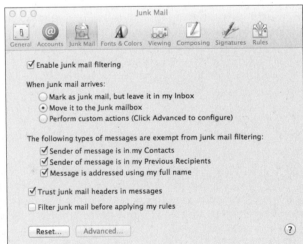

Figure 10-6:
The junkyard.

Most reputable ISPs attempt to fight spam on their own. If you're satisfied with the job they're doing, leave the Trust Junk Mail Headers in Messages check box selected. Apple's Mail program will leverage your ISP's best efforts.

Tips for avoiding spam

You can do your part to eliminate spam, too. Spammers are resourceful and can get your e-mail address through various methods:

- ✔ They employ automated software robots to guess at nearly every possible combination of addresses.

- ✔ They watch what you're doing. Do you fill out online sweepstakes forms? There's a winner, all right — the spammer.

- ✔ Do you hang out in chat rooms and Internet newsgroups? Bingo.

- ✔ Do you post messages in a public forum? Gotcha again.

You can stop engaging in these online activities, of course, but then the Internet won't be nearly as much fun. I have a better idea. Set up a separate e-mail account to use in these out-in-the-open kinds of scenarios. (ISPs such as AOL let you set up myriad accounts or screen names, for example.) You'll still get spam there. Just don't bother using those accounts to send or receive e-mail. Instead, treat your other account or accounts as the sacred ones you share with family, friends, and colleagues.

Setting the rules

As potent as Apple is at filtering spam, you can set up your own filters, or *rules,* for combating junk. You can set rules also to automatically reorganize the messages on hand that are perfectly acceptable. When incoming mail meets certain conditions, such as the subject matter or who sent the mail, the Mail program automatically forwards, highlights, or files them accordingly. For instance, you may want to redirect all the messages you've received from your investment advisor into a mailbox named Stocktips.

To set up a rule, follow these steps:

1. **Choose Mail⇨Preferences, and then click the Rules tab.**

2. **Select Add Rule to open the pane shown in Figure 10-7.**

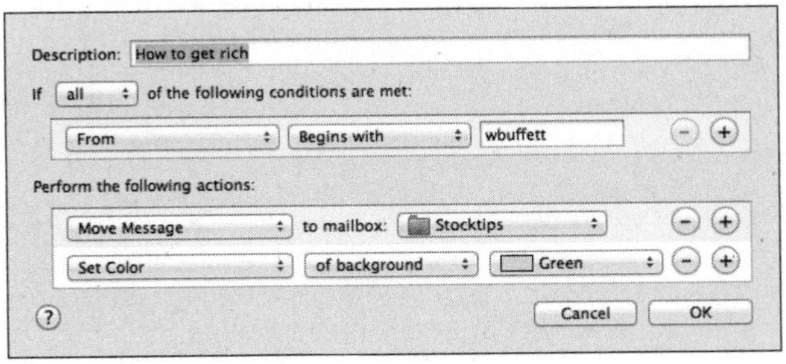

Figure 10-7:
You have
to establish
rules.

3. **Choose parameters identifying which messages are affected by the rule.**

   To redirect e-mail from your financial guru, for example, choose From in the first box, Begins With in the second box, and the name in the third box. Click + to add parameters and – to remove them.

4. **Now choose parameters for what happens to those messages.**

   For example, highlight the messages in green and move them to the Stocktips mailbox.

5. **When you've finished entering parameters, click OK.**

Smart Mailboxes

In Chapter 6, you discover dynamic Smart Folders. Welcome to the e-mail variation, *Smart Mailboxes.* Just as Smart Folders are constantly on the prowl for new items that match specific search criteria, Smart Mailboxes do the same. They are tightly integrated with Spotlight search.

You can set up Smart Mailboxes as a way to organize all mail pertaining to a specific project or all mail from a specific person. For instance, you may want to create a Smart Mailbox containing all correspondence with your boss for the most current fortnight. Mail older than two weeks is replaced by the latest exchanges.

Incidentally, the messages you see in a Smart Mailbox are virtual; they still reside in their original locations. In that sense, they are similar to aliases, described in Chapter 7.

To create a Smart Mailbox, follow these steps:

1. **Choose Mailbox⇨New Smart Mailbox.**

   The screen shown in Figure 10-8 appears.

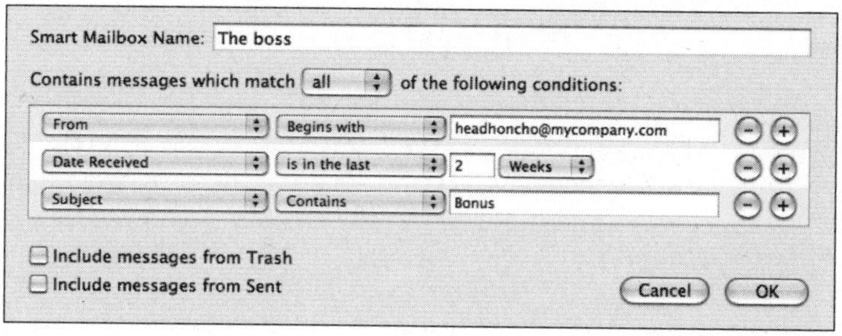

Smart Mailbox Name: The boss

Contains messages which match [all ⬍] of the following conditions:

From ⬍	Begins with ⬍	headhoncho@mycompany.com	⊖ ⊕
Date Received ⬍	is in the last ⬍	2	Weeks ⬍	⊖ ⊕
Subject ⬍	Contains ⬍	Bonus	⊖ ⊕

☐ Include messages from Trash
☐ Include messages from Sent

(Cancel) (OK)

Figure 10-8:
The smart-
est mailbox
around.

2. **Use the pop-up menus and text fields to characterize the parameters of the mailbox.**

   The process is similar to the one you follow when creating a rule. To add criteria, click the + button. To remove a condition, click the – button.

3. **When you're finished, click OK.**

You can create a duplicate of a Smart Mailbox by holding down the Ctrl key while you click the Smart Mailbox. Then choose Duplicate Smart Mailbox, an option that also appears on the Mailbox menu. Why do this? One possibility: You want to create a new Smart Mailbox that uses only slightly different criteria from the mailbox you are duplicating.

Searching mail

With an assist from Spotlight, the Mac's fast and comprehensive search system, you can find specific e-mail messages, or the content of those messages, in a jiffy.

✔ To search within a message you have open on-screen, choose Edit➪ Find➪Find and type the text you're looking for. You can perform a Find to find what you're looking for and (if you want) replace the word you find with another.

✔ You can also search your e-mail backlog. Just enter a search term in the search box at the upper-right portion of the Mail program screen. Use All Mailboxes, Inbox, VIPs, Draft, Sent, or Flagged to determine how to display the results.

You can find messages without opening Mail. Spotlight, in my humble opinion, is the fastest and most efficient way to find wayward messages.

Opening attachments

You already know how to send attachments. But now the tide has shifted, and someone sends you one (or more). Attachments may appear with an icon in the body of the message or as a paper clip in the message header area.

You have a few choices:

✔ Drag the icon onto the desktop or a Finder window.

✔ Double-click the icon, and the attachment should open in the program designed to handle it (for example, Word for a Word file or Preview for an image).

✔ Click Save to save the file to a particular destination on your computer.

✔ Click Quick Look to peek at the attachment without opening it.

Normally, I tell people not to open attachments they weren't expecting, even if they know the sender. Mac users can be a little more relaxed about this than their Windows cousins. While the times they are a-changin', the odds that the attachment will damage the Mac, even if it did carry some type of Windows virus, are low.

If you want to remove an attachment from an incoming message, choose Message➪Remove Attachments.

Making the Most of Your Mail

Before leaving this chapter, I want to introduce other ways to get the most out of your e-mail:

✔ **View a photo slideshow:** Picture attachments are afforded special treatment. By clicking Quick Look, you can view attached images in a lovely full-screen slideshow. From on-screen controls, you can go back to the previous image, pause, advance to the next slide, and view an index of all pictures. You can also click to add pictures to your iPhoto library. (See Chapter 15.) When you're finished with the slideshow, press the Escape key on the keyboard to go back to the original e-mail.

✔ **Pass it on:** Sometimes you get stuff that is so rip-roaringly hysterical (or at the other extreme, tragic and poignant) that you want to share it with everyone you know. To forward a message, click the right-pointing Forward arrow on the toolbar, or the one that appears out of nowhere when you roll the mouse by the line inside a message bordering the header with the body of the message. Enter the recipient's address in the New Message window that pops up. The entire previous e-mail will go out intact, save for a couple of subtle additions: the "Fwd:" prefix in the Subject line and the phrase "Begin forwarded message" above the body of the message. You can add an introductory comment along the lines of "This made me laugh out loud."

✔ **Flag messages:** To call attention to messages you want to attend to later, place a little flag next to them. The easiest way to flag a message is to click the Flag icon on the toolbar. But you can also choose Message➪Flag or press Shift+⌘+L. Repeat Shift+⌘+L to remove the flag or choose Message➪Flag➪Clear Flag. To help you determine the meaning of one flag compared to another, you can assign different colors to your flags.

✔ **Synchronize e-mail:** If you have an iCloud account (see Chapter 12), you can synchronize all your rules, signatures, and other settings across all your OS X computers. You can also synchronize other Mail accounts.

✔ **Archive messages:** Mail that you'd like to stash somewhere but ultimately hold on to is worthy of special backup treatment. That's what archiving messages is all about. First select the messages you want to archive. Next choose Message➪Archive from the menu at the top of the screen. An archive mailbox is created for each account in which you have a message that you choose to archive. You can later retrieve archived messages directly from that mailbox.

✔ **Use parental controls:** You can restrict who junior can correspond with through e-mail to only those addresses you've explicitly blessed. Choose ➪System Preferences and choose Parental Controls. Click the account you want to manage. You have to type your administrative password to make changes. Then click the People tab and select the Limit Mail check box. At your discretion, enter the e-mail addresses (and for that matter, instant messaging addresses) of anyone you'll let your kid communicate with. If you select the Send Permission Requests To option, you'll receive an e-mail plea asking for an okay to send messages to addresses not on your authorized list.

✔ **Use data detectors:** A friend sends an invitation to a dinner party at a new restaurant. A travel agent e-mails the itinerary for your next business trip. Messages typically arrive with fragments of information we'd love to be able to act on. Mail in OS X makes it dirt simple with *data detectors,* which can recognize appointments, addresses, phone numbers, and so on. So when you move your cursor inside the body of a message next to data the program can detect, a tiny arrow signifying a pop-up menu appears. Click the arrow next to an airline departure, for example, and you can add the event to Calendar. Click next to an address, and Mail lets you create a new contact, add to an existing contact, or display a Google map.

✔ **Get rid of mail:** You can dispose of mail in a number of ways. Highlight a message and press Delete on the keyboard. Drag the message to the Trash folder. Or click the Delete button on the toolbar. The messages aren't permanently banished until you choose Mailbox➪Erase Deleted Messages. Apple can automatically extinguish mail for good after one day, one week, or one month, or when you quit the Mail program. To set this up, go to Mail Preferences, click Accounts, choose an account, and select Mailbox Behaviors.

✔ **Get notified:** You can receive alerts of new messages as they arrive, or view the first few lines of a message in Notification Center, the repository for notifications that Apple added to the Mac via Mountain Lion. Notification Center on the Mac behaves in much the same way as Notification Center functions on iOS devices like the iPhone, iPad, and iPod touch. Refer to Chapter 3 for more details.

Take Note (and To-Dos)

Do you frequently e-mail reminders to yourself? I used to, at least before Apple added the handy Notes and Reminders apps. Prior to Mountain Lion, these functions were included inside the Mail app and in the case of To-Dos linked to iCal (now Calendar). They are now discrete apps that are similar to the Notes and Reminders apps in Apple's iOS operating system for the iPhone and iPad Take a moment to read about these now so that you won't have to remind yourself to do so later.

Note-taking 101

If you're like I am, your great thoughts are fleeting. That "ta-da" discovery rises out of the ashes only to disappear just as fast. So I best jot down a note when this brilliant idea is still floating about. Fortunately, creating notes on your Mac doesn't require much effort or any heavy thinking. Just click the Notes icon on the dock — it resembles a yellow legal pad — to summon the Notes app; then scribble (um, type) your musings in the lined yellow notebook window like the one shown in Figure 10-9. You can also dictate your note. If the spirit moves you, you can e-mail the note or include it in an iMessage by clicking the Share button at the bottom of the note. You don't even have to drum up a title for your note — Apple conveniently uses the first line of your note as its subject.

All your notes are listed on the left side of the app. If you're an iCloud member, you can share notes with your iPhone, iPad, or any recent iOS devices you may own. The same goes for other Macs running Mountain Lion and sharing the same iCloud account.

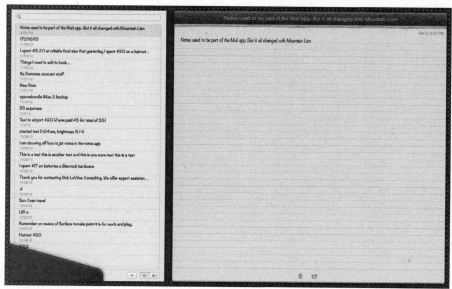

Notes used to be part of the Mail app. But it all changed with Mountain Lion

Figure 10-9:
This is
worth
noting.

And like all the other stuff on your Mac, you can search your notes using Spotlight.

Much ado about to-dos

Creating a to-do is equally easy in the Reminders app that Apple supplies with Mountain Lion.

Click Reminders on the dock to get started. You can add items into the Reminders lists that you create and assign priorities and deadlines for each of the to-dos on your list. (We writers need deadlines!) At your discretion, you can display a calendar inside the Reminders app.

After launching the app, click the + at the upper-right corner of the list you are working with and type in the reminder or task. Then type the circled "i" to assign a date, priority, or, as you're about to see, a reminder or task that kicks in based on your whereabouts.

You heard right. You can receive a reminder when you get to a specific place — a reminder with the number to a taxi you must call upon landing at an airport, for example —. You can also receive a reminder when you leave your current surroundings. Figure 10-10 shows the window where you can enter a date, location, and priority.

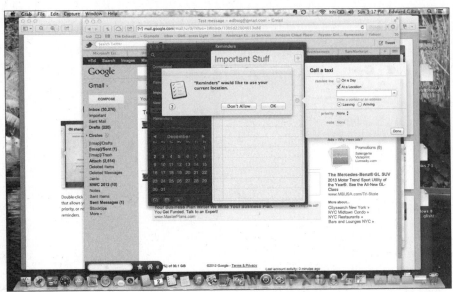

Figure 10-10:
Remind
me when I
leave to . . .

As with Notes, reminders are integrated into iCloud and Notification Center. You can also share Reminders information with third-party calendars from Google, Yahoo!, and others, or just display reminders on your Mac.

Place a check mark in the little box next to a to-do when you've completed a task on your list. And now let me remind you to kindly move on to the next chapter and beyond.

Chapter 11

Caught Up in the Web

In This Chapter

▶ Joining chat rooms

▶ Communicating through Messages

▶ Sharing video chats

▶ Digging through newsgroups and blogs

▶ Socializing through social networking

▶ Finding a mate online

▶ Shopping in the Mac App Store

▶ Playing in Game Center

*F*olks routinely surf the web seeking specific types of information — headlines, stock quotes, vacation deals, weather, homework help, sports scores, technical support, you name it. But as much as anything, the Internet is about meeting and connecting with people. These people could be job prospects or would-be employers. Or people who share your zeal for the Chicago Cubs, sushi, and Macintosh computers. Persuasion takes on a major role in cyberspace, too — as you get on your virtual high horse and attempt to coax others around to your way of thinking.

And, yes, finding companionship, romance, and (under the best of circumstances) long-lasting relationships is part of the cyberexperience too. So is playing games in multiplayer online environments.

Critics have often sneered, "These people need to get a life." But many *Netizens* (citizens of the Internet) have rewarding lives online and offline, thank you very much. And on the Net, they're congregating in vibrant *communities* with individuals of similar interests and passions.

I explore many of these avenues in this chapter.

Chat Rooms

A lot of congregating on the Net happens in *chat rooms,* areas where you can converse in real time on pretty much any topic: quilting, cricket, fad diets, parenting, biotechnology, extraterrestrial sightings, and on and on. The conversing has typically been left up to your fingertips. Indeed, typos be damned; expect to bang away at the keyboard with reckless abandon because text exchanges in chat rooms come fast and furious. You may find dozens of people in a room. Good luck determining who's talking to whom.

As broadband hookups became increasingly common, audio and video chats through the use of small cameras called webcams likewise became more widespread. Built-in cameras are standard issue these days on most new Macs, and are used for FaceTime video chat, discussed later in this chapter, and lots of other purposes.

Chat is also a staple in the online gaming environment, be it poker, backgammon, or the more fantastical corners of the online gaming world. In an immersive three-dimensional virtual fantasy world, for example, you may have your persona — represented by an animated *avatar* — do the chatting for you. One such setting available to Mac users is called *Second Life* (www.secondlife.com). Be aware that the environment sometimes exceeds PG-13 sensibilities.

Some chat rooms are monitored by people who make sure that the discourse remains civil and courteous. In rare instances, monitors may dictate who can and cannot speak, or they may boot somebody out.

The first exposure many people had to chat rooms was inside the virtual confines of America Online. AOL, then a dialup behemoth, established a set of community guidelines, mostly having to do with banning hateful speech as well as threatening or abusive behavior. The same general principles apply, of course, but AOL is no longer behind a subscription-based walled garden, or for that matter as popular as it was in its heyday. The subject categories in chat rooms are quite varied. Such rooms are still found through services such as Yahoo! Messenger. All these chats are descendants of something called IRC, or Internet Relay Chat. But much of the online discourse nowadays occurs on the leading social networks Google+ and especially Facebook, as well as Twitter. And Facebook and Twitter, as noted throughout this book, are all over Mountain Lion.

I tell people visiting a chat group for the first time to say hi to everyone and then take a backseat. Observe. Get a feel for the place. Figure out whether participants are around the same age (or maturity level) as you. Determine whether they're addressing topics you care about — and speaking the same language. Participants in these joints come from all over the planet (and sometimes it seems from outer space).

Communicating One on One: Instant Messaging

You may be speaking (broadcasting really) to dozens of people at a time in a chat room. But what if you strike a bond with the mysterious stranger whose quips catch your fancy? And want to whisper sweet virtual nothings in this person's ear and no one else's? Such intimacy requires a private conversation. It requires an *instant message,* or *IM.*

Instant messages need not originate in chat rooms, and for most people, they do not. Participants once had to rely on dedicated instant messaging *client* software that could be downloaded for free from AOL, Yahoo!, Microsoft, Skype, and others. But you don't always have to fetch separate software for your Mac — Messages, formerly iChat, is a core feature in Mountain Lion. And because I already mentioned Facebook, it's worth pointing out that you can also chat inside the wildly popular social network.

Just as the company did with e-mail, AOL gets the lion's share of the credit for spreading IMing — yes, you can also treat it as a verb — among the masses in the United States. AOL owns the popular *AOL Instant Messenger,* or *AIM,* software, and for a time, the exceedingly popular global IM program, *ICQ.* You can fetch these free at www.aim.com and www.icq.com, respectively. In fact, as you'll see shortly, you need not even download AIM, because Apple's own iMessages instant messaging protocol, which confusingly is part of the Messages program, lets you kibitz with the AIM community.

Instant messaging has become a mainstay in business as well as in social circles. It's a complement to e-mail and in many ways more appealing. Here's why: Just as in a chat room, instant messaging conversations occur in real time, without the delays associated with e-mail. In addition, IM permits the kind of spontaneity that's not possible through e-mail or even an old-fashioned phone call. Through a concept known as *presence,* you can tell not only whether the people you want to IM are currently online but also whether they're willing to chat. Status indicators next to their names on a *buddy list* clue you in on their availability.

Instant messaging has at least one major downside compared to e-mail and the plain old telephone: the lack of *interoperability* among the major IM purveyors. The phone also has the advantage of conveying tone without you having to remember to include appropriate emoticons. For competitive reasons, market leader AOL carefully guards its buddy list, so an AIM member couldn't send a direct instant message to a Yahoo! or MSN user, at least not without techie work-arounds. Think about what would happen if a Verizon Wireless cell phone customer, say, couldn't call a friend who was an AT&T subscriber, and vice versa. But peace is breaking out all the time, so this issue too may be solved by the time you read this.

Just as regular chat has evolved well beyond a text-only communications channel, so has instant messaging. Today's IM programs let you engage in audio exchanges and make free computer-to-computer Internet phone calls. Moreover, if you have a webcam — and owners of most new Macs are blessed with built-in iSight and FaceTime cameras — you can also hold face-to-face conversations. And that leads me right back to Apple's own ever-evolving communication application, Messages, which ties iMessage, text messaging, and instant messaging, into one neat package. But that's not the only way you can communicate through your Mac. Via FaceTime, you can call other people, and see them at the same time.

Messages

In truth, calling Messages an instant messaging program really is selling it way short, kind of like telling somebody that Kobe Bryant knows how to make free throws. The program used to be called iChat AV, with the *AV* part standing for *audio visual* or *audio video,* depending on who you ask, then just iChat. You still find still audio and video in Messages, of course, but these days, it's known by its new name.

For sure, the iMessage component of Messages is a competent instant messenger for handling traditional text chatter. It is also a convenient way to send text messages to somebody's Mac or iOS-based smartphone or tablet. When you communicate with a device capable of handling iMessages as well, you can get a receipt that tells you when your message was delivered and when it was read. You'll also see an indicator that tells you when the person is composing a response. Outside of iMessages, you can also send SMS or text messages to other phones and tablets.

But consider some of its other tricks:

- ✔ You can exchange files while talking with someone.
- ✔ You can have a *free* audio conference with up to nine other people.
- ✔ You can engage in a video conference from your Mac desktop with up to three other people.
- ✔ You can apply funky Photo Booth video effects and backdrops.
- ✔ You can collaborate on presentations during the video conference and even swap *views* (technical in this context, not necessarily opinion-based) and take over each other's computer desktops.

You'll need at least *one* of the following to get going with Messages:

- ✔ **An existing AIM or AOL screen name and password:** As noted, Messages is tied in with AOL's popular instant messaging program.

- ✔ **A Jabber ID:** You can use a Jabber ID to exchange messages with cohorts who share the same Jabber servers. Jabber is an open standard chat system employed in many organizations.

- ✔ **A Google Talk or Yahoo! ID:** You can go to Google's and Yahoo!'s respective websites to sign up.

- ✔ **An Apple ID:** You can use the iCloud.com ID that you got if you signed up for iCloud as your Apple ID. You also have an Apple ID if you signed up for an iTunes store account. Or you can continue to use the mac.com ID or me.com ID you may have had under iCloud's predecessor services known as .Mac (as in dot Mac), and MobileMe. I elaborate on iCloud in Chapter 12. If you don't have an Apple ID, you can create one in Messages.

- ✔ **A local network or classroom using Apple technology called Bonjour, formerly known as Rendezvous:** Through this built-in technology, Messages lets you see who on your local network is available to chat. Bonjour, however, is used for configuration-free networking throughout OS X.

If you want to exploit video, you'll need a fast broadband Internet connection, plus a compatible camera. Apple's iSight or FaceTime camera (standard on most recent models) works well, but any digital camera or camcorder connected to your computer should do, including those you may connect through USB or FireWire.

Hey buddy

Messages is useless without one more essential component: at least one other person with whom to schmooze.

Fortunately, the iMessage service lets you send and receive free and secure messages on your Mac, iPhone, iPad, and iPod touch with folks who have one or more of these devices. They'll either get your message on their mobile device or the next time they open Messages on their Macs. If in return, someone sends you an iMessage, you'll get it on your Mac and any other iOS device you in turn may have, with the caveat that it must be running iOS 5.0 or later.

iMessage provides many benefits:

- ✔ You can send messages to phone numbers or e-mail addresses.
- ✔ You can start a conversation on your Mac or some other device and pick up where you left off on yet another device.
- ✔ You can share attachments of up to 100MB in size, and that includes full high-definition videos and photos.

If you signed up with an AIM, Google Talk or Yahoo! account, your buddy list may already be populated with names of people in those services.

Take a look at the Messages window in Figure 11-1. Any ongoing conversations are listed down the left side of the screen, with the most recent on top. On the right side, you see the exchanges from your current conversation.

To add new people to a new message or conversation, click the + all the way to the right of the To field, as shown in Figure 11-2, and choose a person from your Contacts, your buddies, or any groups you've set up. You can add multiple people to the conversation.

You can choose how you want your buddy names to appear: full name, short name, or handles (their e-mail address or phone number). Go to View➪Buddy Names and make your selection.

Though you don't have to use the buddy list of all your friends and contacts, it can be helpful. Go to Windows➪Buddies, or press ⌘+1 on the keyboard.

To add a new buddy to the list, click the + at the lower-left corner of the Buddy List window and then choose Add Buddy. In the window that appears, type your buddy's AIM, Yahoo!, Gmail, or Mac.com account plus his or her real first and last names in the designated fields. You can also add the new buddy to a group.

Alternatively, choose an entry from your Contacts by clicking the downward-pointing arrow in the lower-right corner of the Add Buddy window. The person's name turns up instantly on your buddy list.

You can also add a group, rather than an individual buddy (perhaps your coworkers, soccer team, and so on). After clicking the + at the lower-left corner of the Buddy List window, click Add Group (as opposed to Add Buddy). Type in the Group name and click Add.

The buddy list has a bunch of visual status cues. Your buddy may have included a mug shot, perhaps through Photo Booth. Or buddies may express themselves through small images called *buddy icons.* You can even animate these icons in OS X.

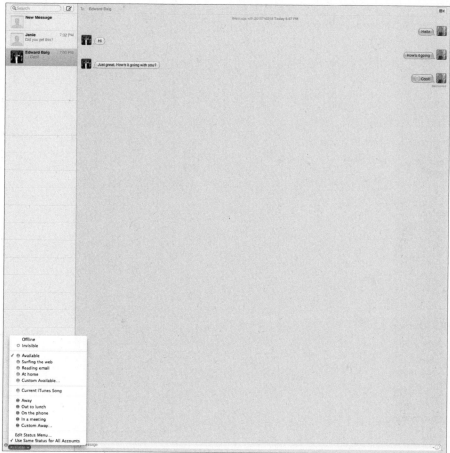

Figure 11-1:
I don't
normally
talk to
myself.
Right, Ed.

How you communicate depends on which of the icons at the bottom of the Buddies list (shown in Figure 11-3) you end up clicking. Click the icon with the "A" to begin a text chat. Click the telephone symbol icon to initiate a voice or audio chat. Click the movie camera icon to connect through video. And click the icon with two rectangles to ask your chat partner if he or she is willing to share his or her Mac screen.

Confusingly, sometimes icons also appear next to an individual's buddy entry. For example, in Figure 11-3, you will see video camera icons next to a couple of the names that indicate that those people are available to chat through video. Click the icon to initiate a video chat with that person.

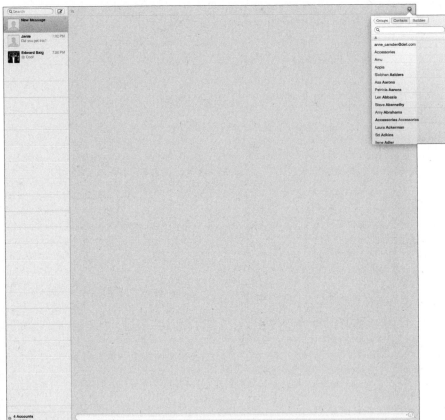

Figure 11-2:
Finding the
people to
communi-
cate with.

Figure 11-3:
Visual cues
let you
know how
to instantly
contact your
buddies.

Mostly you'll be able to tell whether your buddies are online at the moment and willing to give you the time of day. Here's how:

- A green circle to the left of a person's name means that he or she is ready and (presumably) willing to talk.

- A red circle means that the person is online but otherwise engaged. The person is considered Away.

- A yellow circle means that the person on your list is idle and has not used the machine for a while (the window tells you how long the person has been in this state). Your buddy just hasn't bothered to change his or her status from Available to Away.

- If a name is dimmed, your buddy is offline.

You can set your own status for everyone else to see. And you are not limited to Available or Away. Click under your own name and choose Custom from the drop-down menu. You can choose a custom message to appear next to a green or red circle, depending on your particular set of circumstances. Type any message you want, such as, *can chat in a pinch but busy* or *back after lunch*.

Incidentally, if you've been absent from the computer for a while, the Mac will kindly welcome you back to the machine and ask whether you want to change your chat online status from Away back to Available.

iMessage doesn't actually use detailed online statuses like, say, AIM, where you can indicate that you're out to lunch, in a meeting, or otherwise unavailable. (Of course, you can still establish online statuses for the instant messaging programs you use within Messages.) So if you want to stop receiving iMessages on a temporary basis on your Mac (while still receiving messages on your iOS devices), you'll have to disable iMessage on your Mac. In Messages Preferences, select Accounts and select or deselect the Enable This Account check box.

Chatting

To initiate an instant message, double-click a name in the buddy list, which pops up whenever you open Messages. Or highlight a name on the list and click the A icon. Type something in the bottom box. **Hey stranger** will suffice for now.

Alternately, you can choose File⇨New Message and enter the name of the person with whom you would like to chat, assuming the person is among your buddies or contacts. If the individual is not in your buddy list or Contacts, enter the person's e-mail address or phone number in the To field of the Messages window.

What you type instantly appears in a comic-strip bubble in the upper portion of the window. (You can view chats as rectangular boxes instead by making the change on the View menu.) If the person responds, what he or she has to say appears in its own comic-strip bubble. And so on.

You can type in your own smileys and emoticons or check out Apple's own collection by choosing Edit➪Insert Smiley. (I suspect I'll be using the smiley representing "Foot in mouth" more often than not.) And if you need to use currency symbols and other special characters, choose Edit➪Special Characters.

If you look back at Figure 11-1, you'll see yours truly having a silly conversation with yours truly. (Honestly, I don't normally talk to myself. This little exercise is strictly for your benefit.)

Now say that you're having an important IM exchange with your lawyer or accountant. Or swapping tuna casserole recipes with your best friend. You may want a record of your conversation that you can easily refer to later. To create a transcript of your session, open Messages Preferences by clicking the Messages menu and then clicking Preferences. Click the Messages tab and then select the Save History When Conversations Are Closed check box, as shown in Figure 11-4. You can find the appropriate transcript by searching Finder for "chat transcript" under Kind.

To wipe away the record, choose Edit on the menu bar at the top of the screen and then choose Clear Transcript.

Figure 11-4: Chatting the way you like it through Messages Preferences.

Take note of other things you can do in Messages Preferences. For instance, you can change the background color and font.

You can also use iMessages (or other text chat services such as AIM, Google Talk and so on) to send files to your IM buddy (or get a file in return). Not only is it convenient, but unlike with e-mail, you have no size restriction on the file you're sharing. (You can send only one file at a time, however.) Select a name on your buddy list and then choose Buddies⇨Send File. Select the file you want to send. Alternatively, drag a file to a buddy's name or into the area of an open chat window. If you're in a video chat, drag a file to the upper half of the video chat window. And if you're chatting with a bunch of folks at once, drag the file over the name of the person you want to send it to. In a video chat with multiple people, you can also share a presentation or any other files, as you'll discover later in this chapter.

Participants in a chat have the option to accept or reject the incoming file.

While I'm on the painful subject of rejection, if one of your buddies (or anyone else) initiates an IM and you don't feel like talking, click Decline in the window that pops up.

If the person gets on your nerves, click the Accounts tab in Messages Preferences and choose your account. Click Privacy and then select the Block Specific People check box. Click Edit List and add the names of the folks who are on your keep-'em-away list. (Just know that your would-be buddies can do the same to you.)

You can proactively determine who can see that you're online and send you messages. Under Messages Preferences, click the Accounts icon and then click the Privacy tab. Choose a privacy level that you're comfortable with. The options are

- ✔ Allow anyone.
- ✔ Allow people in my buddy list.
- ✔ Allow specific people. If you make this choice, you have to type each person's AIM, .mac.com, iCloud.com, or .me.com address.
- ✔ Block everyone.
- ✔ Block specific people. Again, type the appropriate addresses.

Seeing is believing; hearing too

As I already alluded to, IMing and text chatting in general are kind of yesterday's news (though still darn useful). The twenty-first-century way of communicating is through a video phone call. Apple provides two ways to accomplish this minor miracle: through iMessage and through an innovation introduced on the iPhone called FaceTime. I'll have more to say on FaceTime later in the chapter. (Never mind that a primitive version of this technology was exhibited at the 1964 New York World's Fair.)

Assuming that your camera and microphone are configured to your liking, you can take advantage of twenty-first century innovations by clicking the video camera icon in the buddy list or, for just an audio session, clicking the telephone icon. As usual, your IM partner has the option to accept or decline the invitation. If he or she accepts, you can gaze at each other full-screen. (Your image will appear in a smaller window.)

This stuff is super-slick. In a multiroom conference, participants appear in a virtual three-dimensional conference room with authentic video effects that make people's reflections bounce off a conference table.

And by clicking the Effects button, you can replace the normal background with gorgeous, or bizarre, backdrops from Photo Booth, as highlighted in Chapter 5 and as seen in Figure 11-5. You need Leopard or a later version of OS X and a Mac with a Core 2 Duo or better chip to apply one of these scenes, but pals using older versions of Apple's chat program or AIM will see the backgrounds even if they haven't upgraded to the latest Mac operating system.

Figure 11-5: She's in the clouds, and he's in the falls during this video chat.

Courtesy of Apple

The quality is generally pretty good, though the picture may show some distortion, depending on your broadband connection.

The video used in Messages (and QuickTime) adheres to a video standard known as H.264, or Advanced Video Codec (AVC). It's meant to deliver crisp video in smaller file sizes, saving you bandwidth and storage.

If you have a webcam but your IM buddies do not, they still get the benefit of seeing your smiling face at least. And provided they have a microphone, you still get to hear them.

You can record video chats and share them on your iPod, iPhone, iPad, Sony PSP or a variety of other devices. Choose Video⇨Record Chat. Don't worry: A chat can't be recorded without your permission. To stop recording a chat in progress, click Stop or close the chat window.

Theater

You can share pictures from iPhoto, presentations from Keynote, and even QuickTime movies by turning on the Theater feature (see Figure 11-6), which debuted as iChat Theater in Leopard. It almost looks like you're in a theater when presenting files.

Figure 11-6: Presenting a photo inside Theater.

You can take advantage of the Theater feature in a few ways, provided that your broadband Internet connection is up to the task. During a video chat, do the following: Click the + at the bottom of the screen and then from the drop-down menu, make an appropriate selection:

✔ To share a file, select the Share a File with Theater check box and choose the relevant file from the dialog box.

✔ To share photos, select the Share iPhoto with Theater from the drop-down list and then select the pictures you want to share. You can present an album as a slideshow, provided that you have a relatively recent version of iPhoto on-board. The person doing the sharing has video controls that dictate how the slideshow is being seen at the other end.

✔ To share a web page, select the Share a Webpage with Theater from the list and enter the web address or URL in the box that appears.

✔ To share an application, notably Keynote for making presentations, select the Share an Application with Theater and pick the app from the list.

✔ To share another file, select Share a File with Theater and choose the appropriate file to share.

If you're not sure whether one of your files can be presented in Theater, highlight the item in Finder and choose File➪Quick Look. If you have the ability to peek at it, the person you want to show it to through Theater may be able to see it as well.

Click the X in the upper-right corner of the chat window to stop sharing.

Only the person who started sharing all this stuff can stop sharing.

Screen sharing

It's all well and good that you can make a long-distance presentation through Messages. But suppose you and your buddy want to toil together on a website or some other project from far away. If you both have Macs with relatively recent versions of OS X (meaning Leopard or later), you can work on one or the other's screen — just click back and forth to swap screens. This stunt works with AIM, Jabber, Google Talk, and Bonjour, but notably not with iMessage or Yahoo!.

From the Buddies menu, choose either Share My Screen with *name of person* or Ask to Share *name of person's* Screen. Rest assured that you can politely decline if you're the one being asked. But positive thoughts here, folks, so let us assume that you've given or received the green light. You can each freely run amok on the shared desktop, even copying files by dragging them from one desktop to the other. Messages keeps an audio chat going so that you can let each other know what you're up to.

Not satisfied with what your chat buddy is telling you? Press Control+Escape to put an instant kibosh on the screen-sharing session or click the X to close.

If you're sharing the other person's screen, you'll notice your own Mac desktop in a tiny window, as shown in Figure 11-7.

Figure 11-7:
My screen
or yours?

As you might imagine, this screen-sharing business can get a little too close to home, especially if you don't fully trust the person you're letting loose on your computer. Be especially leery if someone not on your buddy list comes calling with a screen-sharing request. You should also be careful before granting permission to someone on your Bonjour list. They are not always who they say they are.

Face Time for FaceTime

Suppose that you want to talk to a friend who has a late-model iPhone, iPod touch, or iPad. Through FaceTime, you can gab and see them too. FaceTme works from Mac to Mac as well. You need OS X version 10.6.6 or later and an Ethernet or Wi-Fi connection to the Internet. (People at the other end using an iPhone 4 or later, recent iPod touch or iPad 2 or later, or iPad mini can use a cellular connection as well, provided that the devices are running iOS 6 or later.)

You can use the iSight or alternatively the FaceTime camera that is standard on recent Macs. Or you can use an external camera hooked up to your Mac through FireWire, USB, or (via an adapter) Thunderbolt.

Getting started with FaceTime

FaceTime is built in to OS X.

On your initial time out, you have to sign in to FaceTime using your Apple ID, which can be your iTunes Store account or another Apple account, as shown in Figure 11-8. Or, if you'd rather use a new Apple ID, you can create one. You also have to enter an e-mail address; callers will use that address to call you from their Macs or iOS devices.

Figure 11-8:
Sign
in or
create
a new
account to
see me.

If this is the first time you've used this e-mail address for FaceTime, Apple will send an e-mail to that address to verify the account. Click Verify Now and enter your Apple ID and password to complete the FaceTime setup.

If you want to add another e-mail account to associate with FaceTime, open FaceTime Preferences from the FaceTime menu and click Add Another E-Mail. That way, people can reach you via more than one e-mail account.

Making a FaceTime call

FaceTime is closely tied to your Contacts. To initiate a FaceTime video call after you've signed in to the app, click the Contacts button. To call a FaceTime-capable iPhone, click a phone number and/or e-mail address. To call an iPod touch, iPad, or another Mac, again click an e-mail address or, in some instances, a phone number. For you to be able to reach another Mac via a phone number, as of this writing, that other machine must be running Mountain Lion or later.

In most cases, if someone you want to call is not among your contacts, you'll have to add that person to your Contacts before you call him or her in FaceTime. Click the + to add that person to Contacts and by extension FaceTime.

If you're calling back someone you've had a recent FaceTime conversation with, click Recents and then click the person's name or phone number to initiate a call. Under Recents, you can display all FaceTime calls you've made or received lately or just those incoming calls you missed.

You can also add frequent callers to a Favorites list.

You can check out what you look like in a window before making a FaceTime call. Powder your nose, straighten your tie, and put on a happy face. After a call is under way, you can still see what you look like to the other person through a picture-in-picture window that you can drag to any corner of the video call window. You can click a microphone icon (labeled in Figure 11-9) to mute your voice. You'll still be seen. Click the Full-screen button (also labeled in Figure 11-9) to take over the full Mac screen; you'll still see a picture-in-picture window. The Mute, End Call, and Full-screen buttons disappear after a few seconds. To bring them back during a call, move your cursor over the FaceTime window.

If you failed to connect with a recipient through FaceTime, click the green Call Back button in the call window.

Call window shows the person you are talking to

FaceTime with Edward Baig

Figure 11-9:
A FaceTime call in progress — with myself.

How you look to the other person   Mute voice   Go to full screen

Hang up

Receiving a FaceTime call

FaceTime doesn't have to be open for you to receive a video call from a friend. It can open automatically so that your Mac will start ringing and you'll see the caller in the window, as shown in Figure 11-10. Click the green Accept button to answer the call or the red Decline button to reject it.

Figure 11-10:
Please take
my call.

If you failed to reach someone, you can click the Call Back button that appears
in order to try FaceTime with the person again later. (You see a badge next
to the FaceTime icon on the dock showing the number of FaceTime calls you
missed, if any.)

If you don't want to be disturbed by an incoming FaceTime call, open FaceTime Preferences and turn off FaceTime. You can also turn FaceTime off from the FaceTime menu.

More FaceTime tricks

You can do even more in FaceTime:

- **Change orientation:** When you get a call from an iPhone or an iPod touch, the call window on your Mac rotates if the caller changes the orientation of his device. You're not about to rotate the Mac as you would one of those handheld devices. But you can still change the orientation that the caller sees. Choose Video from the FaceTime menu and then select either Use Portrait or Use Landscape.

- **Resize the video call window:** You can make the video call window bigger by clicking Zoom on FaceTime's Window menu. Click Zoom again to revert to the standard-size window. And as with any window, you can expand it by dragging a window edge. And as I indicated, you can go full-screen during a call.

- **Pause a call:** If you need to pause a video call, choose Hide FaceTime from the FaceTime menu or choose Window⇨Minimize. Click the FaceTime icon on the dock to resume the call.

- **Add a caller to Contacts or Favorites:** From the Recents list, click the circled right arrow next to a caller's name or number. In the next screen, click Create New Contact or Add to Existing Contact. Click Add to Favorites to make the caller a favorite and choose the appropriate phone number to use (if more than one exists).

- **Change Caller ID:** You can list any of the e-mail accounts you're using for FaceTime as the Caller ID account that the people you are calling will see. To change to a different account, open FaceTime Preferences, click the right-pointing arrow in the field showing your current Caller ID account, and click any of the other accounts you have associated with FaceTime to select one of them.

Open Notifications settings in System Preferences to arrange alerts for FaceTime calls, and to determine if and how you'll see FaceTime notifications in Notification Center.

If you're traveling in another country, you can arrange it so that any local calls made to iPhone users through FaceTime are using the proper native format for making that call. In FaceTime Preferences, click Apple ID, choose Change Location, and select the appropriate country or region.

Having an Online Voice

You can be heard and seen on the Internet in lots of places. In the following sections, I explore some of them.

Newsgroups

The term *newsgroups* may make you think of journalists retreating to the nearest watering hole after deadline. (Been there, done that.) Or a posse of friends sitting around together watching, I dunno, Bob Schieffer. Newsgroups are defined differently in the chapter you are so kindly reading.

Newsgroups go by numerous descriptors: electronic (or online) bulletin boards, discussion groups, forums, and Usenet (a techie name that dates back to Duke University in the late 1970s). Google acquired the Usenet archives in 2001; through Google Groups, you can read the billions of Usenet postings dating back to 1981.

In a nutshell, people post and respond to messages on everything and anything: pipe smoking, low-carb diets, monster movies, world-class tenors, nanotechnology, canine incontinence, alternative sources of energy, snake charmers. Thousands of these discussions are taking place online.

Newsgroups generally adhere to a hierarchical structure. At the top level, you'll see *comp* for computers, *rec* for recreation, *sci* for sciences, *soc* for socializing, *talk* for politics, *news* for Usenet, *misc* for miscellaneous, *alt* for alternative, and so on. As you move down the food chain, the categories become more specific. So you might start at *alt* and then drill down to *alt.animals,* then *alt.animals.cats,* and then *alt.animals.cats.siamese.*

You'll need a newsgroup reader program to read these posts. If you bought an older version of Microsoft Office for the Mac, it includes a newsreader in the Entourage e-mail program. You can also download free or low-cost shareware newsreaders for the Mac. They go by names such as Hogwasher, MacSoup, MT-NewsWatcher, NewsHunter, and Unison. Keep in mind that your ISP needs to support newsgroup access or you need to subscribe to a fee-based news server such as Giganews, Easynews, Astraweb, or Supernews.

Blogs

Blogs, or weblogs, have become an Internet phenomenon. The blogging search engine Technorati is tracking millions and millions of blogs. Thousands of new blogs pop up every day.

The *blogosphere* has already been exploited by politicians, educational institutions, marketers, publicists, and traditional media outlets. And as you might imagine, you can also find Mac-related blogs, such as `www.cultof mac.com`, `www.tuaw.com` (The Unofficial Apple Weblog), and `www.gigaom. com/apple` (GigaOm's TheAppleBlog).

Some bloggers may dream of becoming journalistic superstars overnight, though only a few achieve such status. And many in the mainstream media fret that bloggers lack editorial scrutiny and journalistic standards, but then again many have become highly respected media outlets in their own right. Still, most blogs are nothing more than personal journals meant to be read by a tight circle of friends and family. Bloggers share their musings, provide links to other content, and invite comments from others.

Destinations for creating and hosting a blog include Google's free Blogger. com service, WordPress (also free), and SixApart's TypePad (starting at around $9 a month).

Blogs and other news feeds are sometimes distributed through technology known as *RSS,* shorthand for *Really Simple Syndication.* Unfortunately, RSS is no longer integrated in the versions of Safari and Mail that came out when it released Mountain Lion. You can still receive RSS feeds through various third-party apps, though, including Google Reader, Reeder, and NewsRack. Search the Mac App Store (more on that particular entity later in this chapter) for these (and other) RSS readers.

Social Networking

Who do you know? Who do your friends know? Who do the friends of your friends know? What's on their minds? Oh, and how can *I* benefit from six (or many fewer) degrees of separation?

That's pretty much what online social networks are all about. By leveraging your direct and indirect contacts, you might find a place to live, broker the deal of the century, or land a recording contract. That's the hope anyway. I hate to be a glass-is-half-empty kind of guy, but none of these outcomes is guaranteed.

Still, social networking sites can help you network and help you be social. They may combine blogs, instant messaging, photo and video sharing, games, music, and a lot more.

Facebook is the leading purveyor of social networking these days with a billion members and counting. Yes, you heard right, billion with a *b.* You can read news feeds from friends, play games, post pictures, opine on any topic left to your imagination, read what these other people are reading, and so much more.

Apple embraced Facebook in a major way starting with Mountain Lion. If you supply your Facebook account credentials to the Mac — do so in System Preferences in Mail, Contacts & Calendars — all your Facebook friends magically show up in your Mac Contacts app, complete with their Facebook profile pictures, e-mail addresses, phone numbers, and whatever else they chose to share. (If you already had set up Contact listings for these folks, the Facebook info is added to any other addresses and phone numbers you may have had for these pals.) What's more, all this stuff is kept up to date. If a Facebook friend, for example, changes his phone number or image through the social network, the change will automatically be applied to his listing in the Mac's Contacts app. Like I said, it's magic.

A similar principle applies to the Calendar. All your friends' birthdays (at least those who share the day of their birth in Facebook) are listed in the Calendar. No more excuses for not getting them a card or present.

As you'll see in Chapter 15, Facebook also makes nice with iPhoto.

Facebook, of course, is listed on the Share menu that shows up in numerous Mountain Lion apps. You can post links from Safari to Facebook as well as photos from Preview, Quick Look, and Photo Booth.

When you do choose Facebook from the Share menu, a so-called *Share sheet* turns up, an example of which is shown in Figure 11-11. If you summon a Share sheet to share a photo in Facebook, for example, you can choose which of your Facebook friends get to see the picture and in which Facebook album it will get posted. At your discretion, you can also choose to make your location "discoverable" when sending the photo.

Another Mountain Lion nicety: You can create a Facebook post directly from Notification Center.

You can find other major social networks, of course, including Google+, which is emerging as a Facebook rival. As of this writing, the once-popular-but-no-longer-hip social network, Myspace, was redesigning its site to focus on creative types such as musicians and artists and hopefully restore some of its lost luster.

Figure 11-11:
You can post to Facebook throughout OS X Mountain Lion.

If you consider video sharing to be social networking, YouTube (owned by Google) has become a cultural phenomenon in its own right and is most representative of the breed. But many other popular examples exist, even if they don't fit the classic definition of social networking, including Craig's List (global communities with free classifieds), LinkedIn (business-oriented), Flickr (Yahoo!'s image-sharing site), Pinterest (pin images on a pin board), and Instagram (another image-sharing site that Facebook has acquired).

Speaking of social communications, read the next section for a Twitter-sized explanation of Twitter, which has become a monster phenomenon in its own right.

Twitter

140 characters is all Twitter gets u. Built around *tweets,* a popular form of *microblogging.* Author's followers can read and reply to tweets.

Tweets are all about the kind of brevity exhibited here because you are indeed limited to 140 characters when you send one of these small bursts of information in real time on its merry way. And sorry to say, a space counts as one of those precious few characters.

You don't have to tweet to get a lot out of Twitter. By following what other people have to say or share, you can get a quick handle on news (often before it's reported in conventional media outlets), ideas, opinions, and what's trending around the world. By clicking on the links that are often included with tweets (and the links are often shrunk to save character space), you can take a much deeper dive into what the person is trying to say or show — through photos, videos, and conversations. You can reply to tweets, *retweet* them (often accompanied by your own wry comments, kept brief, of course), and send someone a direct message.

When you're ready to author your own messages, you may want to mention other folks in your tweet, just to widen the number of people who are likely to see what you have to say — the people following the folks you mention will be exposed to your own tweet. It's a good way to collect followers. You do that by using a Twitter username preceded by the @ sign.

As it did with Facebook, Apple elevated Twitter's presence throughout Mountain Lion. After you sign in to Twitter — again, through Mail, Contacts, and Calendars in System Preferences — you can tweet via *Tweet sheets* from the Share menu that are similar to the Share sheets for Facebook. Figure 11-12 shows what a Tweet sheet looks like.

Figure 11-12:
Examining a
Tweet sheet
in Safari.

Ever mindful of the strict 140-character limit, Apple counts down the number of characters for you as you compose your tweet. You can add your location to a tweet as well, and tweet directly from Notification Center.

If any of your *followers* mentions you in one of his or her own tweets, or if someone sends you a direct message in Twitter, you'll be notified in Notification Center.

If you want to spread the word about an app in the Mac App Store, you can select Share on Twitter from the app's Buy button. You can also share the app on Facebook, in Messages, or by e-mailing a friend.

And by all means, follow me on Twitter @edbaig.

The Virtual Meet Market

As you might have surmised by now, Cupid spends a lot of time on the Internet. You may even run into him in one of the aforementioned social networking sites. But if you're determined to find a mate in cyberspace at all costs, the direct approach is probably best. Dating sites often let you peruse online personals and fill out detailed online profiles for free. With some variation in subscriptions and fees, they typically start charging only when you're ready to get in touch with Mr. or Ms. Right.

Rest assured, you'll find a dating site to fit your lifestyle. Online matchmakers focus on particular communities, political beliefs, sexual preferences, religions, hobbies, and even love of four-legged creatures (check out www.date mypet.com). Leading examples include eHarmony.com, Match.com, Spark. com, True, and Yahoo! Personals. Romantic sparks may fly in Facebook, too, as you reconnect with classmates, coworkers, and campmates from many moons ago.

A few important disclaimers: I take no responsibility for who you meet online through these or other websites (unless it works out and then you can invite me to the wedding). And I can't predict what kind of sparks will fly if a Windows user pairs up with Mac loyalist.

Buying Stuff Online: The Mac App Store

Grandpa, what was it like when people shopped in stores?

I doubt you'll hear such a conversation anytime soon. But more and more, people are purchasing products online, and those products are not just books, music, and software. Increasingly, folks go to the Net to shop for big-ticket items: backyard swing sets for the kiddies, high-definition televisions, even automobiles. Electronic commerce, or *e-commerce,* is alive and kicking, with Amazon.com and eBay.com, the famed auction site, at the top of the virtual heap.

Speaking of commerce, I've already mentioned the App Store for the Mac, modeled after the App Store for the iPhone, iPod, iPod touch, and iPad.

These days, it's Apple's preferred way to sell you software, including the Mountain Lion upgrade itself, which fetches $19.99 if you have the prior version of OS X. Buy it once, and you can install it on any other Macs you own that meet the system requirements.

OS X upgrades are delivered through the Mac App Store as well as updates on any other software you buy through the joint.

When you enter the Mac App Store by clicking its icon on the dock, you're welcomed with a screen that looks like Figure 11-13. I say "looks like" because the content of the store is ever-changing.

Armed with your Apple ID, you're ready to search for Mac apps, purchase and download the ones you like, and if you're so inclined, write a review to let others know what you think of them.

You can use your iTunes Store account to make purchases if you already have one.

Finding apps

You can browse the stores in numerous ways. Your main choices are as follows:

> ✔ **Featured:** Apps that are featured are the new apps that Apple, for one reason or another, thinks merit attention. On the Feature page, you see ad banners that rotate with new offerings. And Apple sometimes lumps apps together in collections to get you to consider programs you might not otherwise stumble upon. For example, the Better Together collection of apps is meant to connect the Mac to its cousins, the iPhone and

iPad. An App Starter Kit features some of the other apps that Apple thinks will help balance the bundle of apps that are preloaded on the machine.

✔ **Top Charts:** Here's where you'll find the top paid apps (those requiring you to part with real loot), the top free apps, and the top grossing apps.

✔ **Categories:** As its name suggests, you can find apps here by category. Numerous categories were available to pore through as of this writing. Ready? Here goes: Business, Developer Tools, Education, Entertainment, Finance, Games, Graphics & Design, Health & Fitness, Lifestyle, Medical, Music, News, Photography, Productivity, Reference, Social Networking, Sports, Travel, Utilities, Video, Weather. Did I miss any? Did Apple?

If you already know the name of the app you're looking for (or think you do), enter it directly in the search box in the upper-right corner of the App Store window.

Figure 11-13:
Lots of rich apps are available in the Mac App Store.

Figuring out whether an app is worth it

You can get an awful lot of information about an app to help you make an informed purchasing decision. Figure 11-14 shows the landing page for Solar Walk 3D Solar System Model. Near the top on the left side you see the app's price — 99 cents in this instance under a special promotion. Move down the page and you can see pictures of what the app looks like and get some information on its category, version number, size, languages, and seller (Vito Technology).

Figure 11-14:
Read all about an app to see whether it is out of this world.

You also see what the app is rated, based on whether it has violence, offensive language, suggestive themes, and so on. Solar Walk carries a 4+ rating, meaning that it contains no objectionable material. The other ratings guidelines are listed as 9+, 12+, or 17+.

Scroll down some more to see customer ratings and reviews from people just like you, sorted as you wish by most helpful, most favorable, most critical, or most recent. Feel free to add your own two cents after playing around with some apps.

Making a purchase

When you're sold on an app, click the app price to buy it. You have to be signed in to the App Store with your store account or Apple ID to complete the purchase. The first time you try and fetch an app from a new computer, you must present your credit card number and billing credentials.

After you are past that and the download commences, you see a progress indicator in Launchpad and Finder that lets you know when you can start playing with the new program.

If you bought the app through the App Store on another Mac, click Purchased. You see a list of all those apps you've purchased in this manner. Apps that are already installed have a grayed-out Installed button to the right of their name and purchase date. Click Install to load any purchased apps that don't reside yet on the Mac you are using. You can also hide an app in the Purchased list by holding down the Ctrl key at the same time you click the app you want to hide. Choose Hide Purchase. (I won't ask which apps you want to hide.)

If you received a gift card — and aren't you lucky? — click Redeem under the Quick Links shown on the Featured, Top Charts, and Categories pages to credit your store account or to fetch the specific app associated with the gift code.

Some apps, frequently games but other types of apps as well, give you the option to purchase add-on features after the fact. These are known as *in-app purchases,* and when you agree to the transaction, they typically unlock features you wouldn't otherwise be able to get to. When you make an in-app purchase, you will again be asked to provide your Apple ID and password.

If and when you grow weary of an app, you can easily uninstall it. In Launchpad, hold down an app's icon until all the icons on the screen start to jiggle. Click the X Delete button on the app you want to get rid of.

None of this will seem foreign to any readers of this book who own an iPhone or iPad. Removing an app on those devices is similar.

You can always reinstall an app by clicking the Install button for the app in the Purchased list.

Check out the book's companion website (www.dummies.com/go/MacsFD12e) for updates on the Mac App Store and other new releases from Apple.

While the App Store is a great place to shop for programs for your app, shopping generally over the Internet affords you many plusses. For example

✔ You avoid crowds and traffic.

✔ You save on gas or commuting costs.

✔ You avoid pushy salespeople.

✔ You can easily compare products and prices across numerous websites, increasing the likelihood that you'll end up with an excellent deal. Visit such longtime comparison shopping sites as www.mysimon.com, www.pricegrabber.com, and www.shopzilla.com.

✔ You can choose from a large inventory of products (which is not to suggest that stuff won't be out of stock).

✔ You can get buying recommendations from your cyberpeers.

Shopping online has a few negatives too:

✔ You can't "kick the tires" or typically inspect the items under consideration.

✔ You typically won't get personal attention from a reliable salesperson either.

✔ You might get spammed.

✔ Without proper safeguards, your privacy could be at risk.

✔ Instant gratification becomes an oxymoron, except on such items as downloadable software and music.

> ✔ You can't make goo-goo eyes with attractive strangers you might meet cruising the aisles.

Managing travel

It used to be that people bought airline tickets and booked hotels over the Internet strictly for convenience. After all, booking online beats languishing on hold, waiting to talk to an airline customer service rep. And you can choose seats and print boarding passes from the comfort of your own keyboard. (Okay, when things get complicated with connections or flying with pets, you might still want to go through an airline staffer or a travel agent.) Nowadays, carriers *want* you to go through the web and take advantage of e-tickets. In fact, you're typically penalized financially for requesting a paper ticket.

Although you can find deals elsewhere, the big three online travel sites — www.expedia.com, www.orbitz.com, and www.travelocity.com — are always worth a visit. Also check out the carrier's own website and ask to get on an e-mail list in which the airline notifies you of last-minute bargains. Other good stops include www.kayak.com, which lets you compare results at other travel sites, www.cheaptickets.com (whose name describes what it is), and www.tripadvisor.com, where you can check out reviews of tourist destinations written by people just like you.

A researcher's toolbox

Imagine if you could take the *Britannica* or *World Book Encyclopedia* and alter or update it at will. You now have some idea of what Wikipedia, found at www.wikipedia.org, is all about. It's billed as a free encyclopedia that *anyone can edit.* At the very least, entries are more timely, and Wikipedia covers a broader topic spectrum than could ever be handled by a print encyclopedia. Moreover, the collaborative global perspective may provide insights lacking in other reference material.

I know what you're thinking. There's a flip side to all this. What if I'm mischievous? What if I'm biased? What if I'm a misinformed know-it-all? Why couldn't I change the text to read that the South won the Civil War or Dewey beat Truman? Yes, it can and does happen, because the very essence of a *wiki* allows anyone with an Internet connection to mess with any of the references. In most instances, blatant vandalism and dubious submissions are corrected by the collective efforts of honest writers and editors from around the world.

But open-sourced wiki entries are organic and never quite finished, and mistakes are introduced, overtly or subtly, consciously or otherwise. One side of an argument might be presented more eloquently than another. You almost always find room for interpretation and debate. So, Wikipedia is a remarkably useful online resource, provided that you recognize its limitations and don't treat everything you come across as gospel.

Showing Your Game Face

You don't have to be connected to the Internet to play games on your Mac, of course. But when you are connected, you can best exploit Game Center, another feature borrowed from the iPhone and iPad. Through Game Center, you can play online games with friends, locally and around the world.

After signing in to Game Center with your Apple ID and password, you can choose whether you want to go with a public profile. If you do opt in by selecting the appropriate check box, your name will be visible to other players inside Game Center. Your nickname will show up on leaderboards and multiplayer games, and Game Center will recommend you to other players with your real name. You can also select a check box to use your Contacts for friend suggestions.

Icons for the top available Game Center games show up on the Game Center screen, which, as you can see in Figure 11-15, looks like a poker table.

In Game Center, click the Friends tab to see not only a listing of your friends' names but also the games you have in common. (See Figure 11-16.)

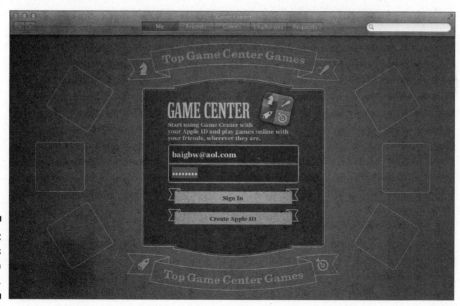

Figure 11-15:
I'm always
ready to
play.

Click Games to see the games you have on your Mac and in iOS. If you don't have any games, click Find Games in the App Store to be transported there directly.

Click Challenges to view any competitive challenges to play a specific game against another person. If you want to challenge the person, click his scores or achievements.

If you receive any Friend requests, they'll turn up when you click the Requests tab.

You can also arrange to receive Game Center notifications in Notifications under System Preferences. And through parental controls, you can restrict your kid from joining multiplayer games.

Playing games on the Internet is a hoot. And playing in general on the Internet is a hoot, too.

Figure 11-16:
Would you
like to play a
game?

Chapter 12

Joining iCloud, the Club That Will Have You for a Member

*W*hen you get right down to it, Apple's iCloud online service represents quite a departure from its immediate predecessor, the subscription service known as MobileMe. For sure, more than a few remnants of MobileMe remain in iCloud, including (but not limited to) mac.com and me.com e-mail accounts, and Back to My Mac, which is a way to remotely control another Mac over the Internet.

At the same time, Apple dumped MobileMe's online Gallery showcase for photos and also shuttered the centralized online iDisk storage repository. While some people indeed miss those features, Apple (through iCloud) giveth more than it taketh away. Even better, iCloud (unlike the $99-a-year MobileMe) is free, though you do have to pay extra to exploit certain aspects of the service.

In this chapter, you take a tour of the iCloud. But if you've been reading right along, you've already seen iCloud in action throughout this book, because it is cleverly woven into apps you use all the time, including Mail, Calendar, iPhoto, Notes, Reminders, iTunes, and more.

As you recall, you were prompted to set up iCloud when you started using your Mac, via a new or existing Apple ID account. But if you refrained from doing so at the time, it's by no means too late to do so.

You can set up iCloud for the Mac (and, for that matter, for a Windows PC as well as for the iPhone, iPad, and iPod touch) on the web at `www.apple.com/icloud/setup`. (The page is shown in all its glory in Figure 12-1.) For the Mac, you need to be running at least OS X version 10.7.4, but to get the full experience, you'll want Mountain Lion version 10.8 or later.

After iCloud is set up on all your devices, the service *pushes* the appropriate information to each and every one of them — that is, the pertinent stuff just shows up on each device, or is at least readily accessible.

The set of Internet goodies you get with iCloud includes tools to keep multiple Macs (and Windows PCs and various mobile devices such as Apple's iPad tablet) in sync, plus backup storage and e-mail.

If you really must know, MobileMe used to be called .Mac, which in turn used to be called iTools. It used to be free too, but then it wasn't (at least partly so). Television was once free as well, of course, but few argue about paying for cable or satellite when you get more viewing choices. So it goes with iCloud. You get a lot gratis. You get more if you fork over extra coin.

Figure 12-1:
Setting up iCloud online is a breeze.

Why Belong?

If you haven't noticed, the whole concept of *cloud computing* is becoming a big deal, not just for Apple but really the entire industry. People ask me all the time what cloud computing is, but there's no need to complicate this stuff. Think of it simply as computing that takes advantage of the Internet.

On a basic level, you get more out of iCloud as you glom onto its features, which I trust will become evident as you explore all the things iCloud can do as you read this chapter. But as I've indicated, most of what really happens occurs in the background. It's not like you actively *think* about calling iCloud into duty; you just benefit from it all the time. Through iCloud, the movies you want to watch and the music you want to listen to are readily available on multiple Macs as well as your other devices. Buy a song in iTunes on your Mac, say, and depending on how you set things up, it can be it instantly downloaded to your iPhone.

You can also access documents you want to work on in the cloud and pictures you want to admire, not to mention reminders, messages, and more. Road warriors who would like to access their computer at home remotely can do that. Another plus: Many of you can take advantage of the extra online storage that comes with membership (5GB when you sign up), though you can pay a premium for extra storage as you'll see.

Meanwhile, for a certain class of users — those with an iPhone, an iPod touch, or an iPad, as well as multiple Macs or Windows computers or both — keeping your calendar, contacts, and Mail inbox up to date may provide the most compelling reasons to sign up.

Your information is stored in that great big Internet server in the sky. As you make changes to your address book on one device or computer, say, those changes are pushed more or less instantly to all your other machines.

 Apple ran into initial snags with sync during the transition from .Mac to MobileMe in the summer of 2008, leading the company to apologize to customers. As part of its, um, MobileMeaculpa, Apple extended subscriptions gratis by a couple of months.

MobileMe is gone now, and the transition to iCloud went a lot more smoothly, though some folks did have to manage the migration of data from the axed iDisk service. Apple is well beyond that now with iCloud. Here's a bird's-eye view of certain key iCloud features, some of which I delve in to in greater detail in this chapter or other chapters:

- **iTunes in the Cloud:** Favorite songs, music, movies, and TV shows are instantaneously synced and accessible on your Macs (and other devices). A pay feature called iTunes Match ($24.99 a year) stores your entire music collection in the cloud whether you acquired those songs from iTunes or not. Read more about iTunes in the Cloud and iTunes Match in Chapter 14.

- **Photo Stream:** MobileMe Gallery is gone, but its core features live on, at least in some respects, through Photo Stream. Take pictures on your iPhone, for example, and you can access those images on your Macs (or PC, other iOS devices, and even Apple TV). Images turn up automatically in your Photo Stream — you really need not do anything. You can also share Photo Streams with designated friends, though the appropriately named Shared Photo Streams feature. Read Chapter 15 for more on Photo Stream.

- **Back to My Mac:** Remotely access and control your Leopard-, Snow Leopard–, Lion-, or Mountain Lion–based Mac from another Mac running Leopard, Snow Leopard, Lion, or Mountain Lion.

- **Find My Mac:** I hope you never have to use Find My Mac. But if you do lose a Mac notebook, you have a fighting chance of getting it back thanks to this very cool location-based feature.

- **Apps:** Purchase an app or program through the Mac App Store on one Mac and you can fetch the app on another Mac using the same store account. From inside the Mac App Store, click the Purchases tab and click to install and download the programs you want to use on this other Mac.

- **Documents in the Cloud:** If you have apps from Apple like Keynote (presentations), Pages (word processing), and Numbers (spreadsheet), you can start working on one Mac and finish the job on another (or once again on an iOS device).

- **Backup:** iCloud backs up data on your iOS devices. But as a Mac owner, you benefit, too, because purchased movies, music, books, apps, and so on are automatically backed up. And you can back up documents, too, as noted previously.

- **Mail:** iCloud provides you with an ad-free, IMAP e-mail account with built-in spam and virus protections.

- **Push e-mail, push contacts, push calendar:** As also mentioned previously, updates to your e-mail, contacts, and calendar are pushed across all your devices and computers. And iCloud works with native OS X applications such as Mail, Contacts, and Calendar. You can share a calendar with friends by entering their names or e-mail addresses. Or, you can check off an option to share a read-only public version of your calendar that anyone with the URL can see. Within the Calendar app, place the pointer over the calendar's name that is listed under the iCloud section of the source list to the left of the calendar and click the broad-cast icon (little waves) that is your signal that the calendar in question resides in the clouds. Alternatively, click the calendar name and choose Edit⇨Share Calendar. Then, in the window shown in Figure 12-2, enter the e-mail address to share the calendar with that individual or place a check mark next to the Public Calendar option if you're comfortable sharing it widely. Your subscribers will receive updates as you make changes. You can also synchronize to-do items. Your calendar remains in sync across all your Macs, as well as PCs, iPhones, and iPads.

✔ **More syncing:** OS X users can also sync Safari bookmarks, so-called iCloud Tabs (open web tabs that are synchronized across all your devices), and Reading List (see Chapter 9), along with notes, remind-ers, dashboard widget preferences, dock items, and System Preferences across the various Macs you own.

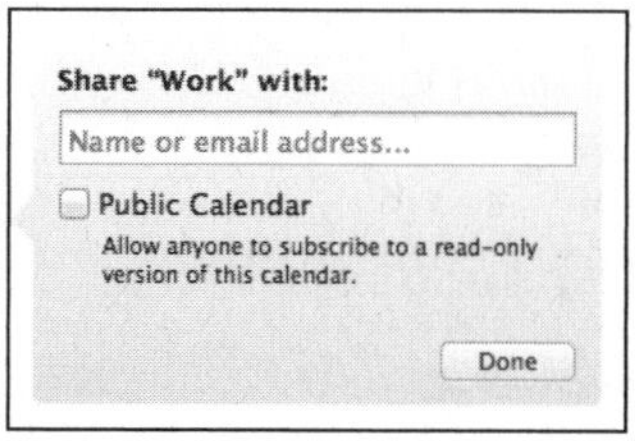

Figure 12-2:
Your options
for sharing a
calendar.

Share "Work" with:

Name or email address...

☐ Public Calendar
Allow anyone to subscribe to a read-only
version of this calendar.

Done

Setting up iCloud on your Mac

So now that you have a good idea of what iCloud is and what it can do, it's time to set it up. My assumption is that you didn't initially sign up for iCloud when given the chance the first time you turned on your Mac. Meanwhile, if you've already set up an iPhone, iPad, or iPod touch to work with iCloud, you're ahead of the game. Either way, proceed to Step 1:

1. **In the Internet & Wireless section of System Preferences, select iCloud.**

2. **If you already have an Apple ID and password that you want to use for iCloud on the Mac, enter it in the fields provided. If not, click Create an Apple ID.**

   You'll have to provide your location and birthday to establish an Apple ID.

3. **After you've signed in, decide whether to accept the defaults to "Use iCloud for contacts, calendars, reminders, notes and Safari," as well as to "Use Find My Mac." Click Next.**

   I see no good reason why you should deselect any of the defaults. Besides, you can always change your mind later, and as you see in Step 4, you can check or deselect iCloud options for specific apps and features.

4. **Click the check boxes to select the items you want to use with iCloud —
Contacts, Calendars & Reminders, Safari, and so on.**

Note the specific options shown in Figure 12-3, and scroll down to see
more options.

If all went according to plan, your contacts and calendars, mail, notes,
reminders, and so on will turn up at iCloud.com. It's not a bad idea to log on
to make sure.

Storage in the sky

Who wouldn't want personal storage in the cloud? That way, if anyone
dropped a bowling ball on your computer, your data is protected. This won't
be the only reference in this book to the importance of backing up your digital treasures.

The now defunct iDisk feature made it easy to access files backed up in your
online locker wherever you happened to be, even from a Windows or Linux
machine. In the Finder sidebar, it appeared to be just another external disk
attached to your Mac. Plus you could easily collaborate or exchange documents with others or access files remotely, especially those files too large
to e-mail.

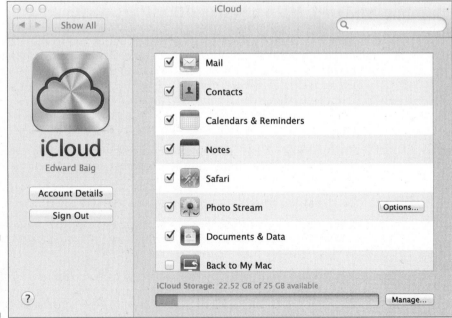

Figure 12-3:
Selecting
items to use
with iCloud.

Alas, iDisk went away, leaving you to rely on third-party services such as Dropbox.

But Apple (through iCloud) still automatically stores stuff in the cloud. I already mentioned that your membership comes with 5GB (gigabytes) of storage space. But that capacity looks even better when you factor in the fact that purchased music, movies, TV shows, apps, and books, as well as photos in your Photo Stream, don't count against that limit. Still, you might eventually need more space. If that day comes, you can boost the storage amount by 10GB (giving you 15GB total) for $20 a year, by 20GB (giving you 25GB total) for $40 a year, or 50GB (giving you 55GB total) for $100 a year. You can change your storage plan whenever you want. On the Mac, visit iCloud Preferences in System Preferences and click the Manage button next to the status indicator telling you how much storage you already have. (Refer to Figure 12-3.) In the Manage Storage window that shows up, click Change Storage Plan.

On the left side of that Manage Storage window, you see a list of apps representing data that you've stored in iCloud. Click Backups to see which of your iCloud-connected devices (such as the iPhone or iPad) are hogging the most online space; you can delete the data from any of those devices that you feel you no longer need to have backed up — if you wish, cherry-picking individual files in some cases. Click Delete to do so, but don't take this step lightly because you can't undo what you started. Or click a specific app in the list — say, TextEdit — and highlight any of the documents in the list that you feel you can live without in a pinch. Click Delete to remove that app from iCloud.

Other backup methods

iCloud is great for keeping your stuff backed up and synced across numerous computers and devices. But regularly backing up your digital keepsakes (pictures, videos, financial documents, and so on) remains vital. I hope I've impressed that upon you by now. (If I haven't, what will it take?) Lecture over.

Even if you spring for extra storage through iCloud, you may not have enough storage for your videos or a sizable multimedia collection. Today's backup arsenal typically consists of recordable CDs and DVDs, external drives, other cloud-storage based solutions, and networks.

In Chapter 13, I discuss Time Machine, a cool way to back up your Mac without having to think too much about it. You'll need to supply the additional drive needed to take advantage of Time Machine.

iCloud Mail

I'd like to tell you that something is extra special about having an iCloud e-mail account, but truth be told, it's like any other web-based e-mail account. Okay, it has a cleaner interface than many online mail accounts, speedy message addressing (through Contacts), and drag-and-drop simplicity. You can click a quick Reply icon to dash off a speedy response to a message in your inbox, without leaving the inbox. And having an iCloud.com suffix is kind of nice too, as in *youraccountname*@icloud.com, with the account name in this case being your Apple ID. You can create multiple e-mail folders and preview messages in a single view. And of course, you can check iCloud mail from any browser. The program also integrates with the Mac's own Mail application or with popular e-mail programs such as Microsoft Outlook. Through iCloud, you can create an e-mail alias in which your actual e-mail address is concealed from the recipient. That's useful when you sign up for mailing lists or buy stuff from an online store. (You can then use your actual e-mail address with family, friends, colleagues, and clients; Apple lets you have up to three e-mail aliases in iCloud.)

Back to My Mac

Suppose that you're using a Mac laptop from your hotel room to prepare a presentation and would like to retrieve a picture from the hard drive or solid state drive of your machine at home. As an iCloud member, you can exploit Back to My Mac, a feature that lets you remotely connect to your Leopard–, Snow Leopard–, Lion=, or Mountain Lion–based computer from another Mac with one of these versions of OS X.

There is some prep work involved. Choose iCloud under System Preferences and select the Back to My Mac check box to ensure that it is enabled. You'll also have to turn on screen sharing under the Share option in System Preferences.

Repeat this procedure on all the machines you want to access; they must share the same iCloud account. You may have to open ports in your firewall for Back to My Mac to work in all its remote computing glory.

Indeed, for Back to My Mac to work, you'll need a router that supports something called NAT Port Mapping Protocol (NAT-PMP) or Universal Plug and Play (UPnP). If you're not sure whether your router stacks up, check the documentation that came with your router or consult the router company's online support. And don't feel bad if you do have your doubts, because the router companies don't make any of this information easily accessible.

Then, to locate the file you want to lift off the home computer, click that home machine (under Shared) in Finder and browse its drive for the file you need. Drag the file to the desktop of the computer you are using for remote access.

You can also share and control your home screen remotely by clicking Share Screen in Finder, as is the case in Figure 12-4. (Before you leave on your trip, remember to select the Screen Sharing option, found when you click Sharing under System Preferences. It sure beats lugging a desktop computer on your travels.)

Figure 12-4: You're never too far away from your home computer.

Find My Mac (iPhone)

I know you care a great deal about your computer. But we're all busy and distracted from time to time, and however unlikely, it's possible that you'd leave a running Mac notebook in the back of a taxi. (C'mon, like you're going to have a running desktop in a cab, much less leave it there.) Or worse, your Mac can be stolen.

The Find My Mac feature (a variant of the similar Find My iPhone feature found on Apple's prized smartphone) increases the odds that you'll get the lost machine back. Make sure that the feature is selected in iCloud Preferences.

Then, if your machine ever does go AWOL, just sign in to iCloud from any web browser or from the Find My iPhone app on an iPhone or iPad. Then click Find My iPhone — yes, that's what it is called, even though you're on a search mission for your Mac.

In a web browser, you see a map like the one shown in Figure 12-5. Each of the green droplets on the map indicates the location of one of your devices — at least its location as close as Apple can pinpoint it. Click the Devices button in the upper-left corner of the screen to see a list of all the devices that you've set up to work with Find My iPhone (or Mac and so on). Hopefully, the computer you're looking for won't be offline. If found, click the Mac in the list, which summons the window shown in the top-right corner of Figure 12-5.

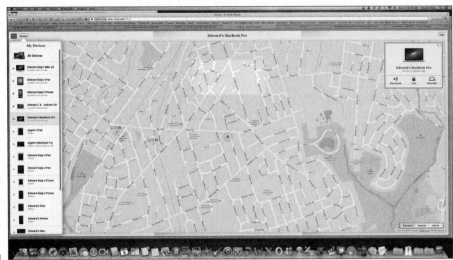

Figure 12-5:
Locating a
lost or
stolen Mac.

But now what are you going to do? How do you alert the Good Samaritan (or crook) who has your machine that you want it back? Your first option is to sound an alarm on your missing Mac, by clicking Play Sound in the window shown in Figure 12-5. But this is really only useful if the missing Mac is actually in your house. (It's a feature that was really designed for such scenarios as an iPhone getting concealed under the cushions of your couch.) An alarm is useless if the person doesn't know how to get in touch with you to return it.

Instead, click Lock in that window. This will let you lock the machine so that the person can't look at any of your private or sensitive information. Using the keypad that appears, enter a six-digit passcode (that you can easily remember) to unlock the computer when and if you do get it back. (You have to confirm the passcode by entering it a second time.) Once you do that, you are provided space to type an optional message that will appear on the lock screen that you hope will persuade the person who has your computer to return it. Offering a reward is not out of the question (unless you're dealing with a thief who is unlikely to cooperate anyway). Click the Lock button when done typing the message.

You'll receive a confirmation e-mail like the one shown in Figure 12-6.

If you come to the conclusion that the machine was indeed stolen, or that the person who now has it has no intention of giving it back, click Erase Mac from Find My iPhone to wipe the contents and settings on the computer clean. Given that this is a pretty major step, Apple requires you to enter your Apple ID before proceeding. Erasing the Mac can take a up to a full day to complete.

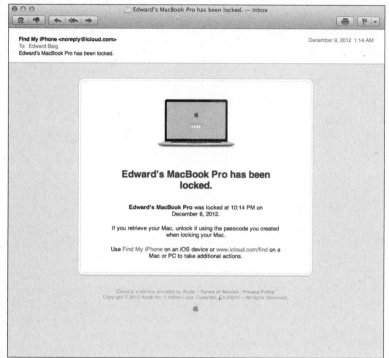

Figure 12-6:
Alerting you
that the
missing
Mac is
locked.

You have several compelling reasons for hanging up in the cloud. The potential to retrieve a lost Mac is right up there with the best of them.

Chapter 13

Mounting a Defense Strategy

· ·

· ·

OS X has generally been immune from the swarm of viruses that have plagued Windows computers through the years. Folks traditionally have needed to call a security specialist for their Macs about as often as you summon the Maytag repair man.

But times change. Heck, Whirlpool bought Maytag. So when it comes to computers nowadays, you can't take anything for granted — even if you own a Mac.

The Truth about Internet Security

Some people suggest that OS X isn't as bulletproof as was once believed. Way back in May 2006, the McAfee Avert Labs security threat research firm issued a report claiming that the Mac is just as vulnerable to targeted *malware,* or *mal*icious soft*ware,* attacks as other operating systems. Although the volume of threats is low, no invisible cloak is protecting Apple's products.

Moreover, the security firm expected malicious hackers to increasingly place the Mac OS in the crosshairs given Apple's transition to Intel chips, and especially as Apple's products gain popularity.

The implication was that the bad guys hadn't spent much time targeting Apple because the Mac had such a miniscule market share. Although that argument may have had some merit, the Mac has become more popular, and the machines have been engineered with your protection in mind. So your operating system is as secure as they come, even more so from Mountain Lion on.

With Mountain Lion, Apple introduced a feature called *Gatekeeper* that can help protect you from inadvertently downloading malicious software when you fetch a program outside the Mac App Store.

Meanwhile, Apple reviews the apps ahead of time that you do buy through the App Store. If any apps do turn out to include malware, they are removed. Apple also ensures that the developers who sell software through the place register with the company first.

As an added safety measure, all apps run through something called the *App Sandbox* in OS X, which ensures that the apps do what they are meant to do, and perhaps more importantly, don't do what they're not meant to do. In other words, apps are effectively isolated from the rest of your system, from other apps they have no business interacting with, and from your data.

But because Macs now double (if you want) as Windows machines, you are advised to take proper precautions.

What then are we to make of the McAfee report? Should Mac owners never turn their computers on? Methinks not. But Mac loyalists shouldn't get complacent either, even though no major security breaches have hit the headlines in the years since the report was issued. For starters, you should install the security updates that show up on your Mac when you click System Preferences under Software Updates or that turn up through the Mac App Store. And you should load software on your computer only from companies and websites you trust.

One other crucial point: Sensible security starts with you. And that means backing up all your important digital jewels, a process a whole lot simpler with the arrival of a feature that would make H.G. Wells beam. It also means paying heed to any OS X updates that Apple delivers periodically. And through Mountain Lion, you'll receive notifications when such updates are available.

But before delving in to the OS X version of Time Machine, let's examine a very real threat that has more in common with Wells' *The War of the Worlds*.

Spies in our midst

Viruses are menacing programs created for the sole purpose of wreaking havoc on a computer or network. They spread when you download suspect software, visit shady websites, or pass around infected discs.

Computer *malware* takes many forms, as viruses, Trojans, worms, and so on. And Windows users are all too familiar with *spyware,* the type of code that surreptitiously shows up on your computer to track your behavior and secretly report it to third parties.

Spyware typically differs from traditional computer malware, which may try to shut down your computer (or some of its programs). Authors of spyware aren't necessarily out to shut you down. Rather, they quietly attempt to monitor your behavior so that they can benefit at your expense.

At the lesser extremes, your computer is served pop-up ads that companies hope will eventually lead to a purchase. This type of spyware is known as *adware.*

At its most severe, spyware can place your personal information in the hands of a not-so-nice person. Under those circumstances, you could get totally ripped off. Indeed, the most malicious of spyware programs, called *keyloggers* or *snoopware,* can capture every keystroke you enter, whether you're holding court in a public chat room or typing a password.

The good news is that as of this writing, no major reports of OS X–related malware have surfaced.

But there's always a first time.

Gone phishing

Dear Citibank Member,

As part of our security measures, we regularly screen activity in the Citibank system. We recently contacted you after noticing an issue on your account. We requested information from you for the following reasons:

We have reason to believe that your account was accessed by a third party. Because protecting the security of your account is our primary concern, we have limited access to sensitive Citibank account features. We understand that this may be an inconvenience but please understand that this temporary limitation is for your protection.

This is a third and final reminder to log in to Citibank as soon as possible.

Once you log in, you will be provided with steps to restore your account access. We appreciate your understanding as we work to ensure account safety.

Sincerely,

Citibank Account Review Department

The text from the preceding e-mailed letter sounds legitimate enough. But the only thing real about it is that this is an actual excerpt lifted from a common Internet fraud known as a *phishing* attack.

Identity thieves, masquerading as Citibank, PayPal, or other financial or Internet companies, try to dupe you into clicking phony links to verify personal or account information. You're asked for home addresses, passwords, Social Security numbers, credit card numbers, bank account information, and so on.

To lend authenticity to these appeals, the spoof e-mails often are dressed up with real company logos and addresses, plus a forged company name in the From line (for example, From: support@ebay.com).

Phishing may take the form of falsified company newsletters. Or you may see bogus requests for you to reconfirm personal data.

So how do you know when you're being hoodwinked? Obvious giveaways included in some fake e-mails are misspellings, rotten grammar, and repeated words or sentences.

No company on the level is going to ask you to reconfirm data that's been lost. And reputable companies usually refer to you by your real first and last names and business affiliations rather than Dear Member or Dear PayPal Customer.

If you have doubts that a communication is legit, open a new browser window and type the real company name yourself (for example, **www.ebay.com** or **www.paypal.com**). Your gut instincts concerning phony mail are probably on the mark.

Bottom line: *Never* click links embedded in suspicious e-mails. When you hover the cursor over a link such as `www.paypal.com`, you'll actually see the true web address pop up, one that leads to somewhere else entirely (perhaps Kazakhstan or some other former Soviet republic).

A similar online fraud, called *pharming,* also involves the use of fake websites. Only this time, traffic is redirected from a legitimate bank or other destination to a bogus website that looks virtually identical. If you smell a rat, proceed gingerly. Don't share personal or sensitive information unless you're 100-percent convinced that the site is legit.

Firewalls

More than likely, if you're connecting to the Internet through a network router (see Chapter 18), you're protected by a shield known as a *firewall.* But OS X also has a software firewall, and you can use it to block unwanted web traffic.

Here's how to access it:

1. **Choose ⌘⇨System Preferences.**
2. **In the Personal section, click Security & Privacy.**
3. **Click the Firewall tab and then click Turn On Firewall.**

   You have to click the lock icon and enter your name (which may already be filled in) and password to make changes. When the firewall is off, all incoming connections to the computer are permitted. When on, all unauthorized applications, programs, and services are blocked.

If you click the Firewall Options button, you'll be able to modify the firewall settings, as shown in Figure 13-1.

You can use your Firewall Options settings to block all incoming connections except those that are needed for basic Internet services. You can also add or remove applications so that their connections can or cannot come through.

You can select the option to allow *signed software* — programs that are securely validated — to receive incoming connections.

You can also operate the computer in stealth mode so that any uninvited traffic receives no acknowledgment or response from the Mac. Malicious hackers won't even know that a machine is there to attack.

And you can help safeguard your machine by selecting various options under Sharing, which is in the Internet & Network section of System Preferences. I touch on sharing in Chapter 18.

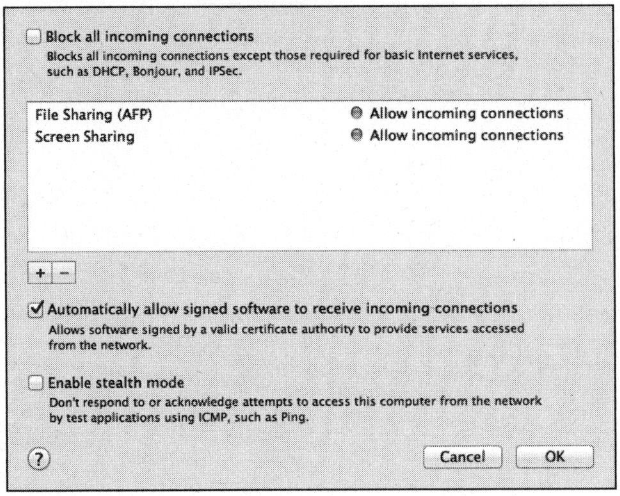

☐ Block all incoming connections
    Blocks all incoming connections except those required for basic Internet services,
    such as DHCP, Bonjour, and IPSec.

File Sharing (AFP)   ⊜ Allow incoming connections
Screen Sharing   ⊜ Allow incoming connections

[+] [-]

☑ Automatically allow signed software to receive incoming connections
    Allows software signed by a valid certificate authority to provide services accessed
    from the network.

☐ Enable stealth mode
    Don't respond to or acknowledge attempts to access this computer from the network
    by test applications using ICMP, such as Ping.

⟨?⟩   [Cancel]   [OK]

Figure 13-1:
Making the
connections
— or not.

FileVault

If your computer houses truly hush-hush information — your company's financial books, say, rather than Aunt Minnie's secret noodle-pudding recipe — you can scramble, or *encrypt,* the data in your Home folder (and only your Home folder) using an OS X feature known as *FileVault.* You know your secrets are protected should thieves get their grubby paws on your machine.

FileVault automatically applies the level of encryption employed by Uncle Sam. It's what nerds refer to as AES-128 (for Advanced Encryption Standard with 128-bit keys). And let me tell you, it's *really* secure. Apple claims it would take a machine approximately 149 trillion years to crack the code. Even if Apple is off by a couple billion years, I'm thinking your system is pretty safe.

The FileVault window shown in Figure 13-2 turns up when you choose Security & Privacy under System Preferences and select the FileVault tab. Each user must enter their password. Apple automatically generates a *recovery key* you can use to unlock the vault. You can store this key with Apple, which will ask you to answer security questions (for example, "What street did you live on when you were 9 years old?") to verify your identity.

As an administrator, you can also set up a safety net *master password* for your system, which you can use to unlock FileVault. This computer-wide password can be used to bail out authorized users on your system who forget their passwords. And it might be a lifesaver if you run a small business through your Mac and have to let a wayward employee go. You'll be able to recover any data left behind in that person's account.

Figure 13-2:
Keeping
your
computer
secure in
System
Preferences.

Heed Apple's warning. If you forget your login password and recovery key or master password, your scrambled data may as well be toast.

If FileVault is turned on and you're not logged in to the machine, other people you normally share folders with on the computer will not be able to access those folders.

It's worth mentioning that FileVault can exact an extreme performance hit on home directories with, say, large iPhoto or iTunes libraries — it can take a long time to decrypt files when you log in and scramble them again when you log out. So while FileVault is a wonderful tool for confidential stuff, be aware of the potentially harsh consequences for folks with little to hide.

Password Management:
The Key to Keychains

Have you stopped to think how many passwords are in your computing life? You probably have so many that you use the same ones over and over, though security experts think that's not such a keen practice.

The pun police will get on me for saying this, but Apple has the key to managing your passwords, account numbers, and other confidential info: a feature known as keychain. A *keychain* can store passwords for programs, e-mail accounts, websites, and more.

You can create keychains for different purposes (one for online shopping, say) by opening Keychain Access in the Utilities folder under Applications. Your keychain password is initially the same as your login password, and for many users, that's the way it'll stay. To add keychain passwords, choose File⇨New Password Item or click the + at the bottom of the Keychain Access window. Fill in the account name, keychain item, and password. Apple will let you know whether you've chosen a wimpy password or one that is bulletproof.

If you ever forget any of the passwords you've used on your Mac (including web passwords), open Keychain Access and click either All Items or Passwords from the pane on the lower left. In the larger pane to the right, double-click the item that has the password that you want to recover. A window will open. Make sure the Attributes tab within that window is highlighted (that is the default) and click to enable the Show Password check box. You will be prompted to enter the username and password that you use to log in to the Mac, or the password you set up to log in to Keychain. Only then will the Mac will reveal the password you are trying to recover, in the field adjacent to the Show Password check box.

Try this simple alternative to recover a web password. Open Safari, click Safari Preferences, and highlight the Passwords tab. Enable the Show Passwords check box. You'll be prompted to enter your Mac username and password. Upon doing so, all your web passwords will be revealed.

Logging In and Logging Out

If you work in an office or other environment where anyone can peek at the monitor to see what you've been up to, log out of your account when you're finished doing what you're doing.

But if you'd rather not bother logging out or you don't think you'll remember to do so, go to the Security & Privacy pane of System Preferences, click General, and select the Require Password after Sleep or the Screen Saver Begins option. You get to choose a timeframe (immediately, 5 seconds, 1 minute, 5 minutes, 15 minutes, 1 hour, or 4 hours). You can also select the Log Out after *x* Minutes of Inactivity option by clicking the Advanced button at the lower-right corner of the window.

You also may want to select the options to Disable Automatic Login under the General tab in Security & Privacy settings. If you're really distrustful, click the Advanced button in Security & Privacy settings and select the Require Administrator Password to Access Locked Preferences check box.

Hiding Your Mac's Whereabouts

Some software that you run on your Mac benefits from knowing where your computer is located. If the Safari browser knows where your Mac is, for example, it can take advantage of *geolocation*-capable sites that might help you find close-by ATMs, coffeehouses, or pizza joints. What's more, by being aware of its whereabouts, a Mac can accordingly set the proper time zone for your machine.

AirPort on the Mac can determine its whereabouts by picking up signals from Wi-Fi networks (assuming that the machine is connected to the Internet). The collected location data isn't supposed to identify you personally.

Still, if this wigs you out, deselect the Enable Location Services check box under the Privacy tab in Security & Privacy Settings to stop providing such information to various applications. Apps that want to use your Mac's location are also listed, so deselect any of the programs that could theoretically benefit from knowing your whereabouts that make you feel uncomfortable.

 You can still forbid a website from using your current location on a case-by-case basis, even if you don't choose to disable Location Services. When coming upon a site that wants to know such location coordinates, you'll typically see a dialog asking for permission on the fly. Click Don't Allow to deny permission or Allow to grant it. You can also select the Request Permission Only Once Every 24 Hours option to give your blessing for a full day.

Securing Your Privacy

Preventing an app from knowing your location is one way to safeguard your privacy. But consider other options. Once again, click the Privacy tab in Security & Privacy Preferences. The pane on the left side of the window lists certain apps and tools; on the right are additional apps that can take advantage of those apps and tools. For example, Contacts appears on the left. On the right are three apps that want to access your Contacts: iBooks Author, Google Chrome, and Skype. You can give permission to such apps by placing a check mark next to their name. Remove the check mark if you have a problem with those apps utilizing Contacts.

In a similar fashion, Twitter and Facebook are listed on the left side of the window. Apps that have requested access to Twitter and Facebook appear on the right. You can determine which apps can access Twitter and Facebook and which cannot by once again selecting and deselecting the appropriate check boxes.

On the left side of the screen you will see a listing for Diagnostics & Usage. Apple's hope is that that you will agree to automatically share information from time to time about how your Mac is working and how you use it. Information is collected anonymously, but if you're not comfortable with the practice either, just say no by deselecting the Send Diagnostic & Usage Data to Apple check box.

Entering a Time Machine

The feature that generated most of the excitement when Apple announced Leopard was Time Machine — and rightfully so. Here, finally, was an effortless way to back up everything on your system. You could gracefully float back in time to retrieve a file that was lost, damaged, or subsequently changed. Why, it's almost science fiction.

To exploit Time Machine, you need to supply a big enough extra drive to store what's on your computer. Time Machine pretty much takes over from there. It automatically keeps backups every hour on the hour for the past 24 hours, and daily backups for the past month. Beyond that, Time Machine goes weekly, at least until the backup drive is packed to the rafters. When you have no more room in the backup drive, Time Machine starts deleting old backups. In Time Machine Preferences, you can choose to be notified after these old backups are removed. (This is a darn good reason why you ought to devote an empty drive for your Time Machine backup.) If you're using Time Machine to back up a laptop, you can determine whether backups should continue while you are using the machine on battery power.

Setting up Time Machine

Plug in that new secondary hard drive or SSD, and your Mac asks whether you want to use it for a Time Machine backup, as shown in Figure 13-3. You won't regret saying yes, and that's really all you need to do, unless you want to customize which files are backed up.

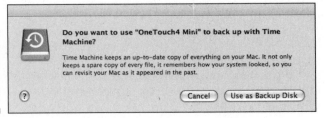

Figure 13-3:
Are you
ready for
time travel?

Do you want to use "OneTouch4 Mini" to back up with Time Machine?

Time Machine keeps an up-to-date copy of everything on your Mac. It not only keeps a spare copy of every file, it remembers how your system looked, so you can revisit your Mac as it appeared in the past.

Cancel   Use as Backup Disk

Apple sells a wireless companion for your Mac called Time Capsule that works nicely with Time Machine. This backup appliance combines a Wi-Fi base station (see Chapter 18) and secondary hard drive. It comes in 2TB ($299) and 3TB ($499) versions.

The Mac begins dutifully copying everything on the computer, including system files. This first copy job is likely to take a while, especially if your Mac is stuffed with files. (I recommend letting the computer do its thing while you're asleep.) Subsequent backups are a lot quicker because by then, the Mac copies only what's changed, such as a manuscript you may have edited.

The results are worth it, because you can go back in time to see what a file or folder looked like on the day it was backed up, using Quick Look if you want a quick preview. Say that you're looking at the batch of photos that make up the Last Import folder in iPhoto (see Chapter 15). When you go back in time with Time Machine, you'll see how the Last Import folder changes on different dates. In other words, the remarkable thing about Time Machine is that it captures multiple copies of your digital belongings.

Although Time Machine is initially set up for automatic hourly backups, you can arrange an immediate backup. Hold the mouse cursor on the Time Machine icon in the dock. Select Back Up Now on the menu that pops up.

I suspect that most of you will choose to back up the full contents of your computer. It's so simple, and if you have the storage capacity, why not? But if your secondary hard drive is crammed or you have stuff you want to keep private, you can omit certain items from being copied. Open Time Machine preferences (see Figure 13-4) and click Options. Then click + under the Exclude These Items from Backups window to add the files, folders, and drives that you want to exclude, or just drag said items right onto the same do not back up window.

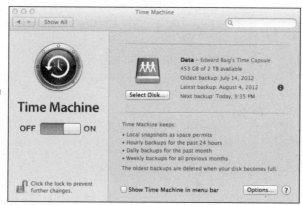

Figure 13-4: I'd keep Time Machine in the On position.

You can also turn Time Machine off altogether in Time Machine preferences by sliding the Off-On switch to the left. Frankly, you won't find many instances where you'd want to flip off the switch, but the option is there nonetheless.

Going back in time

Time travel is way cool. I'm betting that you'll hunt for files from a moment in time just because Apple makes this historical journey such a visually intoxicating experience. Click the Time Machine dock icon, and your current desktop slides out of view. You and whichever Finder-like window was active or frontmost at the time you clicked the icon are now floating in space, as shown in Figure 13-5. So if you know that the particular item you're looking for used to reside in a given folder, open that window before embarking on your journey. Or enter its name in the search box in the Finder window.

You can now venture across the sands of time to discover the lost or altered file. Say that you unintentionally wiped out a critical document several weeks ago that you now hope to recover. Use the timeline along the right edge of the screen or the navigational arrows toward the lower right to go back to the time of the deed. When you click, the windows fly forward or backward for a second or two until landing on the day you chose.

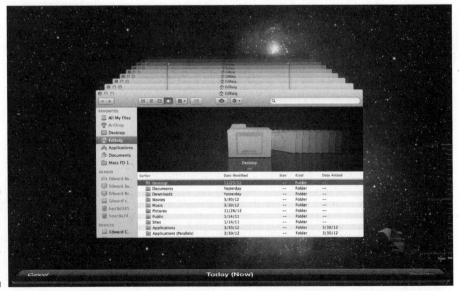

Figure 13-5:
Time
Machine
is on your
side.

If your search-and-rescue mission doesn't immediately uncover the lost file, try typing its name again in the Finder search box. You are searching for the file on that particular date. When you encounter the wayward file, highlight it and click Restore. It's transported back to the present, with Time Machine conveniently dropping the file in its original location. Click Cancel to return to the present.

If the main hard drive (or SSD) on your Mac bites the dust, you can use Time Machine to restore your entire computer. On an older computer, just insert the OS X Install or Restore DVD that came with your Mac (or the USB drive in the case of the MacBook Air) and select Restore from Time Machine. You'll have an option to choose the date from which you want to restore your system. On a machine without an optical drive, connect the backup drive and start up your Mac from the Recovery system by choosing ⌘+R at startup. Use the "Restore from Time Machine Backup" utility.

You can also use Time Machine to transfer important settings, applications, and files to another Mac. Open Migration Assistant (in the Utilities folder under Applications) and choose From a Time Machine Backup when asked how you would like to transfer your information.

Time Machine is unquestionably a great feature. But you still might want to consider backing up your data in the cloud, typically through third-party services such as Carbonite or Mozy. How come? If your Mac and the drive you're using for Time Machine are stolen or damaged, your data is still protected on the Internet. But these services are slow, and potentially (depending on how much you're actually backing up) pricey.

Take some comfort as well that some of your digital jewels are backed up in cyberspace through iCloud.

A nice complement to Time Machine is to make a *clone* backup on yet another external drive. Try such programs as SuperDuper! or Carbon Copy Cloner. Having a clone gives you a fuss-free way to boot up after a disaster.

A couple of additional Time Machine security notes: You can make sure that a given file is not backed up by highlighting it in Time Machine, clicking the Action icon in the Finder window, and then choosing Delete All Backups of *the file in question*. And had you chosen to encrypt files in FileVault (as outlined previously in this chapter), they remain encrypted as part of your Time Machine backup. If you have a Time Capsule and are running Mountain Lion, you can also store encrypted backups there. So even in Time Machine, you'll need a password to get at Aunt Minnie's pudding recipe. What can possibly be more secure than that?

Part IV
Getting an iLife

Check out the article "When iMovie and iDVD Get Together" (and more) online at
www.dummies.com/extras/macs.

In this part . . .

✔ Need to organize your digital music collection? Find out how iTunes can do it for you.

✔ See how iPhoto can help you unleash your inner Richard Avedon.

✔ Find out how you can take home movies to a whole other level with the help of iMovie.

✔ Explore the many features of GarageBand, iLife's gift to all potential American Idols.

✔ Check out the article "When iMovie and iDVD Get Together" (and more) online at www.dummies.com/extras/macs.

Chapter 14

Living in an iTunes Nation

*T*he demographers may have missed it. But a major population explosion took place during the aughts. Everywhere you looked, vast colonies of tiny white earbuds proliferated. They were spotted on subways and on the street. On airplanes, buses, and college and corporate campuses.

Those signature white earbuds, eventually EarPods, of course, were initially connected to iPods, and later their close Apple kin, the iPhones. And there's every chance you're reading a Macintosh book because of them. Although iPods and the iPhone are meant to work with iTunes software in Windows machines as well as on OS X, your first infatuation with the Mac may well have occurred in an Apple store when you ostensibly went to check out the darling of all portable music players.

You also may be thinking that if Apple hit such a home run with the iPod, iPhone, and most recently the iPad, perhaps Steve Jobs and crew knew something about making darn impressive computers too. (Naturally, you'd be right.)

So although this is first and foremost a computer book, forgive this momentary homage to the iPod.

iTunes: The Great Mac Jukebox

As stand-alone devices, iPods, iPhones, and iPads are wonderful examples of exemplary design and superb engineering. But though the iPod name signifies star power, it always had to share (and truth be told probably relinquish) top billing to the maestro behind Apple's musical ensemble, *iTunes* software.

If the iPod was Lennon, Apple's multimedia jukebox program is McCartney. Or Mick to Keith? Rodgers to Hammerstein? You get the drift; the little players and Apple's software make terrific music together. Best of all, iTunes is one of those melodious programs that musical enthusiasts (and everyone else) get just for owning a Mac. It's also freely available to those living in the Land of Microsoft.

Here's a quick rundown on what iTunes permits you to do, with further commentary to come later in this chapter:

- Listen to CDs
- *Rip,* or encode, the songs on a CD into music files that are typically compressed (see the "Compassionate compression" sidebar, later in this chapter) and stored in your digital library
- Add music to the library from the Internet
- Create, or *burn,* your own CDs or DVDs (data or music), with the proper CD or DVD burner, such as Apple's own Super Drive, which frankly used to be included in most Macs but no longer is
- Watch music videos, movies, and TV shows
- Organize your music by name, artist, time, album, genre, rating, play count, and more
- Segregate your music into customized playlists
- Stream or share the music in your library across a network and iCloud — within certain limitations
- Create ringtones for your iPhone
- Transfer music onto an iPod, an iPhone, an iPad, and non-Apple media players
- Download movies and TV shows
- Access podcasts, iTunes U courses, books, apps, and tones

To open iTunes, click its dock icon, which resembles a musical note resting in a blue circle. Upon doing so, iTunes will seek a few answers: Would you like to download music? Import your CDs? Would you like iTunes to search your Home folder for MP3 and AAC music files you already have? (If yes, the songs will be copied to your iTunes Media folder.) Do you want to automatically download album artwork when you add songs to your library? (You'll need an iTunes store account to do so.)

I'll explore some of the iTunes controls, most of which are referenced in Figure 14-1. Depending on the selections you make in the iTunes view options, what you see may vary. In Figure 14-1, you're looking at a Songs view, because Songs is the tab that's highlighted near the top of the screen. (In Figure 14-2, the Albums tab is highlighted.)

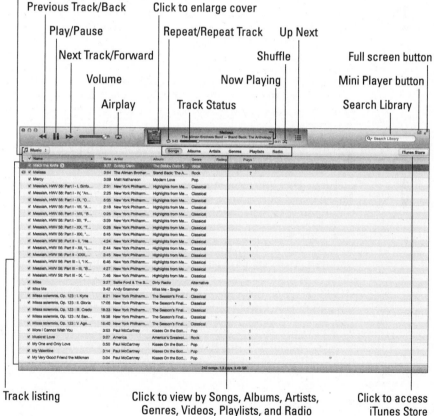

Click column heads to sort

Previous Track/Back

Play/Pause

Next Track/Forward

Volume

Airplay

Click to enlarge cover

Repeat/Repeat Track

Up Next

Shuffle

Now Playing

Track Status

Full screen button

Mini Player button

Search Library

Figure 14-1:
Ode to iTunes software.

Track listing

Click to view by Songs, Albums, Artists, Genres, Videos, Playlists, and Radio

Click to access iTunes Store

Click Artists, Genres, Videos, Playlists, and Radio to see how the look and feel of iTunes changes and, of course, to alter what it is that you're listening to.

Apple frequently changes the iTunes layout, so what you see here, in iTunes 11, may look somewhat different on your own computer. As part of iTunes 11, Apple removed the Cover Flow view that was in prior versions of iTunes. It virtually brought back the idea of rummaging through a stack of record albums. So not everyone was pleased by Apple's decision to do away with Cover Flow. Who knows, maybe Cover Flow will make a comeback. The list that follows highlights some of the key controls and features of iTunes:

- **Back/Forward and Previous/Next track:** The double arrows pointing to the left and right are your Back and Forward buttons, respectively. Place the cursor above these buttons and hold down the mouse button to rewind or fast-forward through a song. If you instead single-click these arrows, you'll advance or retreat to the next or previous track. It's worth noting that you will only go back to the previous track if you're at the beginning of a track; otherwise iTunes rewinds to the beginning of the current track that is playing.

- **Play/Pause:** Click the single arrow pointing to the right to play a song. When a song is playing, the button changes to two vertical bars. Click again to pause the music. Alternatively, press the spacebar to play or pause.

- **Volume:** Dragging this slider increases or decreases the volume, relative to your system volume settings.

- **AirPlay:** This lets you alter the volume and change which speakers you're listening through — your Mac, for example, or your Apple TV or some other AirPlay-capable speakers.

- **Cover art:** Whenever possible, iTunes depicts the album cover of the material you are listening to. In the Songs view shown in Figure 14-1, click the cover art to the left of the Now Playing pane to display the album cover in its own separate window. Roll the cursor over the album image to bring up Play/Pause and Volume controls inside the album window.

- **Album view:** Apple's handsome Album view interface uses album covers too, but you approach it somewhat differently. In iTunes 11, Apple added a feature called *Expanded View* that displays all the songs in an album that you're listening to, and does it in a most elegant way. Apple matches the dominant color scheme of the album cover. In Figure 14-2, The Beatles' landmark *Sgt. Pepper's Lonely Hearts Club Band* is shown in Expanded View. What's more, you can click a button to see songs in the iTunes store that Apple figures you'll find appealing based on what you're playing at the moment.

Figure 14-2:
In Album view, you can admire cover art.

- ✔ **Shuffle:** When the symbol in this little button is highlighted (it turns blue), tracks play in random order. Be prepared for anything. There's no telling when Eminem will follow The Wiggles.

- ✔ **Repeat:** Click once to repeat all the songs in the library or playlist you're currently listening to. Click twice so that the number 1 appears on the button. Only the current track will repeat.

- ✔ **Equalizer:** If you've ever tweaked the treble and bass controls on a stereo, you'll appreciate the equalizer. It allows you to adjust sound frequencies to match the genre of a song, the speakers on your system, or the ambiance of the room in which you are listening. Choose Window⇨Equalizer to display the Equalizer window. You can manually adjust the equalizer by dragging the sliders or choose among more than 20 presets (such as Bass Reducer, Flat, Hip-Hop, or Lounge). To bring up those presets, click the pop-up menu in the window.

- ✔ **Visual effects:** If you were conscious during the '60s, you'll welcome these funky psychedelic light animations and 3D effects that dance to the beat of whatever's playing. And if you're the offspring of a Baby Boomer, you'll arrive at this amazing realization: Maybe Mom and Dad were pretty groovy in their heyday. You can drum up your visual serenade by pressing ⌘+T or by choosing View⇨Show Visualizer. You can also use the View menu to choose the types of visualizer effects you want. And a number of visualizer plug-ins are on Apple's website and other cybersources. For a full-screen effect when the visualizer is active, click the Full Screen button in iTunes. The full-screen icon, which shows up in various apps, is the icon with arrows at each end. It resides in the upper-right corner of the iTunes window (when you're not in full-screen mode) or the upper-right corner of the taskbar (when you are in full-screen mode).

Managing Your Music

So how exactly does music make its way into iTunes? And what exactly becomes of the songs after you have 'em? I thought you'd never ask.

Ripping audio CDs

A remarkable thing happens moments after you insert the vast majority of music CDs into your Mac, assuming of course that the Mac has an internal optical drive or an accessory that you've connected via USB. (Many of the newer models lack the built-in drive.) Typically, iTunes opens, and the contents of the disc — song titles, artist name, length, album name, and genre — are automatically recognized and copied for iTunes to access. The software actually fetches this licensed information from a massive online database run by a company called Gracenote.

Now here's another remarkable feat: Next time, you won't have to keep inserting said CD into the computer to hear its music. That's because you can rip, or copy, the contents onto the Mac's hard drive and then stash the disc somewhere else.

A pop-up asks whether you'd like to copy the album. Agree, and all songs with a check mark next to their name will be copied; be sure to click to deselect any songs you have no interest in before proceeding. In some instances, you'll copy a CD by clicking an Import CD option that shows up in one of two places: Import CD is listed under the Action (gear) pop-up menu below the sidebar if the sidebar itself is visible. It also appears as a downward pointing arrow at the top-right above the content pane. In that spot, it's just to the right of a CD Info icon you can click to learn a little more about the disc at hand, assuming such details as the year the album was produced, the composer, the genre and so on are known. You will only see such Import CD and CD Info options if you've actually inserted a CD into an optical drive that is built in to or connected to your Mac.

As iTunes goes about its business, a gear icon spins next to the song being ripped; the gear turns into a green circle and gains a check mark after the song has been copied. You can monitor the progress of your imports also by peeking at the top display shown in Figure 14-3. It shows you how much time remains before a particular track is captured and the speed at which the CD is being ripped.

Incidentally, you may be able to listen to the CD while ripping a disc, and you can certainly do other work at the same time. After iTunes has completed its mission, remove the CD by pressing Eject if your keyboard has a dedicated Eject button. You can also press the keyboard combination ⌘+E or click the little eject symbol next to the name of the CD you copied. Copied songs are stored in the iTunes library by default. (If that doesn't seem to be happening, open iTunes Preferences, click the Advanced tab and make sure the Copy Files to iTunes Media Folder When Adding to Library check box is selected.)

If you weren't connected to the Internet and couldn't grab song names when copying a disc, you can add that info at a later date. Now, you used to be able to select a song or songs, open the Advanced menu and choose Get Track Names so that iTunes did the grunt work for you. As of this writing, the Advanced menu and Get Track Names feature seemed to be missing in iTunes 11 (although it could get restored by the time you read this).

▲	✔	Name	Time	Artist	Album	Genre
1	✔	All I Really Want	4:45	Alanis Morissette	Jagged Little Pill	Rock
2	✔	You Oughta Know	4:09	Alanis Morissette	Jagged Little Pill	Rock
3	✔	Perfect	3:08	Alanis Morissette	Jagged Little Pill	Rock
4	✔	Hand In My Pocket	3:42	Alanis Morissette	Jagged Little Pill	Rock
5	✔	Right Through You	2:56	Alanis Morissette	Jagged Little Pill	Rock
6	✔	Forgiven	5:00	Alanis Morissette	Jagged Little Pill	Rock
7	✔	You Learn	4:00	Alanis Morissette	Jagged Little Pill	Rock
8	✔	Head Over Feet	4:27	Alanis Morissette	Jagged Little Pill	Rock
9	✔	Mary Jane	4:41	Alanis Morissette	Jagged Little Pill	Rock
10	✔	Ironic	3:50	Alanis Morissette	Jagged Little Pill	Rock
11	✔	Not The Doctor	3:48	Alanis Morissette	Jagged Little Pill	Rock
12	✔	Wake Up	4:54	Alanis Morissette	Jagged Little Pill	Rock
13	✔	You Oughta Know [Alternate Take]	8:13	Alanis Morissette	Jagged Little Pill	Rock

Figure 14-3:
Ripping a
CD.

In the meantime, if you want to edit a song or artist information, select the song in question, choose File➪Get Info, and type in your changes. Look around the Get Info window. You'll see places for song lyrics (if known), a place to add artwork and more.

Although you may have a sizable CD music collection that you want to access on your Mac, physical discs may not be long for this digital world. More and more people are downloading music from the Internet or buying them from iTunes, Amazon.com, and other online emporiums. So that shiny platter may turn into an endangered species.

Importing other ditties

Songs previously downloaded from the Internet can be imported into iTunes with relative ease. The assumption here is that you obtained those music files legally. If you did not, placing them inside iTunes will blow up your computer. (That's not really the case, but I urge you to play by the rules just the same. People's livelihoods depend on it.)

To import audio files from other applications or your desktop, choose File➪Add to Library and then select the file. Or drag the music into the Library, onto a playlist (more coming), or onto the iTunes dock icon.

Adding music from iCloud

Later in this chapter, I tell you how to go about buying music from the iTunes Store. If you're using iCloud, any songs you purchase from iTunes on a different Mac, Windows PC, or iOS device are available to you on the Mac you are using (and all those other devices, too). You don't need to sync anything. You're exploiting *iTunes in the Cloud.*

It's up to you whether you want to turn on automatic downloads to bring those purchases to your Mac. On the one hand, you can't beat the convenience. But be wary if your hard drive or other storage is limited.

To turn on automatic downloads, choose iTunes➪Preferences➪Store. Check off the types of content you want to be automatically downloaded, among music, apps, and books. If your computer had been turned off and you want to see whether any ditties haven't landed yet, choose Store➪Check for Available Downloads.

iTunes Match

You probably didn't get all your music from iTunes. You may have ripped CDs. You may have purchased music from another online service. And (sorry, have to acknowledge the possibility) you may have even obtained it through a file-sharing service whose legal status — I don't pretend to be a lawyer — is dubious.

That's where a premium iCloud feature called *iTunes Match* fills the bill. The service stores all your music in the cloud, no matter how it was obtained, and makes it accessible on up to ten devices and computers, including of course any of the Macs you own with iCloud access — that is, as long as they are running Lion or a later version of OS X.

What's more, matched songs that are available in the iTunes Store — again where you actually obtained them doesn't matter — are made available at what is considered iTunes Plus quality, or in techie terms, 256 kilobits per second. If the song is not available in the iTunes Store, and you'd be hard pressed to find at least mainstream material that isn't, you'll be able to listen in its original audio quality.

Apple charges $24.99 a year for iTunes Match, but if you're a big fan of music (as I am) and boast a sizable music collection, I figure it's well worth it.

To turn on iTunes Match on your Mac, choose Store⇨Turn on iTunes Match and click Add This Computer.

Don't forget to sign in with an Apple ID that is identical to the credentials you used on the first computer you used to set up iTunes Match.

A small cloud icon appears next to any music that is stored on the cloud as opposed to on your computer. Click the song to download it onto your computer so that you can play it when you're offline. But with the arrival of iTunes 11, you can also now stream that song without having to download it, provided, of course, that you have Internet connectivity.

iTunes Match is not available in all countries.

Creating playlists

You listen to music under a variety of circumstances, such as entertaining at a dinner party, soothing a crying baby, setting a romantic mood, or drowning in your sorrows after a painful breakup. In the last situation, you wouldn't want to hear Barbra Streisand belting out "Happy Days Are Here Again," even if the song is otherwise a staple in your iTunes library. With a playlist, you can organize material around a particular theme or mood.

You have several ways to create a new playlist in iTunes 11. The simplest way is to first click the Playlists tab, then click the + button in the lower-left corner of the iTunes window, and finally click New Playlist from the menu that appears (or New Smart Playlist or New Playlist Folder).

If you happen to have to have the iTunes navigation sidebar open on the left — no longer the default view in iTunes, by the way — you'll also see the + button. Whether the Playlists tab is highlighted or not, or whether the sidebar is showing or not, you can also choose File⇨New Playlist or press the keyboard tandem ⌘+N.

A new playlist panel appears along the right side of the iTunes window. Apple inelegantly calls your new playlist, well, *playlist,* but of course you're meant to change it with a more appropriate descriptor, perhaps Jazz Crooners, Dance Mix, Corny Songs, or whatever. Then, as I'm doing in Figure 14-4, you can drag songs or albums to the panel to add them to your playlist. Apple kindly lets you know how many songs reside in the newly named playlist and how long it will take to listen to the whole bunch.

Figure 14-4:
Compiling a playlist.

In iTunes 11, you have another cool new way to add songs to a playlist. In the Songs view (consult Figure 14-1), select a song and drag it to the right. Suddenly out of nowhere your list of playlists appears. Drag the song into the appropriate playlist.

You can also highlight a song so that a right-pointing arrow appears next to the song title. Click the arrow and choose Add To and pick the playlist for your song.

If a song you are adding to a playlist is stored in iCloud, a copy will automatically be downloaded to your computer.

You can sort your new playlist by name, time, artist, genre, rating, and plays, if not the order in which you added songs to the playlist, by clicking the column heading that corresponds to the criteria from which you want to sort the list. You can also change the playlist order by dragging songs one on top of another.

If you're adding multiple songs to the playlist, hold down the ⌘ or Shift key to select a bunch of tracks. You can drag the whole batch over in one swoop. Or select a bunch of songs and choose File⇨New⇨Playlist from Selection. To delete a song from a playlist, highlight it and press Delete. Don't worry; the original track remains in your library. Songs in playlists never really leave the library; the playlist merely functions as a pointer to those files. For the same reason, a particular song can show up in as many playlists as you want without consuming any additional space on your hard drive or SSD.

When playlists get smart

Putting together a playlist can be fun. But it can also take considerable time and effort. Using *smart playlists,* you can have iTunes do the heavy lifting on your behalf, based on specific conditions you establish up front: how fast a song is (based on BPM, or *beats per minute*), the type of music, a song's rating, and so on. You can also limit the playlist to a specific length, in terms of minutes or number of songs.

When you click the + on the Playlists tab to create a playlist, you have the option to choose New Smart Playlist. Or choose File⇨New⇨Smart Playlist. In the dialog that appears, click Add (the + icon) associated with a pop-up menu to choose the parameters on which you're basing the smart playlist from that menu. Click the – button for a menu to remove a condition. You can also set up the smart playlist so that all the criteria you list must be met or *any* of the criteria can be met. Click + or – to add or remove a rule.

A smart playlist is identified in the source list by a gear icon to the left of its name.

Take a look at the smart playlist shown in Figure 14-5. It has iTunes looking for all songs with *Love* in the title that you haven't heard in a couple of months or haven't heard more than 14 times. The song must have been encoded with a bit rate between 128 and 256 Kbps (see the "Compassionate compression" sidebar, later in this chapter). The overall length of the playlist cannot exceed two hours. If you want iTunes to alter the smart playlist as songs are added or removed, select the Live Updating check box.

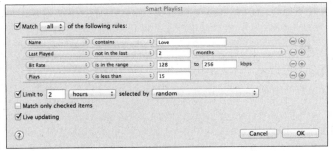

Figure 14-5: Finding the love in a smart playlist.

Figure 14-6 shows the result of this melodious love collection.

Figure 14-6: Love is here to stay in this playlist.

When playlists get even smarter

With the launch of iTunes 8 (again, iTunes was up to version 11 at the time this book was written), Apple unleased a powerful new Genius playlists feature. In a nutshell, it promises to create an instant playlist of songs from your library that (in theory) mesh well with a given song you are listening to. Click the Genius button (refer to Figure 14-4) when listening to that track to generate the playlist. Figure 14-7 shows a Genius playlist created from the "seed song" *A Song for You,* by Donny Hathaway. You can save a Genius playlist and instantly refresh it if you don't like the results. And you can limit the collection to 25, 50, 75, or 100 songs by clicking the arrow next to the number of songs that are in the current list. (Look for the arrow under the Based On heading in the upper-left corner of the playlist window.)

As of this writing, you can generate playlists only with songs you own that are also for sale in the iTunes Music Store. And Genius was a little less smart generating some classical music playlists. That too may change.

Figure 14-7:
This
playlist is
pure Genius.

You'll have to opt in (under the Store menu or by clicking Start Genius by clicking the arrow next to a song title after you highlight it) because to help craft the playlists, Apple anonymously compares data you share from your iTunes library with anonymous data from countless other users. You can also generate Genius playlists on the fly with the newer iPods, as well as the iPhone and iPad.

Genius Mixes

Sometimes you want the Genius inside iTunes to continuously play songs in your library that go great together, as if you were listening to commercial-free radio. That's what the concept of a *Genius Mix* is. iTunes segregates songs into Genius Mix categories, putting, say, a Classical Mix together or a British Invasion or Soundtracks Mix. It's based, of course, on the music that is already in your library. Some of the Genius Mixes iTunes created on my behalf are shown in Figure 14-8.

To get started with Genius Mixes, select Music from the iTunes Library pop-up menu and click Playlists. Click Genius Mix in the list of Playlists, and click the Genius Mix you want to start playing.

Figure 14-8:
Putting a mix of music together is pure Genius.

Up Next?

When we listen to music on the radio, we have an element of unpredictability. You rarely if ever know what the deejay is going to throw at you next, not that there's anything wrong with that. Indeed, you may be one of those folks who loves surprises, which is not only why you frequently listen to radio but also aren't shy about turning on the shuffle during playback.

But then there are the rest of you, the people who don't leave anything to chance. If this describes you, you'll almost certainly appreciate the Up Next feature that arrived with iTunes 11. Up Next is all about letting you know what the next song in your listening queue is, followed by the song after that, the one after that, and so on. You can peek at the list by clicking the Up Next icon to the right of the song that's playing. (It's labeled in Figure 14-1.)

If you see a song in that list that you want to play immediately, click its name in the list. If you see a song in the list that you don't want to play at all, roll the mouse pointer over the track and click the circled X to remove it from the queue.

Moreover, when you moved the mouse pointer over the list, you probably noticed a right-pointing arrow. Click the arrow and you see several additional options. Click Play Next to have the given track jump to the top of the Up Next list. You can also start Genius from here or create a Genius Playlist. And you can seek Genius Suggestions or add the song to an existing playlist. Or you can go directly to the album, song, or artist in your library. Finally, you can show the track in the iTunes Store.

In the Up Next list, you find a tiny icon that resembles a clock. It's just to the left of the Clear button that will clear the Up Next list. If you click the little clock icon instead, the Up Next list morphs into a Previously Played list instead, providing a quick summary of what you've been listening to of late.

MiniPlayer

A lot of times you listen to music in the background while working on other stuff. But you still want to be able to control what you're listening to — and see the Up Next list. The MiniPlayer lets you control and see what you're listening to in a smaller window that doesn't hog more room on the screen. Even so, the version of the MiniPlayer added with iTunes 11 includes the Up Next button. And if you want to listen to something specific, you can search your entire music collection via a search box in the MiniPlayer. Click the MiniPlayer button (refer back to Figure 14-1) to shrink iTunes.

Compassionate compression

iTunes can sing to a variety of audio file formats. Most digital tracks imported into the iTunes database are compressed, or shrunken, so that the music doesn't hog an inordinate amount of space on your hard drive or fill your less-capacious iPods too rapidly. But you generally have a trade-off between file size and sound quality. As you might imagine, larger files offer the finest sonic fidelity — at least in theory.

The best known of these compression schemes is *MP3,* a method in which files are squeezed to a reasonable size while keeping the sound quality at a level perfectly acceptable to all but the most serious audiophiles. Apple prefers an alternate compression method. On Macs with QuickTime 6.2 or later, Apple uses a default encoding scheme known as MPEG-4 AAC (*Advanced Audio Coding*), a compression format that Apple claims is equal, if not superior, to MP3s encoded at the same or a slightly higher bit rate. (If you have an earlier version of QuickTime, MP3 is the default.)

The songs that you purchase at the iTunes Music Store are also in the AAC format. According to Apple, the High Quality AAC setting produces files that take up less than 1MB for each minute of music. But iTunes also recognizes other file formats, among them Apple Lossless, AIFF, and WAV. These last two flavors are uncompressed, so the music is of exceptional quality, but the files gobble up disk space. Apple Lossless is an audiophile format that matches AIFF and WAV in sound quality but takes up half the space. If you're inclined to mess with these file formats, visit iTunes Preferences, click the General tab, and make your choice in the Import Settings section. You can set up the encoder to import using AAC, AIFF, Apple Lossless, MP3, or WAV, and also choose the stereo bit rate. In techie terms, 128 Kbps is the default. Such settings don't apply to songs downloaded from iTunes.

Go in the opposite direction, and make iTunes take over the entire screen, by clicking the Full Screen button (also labeled in Figure 14-1) instead.

Loading tunes onto a portable device

Transferring your songs, playlists, and — as you'll also see — videos, books, and podcasts to an iPod, iPhone, or other portable device is as simple as connecting the device to your Mac through USB or (with a really old iPod and older Mac) FireWire, depending on the model. Each time you connect, the iPod automatically mirrors any changes to your songs and playlists in iTunes. That is, unless you select Manually Manage Music and Videos on the Summary tab in the iTunes window when the device is connected. But wireless syncing options are available through Wi-Fi on the iPhone or iPad.

A connected iPod, iPad, or iPhone shows up in the upper-right corner of the iTunes window. Click the little Eject icon next to the name of your iPod, iPad, or iPhone before disconnecting the device from your Mac. Or click the tab with your device name to summon a page that shows your backup and sync options, including backing up to your Mac.

Burning audio CDs

Knowing how to create a playlist is a handy precursor to burning or creating your own CD that can be played in virtually any standard compact disc player.

Follow these steps to burn a CD (or DVD):

1. **Insert a blank recordable disc in the computer's optical drive. (Obviously it has to have one.)**

   A pop-up window appears, asking you to choose an action.

2. **Choose Open iTunes (if the program is not already open).**

3. **Select a playlist in your library that you want to burn. Make sure that all the tunes you want have check marks next to their names.**

   Be mindful of the length of those tracks; regular CDs have room for either 74 or 80 minutes of music, or approximately 20 songs.

4. **On the File menu, choose Burn Playlist to Disc.**

5. **For the Disc Format field, select Audio CD.**

6. **Select a preferred speed for the burning operation, or better yet, leave the default, which is Maximum Possible.**

7. **Choose the gap between songs (from 0 to 5 seconds; 2 seconds is the default).**

   Keeping the gap at zero means that with live CDs, for example, there's no annoying second or so of silence between songs.

8. **If you want all the songs on the CD to play at the same volume, select Sound Check.**

9. **(Optional) Select Include CD Text.**

   Note that, while certain CD players can display CD track information — the "CD text" that I'm talking about here — most CD players currently on the market can't.

10. **With those preliminaries out the way, click the Burn button in the lower-right corner of the Burn Settings window.**

11. **Click Burn Disc again.**

    Your CD burner chugs away. The entire procedure may take several minutes.

In this example, you burned an audio CD. Apple also gives you the option to burn an MP3 CD. The advantage is that you can store a lot more music (more than 12 hours, or 150 songs) on a typical CD-R disc. The rub: Fewer CD players can handle this type of disc. You can also burn to a data CD or DVD, but again the discs may not play in some players.

Tuning in to Internet radio

Listening to your own CDs and digital tracks is terrific. Presumably a lot of thought went into amassing your collection. But at times, nothing beats the serendipity of radio: not knowing what's coming next, hearing a nugget you haven't heard in decades, or hearing a new jewel for the first time.

You don't have to leave your Mac to revel in this type of experience. In fact, when you click Radio in the source list, you'll have access to a heck of a lot more radio stations than you'll find on AM, FM, or even subscription-based satellite radio. These are *streaming Internet radio* stations, and you can choose from hundreds of them. Apple categorizes these by genre, as shown in Figure 14-9. Click the triangle next to a category name to see all the station options in that genre. Double-click to tune in to a particular station. It starts playing in a few seconds, mercifully minus the static of regular radio.

Pay attention to the *bit rate.* The higher the bit rate number, the better a station will sound, though you're at the mercy of your Internet connection. If you don't see the bit rate, choose View⇨View Options⇨Bit Rate. If not already selected, you can also choose to view Comments and Kind (refer to Figure 14-9).

You can include Internet radio stations in a playlist. Of course, you must still be connected to the Internet to hear them.

Figure 14-9:
You won't
find all
these on
AM or FM.

Stream	Comments	Kind	Bit Rate
WHRO	WHRO 90.3FM is one of the premier classical radio stations, offering the world's greatest music and fine art...	Internet audio...	128 kbps
WKSU	NPR. Classical. Other Smart Stuff.	Internet audio...	128 kbps
WKSU 3 Classical	„Classic‰ Classical - The best of the baroque, classical, romantic and modern eras with a pinch of vocal a...	Internet audio...	128 kbps
WQXR-FM	The Classical Music Station of NYC	Internet audio...	128 kbps
WRTI Classical	Classical	Internet audio...	64 kbps
WSJTHD2	WSJT HD2 Classical Music for Tampa Bay	Internet audio...	64 kbps
WSMR 89.1	All Classical Music ^ 24 hours-a-day	Internet audio...	128 kbps
WWNO-2 - NPR - Classi...	New Orleans	89.9 WWNO ^ 2	Classical Music & NPR	Internet audio...	128 kbps
ZET Chopin	ZET Rock	Internet audio...	96 kbps
ZET Classic	ZET Classic	Internet audio...	96 kbps
104.9 FM XLNC1	Classical Music (San Diego/Tijuana)	Internet audio...	96 kbps
▶ College/University			
▶ Comedy			
▶ Country			
▶ Eclectic			
▶ Electronica			
▶ Golden Oldies			
▶ Hard Rock / Metal			
▶ Hip Hop / Rap			
▶ International / World			
▼ Jazz (231 streams)			
A-JAZZ-FM-WEB	All the JAZZ music : GENUINE-JAZZ / CLASSIC-JAZZ / SMOOTH / FUSION / LATIN / ACID-JAZZ / SWIN...	Internet audio...	128 kbps
ABC JAZZ	pure jazz	Internet audio...	128 kbps
Absolutely Mellow Jazz -...	Relax and unwind to the mellow side of Jazz.	Internet audio...	Unknown
Absolutely Smooth Jazz...	The world's smoothest jazz 24 hours a day	www.sky.fm	Internet audio...	96 kbps
Absolutely Smooth Loun...	Relax and unwind with the smoothest lounge vibes.	Internet audio...	64 kbps
AceRadio ^ Smooth Jazz	Your best bet for Internet Radio.	Internet audio...	128 kbps
AceRadio ^ Vocal Jazz	Your best bet for Internet Radio.	Internet audio...	128 kbps
AddictedToRadio.com -...	Traditional Jazz from the masters like Miles, Thelonius and more	Internet audio...	64 kbps
AddictedToRadio.com -...	Smooth Jazz, the name says it all	Internet audio...	64 kbps

Finding Music (and More) Online

iTunes serves as a gateway to a delightful emporium for music lovers. The iTunes Store is where hunting for songs is a pleasure for all but the most tone-deaf users. Don't believe me? How else to explain the billions of downloads since Apple opened the place? To enter the store, click the iTunes Store button in the upper-right corner of the iTunes window.

Sadly, you won't find every song on your wish list because some performers or the music labels that control the artists' catalogues foolhardily remain digital holdouts. They have yet to put their records up for sale in cyberspace. If you ask me, it smacks of greed. But then don't get me started.

Fortunately, the roster of digital holdouts is shorter and shorter. Even the Beatles, once the poster child for the playing hard to get, eventually relented. The complete Fab Four catalog is available these days in iTunes.

Now that I have that rant off my chest, I'll put a positive spin on buying music online compared to doing so in the physical world. For one thing, your neighborhood record store isn't going to carry the more than 26 million (and counting) tracks found in the iTunes Store. And sadly, many of those physical stores have disappeared, in large part because of the popularity of cyberpurchases. Moreover, every tune in the iTunes joint is always "in stock."

Shopping online for music affords you other privileges. Most notably, you have the opportunity to cherry-pick favorite tracks from an album, without having to buy the entire compilation. Note, however, that some record labels require that some tracks be purchased only as part of a full-blown album.

What's more, you can sample all the tracks for up to 90 seconds, without any obligation to buy. Most of the songs that you wanted to buy used to cost 99¢ a pop, but the most popular material these days more typically fetches $1.29 a track. On the other hand, you can find bargain selections for as little as 69¢. Then you have the matter of instant gratification. You can start listening to the music you buy inside iTunes mere seconds after making a purchase, as you'll see later in the chapter.

Seeking online music recommendations

In a real-life music store, you might find an adolescent clerk willing to recommend an album or artist. (Although why is it you have a sneaking suspicion this kid doesn't speak the same language you do, much less enjoy the same repertoire?) If you get really lucky, you may come across a Julliard graduate moonlighting between gigs. But more often than not, you're browsing the shelves on your own, not that that's a bad thing; I love spending time in record stores.

But face it, we all need a little counsel now and then. You'll find plenty of it in the iTunes Store from Apple as well as from people like you who happen to adore music. If you're interested in finding music, click the Music heading near the top of the screen, when you're in the store. It's to the right of the little Home icon and to the left of menu headings for Movies, TV Shows, App Store, Books, Podcasts, and iTunes U. You'll read more about these later.

The front page of the Music Store is like the window outside a physical record store. You'll see colorful album cover thumbnails, promotions for par-ticular artists, and more.

Store pages are laid out with new and noteworthy releases, What's Hot, Genius Recommendations (based on the music you already have), and lists of top songs, albums, music videos, and more. You may see a few exclusives and other recommendations — presented in the main genre you select by clicking the drop-down menu under Music.

Apple frequently changes the layout and features in the iTunes Store. So don't be surprised if what you see differs from the way it is described in this book.

Figure 14-10 shows the front page of the store when you've selected Classic Hits as your genre.

Figure 14-10:
Browsing
classic
selections in
the iTunes
Store.

Now suppose that you clicked the banner for *Neil Young: Greatest Hits.* You're transported to a page like the one shown in Figure 14-11. In this initial view — the Songs tab — you'll see a list of songs in the compilation. Click any of these to hear 90-second samples. Click the Ratings and Reviews tab to see a review of the album, plus ratings and reviews provided by fans just like you. You can contribute your own rating (based on a five-star system) or click Write a Review. Doesn't some small part of you want to be a critic?

Now click the Related tab. Here's where you see the top albums and songs by Neil Young, as well as other related records that listeners bought. You also see top albums in the genre most people would associate Young with: music.

The search for great music continues

I already mentioned some of the ways you may stumble upon terrific music. Check out the following list for other methods, keeping in mind that the quest can be deeply addictive:

✔ **Search:** A great starting point in your exploration is to search for artists or song titles by entering the name in the Search Store box near the upper-right corner of the screen. As you type characters, iTunes displays possible matches.

Figure 14-11:
You can get Neil Young's *Heart of Gold* for 69¢. You must buy the whole album to also get *Cowgirl in the Sand.*

✔ **Browse:** If you're not starting out with a particular artist in mind, click Browse under Features all the way at the bottom of the iTunes screen. Choose whether you're searching for an app, an audiobook, an iTunes U course, a movie, music, a music video, a podcast, or a TV show, and then select a genre in the drop-down list. To go deeper in the search, choose subgenre. You can then search an artist name and album to find matches in the store.

✔ **Top songs or albums:** If you happen upon an album page but aren't familiar with the performer's music, consult the Top Songs/Top Albums list (under Related) and click to hear your 90-second sample. You can also sample Top Ringtones, if available.

✔ **Listeners also bought:** If you're impressed by what you hear from a given artist, you may also be attracted to other music purchased by fans of the artist's work.

You used to be able to hobnob with the stars — well, not exactly hobnob. But an eclectic cast of the rich and famous — Liv Tyler, Madonna, Mike Myers, William Shatner, Kim Cattrall, Bill Maher, Billy Bob Thornton, Carole King, B.B. King, Nicole Kidman, Russell Crowe, Jennifer Garner, Taye Diggs, Jackie Chan, Smokey Robinson, RuPaul, Andrew Lloyd Webber, Kanye West, Sting, Al Franken, Lebron James, Lance Armstrong, Tim McGraw, Bill Cosby, the Reverend Al Green, and many more — put together lists of their favorite works. The artists usually provided brief descriptions of why they chose certain songs. Regrettably, purchasing songs from these celebrity playlists is not an automatic ticket to stardom. Even worse, Apple no longer provides celebrity playlists as a regular feature. But because of the nature of cyberspace, you can still find links to the celebrity playlists floating out there. Check out `https://itunes.apple.com/WebObjects/MZStore.woa/wa/viewCelebritiesSeeAll?cc=us` to find some of the songs favored by artists who you admire.

When you're ready to buy

So now that you have all these recommendations, you're ready to spend some money. First, though, you have to set up an account with Apple (assuming that you haven't already done so) or use an existing AOL account. Here's how:

1. **Open iTunes, and then choose Store⇨Create Apple ID.**

   You won't see Create Apple ID on the menu if you already have an account.

2. **In the sign-in window, click Continue.**

3. **Fill in the requested name, password, credit card details, and other info.**

   The rest is easy.

4. **Find a song that you want to buy and click Buy Song.**

   You may have to fill in the account credentials again depending on how recently you entered such information.

   To make sure that you really mean it, Apple serves up the warning dialog shown in Figure 14-12.

5. **Click Buy to complete the transaction.**

   In a matter of seconds (usually) the song is downloaded to the aptly named Purchased playlist. But as the nearby "Digital rights police" sidebar suggests, the purchased track may have some restrictions.

Figure 14-12: We're happy to take your money, but...

Are you sure you want to buy and download "Locked Out of Heaven"?

Your credit card will be charged for this purchase and your purchase will begin to download immediately.

☐ Don't ask me about buying songs again.

Cancel   Buy

Once a week, you can download at least one free single, handpicked by Apple, and usually more. The freebies are typically from artists you've never heard of, though the music is often quite good and sometimes someone famous does serve up a gratis tune The downloading experience is identical to buying any track, except you're clicking Free instead of Buy Song.

Apple's generosity has a hidden cost. The company is taking the Lay's Potato Chip "bet you can't eat just one" approach. The expectation is that you'll stick around the Music Store for a while and part with your hard-earned dough at some point. Heck, less than a buck a track doesn't sound like much for those songs you just *gotta* have. But take it from first-hand experience, those 99¢ and $1.29 tunes add up quickly. To find out just how much you're spending, click Account under the Quick Links list in the iTunes Home page, enter your password, and click Purchase History to check out your latest transactions.

If you've cherry-picked the songs you've bought from select albums, Apple lets you buy the rest of the titles on the album at a reduced cost. There's a six-month limit to take advantage of this Complete My Album feature, from the time you first downloaded a song from an eligible album. You see some of your Complete My Album options on the iTunes Music storefront.

Digital rights police

When you buy a regular compact disc, you can pretty much do with it whatever you like. Pop the disc into as many CD players as you have access to. Copy the songs (via iTunes) onto your Mac. Fling the thing like a Frisbee for all anyone cares.

You have more flexibility than ever with the songs you buy in the iTunes Store. But it wasn't always that way. For a long time, you had the rights to listen to given songs on just five "authorized" computers. (This is still the case in certain instances.) If you tried to share the music on a sixth machine, you were told you needed to deauthorize one of the previous five. To do so, you had to make sure that the computer was connected to the Net. Then under the Store menu in iTunes, you clicked Deauthorize This Computer. The five-machine limit applied to Macs as well as Windows machines or any combination. You could also deauthorize all five machines at once by choosing Deauthorize All on the Account Information page, which you can get to from the Store menu by clicking View My Apple ID. (The option only turned up if you had authorized five computers.) On the Account Information page, you will also see the Macs and other devices that are associated with your iTunes in the Cloud account. Quick takeaway: If you are getting rid of an old machine, remember to deauthorize it.

These are the songs purchased through the iTunes Store saddled with DRM (*D*igital *R*ights *M*anagement) restrictions, typically imposed by record labels. In 2007, Apple started offering a selection of DRM-free songs under the name of iTunes Plus. The songs initially cost $1.29, though Apple eventually dropped the 30-cent premium on some. What's more, iTunes Plus songs have been encoded at a higher quality (256-Kbps AAC). You can convert songs you've already bought to iTunes Plus for a nominal fee. Apple has even made special orders to convert music you've already bought to iTunes Plus in one fell swoop based on the number of songs that must be converted. The price is 30 cents per song, which is 30 percent of the current album price. It costs 60 cents a pop to upgrade a music video.

More recently, Apple took it one important step further and made iTunes Plus the standard on iTunes: The company made it so that *none* of the songs offered in the iTunes Store comes with DRM restrictions. Cue in thundering applause, tempered only by the fact that DRM is still associated with video. iTunes Plus music can be burned to a CD as many times you as you wish, and synced to an iOS device or Apple TV and played on any Mac or Windows computers you own.

Look down at Settings under the Account Information page. If you click Manage next to Alert Me "Based on purchases," Apple will send you an e-mail letting you know when artists whose music you've bought in the past have added new music to the Music Store. To do so, select Send Me an E-mail Alert about Artists I've Previously Downloaded. You can also request alerts based on your library content. More ways to get you to part with your money.

Allowances and gifts

If you've bought one too many lame sweaters or neckties over the years as an eleventh-hour birthday gift, iTunes may be your salvation. Click Buy iTunes Gifts under Quick Links to buy something truly valuable. iTunes Gift Certificates can be issued in amounts of $10, $15, $25, $50, or $100. You can e-mail the certificate or print it. You can even give a specific song, TV show, movie, video, or audiobook or create a custom playlist for that lucky person. You can also order iTunes Gift Cards from your Mac, though you'll find such cards for sale at numerous physical retailers.

The whole gift shebang thing takes only a minute or so. It sure beats battling the crowds at the mall.

If you click Allowances instead under Buy iTunes Gifts, you can set up a regular monthly allowance (in the same $10 intervals up to $50) that gets automatically topped off on the first of the month. If all goes well, Junior will learn a thing or two about fiscal responsibility. Unused balances are saved until your kid makes another purchase. Of course, should your son or daughter abuse any privileges, you can pull the plug on his or her iTunes allowance at any time by heading over to the Account Information page.

You can drag songs into a playlist and give them as gifts, even if you don't own the songs. You hear the usual previews; your recipients get the full treatment. Click the arrow next to the playlist and click Give Playlist.

You can also give an entire album inside the iTunes Store by clicking the Buy button for an album and choosing Gift This Album on an Album page.

Note your other drop-down choices here: You can add the album to a wish list, tell a friend about it, copy the link, or share it on Facebook and/or Twitter.

To redeem a certificate you've received, click Redeem under Quick Links and enter the redeem code on your gift card or certificate. You must enter your Apple ID and password to proceed.

Sharing music with other computers

If your Mac is part of a local computer network (see Chapter 18), you can share the music in your library with other machines running iTunes version 4.5 or later. Go to iTunes Preferences, click Sharing, and select the Share My Library on My Local Network option. You can share the entire library or selected playlists. For added security, you can require users of other computers to enter a password. iTunes must remain open on your machine for other computers to access your music. Limits apply, as indicated in the earlier "Digital rights police" sidebar. You can also select the option to look for other shared libraries.

If you want to update play counts in your iTunes library when you play music on other computers in your network, or on an iPod, iPhone, or iPad, select the Home Sharing Computers and Devices Update Play Counts check box.

iTunes: More Than Just Music

It was inevitable that the iTunes Music Store would become just the iTunes Store because, as you know by now, you can purchase a lot more than just music and share it on an iPod, iPhone, or iPad.

Reading books

You can read electronic books on your Mac through various third-party apps, notably Amazon, whose Kindle for the Mac app is free (the books aren't free, of course). As of this writing, however, you couldn't read the so-called iBooks that Apple sells for iOS devices on a Mac. But you can still order such books in iTunes on your Mac that you'll end up reading on those other devices. Click the Books tab in the store to check out the numerous iBook choices Apple makes available.

Listening to audiobooks

From Ernest Hemingway to James Patterson, you can fetch the iTunes equivalent of books on tape and play those on your Mac. You can sample 30-second previews, but the truth is, audiobooks tend to go on for hours, compared to the three or four minutes for your average song, so a 30-second preview probably won't give you more than just the barest hint of how the book reads. Prices vary too. A 22-minute audio of Stephen Colbert's remarks at the White House Correspondents' Dinner costs 95 cents; an 8½-hour audio version of "Papa" Hemingway's *A Farewell to Arms* goes for $23.95. To find audiobooks, click the Books tab.

Mac owners who buy audiobooks from the popular Audible.com service (owned by Amazon.com) can download books directly into iTunes.

Capturing podcasts

Podcasts are another form of Internet radio but are very different from the radio I describe earlier in this chapter. For one thing, many podcasts go beyond "mere" radio by incorporating video, including the Talking Tech video podcasts that I have cohosted with one of my *USA TODAY* colleagues.

Moreover, instead of listening to live streams via the Net, podcasts are downloadable files you can listen to whenever you get around to it.

As you'll see after choosing the Podcasts genre inside iTunes, podcasts cover a broad range of topics (business, politics, sports, TV and film, technology, and so on) and are served up by experienced broadcasters, mainstream media outlets (National Public Broadcasting, *USA TODAY, Wall Street Journal),* as well as ordinary Joe's and Josephine's.

Podcasts are free to download and often commercial-free. You can fetch individual episodes by clicking Free or subscribe to podcasts that arrive on a regular basis by clicking Subscribe. As with audiobooks, you can click to hear (or watch) a sample.

You can find the podcasts you've downloaded by clicking Podcasts in the drop-down Library list.

Catching up on Lost and Family Guy

Quick story. I had never seen the hit series *Lost* before downloading the pilot episode onto iTunes (and then an iPod). I was instantly hooked. I immediately understood the power of iTunes/iPod video.

Lost was among the first handful of TV shows that Apple made available on iTunes. The number of programs quickly mushroomed to incorporate everything from *The Daily Show with Jon Stewart* to *Homeland.* Music videos and short films are also available.

Videos and TV shows inside iTunes typically cost $1.99 to $2.99 apiece; high-definition shows fetch the higher price. As with audio tracks, you can sample 30-second previews and also subscribe to a season for a given series. Or you can rent certain shows for 99¢ each. When you rent a show, you have 30 days to watch it and 48 hours to finish it after you start watching. You can watch rented TV episodes on your Mac, iPhone, iPod touch, iPad, or Apple TV; each device remembers where you left off.

You can drag movie or video files you create yourself or obtain from other sources into iTunes.

Before you can transfer some videos to an iPod, iPhone, iPad tablet, or Apple TV set-top box, you may have to convert the videos to a format those devices recognize. Select the video, choose File➪Create New Version, and then choose Create iPod or iPhone Version, Create iPad or Apple TV Version, or Create AAC Version.

Buying and renting movies

Apple started not only selling motion pictures through iTunes but also renting them, too. Newer films typically cost $14.99 to purchase or $3.99 to rent in standard definition — or $19.99 to purchase or $4.99 to rent in HD. Rented movies come (what, again?) with restrictions. You have 30 days to start watching, just like TV show rentals, but only 24 hours to finish after you've begun playing them.

Through iTunes, you can view the trailer and read plot summaries, the credits, and customer reviews.

You can watch a movie on your computer, of course, and a Mac laptop is a great substitute for a portable DVD player or the dreadful film the airline chooses to show you. But when staying put, you probably want to watch on the widescreen TV in your home theater. Apple sells the aforementioned $99 Apple TV box, which connects to a TV and wirelessly communicates with your iTunes library to show movies, pictures, and videos and play music through the television.

The App Store

If you have an iPhone, iPod touch, or iPad, you can access a gaggle of nifty programs for those devices — covering games, news, productivity, social networking, and a whole bunch more. Apple had something north of 750,000 apps as this book went to press, with the vast majority under $10 and many free. Although you can access the App Store wirelessly on an iPhone or a touch, you can also get there directly via iTunes.

Fetching apps in the App store for your portable devices is very similar to the way you buy Mac apps in the Mac App Store, discussed in greater detail in Chapter 11.

iTunes U

Bet you thought iTunes was all about fun and games. Hey, learning is fun, too. You can take in a lecture on the Roman Empire from a professor at UC Berkeley. Or, find out about Green Chemistry from Yale. iTunes offers thousands of educational audio and video files from top colleges, museums, and other global organizations. K-12 classes are available too. Tuition is free and, better still, you get no surprise quizzes.

Chapter 15

Taking an iPhoto Close-Up

. . . .

. . . .

Disruptive technology is a concept that has been floating around for more than a decade. Loosely defined, it describes how a once-dominant technology gets elbowed aside and is eventually displaced by something new. The idea was coined by Harvard Business School Professor Clayton M. Christensen, and those Ivy educators are pretty darn smart. Disruptive technology is just what seems to be happening in the world of photography, where digital cameras have dramatically overtaken the film side of the picture-taking biz. Ever cheaper and more capable cameras are becoming so pervasive that they're even built in to most mass-market cell phones.

For consumers, digital cameras afford lots of advantages over their film counterparts. Most notably, you can preview shots before you ever snap an image. (Try that one with your old man's Instamatic.) What's more, if you aren't pleased with the results — for goodness sakes, one kid is looking sideways, and the other has her eyes shut — you can erase it on the spot with no harm done and without having to pay to get the shot developed — instantly reclaiming the image storage on your digital roll. Or you can apply filters right on the camera to change the way a picture looks.

With iPhoto, Apple brings its own special smarts to digital photography. The program is part digital shoebox, part processing lab, part touch-up artist, and more. Through this wondrous member of the iLife suite, you can import, organize, view, edit, and ultimately share your masterpieces with an adoring public (or, at the very least, family and friends).

Getting Pictures into the Computer

Taking pictures with most digital cameras is a snap. Taking *good* digital pictures is another matter entirely and beyond the — pun alert — focus of this book. After pressing your digital camera's shutter button, images end up on small (and usually removable) memory cards. Even as the price of memory declines, the capacity on these cards rises. You can now capture many hundreds of pictures on relatively inexpensive and reusable cards.

In the past, it was a challenge to get digital images onto your computer, where the real fun begins. iPhoto and iCloud drastically simplify the process, and so does the fact that many Macs now have slots for SD (Secure Digital) memory cards. For a peek at how iPhoto displays your digital photos after they end up in your computer's innards, gaze at Figure 15-1 (the Events view) and Figure 15-2 (the Photos view). In both cases, you're looking at these images in regular screen mode.

Go to full screen

Figure 15-1:
Zooming in
on iPhoto
Events.

Resize thumbnails   Slideshow   Summon info pane

Search by title, description, date, keyword, or rating   Edit photos in event

Source list (albums appear here)   Create albums books, cards, or slideshow

Add photo to album book or slideshow   Order prints; share using social media; or e-mail

Figure 15-2:
The Photos
view of
iPhoto.

Later you'll see how you can change the look of an already handsome program for the better by clicking the Full Screen button. You find a lot here, which I delve in to throughout this chapter.

Connecting a digital camera

In most cases, you run a direct connection from the digital camera to the Mac by connecting the USB cable supplied with the camera. Turn the camera off and then plug one end of the cable into the camera and the other end into the Mac. Turn the camera back on. (Although not all that common, some cameras must be placed in playback mode, similar to what you do on most camcorders.)

iPhoto opens, assuming that you clicked Yes when the program asked whether you want to use iPhoto to download photos when a camera is connected. (This question pops up the first time you launch the program.) The way iPhoto takes charge, you won't even have to install the software that came with your camera. Consider yourself lucky (at least most of the time).

If everything went down as it should and iPhoto was called into action, skip ahead to the next section. If you ran into a problem, you can try the following:

TIP

✔ Check to make sure that your camera is turned on and you have a fresh set of batteries.

✔ Because every camera is different, consult the instructions that came with your model to make sure that it's in the proper setting for importing pictures (usually Play mode). Don't you just hate when that happens? You want an answer now, and here I am directing you to some manual that was likely translated into English from another language. Translated poorly, I might add.

Importing images from the camera

When you connect a camera and iPhoto comes to life, the camera name (if known) will appear under Devices in the source list to the left of the screen, and your pictures will show up in the main viewing area, as you can see in Figure 15-3. The camera in question in Figure 15-3 is an iPhone.

Figure 15-3: Getting ready to import your pictures.

To transfer images, follow these steps:

1. **Type an event name (for example, Father's Day) in the Add Event Name field in the upper-left corner of the window.**

2. **If the pictures span a few days, select the Split Events check box to split the collection into several different events.**

3. **If you've already imported some of the pictures in the camera, you can select the Hide Imported Photos option. If Hide Imported is already selected, click Show All X Photos to bring them out of hiding, with X representing the number of photos in question.**

4. **Click Import X to transfer all the pictures to iPhoto's digital shoebox, with the X again representing the actual number of pictures ready to be imported.**

   The process may take several minutes depending on a variety of factors, including the number and size of the images being imported (and whether videos are in the bunch). As shown in Figure 15-4, you'll see the images whiz (or crawl) by as they're being copied. A counter at the top indicates how many pictures remain to be copied. If for any reason you want to stop copying pictures, click Stop Import.

   If you'd like to import only selected pictures from this batch, first press the ⌘ key, click all the pictures you want to include, and then click Import Selected.

5. **When the program has finished importing, a dialog gives you the option to delete the originals on the camera or keep them.**

6. **To unmount the camera, drag the camera's name from the source list to iPhoto trash or click the Eject button.**

7. **Turn off and disconnect the camera.**

Seeing double? If iPhoto detects a duplicate photo, it will ask whether you're sure you want to copy it over again. Click Import to proceed or Don't Import to skip this particular image. To avoid getting this question for each duplicate image, select the Apply to All Duplicates option.

iPhoto will also copy over movie clips from your digital camera, provided that they're compatible with QuickTime. These videos are automatically transferred in the same way as still images, except the process may slow you down some more.

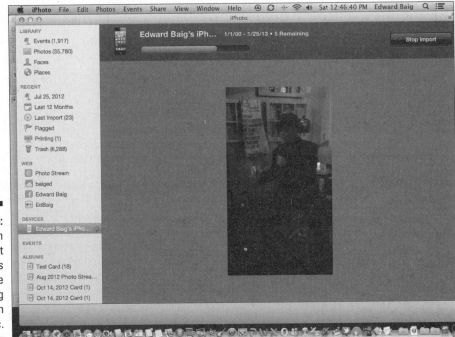

Figure 15-4:
You can
peek at
images
as they're
being
copied on
your Mac.

Importing images from other sources

Not all the pictures in your iPhoto library arrive by direct transfer from your
digital camera. Some reach the Mac by the web, e-mail, CDs or DVDs, flash
drives, or memory card readers. And some of the more recent Mac models, as
mentioned, have SD card slots to handle Secure Digital–type memory cards.

Other pictures may already reside somewhere else on your hard drive.

To get these pictures into iPhoto, simply drag them into the iPhoto viewing
area or onto the iPhoto dock icon. You can drag individual pictures, albums,
or an entire folder or disc.

If you prefer, choose File⇨Import to Library and browse for the files you
want to bring over. Then click Import.

iPhoto is compatible with JPEG and TIFF (the most common image file formats), a photo enthusiast format (available on some digital cameras) known
as RAW, and other formats.

If you haven't bought a digital camera yet and are shooting 35mm film, increasingly rare of course, you can still play in iPhoto's sandbox. Have your neighborhood film processor transfer images onto a CD or post them on the web. Given where the film-processing industry is nowadays, the company will be thrilled to have your business.

Photo Stream

None of the aforementioned ways to get pictures on your Mac are terribly taxing. But then doing next to nothing to have pictures arrive on your computer is even easier. And you'll do next to nothing to take advantage of *Photo Stream*. You do have to ensure that you're all signed up with iCloud. If you take pictures via an iOS-capable device like your iPhone, iPad, or iPod touch, they land more or less immediately on your other machines — iOS devices as well as on your Mac. But if you import pictures from a digital camera or SD memory card, those images can also make it onto Photo Stream.

Even better, because many Macs have reasonably generous storage capacities (depending on the model), you can keep a master set of your pictures on your home computer. Remember that, on an iPhone, iPad, or iPod touch, you can keep a rolling collection of up to 1,000 photos max, all stored for 30 days. Older photos are removed after the 1,000-picture limit is reached. With Photo Stream, the 1,000 most recently imported pictures are uploaded to iCloud automatically, where they can then find their way to your home computer. To make sure that Photo Stream is doing its job and is keeping the best of those images on a permanent basis, connect the device to Wi-Fi at least once during a 30-day period or (on the portable devices) save images to your Camera Roll.

Only JPEG, PNG, TIFF, and RAW photographic file formats can be uploaded into Photo Stream.

On the Mac, Photo Stream is compatible with iPhoto, of course, as well as the optional $79.99 Apple program called Aperture.

To ensure that Photo Stream is turned on in iPhoto, visit iPhoto Preferences, tap the Photo Stream tab, and select (if not already selected) the Enable Photo Stream check box. You can choose to select Automatic Import to include Photo Stream photos in Events, Photos, Faces, and Places, all described later in this chapter. And you can select Automatic Upload to send all new photos to Photo Stream.

Downloaded photos appear in the Photo Stream view in iPhoto and in the Photos app on your iOS devices.

You can manually add a photo from Photo Stream to your iPhoto library by dragging it to the iPhoto source list on the left side of the program.

Meanwhile, you must import a photo that's in Photo Stream to your iPhoto library to edit the image.

To remove photos from Photo Stream, select Photo Stream from the source list, and then do one of the following:

✔ Select the photo (or photos) in the display for that stream and press Delete on your keyboard.

✔ Select the photo and choose Photos⇨Delete from Photo Stream.

✔ Control-click the photo and choose Delete from Photo Stream from the shortcut menu that appears.

✔ Drag the photo to the trash in the source list.

Later in this chapter, I tell you how to share Photo Stream images with designated family, friends, or cohorts through the aptly named Shared Photo Streams feature. You will be able to remove photos from Shared Photo Streams as well. But for now, I take a look at the organizational principles at work within iPhoto.

Finding and Organizing Images

Right from the outset, iPhoto helps you organize pics so that you can more easily find the ones you want to view later. All the imported pictures are stuffed in the iPhoto library, which you can easily access by clicking Events or by clicking Photos in iPhoto's source list. If your pictures have gone through facial recognition, you can access them also through a clever feature called Faces, explained later in this chapter. And if iPhoto knows where pictures were shot through GPS or another method, you can find pictures also through Places, another feature to be, um, addressed (pun intended) later in this chapter. Each option is in the source list under Library. I'll start with the basic Photos view and then move on to the other options.

The Photos view

Your entire image collection shows up in a grid of *thumbnails,* or mini-pictures, in the main viewing area on the right. If you're having trouble making out those thumbnails, drag the zoom slider (near the lower-left corner of the screen) to the right and watch how the thumbnails grow. Cool, huh? Now drag the zoom slider to the left to make the pictures shrink. You can peek at many more pictures in the viewing area that way.

Double-click a photo to make it larger. Double-click again to return to the thumbnail view.

Movie thumbnails appear with a little camcorder icon and the duration of the clip. Clicking a movie thumbnail starts playing the movie in the same window in which you just viewed still images.

iPhoto can accommodate up to 250,000 pictures, depending of course on the available disk space on your computer. That's a very big number for most of us, except maybe if one shoots wedding photos for a living. Of course, if all Apple did was drop all those pictures into one large digital dumping ground, you'd have a heck of a time finding that oh-so-precious shot of your proud kid getting her elementary school diploma. So how do you uncover the very images you want to admire over and over?

For starters, you have the organized Events, discussed in the next section.

Apple automatically creates virtual film rolls on your behalf. For instance, to help you locate the batch of pictures you just imported, iPhoto conveniently places them in a smart album named Last Import. If you click Last Import in the source list, those are the only photographs you'll see.

If you're looking for the pictures you took during, say, the past year instead, click the Last 12 Months roll, also provided as a convenience by your friendly photo processor, Apple.

Go to Preferences on the iPhoto menu and click the General tab if you want to change what's shown in the source list from Last 12 Months to an album containing photos in the Last 1 to 18 Months.

Events planning

All the photos snapped in a given day are lumped into an event. The assumption is that you took a bunch of pictures during the kid's soccer game, a birthday bash, or some other activity. Of course, the smart folks at Apple recognize that life doesn't always work that way. So you might have attended the soccer game in the afternoon and the birthday party in the evening. So now we're talking two events. As you'll see, you can easily split events into two — or, for that matter, merge events that span more than a day (a reunion weekend, say).

Skimming events

It's fabulous that all the pictures attached to a single event are organized in one grouping. But if you're the least bit snap-happy, an individual event may be attached to dozens, if not hundreds, of photos. A very cool skimming feature helps you find the images you want among the others in the given Events pile.

All the photos grouped in an event are represented by a single photo that sits atop an interactive thumbnail. Events are labeled by the name you assigned them or the date. Drag your mouse over the thumbnail and watch how quickly you can skim through all the underlying pictures. No clicking required. Stop rolling the mouse when you land on the image you're looking for.

To change the thumbnail that sits atop the Events stack, skim to the image you'd like to use and press the spacebar. When you move the mouse away, that very image appears on top.

To view all the pictures that make up an event, double-click the thumbnail. Click the All Events button to return to the previous view.

As with the Photos view, you can drag the zoom slider at the lower left of the iPhoto window in either direction to watch the Events thumbnails grow or shrink.

Splitting and merging events

Double-click the event you want to split and then highlight the picture that begins the new event. Choose Events⇨Split Event. Figure 15-5 shows the screen that appears. Double-click Untitled Event and type a name. Click the All Events button at the upper-left corner to return to the main Events view. Click the title under your newly split event and type a new name.

If the pictures you want in your new event aren't adjacent to one another, press ⌘ and click the photos you want to include.

To merge events, drag one thumbnail over the other and click Merge when the dialog shown in Figure 15-6 appears. Then head over to the newly merged event in the display area, click on the event name — at this point probably "untitled event" — and type over it with a new name.

Figure 15-5:
Splitting a
single event
into two.

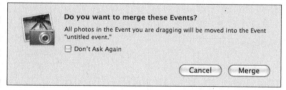

Figure 15-6:
A hot
merger.

Finding pictures by date

Now suppose that you want to display just the pictures you took around a milestone, perhaps when your little angel was born. Click the tiny magnifying glass in the Search box and then click Date to bring up a little calendar. (If just the months but not the days are listed, click the teeny-tiny arrow to display the calendar. Click it again to toggle back to months only.) If a date appears in bold type, iPhoto is holding pictures taken that day. Point to the date to see just how many pictures you're talking about, as Figure 15-7 shows. Click the day to check out those photos. Clicking the little arrow swaps between a display of the days of the month and the months of the year. Months with images are in bold.

Figure 15-7:
Viewing pictures by the month and by the day.

iPhoto captures more than just photos when picture files are transferred over. Through captured *metadata,* the program knows the make and model of the camera used to take the image; the date and time the picture was taken and imported; the size in *pixels,* or picture elements; the aperture setting of the camera; whether a flash was used; and more. Such data is factored into Spotlight searches. Refer to Chapter 6 for more on Spotlight.

Facing up to pictures

How awesome would it be to locate photos based on who is in them? Your wish is Apple's command. The magical Faces feature is based on facial detection and recognition technologies. Although it's off by a few whiskers here and there — iPhoto may fail to recognize a face altogether or falsely match a name to a face — you can't help but walk away impressed, even if it isn't quite up to *CSI* standards.

When you first open iPhoto, the program scans your library in the background to find facial matches. It will also scan faces when you import new photos.

After you click Faces in the source list, the photos that are identified by iPhoto appear on a corkboard. Click the label below the face and type the person's name. Click Show More Faces to find what Apple thinks are more photos with the person you have just named. Click each photo to confirm that Apple got it right or to indicate otherwise. iPhoto gets smarter as you go along and correctly IDs more pictures. You can drag across the images to confirm more than one picture at a time.

In the Faces view shown in Figure 15-8, every person whose face you've correctly identified appears on the corkboard. If you double-click a face, you'll see all the underlying photos of that person that have been identified in your photo library.

You can change the snapshot that appears on the corkboard for a given person. Mouse over the mug that represents all the images of a given face by skimming your mouse pointer over a snapshot and then press the spacebar when the image you want is on top.

You have a couple of ways to identify new faces. After you again click Faces in the source list to get to the Corkboard view, click the Find Faces button at the lower-right corner of the window. iPhoto shows snapshots that it thinks it has properly identified. Click the check mark if Apple correctly identified the person. Click the x if Apple is wrong, and then type the actual name if known.

Figure 15-8:
A Faces
face-off.

On the surface, that "if known" bit seems a tad silly. You'd think you'd know all the people who are in your photos, for goodness sakes. But iPhoto will sometimes show a face of someone who is in the background of a crowded scene, like at a picnic or at a ballgame. And sometimes the face of a picture within a picture will be shown, for instance, if someone you know is posing in front of a movie poster.

A second way to add new faces is to click the Info (i) button on the toolbar. Doing so summons the *Information pane*. Examine the picture. If you see an "unnamed" label below a face, just type in the person's actual name — again if known. If no label appears, click Add a Face in the Information pane. Drag the box that appears over an undetected face, grabbing the corners to make the box larger or smaller as needed. The position and size of the box determine the way the thumbnail images will look on the Faces corkboard. Click to name the person. As you type, iPhoto will suggest names from your Contacts or, for example, your Facebook account, assuming that you've established a link to the latter.

It's all well and good for you to help Apple by naming a person in a picture that iPhoto is having trouble identifying. But consider why iPhoto may be having trouble. Perhaps the image is poorly lit or blurry. Maybe the angle is off or the mug shot is too small. Maybe you had a beard in one picture and were clean-shaven in another. And maybe you have a picture of your kid when she was 2 years old but now, a few years later, she looks completely different. If you're concerned that iPhoto may mismatch other names, you can remove a name from a face. Double-click a snapshot and click the Confirm Additional Faces button. The screen that appears resembles Figure 15-9. Select the photo you want to change so that the green label — in this case, *Ed* — becomes red and says *Not Ed*.

There are places I remember

Many of today's cameras (and camera phones) are so clever they can detect where they are — and, by proxy, where the shooter is — when a picture is snapped. And even if your camera doesn't have such built-in *geotagging* capabilities, you might insert an Eye-Fi memory card that can supply such location data (not all do).

So it stands to reason that, if your camera knows where a picture was taken, iPhoto can exploit location information for your benefit. The way it taps in to geotagging is through the aptly named Places feature, which partly relies on the *Global Positioning System (GPS)* coordinates that your camera captures along with the image.

To get started, click Places in the iPhoto source list (or click the Places button when you're in full-screen view).

A Google map in the main viewing area displays red pushpins that designate spots where one or (more than likely) more than one photo has been taken. Figure 15-10 shows a map where my pictures were shot. Move your cursor over the pin to see the name of the place; click the arrow to summon all the pictures taken there.

You can drag a zoom slider at the lower-left corner of the screen to zoom in or out a map. You can also reveal more of a map by dragging with your mouse, double-click or (via trackpad) pinch to zoom in on an area, or click drop-down menus to look for photos in your library by country, state, city, or point of interest

You can even switch the look of the map to a Satellite view, a Terrain view, or a hybrid of the two.

Even if you hadn't clicked Places, you can check out a photo's location on a map. Click the Info (i) button to open the Information pane, and you can see where the picture was taken on a small map adjacent to the actual photograph. Photo locations work in Events view as well; the map shows pins for all the pix in an event.

Figure 15-10:
The Places
feature
maps your
iPhoto
library.

Don't fret if your camera can't capture location data. You can type your own location information and be as general (such as Chicago) or as specific (Grandma's house) as you like.

You can also add animated maps to slideshows and maps to photo books (discussed later in this chapter).

If iPhoto doesn't seem to be capturing location data, open iPhoto preferences, click the Advanced tab, and make sure that Automatically (as opposed to Never) is displayed under Look Up Places.

If you select the Include Location Information for Published Photos option, any location information captured with your pictures will be included if you share those images via e-mail or on an online photo site such as Flickr. Deselect this item if you don't want to include such information when you share your pictures in cyberspace.

Assigning keywords

Keywords may be the key to finding pictures in the future. These are labels, or tags, applied to a set of photos. Apple provides some keywords right off the bat: Favorite, Family, Kids, Vacation, and Birthday.

Of course, you can type your own keywords for a photo or an event. Select the photo, photos, or events for which you want to assign keywords. Click the Info button (again, it's the little circled *i* on the toolbar). In the pane that appears, click Keywords and then click Add a Keyword. Type your keyword in the Keyword field.

If the Keywords pane doesn't appear, choose View⇨Keywords so that a check mark appears next to that option on the menu.

Alternatively, Choose Window⇨Manage My Keywords and then click the keywords in the window shown in Figure 15-11 that you want to assign to a selected photo or groups of photos. You can also select a check mark to flag all the photos you may assemble for a project. Still another way to create keywords is to select Edit Keywords from the same Keywords window and click the + (Add) button.

You can change a keyword name at any time. Just remember that doing so makes the change in every photo that carries the previously assigned keyword.

Now that the underlying keywords are in place, how the heck do you put them into action? Click Search (the magnifying glass) at the lower-left corner of the viewing area and then click in the Search field near the magnifying glass and tiny downward pointing arrow. That action summons a pop-up list of search criteria. Choose Keyword from the list (the other options are All, Date, and Rating). Choose the keyword that applies to your search.

Figure 15-11:
The key to keywords.

Use keywords as a handy way of finding only the Photo Booth images in your library — or any movies you shot.

Now suppose that you want to display pictures that match one keyword *or* another (Family or Vacation, for example). This time, click the keywords in question while also holding down the Shift key. Again, the viewer will show only the appropriate collection of pictures, perhaps beach scenes that have your kids in them.

If you want to hide pictures with certain keywords — I won't ask, so don't tell — press Option on the keyboard while clicking the keyword or keywords you want to hide. The pictures represented by those keywords are *not* shown.

Apple also supplies one keyword that's not quite a keyword at all. It's a check mark whose purpose is really up to you. You might use a check mark to flag pictures that you're going to round up for a slideshow, a photo book, or whatever.

Assigning ratings

You can also assign ratings to pictures on a scale between zero and five stars. You can do so in several ways with selected images:

- ✔ Choose Photos⇨My Rating and click the number of stars you have in mind.

- ✔ Open the Info pane by clicking the little circled *i* button near the lower-right corner of the screen, and then click the representative dot next to the name of the photo.

- ✔ Mouse over an image until you see a downward-pointing arrow. Click the arrow and click then the number of stars that correspond to your rating.

- ✔ While holding down the ⌘ key, press the 1, 2, 3, 4, or 5 key (representing the number of stars) on the keyboard.

Placing your work into albums

In the film age, really organized people took the time to methodically place prints into old-fashioned picture albums. I admire people like that because I lack this particular organizing gene.

Fortunately, the iPhoto equivalent of placing pictures into albums is much simpler. The process is similar to creating playlists in iTunes (see Chapter 14). So you can place all the pictures from your ski trip in one album, pictures of the high school reunion in another, and so on. Here's the drill: ·

1. **Choose File⇨New⇨Album, or click the Add To button at the lower-right corner of the iPhoto screen.**

2. **In the first example, an untitled album will appear in the source list. In the Add To example, click Album and then click New Album.**

3. **Type a name for your new album (Hawaii Honeymoon, Dance Recital, whatever).**

Now you have to populate that album with pictures, as follows:

✔ Drag entire events or individual photos onto the album name or icon in the source list.

✔ To select a batch of photos to drag over, hold down the ⌘ key while clicking the pictures you want to include.

✔ To select adjoining photos, hold down the Shift key and use the arrow buttons.

✔ To select all the photos between two photos, hold down Shift and click the first image; then hold Shift and click the last image.

As you drag a batch of photos en masse to the album, a little red circle indicates how many pictures you're moving over.

If you want to select the photos *before* creating an album, select the pics and then choose Add To.

Although photos are lumped into albums, the pictures actually remain in the iPhoto library. The images inside albums are merely pointers to the original files. So you can place the same picture in multiple albums. You can also remove pictures from an album without fear that the images will be deep-sixed from the iPhoto library.

After you create a bunch of albums, you can group them into a folder. Choose File⇨New Folder. Give the folder a name (such as Vacations) and drag all the relevant albums into the folder. When you select the newly created folder, you'll see all the pictures stored in all the albums contained in that folder. Folders turn up in the source list.

Creating a smart photo album

Just as you can create smart playlists in iTunes, you can sire *smart albums* in iPhoto based on specific criteria, such as keywords, photos you've rated highly, pictures taken with a particular camera, or the shutter speed. To create a smart album, follow these steps:

1. **Choose File⇨New Smart Album.**

2. **In the dialog that appears, type a name, just as you do with a regular album.**

3. **Select the conditions that must be met for pictures to be included in the smart album.**

   Click the + button to add additional criteria or the – button to remove criteria. As new pictures are imported to your library, those that match these conditions are added automatically to the smart album.

In Figure 15-12, I've set up a smart album seeking only highly rated pictures taken without a flash at the beach since the end of 2010.

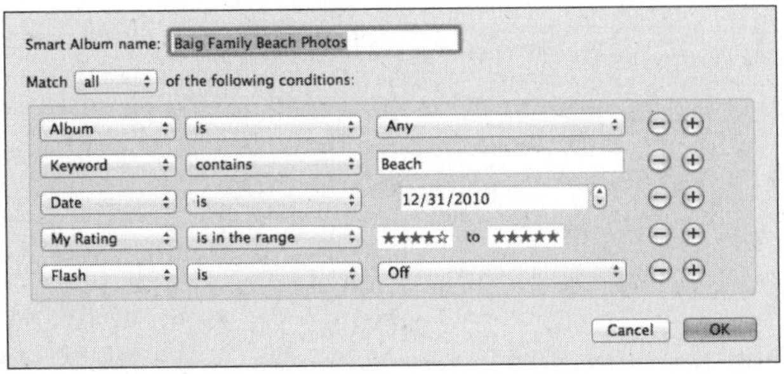

Figure 15-12:
A very smart album.

Smart Album name:	Baig Family Beach Photos		
Match all ◊ of the following conditions:			
Album ◊	is ◊	Any ◊	⊖ ⊕
Keyword ◊	contains ◊	Beach	⊖ ⊕
Date ◊	is ◊	12/31/2010 ◊	⊖ ⊕
My Rating ◊	is in the range ◊	★★★★☆ to ★★★★★	⊖ ⊕
Flash ◊	is ◊	Off ◊	⊖ ⊕
		Cancel	OK

Viewing pictures

In the main Photos viewing area, photos are displayed in the order in which you imported them. If you want to change the order, choose View⇨Sort Photos and then choose an option: By Date, By Keyword, By Title, or By Rating. You can choose whether your selection is in ascending or descending order. It's also worth noting that you have the same options for sorting events or displaying faces.

Something to hide

I'd like to believe every picture I shoot is museum quality. Truth is, I shoot my share of duds that can be easily discarded. But then I find those tweeners — pictures that I don't want to showcase but I'm not ready to get rid of either. You are about to encounter the iPhoto equivalent of shoving something in the closet or under the bed. You have a few ways to hide individual photos. Mouse over a thumbnail so that the downward-pointing arrow appears, click the arrow, and then click Hide. An alternative method is to select the suspect photos and choose Photos⇨Hide Photo. Or after an image is selected, press the keyboard combination ⌘ + L.

To have a picture climb out of its foxhole, choose View⇨Hidden Photos or press the keyboard combination ⌘+Shift+H. An X appears on the thumbnail, reminding you that the picture is still stigmatized with the Hidden tag. To remove the X, select the picture, click the downward-pointing arrow, and then click Show.

Touching Up Your Photos

Here's a dirty little secret. The drop-dead gorgeous models gracing the covers of magazines don't really look like that. (Well, maybe some do, but work with me here.) The unsung heroes are the touch-up artists, who remove a flaw from a picture here, a blemish there. We should all be so lucky to be able to put our own mugs in the best light. And lucky we are for having iPhoto on the Mac.

Now iPhoto is by no means a photo-editing superstar along the lines of Adobe's Photoshop or Apple's own Aperture. But for the mainstream snapshooter, iPhoto comes with several handy editing tools for removing red eye or applying special effects.

I get around to these in a moment. But first, I examine a majestic way to display your images in iPhoto that can help you take advantage of every last pixel.

The full-screen treatment

iPhoto's full-screen viewing option lets you exploit today's large and beautiful computer displays. What's more, Apple lets you edit in this mode. When Apple unveiled iPhoto '11 in the fall of 2010, it made a big push to have you go full-screen. (It's hard to blame the company — the views are stunning.)

To enter the full-screen edit mode, click the Full Screen button (labeled in Figure 15-1). If you go full-screen and select an individual photo, you'll see a strip of thumbnails (see Figure 15-13) at the bottom of the screen. Now click the Edit button at the lower right of the screen. A panel appears along the right side with options to rotate, enhance, fix red-eye, straighten, crop, and retouch the picture. (Again, see Figure 15-13.) I describe these one by one shortly.

You can compare between two and eight photos in the full-screen view. First select the photos you want to view or edit by holding ⌘ while clicking thumbnails in the photo browser. Next, click Edit on the toolbar at the lower right and apply some of the changes that I address over the next several sections.

You can compare before and after versions of pictures that you choose to edit. From Edit view, press the Shift key on the keyboard to see how the picture looked before you applied changes. Release Shift, and the edited image reappears.

To exit the full-screen mode, press the Escape key on the keyboard or click the Full Screen button again.

You don't have to be in full-screen view to edit photos. The same editing options present themselves from the conventional view. Speaking of which, I now take a look at these options.

Figure 15-13:
Editing a picture so that it's just right.

Rotating an image

Sometimes the picture that turns up in the photo library is oriented incorrectly because of the way you rotated the camera when shooting the original. To fix the orientation in iPhoto, select the image, click the Edit button, and then click Rotate on the Quick Fixes edit panel on the right. The image rotates counterclockwise by 90 degrees. Keep clicking until the picture is oriented properly. Press the Option key while clicking to make the picture flip the other way. If you find you have to Opt-rotate a lot, perhaps because you're a southpaw, you can reverse the rotation defaults in iPhoto Preferences.

Cropping an image

Cropping means snipping away at the periphery of an image so that you can get up close and personal to the subject at hand while removing traces of that yo-yo in the background who is sticking his tongue out. Follow these steps to crop an image:

1. **Click the Edit button and click Crop in the Edit pane that appears.**

   If you don't see the Crop button, click the Quick Fixes tab at the top of the Edit pane.

2. **Choose the cropping area by dragging the corner of a selection rectangle to resize it or dragging from the center of the rectangle to move it around the image.**

   To limit the crop area to a specific dimension, select the Constrain check box (if not already selected) and make a selection. Among the choices are 4x6 for a postcard, 20x30 for a poster, or 4x3 if you plan on using the picture in a coffee table book, which I discuss later this chapter. (I recommend examining all your options.) iPhoto puts a border around the potential cropping area.

3. **Click Reset to start over.**

4. **Click Done to save your changes.**

In helping you crop an image, Apple applies a compositional principle known as the Rule of Thirds, a popular guideline in photography and painting. The cropping area you drag around is divided into nine equal parts like a tic-tac-toe grid, as shown in Figure 15-14. The thought is that if you place key elements of the picture in focal points where the lines intersect, you will generally end up with a more interesting photo.

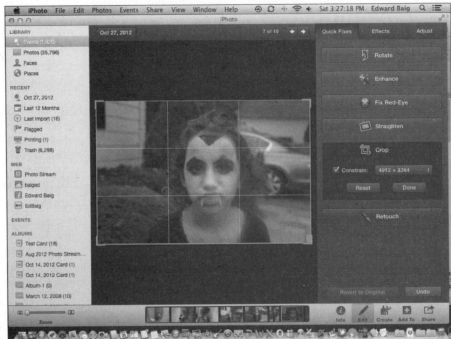

Figure 15-14:
Holy crop.

If you're unhappy with a newly cropped picture, choose Edit⇨Undo (or press ⌘+Z) or click the Undo button. At any time, you can also choose Photos⇨Revert to Original or click the Revert to Original button and pretend like nothing happened.

If you want to crop an image (or apply other edits) *and* keep the original, choose Photos⇨Duplicate. Give the cloned picture a name and use it to do your cropping.

Repairing blemishes

What do you do when that otherwise immaculate portrait is ruined by a small stain on your sweater? Or the sudden appearance on your face of the *zit that ate Cincinnati?*

Click Retouch in the Edit panel to turn on iPhoto's high-tech spot remover or software airbrush. Drag the slider to select a brush size. Then hold down the mouse button as you brush over a freckle, blotch, or pimple. iPhoto paints over these spots using surrounding colors. Use short strokes to avoid smearing an image and making the picture appear even more ghoulish. Alternatively, click over a small spot you want to remove. Click Retouch again when you're finished.

Retouching larger images is easier than doing smaller ones, making full-screen mode all the more valuable when editing thusly. Still (I hate to be the one to tell you this), getting rid of minor defects won't win you a modeling contract.

Straighten

Does the photo you took appear crooked? Or maybe you just can't come to terms with the fact that the leaning tower of Pisa is actually *leaning.* Clicking Straighten brings up a slider that lets you rotate a picture 45 degrees or less in either direction. Some cropping takes place to maintain a rectangular image.

Enhance and adjust

The quick-fix Enhance tool automatically brightens a faded or too-dark image or adjusts one that's too bright by correcting the image's color saturation and tint. Click the Enhance button once, and iPhoto does the rest. The picture isn't always enhanced, but as usual, you have a variety of undo options.

While iPhoto does the work for you inside Enhance, the spotty results you may get could convince you that you have to take matters in your own hands. And that's what Adjust is for; the tools in Adjust put the onus on *you.* To summon the Adjust tools, click the Adjust tab at the top of the Edit panel. Clicking Adjust brings up a pane like the one shown in Figure 15-15. Manually drag the sliders to adjust the exposure, contrast, highlights and shadows, color saturation, and other elements. If you get totally lost after messing with these settings, click Revert to Original to start from scratch.

Reducing red-eye

Flash photography often results in *red-eye,* where it looks like your subject is auditioning for the lead role in *Rosemary's Baby: All Grown Up.* Fortunately, iPhoto, like Visine, can get the red out. The operation is so devilishly simple that you can select an Auto-Fix Red-Eye option (under Quick Fixes) and that mere act may do the trick. Otherwise, click a reddened pupil and drag the red-eye slider to match the red area's size. Click Done to complete the exorcism.

Figure 15-15:
Getting
adjusted.

Special effects

Clicking the Effects tab brings up eight one-click special effects (a ninth button, in the lower right, brings the photo back to its original state. B&W (for black and white), Sepia, and Antique (an aging effect) affect the actual image. So do Fade, which lessens the color intensity in a photo, and Boost, which has the opposite effect. You can repeatedly click the mouse to lay on the effects even more. Clicking Matte, Vignette, and Edge Blur alter the edges of the picture.

While the aforementioned buttons give you those one-click effects, you can repeatedly click other buttons in the Effects pane to achieve the results you're looking for. Options are Lighten, Darken, Contrast, Warmer, Cooler, and Saturate.

Click Revert to Original or Undo to reverse these effects.

Admiring and Sharing Pictures

Until now, I've been speaking of organizing and doctoring images. Enough of that. It's time to sit back and admire your handiwork — and show off your Ansel Adams skills to everyone else.

Creating slideshows

If you're of a certain generation, you may remember having to sit still while your parents pulled out the Kodak Carousel Slide Projector. "There we are in front of the Grand Canyon. There we are in front of the Grand Canyon — *from a slightly different angle.*"

The twenty-first-century slideshow, in care of a Mac, brings a lot more pizzazz. Your pictures can have a soundtrack from your iTunes library. You can slowly pan across photos while zooming in and out employing the Ken Burns Effect, named after the documentary filmmaker.

iPhoto lets you create a couple of different slideshow types: a quick showcase called an instant slideshow or a saved slideshow that will appear in the source list so that you can play it over and over or make changes at a later date.

To create an instant slideshow, follow these steps:

1. **Choose the photos you want to have in your show from an album, an event, or a photo book.**

2. **Click the Slideshow button on the toolbar.**

3. **Choose one of a dozen themes from the slideshow panel that appears.**

   I recommend trying each of these to see what you like or what best shows off your pictures. Among the choices are origami, reflections, and Ken Burns. If you select the Places theme, iPhoto will download the appropriate maps for the pictures you're including and show their location on an animated map. (You can preview these various themes by mousing over their respective thumbnails.)

4. **In the slideshow panel, click the Music tab to change the accompanying soundtrack.**

   You can choose from themed music supplied by Apple, select one of your own iTunes ditties or playlists, or go with one of your own GarageBand compositions. (See Chapter 17.)

5. **Click the Settings tab to change other slideshow settings.**

   Options include showing the title slide, changing how long each slide will appear on the screen, choosing how a caption will appear, and determining whether to play the slideshow as long as the music plays.

6. **Click Play to get on with the show.**

   Press the Escape key to stop playing the slideshow.

Creating a saved slideshow is similar to creating an instant slideshow and involves the following steps:

1. **Choose the photos you want to have in your show.**

   You can select the photos from an event, a Faces or Places group, an album, or a project.

2. **Exit full-screen view (if you're in that view) by clicking Full Screen on the toolbar.**

3. **Click the Create button on the toolbar and then choose Slideshow from the pop-up menu.**

   Alternatively, choose File⇨New Slideshow.

4. **Type a name for your slideshow in the source list where a placeholder for the slideshow name appears.**

5. **If you're happy with the order in which photos appear, leave them be. If you want to change the order, drag them around the photo browser at the top of the window.**

   You can also display photos in random order by selecting that option in Slideshow settings. You can make the controls appear when a slideshow is playing by moving the mouse. The controls are shown in Figure 15-16.

6. **Click the Themes button on the toolbar and choose a theme.**

   Your choices are the same as when you created an instant slideshow.

7. **Click Play to begin the slideshow.**

You can add or remove pictures in a slideshow. To add pictures, select the picture or pictures that you want to include in your slideshow and then click the Add To button on the toolbar. Then click Slideshow from the Add To pop-up list (your other choices were Album, Photo Stream, Book, Card and Calendar). Click New Slideshow to add the selected images to a brand new slideshow collection, or click the name of any slideshow that you have previously created. Your chosen pictures land in the appropriate slideshow.

To remove pictures from a slideshow, select the slideshow in the source list and click the doomed photo in the photo browser at the top of the window. Press Delete.

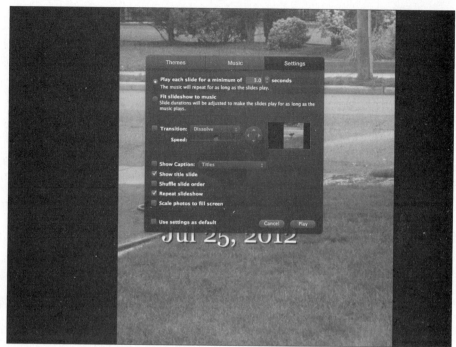

Figure 15-16:
Slideshow
settings.

You can do even more with slideshows. You can burn your slideshow to a CD or a DVD, share it online, or export it to an iPod, an iPhone, an iPad, or Apple TV or for use in other applications on your Mac.

E-mailing pictures

To send pictures using e-mail, highlight an image in your library or an album and, from the menu on top of screen, click Share⇨Email. Alternatively, click the Share button at the lower-right corner of the screen and then choose Email from the pop-up menu. You can hold down the ⌘ key to e-mail up to ten photos.

Pictures are embedded in an e-mail template in one of eight beautifully designed custom themes, courtesy of Apple. Figure 15-17 shows a photo that is almost ready to be e-mailed via the Postcard theme. I say "almost ready" because you'll want to address the message, choose the mail account you're going to send it from, and change the dummy placeholder text by double-clicking it and adding your own. You can also click the picture in the e-mail and then drag a slider to zoom in on the picture. You can also drag the photo around. When everything is to your liking, click Send.

Figure 15-17:
E-mailing
a picture
postcard.

Note the lower-right corner of Figure 15-17. You can send the picture as an attachment in its actual size or choose another size for the photo (small, medium, or large).

You can send the same e-mail to someone else. Select the photo that you previously sent by e-mail and click the Info button. Under Sharing, click the e-mail history and you're returned to the original photo mail. Enter a new recipient's e-mail address.

Smaller files are faster to send and download; larger files boast superior quality but may not slip past the server size limitations or your recipients' ISP.

Booking them

You don't have many guarantees in life. But one of them is that bound coffee-table photo books of the family make splendid presents. Apple makes it a breeze to design these professionally printed 8½-by-11-inch (or other sized) books. And when the grandparents see what *you* produced, don't be shocked if they ask how come you're not working in the publishing business.

From iPhoto, you choose the size and design of these books and the batch of photos to be included. Images are sent over the Internet to a printing plant, which binds and ships the book on your behalf.

The resulting books are gorgeous. As of this writing, Apple's large hardcover photo books start at around $30 (for 20 pages) and go up to $50 for an extra-large (10-by-13-inch book). Large softcover or wire-bound books start at around $20, though smaller-sized books are less expensive.

To make a photo book, you first select the photos you want to include in your book. Then choose Create⇨Book (at the lower-right corner of the screen).

You can choose a book theme, a background color, and a page size and click Create. You can preview your book design by rotating through a carousel and choosing a new theme. iPhoto automatically lays out the pictures in the book for you. You can customize the layout, text, and fonts in your book.

Cards and calendars

Once again, your mission starts when you click the Create button. Only instead of Book, choose either Card or Calendar. You can choose various sizes, of course, with a card costing as little as 99 cents and 12-month calendars fetching $19.99. You need to enter your Apple ID and password to process the order.

You can design customized greeting cards, letterpress cards, and calendars (up to 24 months) by choosing a theme (some with text), a start date, and whether to add national holidays (from about three dozen countries). You can also import your Calendars as well as all the birthdays from your Contacts.

 When you open iPhoto in full-screen mode, click the Projects view to see your books and cards displayed on a wood-grain bookshelf, like the one shown in Figure 15-18. This handsome view might remind you of the bookshelf in the iBooks app on the iPad, iPhone, and iPod touch, if not a real wooden bookshelf in your house. Double-click a book or a card on this virtual bookshelf to open it.

Themed prints

Apple has added lovely borders, mattes, and backgrounds to dress up the photos you print on your home printer. Click Print and then Customize and make selections from the Themes, Borders, and Layouts buttons on a toolbar that appears below the image.

Figure 15-18:
The projects
bookshelf.

Order prints

If you don't want to print pictures on your own, you can order professional prints the old-fashioned way. Click File⇨Order Prints, or click the Share button at the lower-right corner of the screen and then click Order Prints. Each 4-by-6-inch print costs 12 cents. A 20-by-30-inch blow-up costs $14.99. Prices for in-between sizes, of course, vary.

Shared Photo Streams

What if your first child was born recently and you want to share images of the adorable infant with *everyone*. It's not practical to invite them all over to your house to view albums (unless they're willing to take turns changing diapers). And e-mailing the pictures to your entire extended family isn't practical given your lack of sleep.

Apple used to let MobileMe subscribers share pictures online in a MobileMe Gallery. As you know by now, MobileMe is no more, replaced by iCloud. And MobileMe Gallery is also part of history.

Fortunately, you have numerous ways to show off your prized photos in cyberspace, everything from Yahoo!-owned Flickr to Facebook-owned Instagram.

Now I expand on the Photo Stream feature discussed earlier in this chapter. Recall that Photo Stream presents a hassle-free way to make sure that the pictures you've shot end up on all your portable devices like the iPhone as well as on your Macs.

In its infinite wisdom, Apple recognizes that you don't view pictures in a vacuum. You probably want to share your best shots with family and friends. And the result is the aptly named Shared Photo Streams feature, which does share some characteristics with the now defunct MobileMe Gallery. In a nutshell, you can share Photo Streams with the folks you designate — or, in some cases, the general public. What's more, those people you specially invite who happen to have their own Apple devices can comment on your photos and indicate whether they "like" the pictures.

To take advantage of Shared Photo Streams in iPhoto on a Mac, you must be running version 9.4 of the software or later. If that's the case, all you really need to do is open System Preferences, click iCloud, and place a check mark next to Photo Stream. From there, click Options and select the Shared Photo Streams check box as well.

This being a Mac, you have an alternate route for getting there. Open iPhoto Preferences, click the Photo Stream tab, and then select the Shared Photo Streams check box.

Now that you're all set up, here's how to proceed:

1. **Choose the album, event, or batch of photos you want to share.**

2. **Do one of the following to summon the Share window shown in Figure 15-19:**

   a. *On the toolbar at the lower-right of the window, choose Share⇨Photo Stream⇨New Photo Stream.*

   Or,

   b. *Drag photos to Photo Stream in the source list and then click New Photo Stream.*

   Whatever method you choose, you are greeted by the New Shared Photo Stream dialog box you see in Figure 15-20.

3. **In the To field, enter the e-mail address or addresses for each person you'd like to welcome to the Photo Stream.**

   As you can see in Figure 15-20, you have ample room to type in a bunch of addresses.

4. **In the Name field, type in a name for the Photo Stream —** My Adorable Kids **or whatever seems apropos at the time.**

5. **(Optional) To make your Photo Stream public so that anyone, even those without an Apple device, can view your pictures on the web, select the Public Website check box.**

Figure 15-19:
Create a
new Photo
Stream or
add to an
existing one
here.

Figure 15-20:
Choose the
people with
whom you
would like
to share
photos.

New Shared Photo Stream

Photo Streams let you share selected photos with other people.

To:

Name: A Photo Stream For My Friends

☐ Public Website

Allow anyone without an Apple device to view this Photo Stream
on a public website.

Cancel   Share

Without an Apple device, a person can't comment on your photos, read
any comments that you contribute, or read comments posted by others.
But he or she can see the pictures.

6. **Click Share to proceed or Cancel if you change your mind.**

Everyone you've invited will receive an e-mail and notification to subscribe to the stream. If the person with whom you're sharing has a
device running iOS 6 or later, they can view photos inside the Photos

app on that device. If they have a Mac with iPhoto 9.4 or Aperture 3.4 or later, they can view the pictures inside those programs. If they have a Windows PC (Vista or later) and download iCloud Control Panel 2.0, then they can view the images on those computers. If they have a second generation or later Apple TV with software version 5.1 or later installed, they can view the pictures on their televisions. As noted in the previous step, if you selected the public option, folks can also view your pictures on the web, at a URL generated by Apple.

It's quite possible that somewhere down the road you will decide to remove certain photos from the Shared Photo Stream and/or certain individuals from the stream subscriber's list. Here's how to take either action. To delete photos from a Shared Photo Stream, click Photo Stream in the source list and choose the specific Shared Photo Stream in which the doomed photos exist. Select the photos marked for deletion and press Delete.

The photos automatically disappear from everybody's stream.

To remove a subscriber from a stream, select the Photo Stream from the source list, pick the stream in question, and click the Info button on the toolbar. In the Shared section of the Info pane, you see the e-mail addresses for all the people subscribing to the stream. Select each person you are going to drop from the stream and press Delete or click the drop down arrow next to the person's name and select Remove Subscriber from the list of choices. Other choices would let you copy the e-mail address, add the person to Contacts, or resend the Photo Stream invitation.

You can add new subscribers as well. Type in the invitee's e-mail address in the Shared With section of the Info pane. He or she will receive an e-mail invitation to subscribe.

Sharing on Facebook and Twitter

By clicking Share, you can also upload pictures to the wildly popular Facebook social network or add images to one of your tweets. Refer to Chapter 11 for more on Facebook and Twitter.

If you go with the world's largest social network, pictures can end up on your Facebook wall or in designated Facebook albums. You can even change your Facebook profile picture from iPhoto. If your Facebook friends happen to comment on the pictures you've shared in Facebook, you can read those comments right in iPhoto. If Facebook friends tag names of the people in your pictures, those tags are synced to your iPhoto library (and yes, you can add those monikers to Faces). If you name the people in the pictures you've uploaded through Faces, those folks are notified, too.

Highlight the picture, click the Share button, and choose Facebook from the menu that appears. Select where you want the picture to land on Facebook: your wall, an existing album, or a new album. You get a chance to type in a comment before clicking Publish to post.

If you go with the popular microblogging Twitter service instead, your photo will be attached to a Twitter share sheet. You can add your location and type a tweet to go with the picture — up to 119 additional characters.

You can transport your pictures from iPhoto to the Internet cloud in other ways, too. If you click Share, you also have the option to publish photos to the Flickr online photo-sharing site. You'll need a free account for this purpose, which you can set up using your Yahoo! credentials if you have them; Yahoo! owns Flickr.

Apple used to provide a direct way to dispatch photos to its web page and blog creator iWeb. The direct option was removed in iPhoto 9.4 as Apple moves away from iWeb. You can still create an album in iPhoto and separately open iWeb. Using the Media Browser in iWeb, click the Photos option to find the album you've just created. Just know that with Apple migrating from MobileMe to iCloud, it gave the cold shoulder to iWeb.

Preserving Your Digital Shoebox

I've already warned you that I'm going to take every chance I get to ensure that you back up precious files. And what's more precious than keepsake photographs?

iPhoto makes it simple to burn CDs and DVDs. Per usual, select the photos you want to copy (individual pix, albums, events, or your entire library). Choose Share➪Burn and insert a disc into your CD or DVD burner, if your Mac even has one. Depending on the size of your collection and whether you have a CD or DVD burner, you may be able to archive your entire collection onto a single disc.

If you burn pictures inside iPhoto, they can be easily viewed later only in iPhoto. To create a disc that can be viewed also on a Windows machine or elsewhere, choose File➪Export and then choose a file format such as JPEG. Next, choose a location inside Finder. Quit iPhoto and open Finder. Make sure that you have a CD or DVD in your burner and drag the folder with the photos you exported onto the disc icon. After the files have been copied, choose File➪Burn Disk and then click Burn.

Whether you burn CDs or DVDs, you'll thank me if you ever have to retrieve photos from these discs. Losing a lifetime of memories is just the kind of disruption everyone seeks to avoid.

Chapter 16

Shooting an iMovie Screen Test

In This Chapter

▶ Capturing footage

▶ Getting footage onto the Mac

▶ Understanding postproduction

▶ Sharing your movie

▶ Introducing QuickTime X

ooray for Hollywood. Hooray for iLife. Apple's digital media suite —
specifically through iMovie — provides the video editing and other
software tools you need to satisfy your *auteur* ambitions. Then, when the
movie is in the can, you can share it with the awaiting public through a gaggle
of options.

> *"I'd like to thank all the people who made this award possible. The
> wonderful cast and crew, my loving family, my agent. And a special thanks
> to the late Steve Jobs . . ."*

Of course, even if your filmmaking aspirations are of a more modest nature —
producing slick highlights of Johnny or Gillian's soccer games, rather than
anything with genuine box office appeal — iMovie is still a keen companion
for your inner director and producer.

Filmmakers appreciate drama, something Apple provided when it revamped
iMovie back in iLife '08. Not all critics applauded. In an effort to simplify video
editing for newbies, Apple removed some of the most helpful and powerful
editing tools found in the previous version (iMovie HD, to be precise), including the video and audio timeline tracks that some seasoned videographers
came to rely on.

If you were already running iMovie HD, installing iMovie '08 left the program
intact on your hard drive. And if you bought a new Mac with iLife '08, you
could download iMovie HD at no cost.

But now it's time to move on. Apple subsequently released iMovie '09, which brought back some (but not all) missing features. Then in the fall of 2010, Apple unleashed another major upgrade, iMovie '11, still the version in play as this book was being written. The hot killer feature this time around? Hollywood-style movie trailers.

In this book, I spend most of the time with the new version because I suspect that most of you will work with that version. Take a gander at the new iMovie playing field shown in Figure 16-1. You'll get a quick sense of how you view, organize, and edit video.

Okay, then, let's get on with it. Places everyone. Ready? Action!

Figure 16-1:
You oughta
be in
pictures.

Shooting Your Oscar Winner

Legendary filmmaker Alfred Hitchcock is said to have asked, "What is drama but life with the dull bits cut out?" So before sitting in front of the Mac, you have to go out and capture some of that life on video. Trimming the dull stuff and converting your raw footage into worthy home cinema comes later.

Alas, I can't train you to become Hitchcock or Orson Welles or Steven Spielberg. Heck, if I could do that, I'd be sipping martinis in Cannes right about now (or at least authoring *Filmmaking For Dummies*). But I do know enough to send you off to Oz with the right gear. And that gear pretty much consists of a digital camcorder or maybe just a smartphone with a built-in video camera.

Tape, hard drive, and DVD camcorders

Not all digital camcorders sold today are simpatico with iMovie. Most *MiniDV* camcorders using HDV formats make nice with Apple. These compact models, from such leading manufacturers as Sony, JVC, Panasonic, Canon, and Samsung, now start at less than $200; DV camcorders cost under $100 in some cases. Meanwhile, the MiniDV cassettes that you record onto cost less than $2.

Along with MiniDV tape, the latest iMovie works with increasingly popular tapeless models that record onto hard drives and flash memory. Some MiniDVD camcorders work too, but they don't always include USB or FireWire connectivity, and the disks aren't usable in Macs with slot-loading drives, and for that matter fewer Macs have those drives anyway. In scary movie techspeak, the latest iMovie accepts imported video in the high-definition formats. You'll see terms such as AVCHD, MPEG-4, AVC, and HDV. In standard definition, iMovie handles MPEG-2 and DV formats, and supports cinematic 16:9 widescreen and standard 4:3 video. If you don't know whether your video-recording device is supported, use the pop-up menus found at `http://help.apple.com/imovie/cameras/en/index.html?lang=en_US`.

Using a digital camcorder

Sony is credited with producing the first camcorder, the 1983 Betamovie, which used a Betamax cassette. Through the ensuing decades, camcorders handled a variety of media: VHS tapes, VHS-C, 8 millimeter, Hi-8. These *analog* camcorders more than served their purpose for years. But as in almost every other corner of technology, camcorders, too, have gone digital. And why not? Video shot with a digital camcorder doesn't deteriorate when it's copied. Pristine sound is also preserved.

iMovie can exploit only video footage in digital form. The good news for consumers is that prices for most digital camcorders have plummeted in recent years. The most common type of digital camcorder made use of matchbook-sized, 60-minute *MiniDV* tapes. But tape is losing ground to tapeless models, as outlined in the nearby "Tape, hard drive, and DVD camcorders" sidebar.

 I advise searching online for camcorder options. Apple will be happy to sell you models at the store on its website, at `http://store.apple.com/us`. You can generally find excellent prices and a wide selection at `www.bandhphoto.com`. I also recommend a visit to `www.camcorderinfo.com`, a terrific resource for reviews.

When you purchase a camcorder, make sure that you also get the proper USB or FireWire cable to connect to your Mac (or perhaps by the time you read this, a cable that is compatible with the latest Thunderbolt ports). Just keep in mind that cables vary. FireWire-equipped Macs (and there are fewer and fewer of them) may have FireWire 800 ports, and many camcorders are

FireWire 400, so you'll probably also need an adapter cable. Just to confuse you, FireWire also sometimes goes by the name iLink or IEEE 1394.

Even if you haven't gone out and purchased a camcorder, you may well have one. And that's because the latest smartphones — including Apple's own iPhones — double as camcorders, as do state-of-the-art Android phones, Windows phones, and others. Meantime, for a complete list of compatible cameras, click Supported Cameras from the iMovie Help menu.

From Here to Eternity: Camcorder to iMovie

Whether in high definition or not, you've shot scene after scene of amazing footage (what could be more dramatic than junior's first steps?). But remember Hitchcock's observation about getting rid of the dull bits? iMovie can help you do just that. First, though, you have to dump what you've captured into the computer. You can do this in several ways, depending on the type of camcorder, digital camera, or even camera phone you're using. You can also import movies that already reside on your hard drive or solid-state drive. And rest assured that importing video into iMovie does not erase any of the scenes from your camera.

If you're using an iPad, iPhone, or iPod touch, a mobile version of iMovie lets you do some simple cutting-room work before bringing your video into your Mac.

Using a tape-based camcorder

They are not as popular as they once were, not by a long shot. But you still may own or come across camcorders that employ MiniDV tapes, DV, or HDV. These typically connect to a Mac through FireWire, but remember, fewer and fewer Mac models have FireWire connectors, so you may need an adapter. For the moment, though, let's assume you have a Mac with FireWire and a FireWire capable camcorder. Proceed with the following steps:

1. **Connect one end of the FireWire cable to your camcorder and the other to an available FireWire port on the Mac.**

2. **Switch the camcorder to VTR mode — shorthand for *video tape recorder* mode.**

   Camcorders vary; some devices call this Play or VCR mode.

3. **If the camcorder you're using can export high-definition video, you'll see an HD Import Setting dialog; select Large or Full and click OK. If an Import dialog doesn't open, choose File⊃Import from Camera.**

   In most instances, you'll select Large. But for true broadcast quality or if you plan on using Apple's Final Cut Pro X software, go with Full. Just keep in mind that under the Full scenario, you'll be gobbling up more disk space.

4. **Use the mouse to move the on-screen switch on the left side of the Import window to Automatic; then click OK.**

   You'll use this option to automatically rewind the tape and import everything on it.

5. **From the dialog that opens, choose the drive where you want to store the footage, and click to either create (and ultimately name) a new event or select Add to Existing Event to do just that. Click OK.**

   I dig a bit deeper into events later in this chapter.

6. **If you want iMovie to either stabilize the video to smooth things or find people in the footage, choose After Import Analyze For and select the appropriate pop-up menu option.**

   Downside: Stabilization and finding people can take a while.

7. **If you're importing HD video, choose a size from the Optimize Video pop-up menu.**

   I know what you're probably thinking: "Didn't I get to do something similar in Step 3?" The answer is you did, but now you can override that decision. Besides, that HD Import Setting dialog in Step 3 shows up only the first time you import video.

8. **Click Import to rewind the tape to the beginning, import all footage, and then rewind the tape again when finished.**

   You need not stick around and watch at this point, but you can if you want to. Know that you'll only hear the sound through your camcorder.

   In Step 4, I told you to set the switch to Automatic. But if you want to import only a portion of the tape into your camcorder, choose Manual instead. Then use the playback controls in the Import window to navigate to the section of the video where you want to start importing, rather than from the beginning.

Using a DVD, hard drive, or flash memory camcorder

DVD, hard drive, and flash memory camcorders typically use USB rather than FireWire. The biggest distinction compared to their tape cousins is that you don't need to follow a linear structure when playing back a movie on such a camcorder.

When you connect such a camcorder, the Import window opens, only this time it displays all the clips stored on the device. Click Import All if you want to bring aboard the entire batch. To selectively import clips, set the Import window switch to Manual. Then deselect the clips you want to leave behind. Click Import Checked when you're ready.

Most other steps are similar to using a tape-based camcorder, so even if you're using a different type of camera, I recommend reading the preceding section.

If a bunch of clips are selected but you want to import a precious few, first select Uncheck All and then select the clips you are interested in.

Patience is a virtue in the moviemaking business, so be mindful that it may take some time for iMovie to grab all the video and generate thumbnail images of each clip. A progress bar gauges how long your Mac will be at it.

Plugging a DVD camcorder into the Mac might cause DVD Player to wake up. No big whoop. Just close it.

If such a DVD camcorder doesn't have USB or FireWire, and many don't, you need to grab content from a MiniDVD. The process involves finalizing the disk in the camcorder and then using a tray-loading DVD (if your Mac has one or you have an external DVD drive) to import the content to the computer.

Importing videos from other destinations

You may have video you want to use in your final blockbuster that's already on your hard drive. Perhaps it's a project you previously created in iMovie HD or video from a digital still or camera phone that resides in iPhoto. Or maybe you want to incorporate video on a CD or DVD.

To import iMovie HD projects or other videos on your hard drive (or other disks), choose File➪Import➪Movies and search for the location of the video in the Finder window. As before, choose where to stash the recording by making a selection in the pop-up menu. You'll also again decide whether to create a new event or add to an existing one, and choose among Large or Full if an HD Import Setting dialog appears.

The iMovie HD projects have their own submenu item: File⇨Import⇨iMovie HD Project. You'll also see File⇨Import⇨iMovie for iOS Project.

Videos you've already downloaded to your iPhoto Library are readily accessible in iMovie. Merely click iPhoto Videos in the iMovie Event Library list and choose the event you want. The only caveat is that the video must be in a compatible iMovie format.

The first time you open iMovie, you may see the message shown in Figure 16-2. Click Now to generate thumbnails for the video in your iPhoto library or click Later to postpone this time-consuming chore.

Figure 16-2:
You can do
it now or
you can do
it later.

Using an iSight or FaceTime, or other camera to record directly to iMovie

Of absolutely no surprise to anyone, iMovie works fine with video captured by Apple's own iSight or FaceTime cameras, be it the stand-alone version that Apple stopped selling a few years ago or the kind built in to most current Macs.

To record directly from a built-in camera, click the Import button and then click the Capture button on the import window inside iMovie that appears. Otherwise connect your web camera, camcorder, or iSight (if not built-in) and click the Capture button. If more than one camera is connected, select the one you're calling into action from the Camera pop-up menu. Click Capture to start recording your movie, and then follow the by-now-familiar drill of figuring out where to save the footage and determining how to organize it in Event Library.

This may be the time to say thanks that you splurged for an extra-roomy (or additional) hard drive for your Mac. Video consumes about 13 gigabytes for every hour of footage in standard-definition gigabytes — ouch! — and up to 40GB, depending on the format, in high definition. After you finish your movie and put it on a DVD to share with family and friends, discard the unneeded footage so that you'll have plenty of space for the sequel or archive it to an external backup drive or a flash drive in case you need it again in the future.

Mastering Postproduction

Your raw footage is in place — all in a single unified iMovie video library. In the following sections, you find out how moviemaking gets accomplished: by arranging scenes and adding music, pictures, titles, transitions, and more. Get ready to unleash your creative juices. Assembling a movie is where the real joy begins.

Staging events

As you've already seen, the video you import into iMovie is organized into events. I hope you provided reasonably descriptive names for these events: My Little Girl's Ballet Recital, Thanksgiving Pig-Out, whatever. If you didn't type a descriptor, iMovie will substitute one for you, something like New Event 8-13-12. Come on folks; you can do better than that.

The iMovie Library groups all events by a given year (which you can break down by month by choosing View➪Group Events by Month). You can sort them by hard drive instead (assuming that you have more than one, of course) by clicking the little button with a hard drive icon in the upper-right portion of Event Library or by choosing View➪Group Events by Disk.

Here are some of the options you have for putting your own stamp on events:

- **Merge them:** You can take video from multiple sources and place them into one event. Merge events by choosing File➪Merge Events.

- **Split them:** To split one event into two, click the clip you have in mind and choose File➪Split Event Before Selected Clip.

- **Drag them:** To move a clip from one event to another, drag the clip to the title of the new event in Event Library. (Hold down Option while dragging and you copy the clip rather than move it.)

Milking the skimming feature

Skimming is one of the coolest and most useful innovations in iMovie. By mousing over the dynamic filmstrips representing your footage, you can skim through your entire video in a blink — faster than real-time anyway. Images move in both the filmstrips and the larger iMovie viewer. Click the arrows on the keyboard if you'd rather advance or retreat frame by frame. You'll hear sound, too, as you skim through your video; the audio plays backward or forward, depending on which direction you skim.

You can mute the sound while skimming by clicking the Skimming Silencer button on the toolbar (labeled in Figure 16-4 later in this chapter). Click the button again to bring back the audio. You can deselect Audio Skimming also on the View menu.

Turning off Audio Skimming does not affect the sound during normal playback.

Playing around with playback

You can play back your video from any starting point in several ways:

- ✔ Place the pointer where you want to begin watching and press the spacebar.
- ✔ Double-click to start playing from a given spot.
- ✔ Select part of clip and choose View➪Play.

To stop playing a movie, press the spacebar or click anywhere in the iMovie window.

If you want to watch events from beginning to end, select any part of the clip and choose View➪Play from Beginning or press the backslash (\) key on the keyboard.

To admire your video full-screen, choose the part of the video you want to watch and click the Play Full Screen button just below Event Library. As shown in Figure 16-3, the button is next to the Play from Beginning button. Press Escape to leave full-screen mode.

Show/Hide Events list

Play full screen

Play from beginning

Filter video

Figure 16-3:
Controls to
play video.

Working with video

As noted, the individual segments or video clips that make up an entire event look like filmstrips. A typical event has several clips.

The length of a clip has to do with when you (or whoever recorded the video) started and stopped the camera. Video clips are represented by a series of thumbnails, each a frame within a clip. The number of frames that make up a second of video will vary, depending on the video format you chose when shooting. You can select *frame ranges* to determine the video you are working with; the range is designated by a yellow border. If you click a *source video* clip, iMovie selects 4 seconds of video from the point you clicked. You can change this default in iMovie Preferences.

You can expand or shorten filmstrips by dragging a thumbnail slider to the right or the left. And you can drag the yellow selection border to change the frame range as well.

Marking video

No matter how talented you are as a videographer, it will be evident as you skim that some of your footage stands out above the rest, and other footage is at best amateurish. You can mark video gems as favorites while rejecting junk footage. Here's how.

Select the frame range of the video portion you love and click the Mark as Favorite button on the toolbar. It's the star shown in Figure 16-4. A green bar appears at the top of the frame range. If you change your mind, click the Unmark button.

If you want to reject a frame range, click the X on the toolbar. Once again, click the Unmark button if you change your mind. The videos aren't totally eliminated until you move them to the trash (and empty the trash).

In the small pop-up box to the right of the Play buttons, you can sort or filter the video shown in the library. You can show Favorites Only, Favorites and Unmarked, All Clips, or Rejected Only. If you choose Rejected Only, you may charitably give some of those clips a second chance. It's also necessary to display them if you want to trash them.

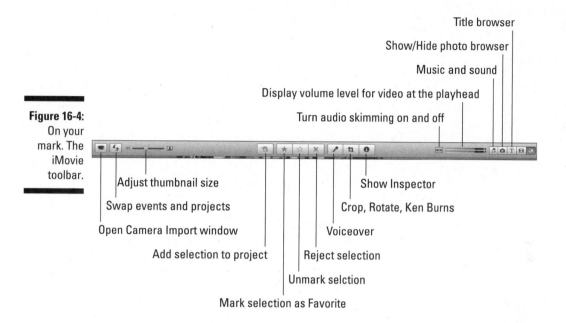

Figure 16-4:
On your
mark. The
iMovie
toolbar.

Title browser

Show/Hide photo browser

Music and sound

Display volume level for video at the playhead

Turn audio skimming on and off

Adjust thumbnail size

Show Inspector

Swap events and projects

Crop, Rotate, Ken Burns

Open Camera Import window

Voiceover

Add selection to project

Reject selection

Unmark selction

Mark selection as Favorite

Cropping video

Even under the best of circumstances — perfect lighting, subjects who actually flash a smile, terrific camera, terrific camera person (that would be you) — your video might need improvement. Here are a few tricks.

Just as you can crop a still image in iPhoto (see Chapter 15), you can highlight an area of a scene or focus in on an otherwise distant subject. Be aware that the crop applies to the entire clip. Follow the steps below to crop video:

1. **Select a clip to crop and click the Crop, Rotate, and Ken Burns button.**

2. **Click the Crop button inside the viewer.**

   A green crop rectangle appears.

3. **Using the rectangle's outer handles, resize it and drag it over the cropworthy portion of the image.**

4. **If need be, click one of the arrows to rotate the entire image in either direction.**

5. **Click the Preview button to see what your newly cropped clip will look like. Or click the Fit button to restore the clip to the full frame and try again.**

6. **Click Done when you are satisfied.**

Your cropped video may look grainy if you used a low-resolution camcorder, shot in low resolution, or crop to a small portion of the frame. Press Fit at any time to undo the cropping.

Improving the sound

Bummer — the sound in one video clip is barely above a whisper, while in another you must turn down the volume. Fortunately, you can tweak the audio in your video so that the sound remains consistent from one scene to the next.

Start by clicking the Inspector button on the toolbar and then click the Audio tab to display various slider controls. If you want to adjust the volume of a single clip, select it and then drag the volume slider to the appropriate level. Click Done when you have it right or select another clip and repeat this little exercise in that one.

You can always restore the volume to its original level by clicking the Revert to Original button.

If you want to normalize the volume across certain clips, select a clip and click Normalize Clip Volume. iMovie makes sure that the clip is as loud as it can be without distortion. Now choose another clip and do the same. The two clips are now within the same normalized range. Keep normalizing clips in this manner until they are all the way you want them.

Now you may want to do something a little more abnormal. You can play around with a so-called Ducking slider to reduce the audio on a given clip when more than one audio clip is playing at the same time — perhaps when you've added a voiceover or music to a video scene that already has sound. You get to choose the clip whose sound you want to emphasize.

While in the Inspector, try tweaking Fade In and Fade Out controls, too, if the use of such controls adds a little garnish to your masterpiece.

Giving birth to a project

The video looks good; the sound is right. And now it's time to bring everything together in a project. Choose File⇨New Project (or go with the keyboard combination ⌘+N). As discussed in the next section, you can select a project theme for your budding blockbuster. But for now, name your budding blockbuster something revealing, like Alex's Amazing Goal or Leslie's Breakthrough Monologue. (Video contained in one or more events tends to be the building blocks of your project. Just select the source video clip and click the Add to Project toolbar button. Alternatively, drag video to the area where you want it to show up in the project.)

Then choose an *aspect ratio,* movie jargon for the way the screen looks. Your choices are

- ✔ **Standard (4:3):** For years, we all watched television this way. If you choose this setting and watch your video on a modern, widescreen high-definition television, you'll see a black space on each side of the video, otherwise known as a *pillar box.*
- ✔ **Widescreen (16:9):** This is the HDTV aspect ratio. If you happen to watch 16:9 video on a standard TV, black spaces will appear above and below the video to form what is known as a *letterbox.*

You'll also get to select the frame rate for your movie. *Frame rate* (frames per second, or fps) is the number of images that flash across the screen as you watch. Select a frame rate that corresponds to the camera you own — typically 30 fps or NTSC for cameras sold in North America, South America, and parts of Asia. Chances are you'll want to go with the PAL format (25 fps) instead if you bought the camera in Europe or Hong Kong.

Now that you've mucked with your video and chosen the right moments for your project, it's time to apply the tonic that turns raw footage into a multi-media marvel.

Pick a theme, any theme

The best way to start is to click one of the Project Themes thumbnails that Apple has so generously provided for your — and your audience's — viewing pleasure. Check out Figure 16-5 for some of your thematic options. With the arrival of iMovie '11, Apple added News and Sports themes, and what's arguably the coolest set of themes, Movie Trailers. I examine those now.

Figure 16-5: The filmstrip selected here is one of the movie project themes you can choose.

Movie trailers

If you go to the movies a lot, you know that the coming attractions are often as entertaining as the movie you're about to see, sometimes more entertaining. The movie trailer themes included as part of iMovie '11 are equally fun to watch.

Apple provides 15 thematic trailer templates to choose from, ranging from film noir (a stylized ode to the films of the 1940s and 1950s) to the supernatural. Each trailer has its own animated graphics, customizable titles, and credits, plus an original soundtrack recorded by no less impressive a collection of world-class musicians than the London Symphony Orchestra. You can preview these trailers in a small movie viewer on the right.

Each trailer tells you how many cast members are needed. Depending on how many folks are in the clips you plan to include in your little movie, this number will help determine which theme to go with. For instance, the romantic comedy trailer calls for two cast members, while the road trip trailer can accommodate two to six.

Think long and hard before committing to one trailer or another. Although you can always edit a trailer later, you can't change themes. As Apple explains it, the required elements from one template won't fit another. If you want to go with a different theme, you must create a new trailer from scratch.

So go ahead and click a theme. If you haven't already typed a name for your project and chosen an aspect ratio and frame rate, do so now.

Click Create and fill in the movie name, cast member name or names, studio name, credits, and any other information in the Outline section of the tabbed interface that appears, shown in Figure 16-6. You simply type over the words that are in the various fields.

Now tab onto the Storyboard section shown in Figure 16-7. The storyboard includes text bars that represent editable on-screen text, along with placeholders for the video clips that will be included in the final project. Click the text to change the words in the various text bars.

To add video clips to the placeholders, click the video (or frame range) in the Event browser. Apple guides you by placing a time stamp on the left edge of the placeholder wells. After adding video to one well, the next placeholder becomes active so that you can add video there too. Try and choose clips that match the style of the placeholder text. If you see a head shot, you'll want a clip with a tight close-up. If the image of a character is on the move, you'll want a similar scene if you have one.

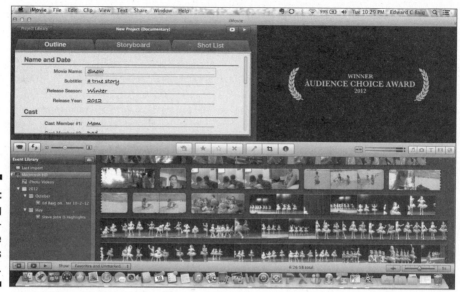

Figure 16-6:
Giving
movie cred-
its where
credit is
due.

iMovie can help you locate an appropriate clip. If you chose to analyze your Event video for the presence of people, click the Keyword Filter button (not shown in Figure 16-3). If you don't see the button, select Show Advanced Tools in iMovie Preferences. In addition to keyword controls, the options in Advanced Tools let you handle such things as cutaways, picture in picture, green screen backgrounds, and chapter markers.

Figure 16-7:
The
storyboard
is where
you dictate
the action.

You can delete a clip on the Storyboard tab by selecting it and pressing Delete. Click Play or Play Full Screen to watch your trailer.

Adding music or sound effects

What would *West Side Story* be without Leonard Bernstein? Or *A Hard Day's Night* without the Beatles? Music is a vital part of most movies (even nonmusicals). Here's how to add a background score or other sound effects:

1. **Click the Music and Sound Effects button, which is on the right side of the toolbar (or choose Window⇨Music and Sound Effects).**

   On the lower right, the Music and Sound Effects browser shown in Figure 16-8 appears.

2. **Click the source of your music or sound effects from the drop-down menu shown at the top of Figure 16-8 (where Classical Music is showing).**

   You have plenty of choices: ditties in your iTunes library, music you composed in GarageBand, and dozens of canned sound effects, including booing crowds, crickets, thunder and rain, and an electric typewriter. Double-click a sound file to hear a preview, or click the Play button in the Music and Sound Effects browser.

Figure 16-8: Adding music and sound effects.

3. **Drag the music or sound effects file to the project background and release the mouse button when you see a green Add symbol (+).**

   A green background appears at the beginning of the first clip and lasts for the duration of the shorter song or video. If the music is longer than the video, the song will still end when the video stops. If the music is shorter than the clip and you want to add to the soundtrack, drag more music to the project background.

4. **If you want to trim the music clip:**

   a. Move your mouse pointer to the Action pop-up menu (it looks like a gear) and choose Clip Trimmer. Choosing Clip Trimmer brings up a magnified display that shows the waveform of the sound or music.

   b. Drag the yellow selection handles in the Clip Trimmer to choose spots where the video starts and ends.

   c. Click Play in the Clip Trimmer to sample your trim.

5. **When you are finished, click Done.**

To remove the background music, select the music by clicking behind the video clips and press Delete. You can also choose Edit➪Delete Selection.

Recording a voiceover

What would your epic be without a James Earl Jones or Patrick Stewart voiceover (you should be so lucky)? You can use your own pipes to narrate a movie and add your voice pretty much anywhere you want in your video.

Click the Voiceover button, which looks like a microphone, and then choose your actual microphone (or sound input device) from the window that appears. Drag the input volume slider so that it gibes with the loudness of your voice. You can select a Voice Enhancement box to electronically make your voice sound swell. Remember that any sound in your video will be heard as you record your own voice unless you mute it. Select the Play Project Audio while Recording check box if you need to hear a clip's sound as you record your voiceover.

When you click the video frame in which you want to speak, the program prompts you with a 3-2-1 countdown. Click anywhere in the project to cease recording. You'll see a purple soundtrack icon in the video where your voice will be heard. Did you stutter (as Jones famously used to)? Click Undo Voiceover and try again.

The cutting room floor

From the get-go, some scenes are obvious candidates for the trash: the ones with blurry close-ups, pictures of your shoes (when you forget to turn off the camcorder), or Grandma hamming it up for the camera.

Fortunately, you can trim unwanted frames from your project clips. Select the frames you want to trim and choose Edit➪Delete Selection or Edit➪Delete Entire Clip. Off they go.

REMEMBER

If you have second thoughts, you can bring them back by choosing Edit⇨ Undo Delete Selection or pressing ⌘+Z.

You don't need to worry about losing the video you've deleted. The video that you remove from a project isn't removed from the event it comes from.

Adding transitions between clips

Moving from scene to scene can be jarring unless you add a smooth bridge. In movie-speak, those bridges are *transitions,* and iMovie gives you two dozen to choose from. Click the Transitions button on the toolbar (refer to Figure 16-4), choose Window⇨Transitions, or press ⌘+4. At your disposal are the various styles in the Transitions pane, which is shown in Figure 16-9.

You may not know the names of all these transitions, but you've undoubtedly seen ones such as Fade to Black and Cross Dissolve in movies and television. You can preview others by placing the mouse pointer over the various Transitions thumbnails.

When you choose the transition you want, drag it between two clips in your project. A small icon represents your transition. You can substitute one transition for another just by dragging another transition over the icon.

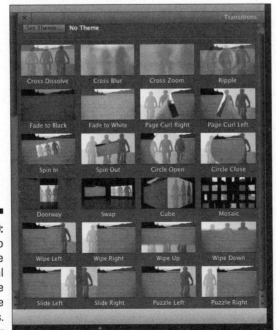

Figure 16-9:
Fade to
Black is one
of several
iMovie
scene
transitions.

Standard transitions are set to one-half of 1 second by default, and a transition can never last longer than half the duration of the shorter clip on either side of it. Themed transitions that go with the theme you may have chosen for your project are 2 seconds long. You can double-click the Transitions icon to change the length of the transitions inside the Inspector. All transitions in your video are the same length unless you dictate otherwise.

Adding titles

Every good movie needs a decent title to hook an audience — even if the film is all about your recent vacation and the only people watching are the ones who took the trip with you. While we're at it, add closing credits. You're the person who put this darn thing together and you want some recognition. Besides, selecting titles is easy. The assumption here is that you haven't selected a movie trailer theme. To add titles, proceed as follows:

1. **Click the Titles button on the toolbar (refer to Figure 16-4) or choose Window⇨Titles.**

2. **Choose a title style from the ones that appear in the Title browser and drag it onto the clip where you want a title.**

   You might choose Formal for a wedding video or Scrolling Credits for the end of a movie. Pay attention to the purple shadow that appears over the clip as you hover. It lets you know whether the title will last for the entire clip or just the first or last third. After you've chosen a title, a blue icon appears above the clip.

3. **Replace the placeholder text in the viewer with your own text.**

4. **Click Show Fonts.**

   You can change the font, color, or style of text by applying selections in the Font window. You can preview your work by clicking the Play button in the viewer.

You can lengthen or shorten the screen time for a title. Move the mouse pointer over either end of the title; when the pointer turns to a cross, drag to the left or right. You can also drag the title to a different part of the clip or have it straddle two clips. Make sure that the pointer turns into a hand before dragging the title.

Adding photos to a movie

Interspersing still photos inside your movie is a great way to show off your artistic prowess. And you can add a bit of pizzazz by adding motion effects to those pictures in what is known as the Ken Burns effect (named for the famed documentary filmmaker and explained in Chapter 15). To do so, follow these steps:

1. **Choose Window⇨Photos, click the Photos button (which looks like a camera on the toolbar), or press ⌘+2.**

    This brings up the Photo browser.

2. **Choose the photo you want from your iPhoto library or elsewhere.**

    You can search for pictures by name in the search field at the bottom of the pane.

3. **Drag the selected picture to where you want it to appear in your project.**

    By default, the picture will remain on the screen for 4 seconds and apply the Ken Burns panning and zooming effect. You can dictate otherwise, as noted in the next steps.

4. **To change a photo's duration, start by double-clicking the photo in your project (which summons the Inspector); then type the new time in seconds.**

5. **To alter the Ken Burns option, select a photo, click Crop, and click Ken Burns.**

    You see a green rectangle that represents where the effect starts and a red rectangle that shows where it will end. Click the double arrow button to swap the two. You can drag and resize the rectangles. Click Allow Black to have a black frame around your image or click Disallow Black to choose otherwise.

Sharing Your Blockbuster

What good would *The Godfather* be if nobody could watch it? So it goes for your classic. Take one last look at the movie you've produced so far. Watch it in full-screen on your Mac. If it's a wrap, it's time to distribute it to an audience — in a suitable format for the device you'll use to view it.

I explore the options in the iMovie Share menu here, noting that some of these options are a prelude to sharing in another app or program:

✔ **iTunes:** Select this option if you plan on watching your finished project on an iPod, an iPhone, an iPad, an Apple TV, or a computer. You'll be presented with various size choices based on the format that most makes sense. The Medium size is recommended for all devices, but you'd probably choose Mobile only if you were planning to watch on an iPhone or iPod touch. Choose Large for an HDTV (through Apple TV) or HD 720p or HD 1080i for a computer. After making a selection, click Publish. Keep in mind that rendering a movie can take a while, especially if you have chosen multiple formats.

If you didn't shoot your original movie in high definition, a Large or an HD-size movie is not an option.

- **Media Browser:** The movies will appear in the size you've selected here, in the Media Browser of iDVD, iWeb, or GarageBand, as noted in Figure 16-10. Again, some size options won't be available if you didn't shoot in hi-def.

- **YouTube:** The wildly popular YouTube site (owned by Google) has come to practically define video sharing on the Internet. Add your YouTube account and password, choose a category for your movie (Comedy, Pets & Animals, and so on), and add the title (if not already shown), description, and any tags. You can make the movie private by selecting the appropriate check box. Apple recommends using the Medium size. After it is published on YouTube, click Tell a Friend to spread the word.

- **Facebook:** Send your movie to the leading social networking site. The movie can be viewed by you alone, by your Facebook friends, by your friends of friends as well, or by everyone.

- **Vimeo:** This is another popular video destination on the web. You can share your work with your Vimeo contacts, anyone at all, or no one.

- **CNN iReport:** The user-generated section of CNN.com is where you get to play the role of reporter.

- **Export Movie:** Once again, you get to choose a size before exporting the movie to another location in Finder.

- **Export Using QuickTime:** With this option, you can play the movie back on other computers that have QuickTime. You have a lot of options for choosing various compression and other settings. These can get extremely technical, depending on your requirements and the requirements of the people receiving your video.

- **Export Final Cut XML:** Use this option to send the finished project to Apple's professional-oriented video-editing program.

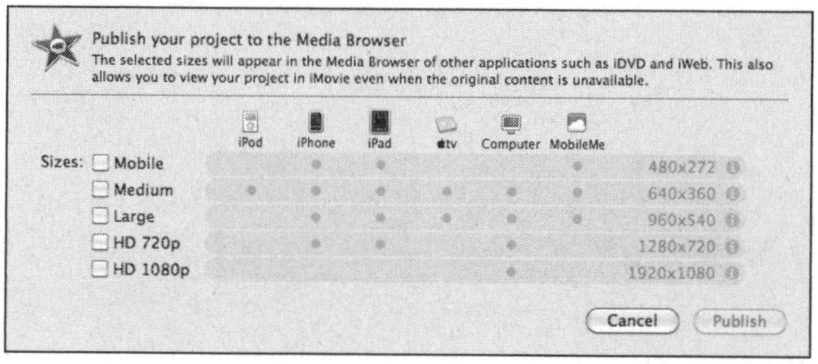

Figure 16-10:
The movie
is in Media
Browser.

Publish your project to the Media Browser
The selected sizes will appear in the Media Browser of other applications such as iDVD and iWeb. This also allows you to view your project in iMovie even when the original content is unavailable.

Sizes:		iPod	iPhone	iPad	tv	Computer	MobileMe	
	Mobile							480x272
	Medium	●	●	●	●	●	●	640x360
	Large		●	●	●	●	●	960x540
	HD 720p		●	●		●		1280x720
	HD 1080p				●			1920x1080

Cancel   Publish

QuickTime X Marks the Spot

As part of Snow Leopard, Apple reinvented QuickTime, its built-in movie player. It called the makeover QuickTime X, and the result was a new, unclut-tered movie-watching experience.

Among its stunts, the QuickTime Player in QuickTime X lets you capture audio and video on your Mac for a podcast or to explain to a friend how to do something on the Mac.

Making a quick QuickTime movie

To make a video recording, launch QuickTime Player and choose File⇨New Movie Recording. Assuming that you're using the built-in iSight or FaceTime camera on your Mac, you'll see your own handsome face. This allows you to fuss with your makeup, adjust the lighting in the room, and so on. When you're all set, click Record. When you're finished, click Record again. It's that simple. Press the Play button (see Figure 16-11) to sample the clip.

The movie is saved in the Movies folder on your Mac.

Go full screen

Figure 16-11: Click the arrow escaping a rectangle to share your movie.

Play button   Share

Shortening the movie

Now suppose that you want to edit your little gem. That's a breeze too. Click Edit⇨Trim. The trimming bar you see in Figure 16-12 appears at the bottom of the screen. Drag the playhead (the red vertical line) to find the footage you can live without. Then use the yellow handles at the start and end of the Trimming bar to select only that portion of the video that is worth preserving. Click Trim and you're finished.

Click the icon with the arrow trying to escape a rectangle (refer to Figure 16-11) for various sharing options: send it off via an Email, Message, or AirDrop. Or post it on Facebook, YouTube, Vimeo, or Flickr.

Figure 16-12:
Getting set
to trim your
movie.

Chapter 17

The Show Must Go On

Do you fancy yourself a rock icon? Your face plastered on the cover of *Rolling Stone* and *Entertainment Weekly?* Groupies stalking you wherever you go? Your band's very own tour bus? I know, it's all about the music. Whatever's driving you, GarageBand is iLife's digital recording studio for making records, creating podcasts, and more.

If you're inclined to skip this chapter because you can't distinguish an F-sharp from a B-flat, take note: You need not read music, play an instrument, or possess a lick of musical talent to compose a ditty through GarageBand. You can even learn to play guitar or piano with GarageBand's assistance as well as take lessons from artists such as John Legend, Sting, and Norah Jones.

Sure, having a good ear helps. And if you actually can belt out a tune, tickle the ivories, or jam with the best of them, all the better. Connect a microphone, piano keyboard, or electric guitar to the Mac, and exploit GarageBand to the max. Although we're only going to scratch the surface of all that GarageBand can help you accomplish, this chapter should provide more than enough impetus to send you on your way to becoming almost famous.

Forming a GarageBand

When you first launch GarageBand, you're presented with the following ensemble of options: New Project, Learn to Play, Lesson Store, Magic GarageBand, and iPhone Ringtone. You can also access any recent projects you've started.

Okay maestros-in-waiting, let's start a new project:

1. **Launch GarageBand.**

   The program is located in the Applications folder. Or click the dock icon shaped like a guitar.

2. **Single-click New Project, highlight the instrument or project you have in mind, and then click Choose.**

   As shown in Figure 17-1, you can click templates for Piano, Electric Guitar, Voice, Loops, Keyboard Collection, Acoustic Instrument, Songwriting, Podcast, and Movie (for a video podcast).

   For the purposes of this primer, choose Piano.

3. **In the dialog shown in Figure 17-2, enter a name for your song and choose a location for the file (the GarageBand folder is the default).**

4. **Set a *tempo*, or constant speed, by dragging the slider anywhere between 40 and 240 beats per minute, or *bpm*.**

5. **Choose a time signature and a scale, or *key*, from the pop-up menus.**

   Don't fret if you don't know what any of these musical designations mean. Just stick with the defaults. You'll learn as you go and can change most of them later.

Figure 17-1: Getting set to play with the Garage Band.

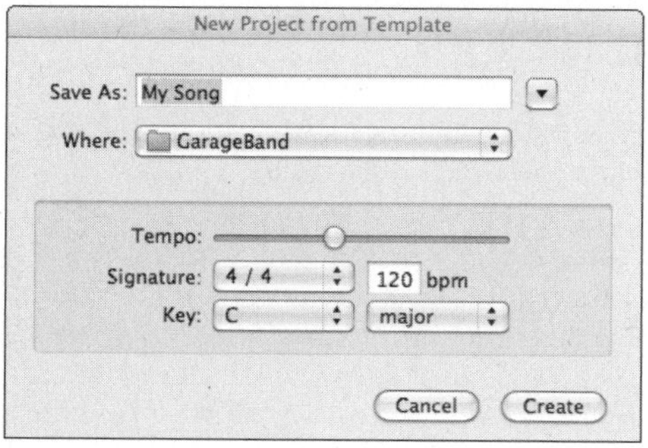

Figure 17-2:
And a one
and a two
and a three.
Creating a
new project.

6. **Click Create.**

The window that opens will look something like what is shown in Figure 17-3.

Figure 17-3:
The main
Garage
Band stage.

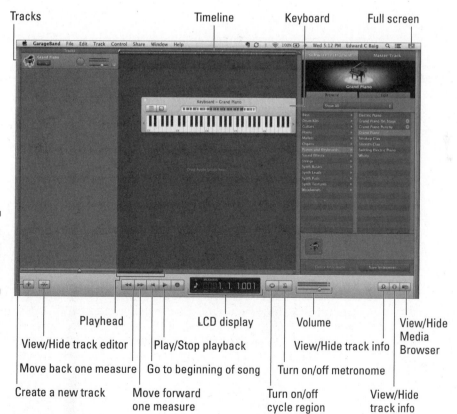

Keeping on track (s)

Mastering GarageBand is all about getting comfortable with tracks (discussed in this section) and loops (see the next section).

Most musical compositions consist of several *tracks,* or layers of individual parts recorded by different instruments. You can connect instruments to your Mac through one of the methods mentioned in the nearby "Connecting real instruments" sidebar or take advantage of more than 100 digitally sampled *software instruments,* heard as you play a small on-screen keyboard by clicking its keys with the mouse. You can choose a wide variety of software instruments, in all the major instrument families (percussion, brass, and so on). You may have to download some instruments from the Internet.

When you open a new project, GarageBand introduces you to the first of these software instruments, a grand piano. It appears by default in the tracks list. It's the instrument you will hear when you play that miniature keyboard.

From the GarageBand Window menu, you can also summon the Musical Typing keyboard. The keys on your computer keyboard are matched to certain notes. Keys in the middle row play the white keys of a piano. Keys in the top row play the black keys.

Follow these steps to add a new track:

1. **Click the Create a New Track (+) button at the lower-left corner of the program, choose Track⇨New Track, or press the keyboard combination Alt/Option +⌘+N.**

   A window slides into view offering the choices shown in Step 2.

2. **Select Software Instrument or Real Instrument (see the nearby "Connecting real instruments" sidebar and Figures 17-4 and 17-5).**

   Odd though it seems on the surface, you can also choose Electric Guitar (a "real instrument" if there ever was one) to record using GarageBand's built-in amps and stompbox effects.

3. **Click Create.**

   A new track shows up in the Tracks list, accompanied in the header by its icon, name (Grand Piano until you change it), and several tiny controls. Among other functions, these controls let you mute the track, lock it to prevent editing changes, make it a solo, set volume levels, and more.

Figure 17-4:
Adding a
software
instrument
track.

In the Track Info pane shown in Figure 17-4, Software Instrument is high-lighted. You can change your instrument selection from Grand Piano to any other available instrument. To do so, choose an instrument category from the left column of the Track Info pane (Pianos and Keyboards in this case, as shown in Figure 17-4) and a software instrument in the right column (Whirly).

You can open the Track Info pane anytime by clicking the little *i* icon at the lower-right corner of the screen. Alternatively, choose Track➪Show Track Info or press ⌘+I.

Figure 17-5:
Adding a
real instru-
ment track.

If the instrument (or loop) you clicked appears dimmed or is not available, a window such as the one shown in Figure 17-6 pops up. You'll have the opportunity to download and install the missing instruments and loops, provided that you have sufficient disk space on your computer.

If you selected a real instrument (refer to Figure 17-5) choose an input (stereo or mono), depending on how the instrument is connected to the Mac. Select Monitor from the pop-up menu to be able to hear the instrument as you play it, with or without feedback.

TECHNICAL STUFF

Connecting real instruments

If you'd rather not use the on-screen music keyboard to control software instruments, you can connect a real MIDI keyboard through a USB cable (on most newer gear) or a MIDI adapter (on older equipment). MIDI is geek shorthand for Musical Instrument Digital Interface, a standard that has been around for years. You can connect other MIDI instruments, including guitars, woodwinds, and drums, and record onto a real instrument track in GarageBand. Click the red Record button when you're ready to rock. Move the playhead to just before where you want to start jamming.

If the high-quality instrument you have in mind is your own singing voice, connect a microphone (in lieu of the Mac's built-in microphone) to an *audio input* port on the computer. Open System Preferences, click Sound, click Input, and then select Line In. Drag the Input volume slider to an appropriate level. Choose Vocals and the instrument that most closely matches your singing style, such as Epic Diva, Helium Breath, or Megaphone. Garage Band will tailor the effects to your voice. (Don't worry if you don't know how to characterize your singing voice; one of your other options is No Effects.) Good microphones, meanwhile, are especially useful when you're recording podcasts, as discussed later in the chapter.

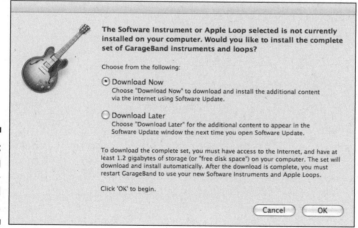

Figure 17-6:
Installing extra instruments and loops.

Getting loopy

Don't let the heading scare you; I'm not advocating alcohol. I'm merely suggesting that you might become artistically intoxicated experimenting with GarageBand *loops*, the professionally recorded (and royalty-free) musical snippets at the very foundation of your composition.

Loops supply drum beats, rhythm parts, melody lines, bass sections, and so on. Apple includes more than 1,000 loop files with GarageBand. You can add thousands more by purchasing optional $99 Jam Packs (covering Remix Tools, Rhythm Section, Symphony Orchestra, World Music, and the most recent addition as of this writing, Voices).

Click the *Loop Browser* button at the lower-right corner of the screen. In older versions of GarageBand, the button resembled the famous CBS eye logo. In more recent iterations of the program, it looks more like a ribbon. You can view the Loop browser by columns, musical buttons (as shown in Figure 17-7), or podcast sounds.

Search for loops inside the browser by instrument (Bass, Guitars, Strings, and so on), genre (Rock/Blues, Urban, Country), mood (Relaxed, Intense, Dark), or combinations of these. Incompatible loop buttons are dimmed.

The list of loop possibilities shows up on the right side of the browser. Click one of them to check it out, conveniently in the project's key and tempo. Most usefully, you can audition loops while the rest of your project is playing to hear how all the tracks blend. If the loop passes muster, drag it onto the timeline. Individual tracks and loops make up the rows of the timeline. To add a new loop, click Reset in the loop browser and make another selection.

Figure 17-7:
In the loops.

The musical patterns in loops repeat (why do you suppose they're called loops anyway?). You can also tug on the right edge of a loop to lay down a track for the entire song. Loops don't have to start at the beginning of a track. And if you want to change the mood midstream, you can add a second loop onto the same track. If you want more than one loop to play in a song (which is typical), create multiple tracks.

The *beat ruler* above the timeline serves as a guide; it displays beats and *measures*. The latter is how the units of musical time are, um, measured.

Building an arrangement

Adding loops or recording your own musical pearls (with real or software instruments) creates a *region* in a track. Regions are color-coded as follows:

- ✔ **Purple:** Real instrument regions you record
- ✔ **Blue:** Real instrument regions created by loops
- ✔ **Orange:** Real instrument regions from imported audio files
- ✔ **Green:** Software instrument regions from recordings, loops, or imported MIDI files

Regions can be cut, copied and pasted, or resized to play as long as you need them to. You can also move regions to another track or another area of the timeline.

The latest GarageBand adds an *arrangement track* to help you organize the structure of your composition. You can define sections (intro, verse, chorus, bridge, and more) and resize, copy, and drag them around in any order that makes sense. When you move a section, all associated tracks for that region move too. Choose Track⇨Show Arrangement Track to get started.

Multitake recording

If you're a perfectionist, you can keep recording part of a composition until you feel your performance is just right. Choose the section of the song you want to work on by clicking the Cycle Mode button (labeled in Figure 17-3). A yellow cycle region appears below the beat ruler. Drag and resize it so that its left side aligns with the area you want to start recording and the right side aligns with where you want the region to end.

Click Record to start recording the appropriate track. The playhead moves across the region and then starts over again and again. Click Play when you want to stop recording.

When you are finished, a circled number appears in the upper-left corner of the cycle region, indicating the number of the active takes or the last take you recorded. So, if you recorded five takes, the circled number is 5. Click Play to hear that take, or click the circled number (5 in this example) and choose another take from the Take menu that pops up. After auditioning all your takes, you can delete the ones you have no use for.

You can take the best performance from one take and combine it with another. To do so, select the cycle region and move the playhead to the point where you want to seamlessly transition from one take to another. Choose Edit⇨Split and then assign each take as before.

You may want to display your composition with standard notes, clef signs, and so forth. Select a software instrument region and open Track Editor by clicking the button at the lower-left corner of the screen. Click the Score View button (it has a musical note on it and is labeled Score) and start composing. The view is displayed in Figure 17-8.

You can print professional-looking sheet music of your composition by choosing File⇨Print on the GarageBand menu.

Staying in the groove

Although Apple makes it easy to lay down tracks and add loops, you won't become Quincy Jones overnight. Even when you match tempos and such, some music just doesn't sound good together. I didn't have much success blending a Classic Rock Piano with a New Nashville guitar. Mixing or balancing all the parts so that one track doesn't drown out another is a challenge as well.

Figure 17-8: Follow the score in notation view.

As part of GarageBand '11, Apple added a groove-matching feature, which Apple compares to a spell checker for bad rhythm. It works across different instrument tracks. To exploit the feature, mouse over the left edge of a track you've decided should function as the *groove track* — the drum major, as it were, for your little marching band. Click the star that appears. Now place check marks next to each track you want to match to the groove track so that everything sounds swell together.

Apple helps you get your timing down too. A *Flex Time* feature that also debuted as part of GarageBand '11 can help you change the timing of audio recorders so that the entire work sounds more professional. You double-click a song region to open an audio waveform editor. You can then click and drag along the waveform to change the timing of notes and beats without influencing other recordings.

Magic GarageBand

If you can read the notes in Figure 17-8, you'll quickly recognize I'm not a real musician or composer. (Hey, I was a great clarinetist in junior high.) I suppose Apple had folks like me in mind when it added the Magic GarageBand feature to GarageBand. The idea is to let you conduct a virtual band.

Choose Magic GarageBand after opening GarageBand and click one of nine icons, representing Blues, Rock, Jazz, Latin, and other styles of music. You can preview a prepackaged song snippet or the entire ditty in the genre of your choice by clicking Play and choosing Snippet or Entire Song.

Click the Audition button to see the instruments used in the song. You can change one or more by clicking an instrument to select it — every time you mouse over a different instrument, a spotlight appears over your selection, as Figure 17-9 shows. Choose an alternative instrument from the list below the stage. When your virtual band is just as you like it, click Open in GarageBand. The regular Garage Band window takes over, with appropriate tracks and regions for your selections.

Figure 17-9:
Behind the
curtain.

Creating Podcasts

Podcasts are like your own Internet radio or TV show, with music (from iTunes or elsewhere), pictures, sound effects, video, or some combination of these. Fans can find your podcasts on the Net (or in iTunes) and subscribe to receive them regularly. Podcasting was introduced with GarageBand 3, so don't try the steps in this section with an earlier version of the program.

Here's how to put a polished podcast together:

1. **From the opening GarageBand screen, click New Project. Then click Podcast to highlight the selection and click the Choose button at the bottom right corner of the screen.**

   The standard Garage Band dialog opens.

2. **Type a name for your podcast.**

   The main screen looks like what is shown in Figure 17-10. It's a little different from the GarageBand screen for music. At the top of the Tracks list is a special Podcast Track to drag photos or other artwork from your iPhoto Library (or elsewhere), accessible through the Media Browser. Next are tracks to optimize for a male or female voice, plus Jingles.

3. **If you haven't already done so, plug in your microphone.**

4. **Choose an audio track (Male or Female), click the red Record button, and then start gabbing, using your finest radio voice.**

You can apply editing tweaks later.

5. **To add a radio-style jingle to your podcast:**

   a. **Open the Loop browser.**

   b. **Select Jingles.**

   c. **Choose a jingle that seems appropriate for your podcast and drag it onto the timeline.**

More than a hundred jingles are included. If you're delivering news commentary, for example, one of the Broadcast News jingles (Long, Medium, or Short) might fit the bill. Just click to hear a sample.

6. **To add extra audio effects:**

   a. **In the Loop browser, choose Sound Effects (everything from an airplane landing to an alarm clock bell) or Stingers (cartoon chipmunk to comedy horns).**

   b. **As with any other loop, drag Sound Effects onto the timeline.**

7. **To add artwork to your podcast, drag pictures from the Media Browser onto the podcast track.**

A chapter marker is added for each picture in a window near the bottom center of GarageBand.

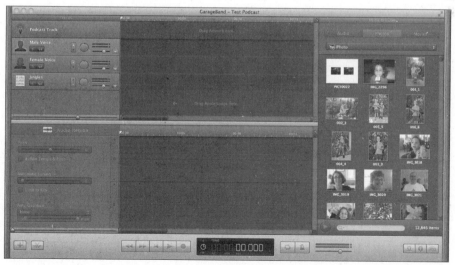

Figure 17-10:
Your podcast broadcast studio.

Folks who listen to your podcast on iTunes, photo-capable iPods, or other devices can see the images. You can add URLs to those pictures. To add a visual title to your podcast, drag the artwork to the Episode drop zone in the lower-left corner of the GarageBand program.

Ducking

TIP

At times, you may want to decrease the volume of your background tracks so that you can hear spoken dialogue— you are the star of your podcast after all. The answer is a, um, quack-pot solution called *ducking*. (Sorry. Couldn't resist.)

Choose Control⇨Ducking. In each track's header, an arrow control appears. Select the up arrow to make a track a *lead* track and the down arrow to make it a *backing* track. When ducking is on, the sound on backing tracks is lowered whenever sound is detected on a lead track. You can adjust the amount of ducking by choosing Track⇨Show Track Info⇨Master Track⇨Edit. At that point you can access a Ducker pop-up menu, which you'll see on the right side of the screen under Master Effects. You can choose various options, such as Fast — Maximum Music Reduction or Slowest — Modest Music Reduction.

Importing video

As part of your podcast, GarageBand lets you either take advantage of the epic you created in iMovie or bring in some other QuickTime-compatible video file on your computer. Use Media Browser in GarageBand to import files located in the Movies folder.

Such files appear as a movie track at the beginning of your GarageBand project — you cannot change this starting position, nor can you have more than one video or movie file in a project. If a movie track is already in the project, you'll have the option of replacing it with the new footage.

As before, you can record narration, add audio, and add music (through real or software instruments). You can also add chapter titles and a URL marker.

Learning to Play

Have you been itching to learn an instrument since you were a kid? GarageBand sends you on your way to your first gig by teaching you guitar or piano. Start by clicking Learn to Play from GarageBand's opening act and choose Guitar Lessons or Piano Lessons. You also find an Artist Lessons option, but skip that for the moment.

You'll have to visit the Lesson Store to download the Basic Lessons that you get as part of iLife '11. Click the right-pointing arrow to visit the joint.

Connect a USB or MIDI-compatible keyboard or guitar, depending on your choice of lessons.

In each full-screen lesson — an example of which is shown in Figure 17-11 — an instructor demonstrates his or her craft. Lessons start simple and become more challenging as you progress.

Lessons include a video glossary and a mixer (to change how you hear the teacher, instruments in GarageBand, or your own instrument). You also find a setup button that leads to options that differ depending on the instrument you're using. If you are learning guitar, you also see a separate tuner button.

In GarageBand '11, a How Did I Play? feature answers that very question with gentle visual feedback. You can check a progress bar that gives you a numeric score; GarageBand keeps a history of your progress. It's like having a music teacher inside your Mac.

If you want your music teacher to be a real headliner, check out the Lessons Store and click Artist Lessons. Sting teaches you to play *Roxanne,* and Norah Jones (see Figure 17-12) explains techniques in *Thinking About You.* Each artist lesson costs $4.99. You can sample an excerpt from these lessons and other artist lessons before purchasing them.

Figure 17-11:
Getting started on piano.

Figure 17-12:
Learning
the piano
from Norah
Jones.

Sharing Your Work

It's great that you're so creative. But what good does it do you if no one notices? Fortunately, you can share your GarageBand jewels with your soon-to-be adoring public in several ways.

Sharing podcasts

When you're ready to share your podcast, you have a few options, each appropriately found on the Share menu. Click Send Podcast to iTunes to do just that. Or click Send Podcast to iWeb to do that. In iWeb, the podcast automatically becomes a blog entry.

iWeb is not preloaded on systems running Mountain Lion. But if you have iWeb from an early version of OS X or iLife, you can still use it with GarageBand, as of this writing. What you can no longer do is publish your podcast to the discontinued MobileMe.

You can also use iWeb to submit your podcast to the iTunes Store. Your podcast is available free to your awaiting public. Here's how:

1. **Click Inspector on the iWeb toolbar (it's at the lower right of the iWeb screen), and then click the RSS button to open the Blog & Podcast window, as shown in Figure 17-13.**

Figure 17-13:
Using iWeb
Inspector
with your
podcast.

2. **Add the Series Artist name and Contact Email.**

   Your e-mail address will not show up in iTunes.

3. **In the Parental Advisory pop-up, indicate whether your podcast is Clean or Explicit.**

4. **Select the Allow Podcast in iTunes Store check box.**

5. **Choose File⇨Submit Podcast to iTunes.**

6. **Enter copyright information, a category for your blog (Kids & Family, Science & Medicine, and so on), and the language (English, German, Ukrainian, whatever), and again indicate whether it is Clean or Explicit.**

   Here's an example where Apple *wants* to be PC, as in politically correct.

7. **Click Publish and Submit.**

You are responsible for owning or getting permission for any copyrighted material associated with your podcast. Apple maintains the right to pull the plug.

You have a few ways to share video podcasts. You can send a movie to Apple's iDVD program by choosing Share⇨iDVD. You can send the podcast to iWeb for publishing on the Internet. Or you can export it as a QuickTime movie.

Apple discontinued iDVD, but you can still take advantage of the program if it resides on your Mac.

Sharing music projects

You can send a song — or an iPhone ringtone (as noted in the nearby "Ring my chimes" sidebar) — you created in GarageBand directly to a playlist in your personal iTunes library.

Choose Share⇨Send Song to iTunes and choose the compression (typically AAC Encoder) and audio settings (Good Quality, High Quality, Higher Quality, or Custom) you want. Then click Share. You can also export the song to a disk or burn it to a CD (assuming you have access of course to a CD burner).

In the case of a ringtone, choose Share⇨Send Ringtone to iTunes.

You can send a single track (or group of tracks) instead of a complete song to iTunes. Just mute all the tracks you don't want to send before sending the ones you do want.

You don't have to export your ditty to iTunes. You can send it as an audio file by choosing Share⇨Export Song to Disk.

Still another option for your composition is to burn the song to a recordable CD. Just place a blank disc in your Mac's optical drive, choose Share⇨Burn Song to CD, choose the settings you want, and click Burn.

You can burn only one song to a CD this way. To burn multiple songs, create or add them to an iTunes playlist first and then burn the playlist to a CD via iTunes.

For more details on GarageBand and other members of the iLife troupe, check out Tony Bove's *iLife '11 For Dummies* (published by John Wiley & Sons, Inc.).

Whichever way you go, remember, the show must go on. Groupies are waiting.

Part V
The Creepy Geeky Section

Check out the article "Deploying Disk Utility" (and more) online at www.dummies.com/extras/macs.

In this part . . .

- ✔ Unravel the mysteries of home networking.

- ✔ Find out how you can make your way in a Windows world from the comfort of your Mac.

- ✔ Learn how to deal with the unexpected (or What To Do When Your Mac Smile Turns into a Frown).

- ✔ Check out the article "Deploying Disk Utility" (and more) online at www.dummies.com/extras/macs.

Chapter 18

Networking Madness

*I*n some ways, a treasured Mac is like a baby. The machine is loved, pampered, even spoiled. But the reality for most of us is that our chosen computer is but one among many. It may very well have siblings, um, other computers in the house. Or your Mac may reside in a company or dormitory, where it almost certainly has to get along with other computers. If you've bitten into one Apple, you've perhaps bitten into others. For that matter, chances are quite good that the Mac must share quarters with a Windows machine. It's such a brave new world that your Mac may even sit next to a computer that runs the operating system known as Linux.

In the ideal computing environment, the various machines can share files, data, music, printers, an Internet connection, and other resources. That's what *networking,* or the practice of connecting multiple computers, is all about. Although networking topics are as geeky as any you'll come across, Apple, in customary fashion, simplifies it as much as possible.

Networking Done Right

You have many right ways and a few wrong ways to network computers. In this day and age, you can set up a wired or wireless network or, more than likely, a combination of the two.

I'll start with the traditional tethered approach to putting together a network. You'll be that much happier when you're liberated from wires later.

The wired way

If the Macs you intend to network are almost always going to stay put in one location, the wired approach is arguably the best way to proceed. Wired networks are zippier, more secure, not as prone to interference, typically less expensive, and arguably the easiest to set up, unless dealing with a mess of wires becomes, well, a real mess.

In Chapter 2, I introduce you to Ethernet, the data cable whose end looks likes an oversized phone plug. Such cables also go by the names CAT-5, CAT-5e, or CAT 6. You may also see terms such as 10BaseT or 100BaseT, which denote networks that use the aforementioned cables. And Intel-era Macs employ blistering fast *Gigabit Ethernet* connections.

To get started with a wired network, plug one end of the cable into the Ethernet port included in any modern Mac that has the connector. (Otherwise you must rely on an optional USB Ethernet dongle accessory.) The other end typically plugs in to an inexpensive network *hub, switch,* or *router,* which in turn is connected to the box feeding your Internet connection, usually a broadband cable modem or DSL.

Although technical distinctions exist between hubs, switches, and routers (and routers usually contain built-in hubs), I'll use the terms interchangeably here. In any case, routers contain multiple jacks, or *ports,* for connecting each Mac (or other computer) or printer that becomes part of your network.

Cutting the cord

Certain benefits of technology are so obvious that they practically explain themselves. Wireless is one of those liberating technologies. By eliminating cables, you can

- ✔ Wander around with a laptop and still hold on to a connection.
- ✔ Drastically reduce the tangle of cables and cords, so the area behind your desk won't be nearly as untidy.
- ✔ Easily add on to the network later, without worrying about connecting cables.
- ✔ Access other wireless networks outside your home or office, through public or private *hotspots* (found in numerous coffeehouses, airports, libraries, parks, and elsewhere). Accessing these hotspots may or may not be free.

Landing safely at the AirPort

All the Macs introduced during the last several years are capable of exploiting wireless networking through radio technology that Apple brands as AirPort. Most of the computing world, including Apple, refers to the core technology as Wi-Fi, as outlined in the nearby "ABCs of Wi-Fi" sidebar.

If you have an older Mac without built-in wireless, you can install an optional AirPort Extreme card, around $49 but no longer sold directly by Apple. Make sure that you have OS X version 10.2.7 or later. Also note that AirPort Extreme is not compatible with Power Mac G5 Dual and Power Mac G5 Quad computers introduced in October 2005. By now, those are practically ancient machines, of course, and not worth dwelling on here.

Macs with built-in wireless communicate over the air — even through walls and at times considerable distances — with a compatible router or *base station.*

As of this writing, Apple sells a $179 AirPort Extreme Base Station with Gigabit Ethernet and a $99 AirPort Express Base Station. Apple also sells two versions of what it calls Time Capsule, which weds an 802.11n AirPort Extreme base station with a wireless Time Machine–capable hard drive for networked backups. (See Chapter 13 for more on Time Machine.) A Time Capsule with 2TB of storage commands $299; a 3TB version, $499.

Apple grounded the first-generation AirPort base station model and cards, though you can still find them on eBay. The cards provide one way to go wireless on an older Mac. You can also purchase option USB dongles for Wi-Fi.

Although Apple would love to sell you an AirPort base station, wireless-capable Macs can also tap in to routers produced by the likes of Belkin, D-Link, Linksys (or parent company Cisco), and Netgear, even if you previously set those up to work with a Windows network. Windows machines can also take advantage of an AirPort base station.

The latest AirPort Extreme has five ports as follows:

- ✔ A single Gigabit Ethernet wide-area network, or WAN, port
- ✔ Three Gigabit Ethernet local-area network, or LAN, ports
- ✔ A single USB 2.0 port (for connecting a USB printer or an external hard drive)

The contraption also incorporates a technology called MIMO. Although it sounds like it ought to be a friend of WALL-E's, MIMO stands for Multiple In Multiple Out. All it means is that you should get excellent range in your home, office, or wherever you are setting up your wireless network. (MIMO exploits multiple antennas to improve reception.) The range and speed of any wireless network are affected by all sorts of factors, including interference from other devices, concrete, and metal walls.

A combination of up to 50 Macs or Windows PCs can simultaneously share a single AirPort Extreme base station.

You can set up a network with AirPort Extreme in several ways. Here is the most common method:

1. **Connect the Ethernet cable hooked up to your cable, FIOS, or DSL modem to the WAN port on the base station.**

   See, not *all* cords are eliminated in a wireless scenario. You'll find no power switch (though you do find a Reset button that you may have to push on occasion); status lights are your only immediate clue that your AirPort has taken off.

2. **Connect any additional Ethernet devices to the LAN ports.**

3. **If you want to network a USB printer, connect it to the USB port on the AirPort. You can also connect a USB external hard drive to store or share files across the network.**

4. **Plug the AirPort Extreme in to a power outlet.**

   AirPort Extreme doesn't have an on-off switch. It will come alive when you plug it in; the only way to shut it down is to pull the plug.

5. **To go wireless, run the AirPort Utility setup assistant software, found in the Utilities folder inside the Applications folder.**

   This step involves responding to a series of questions on what to call your network, passwords, and so on. You may have to enter specific settings from your Internet provider, along the lines of a static IP address or DHCP client ID. Through the AirPort Utility software, you can manually apply various advanced security and other settings.

If you live in an apartment building or are right on top of your neighbors, their routers may show up on your Mac's list. In some instances, the signals will be strong enough so that you may piggyback on their setups, not that I'm advocating doing so. Let this be a lesson that they should have implemented their security settings (requiring robust passwords) and that you should do the same when setting up your Wi-Fi network.

You can determine the signal strength of your wireless connection by examining the radiating lines icon on the menu bar pictured here.

Boarding the AirPort Express

It looks kind of like a power adapter that might come with an older Apple laptop, right down to its built-in plug. But the rectangular, near-7-ounce AirPort Express device is a versatile little gadget. This portable hub has just four ports on its underbelly: two Ethernets (WAN and LAN), USB, and an analog/optical audio minijack.

If you plan on using AirPort Express as a router, plug the device in to an AC outlet and, using an Ethernet cable, connect the Airport Express to your cable modem or DSL. You'll use the same AirPort software as the AirPort Extreme base station.

You'll find no on-off button; status lights clue you in on how things are going. A steady green status light tells you that you've connected with no problem. Flashing amber means that the device is having trouble making a connection and you may have to resort to other means, including (as a final resort) taking the end of a straightened paper clip and holding down a Reset button for 10 seconds.

Here's what the newest AirPort Express can accomplish:

- ✔ As mentioned, connect it to your cable modem or DSL and use it as a wireless 802.11n router, just like its larger sibling.

- ✔ Use it as a wireless *bridge* to extend the range of an existing AirPort network to, say, your attic or backyard.

- ✔ Connect a printer to the AirPort Express USB port to share that printer with any computer on the network.

- ✔ Connect a cable from the broadband box in a hotel room and roam around the room and surf wirelessly.

AirPlay

One more clever feature is available, and it involves the aforementioned audio minijack. If you connect AirPort Express to your home stereo receiver or powered speakers, you can pump the music from your Mac (or Windows) iTunes library through your stereo system. You can use either a ministereo-to-RCA cable or a minidigital, fiber-optic TOSLINK cable, if your stereo can accommodate that kind of connector.

Either way, iTunes detects the remote connection. Through a small pop-up menu, you can click Computer to listen to music through your Mac (or whatever speakers it is connected to), or you can listen through Express and whichever speakers or stereo it is hooked up to. Apple used to refer to this wireless symphony as *AirTunes* when it was an audio-only hookup. The name was changed to *AirPlay* as the technology became more versatile.

If you have an iPhone, iPad, or iPod touch, download Apple's free Remote application from the App Store. It controls AirTunes (along with Apple TV and iTunes).

Apple has built an ecosystem around AirPlay. These days, you can wirelessly stream music, and for that matter other content, to third-party AirPlay-compatible speakers, A/V receivers systems, and stereos.

AirPlay Mirroring

If you have a Mac running Mountain Lion and an Apple TV set-top box, you can display whatever is showing on your Mac screen on a television connected to the Apple TV. It's all through technology called *AirPlay Mirroring*. You can even stream up to the 1080p high-definition video standard.

To take advantage of AirPlay Mirroring, the Mac and Apple TV (second generation or later) must be on the same wired (Ethernet) or wireless network. And you'll need a MacBook Pro dating from early 2011 or later or another Mac model from mid-2011 or later.

If your compatible Mac detects an Apple TV on the same network, the icon highlighted in Figure 18-1 will appear in the status bar of your Mac, signifying the presence of the AirPlay Mirroring menu. If you don't see the icon and think it ought to appear, make sure that the Show Mirroring Options in the Menu Bar When Available check box is selected under the Displays preference in System Preferences.

Figure 18-1:
Show off
what's on
your Mac
on your TV
via AirPlay
Mirroring.

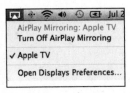

To turn AirPlay Mirroring on, select Apple TV from the AirPlay Mirroring menu to stream stuff from your Mac to the TV. You'll know that it's working when the icon turns blue and when, hopefully, the TV shows the Mac screen. You can also scale the desktop resolution size to best suit the Apple TV or your Mac screen.

If you're playing a movie or TV show through iTunes when you exploit AirPlay Mirroring, you'll enjoy a full-screen AirPlay Mirroring experience on the television.

Having a robust wireless network makes a difference. In my experience, under less-than-ideal networking scenarios, any video that's playing may pause or stutter on the TV.

Testing your network

With all your equipment in place, it's time to make sure that everything works as it should. Fortunately, testing your network is as easy as opening Safari and seeing whether you can browse.

If you run into problems, click the Signal Strength icon on the menu bar and make sure that an AirPort network or other router is in range.

If you're still having trouble, open System Preferences under the menu and choose Network. Click the Assist Me button, and then click Diagnostics in the dialog that appears. You can check the status of AirPort and Network Settings, your ISP, and so on.

Let's Share

Responsible parents teach kids how to share toys. When the youngsters grow up and their toy of choice is a Macintosh, with any luck, they'll still be in that sharing frame of mind.

Anyway, with your networking gear in place, do the following to share some or all of the contents from one computer with another:

1. **Choose System Preferences.**

2. **In the Internet & Wireless section, click Sharing.**

   The pane shown in Figure 18-2 opens. You may want to change your computer name at this point. Calling it *Edward C Baig's MacBook Air,* as I do, makes it sound like "it's my computer, and you can't play with it." Naming it *Basement Air* would help you distinguish the computer from, say, *Bedroom MacBook Pro.*

3. **Select the various sharing preferences you feel comfortable with.**

   If you select File Sharing, users of other machines can access any Public folders on the Mac. If you change your mind about sharing — you may feel uneasy about having just anyone on the Net read those publicly available files — deselect the check box.

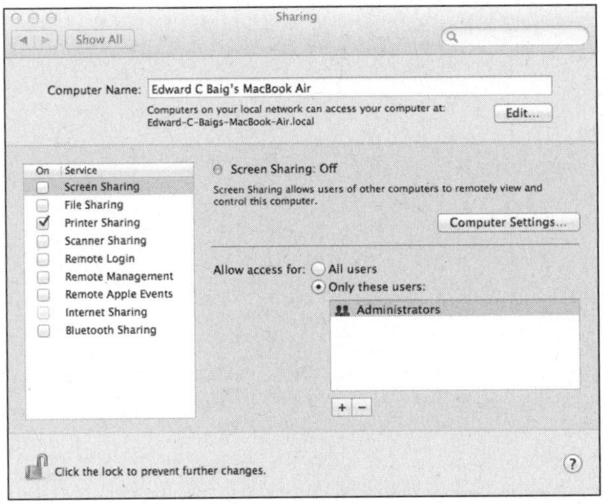

Figure 18-2:
It's polite to
share.

Other Mac users can access your machine by choosing Go⇨Network in Finder.

If you're an iCloud member who plans on taking advantage of the Back to My Mac feature (see Chapter 12), make sure to select the Screen Sharing check box.

AirDrop

If two or more Macs are running Mountain Lion, are connected to Wi-Fi, and are reasonably close to each other, you can share files among the machines, even if they're not on the same Wi-Fi network. No special setup or passwords are required either, though all the machines must have the *AirDrop* feature — the feature that makes all this possible — turned on.

The simplest way to do that is to click AirDrop in the Finder sidebar. Alternatively, press Shift+⌘+R or choose AirDrop from the Go menu in Finder. (Keep on mind that both computers should have Air Drop open.)

Then it's just a matter of dragging the file you want to share onto the picture of the person representing the other computer, as shown in Figure 18-3. You can share text documents, pictures, entire folders, snippets of highlighted text, URLs, audio files, and more.

Apple makes sure that you really want to share the file in question when you drag it over to the picture. And the person at the other end must willingly accept the file. Couldn't be much simpler than that.

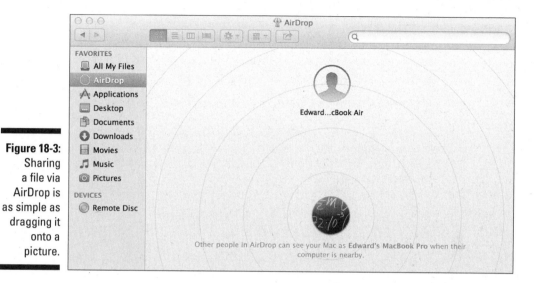

Figure 18-3:
Sharing
a file via
AirDrop is
as simple as
dragging it
onto a
picture.

Close the Finder window when you no longer want your Mac to be visible to other nearby Macs.

Brushing Up on Bluetooth

Of all the peculiar terms you come across in the tech world, *Bluetooth* is probably my favorite. The name is derived from the tenth-century Danish monarch Harald Blåtand, evidently the wireless networking champ of his time. Blåtand was considered a peacemaker in warring Scandinavia, and isn't networking after all about bringing people — or things — together? In any case, Blåtand apparently translates to Bluetooth in English.

Fascinating history, Ed, but I thought I bought Macs For Dummies, *not* European History For Dummies. *What gives?*

Fair point. Here's the drill: Bluetooth (the technology, not the Viking king) is a short-range wireless scheme that lets your Mac make nice with a gaggle of compatible gadgets, from up to 30 feet away.

Among the tricks made possible with Bluetooth:

✔ Connect the Mac to a Bluetooth cell phone. If you don't have access to a Wi-Fi hotspot, you may be able to use the phone as a modem to connect wirelessly to cyberspace.

✔ Wirelessly print through a Bluetooth printer.

✔ Exchange files with another Bluetooth-ready Mac or other computer or gadget.

✔ Schmooze via Messages through a Bluetooth headphone.

✔ Synchronize data with a handheld or other mobile device.

✔ Control a wireless Bluetooth keyboard or mouse.

Newer Macs come equipped with Bluetooth capabilities. Companies such as Belkin, Kensington, Targus, and others sell Bluetooth USB adapters in the $25–$40 range for older computers that lack the capability, with some costing even less than that.

Getting discovered

The path to a meaningful Bluetooth experience starts in System Preferences. Click Bluetooth under the Internet & Wireless section, and you're taken to the area shown in Figure 18-4.

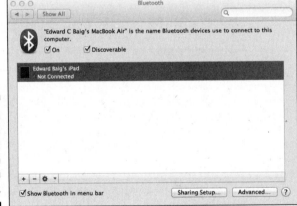

Figure 18-4:
Control everything through Bluetooth preferences.

Before the Mac can communicate with a Bluetooth device or vice versa, the machine's Bluetooth feature must be powered on. To help other devices find your Mac, select the Discoverable option.

Similarly, you'll want your other Bluetooth devices to be placed in a Discoverable mode so that your Mac can communicate with them. But be wary. If you're out in public, you may want to turn off Discoverable mode for security or privacy reasons.

Click Advanced for more control over your Bluetooth behavior. You can

> ✔ Open the Bluetooth Setup Assistant at startup when your Bluetooth mouse or keyboard isn't recognized.
>
> ✔ Allow a Bluetooth keyboard or mouse to wake up a sleeping computer.
>
> ✔ Have your Mac prompt you when a Bluetooth audio device attempts to connect to the computer.
>
> ✔ Share your Internet connection with other Bluetooth devices.

You can also control how the various devices share files with your Mac. Head back to the main System Preferences screen and click Sharing (or click Sharing Setup from the Bluetooth preferences window). Make sure that the Bluetooth Sharing box is selected. You then get to determine other choices, including whether to Accept and Open or Accept and Save items sent from other Bluetooth computers and devices. If you save them, you'll get to choose where to put those items. And select Ask What to Do if you want to make the decision about saving or opening the item on a case-by-case basis.

You can also determine the Public or other folders that Bluetooth devices are permitted to browse on your computer. As one other key measure of security, select the Require Pairing for Security option (described next), which means that a password is required before files can be transferred.

Pairing off

To pair, or set up, Bluetooth devices to work with your Mac, follow these steps:

1. **Choose Bluetooth in System Preferences.**

2. **Click the + at the lower-left corner of the Bluetooth window.**

   Alternatively, if the Bluetooth status icon appears on OS X's menu bar, click the icon and click Set Up Bluetooth Device. Either way, the Bluetooth Setup Assistant appears, as shown on the left in Figure 18-5.

3. **Select the types of device you want to set up, such as a smartphone, tablet, or printer.**

   The given gizmo must be within 30 feet of the computer.

4. **Make sure that Bluetooth is turned on in the selected device.**

   If Bluetooth is not turned on, you may have to dig through the device's menus to find the control that wakes up Bluetooth. (With any luck, the Mac should find it.)

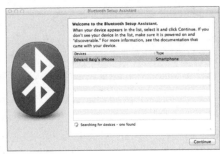

Figure 18-5:
Discovering
and pairing
an iPhone
and a Mac.

5. **Click Continue.**

   The Mac spends a few seconds gathering whatever intelligence it can about the chosen device to determine how to interact with it.

6. **Click Continue again.**

   The device asks you to enter a passkey — it's the code that will complete the process. (See the right side of Figure 18-5.) The documentation for the device may specify what you need to enter for the passcode, but more likely, you'll just see the code on the Mac screen that you need to enter on the other device.

7. **Enter the passkey.**

   The gizmo and the Mac can share a Bluetooth connection.

While you can pair just about any Bluetooth device with your computer, there are limits on what you can do. As of this writing, I could not, for example, send a file via Bluetooth to the iPhone that I paired. Apple hasn't implemented file sharing in its Bluetooth-capable iOS devices.

Still, given all the various ways to network your Mac, you should be pleased that your prized computer is playing so nicely with others.

Chapter 19

Surviving in a Windows World

*I*f it weren't for the fact that their darling computers are so darn special, you might expect loyal Macintosh users to have an inferiority complex. But nothing is inferior about the Mac operating system, and even a market share that has been teeny-tiny is climbing.

Apple has been able to persuade more and more people to switch sides. The runaway successes of the iPod, iPhone, and iPad have helped Apple lure more Windows defectors. So did the clever and funny TV ads Apple ran for a while pitting a hip Mac guy against a nerdy PC counterpart.

The bottom line is that this is, for better or worse, still a Windows-dominated planet. More times than not, the Apple user has to adapt to the Windows environment rather than the other way around. From time to time, the Mac user encounters programs and websites that get along only with the Windows platform, though that's less often the case nowadays. Still, the remarkable Apple-Intel alliance demonstrates that in this topsy-turvy world, anything is possible.

What's more, as you'll see in this chapter, you can actually transform the newest Macs into fully functioning Windows PCs, even ones that run the latest Windows 8 operating system. That bears repeating: *You can actually transform the newest Macs into fully functioning Windows PCs . . .*

What the Mac and Windows Have in Common

For all their differences, the Mac and Windows are more alike than you may initially grasp. And common ground is a good thing:

- Macs and Windows PCs can share the same printers, scanners, digital cameras, mice, keyboards, and other peripherals.

- Both systems are fluent in the common file types, including PDFs, JPEGs, and text.

- Microsoft produces a version of Office for both platforms. So you can work in programs such as Word, Excel, and PowerPoint with little difficulty. The Mac and Windows versions of Office have used the same files since Office 97 for Windows came onto the scene.

- The Mac can read most Windows PC–formatted CDs and DVDs.

- Both sides can easily communicate by e-mail or by using instant messaging services.

- You can access an iCloud account (see Chapter 12) from a Windows PC.

- Versions of QuickTime Player and RealPlayer work on a Mac. Through something called Flip4Mac — free in its most basic version — you can play Windows Media files on your Mac, at least those not saddled with digital rights or so-called DRM restrictions.

- As noted in Chapter 18, the two systems can be on the same wired or wireless network and share files.

- And for several years now, Intel processors are inside both computers.

Making the Switch

Okay, so you've read enough of this book to satisfy your curiosity about the Mac and you're ready to defect.

But frankly, you've invested time and energy over the years in getting your Windows files and preferences just as you like them. Within certain limits, the following sections describe ways to replicate your Windows environment on a new Mac.

Help from Apple

When you buy a new Mac at the Apple Store, you qualify to have a certified Mac technician, not so modestly known as a Genius (see Chapter 20), transfer all your data for free. If you purchased your Mac online or at another retailer, a Genius will still transfer your data, for a fee starting at $50.

The PC must be running Windows 95 or later, and you need to bring your Windows installation disks, any appropriate cables, and the PC keyboard and mouse. Under the free scenario, you have to configure settings on your own.

Burning a disc

Because your Mac can read CDs or DVDs formatted for Windows (assuming that the machine has a built-in or connected optical drive), you can burn your important files onto a disc and copy them onto your Apple. You may not have to burn all your files onto a disc, but a good place to start is in your My Documents (XP) or Documents (Vista or Windows 7) folders on the Windows machine. These folders very well may include photos and videos.

External hard drives

You can exchange files on external USB or FireWire-based hard drives and USB thumb drives.

You can even use an iPod as an external drive by setting it up for disk use. Temporarily dump songs off the iPod to create more room (then add the music back later). Visit `http://support.apple.com/kb/HT1478` for a detailed explanation.

Not all Windows PCs will recognize external hard drives that have been formatted for a Mac.

Using an existing network

Another way to get files from Windows to a Mac is by using a network. Make sure that file sharing is turned on in Windows. Head to the Network and Sharing Center on a Windows Vista machine or the HomeGroup (inside Control Panel) on a Windows 7 PC to start.

Add your Mac to your wired or wireless network (if it's not already part of it) and exchange files as outlined in Chapter 18.

The KVM switch

If you just bought a Mac mini but are holding on to your Windows computer for a while, consider a *KVM* (keyboard-video-mouse) switch. This device uses USB to let the two machines share the monitor and various peripherals. A Belkin KVM switch with all the necessary cables starts at around $45.

Enlisting in Boot Camp

In the preceding section, I touched on various strategies for allowing *separate* Mac and Windows machines to coexist. But if you own Intel-based Macs, you can run OS X *and* Windows on one machine.

It may seem like divine intervention. In fact, it's been possible to run Windows on a Mac for some time — with agonizing limitations. Older Macs loaded with Virtual PC emulation software could do Windows, too, but the program was painfully slow. Even if you find an old copy of the software, it won't work with any current Macs.

Boot Camp software from Apple shook up the computing public upon its apocalyptic arrival in April 2006. Boot Camp graduated from beta, or near-finished, status with the arrival of Leopard. Boot Camp Assistant software is stored in the Utilities folder under Applications.

Boot Camp itself is free. You have to supply your own single-disc, full-install version of Windows; an upgrade disc won't cut it:

It's also important to note that you can use a 32-bit version of Windows XP or Vista on any Intel-based Mac, but you can't use a 64-bit version of XP on any Mac. You can use a 32-bit version of Windows 7 on any iMac or MacBook Pro from 2007 on, or any Intel-based Mac Pro, MacBook, or Mac mini. If you want to use the 64-bit version of Windows 7, you'll need a Mac Pro or MacBook Pro introduced in early 2008 or later. An iMac or MacBook from late 2009 or later will also cut it.

Other requirements follow:

- ✔ An Intel Mac with OS X version 10.6 or later — if need be, run Software Update.

- ✔ At least 16GB of free space on the startup drive for the 32-bit version of Windows 7 or at least 20GB for the 64-bit version of Windows 7. On XP or Vista installations, the requirement is at least 10GB. In all cases, more free space is helpful if you can spare it.

- ✔ A blank CD or USB storage device that you will use for Windows software drivers.

If you don't run into snags, the entire installation (including Windows) should take about an hour.

As of this writing, Windows 8 wasn't officially supported by Apple for Boot Camp, though I suspect that'll change at any time, quite possibly by the time you read this. And even without official support, you can probably install Windows 8, keeping in mind the likely limitations, notably missing or outdated drivers. Windows 8 is also optimized for a touch-screen environment, though you can use it with a standard mouse and keyboard. For now, Macs don't support touch-screen computing. That's not to say the Macs aren't welcoming to touch — as anyone who employs scrolling, pinching or other "gestures" via a trackpad has come to appreciate.

To install Windows 8 via Boot Camp, you still must have a legitimate Windows 8 license from Microsoft and a Win8 installation disc, assuming that you have an optical drive. If you don't have an optical drive, you may be able to create a Windows installer from an *ISO* file downloaded from Microsoft onto a USB flash drive that's 4GB or larger. An ISO file is a disk image file that effectively serves as a stand-in for an entire disk.

Because snags *are* possible, back up all your important information on the Mac's startup disk.

Basic training

Following are the steps to get through Boot Camp. The assumption here is that you haven't already installed Windows through Boot Camp:

1. **Run Boot Camp Assistant (in the Utilities folder under Applications) to make sure that you have the latest *firmware* on your computer.**

   You'll find any updates at www.apple.com/support/downloads. Follow any on-screen instructions if you are updating the firmware. If using a portable computer, make sure to connect the power adapter.

2. **Follow the prompts within Boot Camp Assistant to create a partition for Windows.**

   You are essentially carving out an area of your hard drive for the Windows operating system, as shown in Figure 19-1. This partition must be at least 5GB and can swell to as large as the total free disk space on hand minus 5GB. If you don't plan on doing much in Windows, keep the partition small. If you plan on running graphics-heavy games and a lot of Windows programs, you might devote a more generous chunk to Windows. Drag the divider to set the partitions for both OS X and Windows. Or click Divide Equally to make equal partitions. Still another option: Click 32GB to devote that much to Windows.

If you have a Mac Pro with more than one internal hard drive, you can select which drive to partition. If any of this makes you nervous, know that you can remove the Windows partition later and go back to a single-partition Mac.

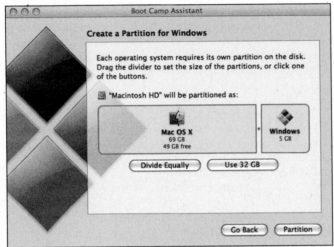

Figure 19-1:
Making
space for
Windows.

3. **Insert the Windows CD or a USB flash drive with the Windows ISO file, and then click Start Installation.**

   If you exited Boot Camp Assistant before installing Windows, open it again, choose Start the Windows Installer, and click Continue.

4. **When asked to choose the Windows partition, select C: if you are running Windows XP or select Disk 0 Partition 3 BOOTCAMP if you are running Vista or Win7.**

   Failure to do so could wipe out your entire Mac OS X startup disk.

5. **Reformat the partition using the Windows installer:**

   • **For Windows XP, format the partition in either the NTFS file system or FAT.**

   FAT provides better compatibility between the two operating systems but is available only if the partition you created for Windows is 32GB or smaller; NTFS is more reliable and secure, but you won't be able to save files to Windows from Mac OS X.

   • **For Vista, format the partition using NTFS — click Drive Options (Advanced), click Format, click OK, and then click Next.**

6. **After Windows is installed, eject the Windows disc.**

7. **Insert the OS X installation disc, and follow the on-screen instructions.**

   At this juncture, you're loading Boot Camp drivers so that Windows recognizes AirPort, Bluetooth, the iSight (or FaceTime) camera, the Eject key on the Mac keyboard, networking, audio, graphics, and so on.

   A Boot Camp control panel for Windows and an Apple Boot Camp system tray item will be added.

8. **When you see the message that the software "has not passed Windows Logo testing," click Continue Anyway.**

   Don't cancel any driver installers. The computer will restart.

9. **Follow any Found New Hardware instructions.**

As with any new Windows computer, Microsoft requires that you activate your XP, Vista, or Win7 software within 30 days.

It's great that you can use Windows on the Mac. But by now, you may be longing to return to the OS X environment. The next section tells you how.

Switching operating systems

You can go back and forth between OS X and Windows, but you can't run both simultaneously under Boot Camp. Instead, you have to boot one operating system or the other, thus the name *Boot Camp*.

Restart your machine and hold down the Option key until icons for each operating system appear on the screen. Highlight Windows or Macintosh HD and click the arrow to launch the operating system of choice for this session.

If you want OS X or Windows to boot every time, choose ⌘⇨System Preferences and click Startup Disk. Choose the OS you want to launch by default.

You can perform the same function in Windows by clicking the Boot Camp system tray icon and selecting the Boot Camp Control Panel. Click either the Macintosh HD or Windows icon, depending on your startup preference.

A Parallels (and Fusion) Universe

As you've just seen, Boot Camp's biggest drawback is its requirement that you reboot your computer every time you want to leave one operating system for a parallel universe. Can anyone spell *hassle?*

Remedies are readily available. Try Parallels Desktop, about $80 from Parallels, Inc., based in Virginia, and VMware Fusion, about $60 from VMware of Palo Alto, California. Their respective software takes the form of a *virtual machine.* The programs simulate a Windows machine inside its own screen within OS X. Or, if you feel like it, go full-screen with Windows. The faux machine behaves just like the real deal. You can add software, surf the web, listen to music, and play Windows games on a Mac.

You can even apply this virtualization stuff with versions of Windows dating back to Windows 3.1, as well as Linux, Solaris, OS/2, MS-DOS, and other operating systems.

Parallels and Fusion differ from Boot Camp because you can run any OS *while* you run OS X, without having to restart. What's more, you can share files and folders between OS X and Windows and cut and paste between the two. The Coherence feature inside Parallels lets you run Windows programs like they were Mac apps.

Check out Parallels at www.parallels.com and VMware Fusion at www.vmware.com/products/fusion. The latest versions support Windows 8.

Virtual or not, you are running Windows on or inside your Mac. So take all the usual precautions by loading antivirus and other security software.

It's also worth noting that while most consumers will do just fine with the virtualized versions of Windows through these programs, you may see some degradation in performance, particularly in 3D-type gaming environments, compared to running Windows on a Windows PC, or even in Boot Camp.

Comforting, isn't it, to know that Macs do well in a Windows world?

Chapter 20

Handling Trouble in Paradise

. . . .

In This Chapter

▶ Fixing a cranky or frozen computer

▶ Getting inside Disk Utility

▶ Finishing off startup problems

▶ Reinstalling the operating system

▶ Repairing common problems

▶ Maintaining the computer

▶ Summoning outside assistance

. . . .

I'm reluctant to morph into Mr. Doom-and-Gloom all of a sudden, but after reading about all the wonderful things Macs can do, it is my unpleasant duty to point out that bad @#$& happens. Even on a Mac.

Fortunately, most issues are minor. A stubborn mouse. Tired hardware. Disobedient software. Under the most dire of circumstances, your computer (or a key component within) may be on its last legs. After all, a Mac, like any computer, is a machine. Still, rarely is a problem beyond fixing. So stay calm, scan through this chapter, and with luck, you'll come across a troubleshooting tip to solve your issue. If not, I provide recommendations on where to seek help.

A Cranky Computer

Your Mac was once a world-class sprinter but now can barely jog. Here are four possible explanations, and a fix to go with each one:

✔ **Your Mac needs more memory.** The programs you're running may demand more RAM than you have on hand. I always recommend getting as much memory as your computer (and wallet) permit. Adding RAM to the recent class of Mac machines isn't difficult (check your computer's documentation for specifics), though it does involve cracking open the case and making sure that you're buying the right type of memory. In some instances — certain models of MacBook Air, for example — the memory you have on-board is all your particular model can handle.

✔ **Your Mac is running out of hard drive space.** This is an easy one: Remove programs or files you no longer use. You must be able to live without something. But if every last bit is indispensable, purchase an additional drive and move large data collections to it (such as your iTunes library, iPhoto libraries, or iMovie data).

✔ **Your Mac's processor, or CPU, is overtaxed.** If you suspect this might be the case, open the Activity Monitor, which is shown in Figure 20-1, by choosing Applications⇨Utilities. Activity Monitor reveals a lot about the programs and processes currently running on your machine. Click the CPU header to display the applications exacting the heaviest workload on your CPU *(central processing unit)*. The most demanding are on top. Quit those that you don't need at the moment.

✔ **The Mac may be trying to save energy.** On a laptop, the Mac may be slowing the processor purposely. If you detect such sluggish behavior while playing a game or editing video, choose ⌘⇨System Preferences and click Energy Saver. Then do one of the following: Deselect the Automatic Graphics Switching option so that your computer will always tap in to high-performance graphics. Or if you have Graphics options, select Higher Performance. You won't see these options on all models. You'll have to log out and log in again for any changes you make to kick in.

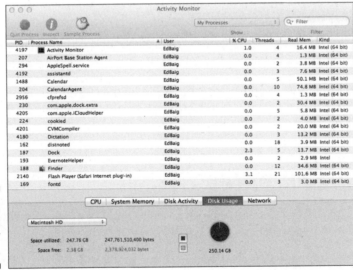

Figure 20-1: Monitoring your activities.

A Frozen Computer or Program

Mentioning beach balls to anyone but a Mac maven usually conjures up pleasant images of the surf, sand, and a glorious summer afternoon. Now Mac people love a day at the beach as much as anybody. But the sight of a colorful spinning beach ball is less welcome on your Apple, at least when that ball never seems to leave the screen. A beach ball that spins — and spins and spins some more — is a sign that a cranky Mac has turned into a frozen Mac or that at least one of the programs on the machine is throwing a high-tech temper tantrum. (In some cases, you may see a spinning gear cursor instead.) Those of you familiar with Windows can think of this as the Mac equivalent of the hourglass that lingers on the screen.

It isn't often that a frozen program will crash the entire system, but it does happen. Your first instinct is to stick a pin inside this virtual spinning beach ball of death, if only you knew how. If you're a model of patience, you can attempt to wait the problem out and hope the spinning eventually stops. If it doesn't, consider the options described in the following sections.

Force Quit

Force Quit is the Mac's common way of telling an iced application, "I'm as mad as hell and I'm not going to take it anymore." (If you're too young, that's a reference to the 1976 movie *Network,* as in television network.)

Choose Force Quit or press ⌘+Option+Esc. A window like the one shown in Figure 20-2 appears. Click the name of the deviant application ("not responding" probably appears next to its name). Under Force Quit, you typically won't have to reboot your computer.

Because you will lose any unsaved changes, Apple throws up a little admonition before allowing you to Force Quit. Alas, you may have no choice.

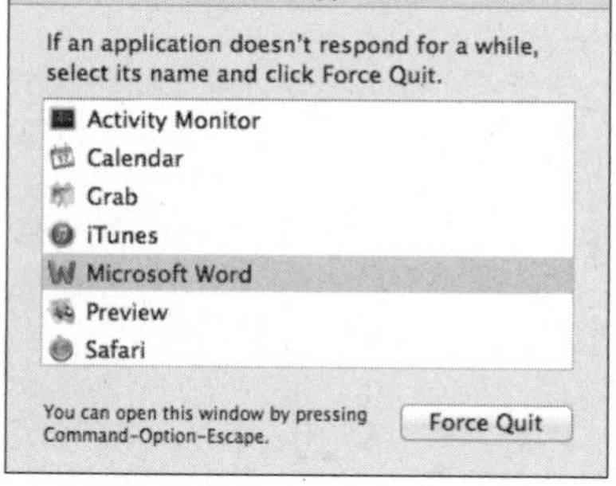

Figure 20-2: Bailing through the Force Quit command.

> ⭘ ⭘ ⭘   Force Quit Applications
>
> If an application doesn't respond for a while, select its name and click Force Quit.
>
> - Activity Monitor
> - Calendar
> - Grab
> - iTunes
> - **Microsoft Word**
> - Preview
> - Safari
>
> You can open this window by pressing Command-Option-Escape.   [Force Quit]

Control-clicking a dock icon brings up a pop-up menu whose bottom item is Quit. If you hold down the Option key, Quit becomes Force Quit.

When a program quits on you

Sometimes, for reasons known to no one, a program keels over. Just like that. You could reopen the app and hope this was a one-time aberration caused by mischievous space aliens en route to the planet Vista. Or you might have a chronic ailment on your hands.

When programs suddenly drop dead, you may see dialogs with the words `quit unexpectedly`. Sometimes the box lets you click Reopen to relaunch the fussy program; sometimes the option is to Try Again. OS X restores the application's default settings (thus setting aside newer preferences settings), in case something you did (imagine that?) caused the snafu.

Assuming that everything went swell from there, you'll be given the option of keeping the new settings upon quitting the program. Your old preferences are saved in a file with a `.saved` extension, in case you ever want to go back. If that is the case, move the newer and current preferences file from its present location and remove the saved extension from the older file.

If the problem continues, it may be time to visit the library. No, not that kind of library. A Preferences folder lives inside your Library folder, which in turn resides in your Home folder. Whew! Got it?

Actually it's no longer even that simple because starting in Lion, Apple decided to hide the Library folder, presumably because it doesn't want you routinely messing with the place. So while it's not exactly off-limits, you do have to run through a couple of hoops to get in the door.

To access the Library, hold down the Option key while clicking the Go menu. The Library option appears.

You can make the Library crawl out of its hiding space on a more or less permanent basis, too, but it involves going through the Terminal, which feels a lot scarier than the rest of Mac-land. Launch Terminal from the Utilities folder (found in Finder under Applications). Then enter the following command: **chflags nohidden ~/Library**. The Library now resides in Finder the way it used to prior to Lion concealing its presence. If you want the Library to go back into hiding, return to Terminal and enter **chflags hidden ~/Library**.

Now that the Library has reappeared, go into its Preferences folder. You will notice that preferences files have the `.plist` suffix. And the files typically begin with `com.` followed by the names of the developer and program, as in `com.microsoft.Word.plist`. **Try dragging a** `.plist` file with the name of the troubled application out to the desktop. If the program runs smoothly, trash the corrupted preferences file. You'll have to reset any preferences you want to maintain.

Forcing a restart

Force Quit will usually rescue you from a minor problem, but it's not effective all the time. If that's the situation you're in now, you'll likely have to reboot. The assumption here is that your frozen computer won't permit you to start over in a conventional way by choosing ⇨Restart.

Instead, try holding down the power button for several seconds or press Control+⌘ and then the power button. If all else fails, pull the plug (or if you have an old enough Mac where you can even do so, remove the battery from a laptop), though only as a last resort.

Safe boot

Starting OS X in *Safe mode* activates a series of measures designed to return your computer to good health. It runs a check of your hard drive (see the next section), loads only essential *kernel extensions* (system files) while ignoring others, trashes what are called *font cache* files, and disables startup and login items.

To start in Safe mode, press the power button to turn on your computer, and press and hold the Shift key the instant you hear the familiar welcome chime. Release Shift when the Apple logo appears. You'll know you've done it correctly because you will see a status bar as the computer boots up, after which the words `Safe Boot` appear in red in the upper-right corner of the login screen. (Before Tiger, the words `Safe Boot` appeared on the OS X startup screen; this feature was not an option before OS X version 10.2.)

Because of its under-the-hood machinations, it will take considerably longer to boot in Safe mode. This is perfectly normal. So is the fact that you can't use AirPort, a USB modem, or your DVD player if you have one. You can't capture footage in iMovie either, and you can't use certain other applications or features.

If the Safe boot resolved your issue, restart the Mac normally next time, without pressing Shift. If not, it might be time to check your warranty or call in an expert, as noted later in this chapter.

Disk Utility

Just about every championship baseball team has a valuable utility player to fill nearly every position. The versatile *Disk Utility* tool on your Mac serves this purpose for all things hard drive–related and many things optical drive–related. At a glance, it gives you a summary of your drives, including disk capacity, available space, and number of files and folders.

I'll concentrate on two of the main tasks that Disk Utility performs: repairing damaged disks and fixing bungled *permissions,* as shown in Figure 20-3.

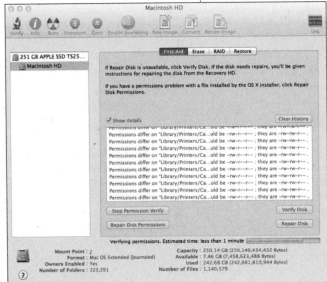

Figure 20-3:
Disk Utility can fix permissions and repair your hard drive.

Permissions granted

As the computer's administrator, you have the right to open, view, and modify programs, folders, and files on your drive at will. Other user accounts on your system (as described in Chapter 5) are given varying privileges to read and change stuff. To regulate who gets to do what, the Mac has established a complex set of permissions.

Sometimes, because of new software you installed or a power glitch, these permissions get messed up, resulting in programs that freeze or fail to open. Disk Utility may be your salvation. Frankly, you may want to run the following steps anyway, as preventive maintenance, particularly if you installed a major operating system update or a new application:

1. **Open Disk Utility in the Utilities folder under Applications, and click the First Aid tab.**

2. **In the pane on the left, click to highlight the name of your disk, volume, or what's called an image.**

3. **Click Verify Disk Permissions to test permissions without changing anything (even if a permissions screw-up is ultimately revealed) or click Repair Disk Permission to test *and* set things straight.**

   As Disk Utility goes about its business, a log of puzzling messages may show up in the results window. Don't try and make heads or tails out of them because they don't necessarily indicate that your permissions were amiss.

You can repair permissions only on the disk used to start OS X.

Repair job

If you suspect that your hard drive is actually damaged (even a reboot doesn't seem to do much good), run Verify Disk to uncover any errors. If you find any, you must be an administrator to authorize a repair. You can't repair (or even test) write-protected disks and nonrecordable CDs and DVDs.

But the most important restriction is this: Although you can use Disk Utility to test the drive you're using (and, as you've seen, fix permissions), you can't repair it until you boot from another disc. This is most likely your Mac OS X installation CD or DVD, which I hope you can easily lay your hands on, if using an older version of OS X. With that in mind, it's a good idea to make a copy of your install disc right now and stash it in a safe place. (On newer systems with Mountain Lion, you no longer have a disc to install the operating system. Shortly, I tell you how to boot up the operating system — and repair the hard drive — without a physical disc.)

After booting with this other disc, open Disk Utility, select your startup disk, and click Repair Disk. Incidentally, booting from the other disc is somewhat tricky. To do so, hold down the C key and wait until OS X boots. Make a language selection and select Disk Utility from the menu.

Get S.M.A.R.T.

After booting from the install disc, you may want to get really S.M.A.R.T. — as in Self-Monitoring Analysis and Reporting Technology. When you select a hard drive in Disk Utility, the S.M.A.R.T. status appears at the bottom of the window. If the status shows `Verified`, your disk is in okay shape.

If `About to Fail` appears in red, you have a ticking time bomb on your hands. Immediately back up your disk and critical files and replace the disk pronto.

Be aware that you can't check the S.M.A.R.T. status of all external drives.

Startup Problems

I just discussed a few ways to get you out of a pickle. But what if you can't even start the Mac? This is a very unusual circumstance. You probably have no power because the plug came loose (blame it on the dog), the switch on the power strip is off, your battery ran out of juice, or a blackout is in your neighborhood. Did you even notice that the lights went out?

On some laptops, you can tell whether a battery needs recharging by pressing a small button on the battery. Lights on the battery let you know how much strength the battery has.

Here's another thing to try: Press the power button and hold down the ⌘, Option, P, and R keys and wait until you hear the startup chime a second time.

If you've added memory, installed an AirPort card, or installed another component and the machine fails to start, make sure that the installation is correct and try again. If your computer still can't be revived, try removing the memory or card you just installed and then give it another shot.

After that, if you still can't restart, you may have to seek warranty service, as discussed later in this chapter.

Reinstalling OS X

If a problem has truly brought your computer to its knees, it may be time to reinstall your favorite operating system. It's bad enough that you have to suffer through the hassle. You're understandably panicked about retaining files and user settings.

Remain calm. Then do the following, if you have an install disc and optical drive:

1. **Insert the OS X installation disc in your CD or DVD drive.**

2. **Double-click the Install Mac OS X icon and go through the usual installation drill.**

3. **When asked, choose your current OS X disk as your destination disk (which in all likelihood is your only option anyway).**

4. **Click Options.**

   You've arrived at an important point in the process.

5. **If you want to salvage existing files and settings, select Archive and Install and then Preserve Users and Networks Settings. If you prefer starting anew, select Erase and Install, keeping in mind that you can't undo this action and those existing files and settings might as well be toast.**

6. **Click Continue.**

7. **To install certain parts of OS X, click Customize. To perform Apple's recommended basic installation, click Install.**

8. **Because the OS X disc you have may not have all the latest tweaks, pay a visit post-installation to Software Update (found on the menu) to bring Snow Leopard, Lion, or whichever version of OS X you're using up to date.**

A retail version of OS X may differ some from the version that was loaded on your computer.

Do not reinstall an earlier version of OS X over a later one. If for some reason you feel compelled to do so, first erase your hard drive completely or select the Erase option in the OS X installer. You'll have to reinstall any software updates.

But what if you don't have an install disc, which is more commonly the case nowadays? Apple has a built-in recovery disk feature that not only lets you reinstall OS X but also enables you to do so while keeping other files and settings intact. Here's what to do:

1. **Make sure that you are connected to the Internet.**

2. **From the menu, click Restart.**

3. **Press ⌘+R when the computer restarts, which summons OS X Utilities.**

4. **Choose Reinstall OS X from the list of options that appears on the screen.**

   Note your other options under OS X Utilities. You can restore from a Time Machine backup, get help online, or visit the Disk Utility toolshed with which you're now familiar.

5. **Click Continue and follow the on-screen instructions.**

If you're running OS X Lion or Mountain Lion, you can create a recovery disc on an external drive that will serve the same purpose as the built-in Recovery tool I've just described. Make sure that the external drive has at least 1GB of free space and download the Recovery Disk Assistant from the following URL: http://support.apple.com/kb/DL1433.

Follow the on-screen instructions from there.

Common Fixes to Other Problems

Sometimes all your Mac needs is a little first aid rather than major surgery. In this section, I consider some minor snags.

A jumpy mouse

Real mice live for dust and grime. And so for a long time did computer rodents. But the optical-style mice included with the most recent Macs don't get stuck like their ancestors because this kind of critter doesn't use the little dust-collecting rolling ball on its underbelly.

Be aware that optical mice don't like glass or reflective surfaces, so if you find your mouse on one, place a mouse pad or piece of paper underneath.

If your mouse doesn't respond at all, unplug it from the USB port and then plug it in again, just to make sure that the connection is snug. If you have a wireless mouse, make sure that it is turned on and that the batteries are fresh.

Meanwhile, if you want to change the speed of your on-screen mouse pointer or want to change clicking speeds, visit Mouse Preferences under System Preferences, as described in Chapter 4.

A stuck CD

It's cool the way most Macs with optical drives practically suck up a CD or DVD. Here's what's not cool: when the drive, particularly the slot-loading kind, won't spit out the disc.

Take a stab at one of these fixes:

- ✔ Quit the program using the disc and then press Eject on the keyboard.
- ✔ Open a Finder window, and click the little Eject icon in the sidebar. Or try dragging the disk icon from the Mac desktop to the trash.
- ✔ Log out of your user account (under the menu) and then press Eject on the keyboard.
- ✔ Restart the computer while holding down the mouse button.

If all else fails, you may have to take the computer in for repair (if possible) or replacement. I know of a least one episode where a toddler stuck an SD memory card in the slot, thereby preventing the DVD that was already inside from escaping. Apple had to replace the drive. In fact, the slot-loading drives that are included on modern Macs can't handle anything but full-size CDs and DVDs.

My Mac can no longer tell time

If your computer can no longer keep track of the time and date, its internal backup battery may have bit the dust. On some models, you can't replace this battery yourself; you'll have to contact the Apple store or an authorized service provider.

Kernel clink

Out of the blue, you are asked to restart your computer. In numerous languages, no less. Your machine has been hit with a *kernel panic*. The probable cause is corrupted or incompatible software, though damaged hardware or a problem with RAM can also unleash this unpleasant situation.

The good news is that a system restart usually takes care of the problem with no further harm. If it doesn't, try removing any memory or hardware you've recently added. Or if you think some new software you installed may have been the culprit, head to the software publisher's website and see whether it's issued a downloadable fix or upgrade.

SOS for DNS

If you're surfing the web and get a message about a DNS entry not being found, you typed the wrong web address or URL, the site in question no longer exists (or never did), or the site or your own Internet provider is having temporary problems. DNS is computer jargon for *Domain Name System* or *Server*. Similar messages may be presented as a *404 not found on this server* error.

Curing the trash can blues

In the physical world, you may try and throw something out of your trash can but can't because the rubbish gets stuck to the bottom of the can. The virtual trash can on your Mac sometimes suffers a similar fate: A file refuses to budge when you click Empty Trash in the Finder menu.

Try junking the files by holding down the Option key when you choose Empty Trash.

A file might refuse to go quietly for several reasons. For starters, you can't delete an item that is open somewhere else on your computer, so make sure that the item is indeed closed. Moreover, you may be trying to ditch a file to which you do not have sufficient permission. Perhaps a file has been opened and temporarily locked by some running application. The other most likely explanation is that a locked file is in the trash. You can unlock it by choosing File➪Get Info and making sure that the Locked box is not selected.

After a program unexpectedly crashes, one or more Recovered Files folders may appear in your trash after a restart. Temporary files are often used and disposed of by your applications, but during a crash, the files may not get disposed of. If any of these files are valuable, drag them out of trash. More often than not, however, it is safe to discard them with the rest of the garbage.

Useful Routine Maintenance

Your computer can use some TLC every so often. The following sections have a few tips for helping it out.

Purge unnecessary files and programs

If you've had your Mac for a while, you've probably piled on programs and files that no longer serve a purpose. Maybe drivers are associated with a printer you replaced a couple of years ago. Maybe you have software you fell out of love with. Even if these files aren't slowing the system, they're hogging disk space. These programs may even be agitating in the background. The Activity Monitor I mentioned earlier in this chapter may clue you in.

Bottom line: It's time to send these files and programs off to retirement for good (with generous severance packages, of course). You already know how to trash files. But it's not always obvious *which* files to dispose of. Some programs leave shrapnel all over your hard drive.

Type the name of the application you are getting rid of inside a Finder search box and do your best to determine whether files shown in the results are associated with the application you want to blow off.

Don't delete files that you know little or nothing about. The consequences aren't pretty if you accidentally trash a crucial system file; you'll need administrative access to get rid of some key files. If you do throw unfamiliar files in the trash, wait a day or so until you're satisfied that you don't need them before you permanently trash them.

Backing up your treasures

I know I've beaten you over the head with this throughout the book. Consider this the final nag. Back up. Back up. Back up. Whether you use Time Machine, Disk Utility, third-party software, or another method, JUST DO IT. SOONER RATHER THAN LATER. There, I've finished shouting.

Consider creating a bootable backup or *clone* of your hard drive by calling on such programs as SuperDuper (free to try, $27.95 to buy at http:// download.cnet.com/SuperDuper/3000-2242_4-46651.html) or Carbon Copy Cloner ($39.95), found at www.bombich.com. By having such a clone, you won't have to spend a lot of time reinstalling OS X and all the data that was on your machine.

Updating software

As a matter of course, visit Software Update under System Preferences on the menu, or arrange to have your Mac download updates automatically. It's a swell idea because upgrades are usually made available for good reasons. I certainly recommend selecting the Install System Data Files and Security Updates check box. If you're passing through System Preferences for any other reason, you can always go to Software Update and click Show Updates to see whether anything is worth fetching on the spot. (Or click Software Update under the menu.) I'll leave it to you whether to select the Automatically Download Apps Purchased on Other Macs check box. If you have enough disk space, and think you will want all the programs on all your Macs, by all means go for it. But if your secondary Mac — a notebook, say — is fairly tight on disk space, you may want to refrain from selecting this check box and just download the apps individually as you see fit.

To see all the applications on your Mac, use System Information.

Head over to the support areas of the websites of the publishers of other software on your computer to see whether they've updated their programs. The download is typically free. You'll often also be notified by a software publisher when an update for its app is available — and may also be made aware of such an update in the Mac App Store.

Summoning Outside Help

Pretty much everything I've described in this chapter up to now is something you ought to be able to handle on your own. But eventually, you'll run into situations beyond your expertise, especially if you face a serious hardware issue. Or perhaps you merely lack the time, patience, inclination, or confidence. I understand your reluctance. Fortunately, you can find help in plenty of places, though the help is not always free.

Third-party software

For all the fine troubleshooting tools included on a Mac, you may at times want to look to outside software. Here are some programs that may bail you out of a jam or help with routine maintenance. Prices and version numbers are subject to change:

- **Alsoft DiskWarrior 4, at** `www.alsoft.com`: A $100 repair utility that warns you of impending drive failure and helps you repair damaged directories (some of which Disk Utility says it can't fix). Check to make sure that DiskWarrior is compatible with your model and OS release.

- **Cocktail, at** `www.maintain.se/cocktail`: This general-purpose utility from Maintain offers a mix of maintenance and interface tweaks. A license for a single computer costs $19, though I've seen it discounted as low as $14. And you can try it before buying.

- **OnyX for Mac OS X, at** `www.onyxmac.com`: A free downloadable program from Titanium's Software that can run a variety of maintenance tasks.

- **Prosoft Engineering's Data Rescue 3, at** `www.prosofteng.com`: A $99 program designed to help you recover files from a corrupt hard drive. (As of this writing, the version of Data Rescue available in the Mac App Store was not compatible with Mountain Lion. The full version, available at the aforementioned company website, does work with Mountain Lion.)

- **Spring Cleaning 11, at** `http://store.smithmicro.com/product details.aspx?pid=12878`: A $50 utility that aims to boost performance by helping to eliminate stray files.

✔ **TechToolPro 6, at** www.micromat.com: A $100 problem solver from Micromat. Apple must be fond of TechTool Pro because it has made some versions available as part of AppleCare (see the next section).

AppleCare

Your Mac comes with 90 days of free telephone support and a year of free support at an authorized Apple retailer. The extended warranty program called AppleCare lengthens the time you can get phone support to three years (from the date of purchase).

AppleCare covers the computer itself plus AirPort Express and Extreme base stations, Time Capsule, MacBook Air SuperDrive, and Apple RAM (used with the Mac, of course). With certain models, including the Mac mini, you can also cover one Apple display if purchased at the same time.

Fees depend on the gear you're covering: AppleCare for an Apple display is $99; Mac mini, $149; iMac, $169; MacBook, MacBook Air, and 13-inch MacBook Pro, $249; Mac Pro, $249; 15-inch and 17-inch MacBook Pro and MacBook Pro with Retina Display, $349. Extended warranties are like any form of insurance — a crapshoot, but a crapshoot worth taking for some folks.

Consulting Einstein

One of the features of the Apple retail store is the Genius Bar. Apple's in-store experts can answer questions about your Mac and, if need be, install memory and handle repairs (for a fee). My own experience leads me to believe that these (mostly) young men and women are quite knowledgeable about the subjects you're likely to hit them with. Judging by blog posts, however, not all of them are ready for Mensa. Now the bad news. You can't exactly mosey up to the Genius Bar. Which leads me to . . .

Making a reservation

Meeting with an Apple-branded Genius requires an appointment. Go to www.apple.com/retail and click Make a Reservation. Then choose the Apple store near you (if one exists), and in the reservation, choose among Genius Bar, Workshops, or Business. (For the purposes of this example, choose Genius Bar and then choose Mac as the product requiring help; you could have otherwise chosen iPod, iPhone, or iPad.)

Available appointments are shown in 15-minute intervals; stake a claim on the next opening. Sign in with your Apple ID or list your first and last names, e-mail, and if you're cool with it, your phone number.

If you're already in an Apple store and it's not crowded, make a reservation on the spot using one of the Macs in the store.

If you had chosen Workshops instead, you could have signed up for a general workshop in OS X Mountain Lion or a class on getting started with iCloud, among other topics. Such workshops are an hour long and free. Apple also offers free workshops for kids 6 to 13. Never mind that the youngsters often know more about computers than their parents. If you need more personalized hands-on help, kindly read on.

One to One Training

A $99-a-year service called One to One Training provides face-to-face tutorials on a variety of topics, from moviemaking to digital photography. Training sessions are at your local Apple store; you can make a reservation online. In fact, when you sign up for One to One training, Apple gives you your own web page to make that reservation, and adds tips and tricks and sample projects.

Help, I need somebody

It sounds like a cliché, but free (or low-cost) help is all around you. Check out these samples:

- ✔ The geeky next-door neighbor, your cubicle-mate, or the friends you didn't know you had on the web.

- ✔ At a social networking site such as Meetup.com, you can search for and perhaps find a Macintosh user group meeting in your neck of the woods.

- ✔ Get referrals from Apple at `www.apple.com/usergroups`. You'll find an events calendar; enter your ZIP Code to find a group close by.

- ✔ For free online answers, poke around the newsgroups and computer bulletin boards, as described in Chapter 11.

- ✔ Check out the troubleshooting articles at `www.apple.com/support/downloads`.

Before leaving a chapter on troubleshooting and the geek section of this book, I'd be remiss if I didn't mention one other avenue for help. It's the Help menu found with most every program you use. In some cases, you will see a "?" indicating that help topics are at the ready.

To be sure, not every one of your questions will be answered satisfactorily, and you have to be careful in how you phrase your question. But before heading on a wild goose chase in search of an enlightening response, give the Help menus a try. Apple often delivers helpful tutorial videos that just might guide you to a solution. They've been right there all along.

Part VI

the
part of
tens

In this part . . .

✔ See the top ten Dashboard Widgets for Mac users.

✔ Check out the top ten indispensable Mac websites.

✔ Enjoy an additional Macs Part of Tens chapter online at `www.dummies.com/extras/macs`.

Chapter 21

Ten Clever Dashboard Widgets

*T*hink of the Dashboard widgets of Chapter 6 fame as a reflection of our busy lives. We're all distracted, pressed for time, going every which way. We generally know what we want, and we want it now. In this fast-food society, snack software seems inevitable.

The truth is that the Dashboard now takes second fiddle to the Mac App Store. Apple hasn't exactly foisted the love on Dashboard since Mountain Lion pounced onto the scene. Even so, the widgets mentioned here are worth it for those quick-hit kind of moments.

In this chapter, I present in alphabetical order a list of ten yummy widgets. With thousands of widgets available as of this writing on Apple's site, you should seek your own favorites at www.apple.com/downloads/dashboard. You can also search cyberspace for other dashboard widgets. Most widgets are free, though donations are often requested.

Alas, a few of my earlier favorite widgets — notably iStat Pro and Wikipedia — weren't functioning in Mountain Lion, at least at the time of this writing. And some other widgets in Apple's Dashboard bazaar have grown stale.

Cocktail

Can you mix an, um, Apple Martini? Kamikaze? Or Piper at the Gates of Dawn? The free Cocktail widget powered by 7.com lets you impress buddies with your mixologist skills. Just type the drink you have in mind. Cocktail's database includes nearly 7,000 drink recipes. Click Feelin Thirsty? for a random selection. With its martini-glass icon, shown in Figure 21-1, Cocktail has one of the better-looking widgets too.

Figure 21-1: I'll have a Cocktail with that widget.

Countdown Plus

Hmm. Steven Chaitoff's simple Countdown Plus widget tells you how much time is remaining until a specified date, such as the newborn's due date, your next vacation, your anniversary, or the day you'll be paroled.

Daily Dilbert Widget

I love Dilbert. And I reckon that if you've worked in an office environment (and even if you haven't), chances are you're fond of Scott Adams' cartoon strip as well. The simple Daily Dilbert widget lifts an RSS feed from Dilbert. com, shown in Figure 21-2. The latest seven comic strips are promised at any given time.

Figure 21-2: Dilbert is a comic strip hero and dashboard widget.

Mac Tips and Tricks

By now, you've caught on that this book is *Macs For Dummies*. So how could I avoid including a Macs-related widget? Mac Tips and Tricks does what's its name suggests — it's a springboard to tips on all things Macintosh, from listening to music through multiple speakers via AirPlay to fine-tuning the volume on your computer. (Okay, I'll tell: Press Option+Shift when pressing the volume keys on your keyboard and you can adjust your volume by smaller-than-typical increments.) Check out the widget for other tricks.

Movies

Want to know the flicks playing in the hood? Want to read a synopsis and view trailers to help you decide which to see? That's just what Movies, a simple film fan widget from Apple, lets you do. Apple supplied the widget with OS X. It even lets you purchase tickets (via Fandango). It's one of the widgets that has exhibited cranky behavior of late, so hopefully Apple will provide the, um, direction, it needs. In the meantime, anyone up for *Hitchcock* (see Figure 21-3)?

Figure 21-3:
A going-to-
the-movies
widget.

Power Switch

Press (or rather click) this single button in the Dashboard to make something happen on your Mac. What that something is depends on what happens when you click the "i" to configure the widget. You can put the Mac to sleep, log out, restart, or shut down, all after that single click. And you can fine-tune these actions. For example, you can place check marks that will close all Finder windows, empty the trash, eject network volumes, and secure the system. You can have the computer announce all these actions out loud too. And by dragging the slider (visible in Figure 21-4), you can delay the start before the behavior takes hold, between 0 and 7,000 seconds after you press the button. The button itself will pulsate leading up to the start of the actions you requested.

Figure 21-4:
A single
button
can con-
trol these
actions.

Quote of the Day

"Silence may be as variously shaded as speech." Edith Wharton said that. "A true friend is one soul in two bodies." Aristotle said that. Start your day with the Quote of the Day widget for these and other pearls of wisdom and a photo or illustration of the person who said them.

Starry Night Widget

Want to know what you're looking at in the evening sky? This interactive planetarium widget can reveal the answers. Click the "i" and then the Time/ Place tab to enter your current whereabouts or some other location. If you place a check mark in the Now box (assuming that it's not already checked), you'll be able to identify the galactic objects in the immediate sky. But you can also enter another date or hour — well into the future or deep in the past — to see how space appeared or will appear at that time. You can also display star and planet labels, and constellations. This stellar widget is shown in Figure 21-5.

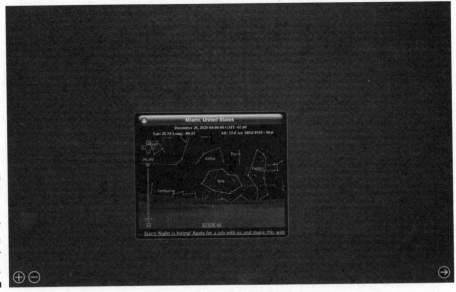

Figure 21-5:
Starry,
starry
night — in
the year
2020.

Translate

Your Mac (well, the notebook models anyway) makes a great world traveler. The machines can converse in foreign languages, too. So if you need to quickly translate a word or phrase, the aptly named Translate widget provides a handy tool. You can translate words to or from English and Chinese (Simplified or Traditional), Dutch, French, German, Greek, Italian, Japanese, Korean, Portuguese, Russian, and Spanish. (I wouldn't go as far as to call the Mac fluent, though. When I requested a French translation of the English phrase "Are you a fan of the Mac?," I received "Êtes-vous un ventilateur du Mac?" in response — "Are you an electric fan associated with Macintosh?," in other words.)

Word of the Day

I'm feeling rather *sedulous*. After all, I'm diligent in my application or pursuit and steadily industrious. Besides, *sedulous* is my word of the day, delivered by a widget of the same name. The app serves up daily definitions from Merriam-Webster.com, Dictionary.com, UrbanDictionary.com, or any of the other sources that developer Code Driven lets you pick from.

Chapter 22

Ten Indispensable Mac Websites

In my line of work, I often get the "how come you didn't" e-mail or phone call, as in "how come you didn't write about my company or product?" So I won't be shocked to hear folks asking about this chapter, "how come you didn't choose my favorite Macintosh website?" Limiting any list to ten is exceedingly difficult — especially when it comes to websites about your trusted computer. Heck, one of my editors wanted me to shoehorn in a mention of www.mactech.com because it's an incredible compendium of Mac-related technology discussions and articles. And how could I possibly leave out www.macdailynews.com? Jeez, I guess I managed to squeeze these in — don't you think I'm cheatin' — and they don't even count against my ten.

AppleInsider

www.appleinsider.com

As with many other comprehensive sites devoted to the Cupertino crowd (including some in this list), you'll find lots of news, forums, and reviews concerning all things Apple. But AppleInsider also wants to solicit your help. You're invited to submit rumors and information to the site — and may even do so anonymously.

Cult of Mac

www.cultofmac.com

This well-regarded daily news site is also on top of the latest out of Apple-land, with forums on the Mac that cover vintage computers to the latest models. Cult of Mac will also happily accept a news tip from you.

MacFixIt

http://reviews.cnet.com/macfixit

When something has gone wrong and you're still seeking answers despite my best efforts in Chapter 20, check out MacFixIt, now part of CNET. This troubleshooting site tackles a gaggle of issues, with help from your Mac brethren. And because of the CNET acquisition, you no longer have to fork over $24.95 a year for a Pro version with tutorials, full access to more than a decade of content, and more. Among the many topics I've came across through the years were making banking sites work with Safari, taming annoying alert sounds in OS X, and iTunes authentication problems.

MacRumors

www.macrumors.com

Apple is one of the most secretive outfits on the planet. Seldom does the company spill the beans on new products in advance; the notable exception is features for the next iteration of OS X. That doesn't prevent numerous Apple watchers from speculating on what might be coming out of Cupertino. Besides, who doesn't love a juicy rumor now and then? Is Apple merging with Nintendo? (Don't count on it.) Is Apple going to add a subscription music plan to iTunes? (Don't count on that either.) Head to MacRumors for the latest dirt, some of which might even turn out to be true.

MacSurfer

www.macsurfer.com

MacSurfer is a wonderful resource for the Apple news junkie. MacSurfer's Headline News sports links to articles on all things Apple, including traditional media, websites, Apple itself, and bloggers. Links are segregated by Apple, OS X, General Interest, Hardware/Software, How-To/Reviews, Op/Ed, Press Releases, Computer Industry, and Finances.

Macworld

www.macworld.com

It's all here at Macworld: news, how-tos, product reviews, discussion forums, and current and past articles from *Macworld* magazine. And one of the places that used to make this top-ten list as a stand-alone site is part of Macworld, too: Mac OS X Hints.

Other World Computing

www.macsales.com

Need more RAM for your computer? Or an extra hard drive, perhaps? Maybe even an add-on that would let you watch TV on your Mac? Other World Computing (OWC) has been specializing in sales of Mac accessories since the first Bush administration. The online retailer has earned a stellar reputation for prompt delivery and reliability. (Hey, I know I'm supposed to mention only ten sites, but if none of my editors are looking, other online retailers worth checking out include MacMall and Small Dog Electronics.)

The Unofficial Apple Weblog

www.tuaw.com

The Unofficial Apple Weblog (TUAW, for short) is an enthusiast's blog that lets people comment on Apple articles and reviews written by the likes of yours truly in *USA TODAY*. (Sure it's a shameless plug for my paper and me, but we are nearing the end of the book. And you'll find plenty of links to articles by other journalists.)

VersionTracker

www.versiontracker.com/macosx or http://download.cnet.com/mac

VersionTracker is a repository for downloadable shareware, freeware, and updates to Mac software. Click a name to discover more about what a program does and to eyeball ratings and feedback. It, too, is now part of the CNET empire, specifically the Mac Software area of Download.com.

And Last but Not Least, Apple.com

www.apple.com

Apple may seem like an obvious place to go. Heck, you probably already landed there just by opening Safari the first time. And you may not love the full blitz of Mac, iPod, iPhone, and iPad advertising and promotions, even if you already drank Apple's Kool-Aid. But presumably most of you already have sweet feelings for the company's products.

As I hinted at in Chapter 20, this website is full of helpful resources, especially for, but not limited to, newbies. You can download software updates and manuals, view video tutorials, post questions in discussion forums, read press releases, and consult the knowledge base. Mostly, I think, you'll walk away with a renewed sense of goodwill for the company responsible for the computer that most of you fancy so much.

Index